WANDERING POETS IN ANCIENT GREEK CULTURE

Although recent scholarship has focused on the city-state as the context for the production of Greek poetry, for poets and performers travel was more the norm than the exception. This book traces this central aspect of ancient culture from its roots in the Near Eastern societies which preceded the Greeks, through the way in which early semi-mythical figures such as Orpheus were imagined, the poets who travelled to the brilliant courts of archaic tyrants, and on into the fluid mobility of imperial and late antique culture. The emphasis is both on why poets travelled, and on how local communities used the skills of these outsiders for their own purposes. Wandering poets are also set within the wider context of ancient networks of exchange, patronage and affiliation between communities and are seen as one particularly powerful manifestation of a feature of ancient life which is too often overlooked.

RICHARD HUNTER is Regius Professor of Greek at the University of Cambridge, and a Fellow of Trinity College. He has published extensively in the fields of Greek and Latin Literature: his most recent books include Plato's *Symposium* (2004), *Tradition and Innovation in Hellenistic Poetry* (with M. Fantuzzi, Cambridge, 2004) and *The Shadow of Callimachus* (Cambridge, 2006).

IAN RUTHERFORD is Professor of Greek at the University of Reading. His principal research interests are Greek lyric, religious practice and state-pilgrimage, and the relations between Greek and eastern cultures. His *Pindar's Paeans* was published in 2001, and he is an editor of *Pilgrimage in Greco-Roman and Early Christian Antiquity: Seeing the Gods* (2005).

WANDERING POETS IN ANCIENT GREEK CULTURE

Travel, Locality and Pan-Hellenism

EDITED BY
RICHARD HUNTER AND IAN RUTHERFORD

CAMBRIDGE UNIVERSITY PRESS
Cambridge, New York, Melbourne, Madrid, Cape Town, Singapore, São Paulo, Delhi

Cambridge University Press
The Edinburgh Building, Cambridge CB2 8RU, UK

Published in the United States of America by Cambridge University Press, New York

www.cambridge.org
Information on this title: www.cambridge.org/9780521898782

© Cambridge University Press 2009

This publication is in copyright. Subject to statutory exception
and to the provisions of relevant collective licensing agreements,
no reproduction of any part may take place without
the written permission of Cambridge University Press.

First published 2009

Printed in the United Kingdom at the University Press, Cambridge

A catalogue record for this publication is available from the British Library

Library of Congress Cataloguing in Publication data
Wandering poets in ancient Greek culture : travel, locality and panhellenism / edited by
Richard Hunter and Ian Rutherford.
p.   cm.
Includes bibliographical references and index.
ISBN 978-0-521-89878-2 (hardback)
1. Poets, Greek.   2. Greek poetry – History and criticism.   I. Hunter, R. L. (Richard L.)
II. Rutherford, Ian, 1959–   III. Title.
PA3095.W36   2008
881′.0109–dc22   2008031296

ISBN 978-0-521-89878-2 hardback

Cambridge University Press has no responsibility for the persistence or
accuracy of URLs for external or third-party internet websites referred to
in this publication, and does not guarantee that any content on such
websites is, or will remain, accurate or appropriate.

Contents

List of figures		*page* vii
Notes on contributors		viii
Acknowledgements		xi
List of abbreviations		xii

1	Introduction *Richard Hunter and Ian Rutherford*	1
2	Hittite and Greek perspectives on travelling poets, texts and festivals *Mary R. Bachvarova*	23
3	Thamyris the Thracian: the archetypal wandering poet? *Peter Wilson*	46
4	Read on arrival *Richard P. Martin*	80
5	Wandering poets, archaic style *Ewen Bowie*	105
6	Defining local identities in Greek lyric poetry *Giovan Battista D'Alessio*	137
7	Wandering poetry, 'travelling' music: Timotheus' muse and some case-studies of shifting cultural identities *Lucia Prauscello*	168
8	Epigrammatic contests, *poeti vaganti* and local history *Andrej Petrovic*	195
9	World travellers: the associations of Artists of Dionysus *Sophia Aneziri*	217

v

Contents

10 Aristodama and the Aetolians: an itinerant poetess and
    her agenda   237
    Ian Rutherford

11 Travelling memories in the Hellenistic world   249
    Angelos Chaniotis

Bibliography   270
Index   307

Figures

1	Map of Greece	*page* 49
2a	Attic red-figure krater, *c.* 420 from Ferrara (Spina), Museo Archeologico inv. 3033, T127. Used by permission of the Museo Archeologico.	71
2b	Drawing of image in figure 2a: Aurigemma 1960: Tavola 6. Photo: Fiona Kidd	72
2c	Detail from figure 2a. Photo: Fiona Kidd	72

Notes on contributors

SOPHIA ANEZIRI is a lecturer in Ancient History and Epigraphy at the National and Capodistrian University of Athens. She has published widely on Greek epigraphy, religion and society, and is the author of *Die Vereine der dionysischen Techniten im Kontext der hellenistischen Gesellschaft* (Historia Einzelschriften 163, Stuttgart 2003) and (in collaboration with others) *Index du Bulletin Epigraphique 1987–2001*, 3 vols. (Meletemata 43, Athens 2005).

MARY R. BACHVAROVA is Assistant Professor in Classical Studies at Willamette University in Salem, Oregon; she has also taught at the University of Manchester and the University of Nottingham. The focus of her research is using Near Eastern material, especially from second millennium Anatolia, better to understand the development of ancient Greek culture.

EWEN BOWIE taught Greek language and literature at Corpus Christi College, Oxford, as E. P. Warren Praelector in Classics from 1965–2007. He has published extensively on the Greek literature and culture of the Roman empire, on archaic and Hellenistic poetry and on Old Comedy. He is currently completing a commentary on Longus, *Daphnis and Chloe*.

ANGELOS CHANIOTIS is Senior Research Fellow in Classical Studies at All Souls College, Oxford. He is senior editor of the *Supplementum Epigraphicum Graecum*. His books include *Historie und Historiker in den griechischen Inschriften* (Stuttgart 1988) and *War in the Hellenistic World: A Social and Cultural History* (Oxford 2005).

GIOVAN BATTISTA D'ALESSIO is Professor of Greek Literature and Language at King's College London; before his current appointment he taught at the University of Messina. He is the author of an annotated edition of Callimachus (Milan 1996, 2nd edition 2007) and has published extensively on Greek lyric and Hellenistic poetry, and on Greek literary papyri.

Notes on contributors   ix

RICHARD HUNTER is Regius Professor of Greek at the University of Cambridge and a Fellow of Trinity College. His research interests include ancient comedy, the novel, and Hellenistic poetry and its reception in Rome. His most recent books are *Theocritus, Encomium of Ptolemy Philadelphus* (Berkeley 2003), *Plato's Symposium* (Oxford/New York 2004), (with Marco Fantuzzi) *Tradition and Innovation in Hellenistic Poetry* (Cambridge 2004) and *The Shadow of Callimachus* (Cambridge 2006).

RICHARD P. MARTIN is Antony and Isabelle Raubitschek Professor of Classics at Stanford University. His publications include *Healing, Sacrifice and Battle: Amēchania and Related Concepts in Early Greek Poetry* (1983), *The Language of Heroes: Speech and Performance in the Iliad* (1989), and *Myths of the Ancient Greeks* (2003), as well as articles on Greek and Latin poetry, myth, ritual and narrative; with a team at Stanford he has produced a CD-based multimedia course on Homer's *Odyssey*. He is currently finishing two books on Homer and a textbook on mythology. Other interests include ancient and modern poetics, Irish language and literature, modern Greek culture, and the study of oral epic traditions worldwide.

ANDREJ PETROVIC is a Lecturer in Greek History at Durham University. Among various publications on Greek history, epigraphy and culture, he has published a book on the verse-inscriptions attributed to Simonides of Keos (*Kommentar zu den simonideischen Versinschriften*, 2007).

LUCIA PRAUSCELLO studied at the Scuola Normale Superiore di Pisa for her MA and PhD and then spent two years at University College London as Momigliano Fellow in Arts. She is now Lecturer in Classics at the University of Cambridge and Fellow of Trinity Hall. She is the author of *Singing Alexandria: Music between Practice and Textual Transmission* (Leiden 2006) and has also published on music, Greek poetry and performance criticism. She is currently working on the 'archaeology' of New Music and its reception.

IAN RUTHERFORD is Professor of Greek at the University of Reading. His principal research interests are Greek lyric, religious practice and state-pilgrimage, and the relations between Greek and eastern cultures. *Pindar's Paeans* was published by Oxford University Press in 2001.

PETER WILSON is the William Ritchie Professor of Classics at the University of Sydney; he has held posts at the University of Warwick and at Oxford. His main research interests are the history and sociology of the Greek theatre, early Greek poetry and society, and Greek music. His publications include *The Athenian Institution of the 'Khoregia': the Chorus, the City and the Stage* (Cambridge, 2000), *Music and the Muses: the culture of 'mousike' in the Classical Athenian city*, ed. with P. Murray (Oxford, 2004), and *Greek Theatre and Festivals: documentary studies*, ed. (Oxford, 2007).

Acknowledgements

The papers collected here were first presented at a colloquium in Cambridge in April 2005. The editors would like to express their gratitude to the British Academy and the Faculty of Classics at the University of Cambridge which both provided generous funding for that event. Michael Sharp of Cambridge University Press offered subsequent encouragement and advice, and the Computer Officer of the Faculty of Classics, Steve Kimberley, laboured tirelessly over recalcitrant Greek fonts.

Abbreviations

Standard abbreviations for collections and editions of texts and for works of reference are used. The following abbreviations for epigraphical collections may be noted:

Ath. Ag. XVI	A. G. Woodhead, *The Athenian Agora.* (*Vol. XVI*). *Inscriptions: the Decrees*, Princeton 1997.
BE	*Bulletin Épigraphique*, in *Revue des Études Grecques.*
CEG	P. A. Hansen, *Carmina epigraphica Graeca.* (2 vols.), Berlin, New York 1983–1989.
CID	*Corpus des inscriptions de Delphes*, Paris 1978–.
CIG	*Corpus Inscriptionum Graecarum*, Berlin 1825–77.
CIL	*Corpus Inscriptionum Latinarum*, Berlin 1863–.
Corinth VIII 3	J. H. Kent, *Corinth VIII 3. The Inscriptions 1926–50*, Princeton 1966.
FD III	E. Bourguet, *et al.*, *Fouilles de Delphes, III. 1–6*, Paris 1929–85.
FdX IX	H. Metzger, *Fouilles de Xanthos.* Tome IX, Paris 1992.
FGE	D. L. Page, *Further Greek Epigrams*, Cambridge 1981.
GDI	H. Collitz, F. Bechtel *et al.*, *Sammlung der griechischen Dialekt-Inschriften*, I–IV, Göttingen 1884–1915.
Guarducci	M. Guarducci, *Poeti vaganti e conferenzieri dell' età ellenistica: ricerche di epigrafia greca nel campo della letteratura e del costume* (Atti della R. Accademia nazionale dei Lincei. Classe di scienze morali, storiche e filologiche, serie 6: vol. 2, 9 (Rome 1929) 629–65.
GVI	W. Peek, *Griechische Versinschriften*, Berlin 1955.
IAG	L. Moretti, *Iscrizioni Agonistiche Greche*, Rome 1953.
IBoT	*Istanbul Arkeoloji Müzlerinde Bulunun Boğazköy Tabletler(inden Seçme Metinler)* [*Boğazköy Tablets in*

List of abbreviations

xiii

	the Archaeological Museums of Istanbul], Istanbul 1944, 1947, 1954, Ankara 1988.
I Cret	M. Guarducci, *Inscriptiones Creticae opera et consilio Friederici Halbherr collectae*, I–IV, Rome 1935–50.
ID	F. Durrbach, P. Roussel, M. Launey, J. Coupry and A. Plassart, *Inscriptions de Délos*, I–VII, Paris 1926–72.
IDid	A. Rehm and R. Harder, *Didyma*, II, *Die Inschriften*, Berlin 1958.
IG	*Inscriptiones Graecae*, Berlin 1873–.
IGR	*Inscriptiones Graecae ad res Romanas pertinentes*, Paris 1911–27.
I. Ephesos	H. Wankel, R. Merkelbach *et al.*, *Die Inschriften von Ephesos I–VII. Inschriften griechischer Städte aus Kleinasien* 11–17, Bonn 1979–81.
I. Erythrai	H. Engelmann and R. Merkelbach, *Die Inschriften von Erythrai und Klazomenai I–II. Inschriften griechischer Städte aus Kleinasien* 1–2, Bonn 1972–3.
I. Iasos	W. Blümel, *Die Inschriften von Iasos. Inschriften griechischer Städte aus Kleinasien* 28 (2 vols.), Bonn 1985.
I. Lindos	C. Blinkenberg, *Lindos. Fouilles et Recherches II: Fouilles de l'Acropole 1902–14. Inscriptions* (2 vols.), Berlin and Copenhagen 1941.
ILS	H. Dessau, *Inscriptiones Latinae Selectae* (3 vols.), Berlin 1892–1916.
I. Magnesia	O. Kern, *Die Inschriften von Magnesia am Maeander*, Berlin 1900.
IMEGR	E. Bernand, *Inscriptions métriques de l'Égypte Gréco-Romaine*, Paris 1969.
I. Olympia	W. Dittenberger and K. Purgold, *Die Inschriften von Olympia*, Berlin 1896.
IOSPE I²	V. Latyshev, *Inscriptiones antiquae orae septentrionalis Ponti Euxini Graecae. Vol. 1* (2nd edn.): *Inscriptiones Tyrae Olbiae Chersonesi Tauricae Aliorum Locorum a Danubio usque ad regnum Bosporanum*, St. Petersburg 1916.
I. Sardis	W. H. Buckler and D. M. Robinson, *Sardis VII. Greek and Latin Inscriptions*, Leiden 1932.
I. Side	J. Nollé, *Side im Altertum. Geschichte und Zeugnisse I: Geographie, Geschichte, Testimonia, griechische und*

	lateinische Inschriften. Inschriften griechischer Städte aus Kleinasien 43, Bonn 1993.
I. Smyrna	G. Petzl, *Die Inschriften von Smyrna I–II. Inschriften griechischer Städte aus Kleinasien* 23–24 (3 vols.), Bonn 1982–90.
Iscr. Cos	M. Segre, *Iscrizioni di Cos* (Monografie della Scuola Archeologica di Atene VI) (2 vols.), Rome 1994.
ISE	L. Moretti, *Iscrizioni storiche ellenistiche. Testo critico, traduzione e commento* (3 vols.), Florence 1967–2002.
I. Tralleis	F. B. Poljakov, *Die Inschriften von Tralleis und Nysa. Inschriften griechischer Städte aus Kleinasien* 36 (2 vols.), Bonn 1989.
KBo	*Keilschrifttexte aus Boğazköy*, Leipzig 1916–.
KUB	*Keilschrifturkunden aus Boğazköy*, Berlin 1921–90.
MAMA VIII	William M. Calder and J. M. R. Cormack, *Monumenta Asiae Minoris Antiqua VIII. Monuments from Lycaonia, the Pisido-Phrygian Borderland, Aphrodisias*, Manchester 1962.
Milet I.3	Rehm, A., 'Die Inschriften', in G. Kawerau and A. Rehm, *Das Delphinion in Milet* [=*Milet. Ergebnisse der Ausgrabungen und Untersuchungen seit dem Jahre 1899*. 1(3)] Berlin 1914, p.162 (n.31–186).
OGIS	W. Dittenberger, *Orientis Graeci Inscriptiones Selectae* (2 vols.). Leipzig 1903–5.
RC	C. B. Welles, *Royal Correspondence in the Hellenistic Period*, New Haven 1934.
RDGE	R. K. Sherk, *Roman Documents from the Greek East*, Baltimore 1969.
SEG	*Supplementum Epigraphicum Graecum*, Leiden 1923–.
SGO	R. Merkelbach and J. Stauber, *Steinepigramme aus dem griechischen Osten* (5 vols.), Stuttgart/Munich/ Leipzig 1998–2004.
SH	H. Lloyd-Jones and P. Parsons (eds.), *Supplementum Hellenisticum*, Berlin/New York 1983.
Syll.[3]	W. Dittenberger, *Sylloge Inscriptionum Graecarum*, 3rd edn. (4 vols.), Leipzig 1915–24.

CHAPTER I

Introduction

Richard Hunter and Ian Rutherford

TRAVELLING POETS

This volume explores the phenomenon of the itinerancy of ancient Greek poets, their movements around and engagement with the cities and cultural networks of the ancient Mediterranean and, more broadly, themes of travel and poetic itinerancy in Greek literature.

Travel and 'wandering'[1] are persistent elements in both the reality and the *imaginaire* of Greek poetry, and intellectual and cultural life more generally, from the earliest days. They are, for example, central to the figure of Orpheus,[2] usually regarded by the Greeks as the first major poet and/or holy man (cf., e.g. Aristophanes, *Frogs* 1030–2), whether in his rôle as a teacher of holy rites, as an Argonaut,[3] or as a lover grieving for the double loss of his wife Eurydice:

> nulla Venus, non ulli animum flexere hymenaei:
> solus Hyperboreas glacies Tanaimque niualem
> aruaque Riphaeis numquam uiduata pruinis
> lustrabat, raptam Eurydicen atque inrita Ditis
> dona querens.

No love, no wedding-songs bent his soul. Alone he roamed over the icy wastes of the Hyperboreans, the snowy Tanais, and the fields which are never free of Riphaean frosts, as he lamented the loss of Eurydice and the gifts of Dis brought to naught. (Virgil, *Georgics* 4.516–20)

In some versions it was that wandering which led to Orpheus' death,

Men say that the wives of the Thracians plotted Orpheus' death, because he had persuaded their husbands to follow him in his wanderings (πλανωμένωι). (Pausanias 9.30.5)

---

[1] For the distinction between the two cf. below pp. 16–17. Some general features of the theme of this book are treated in Schlesier and Zellmann 2004 and Montiglio 2005.

[2] The bibliography is huge: there is guidance in West 1983 and Graf and Johnston 2007.

[3] On Orpheus as an Argonaut cf., e.g., West 2005: 45–6, Graf and Johnston 2007: 165–6.

I

2   RICHARD HUNTER AND IAN RUTHERFORD

Even after death Orpheus' wanderings did not cease, for his still-singing head was believed to have been washed down the river Hebrus and across the Aegean to Lesbos.[4] It is Orpheus whom the Platonic Socrates invokes to describe (with gentle amusement) the crowd of ξένοι whom 'Protagoras [the great fifth-century sophist] brings with him from all the cities through which he passes, enchanting (κηλῶν) them with his voice like Orpheus' (Plato, *Protagoras* 315a7–b1). Plato makes Protagoras himself claim that poets such as Homer, Hesiod and Simonides, and holy men such as Orpheus and Musaeus, were really sophists *avant la lettre* (*Protagoras* 316d, cf. *Republic* 10.600c–d).[5] Six centuries later, Paideia holds out such universal fame and recognition to Lucian as one of the most attractive rewards of sophistic success (*The Dream or The Life of Lucian*), and Philostratus illustrates this many times over in the *Lives of the Sophists*.[6]

Two further examples of the 'Orpheus pattern' will illustrate the range and power of the idea of the 'wandering poet'. Empedocles of Acragas (early-mid fifth century BC), a poet and holy man with perhaps a better claim to reality than Orpheus, addresses his fellow citizens at the opening of his great poem *Purifications* as follows:

Friends, who live in the great city of the yellow Acragas, up on the heights of the citadel, caring for good deeds, I give you greetings. An immortal god, mortal no more, I go about (πωλεῦμαι) honoured by all, as is fitting, crowned with ribbons and fresh garlands; and by all whom I come upon as I enter their prospering towns, by men and women, I am revered. They follow me in their thousands, asking where lies the road to profit, some desiring prophecies, while others ask to hear the word of healing for every illness, long transfixed by harsh pains. (Empedocles fr. 112 D-K, trans. Kirk, Raven and Schofield)

However remarkable the claims, they fall into a familiar and very long-lived pattern. Secondly, there is the (presumably largely fictional) case of the seventh-century poet Magnes of Smyrna which is reported for us by the Augustan historian Nicolaus of Damascus:[7]

Magnes of Smyrna was a very handsome man and noteworthy for both poetical and musical skill. He dressed himself splendidly and, clothed in purple and with his hair formed into a knot by a golden band, he travelled around the cities performing his poetry. Many were in love with him, but Gyges [of Lydia] burned a particular

---

[4] On these myths cf. Faraone 2004. Gallus is a different sort of *poeta uagans* at Virgil, *Eclogue* 6.64–5.
[5] On the fifth-century sophists as 'wanderers' cf., e.g., Montiglio 2005: 105–17.
[6] For the imperial period cf. also the material gathered in Puech 2002.
[7] Jacoby rightly notes in his commentary that some doubt must attach to the poet's name, given the prominent rôle of the Magnesians in this story, but he resists the temptation to replace Magnes by Mimnermus.

Introduction   3

flame for him and was his lover. Wherever he went, he drove all the women mad
with desire, particularly the women of Magnesia, and he slept with them. Their
male relations were angry at the shame this brought, and so they took as an excuse
the fact that in his poems Magnes had celebrated the bravery of the Lydians in
their battle with the Amazons but had made no mention of them, and attacked
Magnes, ripped his clothes, tore his hair and committed extreme violence against
him. Gyges was very upset about this and made many incursions into Magnesia
and finally overran the city; on his return to Sardis he celebrated a splendid festival.
(Nicolaus of Damascus, *FGrHist* 90F62 = *Suda* μ 21)

If aspects of this narrative recall not just Orpheus but also the coming
of Dionysus to Thebes in Euripides' *Bacchae* with the sexual power (and
designs) over women that Pentheus imagines him to have, this will serve –
as also does Empedocles' self-presentation – to remind us that it would be
misleading to try to draw firm and persistent distinctions between 'wandering poets' and other kinds of 'wanderers', whether they be 'wizards'
(γόητες), such as Pentheus imagines Dionysus to be (Eur. *Ba.* 234), or 'historians' or doctors; 'wandering poets' are in fact just one facet of a much
broader phenomenon of Greek culture. The novelistic *Life of Aesop* records
how, once freed, the legendary fable-teller and folk-philosopher 'decided
to travel around the world and he gave lectures in public halls; he made a
lot of money . . .'.[8]

Travelling poets are best attested in the historical (largely epigraphic)
record from the Hellenistic and imperial periods, and the term 'poeti
vaganti/wandering poets' is adopted for this book to honour Margherita
Guarducci, who long ago collected a small corpus of decrees from the third
and second centuries BC commemorating about twenty-five 'poeti vaganti'
who were honoured for their 'presence' (*epidēmia*) and 'behaviour' (*anas-
trophē*) by foreign communities in which they had performed and which,
in many if not all cases, they will have celebrated in their poems;[9] the most
common privileges bestowed upon them are *proxenia*, freedom from tax and
grants of land. Thus, for example, we find the Delians honouring Demoteles of Andros for poetry on 'local myths' and Amphiklos of Chios for poems
that 'brought lustre to the temple and the Delians';[10] the payment of such
honours is, of course, itself an act of piety: the Delphians honour the lyric
poet Kleochares of Athens, who had written a prosodion, a paian and a
hymn to the god, 'so that the city might be seen to honour those who write
something worthy of the god'.[11] As these examples show, the honouring

---

[8] Chapter 101 in the G version, which probably goes back at least to the second century AD.
[9] Guarducci 1929.   [10] Guarducci 1929, nos. viii and ix (p. 650).
[11] Guarducci 1929, no. vii (pp. 649–50).

community was often a city associated with a prominent sanctuary which had attracted the interest of poets – Delphi, Delos, Tenos, Samothrace – but this is certainly not a rule: we might think of the decrees for the poetess Aristodama of Smyrna by the cities of Lamia in Thessaly and Khalaion in Phokis (see Rutherford, this volume). Guarducci's dossier of evidence remains fundamental to this subject,[12] though travelling poets were only a small fraction of the total volume of travelling historians, 'intellectuals' and performers in this period.[13]

The decrees assembled by Guarducci attest to a very lively poetic and performance culture, but are unfortunately usually less forthcoming about the poets themselves or the circumstances of their performances. Only occasionally can we fill in some of the picture, as with Cicero's client Archias of Antioch, whose travels took him through the cities of Asia Minor, Greece and Italy, where – according to Cicero – he was showered with honours and 'lionised' by the cultural and political élite and those who imagined themselves part of it; here too we may feel the resonances of the 'Orpheus pattern':

When he travelled in the rest of Asia [outside Antioch] and all of Greece, his presence was so celebrated that expectation surpassed the reports of his talent, and his actual arrival and the wonder he aroused surpassed expectation. (Cicero, *Pro Archia* 4)

The performers studied by Guarducci were probably professionals, and as such almost certainly members of one of the guilds of 'Artists of Dionysus', though again the decrees do not give details.[14] The songs they performed seem mostly to have been ἔπη, i.e. narrative and encomiastic poems in hexameters, probably recounting local history and traditions; we hear also of hymns and lyric poetry, and, occasionally of drama.[15] On the face of it, the Hellenistic 'poeti vaganti' might seem very different from the more celebrated poets who lived and worked at the Ptolemaic court of Alexandria in Egypt, supposedly secluded within the scholarly confines of the Museum,

---

[12] Chaniotis 1988b was able to make some additions, and cf. also Bouvier 1985, Cameron 1995: 47–9. It is intriguing to find the city of Cos honouring an Ion, son of Menippus, from Chios for poems of praise in a recently published inscription (Bosnakis and Hallof 2003: 204); was this a name which ran in poetic families on Chios? For Hellenistic poetic patronage in general cf. Hunter 1996b: 76–82, 2003: 24–45 (with further bibliography); useful discussion of the phenomenon of 'wandering poets' in Hardie 1983: 15–30.

[13] Cf. Guarducci 1929: 640–4, Chaniotis 1988b, and Chaniotis (this volume).

[14] For the Artists cf. Aneziri (this volume), with further bibliography; several of the contributions to Wilson 2007b contain relevant material.

[15] Guarducci no. xii is an honorary decree for the tragedian Dymas of Iasos from his native city, cf. Rutherford 2007. Cf. also A. Schachter and W. J. Slater, *ZPE* 163 (2008) 81–95.

Introduction 5

but perhaps the differences have been exaggerated. The recently published epigram-book of Posidippus of Pella[16] shows a remarkable engagement with a wide range of cities, both within and without the Ptolemaic orbit, and epigraphic evidence seems to confirm that Posidippus was indeed no immobile composer of epigrams;[17] he was honoured as Posidippus ὁ ἐπι-γραμματοποιός at Thermi and probably also at Delphi.[18] It is as clear as such things can be that Theocritus too was a travelling, if not actually a 'wandering', poet; his poetic activity seems to embrace at least Sicily and the Greek west, Alexandria, and the eastern Aegean. *Idyll* 28 celebrates the poet's journey to Miletus to visit his friend (and patron?) Nicias, and *Idyll* 15 marks (*inter alia*) the coming of Sicilian mime traditions (i.e. the poetry of Theocritus) to Alexandria. At the opening of *Idyll* 16 Theocritus complains that no one will receive his 'Graces' into his home, but everyone sends them away 'without a gift', so that they complain that their journey (ὁδός) has been in vain; *Idyll* 17, a hexameter encomium of Ptolemy Philadelphus, is a surviving example of a type of poetry probably performed all over the Hellenistic Aegean and beyond.[19]

As for Callimachus, the standard picture of him is of a man who travelled once from his home in Cyrene to Alexandria, where he then stayed safe in the Library. We should not give such a picture too much unthinking credence,[20] any more than it is necessary to assume that poems on Cyrenean subjects must have been written in Cyrene. What is important in the present context is that when in the *Aitia* (fr. 178.32–3 Pf.) Callimachus speaks as though ignorant of sea-travel, he is not merely revising a stance associated with Hesiod (cf. *Works and Days* 648–53), the authorising 'model' for the *Aitia*, and situating himself within a specifically Hellenistic discourse about how information is gathered, recorded and disseminated (a discourse about ἱστορίη in fact), but he is also reacting against a very traditional image of how poets operate.[21] Some suggestive evidence from Hellenistic poetry must, however, be treated very carefully. The imagination of Hellenistic poets was filled with a 'sacred geography' of the past in which places were associated with famous poetic figures – Chios of course

---

[16] Bastianini and Gallazzi 2001.
[17] This is not to imply that we know very much about who wrote the thousands of funerary epigrams, of very varying levels of ambition, which survive from the post-classical period; it is normally assumed that they are the work of local ('amateur' or 'professional') poets, but there can be no certainty, and we can hardly discount the possibility that many are the work of 'poeti vaganti', perhaps indeed one of their staple forms of commission.
[18] Cf. Test. 2–4 in Austin and Bastianini 2002, Fraser 1972: I 557, II 796–7. For the geographic breadth of his poems cf. Bing 2005 (with earlier bibliography).
[19] Cf. Hunter 2003.   [20] Cf. Cameron 1995: 49–53.
[21] On these various aspects of fr. 178 cf. Hunter 1996a, Fantuzzi and Hunter 2004: 76–83.

6   RICHARD HUNTER AND IAN RUTHERFORD

with Homer, Mount Helicon with Hesiod, Paros with Archilochus, Lesbos
with Sappho, and so forth; the cults of poets in their home towns and
elsewhere reinforced this map of 'sacred' space.[22] In these circumstances
'travel to' such places can be a matter of literary association and imitation
rather than of physical relocation. Callimachus apparently claims that he
is criticised for writing 'Hipponactean' choliambics although he has never
been to Ephesus, the home of Hipponax (fr. 203.11–14 Pf.); literary 'travel'
can thus take more than one form.[23] The act of reading itself, as the modern
Greek verb διαβάζειν shows, is a movement across space.

An important draw for professional poets and singers at all periods were
musical competitions held at local and pan-Hellenic festivals. These were
particularly widespread in the Hellenistic and imperial periods, though
their origins go back much earlier: the first musical contest of which we
know was that held at the funeral games of Amphidamas at Chalcis in
Euboea, to which Hesiod travelled the short distance from his home and
where he claims to have won a tripod (*Works and Days* 654–7), a claim which
(in part) gave rise to the famous story of 'the contest of Homer and Hesiod'.
Particularly in the early period, the major musical competitions tended to
focus on a limited range of genres and performances, notably kitharody
(which in practice could mean many different forms of poem sung to the
kithara), and rhapsody, i.e. the recitation of Homeric epic. Performances of
drama and choral lyric were rarer at festivals outside Athens (the participation of foreign poets in the dithyrambic contest of the Athenian Dionysia
is a striking exception to general practice), but drama and choral lyric seem
to have figured in the *Sōtēria* at Delphi.[24] In the *Homeric Hymn to Apollo*
we find a visiting poet apparently performing at a festival on Delos and
offering to carry the fame of his hosts 'over all the land which I travel to the
well-ordered cities of men' (vv. 174–5). In Plato's *Ion* Socrates interrogates
a rhapsode just after he has returned from success at the festival of the
Asklēpieia at Epidauros, and Socrates teases him with 'rhapsodising as he
travels around[25] Greece' (541b8). For the early period a distinction between
'poets' who perform their own compositions and 'rhapsodes' performing
the works of others is at best blurred, at least as far as performance at public
festivals is concerned,[26] and it is certainly not to be pressed. The 'Lives

---

[22] Cf. Clay 2004.
[23] Cf. also Nossis, *AP* 7.718 (= *HE* 2831–4), with Fantuzzi and Hunter 2004:16.
[24] On the terms 'rhapsody' and 'kitharody' cf. Ford 1988; for the *Sōtēria* at Delphi cf. Sifakis 1967:
63–85, Nachtergael 1977: 306–8.
[25] περιιών probably plays on Ion's name, cf., e.g., Montiglio 2005:106; cf., however, *Republic* 10.600d7.
[26] Cf. Graziosi 2002: 18–49, with earlier bibliography.

Introduction

of Homer' (of very varied dates) and the 'Contest of Homer and Hesiod' tell us about the alleged travels of Homer himself,[27] but these traditions perhaps reflect as much a belief about the appeal and spread of Homeric poetry as a shaping of Homer after the fashion of subsequent 'wandering poets'.[28]

The itinerancy, both real and imagined, of poets is intimately tied to the ambitions of and for their poetry to enjoy fame and reception all over the world.[29] Theognis' claim to his beloved Kyrnos is perhaps the most celebrated instance of this idea:

> σοὶ μὲν ἐγὼ πτέρ' ἔδωκα, σὺν οἷς ἐπ' ἀπείρονα πόντον
> πωτήσηι καὶ γῆν πᾶσαν ἀειρόμενος
> ῥηιδίως· θοίνηις δὲ καὶ εἰλαπίνηισι παρέσσηι
> ἐν πάσαις κτλ.

I have given you wings, which will carry you easily as you fly over the boundless sea and every land. You will be present at every feast and celebration . . . (Theognis 237–40)

Even after his death, Kyrnos will continue to roam (στρωφώμενος, 247) the Greek world, transported, as are both poems and poets, by the gifts of the Muses. So too, Pindar imagines his song in honour of Pytheas of Aegina travelling over the world and thus spreading the fame of both patron and poet:

> οὐκ ἀνδριαντοποιός εἰμ', ὥστ' ἐλινύσοντα ἐργά-
> ζεσθαι ἀγάλματ' ἐπ' αὐτᾶς βαθμίδος
> ἑσταότ'· ἀλλ' ἐπὶ πάσας
> ὁλκάδος ἔν τ' ἀκάτωι, γλυκεῖ' ἀοιδά,
> στεῖχ' ἀπ' Αἰγίνας διαγγέλλοισ', ὅτι
> Λάμπωνος υἱὸς Πυθέας εὐρυσθενής
> νίκη Νεμείοις παγκρατίου στέφανον κτλ.

I am not a maker of statues, so as to fashion unmoving images which remain standing on the same base. Rather, on every ship and boat, sweet song, go out from Aigina, bearing the news that mighty Pytheas, the son of Lampon, has won the crown for the pancratium at the Nemean games . . . (Pindar, *Nemean* 5.1–5)

No image for the process of composing or enacting a poem is as common as that of a journey, sometimes, as we have seen, a flight above the earthbound, pedestrian (πεζός) world of prose.[30] The idea is strikingly thematised in the *Argonautica* of Apollonius Rhodius in which, as has been

---

[27] These are most easily accessible in West 2003.   [28] Cf. Graziosi 2002.
[29] Cf., e.g., Montiglio 2005: 98–9.   [30] Cf. Becker 1937, Asper 1997: 21–107.

8   RICHARD HUNTER AND IAN RUTHERFORD

well recognised, the wanderings of the heroes are overtly linked to the wandering paths of song and the narrator almost travels as an extra Argonaut himself.

Travelling poets, and honorific decrees for them, continue to be well attested in the Roman Empire and later antiquity; there is a strong sense of continuity with the pre-imperial world. For the earlier imperial period we may cite the case of Paion of Pamphylian Side, who held high office at Pergamum, received citizenship from Tarsos and Rhodes, and whose epigrams, like those of Julia Balbilla, were inscribed on the statue of Memnon at Thebes in Egypt; a surviving inscription describes Paion as 'a poet of very many victories, lyric poet and rhapsode of the divine Hadrian', and another hails him as 'devoted to the Emperor' (φιλοκαίσαρ) and 'a new Homer'.[31] In the early second century Halicarnassus rewarded a poet from Aphrodisias, C. Julius Longianus, who had given 'varied performances (ἐπιδείξεις) of all kinds of poems', with full citizenship and twenty bronze statues to be erected 'in all the most distinguished places in the city, including the *temenos* of the Muses and the gymnasium of the ephebes, next to Herodotus of old'; Longianus' books were also to be deposited in the libraries 'so that the young may be educated by them in the same way as by the writings of the ancients'.[32] Another typical case is Nestor of Laranda in Lycaonia (late second–early third century AD), whom we find honoured at Paphos, Ephesos, Kyzikos and, most notably of all, Roman Ostia;[33] a high-born Roman lady of cultural pretensions (φιλόμουσος) dedicated a statue of him to Aphrodite (and it is perhaps not entirely frivolous to recall the effect which Magnes of Smyrna is said to have had on his female audiences).[34] Of Nestor's many poems very little remains, but he still enjoys a certain notoriety for having composed a 'lipogrammatic' *Iliad*, in which Book 1 contained no α, Book 2 no β, and so on. For the later period, Alan Cameron's study of the phenomenon in late antique Egypt reveals that, even when the poetic competitions had largely died out, many of the same motivations led to poetic mobility, notably the desire to receive commissions for celebrating the antiquities (πάτρια), buildings and local worthies of particular towns.[35]

Dio Chrysostom describes the excitement that the arrival of a 'star' could generate:

---

[31] Cf. Robert 1980: 10–20, Bowie 1989: 202–3, 1990b: 61–6.

[32] *MAMA* VIII.418b, cf. Bowie 1989: 202. Another related inscription (*MAMA* VIII.418c) apparently calls Longianus 'a poet of tragedies'.

[33] Cf. Guarducci 1961, Robert 1980: 20, Weiss 1990: 228–35.

[34] Cf. above pp. 2–3.   [35] Cameron 1965.

Introduction   9

[When I was in Kyzikos] the greatest living kitharode and one, in some people's opinion, not at all inferior to those of the past arrived . . . as soon as people learned that the man was in town (ἐπιδημοῦντα), immediately there was amazing excitement and everyone went off towards the council chamber [where performances would take place]. I myself joined the very front of the crowd, thinking that I too could listen and share with three thousand and more in such a wonderful entertainment . . . (Dio Chrysostom 19.2–3)

The most common form of performance continued to be encomia of the host city and its traditions. The topics of such celebrations in prose and verse are familiar not just from the encomia which survive, but also from the prescriptions gathered together under the name of Menander Rhetor;[36] Dio takes the citizens of Alexandria to task for failing to understand the formulaic and limited nature of such compositions:

Perhaps you enjoy listening to me, and you think that you are being praised when I say these things, as you are by the others who are always flattering you. But I praised water and soil and harbours and places and everything except you yourselves. Where did I call you wise and sensible and just? Was it not rather the opposite? . . . Arrivals and departures of ships, great crowds of people and goods and ships, these are material for encomia of a festival or a harbour or a market-place, not of a city. If someone praises water, this is not praise of men, but of wells; if someone speaks of the good climate, he is not saying that the people are good, but the land; if someone praises fish, he is not praising the city. You, on the other hand, if someone delivers an encomium of the Nile, are as proud as if you yourselves flowed down from Ethiopia. Certainly, most other people also take pleasure in such things, and count themselves blessed if they live, as Homer puts it, on an island which is 'tree-clad' or 'deep-soiled' or in a land which is 'rich in pasture land', 'rich in sheep' or near 'shade-giving mountains' or 'translucent springs'. None of these things belongs to them! Of virtue they take no thought, even in their dreams. (Dio Chrysostom 32.37–8)

For the pre-Hellenistic period, we lack the relative reliability of epigraphic data, and have therefore to rely more on claims made by other writers about poets, or by the poets themselves. Plato certainly assumes a world of itinerant poets. In the *Republic* Socrates explains what would happen to a supreme artist of *mimēsis*:

So then, if a man whose cleverness allowed him to become anything he wanted and to imitate all manner of things were to come to our city, and bring his poems with him, and he wanted to put on a performance (ἐπιδείξασθαι), we would bow before him as being holy and wonderful and a source of pleasure; we would, however, tell

---

[36] Cf. Men. Rhet. 344.15–367.8 Spengel = pp. 28–74 Russell and Wilson, Hendriks, Parsons and Worp 1981: 74–5; for the earlier period cf. Kienzle 1936.

him that it is not lawful for such a man to be in our city, and we would send him off to another city, having poured unguent over his head and crowned him with a fillet of wool. (Plato, *Republic* 3.398a)

The most famous 'wandering poet' of Greek literature, though in a rather special sense, is of course Odysseus himself, and such poets are a familiar feature of the society which the *Odyssey* creates (cf. *Odyssey* 17.382–7).[37] In the *Odyssey* itself, however, poets seem to be tied to specific courts, Demodokos on Phaeacia and Phemios on Ithaca. If there was only a small number of major political centres (as seems likely for the Late Bronze Age), then we might indeed expect poets to have been closely tied to these centres, with very little mobility and catering almost entirely to a local audience.[38] When, however, the arrogant Antinoos delivers a tirade against (wandering) beggars, Homer's Eumaeus (*Odyssey* 17.380–91) points out that invited strangers are most likely to be one of four types of 'craftsmen' (*dēmiourgoi*) who are invited from abroad, and one of these types is the divine singer.[39] If poets are not actually shown travelling, it is clear that poems do. Demodokos has learned a song of events at Troy (from where?, cf. *Odyssey* 8.487–91),[40] and before Odysseus returns to Ithaca Phemios can sing of the 'terrible return of the Achaeans from Troy which Pallas Athena imposed upon them' (*Odyssey* 1.326–7); when Odysseus proudly claims that he is 'known to all men and my fame reaches heaven' (*Odyssey* 9.19–20), he will be thinking of epic song.[41] Odysseus' travels themselves may be read, like the 'Lives of Homer',[42] as a dramatisation of the spread of epic song all over the known (and unknown) world; here again we may recall the promise to the maidens of Delos from the 'blind man of Chios' (*Homeric Hymn to Apollo* 174–6).[43]

As they travelled, poets of the archaic and classical periods carried many different kinds of poetry ('genres') with them, and such travel often led to innovation.[44] Decisive moments in the poetic, as in the cultic, history of a community often came by way of an intervention or arrival from outside, such as is recorded for Olen from Lycia, when he composed what

[37] Cf. further below. For some of the characteristics which distinguish Odysseus from a 'real' bard cf. Scodel 1998.

[38] For the Bronze Age cf. Bachvarova (this volume). These issues of cultural mobility are well summed up by Moyer 2006.

[39] The whole of Burkert 1992 may be seen as an extended gloss on these verses of Eumaeus.

[40] On this passage cf., e.g., De Jong 2001: 214–15.

[41] On this passage cf., e.g., Danek 1998: 160–1.   [42] Cf. above p. 7.

[43] Cf. above p. 6, Martin (this volume) pp. 89–90. For another way in which the 'wanderings' of Homer and Odysseus resemble each other cf. 'Longinus', *On the Sublime* 9.13.

[44] Cf. Bowie (this volume), Martin (this volume) on *polyeideia*.

Introduction

were to become the traditional Apolline hymns at Delos.[45] In her chapter in this volume, Mary Bachvarova suggests that in the Late Bronze Age songs and singers most often travelled in the context of the wholesale relocation of religious cults. Although there is no conclusive evidence that this pattern ever predominated in Greece, in the Bronze Age or in any other period, the idea is very suggestive and some of our evidence would certainly be consistent with that model. What little we know of the seventh-century poet and musician Thaletas of Cretan Gortyn well illustrates the extraordinary 'internationalism' of the archaic period. This musician (and wonder-worker?) is said to have ended a plague at Sparta and then been celebrated in a poem by Polymnestos of Colophon commissioned by the Spartans.[46] Plutarch's history of music at Sparta strikingly suggests the mobility of the archaic period:

The first organisation of music at Sparta was directed by Terpander [of Lesbos]; the principal leaders of the second were Thaletas of Gortyn, Xenodamos of Cythera, Xenocritos of Locri, Polymnestos of Colophon, and Sacadas of Argos . . . (Plutarch, De musica 1134b–c)

So too, Alcman, the most famous poet of archaic Sparta, is often said to have been a Lydian from Sardis, but ancient scholars were unable to settle the matter of his origin; perhaps the status of an 'outsider' was invented, or became important, because it was felt to be an obligatory one for an effective political poet.[47]

The wealthy court of a powerful ruler could draw in poetic talent from a broad catchment area, as Polycrates of Samos attracted Ibycus from Rhegium in the west and Anacreon from Teos. According to Herodotus, Arion from Lesbian Methymna spent most of his time at the court of Periander, ruler of Corinth, although he also travelled to Italy and Sicily where he made a great deal of money (1.24.1). The tyrant Peisistratus is said to have brought (κομίζειν) not only the poetry of Homer to Athens, but also Anacreon and Simonides of Ceos in person;[48] Simonides also spent time at courts in Thessaly and Sicily, and was subsequently portrayed as the archetypal money-grubbing poet, who attached himself to one patron

---

[45] Cf. Herodotus 4.35.3, Callimachus, Hymn to Delos 304–5, Pausanias 10.5.8–9 (who follows the tradition that made Olen a Hyperborean).

[46] Pausanias 1.14.4, cf. D'Alessio (this volume) p. 155. Movement the other way was perhaps less frequent: at Plato, Laws 3.680c the Cretan explains his relative ignorance even of Homer by the fact that 'Cretans are not very familiar with foreign (ξενικά) poems'.

[47] The testimonia for Alcman are conveniently available in Campbell 1988. Cf. also Martin 1992 on Hesiod's 'outsider' status, and D'Alessio (this volume) on Tyrtaeus.

[48] [Plato], Hipparchus 228b–c.

after another, the 'poet as chancer' (cf. Theocritus 16.34–47).[49] This pattern was to persist for centuries – Aeschylus put on plays in Sicily under the patronage of Hieron,[50] Euripides and Agathon are said to have accepted the hospitality of King Archelaos at Pella in Macedonia,[51] Aratus from Cilician Soli enjoyed the patronage of Antigonus Gonatas, and the Alexandria of the Ptolemies played host to the poetic and scholarly world; this was a rôle which it was soon to cede to Rome. The pattern is dramatised in letters written by Alciphron (second century AD) in which the comic poet Menander and his courtesan girlfriend Glykera weigh up the pros and cons of an invitation from Ptolemy I Soter. A different form of poetic travelling is illustrated by the career of Solon of Athens (early sixth century BC); after his political reforms in his own city he travelled widely, and part of his farewell to Soli in Cyprus and its ruler is preserved:[52]

αὐτὰρ ἐμὲ ξὺν νηὶ θοῆι κλεινῆς ἀπὸ νήσου
ἀσκηθῆ πέμποι Κύπρις ἰοστέφανος·
οἰκισμῶι δ' ἐπὶ τῶιδε χάριν καὶ κῦδος ὀπάζοι
ἐσθλὸν καὶ νόστον πατρίδ' ἐς ἡμετέρην.

May the violet-crowned Cyprian goddess send me on a swift ship away from your renowned island. May she grant favour and glory to this settlement and a fair return to my homeland. (Solon fr. 19.2–6 West)

It is lyric and particularly epinician poetry about which we hear most in this context; the great pan-Hellenic athletic festivals offered rich opportunities for the greatest poets, and such opportunities often involved travel, whether to the games, to the victor's home city, or to both. The fifth century before the Peloponnesian War was the golden age of the festivals and the poetry which they inspired. Simonides, Pindar and Bacchylides wrote songs for patrons from all over Greece, and they will have visited many of their patrons' cities (as Pindar represents himself as training a chorus on Ceos in the First Isthmian), although poems were presumably also conveyed to a patron's home by a third party; we know very little indeed about the processes involved in the training of choruses and the delivery of poems when the poet himself was absent. Pindar has a very rich imagery and language of travel for both himself and his poems and this, combined with

[49] Cf. Hunter 1996b: 97–109.
[50] Cf. Griffith 1978, Wilson in Wilson 2007a. For the lure of the west in the archaic period cf., e.g., Ford 2002: 49–52.
[51] Cf. Revermann 1999–2000; for the sceptical case against Euripides' Macedonian stay cf. Scullion 2003.
[52] Cf. Gallo 1976, Lefkowitz 1981: 45, Noussia 2001: 276–80, Bowie (this volume) p. 115.

Introduction

the difficulties of interpreting the first person in his poems,[53] makes the drawing of conclusions from the poems themselves fraught with pitfalls. Even in a case which might seem straightforward, such as the opening of *Pythian* 2, we can hardly be sure that Pindar himself was present in Sicily:

μεγαλοπόλιες ὦ Συράκοσαι, βαθυπολέμου
τέμενος Ἄρεος, ἀνδρῶν ἵππων τε σιδαροχαρ-
μᾶν δαιμόνιαι τροφοί,
ὔμμιν τόδε τᾶν λιπαρᾶν ἀπὸ Θηβᾶν φέρων
μέλος ἔρχομαι ἀγγελίαν τετραορίας ἐλελίχθονος κτλ.

O great city of Syracuse, enclosure of the warrior Ares, divine nurse of men and of horses which delight in steel, I have come bringing you from gleaming Thebes this song which tells of the four-horsed chariot which shook the earth . . . (Pindar, *Pythian* 2.1–4)

At the opening of *Nemean* 9 the Muses are invited by the first-person poetic voice to join a *kōmos* from the temple of Apollo at Sikyon where Chromios had won his victory to the hospitable home of the victor in Sicilian Etna:

κωμάσομεν παρ' Ἀπόλλωνος Σικυωνόθε, Μοῖσαι,
τὰν νεοκτίσταν ἐς Αἴτναν, ἔνθ' ἀναπεπταμέναι
ξείνων νενίκανται θύραι,
ὄλβιον ἐς Χρομίου
δῶμ'.

Let us go in revel, Muses, from Apollo at Sikyon to newly founded Aitna, where the doors, flung open, are thronged by guests, to the blessed house of Chromios. (Pindar, *Nemean* 9.1–3)

As this opening illustrates, poets of the archaic and early classical period tend to represent the relationship between themselves and their patrons as an exchange relationship of *xenia* between two élite friends, but it is likely that financial transactions were in fact fundamental to the 'song culture', even when we have made allowance for the satirical purposes of an Aristophanes, who makes Pindar's *hyporchēma* for the foundation of Sicilian Etna (fr. 105 M) the model performance for the charlatan travelling poet.[54]

The song-culture of Athens might seem to have been relatively autochthonous and to have remained generally independent of the mobility of the rest of the Greek world. Athenian citizenship does seem to have been required for participation in a chorus,[55] but poets could indeed come from

---

[53] For guidance to the huge bibliography cf. Braswell's notes on *Nemean* 1.19–24 and 9.1.
[54] Cf. Martin (this volume). On issues of 'exchange' cf. Kurke 1991: 85–107, Von Reden 1995, with earlier bibliography; for *xenia* cf. Herman 1987.
[55] For drama cf. Kaimio 1999.

abroad; in the *Laws* Plato seems to assume a world in which tragic poets moved freely from city to city (7.817a–c). The early records for Athenian dithyrambic competition attribute victory in fact only to foreign poets, starting with the first (510/8BC) which was won by Hypodikos of Chalcis; the most celebrated in the fifth century were Simonides of Ceos, Pindar of Thebes and Melanippides of Melos. Some of the early tragic poets at Athens were also foreign: Pratinas of Phlius and his son Aristias, Akhaios of Eretria, a celebrated writer of satyr-plays, the versatile Ion of Chios, and Akestor, who was reputed to be a Mysian. On the other hand, comic poets in the fifth century tended to be home-grown, and it is an obvious guess that this is to be connected with the very topical nature of Old Comedy; even here, however, caution is necessary, as there is respectable evidence that some plays of Old Comedy at least found audiences outside Athens.[56] Be that as it may, things certainly changed – as did the nature of comedy – and Alexis from Thurii, Diphilus from Sinope, Philemon (who became an Athenian citizen) from Syracuse or Cilician Soli and Apollodorus from Carystos join the Athenian Menander as the great poets of New Comedy. For the fifth century, the only exception to the home-grown rule seems to be Hegemon of Thasos, better known as a poet of *parōidia*. A surviving fragment of one of his poems provides a vivid account of the pressures that drew him from his island home to seek professional advancement in the big city.[57]

THE POETIC JOURNEY

Singers and poets travel in many societies, perhaps most. Matsuo Basho, the famous seventeenth-century Japanese master, spent much of his life 'on the road', composing epigrammatic *haiku*s about the places he visited; the most famous such work was Oku no Hosomichi ('Narrow road to the Interior'). As in Greek poetry, topographic allusion came to play an important part in Japanese poetics, especially through the device of the 'utamakura' (poem-pillow).[58] In late Medieval Europe, travelling singers and poets are a familiar and much studied phenomenon, notably in Ireland and Provence.[59] By examining the provenance of musicians and singers associated with various German cities in the Middle Ages, Walter Salmen was able to document the economy of travelling poets with a degree of precision greater than is possible from the Greek material; he shows, for example, that the city of

---

[56] Cf. Taplin 1993.
[57] The fragment is preserved by Athenaeus 15.698d–f, cf. Brandt 1888: 42–4.
[58] See Shirane 1998.   [59] See Martin (this volume).

Introduction　　　15

Messestadt-Nördlingen was visited by minstrels from some thirty places, ranging from Denmark in the north to Vienna and Hungary in the south east. The underlying principle here indeed still seems to be that of a market economy: singers travel to where they can find employment, and the best singers migrate to where they will be paid most.[60]

A rather different form of engagement between poets and places emerges from the study of poetic itinerancy in medieval India. A useful case-study here is the movement of religious poets in the southern Tamil area of India, illuminated by the work of Indira Viswanathan Peterson. The poems commemorate the numerous temples in Tamilnadu dedicated to the god Shiva, and it is possible to reconstruct the routes that these poets followed in their worship of the deities, journeys which have been interpreted as a sort of pilgrimage; it is unclear whether the motivation here was wholly religious, or whether there are further factors involved, such as commission and payment. At any rate, the result of this process of poetic itinerancy is the creation of a literature which commemorates the complex sacred geography of the region.[61]

Singers and minstrels still travel in many societies today. In western Africa, for example, griots move around.[62] In the 1970s the Dutch ethno-musicologist Veit Erlmann studied the circulation of musicians and singers in contemporary West Africa, specifically among the Fulani of Diamare in north Cameroon.[63] He collected evidence for the distance and time-table of such travel, and also studied the long-term history of poets' itinerancy, seeing it as reflecting a specific set of historical circumstances, namely the break-up of the Islamic empire in the nineteenth century and the onset of new colonial political structures. Broadly speaking, Erlmann suggests that (a) a century ago these musicians tended to be permanently attached to courts in the larger cities, whereas in more recent decades they have made temporary trips to the centres, being however permanently located in the countryside; and (b) this new relationship between cities and coun-tryside has tended to produce major changes in the nature of the music itself.

Comparative evidence like this can be useful in helping us to understand developments in poetic itinerancy in ancient Greece. With Erlmann's model of poetic change, for example, one might compare the development from the hypothetical poetic economy of the Greek Bronze Age, when poets are supposed to have been attached to royal courts, to the much freer situation of the Iron Age. In general, however, it is the circulating poets of Medieval

---

[60] Cf. Salmen 1960:159 with diagram.　　　[61] Peterson 1983.　　　[62] Hale 1998.　　　[63] Erlmann 1983.

16   RICHARD HUNTER AND IAN RUTHERFORD

Europe who seem to provide the best analogy, whereas the Japanese example
of Basho suggests rather a contrast with the Greek world: Greek poets (*qua*
poets) do not for the most part 'wander' in search of knowledge or spiritual enlightenment, or to perform religious services, though – like other
men – they may travel to cultic sites to witness festivals or be initiated
into mysteries.[64] Where we do encounter figures of spiritual quest in the
Greek world, they tend rather to be 'holy men', like the wonder-working
Hyperborean Abaris,[65] and much later Apollonius of Tyana, whose travels and wisdom fill the pages of Philostratus' *Life*. This is not to say, of
course, that poets never represent the process of intellectual and/or poetical
enlightenment as a journey; this is, for example, clearly one element in the
famous proem of Parmenides' philosophical poem. Here we may also perhaps place the fascinating figure of Aristeas of Proconessus, the seventh- or
sixth-century author of an hexameter *Arimaspeia* which told of his wanderings in the far north of the world and in which he may have presented
himself as a 'shaman' with the ability to travel outside his body.[66]

THE CIRCULATION OF POETRY

Poets, of course, hardly ever literally 'wander',[67] unless perhaps they have
been exiled, as Bacchylides (to the Peloponnese: Plutarch, *De exil.* 605d)
and Sappho (to Sicily: T 251 Voigt) are said to have been.[68] Rather, in
order to understand poetic itinerancy, we have to make some distinction,
however fluid it may be, between 'professional' poets, and men (and occasionally women) for whom composing and performing poetry were not
the principal activities of their lives (cf. Bowie, this volume). Particularly in
the early period some of the best known 'poets' were thoroughly enmeshed
in the political and military life of their societies – Archilochus of Paros,
Alcaeus of Mytilene, Solon of Athens and Theognis of Megara are clear
examples. Such 'poets' might of course travel for the reasons people normally travelled: to trade, to take part in warfare, to found colonies, to visit
friends and contacts within the context of aristocratic guest–friend relations
(Solon's journey to Cyprus perhaps belongs here). This, of course, is not to
say that those who seem to have been 'full-time poets' necessarily avoided
such engagement, or were not caught up in the events which swirled around
them: Anacreon took part in the foundation of Abdera. Even in the later

[64] Cf. Dickie 1998.   [65] Cf. Herodotus 4.36.   [66] Cf. Herodotus 4.13–15, Bolton 1962.
[67] Cf. Erlmann 1983: 203: 'the average professional singer of Fulani society is not a purposeless "rover",
but rather prefers carefully planned trips to selected places'.
[68] On exile cf. Gaertner 2007.

Introduction 17

period of increased professionalisation poets might go on religious missions (cf. Anyte of Tegea, discussed by Rutherford, below pp. 241–2), or – like everyone else – suffer forcible displacement as the result of punishment or enslavement, as was supposed to have happened at the hands of Dionysius of Syracuse to Philoxenus of Cythera in the classical period, and certainly happened to Parthenius of Nikaia in the first century BC.[69] In many cases, however, the question 'poet or part-timer?' is likely to mistake the nature of ancient culture and the place of poetry within it. Heraclitus of Halicarnassus was a poet (one epigram survives) and is celebrated as such in a famous epigram of Callimachus;[70] he is, however, very likely also the Heraclitus who appears on *proxenos* inscriptions from Euboean Histiaia and Chios and was honoured in the sanctuary of Amphiaraos at Oropos in northern Attica; a modern study calls him 'poet and diplomat',[71] and this does not seem unfair.

Professional poets, or poets in so far as they are professionals, travel in order to perform. This was a simple fact of life, though as we have seen it does not exhaust the possibilities of poetic circulation. A poet might hope that his works will be disseminated by other performers or, particularly from the Hellenistic period on, in written form: either of these possibilities would cover Theognis of Megara's promise to Kyrnos (cited above p. 7). Pindar seems occasionally to send a poem to his patron rather than engaging in a performative delivery of it himself.[72] Nevertheless, physical travel remained fundamental to much poetic circulation throughout antiquity. Over time we see a gradual shift towards a more explicit professionalism on the part of the poets and also a shift in generic range: whereas in the classical period poets composed and produced choral songs for local communities and local choirs, in the Hellenistic period we find largely hexameter poetry on the antiquities and famous personalities of the host community. What has changed is the nature of the poetic culture; the practices and phenomenon of 'wandering' remain remarkably stable.

Some of the principal (though obviously not mutually exclusive) contexts for poetic travelling are:

1 Poets travel to perform in cities, expecting to get commissions from individuals and cities along the way; this may have been the most common form of poetic itinerancy at all periods. It is for the most part what the *poeti vaganti* commemorated in the decrees collected by Guarducci were

---

[69] For the evidence and discussion cf. Lightfoot 1999: 3–16.
[70] Cf. Hunter 1992. [71] Swinnen 1970.
[72] Cf, above p. 13. There is one example of this among the 'poeti vaganti' decrees as well: see Guarducci 1929, no. xvi (pp. 654–5).

doing, and must have been the most direct way of making one's poetic repertoire known to the Greek world at large, and of gaining a reputation for oneself as a performer. For understandable reasons, a poet's route might come to resemble a more or less endless circuit.

2 Poets travel to perform in the festivals held at major sanctuaries, and some poets may perhaps have become permanently linked to a specific sanctuary. Festivals might also be a place where a poet could acquire further commissions from those attending, and this might of course involve further travelling; thus a poet of victory odes might receive a new commission during the games and then travel to the victor's home city to perform his composition.

3 Poets travel to other festivals and élite or public gatherings to take part in poetic competitions. Hesiod's performance at funeral games at Chalcis in Euboea is perhaps the best known example. In some cases, poetic competitions may have taken place as part of the process of a public commission for poetry.[73]

4 Poets might travel to the court of a tyrant or king, perhaps as the result of an invitation, and enjoy there a semi-permanent residency. Anacreon's periods at the courts of Polycrates of Samos and Hipparchus of Athens are a good example here, and as we have seen this pattern was a very long-lived one throughout antiquity.[74] Two of Hesiod's examples of intra-craft rivalry are 'beggar v. beggar' and 'bard v. bard' (*Works and Days* 26); it is at least a nice fantasy to imagine two poets squabbling for 'territory' like the beggar Iros and the disguised Odysseus at the Ithacan palace.

5 A city might issue an invitation to a foreign poet to compose a song for a specific purpose.[75] In cases like this it may be relevant that distant experts are sometimes regarded as possessing special knowledge, and cultural capital may be attached to such 'foreigners'. The anthropologist Mary Helms has argued that in many early societies experts who come from a distance are accorded greater respect than locals. In the case of Greece, preference could have been given to poets from other parts of Greece who had already established a reputation in the broader pan-Hellenic community.[76]

6 A poet might travel with a powerful patron. Lysander is said to have kept the epic poet Choerilos of Samos with him at all times, and to have had other poets as well in his retinue (Plutarch, *Lysander* 18.4).[77] Epic poets such as another Choerilos, from Iasos in Caria, and the wholly obscure Agis of Argos accompanied Alexander the Great on his

---

[73] Cf. Petrovic (this volume). [74] Cf. above pp. 11–12. [75] Cf. above p. 11 on Thaletas of Gortyn.
[76] Cf. Helms 1988, Von Reden 1995, D'Alessio (this volume).
[77] For Lysander and Choerilos cf. Huxley 1969.

Introduction

campaigns;[78] Python's satyric play *Agēn* was composed at the Hydaspes River during Alexander's campaign (Athenaeus 13.595e = *TrGF* I 91 F1). Once again the pattern persisted: Ennius followed his Roman patrons during their campaigns in Greece. In a rather different category perhaps is Julia Balbilla who accompanied Hadrian and Sabina to Egypt in 130 AD and whose epigrams, written in an archaising aeolic dialect, were carved on the colossal statue of Memnon.[79]

7 Occasionally poets and musicians seem to have carried out diplomatic activities, as we see in the case of the diplomats from the musical city of Teos who performed music and songs in the course of their stay in Cretan cities, and this pattern may have been more widespread.[80] In the second half of the first century BC, the epigrammatist Crinagoras of Mytilene, obviously a person of high standing in his city, was sent by his city as a member of a diplomatic missions to Julius Caesar and then to Augustus at Rome and elsewhere.[81]

POETS AND PLACES

From the very earliest days, marked for us by the Homeric Catalogue of Ships, a striking element in Greek poetry was the description of locality and the delineation of local traditions.[82] One thinks of archaic hymns, such as Alcaeus' hymn for Itonian Athena (see Bowie, this volume), Pindar's choral compositions for local communities such as Abdera and Ceos (see D'Alessio, this volume), Callimachus' *Aitia*, Hellenistic local epics, such as Rhianus' *Messeniaka*, and local encomia, such as the so-called 'Pride of Halicarnassus', a publicly inscribed encomium of this city in sixty elegiac verses.[83] As the case of Callimachus makes particularly clear, both local and foreign poets played a rôle in celebrating local traditions; there is indeed a degree of productive cross-fertilisation between local traditions and poets from elsewhere, who bring to those traditions an external and pan-Hellenic perspective.

What we call 'ancient Greece' was in fact a loose network of several hundred city-states of varying size, stretching from Ionia to Sicily and from Thrace to Libya,[84] a far from homogeneous area, ethnically, linguistically or religiously, and one lacking major political centres to impose a unified tradition. One of the principal things that held this network together, however, was a loose pan-Hellenic *koinē* of mythological and genealogical

---

[78] Quintus Curtius 8.5.7–8; Arrian, Anab. 4.9.9.   [79] Cf. above p. 8 on Paion of Side.
[80] Chaniotis 1988a, and above p. 17 on Heraclitus of Halicarnassus.
[81] Cf. Gow and Page 1968: 210–12.   [82] Cf., e.g., Kienzle 1936, Vetta and Catenacci 2006.
[83] *SGO* 01/12/02, cf. Isager and Pedersen 2004.   [84] See Hansen and Nielsen 2004.

20   RICHARD HUNTER AND IAN RUTHERFORD

traditions relating to and engaging a broad range of different regions and
cities, the 'collective memory' of the Greeks, to use Jan Assman's terminology.[85] Within these traditions, a balance was maintained between on
the one hand a shared Greek identity, epitomised in the canonical pan-
Hellenic myths (Heracles, the Argonauts, the Seven Against Thebes, the
Trojan Cycle), and on the other hand local traditions, which needed to
be explained by aetiologies within the context of the 'big tradition'. Thus,
one of the main functions of the shared cultural tradition was to provide an ideological fabric connecting the different Greek cities. These key
themes – national identity, local aetiology and connectivity – are ones that
poetic traditions had a key rôle in creating, disseminating and perpetuating. One thinks first, perhaps, of genealogical poetry such as the Hesiodic
Catalogue of Women, which unified by articulating a framework of mythological ancestors linked sentimentally with terrain.[86] In a different way, the
Homeric 'Catalogue of Ships' achieved a similar end, since to recount the
home-cities of the Greek fleet at Troy was to assert the common traditions
of Greek cities in the contemporary world. The same is true of less ambitious poems focusing on a single place and drawing out connections to
other places and to the whole Greek cultural network. Thus, for example,
Pindar's songs for Aegina not only create a cultural tradition for that island,
but also situate it within the overall Greek mythological network.[87]

The circulation of itinerant poets and intellectuals is a factor that
strengthened the cultural pan-Hellenic network in the classical and
Hellenistic periods, and may also have played a rôle in creating that network in the eighth century or before, by promulgating mythological and
genealogical traditions that bound communities together. Itinerant poets
were particularly well suited to play this rôle precisely because they were
perceived as representing a non-local, pan-Hellenic perspective from which
the value of local traditions could best be judged. Some poets may even have
transcended the condition of being tied to any one Greek city and assumed
a supervenient pan-Hellenic identity: the place of Homer, over whom many
cities competed, in the Greek cultural imagination is, as always, the limit
case here.[88]

This book aims to map the terrain over which some poets wandered
and to ask about the history and cultural meaning of such wandering. It is

[85] Cf. Chaniotis (this volume).
[86] Cf. West 1985, Hunter 2005; for other cultures cf. Hale 1998 on griots and genealogical poetry.
[87] Cf., e.g., Burnett 2004.
[88] Hesiod too presents himself as not belonging to any city in particular, but rather as 'metanastic', to
use Richard Martin's convenient term (Martin 1992).

Introduction

divided into three overlapping parts. The first considers the possible history of the phenomenon and the hold that the idea of the 'wandering poet' held over the Greek imagination in both mythical and historical times. Mary Bachvarova explores the phenomenon as one not isolated in archaic Greece, but shared with, and perhaps deriving from, the great earlier cultures to the east, notably Hittite culture. Peter Wilson examines the 'ancient and persistent presence' of Thamyras of Thrace, who competed unsuccessfully with the Muses, but whose unsettling shadow hung over all who laid claim to poetic greatness; in travelling hopefully, poets also commemorated the legendary figures of the past. In historical times too, poets carried baggage with them. Richard Martin considers Aristophanes' presentation of the poet who comes to celebrate the founding of Cloudcuckooland in the *Birds* as an example of the more or less explicit preconceptions which an Athenian audience might be expected to hold and from which humour could be created. Martin's close reading confirms the remarkable persistence of the phenomenon across ancient and modern cultures.

The second section considers various ways in which the relationship between poets and places not their own was negotiated. Ewen Bowie considers how 'wandering poets' of the archaic period presented themselves in the places they visited and the kind of authority which they created for their poetic voices. Giovan Battista D'Alessio turns to what may be considered a special case of the situations treated by Bowie, namely the remarkable use by communities of 'foreign' lyric poets for the composition of poems which, not unlike the Athenian *epitaphios*, spoke to the most pressing issues of local ideology and identity. Such poets speak for the host community in a manner which shows that what is important here is not geographical origin, but a remarkable communicative strategy; this phenomenon can also shed light upon the elegiac poetry of Tyrtaeus and perhaps on the ancient debate as to whether or not he was a Spartan. The meaning of such engagements between foreign poets and host communities could of course change and be re-interpreted over time, and Lucia Prauscello studies the remarkable use of the classical figure of Timotheus of Miletus by Spartans of the imperial period to rewrite and reinterpret their poetic and cultic history. Only rarely can the full significance of the bringing of outside craft into the heart of a community have been so contested as in this striking case. Finally, Andrej Petrovic considers the specific case of public epigrams: who composed them, how were these poets chosen, and was there an audience beyond the local for such poetry? This study concerns the actual process by which 'wandering poets' plied their trade and the local constraints under which they acted.

The final section focuses on the Hellenistic and imperial worlds, to show the range of the phenomenon under consideration. Sophia Aneziri studies the actual operations of the guilds of Artists of Dionysus, who formed the principal organisations governing the movement and conditions of performers; we know much more about the Artists in this period than we do about the 'wandering poets' of earlier ages, and a key question becomes to what extent we can see a systematisation and formalisation of long-established local practice. Ian Rutherford takes on one of the most intriguing case-studies of the Hellenistic period, namely the poetess Aristodama from Asia Minor, of whom we know because of decrees honouring her for performances in central Greece; there is just enough evidence to allow speculation about the political importance of her poetry for the Aetolian League, and here again we may wonder just how typical such a case is: presumably not every 'wandering poet' got caught up in local politics, but poetry on mythical subjects almost always spoke in antiquity to present concerns, and poets presumably soon became very sensitive interpreters of the local climate. Rutherford's essay leads naturally into Angelos Chaniotis' study of how other types of 'performer', such as historians and ambassadors, carried the cultural memory of states with them and used this in their public displays and speeches. Here we see very clearly that the phenomenon of 'wandering poets' is merely one manifestation of a fact about the Greek world which we, with our eyes set firmly on the Athens of classical drama or the Alexandria of Callimachus, too often forget; it would have looked very different to those who were actually there.

CHAPTER 2

Hittite and Greek perspectives on travelling poets, texts and festivals

Mary R. Bachvarova

INTRODUCTION

The *Homeric Hymn to Apollo* presents a vivid picture of how Greek poets reached audiences beyond their home base, from the self-characterisation of the poet as wandering about visiting cities and festivals (166–76), to the description of the Delian festival where spectators from abroad marvel to hear how accurately the Delian maidens mimic the voices and sounds of all humans in their songs,[1] to the narrative of how Apollo compelled a Cretan crew to land at Delphi and become his attendants, performing his paeans in the characteristic Cretan style (vv. 388–end). We have here three ways in which poets moved around: the lone wandering poet, the international festival that can draw both foreign poets and foreign audiences and the involuntary movement of cult personnel. At least two of these must reflect the milieu of the poet who performed this hymn, the final form of which, combining the Delian and Pythian portions and perhaps attributable to a certain Cynaethus, is to be dated to approximately 620 BC, although it is made up of much material that is older.[2] The first method of transmission conforms to the widely accepted model of seers and magicians transmitting their art as wandering craftsmen from east to west during the Orientalising Period, which was presented by Walter Burkert in his *Orientalizing Revolution*. Burkert bases his theory on the comment by Eumaeus in the *Odyssey*, that *dēmiourgoi* are invited into people's houses as *xenoi*, such as 'a seer, or healer, or builder of wood or even a godly singer, who takes pleasure in singing, for these are famous among mortals on the boundless earth' (*Od.* 17.383–6).[3] Clearly this model was believable at the time of the composition of the Homeric poems, and such a method of

---

[1] *HAp* 146–64; πάντων δ' ἀνθρώπων φωνὰς καὶ κρεμβαλιαστύν (v. 162).
[2] See Janko 1982: 102, 112–55, and Burkert 1979a, sceptical of the authorship of Cynaethus, 1987a: 212–15.
[3] Burkert 1992: 41–87, cf. above p. 10. Burkert also mentions itinerant seers who offer purificatory services (Pl. *Rep.* 364 b, e), and see further Burkert 1983. As Burkert's focus is purification and

23

24 MARY R. BACHVAROVA

transmission could have been possible in the Orientalising Period within Greek territory.

However, despite the manifest influence of Near Eastern religion and literature on Greek culture, especially Greek epic, made clear by the pioneering works of Burkert and West,[4] the mechanism by which literature from the Near East reached Greece has not been well studied. Moreover, one can push back the date of possible transmission to Greece of many of the practices that Burkert cites from Mesopotamian sources, and many scholars working on contact between East and West have become more open to considering Anatolia, along with the Levant, as a key locus in which contact could have occurred;[5] so too, some Homeric scholars, such as Latacz, have returned to the point of view espoused by Page,[6] that Homeric poetry, whose roots lie in the Mycenaean age, may reflect – albeit in a very distorted mirror – the very interactions between Anatolians and Greeks in the second millennium that can also be detected in the records from the multilingual archives of Hattusa (modern-day Boğazköy), the capital of the multi-cultural Hittite empire in central Anatolia. The Hittite records match quite closely the time frame of the Mycenaean age (1700–1175 BCE) and attest that the shared rituals which Burkert singles out as evidence of wandering wordsmiths, such as hepatoscopy, substitution rites, disposing

divination, he never explicitly discusses the movements of poets, although his chapter on the parallels between Greek and Near Eastern poetry is entitled 'Or Also a Godly Singer'. This model, which West 1997: 611 cites approvingly (also see his discussion at pp. 606–11), is derived from an article by Grottanelli 1982, who discusses the supposed free-market economy in Greece, as opposed to the Oriental style of production; Grottanelli draws on the argument of Zaccagnini 1983 that in the Near East the movement of craftsmen was tightly controlled. Besides Homer, both cite Herodotus' story of the physician Democedes and Darius (3.125–37), in which the historian describes the Persian emperor's treatment of all those below him as slaves, implicitly contrasting it with the 'freedom' and 'democracy' of the Greeks. Moyer 2006 has subsequently analysed this model of free movement of self-starting craftsmen in Greece as a stereotypical opposition of West vs. Oriental. Yet to be proved is the ability to move freely within Greece.

[4] Burkert 1992, 2004, West 1997.

[5] West seems to change his mind concerning the question of transmission during the course of *The East Face of Helicon*. Compare the opening chapter of this book (also West 1988; and his 'Ancient Near Eastern myths in classical Greek religious thought' in Sasson 1995: 33–42, esp. p. 35), in which he focuses on transmission in the Orientalising Period directly from Semitic sources, with the closing chapters in which he is more open to the possibility of transmission at an early period from the Minoans and via Anatolia (West 1997: 586–90, 607–24). Similarly, Burkert 2005 now includes explicitly the possibility of contacts via Anatolia in the second millennium, although he still discounts Mycenaean Age influence on Homeric epic (2004: 31–2, 47–8). Meanwhile, Bryce 1999 has argued that Anatolian scribes could have brought Near Eastern epic to the Mycenaeans, Morris 2001a, 2001b, has noted Mycenaean era connections between Greece and Anatolia and I have argued that the similarities between Homeric and Hurro-Hittite epic indicate close contact at an early stage between the two poetic traditions (Bachvarova 2005).

[6] Page 1959, Latacz 2004.

Hittite and Greek perspectives on travelling poets, texts and festivals   25

of impurity in the steppe or sea and piglet sacrifices in purification rituals, were being practised in second-millennium Anatolia,[7] while Hurro-Hittite poetry and Hittite prayer show remarkable correspondences with Greek epic and prayer.[8] Thus, transmission of cultural practices – even if they originated in Mesopotamia – via Anatolia during the Mycenaean period, when there is good evidence for contact between Greek-speakers and Anatolians, should be given serious consideration.[9]

My intent here, however, is not to explore systematically the possibility of an east–west interface in Anatolia in the second millennium which had a formative influence on Greek literature, although some of my examples speak clearly in favour of such a possibility. Rather, I will examine the mechanisms by which second-millennium Anatolian singers and other 'masters of the word'[10] made their way from one location to another. Self-propelled, 'wandering' poets unfortunately have left no explicit trace (which does not mean they did not exist), but some forces show clearly in the record that also were in operation in the classical period in Greece and/or appear in Greek myth and/or seem probable for the Mycenaean period. It is against this background that the later phenomenon of Greek 'wandering poets' examined in this book may best be understood.

The examples I discuss provide second-millennium parallels to the displaced Cretans and the Delian maidens of the *Homeric Hymn to Apollo*: a local performer recites or sings in the context of a ritual which either takes place outside his home base or draws an audience which has come from outside. The ritual provides the setting in which other performers may hear him, as well as the reason why his word-smithing skills in a particular local or ethnic tradition are desirable and he therefore finds himself transported or invited to move to a new location. I focus particularly on two related settings: the worship of an imported god and festivals.

---

[7] Hepatoscopy is well attested in the Hittite capital with oracle results and liver models (Güterbock 1987, Meyer 1987: 38–44, Riemschneider 2004, Schuol 1994a, 1994b, Richter 2002: 311–14). On Hittite scapegoat rituals, see Kümmel 1967, Wright 1987: 15–74, Janowski and Wilhelm 1993, Taracha 2000, Bremmer 2001 with earlier refs., and Haas 2003. Burkert 1979b: 59–77 notes the parallels with Hittite substitution rituals, arguing for a typological similarity ('that's how people think'), and connections dating to the Late Bronze Age. On disposal of impurity in the steppe, see D. P. Wright 1987: 269–71. On pig sacrifice see Collins 2006.

[8] Bachvarova 2002, 2005.

[9] The evidence for contact was first discussed by Forrer 1924a, 1924b. Further discussions appear in Güterbock 1983b, 1986, Röllig 1992, Gates 1995, Starke 1997, Niemeier 1998, 1999, Bachvarova 2002: 27–56 and Latacz 2004.

[10] Hitt. *uttanas ishas* (*KBo* 10.23 iii 10''*, ed. Singer 1984: 12).

INVOCATIONS

I begin with an example which makes clear the role of verbal art in effecting the movement of deities, a function which of itself made it necessary to transport its performers, and also demonstrates what I mean by verbal art. My standards are low. I do not think that poetry must be redolent with complex imagery and lovely to the ear. I think that what we call poetry is the by-product of the cognitive processes by which humans make meaning from the world around them through the medium of spoken language[11] and attempt to shape that world to their own desires. Words 'do things', as Austin put it so famously, at least poetry used to before Plato divorced it from its function, or maybe it is better to put it as Tambiah did, that poetry has 'magical power'.[12] I therefore consider the following passage, from a Hittite invocation ritual (*mukessar*) for the disappearing god Telipinu, to be poetry. In this very famous incantation type either the Hattic vegetation god, Telipinu (Hattic 'great son'), or the Hattic goddess, Hannahanna (Hittite 'Granny'), is angered. The house fills with smoke, Telipinu puts his shoes on the wrong feet, or Hannahanna puts her headscarf on backwards, and they rush off and disappear. Telipinu is described as melding with the green steppe. Want grips the land and the gods therefore suffer, so search parties are sent out, but only the lowly bee can find the deity. The bee stings Telipinu awake and he returns, but he is extremely angry. Therefore, soothing offerings including wax are offered to the deity.[13] The passages I have extracted belong to this section of the ritual's *legomena*:[14]

> *kāša galaktar kitta* [*nu* ᵈ *Telipinuwaš ištanza–tiš*]
> *galankanza ēštu kāša parḫ*[*uenaš kitta*]
> *kara̯zš–an tal*ˈ*liyēd* [*du Telipinun*][15]

Here now *galaktar* is **l**ying. Let [your mind, that of Telipinu], be **appeased**. **Here** now *parhuenas*-nut [is **l**ying]. Let (its) **nat**ure pull him, [Telipinu].

---

[11] Jakobson 1956.

[12] Austin 1975, Tambiah 1968. Noegel 2000 presents a thorough and illuminating study of the function of poetic figures in Sumerian and Semitic poetry, including a good survey of the earlier secondary literature on the use of verbal art to empower incantations, based on the assumptions that the connection between signifier and signified is not arbitrary and that phonological parallels produce semantic ones.

[13] See Hoffner 1998a: 14–30 for translations of such incantations.

[14] Abbreviations follow the conventions of the *Chicago Hittite Dictionary* (= *CHD*, ed. Güterbock and Hoffner 1989–). Where possible I convert Sumerograms and Akkadograms into Hittite, contrary to convention. Outside of block quotes I do not use diacritics for Hittite words.

[15] *KUB* 17.10 ii 12'–14' (ed. Laroche 1965, 1968: 32).

Hittite and Greek perspectives on travelling poets, texts and festivals 27

[**paid**]⌐ *du*⌐ *idālu karpiš kard*[*imiyaz*]
[*waštu*]*l šāuwar miyante≈y*[*a≈*(*at* A.ŠA₃-*ni*)]
⌐GIŠTIR⌐ GIŠKIRI₆ *anda lē* **paiz**[*zi*]
dankuwayaš≈⌐*at*⌐ *taknaš* **palšan paidd** [*u*]
dankuwāi taknī ḫapalkiaš⌐DUG**palḫiš kianda**
ištappulli≈šmit šulliyaš kuit≈kan anda
paizzi *n≈*⌐*at*⌐*≈kan namma šarā natta* ⌐ *uiz*⌐*zi*
*anda≈***pat***≈kan* ⌐ *ḫarkzi* ⌐ ᵈ*Telipinu*[*wašš≈a*]
idāluš karpiš kartimmiaz šāuwa[*r*]
waštul idaluš lalaš idaluš **patalḫaš**
anda **paiddu** *n≈at≈kan namma ša*⌐ *rā lē*⌐
uizzi anda≈*at≈kan ḫarkdu*

nu≈za ēt **šanezzi** *eku≈ma* **šanezz**[*i*]
kāša ᵈ*Telipinuwaš* **palšaš**
I₃.DUG₃.GA-*it papparššanza ēšdu*
*nu≈***ššan** *iyaḫḫut* GIŠ**šaḫiš** GIŠ *ḫapp*[*uriyaššaš*]
šašza≈*tiš*⌐*nu*⌐*≈za≈kan š*⌐ *ēški* GI⌐.DUG₃.GAᴵ
maḫḫan ḫandanza z[*ig–a ḫa*]⌐ **ššuit ḫaššu**⌐[**ššarit**]¹⁶
Ḫ*attuši* **kiššan**
ḫandanza ē[*š*⌐]¹⁷

Let evil, fury, anger, [sin] and rage [**go**]. But let it not **go** <u>into</u> the ripe field, forest, (and) garden. Let it **go** along the **pa**th of the Dark Earth.¹⁸ <u>In</u> the Dark Earth lie iron **con**tainers. Their lids are of lead. What **go**es <u>in</u> does not come up again; it perishes <u>in</u> this **ve**ry place. [And] let Telipinu's evil **fu**ry, anger, rage, sin, evil tongues, evil **fe**tters **go** <u>in</u> and let it not come up again. Let it perish <u>within</u>.

Eat **tas**ty things; drink **tas**ty things. Here now! let the **pa**th of Telipinu be sprink**led** with fine oil. Set **out** upon it. Your **b**ed is *sa his* and *ḫappuriyasas* (boughs). Sleep on it. Just as fragrant reed is fitting, so may you be fitting also with the **k**ing and **qu**een and to the land of Hatti.

ᵈ*Telipinuš≈za ḫaššun* **kap***puwit* ᵈ*Telipinuwaš peran*
GIŠ*eya arta* GIŠ*eyaz≈kan* UDU-*aš* KUŠ*kuršaš* **kankanza** *n≈ašta*
anda UDU-*aš* I₃-*an* **kitta** *n≈ašta* anda *ḫalkiaš* ANŠE-*aš*
⌐*wiyan*⌐*aš* **kitta** *n≈ašta* anda GU₄ UDU **kitta** *n≈ašta*
anda MU.KAM.GÍD.DA DUMU.MEŠ-*latar* **kitta**¹⁹

---

¹⁶ I assume here the readings *hassu-* and *hassussara-* for 'king' (LUGAL) and 'queen' (MUNUS.LUGAL), instead of *t/labarna-* and *tawannanna-*. This allows for alliteration of *ha(ss)-*.

¹⁷ *KUB* 33.8 iii 3–22, filled in with *IBoT* 3.141 iii 21–3 (ed. Laroche 1965, 1968: 43–4).

¹⁸ The alliterative expression *danku tekan* ('Dark Earth') has been noted to have Greek and Vedic correspondences, but this kenning for the Underworld also has a Hurrian correspondent. Although Dunkel 1993: 103 discounts the significance of the correspondences in Indo-European languages, Oettinger 1989/1990 and Neu 1996: 247–8, with n. 50, both find it compelling evidence for the calquing of a poetic expression.

¹⁹ *KUB* 17.10 iv 27–31 (ed. Laroche 1965, 1968: 98).

Telipinu **paid** attention to the king. In front of Telipinu a yew (?) tree[20] stands. From the yew is **hang**ing a **h**unting bag of a sheep. In it **lies** fat of a sheep. In it **lie** grain, asses, (and) wine. In it **lie** cattle (and) sheep. In it **lie** long years (and) descendants.

In the first extract, the initial velar of the introductory proximal deictic adverb *kasa*, translated something like 'herewith' or 'here now', is repeated throughout the stanza, strengthening the invocatory power of the incantation. Whatever substance *galaktar* may be,[21] the substantive apparently contains the same root as the participle describing the desired state of the god, *galankanza*, again a word of unknown meaning. The next two paragraphs rely on the alliteration of *pa-* to underline the desired motion of the evils (*paizzi* 'goes', *paiddu* 'let him go'), including *patalhas* ('fetters'), away from the performer into the *palhi-* containers rather than into the cultivated land. In the second extract, *anda* ('inside') is repeated throughout, always close to the verb it complements. The fourth paragraph relies on the alliteration of *s(an)-* to make parallel the desirability of the offerings and the desired state of the god, namely peaceful sleep. Finally the closing section returns to the repetition of velars connecting the desired attention of the god and the desired goods, products of a fertile land, held within the hunting bag, as opposed to the evils contained and buried beneath the earth. Here the repeated *anda* and its associated verb frame the nominal complements.

The parallels between these invocations and Greek myths and ritual are obvious, and most have been discussed before. Some elements are comparable to the story of Demeter and Persephone[22] or Pandora's box,[23] while the *kursa*, a hunting bag made out of the fleece of a sheep or a goat, has been compared to Jason's Golden Fleece, to the flayed skin of Marsyas and to Athena's aegis.[24] I add here that the bedding of boughs spread out invitingly for Telipinu matches the *stibades* spread for the *theoxenia* of Dionysus, who has been connected to Telipinu.[25] However, few scholars other than Calvert Watkins and Jaan Puhvel have been interested in the texts themselves, although they are the chief vehicles by which the stories and practices

[20] This is one plausible possibility for this puzzling item. See Houwink ten Cate 2003: 217, n. 49, for other suggestions.
[21] I like the tentative suggestion by Güterbock 1983a: 71 that *galaktar* may be opium.
[22] Burkert 1979b: 123–42.   [23] Fauth 1974: 120–1, Haas 1993: 78–83.
[24] On the *kursa* as Jason's Golden Fleece see Haas 1975, 1978, as Marsyas' skin see Popko 1975, as the aegis see Watkins 2000 and Morris 2001b: 146–50, and see Morris 2001b and Bremmer 2006 for a survey of previous theories with further interesting suggestions. Less convincingly, Morris 2001b compares the *kursa* to the protuberances decorating the chest of Artemis of Ephesus.
[25] For the use of branches as mats or bedding, see *CHD sub lahhurnuzzi*. See Sourvinou-Inwood 2003b: 79–88 on the *stibades*, and Tassignon 2001 comparing Dionysus and Telipinu.

Hittite and Greek perspectives on travelling poets, texts and festivals 29

would have spread, perhaps in part because they lack meter as defined by classicists and their phrasing is rather jejune.[26]

One particular figure already alluded to here, the repetition of *anda*, has been discussed from different angles by both Watkins and Puhvel. While Puhvel argued that Homeric poets imitated the Hittite use of clause-initial *anda*, substituting *en* + *de*, Watkins compared the phrasing of the description of the contents of the *kursa* in the *mukessar* ritual to Pindaric phrasing, also drawing parallels with the description of Athena's aegis in the *Iliad*:[27]

> ἀμφὶ δ᾽ ἄρ᾽ ὤμοισιν βάλετ᾽ αἰγίδα θυσσανόεσσαν
> δεινήν, ἣν περὶ μὲν πάντη Φόβος ἐστεφάνωται,
> ἐν δ᾽ Ἔρις, ἐν δ᾽ Ἀλκή, ἐν δὲ κρυόεσσα Ἰωκή,
> ἐν δέ τε Γοργείη κεφαλὴ δεινοῖο πελώρου,
> δεινή τε σμερδνή τε, Διὸς τέρας αἰγιόχοιο.

Iliad 5.738–42

And around her shoulders she threw the tassled aegis,
terrible, and around it in every direction Fear has been wreathed,
in it (*en d'*) is Strife, **in it** (*en d'*) is Strength, **in it** (*en de*) is chilling Rout,
and **in it** (*en de*) is the Gorgon head of the terrible monster,
terrible and dreadful, the portent of aegis-shaking Zeus.

Close phraseological correspondences such as these are good indirect evidence of the contact between wordsmiths through whom the phrasing crossed languages. Furthermore, this particular example shows that when cult realia such as the *kursa* bag were imported and adapted to new uses, it may be expected that at least in some cases texts (or perhaps it is better to conceive of them as a repertoire of traditional formulae from which texts could be built) accompanied them in the heads of performers and were translated and modified as necessary.

Moreover, such travelling performers must also have been responsible for the close phraseological and functional correspondences between Hittite *mukessar* prayers (invocations) and Greek literary invocations, such as Sappho 2 Voigt; the 'come from wherever you are' invocation is in fact found only in Hittite and Greek.[28] I draw another Hittite example from a prayer of the New Hittite king Mursili II to Telipinu:[29]

---

[26] See Watkins 1970, 1986, 1995, 1998, 2000, 2001 and Puhvel 1983, 1988a, 1991, 1992, 1993. On Hittite poetry see Eichner 1993, Watkins 1995: 247–51, Carruba 1995, 1998 and Melchert 1998.

[27] Puhvel 1993, Watkins 2000.   [28] West 1997: 589.

[29] *Catalogue des textes hittites* (= *CTH*, Laroche 1971) 377 B = *KUB* 24.2 obv. 10–13 (ed. Lebrun 1980: 180). While the openings of many prayers have been lost, similar invocations are preserved for two

30   MARY R. BACHVAROVA

kinuna⸗tta šanezziš waršulaš ^{GIŠ}ERIN-*anza* I₃-*anza*
kallišdu n⸗ašta appa ^É*karimni⸗tti anda eḫu*
nu⸗tta kāša mukiškimi ^{NINDA}*ḫaršit* ^{DUG}*išpanduzit*
nu⸗ššan parā kalānkanza ēš

Now, let the fine scent, cedar and oil
call you. Come back into your **temple.**
Here now I am calling you with thick bread and libations.
Be **appeased** fully.

The alliteration of velar consonants in significant words connect the act of 'calling' (*kallesdu*), the temple to which the god is called (*karimni*), the traction power of the prayer accompanied by customary offerings (*kinuna . . . kasa mukiskimi*) and the desired state for the god of being soothed (*kalankanza*).

A modified version of this type of invocatory incantation is presented in Sappho 2 Voigt, which calls Aphrodite from abroad to her sanctuary in Lesbos. Albeit in a more sophisticated and elegant form – 'real poetry' – we still see the compelling alliteration of velars (while we might expect the Greek cognate *kalei* as the translation of the Hittite verb *kalles-*, it is replaced by *keladei*), the appealing mention of incense and sleep, the attractive vegetation (although not used as bedding) and the repeated use of ἐν δέ, complicated by the use of ἔνθα δή in the fourth verse:[30]

δεῦρύ μ' ἐκ Κρήτας ἐπ[ὶ τόνδ]ε ναῦον
ἄγνον ὄππ[ᾳ τοι] χάριεν μὲν ἄλσος
μαλί[αν], βῶμοι δ' τεθυμιάμενοι [λι]βανώτῳ,

ἐν δ' ὕδωρ ψῦχρον κελάδει δι' ὔσδων
μαλίνων, βρόδοισι δὲ παῖς ὁ χῶρος
ἐσκίαστ', αἰθυσσομένων δὲ φύλλων κῶμα κατέρρει,

ἐν δὲ λείμων ἱππόβοτος τέθαλεν
ἠρίνοισιν ἄνθεσιν, αἰ δ' ἄηται
μέλλιχα πνέοισιν [
[   ]

ἔνθα δὴ σὺ στέμ‹ματ'› ἔλοισα Κύπρι
χρυσίαισιν ἐν κυλίκεσσιν ἄβρως
ὀμ‹με›μείχμενον θαλίαισι νέκταρ οἰνοχόαισον.

---

prayers to the Sun-Goddess of Arinna (*CTH* 376.A and *CTH* 376.F, trans. Singer 2002: 50, 73), and *mukessar* rituals are used for both chthonic and heavenly gods (Glocker 1997: 124–32).

[30] The text I use of this poem comes from the readable edition of Campbell 1982. See Bachvarova 2002: 151–65 for a more detailed discussion of correspondences between Greek and Hittite invocations.

Hittite and Greek perspectives on travelling poets, texts and festivals 31

(Come) **here** to me from Crete to this holy temple, where lovely for you is a grove of apples, and altars smoking with frankincense,

where cool water sounds (*keladei*) through the apple boughs, and the whole space is shaded with roses, and sleep comes down from quivering leaves,

and where the horse-grazing meadow flourishes with lovely flowers, and the winds sweetly blow . . . .

There indeed you, Cyprian, taking (ritual) branches, pour as wine ambrosia delicately mixed in gold cups for the festivities.

Such material must have been conveyed across time and space from one 'master of the word' to another, each improving on the last as the text developed from 'proto-poetry' to the beautiful stanzas of Sappho. Furthermore, the incantation effects the transportation of the goddess from one location to another, saying, 'Come to the festivities I am celebrating for you. Look, I have all your customary supplies, I can worship you in the style which you prefer.' The invocation itself, which has clear antecedents from mainland Anatolia, can be included among the things that the Cyprian goddess expects in her worship. I need not belabour the fact that Aphrodite is the paradigm example of a goddess who combines Near Eastern, Greek and pre-Greek elements,[31] and that second- and first-millennium Cypriote culture was a melting pot of Anatolian, north Syrian and Aegean elements. The transfer across space of the words must be linked with the transfer of a version of the goddess herself, accompanied by performers.

THE TRANSPORT OF GODS AND PERFORMERS

The process of calling a 'Cyprian' god from Crete to Lesbos provides textual evidence from the first millennium to complement archaeological material which shows that gods, or at least their statues, were being transported from one location to another in the second millennium. Two Near Eastern bronze 'smiting gods', for example, were found in the Mycenaean site of Phylakopi on Melos, along with the bearded 'Lady of Phylakopi', who Elizabeth French suggests was imported from the Argolid[32] and whom I cannot resist comparing to the bearded Ishtar. Could one worship a new god in any way one pleased, or would a foreign god like to be worshipped in the manner to which he or she was accustomed? Certainly, gods in literary and archival texts throughout the Eastern Mediterranean show a distinct preoccupation with receiving their due share of worship, which included

---

[31] Budin 2003.   [32] In Renfrew 1985: 215.

32   MARY R. BACHVAROVA

an attractive home, feasts, singing, dancing and care of their cult images.
When the Myceneans imported the goddess labelled the 'Aswiyan Lady'
from Anatolia,[33] did they import cult personnel with her? Female Anatolian
captives are attested in Mycenean records located in the same area as the
tablet referring to the goddess. Did other Anatolians, so far unattested,
perform in her cult to make the transition easier for her? We now turn to
the evidence in Hittite for performers moving with their gods.[34]

   The Hittite material presents exactly the opposite set of problems from
the Greek material. It has often been said about tragedy, for example, that
we have only a dim reflection of the spectacle that it must have presented,
with only the words and no music, no stage directions, no description
of the costumes. With the Hittite material we have detailed descriptions
of the pageantry of festivals and the *drōmena* of rituals, but for the most
part the festival descriptions (less so the rituals) rarely include the words
spoken, and almost never the words sung. The places in which the verbal
performances occurred may be marked with an *incipit* if we are lucky; the
legomena themselves were typically set down on a separate tablet, and we
have perishingly few of these. For the most part, the words quoted in the
ritual and festival descriptions are not in Hittite, but in less well understood
languages such as Hattic (also called Hattian), the indigenous language
of Anatolia, Luwian, a language related to Hittite and spoken especially
in the south and west of Anatolia (Lycian belongs in the same branch of
Anatolian as Luwian), or Hurrian, a language which may be distantly related
to modern Chechen (its closest attested relative is Urartian), and whose
speakers were one of the main means by which Mesopotamian culture,
texts and religion were brought to the Hittites via north Syria.[35] Therefore,
although we might be able to appreciate their poetic qualities to some
extent (the phonological and morphological figures), we have only the most
imperfect understanding of their content. This of course is exceptionally
frustrating, especially as the barest hints we do have of what the songs
were about are so intriguing. The phrase 'high Wilusa' for example, which
Watkins has noted as a Homeric formula appearing in Luwian,[36] is found
in an *incipit* imbedded in a Hittite description of a festival for the gods of

---

[33] *po-ti-ni-ja a-si-wi-ja* (Pylos Fr 1206), see Watkins 1998: 203 and Morris 2001a with earlier refs.
[34] Morris 2001a: 424–5 discusses from a different angle the transportation of gods from Anatolia to
     Greece, asking, 'Did migrant labor from Anatolia introduce the cult of a goddess from "Asia"?'
[35] Richter 2002 distinguishes between direct transmission in the Old Hittite period and indirect via
     Hurrian intermediaries in later periods. The type of texts examined here are almost never in Akkadian.
[36] *alati Wilusati* (*KBo* 4.11 rev. 46, ed. Starke 1985: 341), Gr. *Ilios aipeinē* (Watkins 1986: 713–15). The word
     *ala/i-*has been translated differently by other Hittitologists (Starke 1997: 473, n. 78), but Watkins'
     interpretation has been accepted by Melchert 1993: 6.

Hittite and Greek perspectives on travelling poets, texts and festivals   33

the town Istanuwa, in which men from Istanuwa and Lallupiya perform a
series of songs in Luwian in their local tradition.[37] The general prevalence
of non-Hittite *legomena* in the festival texts shows the cultural importance
of non-local singers in Hittite cult.

Our direct evidence for the performers of the verbal art, their constraints, motivations, training and personal histories, is extraordinarily limited. When we look at the Greek poets and tragedians, on the other hand,
despite the fact that classicists like to complain about how little we actually know about their real lives,[38] it is possible to discuss these men (and
women) as people. If, for example, Euripides spent time in the Macedonian court, we can imagine the influence of this prestigious art form on
the Macedonian poets who witnessed tragedies, as we can imagine that
Euripides was interested in observing performances by indigenous poets.[39]
A similar situation obtains for Aeschylus and his time in Sicily at the court
of Hiero, where many famous Greek poets spent time,[40] although again
actual evidence for influence in either direction is non-existent, other than
the fact that we know that Aeschylus created a drama involving local characters, *Women of Aitna* (T 1.33–36 Radt). We are in a better position with
Sophocles, who is traditionally claimed to have helped to introduce the cult
of Asclepius to Athens (T 67–73a Radt), and we even have a fragmentary
paean attributed to him (*PMG* 737(b)),[41] while the 'Ode to Sleep' in his
Philoctetes looks distinctly like it is meant to remind his audience of such
paeans;[42] we can thus imagine how a great artist was involved in syncretis-
ing a new god with an old one, using the standard phraseology of paeans
to Apollo for paeans to the closely related god Asclepius.[43] On the Hittite
side, on the other hand, we have much evidence for translating, adapting
and reworking verbal art, and the settings in which these occurred, but
the agents involved are shadowy figures. In the discussion which follows,
therefore, there is necessarily little mention of actual humans, actual poets,
only of the indirect evidence of their movements and how they came into
contact with and influenced each other.

---

[37] On the antiphonal style of singing typical of these performers, see de Martino (2002: 625, with
earlier refs.). An archival shelf list seems to refer to tablets containing these very songs (*KUB* 30.42
i 1, 2, iv 14', ed. and trans. Dardano 2006: 22–3, and also see trans. Hoffner in Hallo and Younger
2002: 69). On the poetic technique employed see Watkins 1995: 144–7.

[38] Lefkowitz 1981.

[39] Texts and translations of sources on his life are conveniently collected by Kovacs 1994. Lefkowitz
1981: 103–4 is sceptical, and cf. above p. 12.

[40] Herington 1986: 29.

[41] See Connolly 1998: 2–4 with earlier refs., for the history of the study of this inscription.

[42] Haldane 1963.   [43] See Käppel 1992: 63 on the re-directing of the paean towards Asclepius.

There is some evidence that trained personnel did at least on occasion accompany their god to his new home, so that he could be worshipped in the manner to which he was accustomed.[44] The Old Hittite king Hattusili I boasts in his Annals that he took back the Storm-god of Aleppo as booty from his campaigns in north Syria (*KBo* 10.1 obv. 38), and this god was subsequently integrated into the Hittite pantheon, appearing in lists of Hittite gods in treaties and referred to as the city god of Hattusa.[45] The appeal of the Storm-god to the Hittite monarch lay in his dual role of bringing on the one hand fertilising rains, embodying the king's responsibility for the prosperity of his land, and on the other violent storms, a symbol of the martial power of the king.[46] The Storm-god of Aleppo, named Adad by the west Semitic Amorites who brought him to north Syria, was syncretised with Teshshub by the Hurrians through whom the Hittites learned how to worship him.[47] By late Middle Hittite, Teshshub is also called Tarhunna/Tarhunt, the Anatolian name for the Storm-god.[48] Thus, while at first the Storm-god of Aleppo was worshipped as a foreign god, he eventually became syncretised with the Anatolian god most like him.[49] His iconography, however, a sub-type of the smiting god type, remained remarkably constant, lasting all the way into Roman times.[50] Aleppo itself was caught between the Hurrian Mitanni kingdom and the Hittites, switching its allegiance at least twice, and by Middle Hittite times it had been turned into a vice-regal kingdom of the Hittites.[51] Thus, the possibility of diplomatic ramifications to the introduction and subsequent elevation of its god, although not recorded in the texts, should not be ignored.

[44] Beckman 1983 has already laid the groundwork for a study of how performers came into Anatolia and what type of evidence can reveal the presence of immigrant wordsmiths. Beckman shows that there is both indirect and direct evidence for the settling of Akkadian scribes in Hattusa, who would have brought with them the Mesopotamian educational tradition, including the copying of 'literary' and 'technical' texts. The Middle Babylonian *Gilgamesh* and epics concerning Sargon the Great and Naram-Sin are found in Hattusa, along with technical genres such as omens and medical texts. As Beckman points out, Hattusa is a key source for Middle Babylonian material. 'Not only do the archives of the Hittite kings constitute the largest single repository of material, but they contain the earliest attested exemplars of several "canonical" Mesopotamian texts' (Beckman 1983: 98). See also Hoffner 1992, 1998b. For discussions of how Mesopotamian prayers were translated and adapted to the Hittite milieu, often through Hurrian intermediaries, see Güterbock (1974) and Archi (1983: 52). Further references may be found in Singer (2002: 3), who sees them as teaching tools for scribes, rather than performed.

[45] See *Répertoire géographique des textes cunéiformes* (= *RGTC*) 6 (del Monte and Tischler 1978) *sub* Halpa, and further Klengel 1965, esp. p. 91, Souček and Siegelová 1974, Houwink ten Cate 1992, Hoffner 1992: 102 and Schwemer 2001: 494–502. Green 2003 provides an interesting study of the Storm-god in the Near East, and Schwemer 2001 provides a detailed survey of the data available.

[46] Klengel 1965: 89, 92.   [47] Klengel 1965: 90.   [48] Bunnens 2004: 60–3.

[49] Taracha 2004: 453–4.   [50] Bunnens 2004.   [51] Bryce 1998: 53–4, 151–3.

Hittite and Greek perspectives on travelling poets, texts and festivals   35

A group of men from the 'palace of Aleppo', which is either in Hattusa or another Hittite town, participates in festivals in his honour held in Hattusa and other towns in the Hittite empire.[52] Furthermore, two archival shelf-lists mention texts by a performer from Aleppo, a ḪAL priest (exorcist) with the Hurrian name Ehal-Teshshub who had a special repertoire of purificatory rituals,[53] and we have a Hurrian prayer addressed to the Storm-god.[54] So it does look as if people with knowledge of the appropriate ritual texts accompanied this god.

Among the many festivals regularly celebrated for the deity from Aleppo is one which was imported along with him, the *hiyar(r)a* festival (more correctly *hiyari* festival). This 'donkey' festival seems to have originated with the Amorites, for whom the donkey was a key means of transport in their nomadic wanderings. The festival is attested in a variety of towns in north Syria in the second millennium, and it is associated particularly with the Storm-god of Aleppo.[55] Although in Hittite territory the *hiyara* festival was perhaps celebrated only by people from Aleppo, and thus served as an identity marker,[56] other Hittite festivals are celebrated for him as well, so the cult of the god was manipulated in different ways according to the needs of his worshippers. We might compare the introduction of the cult of Bendis into Athens, which was first the province of Thracian slaves and metics but was officially adopted by Athens at the beginning of the Peloponnesian War, motivated at least in part by an alliance with the Odrygian Thracians and perhaps in part to build loyalty among the metics.[57] As Garland notes:[58]

The establishment of a cult in honour of Bendis would have been perceived at the time as a highly effective way of consolidating a military partnership, particularly in view of the fact that Bendis' status among the Thracians was such that she effectively personified their military might.

The huntress goddess was easily identified with Artemis, and her sanctuary was placed close to that of Artemis Mounychia (Xen. *Hell.* 2.4.10–11). Yet, her rites must have retained some elements considered to be foreign by the Athenians; at the beginning of Plato's *Republic* (328a1–4), Socrates and his friends remark on the novelty of the mounted torch relay race featured in the festival.

[52] Hoffner 1992: 102, Souček and Siegelová 1974: 44.
[53] *KUB* 30.51 + ii 14'–17', *KUB* 30.56 iii 10'–13' (ed. and trans. Dardano 2006: 126–48, 212–21, and also see trans. by Hoffner in Hallo and Younger 2002: 68–9).
[54] Thiel and Wegner 1984.   [55] See discussion in Cohen 1993: 309–13, 374–5 and Hutter 2002.
[56] Hutter 2002: 194–5.
[57] See Thuc. 2.29.4, and Nilsson 1972: 45–8; 1942. The cult was adopted at least by 429/8 (cf. *IG* I² 310,208).
[58] Garland 1992: 112.

36   MARY R. BACHVAROVA

Just as Socrates differentiates between two groups appearing in
the parade, the Athenian natives (*epikhōrioi*) and the Thracians (*Rep.*
1.327a4–5), so the inscriptions which offer evidence for how the cult was
administrated differentiate consistently between these two groups.[59] Furthermore, the cult is an unusual mix of public and private, foreign and
native, with Thracian *orgeōnes* responsible for a procession that makes its
way to Peiraeus from the *Prytaneion* (*Rep.* 1.327a1, *IG* II² 1283). So, we see
the same process of syncretisation, the same connection between diplomatic relations and religious innovations, and the same official acceptance
of a cult that permits foreigners to maintain their sense of community as
we saw in the case of Adad/Teshshub/Tarhunt.

A Hittite tablet recording the results of a series of oracle-inquiries makes
clear that the Hittites noticed local differences in styles of worship and were
concerned whether a particular god preferred a particular style, a motivation for transporting appropriate performers for the cult of an imported
god. The oracle-result tablet is famous because it alludes to gods from
Ahhiyawa (Achaia) and Lazpa (Lesbos) who were brought to heal the New
Hittite king Mursili II, recording that they would like to be worshipped
in the style of the personal god of the king.[60] This is our best evidence
for cultural exchange between Greek-speakers and Hittites in the second
millennium. The text, however, contains other interesting results concerning the deity of a certain woman named Mezzulla, probably the goddess
Ishhara,[61] who wished to be worshipped in the manner of Ashtata (*KUB*
5.6 + 18.54 i 9–20), a city located in north Syria, subordinate to Hattusa.
Mention is made in this oracle-result of the fact that men came from
Ashtata to advise on how to honour the god (*KUB* 5.6 + 18.54 i 21, 39–40,
44). We know that in each respective region customs from the other have
been imported, as Ashtata (Emar/Meskene) actually has yielded festival
descriptions which show that Hittite-style festivals were imported for gods
with Hittite, Luwian and Hurrian names.[62] Again, there was a connection

---

[59] Simms 1988: 69–72.
[60] Ed. and trans. Sommer 1932: 282–3. The significance of this detail was most recently noted by Morris
2001a: 428. This text further records that the deity Zawalli, who has been hexed along with Mursili
II by an Arzawan named Mashuiluwa, will be cleansed using Arzawan rites (ed. and trans. van den
Hout 1998: 3–5); see Hutter 2001: 228 on the customs of Arzawa, a region in southwest Anatolia.
[61] Prechel 1996: 102–3.
[62] See Hoffner 1992: 103 and Archi 2001 with earlier refs. Typical of Hittite festivals is the repeated
breaking of significantly shaped breads, and the toasting of gods with *rhyta* shaped as totemistic
figures. (These vessels are better called by their Akkadian name *bibrû*, as they do not have secondary
holes through which liquids could be made to flow like a *rhyton*). We can actually distinguish between
distinctive styles of worship, Hittite versus north Syrian, with the Hurrianised southeast Anatolian
city Kizzuwatna having elements from both. For example, the description of the dividing of the

Hittite and Greek perspectives on travelling poets, texts and festivals 37

between newly forged diplomatic ties and the transfer of religious practices (necessarily with personnel) that strengthened a political alliance.[63]

I would compare the examples given above to the displaced Cretans in the *Homeric Hymn to Apollo* (388–end). Just as the performers from Ashtata are summoned from abroad to Anatolia, so the Cretans on a trading voyage are taken off course by Apollo, who announces that they will not return to their families, but henceforth will keep up his newly established cult at Delphi, performing his paean in the characteristic style of Cretans (518). The Cretans were generally connected to the performance of the healing paean, which Thaletas, for example, imported to mainland Greece, a tradition which may have had some basis in fact, as Paia(w)on is attested at Mycenaean Knossos (KN V 52.2, C 394.4).[64] The god of Ahhiyawa brought to Hattusa to heal Mursili II in fact may have been none other than this Paiawon.[65]

The issue of the free will of the performers who brought their healing incantations – that is, whether they travelled on their own impetus or under constraint, an issue which is so important to scholars of the Western world, who look to the democratic ideals of Athens and the competitive drive of pan-Hellenic culture as formative influences on Western civilisation – in truth is less important than the shared conviction, which Mary Helms has shown in illuminating detail is commonly held throughout the world,[66]

that things, information, and experience acquired from distant places, being strange and different, have great potency, great supernatural power, and if attainable, increase the ideological power and political prestige of those who acquire them. Such attitudes underlie the activities of travellers and the influences accorded those who, as shaman-curers/scholars/priests/traders, may arrive at a given locale as learned and experienced 'wise strangers from afar'.

The doctors (both the Akkadian *asûm* [= Sumerian A.ZU] and *āšipu* 'incantation priest') and craftsmen who were sent from one court to another in the second millennium[67] can be compared to the prestige goods that

---

Goddess of Night (ed., trans. and discussion by J. Miller 2004: 259–440), a Kizzuwatnean deity who eventually was worshipped in a variety of cities in Anatolia and was syncretised partially with Ishtar, displays typically north Syrian or Mesopotamian elements, such as leaving water out on the roof at night to absorb the power of the stars. The recorded *legomena* accompanying this rite however make up a typically Anatolian invocation. Miller 2002 notes that the *katra* women who take part in the rites (although the description of their activities includes no mention of their *legomena*) are typically associated with Hurrian rites, so here we may have another example of performers of verbal art embedded in ritual who travel with their rituals.

[63] A more detailed discussion of the political implications of introducing Hittite festivals to Emar may be found in Fleming 1996.

[64] Cf. further West 1992: 140–2 and Rutherford 2001: 14–15, 24–7, Strabo 10.4.16, Pratinas *PMG* 713 iii.

[65] Arnott 1996: 217.   [66] Helms 1988: 263.   [67] Beckman 1983: 106–7.

38   MARY R. BACHVAROVA

were gifted from one king to another.[68] Just as the finished goods produced by imported craftsmen fit the expectations of their patrons even
as their clearly foreign methods added cachet to the product,[69] so too the
songs of imported wordsmiths must have combined foreign and indigenous
motifs.

                         SUPRAREGIONAL FESTIVALS

I move now to parallels to the festival setting described in the *Homeric Hymn
to Apollo*. Typical of Hittite festivals controlled by the capital is the application of a seasonal festival to enforce the hegemony of the king throughout
the core of the Hittite empire.[70] We might compare the development of
the Panathenaia, which grew into a vast and complex affair in which the
overriding message was the superiority of Athens, directed at its allies and at
foreign visitors attracted by the pageantry and competition.[71] For example,
the autumn *nuntarriyashas* festival, the 'festival of haste', was celebrated
when the king returned from campaign; it lasted some forty days, during
which the king, queen and their retinue travelled to and fro between the
capital and various cities in the heart of Hattic country in central Anatolia,
celebrating a series of local and supralocal gods with feasting, toasting and
song.[72] The corresponding spring festival, the AN.TAḪ.ŠUM festival,[73]
also involved travelling around the same area, and both involved transporting the *kursa* bag.[74] The signalling of unification or alliance by such a
procession parallels the procession to Eleusis from Athens for the Eleusinian
Mysteries, or the procession into Athens from Eleutherai during the City
Dionysia. It is not incidental to my comparison that each of these Greek
processions can be connected to the transfer of a local cult to the politically
dominant town. In each case, festivals celebrating the workings of nature
and its management through culture were turned to new uses, whether for
personal salvation or collective solidarity.
   While the AN.TAḪ.ŠUM and *nuntarriyashas* festivals allowed local
singers to remain at home as their supra-local audiences came to them,
the KI.LAM ('gatehouse') festival brought local performers to the Hittite
capital. Its focal points were offerings from the administrators of various towns of grain from their storehouses in the capital, a race with ten

---

[68] Zaccagnini 1983.   [69] Bonatz 2002.   [70] Gilan 2004.
[71] Parker 1996: 89–92, Nilsson 1972: 41–5.   [72] Nakamura 2002: 9–14.
[73] Probably 'crocus festival', see Zinko 2001: 748–51.
[74] The autumn festival also involves transporting the *eya* tree mentioned in the Telipinu invocation.
     On the AN.TAḪ.ŠUM festival see Haas 1994: 772–826, and on the *nuntarriyashas* festival, Haas
     1994: 827–47 and Nakamura 2002.

Hittite and Greek perspectives on travelling poets, texts and festivals 39

runners, a procession viewed by the king before the palace gate-house, and a great assembly (a feast with toasts to more than forty gods accompanied by singing) repeated each day.[75] The procession included dancers, 'masters of the word', priests of the 'tutelary deity', a parade of animal standards and copper(!) *kursa* hunting bags, 'dog-men', a singer or two and other specific classes of men, including men from the town of Anunuwa, and various types of other performers.[76]

The people of Anunuwa later perform a song in Hattic to the accompaniment of the lyre, while spears are clashed.[77] The people from this town seem to be well-respected for their singing, as they turn up elsewhere performing their music, and they provide supplies for festivals along with other groups of craftsmen and cult functionaries, such as the 'wolf-people', who show up in the context of Hattic performances, people from the town of Tissaruliya, who are known to sing in Hattic, and the *zintuhi* women, 'maidens' who performed in Hattic. These females we know were levied from the hamlets of various regions,[78] and one can compare the youthful delegations who came to Apollo's festival, expressing the commitment of Greece as a whole to the pan-Hellenic sanctuary.

It is typical of Hittite documents recording the matters of the centralised official cults of the gods to mention groups of singers from particular towns,[79] such as Ankuwa, which is a stop on the spring AN.TAH.ŠUM festival circuit and whose gods appear frequently in Hittite texts, or Kanesh, modern Kültepe, after which the Hittites named their own language (*nesili*). Singers labelled as being from this town are mentioned very often, although probably this was not a geographic but rather a linguistic designation. Nearly always they perform for Hittite gods.[80] We can compare in Greece the connection between genre, mode of performance and dialect, fossilised in tragedy by the use of normalised Attic for the spoken parts and an *ersatz* Doric for the lyric parts.

If a Greek from classical times dropped in to a Hittite festival from the second millennium, he would find much that was familiar. The obvious

---

[75] On these details of the festival see Singer 1983: 101–4 and Puhvel 1988b: 27. Ardzinba 1982: 248 notes that the presentation of crops by the regional administrators and the gift-giving on the part of the king to the participants imitates a guest–host gift exchange, and that the procedure as a whole is reminiscent of feudal customs. On Hittite feasting, see Collins 1995.

[76] See synopses in Singer 1983: 56–80 and Haas 1994: 748–71.

[77] Is this a weapon dance? See de Martino 2002: 626, and on other Hittite weapon dances see Haas 1994: 686. Perhaps it should be compared to the *pyrrikhē* performed in the Panathenaia (more on this dance below in n. 95).

[78] Rutherford 2004b.

[79] See de Martino 2002 for discussion; attestations in Pecchioli Daddi 1982: 603–8.   [80] Archi 2004.

40   MARY R. BACHVAROVA

similarities have been pointed out by many scholars.[81] Besides singing
accompanied by the lyre, choral dancing, offerings to gods, processions
and athletic competitions, another shared element of Greek and Near Eastern festivals is a staged fight between order and disorder to establish that
now proper order and hierarchy reign.[82] The goal of the fight seems originally to have been to overcome the inconsistency of wild nature, when
winter, drought or infertility was defeated by the Storm-god or a civilising
god such as Ninurta, the Sumerian version of Heracles, who introduced
irrigation after he returned in triumph from slaying a variety of monsters.[83]
The usefulness of such a myth to assert the primacy of the king and his
empire over his enemies is obvious.[84] Among the interesting descriptions of
mock battles and dramatic scenes in Hittite festivals, I discuss further here
two that have connections to the myth of Pythian Apollo, beginning with
the well-known Illuyanka (Hitt. 'snake') tale. Much ink has been spilled
on the snake-killing story, and Gaster has discussed it as an example of the
dramas typical of the eastern Mediterranean, but little to no attention has
been paid to the fact that the festivals themselves, which share such obvious
parallels, were the prime means by which the parallels themselves would
have been transmitted.[85]

   A version of the snake-killing tale is attested iconographically already in
the Old Assyrian colony of Kültepe in eastern Anatolia.[86] It matches in a
fair number of details Apollo's fight with the Python, itself a variation of
Zeus's fight with Typhon in the *Theogony* (820–68), which took place in
Cilicia (as in one of the versions of the Hittite tale), but it matches even
more closely a version of Zeus's fight preserved by Apollodorus (1.6.3–6).[87]

---

[81] See van den Hout 1991–2, Sasson 1973 and Gaster 1961. Carter 1988 and Puhvel 1988b both discuss
   the athletic competitions found in Hittite festivals. Also see Hazenboos 2003 for Hittite descriptions
   of the competitions.
[82] See Gilan 2001, Archi 1973: 25–7 and Bickerman 1967: 199–202. Modern commentators, as Robertson
   2002 remarks, often interpret this fight as reflecting the overcoming of an older indigenous god by a
   new or foreign god, which could be the result of the subjugation of one population by another in the
   temporal world. So Green 2003: 150 for the Illuyanka story, arguing that Illuyanka is an indigenous
   Anatolian god who represents the subterranean waters, a different conception of fertility from the
   sky-god who sends rains. Compare the fight between the Vanir and Aesir in Norse mythology.
   However, such an interpretation of the conflict can only be relatively late.
[83] Annus 2002.
[84] Thus, in one much-cited festival the young men participating were divided into two groups, the men
   of Hatti, who were given sticks, and the men of Masa (a west Anatolian district which did not accept
   easily the hegemony of the Hittites), who were given reeds, and they fought to a predetermined
   victory by the 'men of Hatti' (*KUB* 17.35 iii 9–15, see trans. of Gilan 2001: 120 and interpretation in
   Puhvel 1988b).
[85] Gaster 1961, Watkins 1995: 135–44 has also discussed proto-dramatic elements in Hittite festivals.
[86] Green 2003: 156–60.
[87] On the correspondences, see Fontenrose 1959: 121–9, West 1966: 20–2, Burkert 1979b: 5–10, Watkins
   1992, 1995: 448–59 with other refs., and Bremmer 2006.

Hittite and Greek perspectives on travelling poets, texts and festivals 41

Watkins shows that although the story itself can be shown to have an Indo-European heritage common to both Greek and Hittite, a key peculiarity in the Greek version is best understood as a 'phonetic echo' of a vocabulary item in the Hittite telling.[88] Thus, the binding of the serpent with a rope in Hittite (*ishamanta*) is transformed into striking the ground with a whip in Greek (*himanti*). This is not a re-analysis of a scene communicated pictorially,[89] but a re-analysis of an orally communicated narrative as it moves across a language barrier, from one verbal artist to another, contact which requires *per se* at least one of these artists to travel to a given location such as a supra-local festival.

In fact, Apollo's victory was enacted with the Pythian *nomos* in just such a supra-regional festival, the Pythian games, as was apparently the Storm-god's victory over the snake in the Hittite *purulli* festival, a New Year's festival which renewed the fertility of the land.[90] It seems that the Illuyanka story was mimed in it in some way, as one of the characters in one version of the story, the 'daughter of a poor man', is referred to as cult personnel.[91] The basic thematic correspondences between Apollo's vanquishing of the serpent and the overcoming of Illuyanka that are connected to attempts to control agricultural processes must be linked to the spread of farming itself, by demic diffusion. Therefore, the festivals in their original form cannot be argued to be the means by which the particular practices were spread. However, when a seasonal festival is harnessed to express political dominance or alliance, then it requires a supra-local audience to hear its message, and at this point the festival does become the means by which its *drōmena* and *legomena* are transmitted to new localities as musicians, singers and other performers travel to hear and be heard.

I move from this well-known example of a fight with the Storm-god to one, embedded in the (*h*)*isuwa* festival, which has not yet been brought into the discussion of Greek and Hittite correspondences. This festival for the Storm-god of the mountain Manuzi (whose Hurrian name Eswen explains the name of his festival) takes place in various temples in Hattusa and focuses on purifying the gods and the royal family, and on strengthening the king's martial power. Imported from the Cilician town of Kizzuwatna, the nine-day festival features Hurrian incantations and ceremonies with occasional

---

[88] Watkins 1995: 455.

[89] As Burkert 1987b has argued that representations of Gilgamesh and Enkidu killing Humbaba were turned into Athena, Perseus and Medusa, or Clytemnestra, Aegisthus and Agamemnon, and Morris 1995 that child sacrifice in Near Eastern siege scenes were the basis for the story of Astyanax's death.

[90] On the *purulli* festival see Haas 1988, 1994: 697–747.

[91] Pecchioli Daddi 1987: 368, Haas 1988: 286.

MARY R. BACHVAROVA

Luwianisms, as is typical for Kizzuwatnean rites.[92] Furthermore, the rites make use of a representation of Eswen as a golden eagle, a detail which may best be explained as coming from representations of the rain-bringing mountain as an eagle found a millennium earlier in the north Syrian town of Ebla.[93] This festival therefore represents a regional mix of supra-regional influences. The most peculiar detail of the festival, probably the reason why this particular festival was brought to Hattusa, is the mimed battle that augments the king's military prowess:

> . . . on the [roof], facing the door [. . .], three harpists dance before the god like a battle. They fight with the Storm-god. The harpists sing a *kuwayaralla* of battle and the harpists strike the harp and the tambourine. And one of the harpists stands in the doorway of the god (and) blows the horn. // And one *purapsi* man who is standing on the roof facing the king speaks as following a *kuwarayalla*, 'O King, do not fear. The Storm-god places/will place the enemy and the enemy lands beneath your feet alone. You will smash them like empty vessels of clay. And he has given you, the king, life, prosperity into perpetuity, a victorious weapon, the favour of the gods forever. Do not fear anything. You have vanquished.'[94]

The meaning of *kuwayaralla*, a hapax and apparently a Luwian word, is unknown. The untranslatable name or adverb applied to the song makes clear that the song itself, whose words are unfortunately not recorded, is of a very specific regional variety. The harpists and *purapsi* man mentioned would have had to come from Kizzuwatna in order to perform it. On the one hand, its esoteric quality is what makes the scene effective, on the other, the public enacting of this regional festival at Hattusa on the stage supplied by the temple roof makes it known to a wider audience who could relate it to the more general practice of mimed battles, while those performers from the temples in Hattusa who witnessed it could choose to make use of some of the original details of performance in their own subsequent performances.

Like the battle with the snake Illuyanka, this mimed battle with its musical accompaniment including harp, tambourines, horn and singing may be compared to the *nomos Pythikos*, in which various rhythms represented the various events in the contest and helped to characterise the snake. The encouraging words of the Hittite performers may be compared to the encouragement of the Greek spectators, as they shouted, '*Hiē Paiōn!*'[95]

---

[92] See synopses in Dinçol 1989: 4–9, Wegner and Salvini 1991: 6–11 and Haas 1994: 848–75, also de Martino 2002: 626.

[93] Haas 1981.

[94] *KBo* 15.52 + *KUB* 34.116 v 2'–15, with duplicate *KBo* 20.60. A partial transliteration is provided by Gilan 2001: 119, n. 37. My translation was aided by *CHD* sub *nah-*, *pariparai-*, and *purapsi-*.

[95] Strabo *Geo.* 9.3.10, [Plut.] *Mus.* 1131d, Poll. 4.84, see Rutherford 2001: 25–7, who compares a Vedic example. Also comparable is the *pyrrikhē*, an *enoplios orkhēsis* (Dion. Hal. *Roman Antiquities* 7.72)

MYCENAEAN PARALLELS

I close now with a brief discussion of evidence from the Mycenaean side that imported gods and festivals dedicated to the gods were a means by which supra-local audiences were exposed to local poetic traditions in second-millennium Greece. Recent work on the Mycenaean feast has focused on identity formation,[96] the competition for prestige and clientage among humans, differentiating between diacritical, exclusionary and inclusionary feasts,[97] and looking at the monopoly of prestigious imported goods as a means of acquiring or maintaining political dominance. We can see, however, that the relationship between local cult and central authority shares many similarities with that of the Hittite empire. We see tight accounting control over disbursement of supplies for regional festivals such as a Pylian festival for Poseidon in Messenia,[98] as well as central festivals and collecting of supplies from various regions for large-scale centralised feasting.[99] We also have frescoes depicting song and music in processions, as recorded for the KI.LAM.[100]

Furthermore, we also have some evidence that regional traditions were kept separate yet available to be viewed by outsiders, not only from the attestation of the Aswiyan Lady, who appears in a cache of tablets which also produced mentions of people from Asia, but also in a single tablet (KN V 52) from the so-called Room of the Chariot Tablets at Knossos. This is a deposit of texts dated to Late Mycenaean II, listing a series of deities who are attested as gods in later times: not only Paiawon, but also the pre-Greek Enuwalios and Erinus, the Indo-European Poseida(on), and the hapax *a-ta-na-po-ti-ni-ya* or *Athānāi(/-ās?) Potniāi*. These gods fit the martial and equestrian character of the rest of the tablets found in the room.[101] This find is striking because it shows an awareness that these gods, all of whom seemingly belong to the imported, already syncretised Mycenaean pantheon rather than to the Minoan one, should be grouped together, and it indicates that the gods arrived with at least some of their well-known characteristics. Finally, Athena is clearly noted as a regional god, one of many *potniai*, in the same way that Sappho 2 Voigt indicates that Aphrodite is an imported

---

which was performed at the Panathenaia (Lys. 21.2, 4), among other venues. There were a variety of interpretations of this dance in ancient times. When associated with Athena, it was explained either as her victory dance after the Titans were destroyed (= Gigantomachy? Dion. Hal. 7.72) or as the dance she performed upon emerging from the head of Zeus (Lucian *D. Deor.* 13). Cf. Borthwick 1970, Ceccarelli 1998.

[96] Wright 2004a.   [97] Borgna 2004.   [98] Palaima 2004: 110–11.
[99] Palaima 2004: 112–16, Stocker and Davis 2004: 72–3.
[100] Bachvarova forthcoming.   [101] Gulizio, Pluta, and Palaima 2001.

god, and the Hittites distinguished deities by their hometowns. Like the Potnia from Assuwa, these mainland gods could have been accompanied by performers in their cult when they were brought to Crete.

Given these gods' role in the means of domination, one would surmise that songs and other performances for their sake could share similarities with the mock battles found in the Hittite material. Furthermore, in the atmosphere of public performance and jockeying for position detected by Mycenologists, it is hard to imagine that verbal art purporting to be directed at a god, but also having implications for humans, did not play a major part in the process of negotiating for power, and that local poets were not highly motivated to take the best from what they witnessed of others' performances and incorporate it into their own. So, I think we can assume that feasts/festivals were also a key setting for the communication of local verbal art within Greece in the second millennium, attracting performers and audiences to the palaces.

CONCLUSION

I hope to have shown that festivals from Anatolia and other parts of the Near East shared much in common with Greek festivals of the first millennium, not only in the particular events of the festivals, such as processions within the town and between towns, athletic competitions, musical performances and mimed battles, but also the application of seasonal rites for political ends, whether to vaunt one's military superiority, to strengthen the king against his enemies, or to express solidarity among various towns or countries, or between the king/state and vassals. The supra-regional audience and performers drawn to these festivals would have been an important vehicle by which the particular *drōmena* and *legomena* witnessed would have spread to new locales. While some of the shared details could simply be explained as typological, the very similarity between the festivals, whatever their reason, would make it easier for an outsider to appreciate the regional variations and inspire him to repeat and adapt those elements he found particularly compelling when he returned home to perform in the rite he considered to be equivalent. Thus, one of the means by which poets came into contact with new audiences and new ideas in the second millennium in Anatolia was similar to the pan-Hellenic festival circuit of the first millennium.

The mythical voyages of gods such as Apollo in some cases reflect the transfer of divine cult, and are paralleled by the voyages of the men (and women) who told their stories, whether their movements were voluntary

Hittite and Greek perspectives on travelling poets, texts and festivals   45

or constrained. Like Apollo, who honoured the little island of Delos by his birth there after his mother's extended wandering, and who arrived at Delphi to slay the serpent and open the land to cultivation, the seventh-century BC performer Cynaethus honoured and educated the spectators and other singers at the Delian festival by his superb and memorable performance. Just as Apollo came from afar to heal his worshippers, so in the second millennium BC, as in the first, doctors equipped with esoteric invocatory incantations to summon healing gods travelled or were sent as diplomatic gifts from one king to another.

CHAPTER 3

Thamyris the Thracian: the archetypal wandering poet?

Peter Wilson

'The only itinerant poet mentioned in Homer is the Thracian Thamyris': thus Bruno Gentili, in a book that perhaps more than any other indicated the road to understanding the social meaning of poets in early Greece, whether wandering or not.[1] The assertion is not quite true. In the *Odyssey*, the swineherd Eumaeus enunciates the general principle that one would not 'seek out and summon a stranger from abroad, unless it be one of those *dēmioergoi*' like a prophet, a healer, a carpenter – 'or a divine *aoidos*, who gives pleasure with his song. For these men are summoned all over the boundless earth' (17.382–5). Eumaeus seems to have an eye for professionalism that his social superiors lack: he is the only person in Homeric epic to remark that *aoidoi* are specialists from outside a community akin to the prophet, healer or builder. It is, however, certainly true that Thamyris is the only *named* wandering poet-singer in Homer, and the only one about whose story we hear anything of note. For that reason, and for the priority of his mention in the older epic, he has a claim to the title of archetypal 'wandering poet'. But he is, to say the least, a difficult rôle-model.

Thamyris is in some ways a marginal figure in Greek myth and literature, at least as it survives. But his is an ancient and persistent presence all the same. Like so many other figures important to Greek musical myth and history, he is from the margins of the Hellenic world.[2] He has affinities with

---

Thanks to Richard Hunter, Leslie Kurke, Luigi Battezzato, and audiences in Dublin, Armidale, Sydney, Otago and Cambridge for valuable comments and criticism. I am especially grateful to Grazia Merro for allowing me access, prior to publication, to her important work on the scholia to the *Rhesos*, and to Giovan Battista D'Alessio for informing me of it.

[1] Gentili 1988: 285.

[2] Beschi 1991; Restani 1995. Thrace and Thracians became increasingly familiar to classical Athenians with the founding of Brea (440), re-founding of Amphipolis (437), granting of citizenship to Sadakos son of Sitalkes (431), introduction of the cult of Bendis (429), on top of the presence of significant numbers of Thracians in the city throughout the century. Cf. Parker 1996: 173–4 on the status of Thrace in Athens in the fifth century (p. 174): 'a savage country and home of a savage people, but

Thamyris the Thracian: the archetypal wandering poet?   47

his fellow countryman and musician, Orpheus, but important differences too. The most striking of the latter is the competitive ambition that drives him to his destruction. And, although Orpheus is sometimes represented as religiously negligent (in his failure to recognise Dionysus in Aeschylus' *Bassarai*, for instance), he does not exhibit the relentless defiance shown by Thamyris to the Olympian Muses. That characteristic defiance makes of Thamyris a useful model of opposition – a figurehead, as I shall argue, for a religious tradition that ran against the current of the mainstream Olympian religion of the *Iliad* as well as for a mode of poetic performance that challenged that of Homeric epic itself. And, in a later age, tragic Thamyris served a society enthralled and troubled by the rapid changes in its poetic and musical culture to think through those changes; moreover, around the same time, the Thracian hero's record of defiance appealed to embattled musicians of the *kithara* contending in a world of ever-increasing specialisation, competition and professionalism.

THAMYRIS AND EARLY EPIC: A WANDERING CONFLICT

Thamyris first wanders into our view in the *Iliad*. His entry already has a distinct air of the metapoetic about it – or perhaps 'meta-aoidic' is strictly the more accurate term. He has a walk-on moment in the 'Catalogue of Ships', under the record of the contingent from Pylos at Troy (*Iliad* 2.591–600). We find him remembered at the mention of Dorion, the last named place in the list of Pylian cities who sent ships. It was in Dorion that the Muses met Thamyris, *en route* from Oikhalia and the house of Eurytos:

> οἳ δὲ Πύλον τ' ἐνέμοντο καὶ Ἀρήνην ἐρατεινὴν
> καὶ Θρύον Ἀλφειοῖο πόρον καὶ ἐΰκτιτον Αἰπὺ
> καὶ Κυπαρισσήεντα καὶ Ἀμφιγένειαν ἔναιον
> καὶ Πτελεὸν καὶ Ἕλος καὶ Δώριον, ἔνθα τε Μοῦσαι
> ἀντόμεναι Θάμυριν τὸν Θρήικα παῦσαν ἀοιδῆς,
> Οἰχαλίηθεν ἰόντα παρ' Εὐρύτου Οἰχαλιῆος·
> στεῦτο γὰρ εὐχόμενος νικήσεμεν, εἴ περ ἂν αὐταὶ
> Μοῦσαι ἀείδοιεν, κοῦραι Διὸς αἰγιόχοιο·
> αἱ δὲ χολωσάμεναι πηρὸν θέσαν, αὐτὰρ ἀοιδὴν
> θεσπεσίην ἀφέλοντο καὶ ἐκλέλαθον κιθαριστύν·

one with which it was indispensable for economic and strategic reasons constantly to grapple. . . . a land of promise and peril'. Cf. also Tsiafakis 1998 on the prominence of Thracian figures in classical Athenian iconography.

48   PETER WILSON

> And they who dwelt in Pylos and lovely Arene
> and Thryon, the ford of the Alpheios, and well-built Aipy
> and who lived in Kyparisseis and Amphigeneia
> and Pteleos and Helos and Dorion, where the Muses
> met Thamyris the Thracian and made an end of his singing,
> as he was journeying from Oikhalia, from the house of Eurytos the
>   Oikhalian:
> for he declared with boasting that he would win even if the
> Muses themselves were to sing against him, the daughters of Zeus
>   the aegis-bearer;
> they in their wrath maimed him, and took from him
> his wondrous singing, and made him forget his playing.
>
> Homer, *Iliad* 2.591–600

This might seem a curious way to embellish the traditions of the Pylians who, as we know from the loquacious old man Nestor, had plenty of other things to boast about.[3] And Thamyris was, after all, just passing through their region. Suspicions have been triggered by the fact that he should be described as meeting the Muses in *Dōrion* – which was in northern Messenia – when *en route* from Eurytos' city Oikhalia, which Homer himself places in distant Thessaly (see figure 1) only some hundred lines later.[4] Thamyris is certainly '*vagante*' – perhaps he is even lost.

   The localisation of this event exercised ancient scholars.[5] The Thessalians did indeed also lay claim to it, and this tended to stick. In the Hesiodic *Catalogue of Women* it took place Δωτίωι ἐν πεδίωι, 'on the *Dōtion* plain' near the Boibean lake.[6] Modern scholars have certainly felt more comfortable with the Thessalian localisation of this encounter. Geoffrey Kirk spoke for a modern consensus when he wrote that this 'is a more likely place for bumping into the Muses than the south-western Peloponnese'.[7] This has led some to suppose that Homer himself is a bit lost, and has confused Messenian *Dōrion* with Thessalian *Dōtion* because of the similarity in their names.[8] But it is clear that we are dealing with evidence of a struggle, rather than of a nodding Homer. As much is suggested by the fact that further

---

[3] Sufficient indeed to have constituted an independent epic tradition, in the view of many: Vetta 2003; cf. Kiechle 1960.

[4] *Iliad* 2.730.

[5] The debate is especially evident in the scholia to the passage of the *Iliad*; cf. also Paus. 4.33.7, with Musti and Torelli 2000: 264–5; Brillante 1991: 429–31.

[6] Hes. *Ehoiai* fr. 65 M-W; cf. fr. 59.2. The Hesiodic account is also explicit about the blinding: cf. αὐτὸν τετυφλῶσθαι, *ad* fr. 65.

[7] Kirk 1985: 216. In the post-Homeric tradition, Oikhalia was often placed in Messenia (or Euboia: see esp. Strabo 9.5.17 and Aristonikos II, p. 311, 61f Erbse [*ad Iliad* 2.596]).

[8] Burr 1944.

Thamyris the Thracian: the archetypal wandering poet?

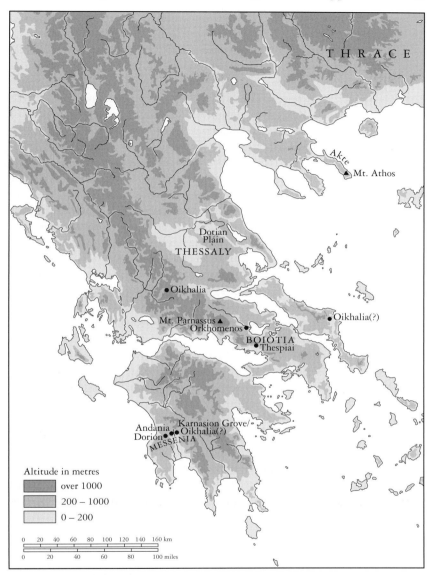

1 Map of Greece

50 PETER WILSON

places also claimed the event – one or more in Boeotia, and probably Eretria in Euboia among them.[9]

That there was an early struggle over where Thamyris met the Muses is telling in itself. It was an event worth struggling for, or arguing about. And it suggests that he was a figure with a larger rôle to play in early Greek tradition than we are now able to see. The existence of multiple claims *on* Thamyris may also imply the existence of multiple claims *about* him. The *Iliad*'s casual dismissal masks an aggressive rivalry, as recent critics have stressed. Therefore it is likely to mask a more 'favourable', or at least a different, tradition. I suspect there may even be traces of this embedded under the surface of the *Iliad*'s account. Consider line 599: αἱ δὲ χολωσάμεναι πηρὸν θέσαν, αὐτὰρ ἀοιδήν. . . . Had this been a rogue papyrus fragment, we might have expected it to continue something along the lines of – 'In their anger they maimed him, but *left him* his power of song.' αὐτάρ normally marks a strong contrast, but in the passage as we have it, it is necessary to understand it in the much less common 'additive' usage, 'to mark a rapid succession of details' (*LSJ s.v.*).[10] Ancient critics already noted that the line is morphologically parallel to *Odyssey* 8.64, describing Demodokos, where the Muse is the subject: ὀφθαλμῶν μὲν ἄμερσε, δίδου δ' ἡδεῖαν ἀοιδήν 'she took away his eyesight, but gave him the power of sweet song'. This pattern of bad balanced by good at the hands of a Muse invites us to expect that αὐτάρ will indeed introduce a contrast in the *Iliad* passage.[11] But if it were ever there, it has otherwise been thoroughly edited out, and Thamyris' relation with the Muses becomes the reversal of the 'good' encounter, as exemplified by Hesiod and Archilochus.

There are however other reasons to think that the story of Thamyris was told differently. His very name implies a figure more akin to the useful *dēmioergos* of *Odyssey* 17, the skilled stranger called in from outside. In old Aeolic, the word θάμυρις (*thamyris*) meant a 'festal assembly' (πανήγυρις) or a 'gathering' (σύνοδος), while the verb θαμυρίζειν meant 'to bring together', 'to assemble'.[12] The adjective θαμυρός was used to describe highways, 'roads that carry people' as Hesychius' gloss puts it (καὶ ὁδοὺς θαμύρας τοὺς λεωφόρους). 'Thamyris' thus looks like an ancient

---

[9] For Thamyris in Boeotia see Paus. 9.30.2 and the further evidence mentioned in note 17 below; for Eretria, the suggestion rests on the presence of the city of Oikhalia there (Paus. 4.2.2, with note 24 below), and the assumption that it brought with it the story of Thamyris.

[10] Leaf 1900: 96: 'αὐτάρ is additive'.

[11] See schol. *ad Iliad* 2.599 Dindorf. Buxton 1980: 27 points to a tradition preserved by schol. *ad* Ovid *Ibis* 272 that Demodokos was blinded after losing a contest with the Muses, and asks whether Homer knew of this and chose to ignore it.

[12] Hesychius θ90, θάμυρις· πανήγυρις, σύνοδος; θ91, θαμυρίζει· ἀθροίζει, συνάγει. West 1999: 376.

Aeolic name for a special form of communal gathering, for supra-local meetings at a religious centre. The Thracian's mythic identity must somehow be founded on this idea, as the embodiment or instigator of such unions, probably as 'the one who brings people into a group *through song*'. That the adjective was used in particular of roads brings us into the same semantic field as οἴμη, used of the 'ways' of epic song in the Homeric tradition. But the 'roads' of Thamyris suggest the centripetal force of song, the gathering into union and collectivity; while the Homeric paths are, as Andrew Ford has put it, the open avenues of the singers' resource, poetic 'paths' that stand for 'themes', a wide array of possibilities 'whose relative fixity and stability . . . was figured in Homeric language by describing them as if they were tracks cut into some landscape'.[13] If then the image of the road looks like being rather different in the worlds of Thamyris and Homer, its presence in both reflects a shared, but rivalrous, conception of their traditions and authority.

So too do the very names of Thamyris and Homer. Martin West has argued that 'Homer' might be 'as fabulous a figure as Orpheus and Musaeus',[14] and that the Homeridai were a professional group who 'retro-invented' the name 'Homer' and whose own name is to be associated with the very same idea of a large public gathering or festival assembly, a hypothetical *ὅμαρος or *ὅμαρις, traces of which can be seen in the name of the Achaian Homarion near Helike.[15] Durante suggested some time ago that the name Thamyris similarly derived from a collective group, the Thamyridai or Thamyradai, and Boeotian epigraphy provides an astonishing classical example of θαμυρίδδοντες.[16] These were officiants in a cult in Thespiai which had connections to political power. The cult might have been a hero-cult for Thamyris himself in the valley of the Muses; the name of its officers probably combined the sense of 'the gatherers' with that of 'Thamyrists'.[17]

---

[13] Ford 1992: 42.   [14] West 1999: 373.

[15] West 1999: esp. 373–7; West here reprises important theses of Durante 1976.

[16] Durante 1976: 195–202.

[17] The inscriptions testifying to a cult at Thespiai: *SEG* 15, no. 320; 32, no. 503; Durante 1976: 202: 'i cantori delle riunioni festive'; Roesch 1982: 138–42, 140: 'une association de Thamyristes'; Schachter 1981–94: vol. 4, 41; Bonnet 2001: 55: 'compagnie d'artistes vraisemblablement chargée de l'organisation des fêtes en plus spécifiquement cultuelles qui avaient lieu dans le sanctuaire'. Brillante 1991: 445, citing Amphion of Thespiai (*FGrH* 387 F1), the author of a work on the sanctuary of the Muses on Helikon, proposes musical contests for boys within the cult (Amphion speaks of παίδων ὀρχήσεις, boys' or children's dances), with an initiatory character overseen by the mythic figurehead of Thamyris. Pausanias 9.30.2 describes a statue of Thamyris at Thespiai 'already blind and holding his shattered lyre'. Thamyris was represented in a lost statue group by Kephisias of Boeotia, from the Valley of the Muses. It was erected before 241 by Philetairos son of Eumenes of Pergamon: see *BCH*

52   PETER WILSON

It thus looks as though Thamyris may be the name of an ancient tradition, associated with the Aeolian sphere, now lost or at least submerged and misrepresented, and that it may have posed a challenge to the Homeric tradition on the pan-Hellenic, or pan-Hellenising, stage. Is it possible to excavate any further into this tradition, before returning to the *Iliad* to see how that epic's thinly-veiled aggression deals with it? Some indications, however fugitive, may come from a trip back to Oikhalia.

THAMYRIS, OIKHALIA AND THE MYSTERIES OF ANDANIA

Thamyris was by no means so out of place in Messene as Kirk thought. As I indicated, the mainstream of all modern and much ancient tradition thinks that Thamyris really 'ought' to have met the Muses on his way from the better-known Thessalian Oikhalia – and so in the region that lay between Parnassos and Thrace, his own home and that of the Muses. But ancient scholars identified up to five Oikhaliai, most or all of them associated at some time with Eurytos, the master archer and/or with Thamyris, the master singer and kitharist. And Eustathius shows that the question as to just which Oikhalia Thamyris had left when he ran into the Muses had been a kind of meta-*agon* in earlier scholarship, an *agōn* that he says was won by the Arcadian claim: νικᾷ δὲ ἡ Ἀρκαδική as he put it.[18] And by 'Arcadian' he certainly means the Oikhalia in northern Messene, which was on the road to Arcadia.[19] But there were at least three places that made loud claims in this debate: Thessaly, Messenia/Arcadia, and Eretria. And while we do not hear of an Oikhalia in Boeotia, the Thamyris story was certainly prominent there, and probably localised in Orkhomenos among other centres, as the presence of Thamyris in the *Minyas* suggests.[20] This

---

26 (1902–8) 155–60; Roesch 1982: 140–1. In the first century the poet Honestos added a distich to it that has Thamyris 'show remorse': τὸν θρασὺν ἐς μολπὴν ἄφθογγον νῦν μ' ἐς ἀοιδὴν / λεῦσσε. τί γὰρ Μούσαις εἰς ἔριν ἠντίασα; / πηρὸς δ' ὁ Θρῇξ Θάμυρις φόρμιγγι πάριμι / ἀλλά, θεαί, μολπῆς γ' ὑμετέρης ἀίω. 'Look at me, once brazen in music, now with no voice for song. Why did I oppose the Muses in competition? Here I am with my *phorminx*, lame Thamyris of Thrace; and now goddesses, I attend to your music.'

18 See Eustathius *ad Iliad* 2.596 in van der Valk 1971–87: 461: ὃ καὶ ἀμφιβολίαν, φησί, ποιεῖ, πόθεν ὁρμηθέντα τὸν Θάμυριν ἀοιδῆς ἔπαυσαν αἱ Μοῦσαι 'and this leaves it ambiguous as to the place from which Thamyris was setting out when the Muses stopped his song'. The fact that Eustathius declared the Arcadian Oikhalia the 'winner' will owe something to its place in the *Iliad*, but there are likely to have been other reasons now unrecoverable for his decision.

19 Paus. 4.2.3; Pherecydes fr. 82a Fowler *ap.* schol. Soph. *Trach.* 354: ᾠκεῖτο δὲ αὕτη ἐν Θούληι τῆι Ἀρκαδίας. For ἐν Θούληι Bölte (in *RE s.v.*, col. 2097) proposes: ἐνθ' οὖν δή, 'wo auch immer'. See now Fowler 2000: 318 for other readings. (He prints †ἐν θούληι†). Musti and Torelli 2000: 207–8. Cf. Strabo 9.5.17 (Oikhaliai in Thessaly, Euboia, Arcadia).

20 Paus. 4.33.7; 9.5.8. See *EGF* fr. 4 Davies. See also above note 18 on the cult of Thamyris in the Valley of the Muses.

Thamyris the Thracian: the archetypal wandering poet?   53

wandering of Oikhalia is far from random. All these regions share mythic and ethnic traditions and – Euboia aside – they represent the spread of the Aeolian sphere.[21] The only major Aeolian region not attested is the northern Aegean, in particular Lesbos, and it would not surprise us to learn one day that his story was somehow present in that home of *kitharōidia*.

Though the *Iliad* later (2.730) puts Oikhalia in Thessaly, to my mind, the Pylian passage of the 'Catalogue of Ships' (2.596) certainly suggests knowledge of the Oikhalia in Messene.[22] This was a very ancient site, probably the Okara₃ named on Pylos tablets.[23] It lay on the western side of the river Electra to the east of which was the Homeric Dorion. If this is where the Iliadic Thamyris had been in the house of Eurytos, he had not travelled very far at all when the Muses came upon him. At some point this Oikhalia (like the others) was destroyed, and the name of the site became the Karnasian grove (Καρνάσιον ἄλσος).[24] The likely context for such a change is the Spartan invasion of Messenia in the eighth century.[25] This was the site of the second most important mystery-cult in all Greece, after the Eleusinian – the Andanian mysteries, which were named after the place Andania whose ruins Pausanias says lay just 1.5 kilometres (8 stades) away from the grove and the site of ruined Oikhalia. A number of ancient sources directly identify Andania with Oikhalia.[26] This cult was central to the religious life and identity of the Messenians, and it is generally thought to have long predated the arrival of the Spartans.[27] The renaming clearly reflects Spartan efforts, subtle or otherwise, to inveigle themselves into this most ancient of Messenian cults, for it is likely that Apollo Karneios was

---

[21] It is explicitly stated that the Euboian claim is a later one, made by οἱ νεώτατοι: e.g. Aristonikos *ad Iliad* 2.596, I, p. 311, 61f Erbse. The authority of Hekataios of Miletos was however adduced for the Euboian claim at some time: see note 24 below.

[22] Note too that at Hom. *Od.* 21.15 Odysseus meets Iphitos 'in Messene'. Long ago Leaf 1900: 95 objected to the attempts of commentators to save the consistency of the Catalogue and Homer by supposing that Thamyris was a wandering bard who found himself far away from Thessalian Oikhalia: 'this is clear evidence that the Oichalia legend . . . was localized in the Peloponnesos as well as in Thessaly'.

[23] Talamo 1975: 29. This continuity of name over so long a period would *prima facie* give Messenian Oikhalia a certain precedence.

[24] Paus. 4.33.4. This is the Messenian tradition, which Pausanias supports. At 4.2.2 Pausanias records the debate over where Oikhalia was: Thessalians say it was what is now the (abandoned) site of Eurytion, while the Euboians have Kreophylos' *Heraklea* and Hekataios of Miletos on their side in saying that there was an Oikhalia in Skios, a part of Eretria.

[25] Some may say rather that the Spartan invasion is a likely context for the – (?) Messenian and/or Spartan – invention of the tradition of Oikhalia in Messene, and of Thamyris' association with it.

[26] For Demetrios of Skepsis, Oikhalia is the old name for Andania: see Strabo 8.3.6, 8.3.25, 8.4.5; Scarpi 2004: 103–4; Livy 36.31.7.

[27] One of the thrusts of Luraghi's recent work on Messenian identity (see esp. Luraghi 2002) is to suggest that the idea of a pre-conquest genuinely 'Messenian' identity is a chimaera; contrast Zunino 1997, Deshours 1993, 1999.

54   PETER WILSON

superimposed onto a Messenian Apollo already in the sanctuary.[28] It was
a cult of Apollo, Hermes and Hagne – whom Pausanias identifies as the
daughter of Persephone. And the preliminary act of these mysteries was a
sacrifice to the hero whose house Thamyris had just left as he encountered
the Muses in the *Iliad* – Eurytos. His bones were kept at Oikhalia.[29]

What light might all this throw on the early tradition of Thamyris and his
reception within the *Iliad*? Thamyris' father was Philammon (the tradition
is virtually unanimous in this respect), the founder of another great mystery-
cult, that at Lerna in the Argolid,[30] and according to one report, another
of Philammon's sons was Eumolpos.[31] The family starts to look like a
dynasty of founders of mystery-cult. To an audience who knew of the
rôle of Oikhalia and of Eurytos in the mystery-cult, the very emphatic
description of Thamyris' progress in line 596 (with its somewhat incantatory
sound) – Οἰχαλίηθεν ἰόντα παρ' Εὐρύτου Οἰχαλιῆος – may have carried
a very different charge, though the victory of the Olympian Muses and
the Homeric tradition give us little hope of reconstructing just what that
might have been. What did it mean for Thamyris to 'come from the house
of Eurytos'? Might Thamyris have been a kind of mythic mystagogue in
Andania? Some sources ascribe a theology or a cosmology to Thamyris
of the sort we more often associate with his mystic fellow countryman,
Orpheus.[32] Given his identity as a Thracian, as a miraculous singer and a
wanderer, perhaps most likely is a rôle as the 'importer' of the cult itself, or
as the mythic 'convenor' of its gatherings.

Pausanias tells us that you cross a river called Balyra on your way between
Messene and Andania – the river taking its name from the 'casting of the
lyre' (βάλλειν λύραν) of Thamyris after his maiming.[33] The conflict in
some form (probably with the Apollo of the shrine, or his 'local' Muses?)[34]
may thus be organic to the Messenian cult. Perhaps Thamyris' fate was seen
as a kind of symbolic death that might be fitting for a mystery context. And
the city of Oikhalia, wherever it was placed, is a city destined for disappearance, to exist mythically to be destroyed. Ziehen argued persuasively that

[28] See esp. Paus. 4.26, with Musti and Torelli 2000: 242–3; Zunino 1997: 321; Figueira 1999.
[29] Paus. 4.2.3, 4.3.10, 4.33.5.
[30] Philammon: Apollod. *Biblioth.* 1.16–17; scholl. Hom. *Il.* 2.595; Eustath. *ad Il.* 2.594ff.; *Suid.* θ41, φ300.
     The only variant is that the schol. Hes. *WD* 1 (= Gaisford 24–6) cites Aethlios as an alternative to
     Philammon.
[31] Paus. 2.37.2.
[32] Cf. *Suda* θ41: φέρεται δὲ αὐτοῦ Θεολογία εἰς ἔπη τρισχίλια 'a *Theology* by him of 3,000 verses is
     transmitted'; for the cosmology: Tzet. *Chil.* 7.95.6.
[33] Paus. 4.33.3.
[34] The Messenians had Muses of their own: cf. the Muse 'dear to Ithome' from the (probably) early
     prosodion of Eumelos, Paus. 4.33.2 and 4.31.10–12 with Zunino 1997: 178 n. 128, 185–6.

Thamyris the Thracian: the archetypal wandering poet?

its very name evokes as much, with its echo of οἴχεσθαι, 'to be gone'.[35] In *Iliad* 2.596, Thamyris is thus 'coming' (ἰόντα) from the place that is 'gone' (Οἰχαλίηθεν), or perhaps from the place of 'the departed'. This could serve well as an (encoded) way of speaking of a return from the Underworld.[36] Oikhalia is a place associated with heroes who are made to disappear or to be blinded for their presumption, whose powers in the two great areas of Apollo's mastery – bow and lyre – bring them close to, and so inevitably in conflict with, Apollo.[37] The cult of Apollo in the Karnasian grove certainly incorporated the god's 'enemy' in the bow, Eurytos, and may have likewise included his musical antagonist too. The very defiance of these heroes, perpetuated in myth, cult and music, keeps them alive, makes them repeatedly to be reborn.

I suggest that Thamyris shared with his fellow countryman and musician Orpheus an early rôle as the figurehead of, and agent in, mystery-cult and its associated myth. That the text of the *Iliad* is cognisant of this rôle can only be a hypothesis, but one with important ramifications for our view of the epic's religious framework and vision. Thamyris' association with Andania, and with a possible network of mystic cult and performance, may date to the eighth or seventh century, but we cannot simply retroject thither the hints we have of it from a later age.[38] If however we admit the possibility that Thamyris in the *Iliad* may have represented a tradition of religious song that proffered the hope of an afterlife radically different from that implied by the *Iliad*, the passing story of his encounter with the Muses takes on a very different character. Thamyris' claim that he could defeat them in song becomes so much more than the boast of a musical rival. It becomes a religious claim as much as a performative one; the blinding of the singer and destruction of his instrument becomes not a retort of the wounded pride of a professional but an assertion of cosmic authority and order. Like Orpheus, Thamyris was not merely a rival to the singers of Homeric poetry, or to their authority-figures in myth, be they an archetypal

---

[35] 'Denn O., das Ziehen . . . mit οἴχομαι "sterben" zusammengestellt hat, ist das Reich der Abgeschiedenen, und Eurytos, der überall mit O. zusammengehört, ist der Herr dieses Reiches': Ziehen, as quoted in *RE* 17.2099 *s.v.* 'Oichalia'.

[36] Thamyris himself was placed in the Underworld in the epic *Minyas* (Paus. 9.5.8), as too in the representation of the Underworld by Polygnotos in the Delphian *leskhē* of the Knidians (Paus. 10.30.8).

[37] Nagy 1979. The parallel with the only hero in the *Iliad* who plays a stringed instrument – Akhilleus – is evident.

[38] It is possible that some of this is retrojected tradition, in part developed out of the passage of the *Iliad*. Musti and Torelli 2000: 207 suggest that the localisation of Oikhalia in Messenia in the early period, as a secondary regional 'capital' after Pylos, was due to its proximity to Andania, and to a desire to give it an 'epic chronology'.

PETER WILSON

Homeros, or the Muses of Olympos. Early music and poetry did not form an autonomous sphere of artistic excellence and competition. Differences in music implied differences in world-view, and in particular, in religious outlook.

Did a promise of an afterlife through a mystery-cult to which music was central thus represent a threat to the kind of afterlife promulgated by Homer?[39] Richard Buxton demonstrated that blinding in myth takes place 'by virtue of extraordinary power or insight' of the individual blinded, who 'threatens to blur the distinction between god and mortal'.[40] The extremity of Thamyris' punishment (which troubled ancient critics) clearly makes sense in a context where his actions had seriously threatened that divide. In the *Iliad*, the Muses, 'daughters of Zeus the aegis-bearer', impose a poetic and religious authority whose main aim seems to be to put this figure, who was so prominent on the Messenian horizon, and perhaps in a wider, ancient Aeolian network, well and truly in his place. It is in fact not even clear that Thamyris was given his chance to sing against the Muses in the *Iliad*. We are simply told that he boasted of victory '*even if* the Muses themselves should sing against him . . .' and then, with no mention of an actual contest 'they in their wrath maimed him . . .'

EPIC POET VS. THRACIAN SINGER

If the case for a religious point of difference between Homer and Thamyris must remain a hypothesis, there can be no doubt that powerful antagonism of some sort underlies this encounter. Suggestive commentaries on these dynamics of antagonism have recently been given by Richard Martin and Andrew Ford. Martin has argued that this is Homer's way of obliterating poetic rivals in passing and (as it were) in advance. He sees the reference to a singer coming 'from Oikhalia' to mean the epic tradition that included the *Sack of Oikhalia*, and so to refer to the whole nexus of (rival) epic tradition that gave Herakles the most privileged rôle. By depicting Thamyris as the mythic progenitor of this tradition, and as having had this dreadful encounter in the distant past, he is in effect asserting that *that* current of the epic had long since been definitively shut off.[41] Ford, on the other

---

[39] Given its possibly mystic colouring, the Thamyris tradition may pose the sort of 'threat' that 'Orpheus' did. Cf. Albinus 2000: 104: 'Orpheus was a legendary poet like Homer but, contrary to Homer, it was the story of his life and death, more than the authority of Apolline inspiration, that defined the power of his song.' See Hardie 2004 for a powerful case that music featured prominently in the exegesis of Greek mystery-cult, and more broadly on the relation between music, the Muses and mysteries.

[40] Buxton 1980: 27.   [41] Martin 1989: 229–30. Cf. Grandolini 1996: 42–5.

Thamyris the Thracian: the archetypal wandering poet?   57

hand, argues that Thamyris is made to stand for all earlier poets; his fate is a lesson in poetic and religious respect: 'Thamyris, the only named and identified singer in the *Iliad*, stands in that poem for preceding poets, and his contest shows that mere temporal earliness is not enough to guarantee a strong transmission of song if the Muses are not honoured.'[42] On this reading – and, in fact, on any reading sensitive to the dynamics of poetic composition and contest – the precise positioning of the event in Book 2 should be related in part to its proximity to the great re-invocation of the Muses with which the 'Catalogue of Ships' begins, just a hundred lines earlier. This demonstrates a markedly respectful attitude to the Muses: 'You are goddesses and know all things, but we hear only a rumour and know nothing . . . the multitude I could not tell or name, not even if ten tongues were mine and ten mouths and a voice unwearying, and the heart within me were of bronze, *unless* the Muses of Olympos, daughters of Zeus . . . call to my mind all those who came beneath Ilios' (2.484–92). This is close enough in the narrative to make the contrast with Thamyris abundantly clear: the poet of the *Iliad* has a respectful, intimate and authoritative relationship with the Muses.

However, rather than being simply annihilation by mythic means of another current of the epic tradition, or a reminder of the need for a pious attitude to the Muses, this use of Thamyris should, I think, be seen as one means by which hexameter epic positions itself in relation to a rival *performance* tradition – to a more fully *musical* tradition, of fully-fledged song to the kithara, *kitharōidia*. The short description lays great emphasis on the medium of song and on Thamyris' instrumental skill, and it includes the epic's sole use of the rare abstract term *kitharistus*.[43] That performance rivalry might be at issue here is also suggested by the fact that, in the *Homeric* tradition, physical blindness is far from incompatible with the power of song; whereas in Thamyris' case, blindness (if that is what πηρός means) is made a mark of extra humiliation rather than of honour or special 'inner' vision.[44]

Bruno Gentili and Gregory Nagy have done a great deal to demonstrate that the image of radical historical progression from epic to lyric is in

---

[42] Ford 1992: 97.

[43] Stress on his *song*: 595, 598, 599. The *schol. vet.* comment of *kitharistus* that it is an Aeolic formation (ὁ δὲ σχηματισμὸς τῆς λέξεως Αἰολικός). This passage of the *Iliad* and its commentators aside, the only other usage of the word seems to be in the third-century elegy of Phanokles, fr. 1.21 Powell, where it is used of the post-mortem music of Orpheus.

[44] Aristarchus (schol. *ad loc.*) saw that blinding was not of itself a particularly effective way to punish a singer, and glossed πηρὸν as τῆς ὠιδῆς πηρόν ('lame of song').

58   PETER WILSON

large part an optical, or perhaps a textual, illusion.[45] The fourth-century
'history of music' (*Synagōgē*) of Heracleides Ponticus placed *kitharōidia* and
kitharōidikē poiēsis, invented by Amphion, at the very origins of all music
and poetry.[46] In its next age came Thamyris and Demodokos. Gentili
took the latter as an avatar of the pre-Homeric kitharode, but Thamyris
might be just as promising a candidate. Heracleides identified him as the
'one who sang with the most beautiful and melodious voice of all men of
that time',[47] and this emphasis on the musical quality of his voice seems
important.[48] Recent work on the earliest Greek musical resources suggests
that there were two distinct but interacting traditions in Dark Age Greece,
which we might call broadly 'melic' and 'epic': the former based on a
heptatonic system of tuning of great antiquity, the latter on the more
limited musical resources implied by and probably founded on the system
of linguistic pitch.[49] The conflict between Thamyris and the Muses, seen
as a displacement for a conflict between Thamyris and Homer, looks to
me like a representation of this clash between two musical traditions that
expressed themselves ultimately in the different generic performance-types
of hexameter epic and kitharodic lyric.[50]

---

[45] Gentili 1988: 15; Nagy 1990a.

[46] Fr. 157 Wehrli = [Plu.] *de Mus.* 3, 1132b. Heracleides (according to *de Mus.* 1132a) famously referred
to the *anagraphē* in Sikyon (*FGrH* 3 B550, p. 536) to support his history.

[47] He adds that 'it is recorded that he composed a *War of the Titans with the Gods*' – another title
suggesting an intriguingly cosmological, or at least primordial, pre-Olympian subject.

[48] It is also worth noting that Thamyris is one of the various mythic figures to whom the invention of
the Dorian *harmonia* is ascribed: see e.g. Clem. Alex. *Strom.* 1.16.76; Eustath. *Hom.* 297.38 (*ad Il.*
2.594). The ascription is made in connection with the Homeric localisation of the meeting with the
Muses in *Dōrion*. But rather than being the idle invention of a scholar spun out of that passage, it
is more likely to represent the strategic interpretation of the passage on the part of a group whose
interests were served by endowing Thamyris with the authority to be derived from the invention of
this cardinal musical mode. The attribution of the *orthios nomos* to him comes as less of a surprise
(gloss on Hdt. 1.24 in Latte and Erbse 1965: 197, Ὄρθιον νόμον Θαμύρα. ὁ κιθαρωιδικὸς τρόπος
τῆς μελωιδίας, ἁρμονίαν ἔχων τακτὴν καὶ ῥυθμὸν ὡρισμένον).

[49] Franklin forthcoming b: cuneiform texts suggest that there was a whole Mediterranean 'metaculture'
with heptatonic tunings long before their codification in fourth-century Greece. The work of Nagy
(1990a: esp. ch. 1) is important here, too, for the argument that an earlier, undifferentiated form of
'song' was differentiated into melodic and non-melodic types, with Homeric epic most prominent
among the latter.

[50] One tradition makes Thamyris the father of Homer (*Cert. Hom. et Hes.* 22, Tzet. *Proom. Alleg. Hom.
Il.* 64 = Matranga *Anecd. Gr.* i, p. 3: I owe these references to Merro 2006). The claim is likely to
mask (and to have promoted) poetic polemic between these two traditions, by granting Thamyris the
symbolic seniority that goes with paternity. Although it appears centuries after the relevant period, it
is worth noting that the subject matter of the *Sack of Oikhalia*, normally associated exclusively with
hexameter epic, found expression in strictly lyric form. A couple of interesting fragments of a lyric
Οἰχαλίας ἅλωσις, probably by Pindar, were published in 1968, but never made it into *Supplementum
Lyricis Graecis*: *P. Oxy.* 2736 (vol. 35, ed. Lobel). See Lavecchia and Martinelli 1999. On the epic –
'Kreophylean' – *Sack*, generally dated in the second half of the seventh century, see esp. Burkert
1972.

Thamyris the Thracian: the archetypal wandering poet?

Whatever meanings the representation of Thamyris in *Iliad* 2 was made to carry, there is no doubt that, for us, he begins his poetic life as the musical competitor *par excellence*. His claim to defeat anyone in song, even the Muses, is the *reductio ad absurdum* of the agonistic mindset.[51] The Delphian records had him on their lists among the earliest victors at the Pythia and this quality – which distinguishes him sharply from his fellow Thracian, the otherworldly Orpheus – will continue to be important in the fifth century.[52] Thamyris is not the only wandering poet in Homer, but he is the only one who talks openly about *competition* – εὐχόμενος νικήσεμεν. But that also means that, for all its coyness on the matter, the Homeric tradition itself is well aware of agonistic poetics. Its decision to elide its own competitive environment and ambitions, and to represent its one musical agonist as a transgressive extremist, cannot be neutral. It begins to look like a form of misrecognised competitiveness of its own, one that seeks to conceal itself, or to engulf all rivals in such a way as to do away with contest altogether.[53]

TRAGIC LYRIC: THAMYRIS ON STAGE

Already in Homer, Thamyris has the air of the heroic, competitive musician who asserts the independence of his musical skills from their (or at least from one authoritative) divine source.[54] That assertive stance clearly struck a chord with the tragedians. The Thracian and his musical contest with the Muses were once thought to have featured prominently in a tragedy (or satyr-play) of Aeschylus, but the slender foundations on which that belief was based have very recently been removed.[55] Nonetheless, in addition to

---

[51] Schadewaldt 1965: 64; Weiler 1974: 59, 66–72.

[52] Paus. 10.7.2–3. Unless the new fragment of Eumelos in *P. Oxy* 53, 3698 is correctly restored by Debiasi (2003) to suggest that he was otherwise in the *Korinthiaka*, Orpheus is characteristically not a competitor; but cf. also fr. 8 Bernabé, in which Orpheus is apparently the victor with kithara in the musical contest at the first Isthmian Games, in which the Argonauts took part.

[53] Ford 1992: 96–9 makes a similar point about the way this passage allows the 'agonistic underpinnings' of the epic to show through, even though 'muted to near inaudibility' (p. 97).

[54] Again, unlike the pious Orpheus, whose failure to acknowledge Dionysus in Aeschylus appears to have been negligence: *Bassarai TrGF* 3, pp. 138–40.

[55] The evidence was a fragmentary page of the codex *Vat. Gr.* 909, with scholia on Euripides' *Rhesos* 916 and 922 (published by Rabe 1908 = *TrGF* 3, F376a). Part of the scholion on 916 was restored by Rabe to read 'the story of Thamyris and [the Muses] received more [detailed] exposition in Aeschylus' (παρ' Αἰσχύλωι δὲ τὰ περὶ τὸν Θάμυριν καὶ [τὰς Μούσας ἀκριβέσ]τερον ἀφήγηνται). Some (such as Hall 1989: 134–6) argued that the plot summary that the scholar goes on to quote from Asklepiades' *Tragōidoumena* (= 12 *FGrH* F10) was meant to explicate an Aeschylean play fully centred on Thamyris (others had envisaged a reference within the *Edonians* or *Bassarai*: see *TrGF* 3, 376a). Work by Grazia Merro 2006 on this page has produced a superior text which reads at the crucial

60   PETER WILSON

the famous Sophoclean tragedy devoted entirely to him, Thamyras features prominently in the lament of the Muse which closes the *Rhesos*, where he is described, intriguingly, as 'that Thracian sophist' (p. 924).[56] He also returns to the stage – this time the comic stage – in the fourth century, in a work by Antiphanes named after him. It is quite likely that Antiphanes' work interacted with its famous tragic predecessors.[57]

What issues in contemporary Athenian *mousikē* does this mythic musician serve to focus – at once an honoured figure of earliest musical history and an arch transgressor? The central and immutable fact of Thamyras' existence (as we know of it) is his musical arrogance, the boast that he could defeat the Muses in song, which led to their making him blind, lame, mute, mad or oblivious of his skills – or some combination of these. Hellenistic scholars argued over how to translate the crucial Homeric adjective, πηρός.[58] But it is too easy, I think, to assume that the story simply appealed to Sophocles as a variant on the pious theme of hybris punished.[59] When the hero facing ruin is a colleague – however remote – of the tragic poet, there must be something more at stake.

The Sophoclean *Thamyras* was one of his most famous plays. The tradition that Thamyras was one of the few rôles Sophocles acted himself as protagonist, and that he was painted in the rôle in the *Stoa Poikilē*, suggests that some sort of affinity was felt between the Thracian singer and his tragic creator.[60] If true, Sophocles will have had to demonstrate his *vocal* and *instrumental*, as well as his Thespian, powers.[61] But I suspect that, behind the story in the biographical tradition that Sophocles soon gave up

passage 'some treated the story of Thamyris and [the Muses] more . . .'. Reference to Aeschylus is an impossibility: Merro 2006: 'nel punto in cui Rabe scorgeva . . .>σχύλωι si legge in verità ἔνιοι'. Hall 1989: 102–38 remains the most important treatment of 'the Thracian' in tragedy.

[56] Hereafter I shall use the spelling Thamyras, the Attic form of the name: cf. Lex. Cyr. *ap.* Cramer *Anecd. Gr. Paris.* 4.183.13: ὁ Θάμυρις . . . Ἀττικοὶ δὲ Θαμύρας. '"Thamyris" . . . and "Thamyras" in Attic authors.' Philammon may have been called a σοφιστής in the Sophoclean play (see note 131 below). I would suggest that the word so used invites an association with the group of cultural innovators prominent in Athens of the last third of the fifth century whose spheres of expertise included not just rhetoric but, among others, music. Cf. Wallace 1998.

[57] *PCG* 2, 104, with Kassel and Austin *ad loc.* on signs of possible Euripidean imitation.

[58] Mad: schol. B Hom. *Il.* 2.599; πηρόν: ἔνιοι δὲ πεπηρωμένον καὶ βεβλαμμένον αὐτοῦ τὴν διάνοιαν; '*pēros*: according to some this means incapacitated and wounded in his mind'; Plin. *NH* 35.144 (fourth-century Theon of Samos painted a mad Thamyras); Hesykh. θ92, *Suda* θ42: Θάμυρις μαίνεται as a proverbial expression. Ameis and Henze *ad loc.* opt for 'stumm', in the sense of 'deprived of song'. See Aristarchus, quoted in note 44 above.

[59] Thus Cillo 1993: 208.

[60] In fact, the sources say only that 'he took up and played the kithara only in the *Thamyris*, as a result of which he was painted with kithara in the *Stoa Poikilē*' (*Vita*, TrGF 4 T1); while Athenaios (1.20e = TrGF 4 T28) explicitly says that 'when he was producing the *Thamyris* he himself played the kithara'. In other words, neither actually states that he acted as protagonist, only as kitharist.

[61] On the latter cf. Eust. *Il.* 381, 8 = TrGF 4 T29, καὶ κιθαρίζειν ἄκρος.

Thamyris the Thracian: the archetypal wandering poet?   61

acting because of his weak voice, we might detect the shaping contours of myth – as though, in playing Thamyras, the poet had himself suffered the Thracian's fate and lost the power of song.[62] Whatever the correct proportions of myth and history, the story suggests a perceived analogue between the tragic poet and the mythic musician.

The first performance appears to have made a striking and lasting impression. We can point to a number of factors that played a part in this. At the dramaturgical level, there is the probable use of the innovative 'blind' mask that, when used in alternate profile, visually rendered the awful transformation of the singer at the moment of reversal. One side had a seeing eye, the other a blinded eye. Secondly, there is the fact that Aeschylus' son, the tragic actor Euaion, may have played Thamyras' mother Argiope, alongside Sophocles himself as Thamyras (if we give credence to the biographical tradition): a wonderful interlacing of theatrical and mythic generations.[63] The iconographic evidence for Euaion acting the rôle of Argiope at a date when he could be lauded as *kalos* on a vase is also (sadly) our best indication to the date of the *Thamyras*.[64] The grounds for the 'traditional' early date of the 460s were never very strong: the belief that Sophocles acted the rôle before giving up on acting; the claim that he was represented as Thamyras in the *Stoa Poikilē*, completed *c.* 460 (but see note 60), and the likelihood that Euaion played Argiope as a young man.[65] I have already indicated significant problems with the first two points. As to the last, Green (2002: 96) notes that Euaion should have been a young (and *kalos*) actor in the 440s.[66] That then is the most likely period for the play on the evidence currently available.

We cannot go far in safe reconstruction of the play, of which we have some ten short fragments.[67] We can however say with some confidence that it was set on the Thracian Chersonese, perhaps on the eastern coastal region of Mount Athos.[68] In other words, Thamyras was in Thrace, in his homeland. This may be something of a general tragic reversal. In the *Iliad*, Thamyris was himself on the move, and certainly somewhere other

---

[62] *Life* 5.24ff. = Radt *TrGF* 4 T1. Thus also de Martino 1995: 22–4.

[63] For the profile 'blind' mask, based on Pollux 4.141, cf. Trendall and Webster 1971: 69; the thesis has been supported more recently by recourse to vase-imagery: Lesky 1951; Séchan 1967: 193–8; Cillo 1993: 209; Brillante 1991: 434 expresses some doubts. Euaion as Argiope: Webster 1969: 205; Green 2002: 95–6.

[64] Attic hydria *c.* 430 Vatican Museo Etrusco Gregoriano. Trendall and Webster 1971: III 2.9.

[65] Hauser 1905; Webster 1969: 6–7; Trendall and Webster 1971: 69–70; Cillo 1993: 206–7.

[66] See now Krummeich 2002.

[67] For relevant suggestions see Pearson 1917; Sutton 1984.   [68] See *TrGF* 4 fr. 237.

62   PETER WILSON

than Thrace.[69] In Sophocles' *Thamyras*, as well as the *Rhesos*, the Muses are the mobile agents, finding Thamyras in his homeland (following the sound of his music?). These mobile Muses might incline us to associate the intriguing account given of Thamyras' story by Asklepiades of Tragilos – probably deriving from his compendium of tragic mythography, the *Tragōidoumena* (12 *FGrH* F10) – with the Sophoclean play.[70] Asklepiades explains that the Muses came to Thrace (ἀφικομένων δὲ τῶν Μουσῶν εἰς Θραίκην), where Thamyras challenged them to a singing contest in which if he won, his chosen prize would be to cohabit with all nine Muses; if they were victorious, they could do with him what they would. In the outcome, they won and blinded him.

The association of this narrative with Sophocles' play is entirely conjectural. Before Grazia Merro produced a superior edition of the scholion to the *Rhesos* which preserves this quotation of Asklepiades, some were inclined to see the passage as preserving the plot of a lost Aeschylean *Thamyras*.[71] With the removal of all reference to Aeschylus in the new text, the scholiast in fact cites Asklepiades to substantiate his remark that 'Some treated the story of Thamyris and [the Muses] more [? fully].' The fact that in Asklepiades' version the Muses go to Thrace (as they do in the *Rhesos*) is hardly sufficient to give much confidence in a Sophoclean basis to the digest.[72] So it remains no more than an intriguing possibility that the Sophoclean play and hero had the characteristics listed by Asklepiades: a Thamyras of 'amazing appearance' (περὶ τὸ εἶδός φασι θαυμα<στ>όν), and apparently wall-eyed before the blinding (τῶν δὲ ὀφθαλμῶν τὸν μὲν δεξιὸν λευκὸν εἶναι, τὸν δὲ ἀριστερὸν μέλανα). Most fascinating of all is the sexual voraciousness – or at least a cultural inclination to polygamy – shown by this Thamyras. Athenian ethnic stereotyping of Thracians as generally voracious and sexually polygamous would appear here to be intriguingly entwined with Thamyras' musical skills. Pride in his own performance capabilities

---

[69] As my discussion of the Homeric material suggested, it is possible that the *Iliad* knew of a tradition according to which Thamyris in Dorion could be seen as 'at home' in the region by virtue of his place in a local cult, yet nonetheless still a 'wandering singer' by virtue of his ethnic origins.

[70] The explicit reference of the citation to the *Tragōidoumena* can no longer stand in the scholion to *Rhesos* 916 (the text reads merely 'Asklepiades, in the second book', ὁ Ἀσκληπιάδης ἐν τῶι δευτέρωι), but as Merro 2006 indicates, this presents no problem of clarity, especially given the full reference to the *Tragōidoumena* just above in the scholion to 895.

[71] See above note 55; Hall 1989: 134–6.

[72] On the other hand, Asklepiades' version is unlikely to have been based on the known comic treatment by Antiphanes, and we cannot cite any other lost tragic work known to have dealt so fully with Thamyras. Weiler 1974: 68 believes that the erotic motif could only have appeared in a comic treatment. Hall 1989: 134–6 comes close to suggesting it was a tragedy, but pulls back at the last minute and thinks of a satyr-play. I see no problem with the inclusion of the sexual element in a tragedy.

Thamyris the Thracian: the archetypal wandering poet? 63

seems to underlie his bravura claim that he could take all the Muses as partners, as well as a wish to outdo Zeus' original nine nights of intercourse that produced the Muses in the first place (Hesiod *Theogony* 56–7).[73] A test of musical prowess is used to adjudicate the quarrel. This looks like an early attestation of a semantic and symbolic overlap between musical and sexual activity which surfaces more clearly around 430, in the 'New Musical' environment. We find the 'loosening' of strings symbolic of sexual mastery, κιθαρίζειν – 'to play the kithara' – available for a number of innuendos, and the specific superlative adjective 'very kitharodic' – κιθαρωιδότατος – used as a term of abuse suggestive of excessive sexual indulgence.[74] In a famous fragment of Pherecrates' comedy the *Kheirōn*, Music (*Mousikē*) ascribes her ruined (sexual) state to the activities of those 'new' musicians of the kithara and of dithyramb, Kinesias, Phrynis, Timotheos and co. (fr. 155 K-A). The possible parallel, across genres, with Sophocles' *Thamyras* is striking: Muses (rather than *Mousikē* personified) threatened with sexual mastery by a boastful and brilliant kitharode.

The play very probably brought the Muses themselves on stage. The recorded Sophoclean title *Mousai* may well be a doublet for the *Thamyras* and, for that and other reasons, it is likely to have had a chorus of Muses – a potent form of dramatic representation indeed, to imitate that ultimate choral source of *mousikē* in the very physical embodiment of a tragic chorus.[75] And all the more potent, given that these were violent Muses. In typical tragic fashion, the play foregrounded that violence within their make-up that is normally concealed from view or, in the case of the *Iliad*, that is passed over in discreet narration in a hexameter or two. Moreover, it will also have been in keeping with generic expectations if Sophocles emphasised the genealogical link between Thamyras and his punishers. Thamyras' mother Argiope was a nymph born on Parnassos.[76] These violent Muses were attacking a relative.[77]

---

[73] Cf. Catullus 32.8.

[74] Pherecrates fr. 155.3–5, with Dobrov and Urios-Aparisi 1995: 143, 155–7 and Hall 2000; cf. Eupolis fr. 311; Aiskhines, *Against Tim.* 41 with Fisher 2001: 171–2; Prauscello 2004: 336–8; Wilson 2004: 286–7.

[75] A Muse chorus: Trendall and Webster 1971: 69–70. Cillo 1993: 208 regards it a certainty, on the basis of the twin *hydriai* of the Phiale Painter (*ARV*² 1020, 92; 1020, 93), on one of which, above two Muses who are watching Thamyras (thus in the Attic form of his name), is inscribed XOPONIKA. If, as Lloyd-Jones (1996: 103) and others believe, the play Μοῦσαι (*Muses*) is an alternative title for the *Thamyras*, the collective form of the name may point to a chorus of Muses. See Sutton 1984: 78 on the *Muses*. Muses in any case form a 'natural' chorus, from at least the time of Hes. *Theog.* 7. Schneidewin suggested that the chorus of the *Thamyras* was made up of followers of Thamyras: Pearson 1917: 178. Sutton 1984: 139 thinks of Thracian locals.

[76] Konon *FGrH* 26 F1 (7); Paus. 4.33.3. Brillante 1991: 433–4.

[77] A number of sources give Thamyras a Muse for mother: schol. Hes. *WD* 1 (= Gaisford 24–26); schol. D *Il.* 10.435.

64   PETER WILSON

It is also likely – from both the fragments and iconography – that the
contest, the blinding of Thamyras and the destruction of his instrument
actually took place on stage. A famous *hydria* in the Ashmolean shows
Thamyras, uniquely, in right profile (to signal his blinding), his lyre flying
from his hand just as the punishment has taken place, watched by his
distraught mother and a Muse.[78] This was in other words a spectacular
production. Its probable full theatrical staging of a mythic, musical *agōn*
between singer and Muses pre-empts the sort of thing that is found –
and reckoned spectacularly innovative – in the 'new' dithyramb later in
the century. In that context, the parallel musical contest between Marsyas
(playing the *auloi*) and Apollo (on the lyre) seems to have received a quasi-
dramatic enactment in dithyramb.[79]

Even though they are preserved by a variety of routes, most of the handful
of surviving fragments treat 'musical' matters to a remarkable degree, and
are themselves metrically varied. If they are an even vaguely representative
selection, this tragedy was clearly hyper-musical, both in its form and in its
preoccupations. Kitharodic song is likely to have featured prominently –
both in the exemplary and competitive performances of Thamyras before
the disaster and, it has been suggested, in the form of a lament after the
blinding by the Muses. The Muses, too, will presumably have sung in
choral and/or solo performance – a challenging rôle for any group of mortal
amateurs.

Fragment 240 has resolved tetrapodies, their only occurrence in
Sophocles:

πρόποδα μέλεα τάδε σε κλέομεν
τρόχιμα βάσιμα χέρεσι πόδεσι.

These tunes by which we celebrate you get the feet forward, running, moving –
hands and feet.

The mimetic power of this trochaic rhythm is clear, as it well and truly lives
up to its name.[80] The apparent element of ritual self-description here very
strongly implies choral performance with energetic dance, perhaps even an
entrance-song. This might militate against the view that the play had a
chorus of Muses, for these words are more likely to come from the mouths
of supporters of Thamyras, as Schneidewin proposed.[81] We could however
perhaps think of the Muses addressing their leader Apollo (σε κλέομεν)
in an opening entrance-hymn, though the metre seems less appropriate

---

[78] Oxford Ashmolean 530; *ARV²* 1061, 152.   [79] See Csapo 2004: 213.
[80] See Gentili and Lomiento 2003: 120–30, esp. 120 on the close relation between trochaics and the
  khoreios (χορεῖος), 'perché si prestava facilmente agli movimento della danza'.
[81] Reported by Pearson 1917: 178.

Thamyris the Thracian: the archetypal wandering poet? 65

for the Olympian. Alternatively, we could envisage a secondary chorus of Thamyras' supporters, as in the *Hippolytos*.[82] We are told on good authority that the trochaic rhythm was especially characteristic of the *Phrygian* mode in music, and Sophocles himself was said to have introduced this mode into tragedy, in a 'dithyrambic' manner.[83] The music that accompanied fr. 240 could very well have been an instance of such 'dithyrambic' Phrygian.

Fragment 242, describing Thamyras' maternal grandmother Philonis, is by contrast in hexameters:

ἐκ μὲν Ἐρίχθονίου ποτιμάστιον ἔσχεθε κοῦρον
Αὐτόλυκον, πολέων κτεάνων σίνιν Ἄργει κοίλωι.

She had at the breast a boy by Erikhthonios, Autolykos, plunderer of many possessions in hollow Argos.

Wilamowitz imagined that these were lines sung by Sophocles as Thamyras – a nice idea, although the hexameter is unlikely to have been the only metrical form used for Thamyras' kitharody. If this is from Thamyras, he is evidently chanting the catalogue of his own genealogy, and tracing his ultimate descent from the divine inventor of the lyre, Hermes (also known as Erikhthonios).[84] At least one other fragment – the frustratingly incomprehensible fragment 241 – may be from a sung lament by Thamyras after the blinding by the Muses and what seems to have been his own destruction of his instrument. To that extent his suffering was, Oedipus-like, a composite affair in which his own hand added the destruction of his instrument to the divine work of blinding.[85] Before lapsing into unrecoverability, this fragment begins: 'Gone are the plucked melodies of *pēktides* [harps]' and it goes on to mention lyres and *monauloi*, a kind of single pipe or flute. Yet another fragment (fr. 238) also describes musical instruments. This lays much emphasis on their materiality, and happens to give us our third example of *melos* in so very few fragments:

πηκταὶ δὲ λύραι καὶ μαγαδῖδες
τά τ' ἐν Ἕλλησι ξόαν' ἡδυμελῆ

joiner-made lyres and harps that give octave concords, and the instruments carved from wood to give sweet music among the Greeks.

It is difficult to tell how strong a contrast, if any, is intended here between the complex lyres and harps of evidently Lydian origin in the first line, and the wooden instruments used among *Greeks* in the second: the τε looks

---

[82] A suggestion already made by Lammers 1931.
[83] Aristoxenos fr. 79 W; Psell. *de trag.* 5; cf. West 1992: 181.
[84] *Et. Mag.* 371, 49: Ἐριχθόνιος· ὁ Ἑρμῆς.
[85] Fr. 241 with Pearson 1917: 181 for various suggestions for ordering the confusion in the latter part of this fragment.

66   PETER WILSON

like it simply continues the list, and if that is so, this fragment does not so
much capture an ethnic contrast between Greece and the east as expressed
in musical instruments, but in fact the 'instruments carved from wood to
give sweet music among the Greeks' are given something of an outlandish
sound in this company, and may well describe non-Greek instruments.
This is the only instance of *xoanon* used of a musical instrument.[86]

   We should perhaps place the two single-word fragments 239 and 239a
in the same general context. These are the words τρίγωνος (*trigōnos*) and
φοῖνιξ (*phoinix*), both used of musical instruments. It is especially striking
that these two regularly appear on the list of banned instruments drawn
up by the musical conservatives Plato, Aristotle, Aristoxenos and co. I shall
return to the *phoinix*. The *trigōnos* was a variety of harp plucked with the
fingers rather than struck with a *plēktron*, and it is usually associated with
Phrygia (further evidence of 'Phrygian' music in the *Thamyras*). According
to the Socrates of the *Republic*, it had too many strings. Aristotle included
it among those instruments that were taken up by Greeks in their over-
excitement at winning the Persian Wars, and with too much time and
money on their hands. They later saw the error of their ways and rejected it
when they were in a better position to judge what was conducive to virtue,
since the *trigōnos* promoted only pleasure.[87]

   Fragment 244 shows us the very moment of crisis for singer and instrument, describing (in lyric metre) someone – surely Thamyras himself,[88]

          ῥηγνὺς χρυσόδετον κέρας,
          ῥηγνὺς ἁρμονίαν χορδοτόνου λύρας

breaking the horn bound with gold, breaking the harmony of the strung lyre

The correlation between the physical construction of the instrument and
the harmony of its music is widespread in Greek thinking about the lyre.
Here it is underscored by the phonic and metrical similarity between
χρυσόδετον and χορδοτόνον. It is characteristic of tragic *mousikē* to focus
on that union at the moment of its disintegration. It looks as though
Thamyras' active choice to destroy the lyre may have been a focus of special dramatic attention.

---

[86] See further below note 104 on this.
[87] On the Phrygian associations of the *trigōnos* see also Soph. fr. 412, with Barker 1984: 50 and Gentili
and Lomiento 2003: 85. Pl. *Rep.* 399c–d; Arist. *Pol.* 1341. Aristoxenos (fr. 97 W *ap.* Athen. 177f)
described both as 'alien instruments' (ἔκφυλα ὄργανα).
[88] Reiske thought Thamyras the speaker; Beazley, the chorus: see Pearson 1917: 183.

Thamyris the Thracian: the archetypal wandering poet? 67

It is fragment 245 however – the longest extant (a whole eighteen words) – that gives us the best idea of how Thamyras' music was treated in Sophocles' tragedy.

> μουσομανεῖ δ᾽ ἐλήφθην
> ἀνάγκαι, ποτὶ δ᾽ εἴραν
> ἔρχομαι, ἔκ τε λύρας
> ἔκ τε νόμων, οὓς Θαμύρας
> περίαλλα μουσοποιεῖ.

[2] ἀνάγκαι Lloyd-Jones 1994: δαν καὶ το *codd.*: δακέτωι Radt δ᾽ εἴραν Campbell; ποτὶ δειράν, ποτίδειραν *codd.*
[3] ἔρχομαι aABMon.: ἔχομαι Blaydes: ἄγχομαι Sheldon

> And I was seized by a compulsion
> to be mad for music, and went
> to the place of assembly*, under the force of the lyre
> and the force of the measures, with which Thamyras
> makes music supremely.

* *or* 'and I was stricken at the throat'

The speaker describes the effect of Thamyras' music on him – or her – as a form of madness (μουσομανεῖ), of physical seizure (ἐλήφθην) by a *force majeure* (ἀνάγκαι). This is force, not persuasion, nor even the mighty *thelxis* of Orpheus. The translation 'to be mad for music' is too weak, suggesting the hobbyist rather than someone driven insane by a desire to hear Thamyras, or perhaps even driven insane *by* the music of Thamyras – the force of μουσομανεῖ is ambiguous.[89] The agents of this music are presented with clarity: its instrument – λύρα – and its tunes – νόμοι. But the manner of the description, with its repeated and emphatically positioned use of ἐκ, hints at excess, of 'going beyond' limits. The effect is promoted by the way this clause describing the agents of the music-madness is itself delayed by the interposition of a new clause,[90] – 'and I went to the place of assembly' – ποτὶ δ᾽ εἴραν ἔρχομαι. And it is perhaps more strongly felt in the second case, where ἔκ τε νόμων more naturally suggests 'beyond' or 'outside of the laws'. The pun is easy and common, and the irony would be characteristically Sophoclean.[91] The certain presence of cannabis in this drama – we have the single-word fragment κάνναβις (fr. 243) – has led Bremmer (2002: 31)

---

[89] The adjective is extremely rare and the verb μουσομανεῖν is attested only late: Luc. *Ner.* 6; Athen. 4.183e.
[90] A practice favoured by Euripides: Diggle 1994: 428–9.
[91] From as early as Hes. *Th.* 66, the Muses are responsible for singing *nomoi* (in that case, *nomoi* of the gods). The sense there is probably 'ordinances', as West 1966: 178 argues. It is unclear when the

68   PETER WILSON

to make the very plausible suggestion that 'Sophocles somehow connected
the Thracian Thamyras with an ecstatic use of cannabis'. It is extremely
likely that Thamyras' ecstatic use of cannabis was within the context of
the 'alien' music and dance he promoted and of which even these meagre
fragments give us some glimpse.

Lloyd-Jones has done much to bring order to this *fragmentum vexatum*,
and I have basically reproduced his text.[92] But there remain two significantly
divergent possibilities for that second, interposed, clause: 'I went to the
place of assembly' – *or* – 'I was stricken at the throat.' Thamyras' lyre-
playing either induces political gatherings or hysterical singing.[93] The latter
possibility would fit into the wider trope of being gripped by a desire
to sing, as expressed for instance, with practised spontaneity, by girls in
Alcman's choruses.[94] The Sophoclean variant would however represent a
far stronger alternative. It would continue the emphasis on the very physical
grip exercised by Thamyras' music, and imply perhaps that it led to a kind
of hysterical vocal contagion in its hearers.[95]

Nevertheless, hurrying to the 'place of speech' seems, on balance, to be
what happened. Lloyd-Jones revived Campbell's clever suggestion that the
rare word εἴραν was lurking in the text. This is certainly the *lectio difficilior*.
The noun, meaning 'a place of speech', occurs at *Iliad* 18.531, where
Eustathius (*Hom.* 1160.35) interestingly notes that it means 'the place of
assembly and prophecy' τὴν ἐκκλησίαν καὶ τὴν μαντείαν.[96] It would be
entirely consistent with all else we know of Thamyras if the songs which
drew his hearers to him also had an oracular character. This 'place of

---

more strictly musical meaning of *nomos* begins. It can be no more than a guess that Sophocles may
have likewise punned, with etymological force, on the name of Thamyras at some point in the play,
associating the idea of 'populous gathering' with him *via* terms such as θαμά, θαμέες, θαμίζω. The
example of Ajax (see esp. Soph. *Aj.* 430–3 with Garvie 1998: 165) could be adduced.

[92] Lloyd-Jones 1994: 135–6. Note the enthusiasm of Easterling 1998: 212 for Lloyd-Jones' reading
ἀνάγκαι.

[93] As Luigi Battezzato points out to me, ποτὶ δειράν / ἔχομαι – 'I am stricken [or 'gripped'] at the
throat' – may rather suggest restriction, an inability to sing (listeners to Thamyras' music struck
mute despite the urge to sing?). It would certainly be so with ἄγχομαι, 'I am strangled.' This in
many ways attractive suggestion (especially after Lloyd-Jones' ἀνάγκαι) was made to me by John
Sheldon, but it would introduce a verb apparently not elsewhere used in tragedy.

[94] E.g. Alk. *PMG* 3.1ff. = 26 Calame; cf. Calame 1983: 396 for discussion and other examples.

[95] Aristoxenos reports that at a spring festival in Rhegion there were sixty days of paian-singing to
Artemis Phakelitis, at perhaps twelve paians per day: fr. 117W, with West 1990. This punishing
régime was said to have been prescribed by oracle as a cure for a sickness that made the women
of Rhegion and Lokris flee the city as they sat eating, thinking they heard a voice call them: an
intriguing (re-)combination of elements possibly present in the passage of the *Thamyras*.

[96] Cf. also Aristonikos 4.548 Erbse, ὅτι εἴρας λέγει τὰς ἀγοράς 'by *eiras* he means the agoras', *E.M.*
s.v. εἴρα: ἀγορά, Lloyd-Jones 1994: 136, noting that the word has been restored also at Hes. *Theog.*
804, Pind. *Nem.* 3.14.

Thamyris the Thracian: the archetypal wandering poet? 69

assembly' – and perhaps of prophecy – will be where Thamyras played his lyre, in the agora of the town near Mount Athos. Were his lyric *nomoi* characterised as having a political or socialising force, bringing a form of civic cohesion through the 'legislative' power of music, and its physical impulse to gather? Or perhaps, given the violence of the language used, these *nomoi* drove people together with a commandeering, tyrannical force? Either way his music offers a fascinating inversion of the standard Dionysiac pattern, driving people *to*, rather than away from, the urban centre. This image of hearers gathered in an assembly in the grip of a kind of madness, under the sway of a charismatic individual, may also have had a specifically political resonance for an Athenian audience – at any time, but perhaps all the more so in the later in the century we date the play.

A number of other factors encourage us to see a link between Thamyras' musical and political power – among them, the linguistic and epigraphic evidence for the meaning of the name Θάμυρις itself that I have already discussed, as well as a range of other historical and mythical instances where political and musical power come together.[97] The paradigm of the musician-poet brought in from outside a community to assist it in matters of civic harmony, and who often goes on to attain special status within it, is pervasive and persistent, and lies at the heart of any definition of the *poeta vagante*. Stesichorus and Terpander are two early more or less historical examples.[98] It seems likely that Sophocles was following a tradition, known from the Hellenistic scholar Konon, that Thamyras' musical powers led to his being given royal power. According to Konon, 'when he grew to manhood he reached such attainment in *kitharōidia* that even though he was an outsider, the Scythians made him their king'.[99] The outsider becomes

---

[97] A rough selection of examples might include: the Singers (*Molpoi*) of Apollo Delphinios, the institution of whose processional ritual of songs along the sacred way from Miletos to Didyma marked the end of an exhausting period of civil war and repeated Lydian interference in Miletos, and who seem also to have been élite civic officers of state (*LSAM* 50); the theory that the name Apollo may be a formation in –ων formed from ἀπέλλα (a kind of assembly: Burkert 1975); the way cities use musical symbolism or practice to organise themselves, as in the arrangements of the civic divisions and perhaps of the very streets of fifth-century Kamarina: see Cordano 1994; Wilson 2003b, 2004.

[98] Stesichorus: *PMG* 281c = Philodem. *De mus.* 1, fr. 30.31–5, p. 18 Kemke; Terpander 'made the Lacedaemonians stop from their discord by singing in their messes' (Philodem. *De mus.* 1, fr. 30.31–5, p. 18 Kemke = Gostoli 1990: T14a). Philodemos was sceptical, but still had to point out that 'very large numbers of music maniacs (μουσόληπτοι)' all agreed about this (Philodem. *De mus.* 4, Pap. Hercul. 1497, col. 19.4–19 = Gostoli T14b). See further Gostoli 1990. Pythagoras advised the citizens of Kroton to set up a sanctuary of the Muses and so brought *homonoia* (civic concord): Iambl. *de vita Pyth.* 9.45.

[99] *FGrH* 26 F1 (7): ὃς ἡβήσας ἐπὶ τοσοῦτον ἧκε κιθαρωιδίας ὡς καὶ βασιλέα σφῶν καίπερ ἐπηλύτην ὄντα Σκύθας ποιήσασθαι. Kanne 1798: 83 suggested that Konon confused Scythians with Thracians. I owe this reference to Brown 2002: 91.

70   PETER WILSON

king through his power of song and string: such a correlation looks likely
to be present in Sophocles, if not quite in the particular form it takes here,
among the Scythians. Did Thamyras exercise royal power in Sophocles'
play as a *mousikos*? In the authoritative Hesiodic *Theogony*, the Muses have
tutelage of kings as well as singers.[100] If Sophocles' Thamyras was both singer
and king, his conflict with the Muses will have represented a spectacular
perversion of that proper relationship on both scores.

As fate would have it, fragment 245 of Sophocles' play is framed by
'muses', through its first and last words – μουσομανεῖ – μουσοποιεῖ. In a
tragedy where Muses play a major rôle, the repetition can hardly be idle. It
draws attention to Thamyras' enemies even as it describes his own power.
It underlines the awful paradox of having as enemies the very source of
his power – a paradox that may well have featured prominently in Sophocles' treatment.[101] The second of these compounds is especially interesting:
μουσοποιεῖ. This is the first of an extremely small number of occurrences
of this verb or the related noun μουσοποιός. Thamyras 'muse-makes' his
lyrical *nomoi*. This conjunction of the 'muse' with the verb of 'making'
points to a problem at the heart of the story of Thamyras. It describes him,
for want of a better word, as a 'creative artist'. He is the agent, working on
the Muse. This is very unlike the epic vision of the poet-singer's relation
to divinity, which figures the *aoidos* as little more than a conduit for the
all-encompassing knowledge of the Muses. Thamyras turns the Muse into
his own *nomoi*.[102]

        SOPHOCLES, THAMYRAS AND THE 'NEW MUSICIANS'

There is a debate locked within this word *mousopoiein* and in the fate of
Sophocles' Thamyras, that is to be taken up not many years later in the fifth
century. That debate is over the question as to where mortal power over
images should cede sovereignty to the divine. An Attic red-figure krater
from around 420 presents an unusual and very striking representation of
Thamyras, the Muses and the contest (see figure 2).[103] On one side, the
contest is taking place. Thamyras, looking rather like a kitharode in a

---

[100] Hes. *Theog.* 80–103; Bertolini 1995.
[101] Cf. Buxton 1980: 28 on the story told of the tragic poet Akhaios: 'In being blinded by bees a poet
    is being weakened by the very agency which represents his strength.'
[102] Ford 2002: esp. 137–8 discusses tragedy's avoidance of the language of 'making' in relation to song.
    See further below.
[103] Ferrara (Spina) Museo Archeologico inv. 3033, T127 Aurigemma 1960: 1.37–43, tavv. 1–16; Alfieri,
    Arias and Hirmer 1958: 80–1, figures 108–9; in what follows I am much indebted to the excellent
    article of Brillante 1991.

Thamyris the Thracian: the archetypal wandering poet?

2a Attic red-figure krater *c.* 420 from Ferrara (Spina). Thamyras plays the kithara in the presence of Apollo and the Muses

2b Drawing of image in figure 2a

2c Detail from figure 2a. Nine small female figures (*xoana*) above an altar: to the left a Muse watches in surprise as Thamyras seeks to animate these with his music

Thamyris the Thracian: the archetypal wandering poet? 73

mousikos agōn, is depicted in the act of playing his instrument (a *kithara*) in the presence of Apollo (beside a large tripod) and the Muses, variously arranged and equipped with instruments. In the top right-hand zone of this image there is an altar, a lyre leaning against it, while above it, nine small female figures are gathered in a close, neat single-file row. On Carlo Brillante's convincing interpretation, Thamyras is here attempting not simply to display his musical virtuosity, but to animate with his song this chorus of nine female *xoana*, his own personal substitutes for the nine real Muses, the latter being his adversaries rather than aids.[104] Alongside and observing these nine inanimate figures – which we are probably to imagine as having begun to move in choral dance around the altar – is a female figure expressing surprise and horror. This is doubtless one of the 'real' Muses, suitably shocked.[105] The act befits a magic-man or mystic, and it is a challenging image of Thamyras the *'muse-maker'* indeed.[106]

The other image on the body of this krater treats Hera and Hephaestus, and apparently shows the craftsmen's god liberating Hera from the magic throne to which she was bound by invisible chains.[107] This scene includes a number of satyrs, one of whom prominently carries a torch, thus echoing the imagery of the vase's neck, which is that of a human torch-race conducted in a non-mythological, agonistic context. This combination has encouraged an association with the Athenian festival of Hephaestus, with

---

[104] Brillante 1991: 442. Other interpretations see in the nine figures simply a circular chorus dancing around the altar (Ferri 1931); Alfieri *et al.* 1958: 81 hold the view that these *xoana* are a chorus with which Thamyras hopes to oppose the rival chorus of the Muses; Koller 1963: 40 takes this up, but sees the figures as human girls, guided by Thamyras. Brillante 1991: 438–9 demonstrates the problems with these interpretations. We should not press this image unduly for an association with the Sophoclean tragedy. It is nonetheless intriguing that one fragment (fr. 238, see above) includes an apparently unique usage of the word ξόανον to describe a wooden musical instrument. Could τά τ᾽ ἐν Ἕλλησι ξόαν᾽ ἡδυμελῆ refer to Thamyras' 'substitute' Muse-*xoana*: 'the *xoana* that give sweet music among the Greeks'? The usage of the term *xoanon* of the effigies depicted on the Spina krater is of course modern, and influenced by the classification of images adopted by Pausanias (Pirenne-Delforge 2004: 813). It is however entirely plausible for the classical period: cf. e.g. *Xoanēphoroi*, the '*Xoana*-bearers', a title of a Sophoclean drama *TrGF* 4: 374; Eur. *Ion* 1403.

[105] Others (e.g. Trendall and Webster 1971: 4) interpret this woman as Thamyras' mother, Argiope. Among other reasons for rejecting this view (cf. Brillante 1991: 439) is her iconographic similarity to the other Muses. In her horror she has abandoned the instrument she was, like her fellows, holding.

[106] Brillante 1991: 441: 'in questo contesto, ispirazione e animazione non sono dissociabili. Col suono della cetra Thamyris si proponeva di realizzare sia l'una che l'altra.' The fact that the fringed garment worn by the chorus of *xoana* has been identified with the woollen ἀγρηνόν worn by prophets, in particular, and members of Bacchic choruses (Pollux 4.116; Hesykh. α777; *Etym. Mag.* 14.2 Gaisford; cf. Brillante 1991: 440) does little to bring the image into a specifically dramatic environment. Brillante's case for these *xoana* being 'substitute Muses' could be further bolstered by the fact that such unusual *xoana* – usually in threes, but in one case nine – appear in the iconography of the Muses and their sanctuaries *only* in connection with Thamyris: Nercessian, *LIMC s.v.* 'Thamyris/Thamyras': 904.

[107] Alfieri 1979: 80.

74   PETER WILSON

its famous torch-races. At just this period – in the year 421/420 in fact –
this festival was reorganised, with the inclusion of significant musical
events.[108] *Kitharōidia* was almost certainly one of them. This expansion
of Athenian musical contests to the Hephaistia in the 420s, probably on
the model of the Panathenaic events, is an important part of the growing
economy of theatrical and musical performance, to which new professional
and virtuosi on the *kithara* were key. Sophocles' play is more than likely
to have mused on the limits of musico-poetic power; perhaps, too, on the
relation between musical and *political* power. I would also suggest that
it involved an engagement by one musical art – that of tragedy – with
another – that of *kitharōidia*. Unlike all of its fifth-century colleagues and
rivals in poetic *sophia*, tragedy has trouble engaging in the meta-poetic, or
meta-musical. Comedy revels wildly in exactly this potential, at times turning itself into a kind of aggressive, megalomaniacal rage against all other
mousikoi. But even the purely choral form of dithyramb could engage in
this way, as could the solo lyric form, the kitharodic *nomos*, whose final
sphragis allowed the musician's voice to sing out in its closing phrases.[109]
The fully mimetic, polyphonic mode of tragedy isolated (or protected) its
practitioners from such direct engagement in their own name, or in some
stylised persona built upon their own name. Yet the need was there to
engage or risk marginalisation. Comedy also demonstrates in a general way
the ongoing need of each poetic form to enunciate its claims to *sophia*,
personal and generic, and to engage in the broader issues of musical and
political authority in the city, where rhetoric, philosophy and other *sophiai*
and *tekhnai* were more and more insistently clamouring at the doors of
traditional cultural authority.

   An important means by which tragic poets could engage in these issues
is provided by the rich resource of pan-Hellenic musical myth. Thamyras
belongs to a small but significant group of figures from that world who
found themselves on the fifth-century Athenian stage, and we ought to look
to these to see what tragedy made of those issues that ran through its *own*
broad medium, namely of *mousikē*. For there can be no doubt that it was a
turbulent and charged field. The idea that figures like Orpheus, Thamyras
of Thrace and Amphion of Thebes were one means open to the tragic poet
to engage in the ongoing 'debate' about his medium is supported by the fact
that comic poets seem to have responded with particular energy to them.
Cratinus composed a comedy called *Euneidai* that somehow treated the

---

[108] *IG* I³ 82, esp. line 14. Cf. Froning 1971: 67–86, arguing that the vase reflects a dithyramb on the
     subject at the Hephaistia.
[109] See Timotheos *PMG* 791. Cf. *PMG* 802.

Thamyris the Thracian: the archetypal wandering poet? 75

Athenian clan of musicians who claimed descent from Euneos, who starred in Euripides' *Hypsipyle* and was taught the Asiatic kithara by Orpheus; Euboulos produced an *Amphion* that clearly responds to the Euripidean treatment;[110] and as I have indicated, Antiphanes returned to Thamyras, with a comedy of that name.

The fifth-century history of *kitharōidia* is almost a black hole. A little light appears in the last decades of the century, when practitioners like Phrynis and Timotheos set to work on what was once a rigidly structured form (the kitharodic *nomos*), to make of it – along with dithyramb – a hotbed of innovation.[111] It is usually, and quite understandably, to Euripides that one is directed to observe the influence which these innovators in lyric poetry exercised on tragedy, but Sophocles' *Thamyras* is, I would suggest, a harbinger of that revolution, or at least reflects on its approach.

Thamyras' musical instrument in Sophocles is described as a lyre.[112] But this certainly does not mean that he and his story could not be made to say things about the music of the kithara. For it may have felt jarringly anachronistic to introduce the kithara itself (at least the word) into the world of tragic myth, and the use of the term λύρα (*lyra*) in tragedy is far from precise.[113] The instrument used on stage could well have been a concert-kithara, or something very like it. In fact, much has been written about Thamyras' instrument, especially as it appears in iconography. It is never the simple traditional tortoise-shell (*khelys*) lyre, but a special, somewhat longer-armed variety with a larger resonating-box that art historians have named the 'Thracian lyre' in his honour.[114] He was probably given this special type not because 'real' Thracians used it, but so as to mark his instrument as different from the standard tortoise-shell lyre that every good Greek boy learned to play. And the difference moves his instrument in the direction of the concert kithara.

In the last thirty years of the fifth century, there is an explosion of Attic vase-images of Thamyras, among them the krater from Spina already discussed. Some ten or fifteen years after the production of Sophocles' play,[115] the type of instrument he is found playing, and the scenes in which he plays it, change significantly. He starts to play a larger, more elaborate version of the 'Thracian kithara', much closer to the grand concert-kithara.

---

[110] Wilson 1999/2000: 432.   [111] West 1992: 356–64; Csapo 2004.

[112] Note the use of λύρα in frr. 238, 241 and esp. 245; Cillo 1993 for the possibly relevant vase-images.

[113] Cf. e.g. Eur. *Pho.* 822–3; West 1992: 51; Maas and Snyder 1989: 79–80; Wilson 1999/2000: 445 n. 66.

[114] Wegner 1949: 45–7; Cillo 1993: 222–42; Bundrick 2005: 27–8.

[115] For my view of the date see above p. 61.

76   PETER WILSON

Sometimes it has more than the traditional number of seven strings.[116]
Moreover, around 425 the Thracian appears standing on a concert podium
in a fully mundane, agonistic context; and thereafter looks more and more
like a well-dressed young Athenian kitharist of his day.[117] One image of
this date – in which a vast decorated tripod stands between Thamyras
and Apollo – has generated the plausible hypothesis that behind it lies
a dithyramb (hence the prize tripod) in which Thamyras the kitharist
figured. This kind of interaction between the traditionally choral, *aulos*-
based form of dithyramb and the myths and instruments of *kitharōidia*
would be entirely plausible for the 'new' music of the age.[118] But, as I have
suggested, Sophocles' tragedy, with its staged mythic musical *agōn*, had
already gone some way in this direction in terms of musical theatrics, as
well as its likely thematics.

The perceived fate of stringed instruments was at the centre of the
debate surrounding the so-called 'new music'.[119] The major technical
developments introduced at this time in large part consisted in exploring the full potential of what Plato called that *polykhordotaton* or – 'very
many-stringed' – instrument, the *aulos* (pipe), and then extending the new
range of notes, scales and musical effects from the *aulos* to the kithara, which
had some four new strings added to it to increase its range. This was the
more shocking since the stringed instruments had long been the preserve
of the élite, their practice laid on solid foundations of an amateur ideal.
The increasingly virtuoso style of music for the kithara, now practised by
professionals drawn from diverse social backgrounds, was thus repugnant
to the 'Old Guard', and exceedingly successful in the theatres.

It looks to me as though the myth of Thamyras was at some point tailored
to the needs of these new musicians, perhaps even forged into an emblem
of their professional pride. His very history of defiance of the highest Establishment powers and magnificent suffering may have appealed to them, as
the similar story of Marsyas evidently did to the new practitioners of the
aulos in the same period. The 'Thamyrists' (Θαμυρίδδοντες) whose activity
in fourth-century Boeotia I noted above seem to have been officers of cult
and civic service rather than musicians who looked to the Thracian hero
as a figurehead for their activities, ascribing their music directly to him;
but it is quite possible that they were both these things. The 'Timotheasts'
(Τιμοθεασταί) we find active in a contest of the Great Didymeia in the
third century AD (*IDid* 181) may offer a partial parallel.[120] A Timotheast is

---

[116] Cillo 1993: 232–3.   [117] Cillo 1993: 215.   [118] Froning 1971: 75–86.
[119] See esp. Csapo 2004; Wilson 2004.   [120] See Prauscello 2006: 115 n. 369.

Thamyris the Thracian: the archetypal wandering poet? 77

presumably a specialist interpreter and performer of the works of Timotheos of Miletus – who, by *c.* 230 (the date of the relevant inscription), was already so distant a classic as to perhaps have had something of a mythic status himself.[121]

The indications are that it was for *kitharistai* in particular that Thamyras served this rôle – that is, for the pure instrumentalists who did not sing. Plato's rhapsode Ion knows Thamyras as the nonpareil of *kitharistikē*, of whom one says 'second to none in *kitharistikē*'.[122] In Athens and elsewhere, kitharists stood lower on the hierarchy of cultural and economic capital that their musical expertise could bring than their singing-and-playing colleagues the kitharodes (at the fourth-century Panathenaia the first prize for *kitharistikē* was exactly one third as valuable as that for *kitharōidia*), and a figure like Thamyras would have suited their somewhat inferior position in the performative hierarchy.[123] There was evidently rivalry between these two musical *tekhnai*. Witness for instance the comment by a contemporary kitharist, quarrelling with a rival musician, who was a kitharode, to the effect that the kitharode was 'a pygmy in a great craft, while I am a giant in a small one'.[124]

The Homeric archetext of *Iliad* 2 was even, I tentatively suggest, interpretable to the effect that the singer's conflict with the Muses had deprived Thamyris of his power of *song*, but left him with his *instrumental* skill in tact. As I have said, the precise nature of the punishment in *Iliad* 2 was much discussed by ancient scholars, who were most confused by the idea that *blinding* should be used to punish a singer: cf. Demodokos![125] And back some of them went to πηρός in line 599, and insisted it must mean 'lame of mind' – or '*mute*'. One strand of interpretation envisaged the punishment as blinding, loss of voice and a form of madness, but with no mention of loss of *playing* power.[126] Such a view can only be based on a reading of the last element in the list – καὶ ἐκλέλαθον κιθαριστύν (line 600) – as though ἐκλέλαθον were not causal, but referred to the Muses' own forgetfulness: that is to say, 'They made him lame of mind, took away his wondrous song,

---

[121] On Timotheos' *Nachleben* see Prauscello (this volume).

[122] Plato, *Ion* 533b; cf. Dio Chrys. 12.21. Pliny *NH* 7.204 expresses it most clearly by describing Thamyras as the inventor of the art: *cithara sine uoce cecinit Thamyras primum*.

[123] Cf. Cillo 1993: 216. Panathenaic prizes: *IG* II² 2311. Note Martin's recent (2001) compelling argument on the basis of the *Ion* passage that contemporary rhapsodes attributed their material to big names of the mythic past. He is interested in Orpheus, but kitharists may well have done the same with Thamyras. We also hear of a performer, of unknown type (perhaps a kitharist?), called Claudius Thamyris in the first century AD: Stephanis 1988: no. 1126.

[124] Nikostratos (possibly Stratonikos?): Aelian *VH* 4.2.

[125] See esp. Ven. A. schol. *Iliad* 2.599, with Whallon 1964. Cf. Brillante 1991: 431–2.

[126] Eustathius: see van der Valk 1971: 461 *ad Iliad* 2.596.

78   PETER WILSON

and forgot about his kithara-playing.' This would certainly be a challenging 'reading against the grain' – and against the grammar – leaving us with
Muses deficient in the most embarrassing way, in *memory*. But it would
also serve as an excellent charter myth for embattled kitharists.[127]

Sophocles may have been εὔκολος – 'easy-going', as Aristophanes'
Dionysos describes him (*Frogs* 82). But we should not be mesmerised by
that myth of the genius sublimely elevated above the rivalries of his day
into thinking he was above the tumultuous concerns that were making
themselves felt through his own medium of *mousikē*. We know far too little
about the *Thamyras* to state categorically that in it he was treating some of
these issues in a tragic key. But my interpretation of fragment 245 gives us a
strong hint of that, in the way it spotlights the issue of the proper 'mortal'
limits of music. In conclusion, I would add a few further indications in this
direction.

Radt had some doubts as to whether the extremely rare verb μουσοποιεῖ
used of Thamyras' activities – the last word of fragment 245 as he prints it –
should in fact be included as genuinely Sophoclean. Ford endorses these
doubts in building his own argument that tragedy avoids the language of
'making' in relation to song.[128] But they seem unfounded, and Ford himself
has to make an exception of 'a few ironic passages in Euripides'.[129] It is,
however, very striking that the verb *mousopoiein* appears in one of its very
few other classical occurrences at Aristophanes' *Clouds* (334) to describe
the artistic activity of those 'composers of convoluted songs for circular
choruses, men of airy quackery, lazy idlers' – that is, precisely poets of the
'New' music.[130]

Thamyras' father Philammon may have been referred to in Sophocles'
drama as a σοφιστής ('sophist')[131] – a description that, with a hint of
anachronism, associates him with the various 'new thinkers' of the period,
among whom were musical theorists and practitioners.[132] I noted that many
of the instruments mentioned in this extraordinary work were precisely the
ones which feature on the proscribed list of arch conservatives. I did not
dwell at any length on one of these, the φοῖνιξ (*phoinix*, fr. 239a). This is

---

[127] Cf. Cillo 1993: 241.   [128] Ford 2002: esp. 137–8.

[129] Ford 2002: 138 with n. 28. Eur. *Suppl.* 180 (*hymnopoios*) should be added to Ford's 'exceptions'.

[130] It also appears in Trag. adesp. 496: μὴ μουσοποίει πρὸς τὸ νηπιώτερον· / πόρρω γὰρ ἑστὼς ὁ
θεὸς ἐγγύθεν κλύει.

[131] Welcker plausibly assigned Soph. adesp. 906 to the *Thamyras* (see *TrGF* 4, 578). It describes a
kitharode as: . . .σοφιστὴν ἐμόν. Thamyras himself is a 'Thracian sophist' in *Rhesos* 924; see further
note 56 above.

[132] An unusual image of *c.* 430 associates Thamyras (holding an eight-stringed kithara) with the 'new'
(to us at least) and young Muse named *Sophía*: Philippaki 1988.

Thamyris the Thracian: the archetypal wandering poet? 79

the play's latest arrival, having been added to it by Radt on the basis of a new manuscript of the *Lexicon Cyrilli*.[133] All we know of the *phoinix* as an instrument is that it was a type of lyre that had long arms made from the twisted and hollow horns of a kind of antelope, the *oryx*. And that it was later said to have been used specifically 'by Thracian princes at their feasts'.[134] It has been argued that these made a new range of timbres possible on the instrument, and were probably exploited for this very reason by the new musicians. If true, and if this was an instrument used by Sophocles' Thamyras, he comes one step closer to presaging the New Wave.

[133] Naoumides 1968.
[134] Hdt. 4.192; Cillo 1993: 231–2. Nikomedes *ap*. Athen. 14.637a–b; cf. Hall 1989: 130.

CHAPTER 4

Read on arrival

Richard P. Martin

The international community of vagrants calling themselves Classicists can well appreciate at least one problem faced by the poets whom they study. Wittingly or not, modern scholars have replicated the complicated itineraries, competitive atmosphere, quest for patronage and desire for publicity that were all known to ancient Greek performers. They may not get mugged like Ibycus or have to jump ship like Arion but, eventually, as did the ancients, they face the rhetorical dilemma: what should I say when I get there?[1]

My solution to the dilemma (at least for this paper) is to take a look at *their* solutions. Rather than pick one synchronic slice in the long history of Greek poetic practices, I shall attempt to make a diachronic cross-cut. By examining the poetic strategies of those figures who were represented as performers who moved from place to place, we can nail together a rough typology. That typology, in turn, can enable us to explore further the poetics of a number of genres, beyond those that are explicitly connected with travelling poets. In fact, just as heroes and outlaws usefully trace for us the outlines of the possible, wandering poets are most beneficial when they force us to scrutinise the habits of the stable and stay-at-home.[2]

This dynamic, the give-and-take between centre and periphery, may sound like another version of metanastic poetics, a term proposed some years back to describe the workings of Hesiodic composition.[3] But what I would like to sketch here, while related, is not the same. The ideal

---

[1] My thanks are due to Richard Hunter and Ian Rutherford for placing me in the jaws of this dilemma and making the experience so pleasant. Perhaps the tales told about Ibycus (*Suda* ı 80 = ii 607 Adler; *Anth. Pal.* 7.745) and Arion (Hdt. 1.24) originated in *autobiographical* discourses, worked into the performance commentary or even into the poetic compositions of these poets. An alternative source for the details of personal misfortune could be folktale-style narratives told later (and sometimes concocted from poetic remains, as in the stories of the death of Euripides elaborated via his *Bacchae*): for the phenomenon see Lefkowitz 1981.

[2] Three exemplary studies of the uses of such figures: Nagy 1985, Ó hÓgáin 1985 and Brown 2003.

[3] Martin 1992.

80

metanastic figure has acquired a sort of one-way ticket. Hesiod, except for the odd trip to Chalkis, is not going anywhere, yet his status in Ascra is that of a semi-outsider, a marginal figure who is by virtue of that position empowered to speak his mind.[4] Anacharsis the Scythian, so totally out of the loop that he can even question the value of gymnastics in Greek culture, gives us a similar figure, from the prose tradition.[5] He does eventually go back home, but the essence of the tradition about him centres on his foreign residency – what he sees and then misinterprets (for our ultimate benefit) while staying in a place not his own.

In contrast to the metanastic stance, the poetic strategies of wandering poets have to do with the realities of short-term encounters. Instead of a one-way ticket, these types, as they are represented to us, have obtained the equivalent of a long-term Eurail pass. The social context is different. It resembles less resident alien status, more a whistlestop campaign. How do you present yourself, and continue to operate successfully, in the cultural situation of licensed itinerancy? What are the pressures and what techniques exist to deal with them? What are the rules – which is to say, in terms of verbal art, the poetics – of this mode? Let us call these rules, for the sake of complementarity and Greek derivation, 'planetic poetics'.

An investigation of wandering poetics might trail all over the map. As it is, we have a fairly good pilot for part of the journey in the form of a parodic passage from Aristophanes. At *Birds* 904–57 Peisetairos has just dismissed the priest and undertaken to sacrifice to the avian gods himself, when a wandering poet interrupts him:[6]

ΠΟΙΗΤΗΣ

	Νεφελοκοκκυγίαν	
	τὰν εὐδαίμονα κλῆσον, ὦ	905
	Μοῦσα, τεαῖς ἐν ὕμνων	
	ἀοιδαῖς.	
{Πε.}	τουτὶ τὸ πρᾶγμα ποδαπόν; εἰπέ μοι, τίς εἶ;	
{Πο.}	ἐγὼ μελιγλώσσων ἐπέων ἱεὶς ἀοιδὰν	
	Μουσάων θεράπων ὀτρηρός,	
	κατὰ τὸν Ὅμηρον.	910
{Πε.}	ἔπειτα δῆτα δοῦλος ὢν κόμην ἔχεις;	
{Πο.}	οὔκ, ἀλλὰ πάντες ἐσμὲν οἱ διδάσκαλοι	

---

[4] On the self-representation of 'Hesiod' in terms of his relation to Perses and the community, see now Edwards 2004: 176–84. For the poet's various poses as displays of poetic *sophia*, see most recently Steiner 2005.
[5] Martin 1997.   [6] Text as in Dunbar 1995: 96–7. Translation mine.

Μουσάων θεράποντες ὀτρηροί,
κατὰ τὸν Ὅμηρον.

{Πε.}   οὐκ ἐτὸς ὀτρηρὸν καὶ τὸ ληδάριον ἔχεις.   915
ἀτάρ, ὦ ποιητά, κατὰ τί δεῦρ' ἀνεφθάρης;

{Πο.}   μέλη πεποίηκ' εἰς τὰς Νεφελοκοκκυγίας
τὰς ὑμετέρας κύκλιά τε πολλὰ καὶ καλὰ
καὶ παρθένεια καὶ κατὰ τὰ Σιμωνίδου.

{Πε.}   ταυτὶ σὺ πότ' ἐποίησας; ἀπὸ ποίου χρόνου;   920

{Πο.}   πάλαι πάλαι δὴ τήνδ' ἐγὼ κλῄζω πόλιν.

{Πε.}   οὐκ ἄρτι θύω τὴν δεκάτην ταύτης ἐγώ,
καὶ τοὔνομ' ὥσπερ παιδίῳ νυνδὴ θέμην;

{Πο.}   ἀλλά τις ὠκεῖα Μουσάων φάτις
οἷα περ ἵππων ἀμαρυγά.   925
σὺ δὲ πάτερ, κτίστορ Αἴτνας,
ζαθέων ἱερῶν ὁμώνυμε,
δὸς ἐμὶν ὅ τι περ τεᾷ κεφαλᾷ θέ-
λῃς πρόφρων δόμεν.   930

{Πο.}   τουτὶ παρέξει τὸ κακὸν ἡμῖν πράγματα,
εἰ μή τι τούτῳ δόντες ἀποφευξούμεθα.
οὗτος, σὺ μέντοι σπολάδα καὶ χιτῶν' ἔχεις·
ἀπόδυθι καὶ δὸς τῷ ποιητῇ τῷ σοφῷ.
ἔχε τὴν σπολάδα· πάντως δέ μοι ῥιγῶν δοκεῖς.   935

{Πο.}   τόδε μὲν οὐκ ἀέκουσα φίλα
Μοῦσα τὸ δῶρον δέχεται·
τὺ δὲ τεᾷ φρενὶ μάθε
Πινδάρειον ἔπος.

{Πε.}   ἄνθρωπος ἡμῶν οὐκ ἀπαλλαχθήσεται.   940

{Πο.}   νομάδεσσι γὰρ ἐν Σκύθαις ἀλᾶται στρατῶν
ὃς ὑφαντοδόνητον ἔσθος οὐ πέπαται.
ἀκλεὴς δ' ἔβα
σπολὰς ἄνευ χιτῶνος.
ξύνες ὅ τοι λέγω.

{Πε.}   συνίημ' ὅτι βούλει τὸν χιτωνίσκον λαβεῖν.
ἀπόδυθι· δεῖ γὰρ τὸν ποιητὴν ὠφελεῖν.
ἄπελθε τουτονὶ λαβών.

{Πο.}   ἀπέρχομαι,
κἀς τὴν πόλιν γ' ἐλθὼν ποιήσω τοιαδί·
κλῇσον, ὦ χρυσόθρονε, τὰν τρομεράν, κρυεράν·   950
νιφόβολα πεδία πολύπορά τ' ἤλυθον.
ἀλαλαί.

{Πε.}   νὴ τὸν Δί' ἀλλ' ἤδη πέφευγας ταυταγὶ
τὰ κρυερὰ τονδὶ τὸν χιτωνίσκον λαβών.
τουτὶ μὰ Δί' ἐγὼ τὸ κακὸν οὐδέποτ' ἤλπισα,
οὕτω ταχέως τοῦτον πεπύσθαι τὴν πόλιν.

Poet	Cloud-cuckoo-land the blessed, celebrate, O Muse, in your hymn-songs.
Peisetairos	What is this annoyance? Where is it from? Tell me, who are you?
Poet	It is I, the one who sends forth the song of honey-tongued words, zealous servant of the Muses, according to Homer.
Peisetairos	So you're a slave . . . and you wear long hair?
Poet	No, but in fact all we producers are zealous servants of the Muses, according to Homer.
Peisetairos	Well, that's a hol-ey zealous little cloak you've got, too. But, poet, why have you turned up here?
Poet	Songs have I composed in honor of your Cloud-Cuckoo, many and splendid circle-dances and parthenia and things after the manner of Simonides.
Peisetairos	Just when did you compose them? Since what time?
Poet	Long, long now have I been celebrating this city.
Peisetairos	But am I not right now sacrificing for its tenth-day and haven't I only just named it, like a baby?
Poet	Like the flash of steeds, swift is the Muses' report. Thou father, Aitna-founder, namesake of god-filled holy rites, give to me whatsoever you will to give, by your head's assent.
Peisetairos	This wretched thing will cause us problems if we don't get rid of him by giving something. *(To assistant)*. You there, you've got a jerkin as well as tunic. Take it off, give it to the wise poet. *(To the poet)*. Have this jerkin. You do seem chilly.
Poet	Not unwillingly does my dear Muse accept this gift; but let thy mind learn the Pindaric saying.
Peisetairos	The man just will not shove off from us.
Poet	'For among the nomad Scyths, he wanders apart from the host, who acquires no woven-whirled garment. Unglorified goes a jerkin without tunic.' Understand what I say.
Peisetairos	I understand that you want to get the little tunic. *(To assistant)*. Take it off. We have to help the poet. *(To the poet)*. Here it is – take it and get out.
Poet	I am going, and having gone to the city I will make such verses: you of the golden throne, celebrate the shivering, freezing one; to snow-blasted many-wayed plains have I come. *Alalai!*
Peisetairos	By Zeus, you're away from the chills already, since you got the tunic. This pain, by Zeus! I never expected this guy could learn so quickly about the city.

The hermeneutically useful aspect of parody is that the joke once had to work: that is, in order for an audience to find humour, actual traits of style and character must have been presented, albeit in exaggerated

84 RICHARD P. MARTIN

form.[7] Therefore, we can use this passage as a kind of evidence (albeit stylised) for the typical behaviour one might expect from a certain kind of Greek poet encountering a potential patron in the later fifth century. The following microanalysis of the discourse will take each strategic 'move' in the order it comes. Under each heading I will then glance at the related evidence from a range of other Greek poems, some planetic, others not. While the conclusion may not end the way this passage does, with the wandering scholar, like the poet, getting a new coat, I shall be content if we arrive at a new appreciation of the systematicity underlying an important set of data in Greek culture.

To start with the opening gambit: if one were compiling a best-selling handbook for would-be wandering poets, this strategy would be titled 'praise the place, and let the people come later'. Of course there already exists such a handbook from antiquity, in the form of the guide to epideictic oratory by Menander Rhetor, who goes into great detail on how to praise a city, a harbour, or a citadel. He even advises one on how to praise such an encomiastically challenged location as Hesiod's Ascra (you should say 'the inhabitants must perforce be philosophical and enduring' – sect. 347.27–30).[8] Menander is writing for the local intelligentsia of the imperial age, but the basic rhetorical practices and the situations that call for them are surely much older.[9] His prescriptions are extensive, but oddly enough he never advises that the encomiast call a city 'blessed'. Perhaps there is something more fundamental happening in the *Birds* parody.

Of the eight times that Pindar uses the adjective *eudaimōn*, only once, towards the end of *Pythian* 4, does it modify the name of a city (275–80):[10]

> τὶν δὲ τούτων ἐξυφαίνονται χάριτες.
> τλᾶθι τᾶς εὐδαίμονος ἀμφὶ Κυρά-
> νας θέμεν σπουδὰν ἅπασαν.
>
> τῶν δ' Ὁμήρου καὶ τόδε συνθέμενος
> ῥῆμα πόρσυν· ἄγγελον ἐσλὸν ἔφα τι-
> μὰν μεγίσταν πράγματι παντὶ φέρειν·

> But for you the blessings of such things are unfolding
> Dare to devote all your serious effort
>   to the cause of blessed Kyrene.

> And among the sayings of Homer, take this one to heart
> and heed it: he said that a good messenger
>   brings the greatest honor to every affair.

---

[7] Rose 1993 presents a useful theoretical overview.   [8] Text in Russell and Wilson 1981: 34.
[9] On his milieu see now Heath 2004.   [10] Translation from Race 1997a: 295.

Read on arrival 85

It is perhaps significant that the word's deployment comes within the one passage in Pindar where we see the poet most directly asking for a favour. In this *envoi*, Pindar pleads with his addressee Arkesilas IV, ruler of Cyrene, to call back from exile the young man Damophilos. Furthermore, the entire close of *Pythian* 4 is constructed as advice on how to handle a city. Arkesilas is compared at line 270 to a healer (*iatēr*). In other words, he is a fellow *dēmiourgos*, if we recall the famous list of travelling craftsmen (seers, doctors, carpenters and singers) at *Odyssey* 17.382–6:

τίς γὰρ δὴ ξεῖνον καλεῖ ἄλλοθεν αὐτὸς ἐπελθὼν
ἄλλον γ᾽, εἰ μὴ τῶν, οἳ δημιοεργοὶ ἔασι;
μάντιν ἢ ἰητῆρα κακῶν ἢ τέκτονα δούρων,
ἢ καὶ θέσπιν ἀοιδόν, ὅ κεν τέρπησιν ἀείδων.
οὗτοι γὰρ κλητοί γε βροτῶν ἐπ᾽ ἀπείρονα γαῖαν·

For who goes and calls another, a stranger, from elsewhere
unless it be one of the public workers?
A seer, or healer of ills or shaper of wood
Or even inspired singer, who can delight with song –
For these among mortals are ones summoned upon boundless earth.

Pindar, the out-of-town poet, and his royal addressee are therefore placed on the same level, at least in the imaginary.[11] And one senses that in this relationship Pindar has the upper hand: the seemingly generic line 275 (τὶν δὲ τούτων ἐξυφαίνονται χάριτες) as translated by Race ('For you the blessings of such things are unfolding') misses the Pindaric specificity of both noun and verb. *Kharites*, in Pindar, can mean favours or blessings but is also, quite commonly, used to mean poems, songs or the glory one gets from poetry.[12] And *exuphainō*, in its only other Pindaric attestation, refers to the creation of praise poetry, when the poet calls to his lyre '*exuphaine . . . melos*' (weave out this song,' *Nem.* 4.44).[13] We need not enter here into the further resonances of *huphainō*, other than to say that it was taken even in antiquity as the root of the noun *humnos* 'hymn'.[14] In brief, the double-edged message of *Pythian* 4.275 is 'you are blessed' and 'you are getting poetic praise created for you'. In this immediate context, the next line: 'Dare to devote all your serious effort to the cause of blessed Kyrene' can be read as a summary *quid pro quo*: *because* you are praised so extravagantly, *act* in a way to deserve praise. Finally, if this is indeed the sociopoetic exchange

[11] In the same section, Pindar also likens himself to a herald (lines 278–9) – the only other trade designated *dēmiourgos* in Homer (*Od.* 19.135).
[12] See the nine instances in Slater 1969: 542 *s.v. kharis*, 1.b (a and b). Slater puts *kharites* at *Pyth.* 4.275 under the heading 'favour, blessing'.
[13] Slater 1969: 180.   [14] On the word's etymology and semantics see Nagy 2000.

86   RICHARD P. MARTIN

being transacted, the adjective *eudaimōn*, applied to Kyrene, is proleptic, anticipating the desired outcome. Act this way and Kyrene *will* be 'blessed'.

This might seem like a lot of semiotic baggage to tote back to the first lines of our bardic *Birds* passage. But it is the sort of comparison we especially need when dealing with the highly stylised and well-known set of poetic codes underlying ancient Greek praise-poetry. What further meanings do we obtain on taking the *Birds* poet as a potential partner in an exchange with Peisetairos? First, the stakes are raised because what is in question is civic identity. Whereas Peisetairos might be expected to eject him for asking a personal favour, the ragged poet has already ensured himself a reward by blessing the city rather than an individual; to call it *eudaimōn* is both to wish for it to be so and to make it happen. This is the ultimate performative utterance. And second, the utterance promises to resound into the future, because it is the Muse who performs the praise. Cloud-cuckoo-land, like it or not, has become matter for song. The implicit bargain is that its *kleos* will spread, through the medium of *mousikē*. Just as Pindar's allusion to the blessings of Arkesilas foregrounds the continuing rôle of his own art in the eventual successes of ruler and city, the anonymous poet's invocation of the Muse in Aristophanes' play hints at the potential of reperformance.[15] The encomiastic command has produced a song.

The initial strategy of generalised praise does not immediately captivate Peisetairos. 'What and from where is this annoyance? Tell me, who are you?' he exclaims. Yet even when asked directly for identification, the poet prefers to describe himself in a periphrasis. For that matter, he himself does not pause to ask who his audience is either, which might imply that he could never imagine stooping to flatter them. In our handbook on the habits of highly effective vagrants, this move would be bullet-point no. 2: 'make yourself the voice of tradition'. Several facets of the bard's self-description catch the eye. First, by calling himself *Mousaōn therapōn* ('servant of the Muses') the anonymous singer not only blends himself into the poetic past, but activates a deeply traditional set of associations through which poets are equated with cult heroes. Gregory Nagy fully explicated this trope in *The Best of the Achaeans*, with reference especially to the phrase as it operates in the Hesiodic *Theogony*.[16] Let me point out that Bacchylides in 476 BCE can still use the term to introduce himself in the opening of his *epinikion* for Hieron, while specifying that he serves the Muse Ourania (Bacch. 5.7–14):[17]

---

[15] On the important notion of reperformance in archaic poetic composition, see Nagy 1996: 7–23, 53–8.
[16] Nagy 1979: 292–7.   [17] Translation from Campbell 1992: 139.

Read on arrival

δεῦρ᾽ ἐπάθρησον νόῳ,
ᾗ σὺν Χαρίτεσσι βαθυζώνοις ὑφάνας
ὕμνον ἀπὸ ζαθέας
νάσου ξένος ὑμετέραν πέμ-
πει κλεεννὰν ἐς πόλιν,
χρυσάμπυκος Οὐρανίας κλει-
νὸς θεράπων·

Turn your thoughts this way;
With the help of the slim-waisted Graces your guest friend,
the famous servant of Urania with her golden headband,
has woven a song of praise and sends it from the sacred island
to your distinguished city.

As Nagy demonstrated, the *Lives* traditions concerning Homer, Archilochus and Hesiod fit the pattern of such cult heroes.[18] In this light, it is significant that the anonymous *therapōn* in the *Birds* chooses to describe himself further as 'uttering a song of honey-tongued words' (μελιγλώσσων ἐπέων ἱεὶς ἀοιδάν). For the last two words of this phrase could be taken as a gloss on the very name 'Hesiod', which has been plausibly etymologised as a speaking-name: 'he who emits the voice' (from *hiēmi* and *audē*).[19] In the *Birds* phrase, the dictional choice of *aoidē* 'song' simply makes use of a surface lexical renewal within the same semantic field; furthermore, *aoidē* and *audē* function as synonyms already in Hesiod.[20] In effect, this wandering bard names himself in terms of his function, and in coded bardic fashion, in words that recall the famous hymnist of the gods.

I have been trying thus far to reach beyond the superficial concepts of 'cliché' or 'well-worn tropes' to which commentators on the *Birds* passage have inevitably resorted.[21] Instead of these reactions, we might imagine that the Aristophanic parody of a *Mousaōn therapōn* accurately, albeit with comic exaggeration, captures the actual discourse of praise-poets in the fifth century BCE. That the poets seen so far in this portrait range from Hesiod to Pindar and Bacchylides could be taken as an accident. But the alternative is more poetically intriguing and also practicable. In generic terms, the figure of Hesiod, poet of the *Theogony*, *was* a praise-poet. In genetic terms, Pindar and Bacchylides can consciously be modelling themselves on

---

[18] In addition to Nagy 1979: 297–308, see now Clay 2004.

[19] Nagy 1979: 296–7. On the Indo-European mythopoeic traditions behind *meliglōssos*, see Bader 1989: 31–2.

[20] Cf. within the same scene of poetic induction, line-final *aoidē* at *Theogony* 22 and 44, with line-final *audē* at *Theogony* 31 and 39, all describing songs of praise.

[21] The most recent examination, by Loscalzo 2005, also views the passage as a pastiche with no specific target or parodic method.

88   R I C H A R D   P.   M A R T I N

Hesiod (as would many Alexandrian poets to come).[22] To go even deeper, Homer, Hesiod and the varieties of Greek praise-poetry are all evolutionary off-shoots of Indo-European praise-poetry traditions.[23] What might seem problematic is that none of these poetic predecessors to our *Birds* bard seems to represent *himself* as a *planetic* poet. This will be dealt with at the end of the paper.

A final observation on this second gambit – 'blend into tradition' – before we move on. When the commentators offer Bacchylides for a parallel to the use of the word *meliglōssos*, it is similarly in the same *pro forma* tone, pointing to a surface phenomenon. But let us examine the *function* of the conclusion of Bacchylides' praise-poem, where the word occurs (3.90–8):

> ἀρετᾶ[ς γε μ]ὲν οὐ μινύθει
> βροτῶν ἄμα σ[ώμ]ατι φέγγος, ἀλλά
> Μοῦσά νιν τρ[έφει.] Ἱέρων, σὺ δ᾽ ὄλβον
> κάλλιστ᾽ ἐπεδ[είξ]αο θνατοῖς
> ἄνθεα· πράξα[ντι] δ᾽ εὖ
> οὐ φέρει κόσμ[ον σι]ω-
> πά· σὺν δ᾽ ἀλαθ[είαι] καλῶν
> καὶ μελιγλώσσου τις ὑμνήσει χάριν
> Κηΐας ἀηδόνος.

> Of human excellence, the gleam
> does not shrink with the body. Instead,
> a Muse nurtures it. Hieron, you showed
> to mortals the finest flowers of wealth.
> To one who has done well, silence
> is not what brings adornment. The truth
> about your noble deeds someone will sing
> and thus will hymn the grace of a sweet-tongued
> Cean nightingale.

The gnomic cap, 'silence does not bring adornment to one who has done well', leads into the final declaration that the poet's *kharis* – both his graceful song and his grateful recompense – will itself become a topic of song. Bacchylides might well be imagining two related sociopoetic phenomena. First, his *poem* will be re-performed (a fact that the Aristophanes parody in effect confirms); and second, the further story of his *relationship* with

---

[22] On some of the varied uses of Hesiod in Hellenistic poetics, see Stephens 2003: 163, 252–7. Cameron 1995: 362–86 makes useful distinctions concerning Hesiodic influence on Alexandrian writers.

[23] On Homer and praise-poetry, see Nagy 1990a: 146–214. On this function of the poet in Indo-European culture, see Watkins 1995: 68–84.

Read on arrival

89

Hieron will be told, perhaps in the form of another poem, or in stories that embed the poems. That is to say, Bacchylides is aware of the ongoing process of mythologising the performer. That such ancient para-poetic traditions did exist is attested by the various *Lives* traditions, from the *Contest of Homer and Hesiod* to the Mnesiepes inscription about Archilochus. I would argue that, given the Greek and the comparative evidence, no traditional poetry ever travels *without* such contemporaneous para-poetic traditions. I think especially of medieval Celtic prose tales concerning poets, but also of Provençal troubadour *vidas* and *razos*, the anecdotes that explain how a song came to be.[24]

Bacchylides' assertion is that his true poetic telling of Hieron's deeds (σὺν δ᾿ ἀλαθέαι καλῶν) will result in his own story being told. But he does not say 'my story'; he refers to 'the *kharis* of the nightingale of Keos'. It is the periphrasis that should interest us. The two parallel passages that feature similar tropes of poet–patron symbiosis simply refer to the poet in the first person: Pindar in *Olympian* 1 prays for fame in *sophia* (115–17):[25]

εἴη σέ τε τοῦτον ὑψοῦ χρόνον πατεῖν,
ἐμέ τε τοσσάδε νικαφόροις
ὁμιλεῖν πρόφαντον σοφίᾳ καθ᾿ Ἑλ-
λανας ἐόντα παντᾷ.

May you walk on high for the time that is yours,
and may I join victors whenever they win
and be foremost in wisdom among Hellenes everywhere.

Similarly, Ibycus in his ode to Polycrates mentions his own *kleos* (*PMG* 282.45–7).[26] By contrast, Bacchylides awards himself a praise-name, the sort of phrase that we expect from the later generations who will refer to him, not from the poet himself. He is in effect already collaborating in the work of memorialisation, doing his own public relations. Keeping in mind the poetic periphrasis 'one who utters the song' (ἱεὶς ἀοιδάν) of the bard at *Birds* 907, we can triangulate the bird-like Bacchylides with a third poet, also periphrastically self-described. In an often-cited departure scene in the *Hymn to Apollo*, the performer of the hymn bids farewell to the Delian maidens (166–75):[27]

---

[24] For an introduction to the range of such Celtic tales, see the essays in Nagy and Jones 2005; on Provençal tales, see Poe 1995 and VanVleck 1991: 40–7, 56–60.
[25] Translation from Race (1997a: 59.
[26] On the intertextual relations of his assertion, see Steiner 2005.
[27] Translation mine (with the reading ἀμφ᾿ ἡμέων).

90 RICHARD P. MARTIN

χαίρετε δ' ὑμεῖς πᾶσαι· ἐμεῖο δὲ καὶ μετόπισθε
μνήσασθ', ὁππότε κέν τις ἐπιχθονίων ἀνθρώπων
ἐνθάδ' ἀνείρηται ξεῖνος ταλαπείριος ἐλθών·
ὦ κοῦραι, τίς δ' ὕμμιν ἀνὴρ ἥδιστος ἀοιδῶν
ἐνθάδε πωλεῖται, καὶ τέῳ τέρπεσθε μάλιστα;
ὑμεῖς δ' εὖ μάλα πᾶσαι ὑποκρίνασθ' ἀμφ' ἡμέων·
τυφλὸς ἀνήρ, οἰκεῖ δὲ Χίῳ ἔνι παιπαλοέσσῃ,
τοῦ πᾶσαι μετόπισθεν ἀριστεύουσιν ἀοιδαί·
ἡμεῖς δ' ὑμέτερον κλέος οἴσομεν ὅσσον ἐπ' αἶαν
ἀνθρώπων στρεφόμεσθα πόλεις εὖ ναιεταώσας·

Farewell to you all. And remember me hereafter,
when some man of the earth, a stranger much-enduring,
comes and asks 'Girls, who is the sweetest singer hereabouts,
Who delights you most?' All of you, answer well of us:
'A blind man, he lives in rocky Chios; it's his
songs, all of them, that are best in later times.'
And we will bring *your* fame as far on earth
as the well-inhabited cities on our circuit.

This, too, is a *kleos*-bargain: you praise me, and I shall spread your praises.
But the *Hymn* poet also carefully chooses to rehearse the maidens in what
they are supposed to say when another wanderer (some weary *xeinos*)
encounters them. He is a blind man who lives in Chios, and whose songs
are the best ever. Why is the blind man nameless? Several practical functions
are fused within the periphrastic strategy. The mechanism enables mimesis
of the poet by performers who are not the 'original' first-person speaker.[28]
At the same time, the coded signature implies that the composer is already
far beyond seeking fame – the masked man never has to utter 'I am Zorro.'
But most of all, this sort of self-characterisation naturalises the poet as the
voice of tradition by making him part of the accepted canon, the 'songs
that are best in later times'. The *Birds* bard is the essence of a certain type
of poetry, but not just in Aristophanes' parodic vision: it is an important
feature of the poetry's own essentialising.

Two of the aforementioned three self-effacing self-praisers are explicitly
depicted as wandering poets. Bacchylides would seem to be the odd man
out (but more on that later). We can also note that the *Birds* praise-poet
does in fact name *someone*: he has an annoying tic of referring to Homer,
when using the phrase *therapōn otrēros*. Even the scholiast *ad loc.* noted

---

[28] A similar merging of multiple performers can occur in Provençal poems: on the tension between
assuring transmission and preserving authorial claims, see VanVleck 1991: 164–77. On the Homeric
rhapsode as a 're-composed' performer, and the Delian maidens as a model for re-enactment, see
the extended discussion in Nagy 1996: 61–82.

Read on arrival 91

'some say these are too much'.[29] It does strike us as the desperate move of an insecure poet, or at least, as a gesture of secondariness. It reminds me how certain singers of short poems when interviewed on their home turf, in the White Mountains of western Crete, asserted the authenticity of their performances by bringing out tattered song-books to show that their texts matched that on the old page.[30] Homer was credited with the phrase *Mousaōn therapōn*, from the opening of the *Margites*, but the comic point here is not that the *Birds* bard has to go around citing a text of that poem.[31] Instead, I submit, he is doing what praise-poets actually do, citing Homer by name.[32] The Pindar passage cited above (*Pyth.* 4.277–8) is a good example (τῶν δ᾽ Ὁμήρου καὶ τόδε συνθέμενος ῥῆμα πόρσυν᾽).

You might say that Pindar cites Homer for an idea, not a stylistic nicety, but the parodied bard is doing the same, making an assertion that poets are indeed *Mousaōn therapontes* (*kata ton Homēron*). At least, this is the point that Peisetairos takes up for the next joke, misunderstanding *therapōn* in its debased sense: if you're a slave, how come you have long hair? The bard's reply – no, all of us *didaskaloi* are *Mousaōn therapontes* – casts him as a choral instructor in the mode of a dithyramb-writer, or even a dramatic poet. As it turns out, an actual dithyrambic poet, Kinesias, will turn up in Cloud-cuckoo-land some 400 lines after this point (vv. 1373–1409). He will identify himself as a *kukliodidaskalos*, one who is the object of competition by the tribes (v. 1403). The contrast is instructive. The Kinesias scene depends for its humour on a critique of the airy, new-fangled, Timotheus-style dithyrambic language.[33] Kinesias, however, is not a wandering poet, but already deeply embedded in civic *agōnes* (where all know of his talents and therefore want him to train their tribe's chorus). His flying fantasy is

---

[29] *Scholion ad* 913 in Dübner 1877: περισσά τινες ταῦτα. Cf. Rutherford 1896: 505 who takes the phrase as indicating possible interpolation. The upshot is the same, whether the words denote content ('excessive') or repetition ('redundant').

[30] Personal fieldnotes and audiotape from Karanos, Crete, June 1996.

[31] Dübner 1877: *ad Birds* 913, 'Homer was also believed to have written the *Margites*, in which the phrase "servant of the Muses and far-shooting Apollo" appears.' From a papyrus fragment (West *IEG*² 'Homerus' 1) it appears the line comes from the proem, telling how an old poet came to Kolophon; apparently this mention (like *Hy. Ap.* 172–4) was widely taken to be a self-portrait of 'Homer'. For Homer's relations with Kolophon, as depicted in the *Vitae*, see below.

[32] Around 100 BCE, the *grammatikos* Dioskourides of Tarsos is commemorated by an inscription at Delos for having composed for the people of Knossos in Crete an *enkōmion kata ton poiētan* about their city. The striking continuity of this poetic strategy, three centuries after Aristophanes parodied it, might even have extended to an explicit citation of Homer by name in the composition of Dioskourides (whose pupil, Myrinos, a melic and epic poet, actually performed the encomium): for text and commentary see Guarducci 1929: 637–8 and 655, who suggests that the poet might have elaborated the praises of Crete found in e.g. *Od.* 19.172–9.

[33] See Csapo 2004 for the fullest account of this style and its ethos.

92   RICHARD P. MARTIN

like a sublimated form of wandering – it is all in the mind and words, an
escape from his more mundane task as *didaskalos*.[34] And his plan of getting
wings from Peisetairos abruptly ends when the city-founder offers him the
scrawniest *khorēgos* and a tribe of birds to train.

   The wandering bard, as opposed to the would-be nightingale Kinesias,
actually gets what he wants. Why does he succeed? Obviously, he has read
the vagrant's handbook, strategy no. 3 – 'for success, don't dress'. Well-
known dithyrambic court-supported poets, like Arion, dress sumptuously.
Even *aulos* players and *chorēgoi* associated with this sort of poetry are always
well turned out.[35] But the wandering *didaskalos* dresses down. Peisetairos,
picking up on the poet's adjective, remarks at lines 915 'no wonder you've
got an *otrēron lēdarion* – 'nimble little tunic.' As Dunbar points out, he
is making a pun on words like *trēma* 'perforation' – in other words, the
poet's garb is '(w)hol(l)y in fashion' for dirt-poor warblers. This is the basis
for the ensuing dialogue, to which we might now skip ahead. The poet
comes on with a rather direct request: 'give to me whatsoever you will to
give, by your head's assent' (τεᾷ κεφαλᾷ). Though Dunbar thinks that
this phrase is 'deliberately odd, showing the poet's want of skill', a closer
look at Pindar shows that this is in fact highly exact technical language for
a transaction involving supplication, honour and oaths.[36] Peisetairos gets
the picture and, to prevent further trouble from 'this bad thing', orders a
companion to hand over his jacket, since the sidekick still has a *khitōn* to
wear. There is general agreement that the scene evokes Hipponax (esp. fr.
32 *IEG²*), and we could leave it at that.[37] But the poet's gracious reply opens
up further possibilities for interpretation. In a neat μέν / δέ construction, he
takes and gives: 'Not unwillingly does my dear Muse accept this gift (μέν);
but let thy mind (δέ) learn the Pindaric saying.' Like all good comedy, this
moment gets its punch from a serious potential breach in social relations.
Peisetairos thinks he can banish his problem by a quick payoff, the way one
gets rid of roaming accordionists at outdoor restaurants. But the paid poet
is working with a different perspective of the exchange relationship. He has

---

[34] On the biographical details, including his victories, see Dunbar 1995: 660–1. On the imagery of
flying, see Loscalzo 2005: 230–1.
[35] For Arion: Hdt. 1.24. On aulete costuming, see P. Wilson 1999: 72–7, and on the Aristophanic play
with this convention within the *Birds*, see Barker 2004: 198–202. For the finery of the *chorēgos*, as
part of the *lamprotēs* and *megaloprepeia* associated with the agonistic event, see Wilson 2000: 136–43.
[36] Dunbar 1995: 534. Compare the contexts of *heai kephalai* in *Ol.* 6.60 ('asking for some honour to
nourish the people, for/by his own head') and *Ol.* 7.67–8 ('to agree [literally nod] with the son of
Kronos that [the island] would be for his head/by her head a prize of honour ever after').
[37] Cf. Dunbar 1995: 535, Loscalzo 2005: 232–3.

Read on arrival 93

been paid (μέν) and so he will *re*pay in his own verbal medium (δέ); which then of course would require counter-payment.

An interesting parallel appears in Thomas Hale's volume on west African griots or *jeliw*. In a section covering griot financial arrangements called 'Rewards at home *vs.* rewards on the road', Hale says: 'The traditional patron who gives the griot anything – a blanket, $10, a goat – seals an unwritten life contract with the bard. The griot may now ask the donor for anything at any time, and the patron is normally under the obligation to do his or her best to accede to the request.' He continues, 'The concert promoter, on the other hand, gives the griot a check for $750 and may not see the performer again for several years, if at all. The relationship is not personal; it is commercial.'[38] To put the *Birds* scenario into these terms, the bard, although on the road, is looking for a long-term patron with whom he can settle down; Peisetairos, on the other hand, wants to cut the cord with a cheque. In a small way, we can glimpse here the clash of symbolic and monetary exchange cultures that Leslie Kurke has explicated in her *Coins, Bodies, Games, and Gold*.[39] In this, too, the anonymous bard is more like Pindar than Pindar would ever admit.

A wandering poet cannot loiter, because he presents an implicit threat: either he becomes a drain on the economy, with his continuous high-priced praise and advice, or worse, he can turn mean. Plenty of comparative evidence exists concerning praise poets who get outrageous payoffs by turning to satire. Among the Hausa, for example, Ruth Finnegan tells of the virtual blackmail tactics of roving solo singers, who come into town, apostrophise the local big-wig in praise-verses, and then, if not paid, gradually shift stanza by stanza into harsher innuendoes about his occupation, reputation and political integrity.[40] The Middle Irish story of the Ulster poet Aithirne Ailgesach ('Aithirne the demanding'), who obtained as payment the (only remaining) eye out of the head of the Connaught king Eochaid, paints a similar picture.[41] The *Birds* bard seems relatively tame, by these standards, at least on the basis of what he says. It could be that in a context of patronage-hunting and its protocols, he does not need to say any more. As it turns out, the counter-gift, consisting of the bard's treasured Pindaric *epos*, features further innuendo that cannot be ignored. The lines run (941–5):

---

[38] Hale 1998: 302.   [39] Kurke 1999, especially 101–65.   [40] Finnegan 1970: 92–8.
[41] Book of Leinster folio 114b1–30 (the opening of the eleventh-century tale *Talland Étair*); summary and further bibliography in Ó hÓgáin 1991: 22–3.

94   RICHARD P. MARTIN

'For among the nomad Scyths, he wanders apart from the host, who acquires no woven-whirled garment. Unglorified goes a jerkin without tunic. Understand what I say.'

Peisetairos gets the point, hands over his companion's tunic in addition to what has gone before, and tells the poet to take it and get lost (*apelthe – labōn*). The comic business with the clothes is fast and funny enough that we may not catch all the artfulness of this turn. First, there is the lovely pathetic irony of a marginal wandering type implicitly comparing himself to a marginal type among a marginal people – not just a Scythian but a Scythian *outcast*. Next, there is the implied threat – the 'jerkin' going 'without glory' is a barely coded way of saying 'no one will ever get my transmitted *kleos* about you and your city unless you give me more'. We may be reminded of similar exchanges within the Phaeacian episode of the *Odyssey*, which is after all our first extended representation of another extortionist wandering poet who controls the threat of ill fame (see especially *Od.* 11.333–84).[42]

Finally, when we hold up this passage against the original Pindaric *hyporchēma* the innuendo gets sharper. As we have it (thanks largely to scholiasts explicating this very passage in the *Birds*), the Pindar passage ran (fr. 105a–b):[43]

σύνες ὅ τοι λέγω,
ζαθέων ἱερῶν ἐπώνυμε
πάτερ, κτίστορ Αἴτνας.
νομάδεσσι γὰρ ἐν Σκύθαις ἀλᾶται στρατῶν,
ὃς ἀμαξοφόρητον οἶκον οὐ πέπαται.
ἀκλεὴς <δ'> ἔβα.

Understand what I tell you,
you whose name means holy temples,
Father, founder of Aitna.
For among the nomadic Scythians the man is excluded
from the folk who does not possess a house borne on a wagon,
and he goes without glory.

Modern commentators like Kugelmeier and Dunbar innocently resist, but Tzetzes long ago saw this as disparaging, and not just parodying, Pindar. διασύρει τὸν Πίνδαρον says the Byzantine scholar: 'he rips him apart'.[44]

---

[42] Cf. above p. 10. On the metapoetic nuances of the hero's interaction with his Phaeacian patrons in this so-called *intermezzo*, see Doherty 1991, Wyatt 1989 and Martin 2001.

[43] Text and translation Race 1997b: 336–8.

[44] *Ad Birds* 930 in White 1901: 85. Kugelmeier 1996: 115 thinks there is no parody of Pindar intended, but that the lines are simply convenient for the beggar.

Read on arrival 95

Aristophanes has cleverly taken the first line of the *hyporkhēma* (σύνες ὅ τοι λέγω) and placed it *after* the lines about the poor garment-less Scythian, which the bard has pointedly used to get himself a tunic. This way, the original phatic utterance of Pindar to Hieron ('now hear this') becomes much more mercenary ('now hear *this* – give me *that*'). But the ultimate satiric point is that Pindar *himself* in his poems to Hieron was angling for bling. What kind of accessorising did he have in mind? The *Birds* poet just wants some clothes, but the phrase ὑφαντοδόνητον ἔσθος is a metapoetic (and partially rhyming) rewording of Pindar's original which mentions a house on a wagon (ἀμαξοφόρητον οἶκον). Is Aristophanes implying that the real Pindar was hitting up Hieron for a sort of Scythian suburban utility vehicle?[45] At the risk of making a parodic interpretation of this parody, I will simply point to a fragment of another *hyporkhēma* in which Pindar reminds Hieron that, while other places are good for various goods, Sicily is the world leader in production of the fancy mule-car (*okhēma daidaleon*, fr. 106.6). Perhaps the roving Pindar really needed new wheels and not so subtly told Hieron to improve his ride.

One cannot help falling into this language of hip-hop, because there are many structural similarities between ancient and modern pay-per-poem performers. The constant threat of public blame for disrespect (i.e. non-payment) has already been mentioned. Self-mythologising is another (cf. among rappers, anyone from Eminem to Fabolous). Tied up with the presentation of self are the next two maxims for wandering poets: no. 4 'inflate your worth' and no. 5 'diversify'. In the poet's case they are connected to the essentially unregulated and open-ended nature of his occupation, as opposed to that of the stay-at-home performer. It is precisely because he appears out of nowhere, and can say anything about where he has been and is going, that the planetic poet can make his initial encounter into an investment tool. An excellent way to show how important you are is to mention the exciting, exotic or simply better places to which you must be moving on. In planetic discourse, this can be used to imply that the locals are stingy but over in (*insert name of next town*), boy, do they ever pay big. A neat example of this strategy occurs in the novelisation of Homer's life attributed to Herodotus.[46] The young and newly blind Homer has

---

[45] Rogers 1906: 129–30 notes that the scholiast implied that Pindar's original poem embodied his own request, and that the fragment was thus understood by Schneider in his commentary. Rogers himself cautiously suggests that 'it would certainly make the Aristophanic adaptation more pungent, if Pindar was begging the additional present on his own account'.

[46] Graziosi 2002 provides a sophisticated reading of this and other *Lives*, in the context of later ancient 'inventions' of an author to accompany the reception of Homeric verse.

96 RICHARD P. MARTIN

wandered from Kolophon to Smyrna and thence to Neon Teikhos where
he finds a gig at a cobbler's shop, entertaining people with hymns and tales
from the Theban cycle. He makes a living (*mēkhanē*) that way but then
starts falling short of cash and decides to head for the metropolis, Kyme.
Before he departs he says (lines 127–8 Allen):[47]

> αἶψα πόδες με φέροιεν ἐς αἰδοίων πόλιν ἀνδρῶν·
> τῶν γὰρ καὶ θυμὸς πρόφρων καὶ μῆτις ἀρίστη.

> May my legs bring me soon to a respectful town:
> the heart of such men is willing, their devices the best.

While it is an indirect snub, the operative words *aidoios* and *prophrōn*
(appearing at emphatic caesural points in the line) are keys to the mercenary
implications of the couplet (recall here *prophrōn* in the request at *Birds* 930).
As Markwald has shown in his extensive study of the Homeric epigrams,
these words are used in formulaic fashion in scenes of encounter in the
Odyssey, in which the hero is seeking a kindly reception.[48] Within the
pseudo-Herodotean *Life*, the formula αἰδεῖσθε ξενίων κεχρημένον ('have
respect for the man who needs guest-friendship') has in fact already been
used by the blind Homer when he first encounters the people of Neon
Teikhos (a poem we shall examine shortly). Alas, no one rushes out with
cash in hand to prevent Homer from leaving Neon Teikhos. The *quid pro
quo* he has in mind is revealed when he gets to Kyme and frankly tells the
governing council that, in return for public support (*dēmosiēi trephein*),
he will make their city as famous as possible (*eukleestatēn*). In the case of
the *Birds* bard, this bargain is never as explicit but must lie just under the
surface. In the Homeric life, the Kymaeans' refusal of support leads to an
outcome that we might have predicted, based on the African and Irish
parallels to which I have referred: Homer, in verse, bewails his ill treatment
in the presence of the presiding council member, promising that he will
leave immediately for a different polis:[49]

> Aeolian Smyrna, seaneighbor, holy shore,
> traversed by the bright water of holy Meles –
> going forth from there Zeus' daughters, his glorious children,
> desired to celebrate a noble land and city of men,
> but they in their folly refused the holy voice, the word of song
> (ἱερὴν ὄπα, φῆμιν ἀοιδῆς).

---

[47] Translation from West 2003: 365.
[48] Markwald 1986: 24–5, 30.   [49] Text and translation from West 2003: 369.

Read on arrival   97

Homer refashions the council's refusal into an insult to the Muses themselves, who have come from Smyrna (a coded reference to his own poetry). With the self-important phrase ἱερὴν ὄπα, φῆμιν ἀοιδῆς he adheres to rule no. 2 – 'make yourself the voice of tradition'. The poem also contains a threat that he will get pay-back, and the subsequent prose tells us that he laid a curse on the people of Kyme, that they never produce a great poet (probably, as West suggests, an allusion to the lore that Hesiod's father came from Kyme – in which case this is a slap at the poetic tradition that most rivalled the Homeric).[50] Praise-poets can be touchy.

If we take this *Life* of Homer as articulating a basic strategy whereby poets allude to their value by mentioning greener pastures where they can get 'respect', then Aristophanes' stylisation of planetic discourse becomes all the funnier. At *Birds* 948, the poet takes his new clothes and says, 'I'm off.' This is a crucial moment because the audience will now expect to hear whether the wandering bard intends to go somewhere else where he will get better treatment and denigrate Cloud-cuckoo-land, or instead, go off content and spread the *kleos* of the new city, as his re-payment for their hospitality. But the expectation is jilted. What he says is: 'And going into the city I will make such verses as the following.' What city? Says Dunbar, 'the juxtaposition of prepositional phrase and *elthōn* suggesting going into the city when he is now about to leave it, is awkward, but may be another example of the hack poet's ineptitude'. Far from it, I think. The whole joke must be that the poet has been paid and therefore will *stay* in this very city of Cloud-cuckoo-land – the outcome that Peisetairos had feared from the start. But – even funnier – he's now shifting gear into what is obviously a different poetic register, that of new-dithyramb (compare the later Kinesias poem). And joke no. 3: using the planetic strategy of saying 'I'm off to greener pastures now', he tells us that he intends to praise the city as being freezing cold, snow-struck and full of passage-ways (*polupora*). Not too attractive, but it fits the aerial locale perfectly, while hinting heavily that he requires another anorak. *Polupora* must be another hint that this boundless cloud-city offers endless opportunities for his extortionistic-encomiastic 'ways of song', for *poros* in late fifth-century usage often refers to monetary 'ways and means'.[51]

As my own ways of song are not endless, I will not delay over the evidence that Solon and Xenophanes knew and used strategy no. 4.[52] Instead, let me

---

[50] West 2003; cf. the *Contest of Homer and Hesiod* (West 2003: 318–53).   [51] LSJ⁹ *s.v.* II.3.
[52] See West *IEG*² Solon fr. 19 (his departure from Soloi); Xenophanes fr. 6 (a threat to spread rumours about a cheap patron?).

98   RICHARD P. MARTIN

turn now to the penultimate gambit no. 5 – diversify. Once again, the
pseudo-Herodotean *Life* is a good place to start. A simple inventory of the
poems embedded within this composition, or alluded to therein, yields a
range of thirteen different genres: praise/supplication (*epigr.* 1, 9; *Eiresiōnē* =
epigr. 15); blame (*epigr.* 16 – to the riddling boys); epic (ch. 16 = *Little Iliad*
fr. 10, ch. 9 = *Expedition to Thebes*); epic as praise-poetry after the fact
(chs. 26, 28); local history (ch. 16 Phocais); parainetic (*epigr.* 5, 1, 13 – the
last-named also a begging poem?); propemptic (to himself = *epigr.* 2, 4, 6);
epitaph (*epigr.* 3 for Midas' tomb); plaint (*epigr.* 7); threat/curse (*epigr.* 8,
12, 14); oracle (*epigr.* 10); hymns (ch. 9); *paignia* (ch. 24).

   The composer of the *Life* sometimes places Homer in fairly far-fetched
situations simply to explain how a particular (most likely pre-existent) poem
has come to be attributed to him. But we should not dismiss the prose as
padding. Like the Provençal *razos*, and medieval Irish bardic romances (such
as the story of Cearbhall and Fearbhlaidh), the anecdotal tradition travels
with the poetry; it can be as informative (and authentic) as the compositions themselves.[53] Certainly, Homer is being credited with the use or even
invention of almost all important non-melic genres.[54] In this, he encapsu-
lates the essence of rhapsodic performance as we can reconstruct it from
other sources. He is also made into the essence of folk tradition, with the
remarkable assertion that it was Homer who invented the *Eiresiōnē* song and
custom while wintering in Samos. His invented tradition continued forever
after, as a children's performance at a local feast of Apollo. The composition is itself a perfect illustration of the dynamics of planetic discourse. In
company with children, Homer would approach the most well-off houses
and praise the occupant for his wealth and power, then switch to requests
for hand-outs (*epigr.* 15, lines 3–7, 11–15):[55]

> αὐταὶ ἀνακλίνεσθε θύραι· Πλοῦτος γὰρ ἔσεισιν
> πολλός, σὺν Πλούτῳ δὲ καὶ Εὐφροσύνη τεθαλυῖα,
> Εἰρήνη τ' ἀγαθή. ὅσα δ' ἄγγεα, μεστὰ μὲν εἴη,
> κυρβα<σ>ίη δ' αἰεὶ μάζης κατὰ καρδόπον ἔρποι.
> νῦν μὲν κριθαίην εὐώπιδα σησαμόεσσαν . . . . . .

---

[53] On the Irish tale, see Doan 1985.
[54] The relationship of this fact to his 'first' name *Melesigenes* (cf. ps-Herodotean *Life* ch. 3) bears
    further scrutiny. The successive names of Homer suggest an evolutionary perspective on the level of
    individual performance career, which can in turn be taken as metonymic for the greater span of the
    development of distinctive genres out of an originally indeterminate category of 'song' (*melos*). For
    this evolution on the macro-level, see Nagy 1990a, esp. 33–51.
[55] Text and translation from West 2003: 394–7. On this poem and the very similar *Korōnisma* attributed
    to Phoenix of Kolophon, see Furley 1994.

νεῦμαί τοι νεῦμαι ἐνιαύσιος ὥστε χελιδών·
ἕστηκ᾽ ἐν προθύροις ψιλὴ πόδας· ἀλλὰ φέρ᾽ αἶψα.
<ὑ>πέρ σε τὠπόλλονος, <ὦ> γύ<ν>αι τι δός.
κεἰ μέν τι δώσεις· εἰ δὲ μή, οὐχ ἑστήξομεν,
οὐ γὰρ συνοικήσοντες ἐνθάδ᾽ ἤλθομεν.

Open up, doors, all on your own: Wealth is coming in
lots of it, and with Wealth, flourishing Good Cheer
and Peace the good. Let all the jars be filled!
May the mound of dough creep atop the trough.
Now for some fair-faced barley meal-and-sesame. . . .

I'll return, I'll return every year, like the swallow.
Here I stand at the forecourt, barefoot. Bring quickly!
For Apollo's sake, woman, give something!
If you give . . . good; if not, we will not stand here:
for we did not come to live with you.

Homer's generic versatility is given pragmatic grounding by the realistic
depiction of the various contexts that surround his compositions. We can
go even further and speculate that the anecdotal tradition preserves some
memory of actual occasions when real wandering poets – and not just
their stylising rhapsodic descendants – found a use for verse. In this it
helps to triangulate the generic diversity of wandering bards with information from Egypt, both in early and modern times, and nineteenth-century
Ireland. Alan Cameron, in his justly famous article on poets of Byzantine
Egypt, observes that one of the characteristics of Pamprepius, Horapol-
lon, Christodorus and their kin was the ability to handle a whole range
of material, from invective to encomia, epithalamia to epic, and especially
local histories – for which they seem to have been paid by the locals.[56]
I am reminded of the *Life*'s picture of Homer's dictation of the *Phocais*
(ch. 16). As Cameron stresses, the *Gelegenheitsgedichte* of such poets have
to be distinguished from productions of the non-wandering scholar-poets;
in most cases, the very occasionality of the *vaganti* verses has led to their
disappearance, while big-ticket scholarly poets like Nonnus survive. No
doubt the same applies to the bulk of the verse performed by wandering
Greek poets of all eras.[57]

From fifth-century Egypt to nineteenth-century Ireland is not that far,
in terms of poetic practices. The sociopolitical landscapes also look similar:

[56] Cameron 1965.
[57] In this connection, it is interesting to see the range of genres performed by the poets referred to in
epigraphic evidence collected by Guarducci 1929; see for example her no. 7, in which Kleokhares of
Athens is commemorated at Delphi in 230 BCE for composing a *prosodion*, paean, and hymn to be
sung yearly by children at the *Theoxenia*.

in both cases, as the result of régime change, men educated in a millennia-old poetic tradition were no longer readily employed; they take to the road, seeking patronage, meanwhile making a living as *grammatici* or as hedge-school masters, turning out polished poems according to the canons of their ancestors. In the case of Irish tradition, it was only the efforts of antiquarians and the nationalist stirrings of such scholarly collectors as Douglas Hyde that preserved the words of the last poet in this wandering tradition, Antoin Ó Reachtúire (Raftery, in English). Having lost his sight as a child, this illiterate performer spent most of his 51 years wandering around Galway between Athenry and Loughrea. In his edition Hyde notes the generic range of the surviving verses: 'Raftery made songs in praise of people who helped him, or whom he liked, or in praise of the places in which they lived; he made political songs spurring the people against the Galls, or English enemy, and helping Daniel O'Connell's party. He made an occasional love song, and an occasional religious song, and now and again a song of dispraise, a satire or "*aer*" as the old Gaels used to call it.'[58] Many points here could be paralleled with the *Life* of Homer tradition: I choose just one such *aer*, which Raftery made upon a farmer's wife. The woman was preparing dinner, and Raftery smelled the beef and cabbage, but she told the blind man there was not a bite to eat in the house, at which point he said:[59]

> Cluinin an torann, ach ní fheicim an bia:
> An té' dhéanfas leathchuma orm, nár fheice sí Dia.

> I hear the noise, but I see no food:
> Who keeps me deprived, may she never see God!

We might compare Homeric *Epigram* 12 and the accompanying story. Homer, on the way to celebrate the Apatouria on Samos, encountered some women sacrificing to Kourotrophos at a crossroads. When the priestess told him to keep away from the ritual, Homer cursed her:[60]

> κλῦθι μοι εὐχομένῳ Κουροτρόφε, δὸς δὲ γυναῖκα
> τήνδε νέων μὲν ἀνήνασθαι φιλότητα καὶ εὐνήν,
> ἡ δ' ἐπιτερπέσθω πολιοκροτάφοισι γέρουσιν,
> ὧν ὥρη μὲν ἀπήμβλυνται, θυμὸς δὲ μενοινᾷ.

> Hear my prayer, Kourotrophos, and grant that this woman
> refuse the love and bed of younger men:
> let her fancy be taken by old men grey at the temples,
> whose vigour is blunted away, though their hearts still hanker.

---

[58] Hyde 1903: 15. [59] Text and translation in O'Flynn 1998: 214–15.
[60] Text and translation from West 2003: 390–1.

Read on arrival   101

The main point, however, is simply that poetic diversity – the ability to
handle many genres – is an evolutionary survival response to the dilemma
of the wandering poet. The further consequences of this multi-tasking
mechanism might be worth exploring at some other time. For instance, it
could be shown that such flexibility enables formulas and motifs to pass
easily from one sort of composition to another, as they are all in the same
poet's head. Furthermore, it is likely that this ability – reflected in the
concept of *polyeideia* – is what Callimachus and later poets are striving to
reclaim in their own production. Ion of Chios, one of the classical models
for Callimachus, seems to have enjoyed the skill, but probably even he is
just archaising: it is poets like Hipponax (another emblematic figure for
Callimachus) who are more likely to have really required and displayed
generic diversity in their travels.[61] Circling back to the *Birds* passage, we
can now see that the bard's declaration on entry – that he has many melic
songs for Cloud-cuckoo-land – is an entirely logical assertion for a poet
seeking employment. He mentions dithyrambs (*kuklia polla*), *partheneia*
and songs in the style of Simonides – in other words, civic poetry.[62] The
last-named figure is a further hint at two facts: first, Simonides himself is
emblematic of a huge range of genres, including hymns, *thrēnoi*, encomia,
epigrams, paians, *prosodia*, dithyrambs and even tragedies (if one believes
the *Suda*).[63] Second – and certainly not unrelated – Simonides, according
to a body of lore about him, was a money-obsessed, skinflint poet-for-
hire.[64] So to say you can do things *à la* Simonides is both a compelling
advertisement and a warning signal.

We arrive finally at the last handbook strategy, which might also explain
this paper's title, 'Read on Arrival'. To put it in the words of the New Yorker
who was asked by an out-of-towner how to get to Carnegie Hall: 'practice,
practice, practice'. The most amazing part of the *Birds* bard's pitch is that
he has *already* composed songs (μέλη πεπόηκ᾽ εἰς τὰς Νεφελοκοκκυγίας)
for a city that has barely been founded. 'When did you do that?' asks
Peisetairos, naturally. The poet answers 'For a long long time now I've
been celebrating this city.' Like the flash of steeds, swift was the Muses'
report that came to him, says the poet. And then, just before asking for a
gift, he addresses Peisetairos at line 925–6 as 'Thou father, Aitna-founder,
namesake of god-filled holy rites.' This, say the scholiasts, is a quotation

---

[61] On the concept of *polyeideia* and its extensive repercussions, see Acosta-Hughes 2002.

[62] On this point see Loscalzo 2005: 225, who stresses the appropriateness of a poet not seeking private
patronage from the city founders.

[63] For an overview stressing the poet's generic variety, see Bowra 1961: 308–72.

[64] On the stories, see Bremer 1991: 49 with further bibliography. I owe this reference to Felix Budelmann.
Cf. further above pp. 11–12.

102   RICHARD P. MARTIN

of the Pindaric *hyporchēma* mentioned earlier (fr. 105), in which Pindar
puns on the name of his tyrant addressee, Hieron the First. Once again,
we can choose to see this as a bit of comic bungling and leave it at that.
But the parody must go deeper. Aristophanes, in sketching the wandering
poet, has given us a performer with a *modus operandi* in every other respect
consistent with what we know of other wandering bards, real or imagined.
What he is making comically obvious is that *this* bard – and by implication
others – uses canned material. New to the area and short on details? No
problem – a sixty-year-old praise-poem for Hieron can be recycled. This
is a *rehearsed* performance, and the material has indeed been around *palai
palai*. The bard has practised and practised this all before. As it happens,
we have an interesting piece of evidence that might confirm the practice
in question. The first epigram in the pseudo-Herodotean *Life* of Homer
represents the wandering Homer's first plea for support. In good planetic
fashion he praises the place (see rule no. 1). But what place *is* this? The prose
introduction clearly states that the poet came to Neon Teikhos a colony of
Kyme, and said these lines. But the codices of the *Lives* unanimously make
it sound as though he has arrived at *Kymē* (the next stop on his itinerary),
'Kymē the fair daughter'. The Greek as printed in Allen's text runs (lines
101–5):

> αἰδεῖσθε ξενίων κεχρημένον ἠδὲ δόμοιο,
> οἳ πόλιν αἰπεινὴν Κύμην ἐριώπιδα κούρην
> ναίετε, Σαρδήνης πόδα νείατον ὑψικόμοιο·
> ἀμβρόσιον πίνοντες ὕδωρ θείου ποταμοῖο
> Ἕρμου δινήεντος, ὃν ἀθάνατος τέκετο Ζεύς.

> Have Respect for one in need of house and hospitality
> you that dwell in the steep city, *the fair-eyed daughter Kymē*,
> on the lowest spur of high-forested Sardene,
> drinking the ambrosial water of the divine river,
> the eddying Hermus, born of immortal Zeus.

Martin West, on whose recent Loeb edition of the *Life* the above translation is based, prints at the end of the second line νύμφης ἐριώπιδος
Ἥρης, 'of fair-eyed Hera the Bride', a phrase he constructs on the basis of
another version of this short poem (one that completely avoids the place-
name) found at the end of several manuscripts of the *Homeric Hymns*.[65]
Pauw's emendation Κύμης (the genitive) might seem the sanest solution,
and that is what Markwald prints. According to the latter, the geographical

---

[65] West 2003: 363. The hymn version has νυμφῆς ἐρατώπιδος Ἥρης. On this poem as an *envoi* to the
Hymns collection, see Allen, Sikes and Halliday 1936: 442–3.

Read on arrival

detail about proximity to the river Hermos can only fit Neon Teikhos, the new city, not older Kyme, and so the poem should say 'the daughter (i.e. daughter-city) of Kyme.'[66] But I wonder whether it is not safer to stick with the received text. The psychological error was not scribal but bardic, an authentic performance fault rather than a wrong-headed transcription. Homer, practising for his reception in the bigger town of Kyme, got ahead of himself, or did not shift his formulas to fit changed circumstances.[67]

For a card-carrying oralist the scripsist title 'Read on Arrival' might seem regressive. But the process I have been describing as endemic to wandering poetics seems to require a kind of temporary textualisation of one's repertoire, ready to be 'read' under any circumstances, as much as it requires the fluid, composition-in-performance strategies of oral tradition. The successful roaming poet will be one who makes the memorised look spontaneous.[68] I am not suggesting that *poeti vaganti* were the key to the writing down of early Greek verse, but they were certainly part of the cultural conditioning that accepted and encouraged re-performance in increasingly familiar forms.

This brings us at last to the apparent target of the *Birds* in its parodic portrait. Like Aristophanes' portrait of Socrates in the *Clouds*, the whole caricature can be easily dismissed as a comic composite of several types – Hipponax, Simonides and Pindar. But it could also be a clear-headed de-mystification of Pindaric pretence and its dangers.[69] No matter how often Pindar in his odes professes inspired spontaneity, going so far as to adopt the conversational style that Andrew Miller has so well delineated, these

---

[66] Markwald 1986, *ad loc.*

[67] That the performance of prepared encomiastic poems was acceptable, at least in post-classical times, seems clear from such inscriptions as Guarducci 1929, no. 12, commemorating the young Ariston of Phocaea for his several *akroaseis* in the assembly and theatre at Delos in 146/5 BCE, at which he read aloud (ἀναγ]νούς) poems already made πεπραγματευμένα ἐ[γκώμια, line 10) and also hymned Apollo.

[68] It must be stressed that the existence of such units in no way detracts from the overall phenomenon of live composition-in-performance; the units function like formulaic phrases, or at the higher level, like 'themes', as aids to rapid verse manufacture. In this way, pre-fabricated sections actually confirm the habits of oral composition, for otherwise such devices would not be needed.

[69] MacDowell 1995: 210, like most, veers away from direct attack, proposing instead a generic target: 'Evidently there were in fact poets in Athens at this time who offered for sale songs for special events, like Pindar's odes at an earlier date, and Aristophanes is mocking them here.' One objection to seeing the historical Pindar as the parodied poet is of course that the audience of 414 BCE would have been a generation removed from his activity. But it can be argued (1) that a similar generation gap did not prevent Aristophanes from parodying Aeschylus (e.g. in the *Frogs*); (2) that there is a strong possibility that Pindaric poetry would have been familiar from *reperformance* in Athens and elsewhere, on which see now Currie 2004; and (3) that there were good contemporary motivations in 414 BCE for a comic attack on Pindar (and, metonymically, any patron-paid poets), on which see below.

poems are paid commissions, prepared in advance, rehearsed – most likely –
and performed by trained choruses.[70] Pindar had no Plato to play the part
of his apologist, but everyone, starting from his original patrons on down,
willingly collaborated with his high-minded conceit that his praise is non-
mercenary *kharis*, and his status as wandering poet really that of a guest-
friend, a *xeinos*. To act otherwise would be to question the basis of the entire
system that produced the precious praise commodity and its aristocratic
bases.[71] But, by contrast, as a citizen from Kydathenaion, a deme in the
heart of democratic Athens, working in a poetic medium finally and for
the first time freed (thanks to state support) from the total control of any
one powerful individual, in which one-time high-risk productions were
the rule, Aristophanes transcends the lot of would-be court poets. His is a
tougher art-form (though at least he does not have to travel to get work).
Thus, he can cast a cold eye on his predecessors in the craft of verse-making.

Why would he want to? Perhaps because tragedy itself, the complement
and rival to Aristophanic drama, *was* (so it seems) regularly subject to the
pressures of political patronage. We know of the rôle played by prominent
khorēgoi who happened also to be ambitious public figures (Themistocles,
Pericles). Bremer's evidence for payments to tragedians (and also come-
dians) raises the much larger issue of Athenian drama's relationship to
traditional patron-supported encomiastic poetry, out of which it may in
fact have grown under the Peisistratids.[72] In addition, we must factor in
the age-old tendency for politicians to take advantage of all possible poetic
outlets. In this regard, the *epinikion* composed by Euripides in honor of
Alcibiades, on the occasion of his Olympic chariot victory, stands out. As
it happens, the victory took place in 416 BCE and the poem about it must
have followed shortly thereafter – that is to say, not long before the *Birds*
went into production.[73] While piling the clothes onto his Pindar-stand-
in, Aristophanes may have been making yet another stab at Euripides and
stripping bare a poetic genre that still posed a threat to democracy.

---

[70] Miller 1993.   [71] Kurke 1991 remains the best articulation of the full system and its ideology.
[72] Bremer 1991, esp. 54–60.
[73] Testimonia and fragments: *PMG* 755 and 756. The latter (from Plut. *Dem.* 1.1) quotes Euripides as
saying that requisite for the fortunate man (*eudaimōn*) is a glorious (*eudokimos*) city. Cf. *Birds* 905.

CHAPTER 5

Wandering poets, archaic style

Ewen Bowie

In this paper I explore archaic wandering poets' representation in their poetry of themselves and of their performances. I confine myself (some *comparanda* apart) to non-hexameter poetry of the period down to 500 BC and to pieces that I take to be in the first instance for monodic rather than choral performance. That is one of the reasons I have decided to exclude Stesichorus; another is that in his surviving poetry itself there is almost nothing that contributes to the issues I investigate. My cut-off date of 500 BC is partly to legitimise my exclusion of Bacchylides and Pindar. But another, and better, reason for that exclusion is that even their surviving *epinikia* on their own merit a separate treatment, and I am pursuing some related issues concerning them in another volume.[1]

A high proportion of the surviving poetry whose audience of first performance can be identified purports, at least, to be delivered to an audience outside the poet's polis. To some extent the bare data may be misleading: a huge proportion of the surviving poetry bears no unambiguous indication of the location of its first audience, and when we can be sure, or almost sure, that this audience is not in the poet's own polis, it is because there is either an identifying vocative plural address or a clear marker of some other sort – e.g. the poet praises an overseas host – features that we have much less right to expect in poetry composed for a poet's regular Friday-night drinking-companions in his own community. Thus it would probably be right to guess that a fair proportion of poetry attributed to a poet from Ephesus, Mytilene, Thasos or Athens was indeed composed for audiences in these cities despite the absence of clear markers of this location in our fragments. Even after allowances are made for this bias, the number of pieces that on one ground or another can be tied down to a place other than the poet's polis remains impressive.

---

[1] P. Agócs, C. Carey and R. Rawles (eds.), *Reading the Victory Ode* (in preparation).

105

EWEN BOWIE

This is not, in the seventh and for most of the sixth century, because elegiac, iambic or even melic poets are travelling *in order to* perform, or are seeking and accepting specific 'commissions'. Rather it is because most poets are a species within the genus 'member of a local élite', men who were much involved in what has conventionally been called colonisation and in associated trade and travel. The distances that a sympotic elegiac singer might well have travelled are brought out in some lines from just after the end of my period – precisely from 480 BC, if the lines in question, *Theognidea* 783–8, do indeed belong with the preceding lines 773–82, a prayer by a Megarian singer, perhaps Philiadas, to protect his city from the Medes.

> ἦλθον μὲν γὰρ ἔγωγε καὶ εἰς Σικελήν ποτε γαῖαν,
>   ἦλθον δ᾽ Εὐβοίης ἀμπελόεν πεδίον,
> Σπάρτην τ᾽ Εὐρώτα δονακοτρόφου ἀγλαὸν ἄστυ·
>   καί μ᾽ ἐφίλευν προφρόνως πάντες ἐπερχόμενον·
> ἀλλ᾽ οὔτις μοι τέρψις ἐπὶ φρένας ἦλθεν ἐκείνων·
>   οὕτως οὐδὲν ἄρ᾽ ἦν φίλτερον ἄλλο πάτρης.

Theognidea 783–8

> For I have once gone even to the land of Sicily,
>   and I have gone to the viney plain of Euboea,
> and to Sparta, the glittering city of the reed-nurturing Eurotas:
>   and they all showed me eager affection when I arrived;
> But no pleasure from these things went into my heart;
>   so true is it that nothing, it seems, is dearer than one's home country.

Here we have a singer keen to evoke places he claims to have visited in his travels,[2] though his purpose in listing them is priamel-like, in order to lead up to his closural γνώμη that home is best. For us, however, the potential extent of a Megarian symposiast's travel is illuminating.

We cannot tell *why* this singer travelled. But some travellers were men whose part in their city's political in-fighting had led to departure elsewhere, with or without ἑταῖροι, departure that might in some cases be, or come close to being, 'exile'. This phenomenon must be factored in judiciously.[3]

---

[2] Cf. the marble base from the Piraeus *c.* 475–450, presumably once bearing a herm, which picks out the dedicator's wide travels (*CEG* 316): Πύθων Ἑρμῆι ἄγαλμα Ἑρμοστράτο Ἀβδηρίτης ἔστησεμ πολλὰς θησάμενος πόλῃας. Εὔφρων ἐξεποίησ᾽ οὐκ ἀδαὴς Πάριος ('Python son of Hermostratos from Abdera set up for Hermes the object of delight after gazing upon many cities. Euphron fashioned it, not unskilled, from Paros').

[3] In Bowie 2007 I discuss representations of exile and displacement in archaic poetry (including hexameter epic), limiting myself to cases where that displacement is more or less involuntary. In the present piece I address poetry that offers evidence of voluntary wandering, but given the nature of our evidence attribution to one or other category is not always certain.

Wandering poets, archaic style

For example, we are told that Semonides of Samos led a group of Samians to join the existing Naxian settlement on Amorgos. It is not clear whether the Samians went to all three of the Naxians' settlements, Arkesine, Aigiale and Minoa, or only to Minoa where their presence is more fully attested archaeologically. It would probably be wrong to seek out an emigré perspective in our disappointingly scanty remains of Semonides' poetry. As we shall see, remains of one of his poems do bear upon my investigation, but as far as I can detect they are not affected by being composed by the Samian oecist of Amorgos (and may of course have been composed on Samos before Semonides jumped, fell or was pushed out). Much the same applies to *some* of Archilochus' poetry: once on Thasos he seems to see the world chiefly from a Thasian perspective, though here there are one or two much-cited lines which do reflect his change of domicile.

Let me move from these general considerations to particular cases. My discussion is articulated by genre (iambic, elegiac and finally melic poetry) because the conditions of composition, performance and circulation of poetry in each of these genres is different in ways that might be significant for this enquiry. For example, iambic and elegiac poetry could be readily composed by an amateur performer, even one with modest skills, and might be performed on any sort of sympotic occasion, at least (in the case of elegy) where an *aulos*-player might be expected to be present. Once performed they might well be transmitted without the tune to which (again in the case of elegy) they had first been sung. Performing most melic poems would require more preparation, and a composer-singer whose vocal skills combined with his (or her) skill on a stringed instrument were good enough to make his (or her) performance special. There was much greater opportunity for a gap to open up between amateur and virtuoso, and between virtuoso and professional. Moreover, when a melic performance was a 'hit', it will partly (to us incalculably) have been due to the effectiveness of the 'accompanying' music, and it will have been to that music that both the composer-poet and others reperformed the poem.

TRAVELLING IAMBIC POETS

First, Archilochus. The narrative later told about Archilochus was that he was the son of a Parian, Telesicles, who left Paros to found a colony on Thasos; that Archilochus himself went to Thasos, perhaps not with his father but later, and was active there as a citizen, both fighting against Thracians and Naxians for control of the Thracian Peraea to which Thasos gave ready access and embroiled in political in-fighting in the new polis

108   EWEN BOWIE

of Thasos.[4] His situation as a man who had been a youth (νέος) in Paros
and who in some poems is addressing an audience which is now, like him,
Thasian comes across only in a few of his surviving fragments:

> ἔα Πάρον, καὶ σῦκα κεῖνα, καὶ θαλάσσιον βίον
>
> Archilochus fr. 116 West

To hell with Paros, and those figs, and its sea-bound life!

> ὡς Πανελλήνων ὀιζὺς εἰς Θάσον συνέδραμεν
>
> Archilochus fr. 102 West

How the misery of the whole of Hellas has flocked together to Thasos!

> ἥδε δ᾽ ὥστ᾽ ὄνου ῥάχις
> ἕστηκεν ὕλης ἀγρίης ἐπιστεφής
>
> Archilochus fr. 21 West

But this island, like the spine of a donkey,
Stands up, crowned with wild woodland.

> οὐ γάρ τι καλὸς χῶρος οὐδ᾽ ἐφίμερος
> οὐδ᾽ ἐρατός, οἷος ἀμφὶ Σίριος ῥοάς
>
> Archilochus fr. 22 West

For it is not a beautiful place, nor attractive,
Nor desirable, like the one by the streams of the Siris.

Of these lines the tetrameter fr. 116 West is clearly dismissive of Paros, and
it certainly suggests a non-Parian audience; that it is a *Thasian* audience
can only be a guess. As to fr. 21 West, we can be confident from Plutarch's
quotation that it is about Thasos; and from the way that Athenaeus cites
fr. 22 West we can be fairly confident that the poem compared Thasos
unfavourably with a settlement on the river – perhaps the south Italian
river – Siris. If we then judge it probable that these formed part of the
poem beginning with fr. 19 West – οὔ μοι τὰ Γύγεω τοῦ πολυχρύσου
μέλει ('I have no interest in the affairs of gold-rich Gyges') – we can conclude
from Plutarch's quotation of fr. 19 that they were all spoken in the *persona*
of a Thasian. We thus get an *iambos* in which the Thasian speaker (known
from Aristotle to have been the carpenter, τέκτων, Charon) is critical of
(ψέγει) the island that both he and presumably his audience have settled

---

[4] Much of this is a Parian narrative, found in the inscriptions erected in the Parian Archilocheion by
Mnesiepes (third century BC, *SEG* 15.517) and Sosthenes (first century BC, *SEG* 15.518). We cannot
be sure that it was fully supported by the surviving poetry, far less that Thasians accepted the same
tradition. See most recently Clay 2004.

Wandering poets, archaic style

on, and praises the grass on the other side of the Greek colonial world. The stance is certainly modulated by the fact that neither the poet, nor presumably his *persona loquens*, nor indeed much of his audience, have *started* life on Thasos, but have all gone there, more or less by choice, rather than to another overseas settlement (ἀποικία).

Another quoted fragment of Archilochus also plays the Parian emigré card. We know from its quoter, the allegory-hunter 'Heraclitus', that fr. 105 West was uttered by an Archilochus who presented himself as 'cut off in a critical military situation in Thrace' (ἐν τοῖς Θρᾳκικοῖς ἀπειλημμένος δεινοῖς):

> Γλαῦχ’, ὅρα· βαθὺς γὰρ ἤδη κύμασιν ταράσσεται
> πόντος, ἀμφὶ δ’ ἄκρα Γυρέων ὀρθὸν ἵσταται νέφος,
> σῆμα χειμῶνος, κιχάνει δ’ ἐξ ἀελπτίης φόβος.
>
> Archilochus fr. 105 West

Look, Glaucus: already to its depths do waves churn up
the sea, and about the heights of Gyrae there stands, right above them, a cloud
the mark of a storm; and from its unexpectedness there comes fear.

There can be little doubt that Archilochus' address to his comrade (ἑταῖρος) Glaucus (one of many to him) is the address of one fighting Thasian citizen (πολίτης) to another, and that it belongs to one of several tetrameter poems describing and perhaps *pre*scribing details of fighting in Thrace, in another of which Glaucus is criticised (fr. 96.1–3 West).[5] But in this address their shared Parian past is exploited. As Sandbach demonstrated many years ago,[6] the 'heights of Gyrae' (ἄκρα Γυρέων) are almost certainly the high mountains at the south end of Tenos. These are some 50 km / 30 miles from Paros town, and clearly visible from the Delion on the hill just north of its harbour: they are some 375 km / 225 miles from the nearest point on the Thracian shore (περαία) that the Thasian Greeks were fighting to annex. There is no way they could be a literal weather sign for Thasian or coalition Greek fighters in Thrace. Two points follow: first, in this case at least 'Heraclitus' seems to be right in diagnosing allegory; second, in choosing his allegory Archilochus picks a landmark and a weather sign familiar to himself and his addressee Glaucus – and no doubt to others of their generation who heard and may have reperformed the poem – as Parian emigrés. He uses this possibly nostalgic recollection as a little-disguised lever to assist male bonding. Archilochus and his co-eval comrades might well remember from their boyhood checking the clouds over Tenos before

---

[5] On these see Bowie 2001.   [6] Sandbach 1942.

deciding if it was a good day to go out fishing, or whether it was better to stay on land plucking figs or trying to pick up the daughters of their fathers' political enemies. I shall return to Archilochus when I discuss elegiac fragments.

The evidence for an itinerant Semonides is much scantier and somewhat different. As I noted earlier, nothing that survives presents him as a Samian on Amorgos, or indeed as a Samian anywhere or an Amorgan anywhere. Twice, however, his Samian origin may season his story: an eel from the river Maeander at fr. 9 West, a goose from the Maeander at fr.11 West. Samos town (now Pythagorion) is a mere 15 miles / 24 km from the modern mouth of the Maeander, while the north-eastern end of Amorgos is five times that distance. Did Samians on Amorgos retain a liking for Samian luxuries, and is Semonides also playing the emigré card; or do these fragments simply come from poems composed on Samos anyway? We cannot tell.

More however can be got from frr. 22 and 23 West.[7] Fr. 22 West, which we know from Athenaeus to be the first line of an *iambos*, runs:

<ἦ> πολλὰ μὲν δὴ προυκπονέαι, Τηλέμβροτε,

Indeed you have gone to a lot of trouble preparing, Telembrotus.

This seems to have been followed, perhaps immediately, by fr. 23 West:

ἐνταῦθα μέν τοι τυρὸς ἐξ Ἀχαίης
Τρομίλιος θαυμαστός, ὃν κατήγαγον . . .

Here for you is a cheese from Achaea
A Tromilian cheese, a marvellous one, which I have imported . . .

We cannot be sure that the action asserted by fr. 23.2 West 'I have imported' (κατήγαγον) was that of Semonides himself rather than of a *persona* he has created; and it is indeed possible that this opening speech was followed by a framing coda, as in Archilochus fr. 19 West, which disclosed that the speaker was a named person quite different from the poet or *persona loquens* of the poem as a whole. But there is also some chance that this is a poem complimenting a host, Telembrotus, and that it is for performance by Semonides himself in a ξενία (hospitality) situation in which he finds himself. Whichever of these is correct, the speaker presents himself as producing as his contribution (ἔρανος) a cheese which he has brought back from Achaea: he thus uses his travels as a way of showing how his attention to bringing an interesting contribution might be seen to match his host's attentive preparations, and of course in doing so he adds décor to his poem.

---

[7] I have discussed these fragments from a different perspective in Bowie 2001.

Wandering poets, archaic style

I have not observed other iambic poems where the speaker uses exotica in this way to mark himself as a traveller.[8] But the third of the three canonical iambists, Hipponax, also presented himself as a traveller familiar with topography some way from his city, Ephesus, perhaps partly to evoke recognition in the members of his audience, doubtless numerous, who also knew their way round the area. Hipponax's ploy is to list landmarks on the road to Smyrna

  . . . . τὴν ἐπὶ Σμύρνης
ἰθὺ διὰ Λυδῶν παρὰ τὸν Ἀττάλεω τύμβον
καὶ σῆμα Γύγεω καὶ [Σεσώ]στρ[ιος] στήλην
καὶ μνῆμα Τωτος Μυτάλιδι πάλμυδος,
πρὸς ἥλιον δύνοντα γαστέρα τρέψας . . .

Hipponax fr. 42 West

The road towards Smyrna
Straight through Lydian country, along by Attalus' tomb
And the gravemarker of Gyges and the stele of Sesostris
And the memorial of Tos, the machtig Führer,
To the setting sun turning your belly . . .

It is hard to fit all these monuments into the road between Ephesus and Smyrna, most of which anyway runs north-north-west, so the setting of the poem from which these lines come seems likely to be some other city, possibly Sardis itself. A fuller text might have allowed us to decide where indeed the poem was intended for first performance and how far, if at all, Hipponax was presenting himself as an Ephesian.

Hipponax certainly composed at least one *iambos* for a non-Ephesian audience, that *iambos* which very probably opened the first book of his *iambi* in the Alexandrian edition:

ὦ Κλαζομένιοι, Βούπαλος κατέκτεινεν . . .
Hipponax fr. 1 West

O men of Clazomenae, Bupalus has killed . . .

No doubt there were other pieces of poetry which bore marks of a Clazomenian performance-context and which contributed to the tradition found in the *Suda* that Hipponax was thrown out of Ephesus by tyrants Athenagoras and Comas and settled in Clazomenae. We cannot tell whether in the continuation of fr. 1 West Hipponax marked himself as Ephesian, but we

---

[8] An outward-looking veneer can be imparted by mentioning food and drink in a way that serves something of the purpose of the Tromilian cheese. Hipponax fr. 124 West introduced Lebedian figs from Camandolus, a line apparently used to establish that Camandolus was in the territory of Lebedos: but this is just up the coast from Ephesus, so not especially exotic.

112   EWEN BOWIE

do once find him trading on his familiarity with its urban topography, if
Strabo is right to insist that fr. 50 West (which he alone cites, 14.633) is to
do with the topography of Ephesus and not of Smyrna:

οἴκει δ' ὄπισθε τῆς πόλιος ἐν <τῇ> Σμύρνῃ
μεταξὺ Τρηχέης τε καὶ Λεπρῆς ἀκτῆς.
                                        Hipponax fr. 50 West

and settle behind the citadel in Smyrna
between the Rugged and the Rough cliff.

Although it is almost impossible to assess the point of this topography out of
context, what we have seen involves a different technique from that which
we saw in Semonides. Hipponax is not flaunting overseas connections but
playing upon an audience's presumed familiarity with the topography of
the triangle Clazomenae – Ephesus – Sardis, and presenting himself as
one of those who know their way around it. For this sort of an audience
exoticism is generated rather by reference to a eunuch in the distant Persian
administrative centre of Lampsacus (fr. 26.3 West).

                    TRAVELLING ELEGIAC POETS

Exploitation of the poet's place of origin or of his being a ξένος in his
place of first performance is less obtrusive in elegiac poetry, but not so
much so that claims about generic difference can be pressed. Nothing in
surviving Archilochian sympotic elegy shows him playing what I earlier
called the Parian card. Fr. 3 West has him looking ahead to a battle against
Euboeans, and that could be a battle *on* Euboea, as some commentators
have supposed (though of course need not have been). Even if that were
so, it would be a further speculative jump to suppose that the poem was
composed for first performance on Euboea by Archilochus to fellow Thasian
(or Pario-Thasian) invaders: it remains a possibility, but no more, and the
probability is not increased now that we know, thanks to Ben Henry, that
adespota elegiaca 61 and 62 West belong to Archilochus too, so that we can
also draw in some reference to Carystians and the territory of the Eretrians
in fr. 62.6–7 West.[9] Archilochus' story of his shield that has fallen prey to
some Saian (fr. 5 West) implies a battle somewhere in the Thracian Peraea,
but the implication is 'Look! I am back from fighting the Thracians' not
'Look! Here we are fighting the Thracians.'

[9] As to something Thessalian in fr. 61.8 West.

The elegiac poetry of Archilochus' mid-seventh-century contemporaries more often attests a migratory past for their communities than an itinerant present for them as individuals. Tyrtaeus' fragments offer nothing to support the smear of Callisthenes (*FGrH* 124F24) that he was an immigrant from Athens – in particular, according to Philochorus (*FGrH* 328F215) in the early third century, from Aphidna – or its development reported by Pausanias (4.15.6) that he was a lame Athenian schoolmaster.[10] Rather, as Strabo spotted (8.4.10), Tyrtaeus' use of the first person plural in fr. 2 West, ascribed by Strabo to the *Eunomia*, supports – though it cannot prove – his Spartan ethnicity:

]ῳ πειθώμεθα κ[
]άν ἐγγύτεροι γέν[εος
αὐτὸς γὰρ Κρονίων καλλιστεφάνου πόσις Ἥρης
  Ζεὺς Ἡρακλείδαις ἄστυ δέδωκε τόδε,
οἷσιν ἅμα προλιπόντες Ἐρίνεον ἠνεμόεντα
  εὐρεῖαν Πέλοπος νῆσον ἀφικόμεθα

Tyrtaeus fr. 2.10–15 West

]let us obey [
]nearer to the kin[
for the son of Cronos himself, the husband of Hera of the lovely garland,
  Zeus, gave this city to the children of Heracles,
together with whom we left windy Erineon
  and arrived in the broad island of Pelops

The same identification of poet and migratory community informs a fragment of Mimnermus of Colophon and Smyrna. Mimnermus fr. 9 West, ascribed by Strabo to his *Nanno*,[11] uses perhaps clichéd eroticising language to talk up both Colophon, where he claims the emigrés fom Pylos first settled, and also their final home Smyrna:

αἰπὺ <   > τε Πύλον Νηλήιον ἄστυ λιπόντες
  ἱμερτὴν Ἀσίην νηυσὶν ἀφικόμεθα,
ἐς δ' ἐρατὴν Κολοφῶνα βίην ὑπέροπλον ἔχοντες
  ἑζόμεθ' ἀργαλέης ὕβριος ἡγεμόνες·
κεῖθεν δ' Ἀστήεντος ἀπορνύμενοι ποταμοῖο
  θεῶν βουλῇ Σμύρνην εἵλομεν Αἰολίδα . . .

Mimnermus fr. 9 West

---

[10] On Tyrtaeus cf. further D'Alessio (this volume) pp. 150–6.

[11] Strabo omits to point out that Mimnermus' silence on an early occupation of Smyrna does not support his schema of settlement in Smyrna – expulsion to Colophon – return to Smyrna. The overlap of this subject-matter with what we might expect to have been in the *Smyrneis* may perhaps be better explained by seeing these lines as a reworking for sympotic performance of a part of the *Smyrneis* than by the supposition that Strabo is wrong to ascribe them to *Nanno*.

leaving Pylos, the steep city of Neleus,
    we arrived in our ships at desirable Asia,
and bringing our overpowering might to lovely Colophon
    we settled, leaders of inexorable violence:
and from there, setting forth from the river Asteeis,
    by the will of the gods we captured Aeolian Smyrna . . .

The only wanderings the poet here admits to are those of or with his
Smyrnaean ancestors, and it is most probable that the first performance
was addressed to a Smyrniote audience.

If Strabo (14.1.4, 633C) is to be believed, Callinus frr. 2 and 2a West
also offered identification of a poet with his own community, in this case
Ephesus. Strabo quotes lines found in a work he calls 'The address to Zeus'
(ἐν τῷ πρὸς Δία λόγῳ)

> Σμυρναίους δ' ἐλέησον
>
> Callinus fr. 2 West

and pity the Smyrnaeans

> μνῆσαι δ, εἴ κοτέ τοι μήρια καλὰ βοῶν
> <Σμυρναῖοι κατέκηαν>
>
> Callinus fr. 2a West

And remember, if ever for you beautiful thighs of cattle
<have been burnt by the Smyrnaeans>

This is part of the argument of Strabo we have already encountered that
Ephesus or a part of it was once called Smyrna. Other parts of that argument
may or may not work, but this detail is quite unconvincing: are we to believe
that both Ephesus and Smyrna were known as Smyrna in the 650s BC?
Besides, is it to Zeus we would expect Ephesians to turn in a crisis? The fact
that the πολιοῦχος θεός of Ephesus is Artemis, whereas in Smyrna there
was a major cult of Zeus, counts strongly against Strabo's interpretation.[12]
More probably – and certainly more interesting for this volume – Callinus
of Ephesus has either been 'commissioned' by neighbouring Smyrna to
compose an elegiac hymn to Zeus, or has found himself in a Smyrniote
symposium and offered as one of his contributions an intercessionary hymn
to his hosts' divinity.[13]

That, then, might be my first decisive testimony to an elegiac *poeta
vagans*. The second is likely to be the song of a more distant traveller,
this time singing at the point when he returns home, found in Solon's

---

[12] Cf. Cadoux 1938.   [13] Cf. Alcaeus and Anacreon discussed below.

Wandering poets, archaic style

self-propempticon when he takes his departure from Philocyprus of Soloi (fr. 19 West).[14] Again the surviving lines are articulated around a prayer – indeed a wish and three prayers, with two prayers to Aphrodite for his own safe return enfolding a third asking for favour and distinction for the city he is leaving:

νῦν δὲ σὺ μὲν Σολίοισι πολὺν χρόνον ἐνθάδ᾽ ἀνάσσων
  τήνδε πόλιν ναίοις καὶ γένος ὑμέτερον·
αὐτὰρ ἐμὲ ξὺν νηὶ θοῇ κλεινῆς ἀπὸ νήσου
  ἀσκηθῆ πέμποι Κύπρις ἰοστέφανος·
οἰκισμῷ δ ἐπὶ τῷδε χάριν καὶ κῦδος ὀπάζοι
  ἐσθλὸν καὶ νόστον πατρίδ᾽ ἐς ἡμετέρην.

Solon fr. 19 West

But now may you, ruling here for many years over the Solioi,
  dwell in this city, and your family too:
but may I with a swift ship from your famous island
  be sent unharmed by the Cyprian goddess of the violet garland;
and on account of this foundation may she bestow on me her favour,
  and glory
    that is noble, and return to my native land.

Herodotus also knew hexameters or elegiacs – more probably, like fr. 19 West, elegiacs – in which there was warm praise of Philocyprus, 'this Philocyprus whom Solon the Athenian greatly praised in verses when he came to Cyprus' (Φιλοκύπρου δὲ τούτου τὸν Σόλων ὁ Ἀθηναῖος ἀπικόμενος ἐς Κύπρον ἐν ἔπεσιν αἴνεσε μάλιστα, Hdt. 5.113.2). I take the pattern here to be one that we find not much later with melic poets: a distiguished figure from another city, well-known for his wisdom or his poetry (and in this case both), visits a leading member of another city's élite (in this and some other cases a 'tyrant', τύραννος), praises him in sympotic poetry and prays for his and his community's good fortune.

From later, or probably later, we have one or two more cases in the *Theognidea* (which I discuss in line-order given the uncertainty of their chronology).

The first, by chance, is likewise a prayer. The brief invocation at *Theognidea* 11–14 seems to be addresssed to the Artemis whose cult at Euboean Amarynthos we know from Callimachus: it could of course be composed by a resident of Amarynthos, but a traveller seems more likely:[15]

---

[14] It is of course possible that, as argued by Lardinois 2006, fr. 19 West is not by Solon but is an intruder into one of the ancient collections of Solon's poetry. I do not think the grounds for scepticism about the Solonian authorship of this fragment are any greater than for other poems of Solon or indeed of most archaic elegiac poets.

[15] Cf. van Groningen 1966 *ad loc.*

Ἄρτεμι θηροφόνε, θύγατερ Διός, ἣν Ἀγαμέμνων
    εἷσαθ᾽ ὅτ᾽ ἐς Τροίην ἔπλεε νηυσὶ θοῆς,
εὐχομένῳ μοι κλῦθι, κακὰς δ᾽ ἀπὸ κῆρας ἄλαλκε·
    σοὶ μὲν τοῦτο θεὰ σμικρόν, ἐμοὶ δὲ μέγα.

Theognidea 11–14

Artemis, beast-slayer, daughter of Zeus, whom Agamemnon
    established when he sailed to Troy with his swift ships,
hearken to me as I pray, and drive off evil fates:
    for you, goddess, this is a small thing, but for me a great thing.

Such a traveller's song may also be found in the address to the Dioscuri
at *Theognidea* 1087–90:

Κάστορ καὶ Πολύδευκες, οἳ ἐν Λακεδαίμονι δίῃ
    ναίετ᾽ ἐπ᾽ Εὐρώτᾳ καλλιρρόῳ ποταμῷ,
εἴ ποτε βουλεύσαιμι φίλῳ κακόν, αὐτὸς ἔχοιμι·
    εἰ δέ τι κεῖνος ἐμοί, δὶς τόσον αὐτὸς ἔχοι.

Theognidea 1087–90

Castor and Polydeuces, who in divine Lacedaemon
    dwell by the Eurotas' fair-flowing river,
if ever I were to plot some evil against my friend, may I be
    ensnared by it myself;
        and if he were to plot anything against me, may he get
            twice as much himself.

Again, like *Theognidea* 11–14, this could be by a resident, and has mostly
been taken to be so. But the lightly applied praise of Lacedaemon and the
Eurotas would also suit a well brought-up visitor.

The stance of a traveller is unambiguously adopted in six lines which
compare the singer to Odysseus:

μή με κακῶν μίμνησκε· πέπονθά τοι οἷά τ᾽ Ὀδυσσεύς,
    ὅς τ᾽ Ἀΐδεω μέγα δῶμ᾽ ἤλυθεν ἐξαναδύς,
ὃς δὴ καὶ μνηστῆρας ἀνείλετο νηλέι θυμῷ
    Πηνελόπης, Εὔφρων, κουριδίης ἀλόχου,
ἥ μιν δῆθ᾽ ὑπέμεινε φίλῳ παρὰ παιδὶ μένουσα
    ὄφρά τε γῆς ἐπέβη δειμαλέους τε μυχούς . . .

Theognidea 1123–8

Don't remind me of my misfortunes: I tell you, I have gone through
    the sorts of things Odysseus did,
        who came back after getting out of the mighty house of Hades,
he, indeed, who also killed with ruthless spirit the suitors of
    Penelope, Euphron, his wedded wife,
who waited long for him by the side of his dear son,
    and when he set foot on his land and its fearful recesses . . .

Wandering poets, archaic style 117

More is going on here than can be explored in this paper.[16] The *persona* of a long-absent traveller who has returned from extreme peril and picks out for especial highlighting Odysseus' murder of Penelope's suitors might be taken as a warning to the singer's drinking companions that he takes his marriage seriously. We may have lost further lines, but in what we have it is the analogous perils and deeds of Odysseus that the singer chooses to present, perhaps allegorically, not the landscapes of his travels nor those of the city or country that he has left or arrived at.

It is possible that another elegiac sequence is also for performance by a travelling poet, *Theognidea* 879–84:

> πῖν᾿ οἶνον, τὸν ἐμοὶ κορυφῆς ὕπο Τηϋγέτοιο
>   ἄμπελοι ἤνεγκαν, τὰς ἐφύτευσ᾿ ὁ γέρων
> οὔρεος ἐν βήσσῃσι θεοῖσι φίλος Θεότιμος,
>   ἐκ Πλατανιστοῦντος ψυχρὸν ὕδωρ ἐπάγων.
> τοῦ πίνων ἀπὸ μὲν χαλεπὰς σκεδάσεις μελεδῶνας,
>   θωρηχθεὶς δ᾿ ἔσεαι πολλὸν ἐλαφρότερος.
>
> *Theognidea* 879–84

> Drink wine which under the peaks of Taygetus
>   has been produced by vines which the old man planted
> in the mountain glens – old Theotimus, dear to the gods,
>   channelling cool water to them from Platanistous.
> Drink some of this, and you will scatter dire cares,
>   and well fortified you will be much lighter at heart.

It is only a guess that they were first sung by a traveller – if so, a travelling Laconian who brings with him some of his own *appellation* to improve the party and allow him to praise his home – something he does with concise sensitivity, evoking Taygetan glens, cold water and the speaking toponym Platanistous. The reference to the provenance of the vines might also allow him to establish a connection with the Churchillian figure of the Spartan king Theopompus, if we think that θεοῖσι φίλῳ Θεοπόμπῳ at Tyrtaeus 5.1 West permits us to emend 881 from θεοῖσι φίλος Θεότιμος (Theotimus, dear to the gods) to θεοῖσι φίλος Θεόπομπος (Theopompus, dear to the gods). If sung first by a traveller, it resembles Semonides' address to Telembrotos (frr. 22 and 23 West), but with greater elaboration of provenance than in what survives of Semonides' poem. It remains possible, however, that we simply have the song of a Laconian host to a guest who himself might be Laconian or not.[17]

---

[16] For a proposal that this is a piece of Archilochus, and that Euphron is a proper name, see Bowie 2008.

[17] Van Groningen 1966: 336 argues that if the speaker had been a visitor there would have been warmer commendation of the host's hospitality: there may well have been in lost lines preceding our

118 EWEN BOWIE

Within elegy, then, there is much attesting the movement of poets singing songs generated by their xenic status in a context that, where identifiable, appears to be sympotic. What, then, of lyric? I approached the material expecting to find much more exuberance, and more that could be imagined to be a virtuoso or professional development of themes provoked by the poet's situation as a visitor.

TRAVELLING LYRIC POETS

Alcaeus

I set aside Alcaeus' storm-poems, perhaps arbitrarily, from this discussion, though any non-allegorical storm-poem is some evidence of an Alcaeus *vagans*. That Alcaeus *did* wander is manifest both from internal evidence and from the ancient biographical tradition. Some at least of these wanderings were involuntary, occasioned by exile resulting from his hyperactive participation in Mytilenean *stasis*; of these exiles, at least one took him no further than parts of Lesbos outside a Mytilenean junta's writ, and there, indeed, it is clear that frr. 129 and 130 Voigt were first sung.[18] But the later tradition has hints of him fleeing Lesbos, and it is worth asking whether a group of well-known poems might have been composed precisely for performance during overseas travel, whether voluntary or otherwise.

The first is fr. 347(a) Voigt:

τέγγε πλεύμονας οἴνῳ, τὸ γὰρ ἄστρον περιτέλλεται,
ἀ δ' ὤρα χαλέπα, πάντα δὲ δίψαισ' ὐπὰ καύματος,
ἄχει δ' ἐκ πετάλων ἄδεα τέττιξ. . . .
ἄνθει δὲ σκόλυμος· νῦν δὲ γύναικες μιαρώταται,
λέπτοι δ' ἄνδρες, ἐπεὶ <δὴ> κεφάλαν καὶ γόνα Σείριος
ἄσδει . . .

Alcaeus fr. 347(a) Voigt[19]

Wet your lungs with wine, for the star is coming into its place,
and the season is harsh, and everything is thirsty because of the heat,
and from the leaves the cicada sings sweetly . . .
and the artichoke is in bloom: now women are at their most wicked
but their men are weak, for indeed their head and knees
are parched by Sirius . . .

---

fragment. Harrison 1905: 329 suggested the poem was a letter accompanying a gift of a Laconian wine.

[18] For more detailed discussion of fragments relating to Alcaeus' exile in Lesbos see Bowie 2007.

[19] It is possible that fr. 347(b), three lines on the cicada, belong after line 3 of fr. 347(a).

Wandering poets, archaic style 119

The linkage here between drinking and the hot summer days is an ecphrastic *mimesis* of Hesiod, *Works and Days* 582–96. Alcaeus is upstaging as well as reworking Hesiod: the linkage with drinking is moved to the opening of the poem (if it is the opening) – Hesiod had drinking as the closure of this section of *his* poem – and Alcaeus' other *sympotika* suggest that this song is for indoor drinking, whereas Hesiod's lines envisaged toping in a pastoral outdoors, with a shady rock and a spring (589, 595–6). The observation that in this season women are 'most lustful', μαχλόταται (Hesiod), or 'most wicked', μιαρώταται (Alcaeus), has more immediate relevance in a symposion with *aulos*-players, αὐλητρίδες, and the like than on the goat-grazed slopes of Helicon. But is this all? Is Alcaeus simply repatriating to the Aeolian soil of Lesbos some lines composed by the son of a man originally from Aeolian Cyme?[20] Such a song would be an elegant compliment to hosts in Thespiae or indeed any Boeotian city within range of Ascra, and I suggest that first performance in a Boeotian symposium ought to be treated as a strong possibility.[21]

Two other poems also point to a visit by Alcaeus to Boeotia, his hymns to Athena Itonia, worshipped at Coronea (fr. 325 Voigt), and to Eros (fr. 327 Voigt), a god whose only significant Greek cult was at Thespiae. Both of these fragments are conceded by the selectively sceptical Page to indicate a visit to Boeotia. I would take the former to be the opening of a short hymn for sympotic performance similar to the short elegiac hymns from the *Theognidea* that have been discussed:

> ὦνασσ' Ἀθανάα πολεμάδοκε
> ἄ ποι Κορωνήας μεδ[
> ναύω πάροιθεν ἀμφι[. . . .]
> Κωραλίω ποτάμω παρ' ὄχθαις . . .

> O lady Athena, sustainer in war,
> who ru[les], we know, over Coronea[. . . .]
> in front of the temple around [. . .]
> by the banks of the river Coralius . . .

Much more can perhaps be said about Alcaeus' hymn to Delphian Apollo, which apparently teemed with descriptions that set celebratory men, animals and inanimate nature in the context of a Delphic festival welcoming Apollo's return from the Hyperboreans. The *communis opinio*

---

[20] Hes. *Works and Days* 636.
[21] Contra Page 1955: 306: 'There is neither reason to seek, nor opportunity to find, any ulterior purpose in Alcaeus' poem. It pleased him to repeat to his convivial companions a passage of Hesiod translated into the native dialect and metre.'

120 EWEN BOWIE

takes Himerius, *Oration* 14.10–11 (= fr. 307(a) Voigt) to be a fair reflection of its content, and I see no good reason not to go along with that. Alcaeus, it seems, described the Delphians composing a παιᾶνα, paean, and a μέλος, song, and establishing χοροὺς ἠιθέων, 'choruses of young men', around the tripod in their successful attempt to recall Apollo from the Hyperboreans; then his actual return in a swan-drawn chariot in midsummer welcomed by the music of lyres, nightingales and cicadas and marked by Castalia flowing with silver, with even the relatively distant river Cephisus rising in recognition.

Although much has been written about this poem it seems to me that points have been missed. Alcaeus' description of public festival, with singing and dancing to the αὐλός (probably specified by Alcaeus, as we know from Ps-Plutarch *de musica* 1135f = Alcaeus fr. 307(b) Voigt) was balanced by one of lyre-playing,[22] and that led into an account of music-making by winged creatures which are common as figures for a poet, the nightingale and the cicada. I agree with Ian Rutherford that we cannot tell whether this was itself a paean or a lyric hymn, but my *guess* is that it was the latter, and I take the reference to the lyre and the images of winged musicians to be self-referential to Alcaeus' own performance of this hymn, and that performance to be sympotic. I also agree with Rutherford that the hymn 'could well have been intended for performance at Delphi';[23] if we have indications of Alcaeus' presence in Thespiae and Coronea, a further sixty kilometres to Delphi is a relatively short journey. However, I think Himerius' insistence that the season is the height of summer – ἦν μὲν οὖν τὸ θέρος καὶ τοῦ θέρος τὸ μέσον ('now it was summer, and the middle of summer') – does not allow us to see Alcaeus' festival as the *theoxenia*,[24] which was a spring festival. If Alcaeus was in Delphi at the time of a summer festival, that must be either the *Septērion* or the *Pythia*. The emphasis on Apollo's rôle as a catalyst of music surely makes the *Pythia* more likely: I imagine (though imagination is always dangerous) a hymn by a sympotically competitive Alcaeus which blends allusion to the earlier spring festival of the *Theoxenia* with evocation of the musical excitement occasioned by the contemporary ἀγὼν μουσικός, musical competition, of the *Pythia*. Alcaeus, on this hypothesis, has travelled by Boeotia, which may do something to explain the tumescent response attributed to the river Cephisus and his seeming claim (according to Pausanias) that Castalia's water is a gift of the Cephisus: ἤκουσα δὲ καὶ ἄλλο τοιόνδε, τὸ ὕδωρ

---

[22] Cf. below on Ibycus fr. S166.5 Davies.
[23] Rutherford 2001: 27.   [24] So Rutherford 2001: 28 n. 21.

Wandering poets, archaic style

τῇ Κασταλίᾳ ποταμοῦ δῶρον εἶναι τοῦ Κηφισοῦ. τοῦτο ἐποίησε καὶ Ἀλκαῖος ἐν προοιμίῳ τῷ ἐς Ἀπόλλωνα: ('and I heard another story to this effect, that the water was a gift to Castalia of the river Cephisus. This is also what Alcaeus composed in his prooemion to Apollo').[25] Alcaeus' Delphic cicadas also recall the Hesiodic cicadas reworked in that other poem of hot summer, 347(a) Voigt. In both poems the time of year is unambiguously the same. The year itself is irrecoverable, but it would be unadventurous not to point out that Alcaeus' major period of over-seas exile seems to have been when Pittacus ran Mytilene for ten years as *aisymnētēs*, conventionally 589–579 BC, and that the reorganisation of the Pythia to make it a major ἀγὼν μουσικός seems to have happened in 586 BC. The *Pythia* of 586 BC, attended by Cleisthenes of Sicyon (whose char-iot was victorious in the chariot-race)[26] and doubtless by other powerful figures, would be an excellent place for an exiled aristocrat to hang out and network.

Two more fragments of Alcaeus can get only a glance. First, fr. 45, the beginning of a cletic hymn or prayer to the river Hebrus.

<blockquote>

Ἔβρε, κ[ά]λλιστος ποτάμων πὰρ Ἄ[ἶνον
ἐξί[ησθ' ἐς] πορφυρίαν θάλασσαν
Θρᾳκ[ίας ἐ]ρευγόμενος ζὰ γαίας

4   .]ιππ[.]. [. .] ι·

καί σε πόλλαι παρθένικαι 'πέπ[οισιν
κὰκ κά]λων μήρων ἀπάλαισι χέρ[σι
χάρμα]· θέλγονται τὸ σὸν ὡς ἄλει[ππα

8   θή[ἶον] ὕδωρ

9   [. . . . .]

</blockquote>

Alcaeus fr. 45 Voigt

<blockquote>

Hebrus, it is as the fairest of rivers that by Ainos
you stream out into the dark-red sea
roaring through the Thracian land

4   [. . . . .]:

And you are frequented by many maidens,
for their soft hands [stroking their fair thighs]
[a joy]: they are bewitched, as, like an ungent, your

8   divine water

9   [?they pour upon themselves]

</blockquote>

---

[25] Paus. 10.8.10, cf. Strabo 8.7.5 = Alcaeus fr. 307(d) Voigt).   [26] Paus. 10.7.5–6.

I am not reluctant to join those labelled by Page as 'imprudent'[27] who would associate this hymn with some visit by Alcaeus to Mytilene's colony at the mouth of the Hebrus, Ainos (and I have a quite different idea from Page of how the poem went on). Of course, an Ainian location can be no more than conjectural, but if accepted it would show another way in which a travelling singer might draw on local colour to create a new poem and to compliment his hosts.

Finally Alcaeus fr. 140 Voigt, beginning

μαρμαίρει δὲ μέγας δόμος
χάλκωι, παῖσα δ᾽ Ἄρηι κεκόσμηται στέγα
3 λάμπραισιν κυνίαισι. . .

Alcaeus 140 Voigt (= 203, 357.2–4 L-P)

the great hall glitters
with bronze, and it seems that the whole house is finely adorned (for Ares?)
with brilliant helmets . . .

This is a version of self-referential description of a sympotic location, but one that picks out for *ekphrasis* the weapons necessary to prosecute the stasiotic battles to which Alcaeus and his *hetairoi* are addicted. It might add a modest datum to a dossier on Alcaeus' movements – is this for first performance in the *andrōn* of his own house, or is it rather, as I would like to suggest, for a symposium in that of an *hetairos*, and so something to classify alongside Semonides' praise of his host's preparations (frr. 22 and 23 West)?

Ibycus

Whereas some poetry of Alcaeus is firmly tied to a Mytilenean context, even if not to performance within the walls of Mytilene, Ibycus' own city Rhegium remains one that has not yet been documented as figuring in his songs, unless it is to Rhegium that the Chalcidian colony of S227 Davies (= *P. Oxy.* 2637 fr. 7) refers. To the long-known and much-debated papyrus fragment which praises a Polycrates, surely of and presumably on Samos (S151 Davies = *P. Oxy.* 1790 fr. 1), have now been added others which have revealed Ibycus as poetically active in connection with another Chalcidian colony, Leontini (S220 Davies = *P. Oxy.* 2637 fr. 1(a) 1–31), and Sparta (S166 Davies = *P. Oxy.* 2635 fr. 1). Barron has also argued for a visit to Sicyon.[28] Quoted fragments had already preserved references to Syracusan

---

[27] Page 1955: 288. I print the text and follow the interpretation of Gentili and Catenacci 2007: 198–200, though I am less open than they (p. 198) to the idea that the setting is in some way ritual.
[28] Barron 1961.

Wandering poets, archaic style 123

topography, Ortygia (fr. 321) and Arethusa (fr. 323). A neglected anecdote in Himerius transmits a tradition that Ibycus had a road-accident between Catana, 30 kilometres south of Leontini, and Himera.[29]

The ancient biographical tradition surviving in the *Suda*[30] has Ibycus visiting Samos, and it is most plausible to suppose that the song to Polycrates was sung there, that the song praising somebody in a Laconian context was sung in Sparta, and that those with Sicilian links were sung in Sicily, though of course it is formally possible that at least the Sicilian songs were sung in Rhegium in praise of Sicilian guests (ξένοι). In what sequence should such visits be supposed to have occurred, and in what capacity should we imagine Ibycus to have made them?

Bowra proposed a model in which Ibycus began his career composing long, Stesichorus-like mythological poems in the West, and only took up shorter erotic poetry when he encountered it at the court of Polycrates on Samos.[31] Not inherently persuasive when formulated, this hypothesis has become increasingly unattractive as papyrus fragments accumulate. It now seems quite unlikely that Ibycus ever did compose long Stesichorean heroic narratives, which are anyway not suggested by the Alexandrian edition of Ibycus, since it arranged his poems by numbered books rather than (as for Stesichorus) giving them titles,[32] and his exploitation of mythology often seems to have an erotic aspect.

The case of a long-known quoted fragment, fr. 289 Davies, both illustrates how mythology might have operated in a poem praising an attractive youth and has some claim to be Sicilian in its location. This is a statement in the scholia on Apollonius of Rhodes claiming that *Argonautica* 3.158–66 paraphrase what Ibycus said about Ganymede's abduction 'in his song to Gorgias', ἐν τῇ εἰς Γοργίαν ᾠδῇ. Comparison with Ganymede, then, explicit or simply implied, could allow a song of praise to benefit from αὔξησις in the form of mythological narrative. But whence was the *laudandus* or ἐρώμενος of this Ibycan song, Gorgias? The name is not as common as Hutchinson suggests,[33] and one of its attestations is of course in Leontini, borne by the famous sophist whose life began in the 480s: I would guess that an earlier member of this élite family of Leontini, perhaps his grandfather, also had the name Gorgias and caught Ibycus' eye. Since I

---

[29] Ibycus fr. 343 Davies = Himerius *Oration* 69.35.

[30] *Suda s.v.* Ἴβυκος (2.607 Adler) = TA1 Davies, cf. below n. 43.   [31] Bowra 1961: 241–67.

[32] The *Funeral games for Pelias* (Ἄθλα ἐπὶ Πελίᾳ) remain a puzzle, though this would be resolved if we simply concluded that a Stesichorean poem with this title (perhaps unusually short) was ascribed to Ibycus in error, cf. Hutchinson 2001: 230 with n. 4.

[33] Hutchinson 2001: 229 n. 2.

124   EWEN BOWIE

first made this guess long ago, an Oxyrhynchus fragment, S220 Davies =
P. Oxy. 2637 fr. 1(a) 1–31, has shown, as noted above, that Leontini did
indeed figure in Ibycus' poetry, with mention of 'glens of Kronios', Κρο-
νίου πτυχαί (modelled on Homeric πτύχες), said by the commentator
to be at Leontini and linked with somebody's frequent visits for hunting.
The same commentary goes on to discuss an apparently erotic poem entitled 'Callias' (S221 Davies = *P. Oxy.* 2637 fr. 1(a) 32–42), and this sequence
might be taken as some, admittedly very fragile, support for the idea that
the Leontini passage was also from an erotic poem, perhaps precisely from
that for Gorgias.[34]

    Much of this is precarious. But what stands out is a recurrent intertwining
of mythology with praise of beauty, and, on at least one occasion, with a
declaration of desire, ἔρως (S222 Davies = *P. Oxy.* 2637 fr. 1(b)). At the
same time the praise in S220 Davies, the Spartan song, seems to have
been of athletic achievement, inviting classification as (proto?)-epinician.[35]
How does all this fit together? Does Ibycus 'make a name for himself' as a
poet of praise, and is then 'commissioned' to compose praise for athletic
victors in cities first in the West, then in the Peloponnese – and in due
course invited to compose praise poetry for Polycrates? Or is he simply
an accomplished aristocratic singer whose virtuosity might encourage a
host to invite a composition praising an athletic success in the family and
whose erotic inclinations might prompt him to praise attractive young men
wherever he found them? The former model might cohere well enough with
a supposition that once Ibycus reached Samos he stayed, at least for some
time, as a 'court poet': but it does not entail it. The latter model would
encourage us rather to believe that Ibycus could well have travelled from
the Ionian to the Aegean sea and back, perhaps indeed more than once,
and that his visit to Polycrates was just one, albeit the most spectacular,
among many visits to aristocratic houses in various Greek cities, visits in
which his primary status was that of a ξένος.

    In favour of the first model might be the possible performance of some
of his poetry by a chorus and to the accompaniment of the αὐλός. So far we
have only inconclusive hints in this direction. The similarity of some of his
metrical units to those of Stesichorus, the triadic structure of many of his
poems, the possible first-person plural ἀείδο[μεν?] in S166.5 Davies and the
mention of an αὐλός-player, α]ὐλητῆρος, in the same line – these might all
support choral performance.[36] But we are not entitled to take S166.5 Davies

---

[34] Cf. a Gorgias also in S226 = *P. Oxy.* 2637 fr. 32.   [35] Barron 1984.
[36] An αὐλός also appears in S257(a) fr. 27.

Wandering poets, archaic style 125

as certainly self-referential: as in the *Homeric Hymn to Apollo* 156–66, one sort of musical artist can describe the performances of another.[37] Moreover we may not be entitled either to assume that a poet training a chorus in a city he is visiting establishes that his status is that of a 'professional' rather than of a virtuoso aristocrat.

In favour of the second model might be a detail in the secondary tradition of which little has been made. There was a proverb 'dumber than Ibycus' (ἀρχαιότερος Ἰβύκου) which is explained as being something said 'about simple-minded people' (ἐπὶ τῶν εὐηθῶν): 'for although he could have been tyrant he left his city' (οὗτος γὰρ τυραννεῖν δυνάμενος ἀπεδήμη-σεν).[38] The quality of this information cannot be assessed, and it must be admitted that it could be worthless. On the other hand, it has about as much chance as the *Suda* entry of preserving some information about Ibycus' life. If it does, then Ibycus was from the politically active stratum of Rhegian society – almost certainly, that is, a member of the élite like Archilochus, Alcaeus and Solon – and one motive for at least some of his travelling was to distance himself from the political turmoil of Rhegium. This is a context we should explore for the arrival of Ibycus at Samos: politics in Rhegium may have been complicating relations with hosts in Sicilian cities, a visit to Sparta may have offered contacts in Samos and an opportunity to extend Ibycus' ξενία-network,[39] and after a visit to Sicyon, as proposed by Barron,[40] and Euboean Chalcis (nowhere attested, but how could Ibycus resist visiting the mother-city of Rhegium?) Samos would be an easy move.

What did Ibycus find on his arrival at Samos? The praise of Polycrates' κάλλος, 'beauty', in S151.46–8 Davies is delicate but insistent: 'These men have forever a share in beauty, and you, Polycrates, will have deathless fame, even as my fame is in respect of my song.'[41] Insistent too, however, is the implication of the word κλέος, 'glory' characteristically, as has been heard in the clipped Trojan narrative, acquired in war. Polycrates may expect to acquire this κλέος in the traditional manner in due course. The future tense, like the indirect praise of his κάλλος, requires a context quite early in Polycrates' career. This is not to say, however, that he is not yet a tyrant.[42] If we accept the *Suda* statement (as emended by von Gutschmid) that

---

[37] Cf. also above on Alcaeus fr. 307(a) Voigt.
[38] Diogenianus 2.71 = Test. 4 Davies: one MS (B) adds 'to Ionia' (εἰς Ἰωνίαν); Diogenianus 5.12 has the variant proverb 'stupider than Ibycus' (ἀνοητότερος Ἰβύκου).
[39] Cartledge 1982, cf. Hutchinson 2001: 231 n. 5.   [40] Barron 1984.
[41] It is even more insistent and direct if we translate 'Along with these you too, Polycrates, will always have deathless renown for beauty', as argued for e.g. by Hutchinson 2001: 253–4, perhaps correctly.
[42] *Pace* Hutchinson 2001: 232, what we find here is not 'praise for beauty alone'.

126 EWEN BOWIE

Ibycus 'came to Samos when the father of the tyrant Polycrates was its ruler' but at the same time reject (as other evidence shows we must) the *Suda* entry's synchronism with Croesus and the 54th Olympiad (564–1)[43] we have an Ibycus arriving, probably, in the 530s BC, perhaps not long before Polycrates became tyrant.[44] If the *Suda*'s term ἦρχε, 'was its ruler', is taken to have some basis of truth, then Polycrates' father, Aeaces, was either *de facto* top dog in the current Samian aristocratic power-struggles or perhaps was actually holding an elected office.[45] In either case he need not have been perceived either by himself or by others as a 'tyrant' – Herodotus' narrative (3.39.1) counts strongly against any other person than Aeaces being Polycrates' father and against Aeaces himself being 'tyrant' – and whatever powers he had may well not have been easily passed on to his sons. Such a figure's death before the family's grip on power had been secured by the next generation could indeed precipitate a crisis for would-be successors, and the 'coup' asserted by Herodotus is wholly intelligible if young Polycrates and his brothers did not relish spending years or more in a political wilderness. The analogies of the actions taken by Alexander on the death of Philip, or by Octavian on the death of Caesar, support the likelihood of such a move by a youthful Polycrates.

In this (of course imaginary) scenario, S151 Davies would fit just as well in the months before Aeaces died or those immediately succeeding Polycrates' coup: in either case Polycrates' youthful beauty can without embarrassment be praised by a poet who seems to have uttered such praise wherever he went, and his expectation of glory can be introduced by a statement about the future.

What does S151 Davies tell us of the stance taken by the poet Ibycus in his current stopping-point? He and his audience share a preoccupation with beauty. As in some other fragments, that is interwoven with mythology – here the part of beauty in precipitating the Trojan War is stressed (ξα]νθᾶς Ἑλένας περὶ εἴδει, 5; χρυ]σοέθειραν δ[ι]ὰ Κύπριδα 9) before the presence of beautiful people in the conflict is picked out (τανίσφυρ[ον] . . . Κασσάν-δραν, 12, Cyanippus 37, Zeuxippus 40, Troilus 41). But the wandering eye

---

[43] *Suda s.v.* Ἴβυκος (2.607 Adler) = TA1 Davies: ἐνθένδε (sc. from Rhegium) εἰς Σάμον ἦλθεν ὅτε αὐτῆς ἦρχεν ὁ τοῦ Πολυκράτους τοῦ τυράννου πατήρ: the manuscript reading is ὁ Πολυκράτης τοῦ τυράννου πατήρ. Von Gutschmid's emendation, in H. Flach, *Geschichte der griechischen Lyrik* 1884, 524 n. 4, was convincingly argued for by West 1970: 208 against Barron 1964: 223 n. 1 (who proposed Πολυκράτης ὁ τοῦ τυράννου πατήρ, and argued for a father and son both bearing the name Polycrates).

[44] Hutchinson 2001: 258 n. 3

[45] Like Hutchinson 2001: 232 n. 7, I am inclined to take the ἐπιστάτης Aeaces who dedicated ML 16 as Polycrates' father.

Wandering poets, archaic style

of Ibycus has also picked out a martial detail that would not displease his principal host (be it Aeaces or Polycrates): the best of the Achaeans at Troy were Achilles and Ajax (32–5). Of course that pre-eminence was not controversial (at least until the award of Achilles' arms to Odysseus). But it can be said with especial force in the house of Aeaces, because with that name it is very probable that the family is claiming kinship with the Aeacus who was grandfather to both these heroes.

Anacreon

Anacreon's travels are more firmly documented than those of Ibycus, but his status and self-representation in the places he visited is almost as problematic. He seems to have been part of the Teian community that left Teos to refound Abdera *c.* 545 when the Mede Harpagus attacked Teos (Hdt. 1.168); it is presumably in the late 530s or early 520s that he went to Polycrates' 'court' on Samos, even if we treat as unreliable Himerius' account of his being summoned as tutor by his father to the young Polycrates[46] – which would seem to require Anacreon both to be there at the start of Polycrates' reign and, as the more probably reliable Herodotus has it (3.121), at its end. Of course if we allow that Anacreon might (as suggested above for Ibycus) have come and gone, the oddity of this is lessened. It was presumably on the murder of Polycrates by Oroetes that, according to the Ps-Platonic *Hipparchus* 228b–c (cf. [Aristotle] *Ath. Pol.* 18.1), Anacreon was taken from Samos to Athens by a Peisistratid penteconter.[47]

Linking surviving fragments and these places is mostly conjectural. In some poem Anacreon may have presented himself as one of the Teians involved in refounding Abdera, hence its dating by reference to him in Strabo 14.1.30. An iambic trimeter quoted here by Strabo (= fr. 505(a) Page) – 'Abdera, the beautiful colony of the Teians' (Ἄβδηρα καλὴ Τηίων ἀποικίη) – may indeed be by Anacreon, but is not certainly his; Strabo's phrase 'not enduring the Persian violence' (οὐ φέροντες τὴν Περσῶν ὕβριν) has a poetic colour[48] and may be drawn from the same poem. We may also speculate that Anacreon's description of Teos as Athamantian (fr. 463 Page = Strabo 14.1.3) and the lines in which he 'adorns the city of Teos with his songs, and brings the Erotes from there' (κοσμεῖ . . . τὴν Τηίων πόλιν τοῖς μέλεσι, κἀκεῖθεν ἄγει τοὺς Ἔρωτας: fr. 490 Page = Himerius

---

[46] Himerius *Or.* 29.22 Colonna = fr. 491 Page, best read in the text printed by Campbell 1988.

[47] For an excellent discussion see Hutchinson 2001: 256–60.

[48] Cf. Mimnermus fr. 9.4 West (discussed above pp. 113–14), *CEG* 100.2, 179.1 = ML 15.1 (Athens *c.* 506 BC) and στρατὸν ὑβριστὴν Μήδων *Theognidea* 775.

128   EWEN BOWIE

27.27 Colonna) belong to poetry in which he celebrated Abdera's Teian origins.[49] It has also been suggested by Hutchinson that both fr. 347 Page (on the cutting of the Thracian Smerdies' beautiful hair) and fr. 417 Page (flirtatiously chiding the 'Thracian filly') should be thought to be Abderan poems because of Abdera's Thracian location. But Thracians, especially slaves, found their way to many parts of the Aegean, and locating fr. 347 Page in Abdera involves discarding one ancient tradition that made Polycrates Anacreon's rival for the favours of Smerdies.[50]

It is clear that at least some of the poems praising pretty boys for which Anacreon was later notorious had a Polycratean context, e.g. poetry about Bathyllus, cf. Apuleius *Florida* 15.51, 54 (test. 5 Campbell), or about Smerdies and Cleobulus as well as Bathyllus (Maximus of Tyre 37.5 = fr. 471 Page) or about Megistes (Athenaeus 671ef, 673d = fr. 352 Page).[51] The surviving expressions of homoerotic desire – 347 Page for Smerdies (by implication), frr. 357 and 359 Page for Cleobulus – suggest a sympotic performer whose age did not prevent him exploiting his musical and verbal gifts to attract the young and whose relationship with his host Polycrates, to my mind one of ξενία, did not inhibit competition with him for some of these boys' favours.

Alongside freedom of sexual action within Polycratean symposia, Anacreon may also have arrogated freedom of expression. We have not simply wry innuendoes at the expense of a girl from Lesbos reluctant to come his way (fr. 358 Page), who may anyway not be of high status (was perhaps even a slave), or obscenity directed at Herophile and Smerdies, perhaps by then lost causes (frr. 346.13 and 366 Page), or elaborate and prolonged invective against Artemon (fr. 388 Page), who is more successful with Eurypyle than Anacreon ('and blonde Eurypyle fancies litter-lounger Artemon', ξανθῇ δ' Εὐρυπύλῃ μέλει / ὁ περιφόρητος Ἀρτέμων, fr. 372 Page).[52] As well as these barbs there is perhaps gossip, whose power against himself Anacreon recognises, in fr. 354 Page: 'and you will make me notorious among the neighbours' (καί μ' ἐπίβωτον / κατὰ γείτονας ποήσεις).[53]

Some gossip may have been at the expense of a married woman in Polycrates' entourage. Lines 11ff. of the poem expostulating at a boy's cutting of his Thracian hair (fr. 347 Page: most probably Smerdies) have baffled scholars since Lobel's publication of the papyrus. Anacreon's rhetorical question

---

[49] Cf. Tyrtaeus fr. 2 West, Mimnermus fr. 9 West.
[50] Athenaeus 540e, Aelian *VH* 9.4, printed with fr. 414 Page but dismissed by Hutchinson 2001: 264.
[51] For Megistes (also addressed in fr. 353 Page) and Bathyllus as ἐρώμενοι of Anacreon cf. Leonidas xxxi G-P = *Anth. Plan.* 306.5; for Megistes cf. Antipater of Sidon xv G-P= *Anth. Pal.* 7.27.5.
[52] For Anacreon's own interest in Eurypyle cf. Antipater of Sidon xv G-P= *Anth. Pal.* 7.27.5
[53] Cf. Semonides fr. 7.110–11 West, Archilochus fr. 196A. 34 West.

Wandering poets, archaic style 129

in the voice of the *persona loquens* 'for what will one do if one has not even been successful on behalf of Thrace?' (lines 9–10: τί γάρ τις ἔρξῃ | μηδ᾽ ὑπὲρ Θρήικης τυχών;) is followed by a claim to have heard that a 'famous woman' is distraught: 'indeed I hear that piteous thoughts are entertained by the famous woman, and that she often says this, blaming her misfortune . . .' (lines 11–12: οἰκτρὰ δὴ φρονεῖν ἀκου[- | τὴν ἀρίγνωτον γυναῖ[κα | πολλάκις δὲ δὴ τόδ᾽ εἶπ[εῖν). ἀκου[- is most readily and most often supplemented ἀκούω – and that offers a suitably arch expression for introduction of a damaging or amusing testimony. But who is this 'famous woman'? Attempts at solution range from a well-known *hetaira*, to the mythological Helen (requiring line 11 to begin a new poem, something the papyrus in no way signals), to a personification of Thrace.[54] The crucial difficulty is that a description of the form 'the well-known *x*' is quite inadequate to allow identification ('Do you know the well-known joke?'). That difficulty can be overcome by a trivial emendation: for ἀρίγνωτον read Ἀριγνώτου (the genitive of the proper name). The accusative will have been written by mistake for the genitive because it lies between τὴν and γυναῖ[κα. Lines 11ff. acquire sense and teeth. The wife of Arignotus is not simply upset, like Anacreon, but distraught, wishing for death in heroic language.[55] That a married woman should be exposed as reacting in this way to the loss of Smerdies' lovely locks brings shame upon both husband and wife and *Schadenfreude* to their neighbours: Anacreon has turned what started as apparently a poem of self-pity into a sceptic *tour de force.*[56]

Against the poet's self-representation as a desiring, drinking, jesting, autonomous and parrhesiastic member of a sympotic group, of which Polycrates also just happens to be a member, there is no hint in what survives that Anacreon made poetic moves to reinforce his status by reference to his own origins, and only a few that he complimented his host's (or hosts'?) generosity or hospitality. Strabo claims his poetry was 'full of references to Polycrates' (πλήρης ἐστι τῆς περὶ αὐτοῦ μνήμης), and Himerius that he sang of Polycrates' good fortune (τύχην) when the Samians were making offerings to Hera (this might be in a *prosodion* or in a sympotic hymn).[57] It may be the chance of survival, but a description of Samos as a 'city of

---

[54] Thrace was Lobel's own suggestion: for good discussion of proposals see Hutchinson 2001: 269–71, rightly expressing doubt about all.

[55] Lines 15–18, see Hutchinson 2001: 272–2.

[56] Anacreon is likely to have known fr. 7 West of Semonides of Samos and Amorgos, also exposing the *uitia* of the wives of those present (cf. Osborne 2001). Perhaps this trochaic tetrameter poem sets out to be in that tradition.

[57] Strabo 14.1.16 and Himerius *Or.* 28.2 = fr. 483 Page.

the Nymphs' (ἄστυ Νυμφέων, fr. 448 Page), perhaps a compliment to some Polycratean hydragogy, must be reckoned thin pickings. Of course the praise of Teos, fr. 505(a) Page (if this is by Anacreon), *could* have been uttered in a Samian context, but Strabo's citation counts against that (see above).

Perhaps Anacreon was justified in focusing attention on his own poetic *persona* and skills. In Peisistratid eyes, he was a catch, and the impact he made in Attica vindicated their judgement.[58] But here too he was not the tyrant's poodle. It may be worth recalling that whereas the Ps-Platonic *Hipparchus* says (228bc) that Simonides was lured to Athens 'by large rewards and gifts' (μεγάλοις μισθοῖς καὶ δώροις), no such claim is made for Anacreon. Once in Attica it was not only for the Peisistratids that he was active. A Critias son of Dropides, ancestor of the late-fifth-century oligarch and elegiac poet, was praised in a poem that was presumably amatory (Pl. *Charmides* 175e4–7).

Simonides

The last great lyric poet already active in the sixth century is Simonides.[59] The secondary tradition about his poetic activity and his relations with those whom he praised in his poetry is more voluminous than that concerning either Ibycus or Anacreon, but even fewer fragments survive which allow us to perceive how he presented himself and his relationship to his audiences. In what follows only some details of the secondary tradition will be drawn into my discussion, and this will base itself on the one or two fragments that might contribute to this investigation.

First, the posture of praise is now firmly established as related to victory in ἀγῶνες, prompting Alexandrian editors to classify many poems as *epinikia* (arranged by contest).[60] Praise is also likely to have been found in *Laments*, Θρῆνοι, though the only clear case is in the fragment of a poem on the dead at Thermopylae, fr. 520 Page, not certainly a θρῆνος. Within both *epinikia* and θρῆνοι aphorisms, γνῶμαι, had a significant rôle (as in the *epinikia* of Bacchylides and Pindar), though hardly as significant as their frequent later quotation might suggest. Only recovery of a complete poem

---

[58] For Anacreon's name and person on Attic vases cf. Hutchinson 2001: 259. At some date a bronze statue was cast (?by Pheidias or his workshop), and in Pausanias' day was on the acropolis, Paus. 1.25.1.

[59] For the complications of his chronology, and an excellent brief introduction, see Hutchinson 2001: 285–91.

[60] Frr. 506–19 Page, with praise in frr. 506–7, 509–10, 513.

Wandering poets, archaic style　　　131

will show just how these aphorisms, γνῶμαι, functioned in a Simonidean poem, but even what we have points to their greater prominence than in Ibycus, where only fr. 313 Page looks like a γνώμη, with perhaps a hint at moralising in fr. 310 Page.[61]

The fragment that seems most likely to help us is the substantial sequence from a poem addressed to Scopas quoted and discussed in Plato's *Protagoras* (fr. 542 Page, in Pl. *Protag.* 339a–346d). There is no agreement on how the three-line γνώμη first quoted by Plato relates to a similar γνώμη described as 'the maxim of Pittacus' (τὸ Πιττάκειον, fr. 542.11 Page), or how Simonides' own conclusion differs from the latter. Fortunately, this does not matter here. What is important is that Simonides devotes 40 lines to arguing for and proclaiming what he presents as *his* idea of the good man, and does so in a poem addressed to a Thessalian tyrant who was presumably lavishing, at the very least, hospitality and, on most views, further rewards in cash or kind, on the outspoken poet. Nowhere in Pindar or Bacchylides, far less in earlier lyric poetry, do we encounter such sustained moral argumentation. A similar mode is found in fr. 541 Page, whose preservation on a second-century AD papyrus gives us no clue as to context.[62] What remains frustratingly unknown is how large a proportion of a poem either fr. 541 or fr. 542 constituted, what the rest of the poem contained, and to what genre it belonged.

Other uncertainties abound. Nothing indicates that Simonides ever explicitly presented himself as a Ceian, or himself (or his poetry) as a visitor or ξένος at a particular place; yet from the poetry of Bacchylides and Pindar one would infer that he is likely to have done so in his *epinikia*, and the story of the collapse of Scopas' palace after his prevarication over payment for an *epinikion* (fr. 410 Page) might suggest a source, albeit perversely interpreted, in which both Crannon and Simonides' presence there were mentioned.[63] As likely as not, then, the absence of these topics is due to the accident of survival. Certainly in other contexts Simonides is far from shy about introducing named places: Athens and Parnes in fr. 519 fr. 35(b) Page, Delian daughters in fr. 519 fr. 55(a) Page (?both paeans); Thermopylae, Hellas and Sparta in the nine lines of fr. 531 Page; six or more place names in the last 16 lines of the 'Plataea' elegiac fragment 11 West². If we turn to that and to the other longer elegiac fragments published in 1992 we immediately gain a broader perspective.

---

[61] Aphorisms are also found in poems whose genre is uncertain: as well as in frr. 541 and 542, discussed below, cf. frr. 579, 581, 584, 590, 598, 602–4,? 605.
[62] On this fragment see Johnstone 1997.　　[63] As too might fr. 529 Page = Schol. Theoc. 16.36–7.

132   EWEN BOWIE

In one, frr. 19 (Stobaeus 4.34.28 lines 1–5) and 20 West (Stobaeus 4.34.28
lines 6–13 overlapping *P. Oxy.* 3965 fr. 26), it emerged that the moralising that had been known from Stobaeus was an abbreviated version of a
longer argumentative sequence – a sequence that we already knew from
Stobaeus led to the injunction to enjoy life while we can: 'but learning
this lesson persist to the end of your life indulging your heart with good
things' (ἀλλὰ σὺ ταῦτα μαθὼν βιότου ποτὶ τέρμα / ψυχῇ τῶν ἀγαθῶν
τλῆθι χαριζόμενος, fr. 20.11–12 West). In a sympotic context, then, the
moral argumentation of these elegiacs had a pertinent function, and there
are plenty of elegiac precedents for the movement of thought, if not for
the proportion of argumentation to conclusion. This might lead us to speculate that the strong moralising streak in some of Simonides' lyric poetry
may be a contamination from his elegiac activity.[64]

The next poem of interest comes to us from a combination of *P. Oxy.*
2327 and *P. Oxy.* 3965, giving fr. 22 West². The singer imagines a journey
to an idyllic island where he may see blond Echecratidas, take his hand
and experience the desire that drips from his eyes; then he could have a
good time with this παῖς, 'boy', shedding his own white wrinkles – a party
in a flowery landscape where garlands will be woven and songs will be
sung:

```
                           ] . οιο θαλάσσης
                           ]ρουσα πόρον·
                           ]μενος ἔνθα περανα[
                           ]
    5                      ]οιμι κελευθο[
                       ]ν κόσμον ἰος[τ]εφάνων
                   ]ἕδος πολύδενδρον ἱκο[ίμην
                ἐσ [. . . .] εὐαέα νῆσον, ἄγαλμα β[ίου·
                κα[ί κεν] Ἐχεκ[ρατί]δην ξανθότρ[ιχα
    10          ὀφ[θαλμοῖσιν ἰδ]ὼν χεῖρα λάβοιμ[ι
                ὄφρα νέο[ν] χ[αρίεντ]ος ἀπὸ χροὸς ἄν[θος
                λείβοι δ' ἐκ βλ[εφάρ]ων ἱμερόεντα [πόθον.
                καί κεν ἐγ[ὼ μετὰ πα]ιδὸς ἐν ἄνθε[σιν ἁβρὰ πάθοιμι
                κεκλιμένος, λευκὰς φαρκίδας ἐκτ[ανύσας
    15          χαίτ[ησι]ν χαρίε[ντ]α νεοβλάστ[
                       . [      ] εὐανθέα πλε[ξάμενος στέφανον·
                                 ] of the sea
                            mak?]ing a journey
```

[64] The same suggestion (independently), preferring conscious to unconscious contamination, in
Hutchinson 2001: 292, pointing out the precedent of Solon fr. 13 West.

Wandering poets, archaic style

```
              ]ing, where to complete
     ...              . . . . . . . . . .]
5                  I may [. . .]paths
           ]adornment of violet-garlanded
           ]to a spot with many trees might I come
           to?[. . . . . . . .]an isle with fair breezes, an enhancement of life:
     and Echecratidas with his blond hair would be [ ]
10         seen by these [old?] eyes of mine, and I could [again?] take his hand
     so that he might [diffuse?] the young bloom from his graceful skin
           and pour desire-arousing longing from his lids.
     And I could [with the b]oy amid the flowers [have a pleasurable time
           reclining, my white wrinkles smo[othed out
15   for (his?) hair charming new-blown [
           [. . . . . .] plaiting from beautiful flowers [a garland
                                    Simonides 22.1–16 West²
```

The most persuasive interpretation of these lines supposes that Echecratidas and the 'boy' are identical, that Echecratidas is dead, and that Simonides is fantasising about a journey to somewhere like the isles of the blest.[65] Echecratidas' identity is contested, but in my view he is most probably the son of the Thessalian Echecratidas and Dyseris whose other son, Antiochus, is attested by Aelius Aristides (31.2 Keil = fr. 528 Page) as having been greatly lamented by Dyseris, and by the scholion on Theocritus 16.34–5 as having been said by Simonides to be the son of Echecratidas and Dyseris. Our poem would then be a composition for first performance in the house of the surviving parent or parents of Echecratidas – that Aelius Aristides mentioned only Dyseris might indicate that her husband, Echecratidas the father, was no longer alive when their son, Antiochus, died.

Several conclusions of interest can tentatively be drawn. First, Simonides had formed and declared a romantic interest in the young Echecratidas before he died. This seems in no way to have compromised his relationship with Echecratidas' mother Dyseris, whether we take this poem about Echecratidas or the lament for the dead Antiochus (on this view his brother) to be earlier. There is a later parallel in the erotic response expressed by Pindar towards Thrasybulus, son of Xenocrates of Acragas.[66] Whatever rewards may have been offered to or requested by Simonides for *epinikia* or θρῆνοι for the Thessalian family, Simonides' behaviour in their house or palace was that of a ξένος, just as had been that of Ibycus and Anacreon.

---

[65] Cf. esp. Mace 2001.   [66] Cf. Pindar *Pythian* 6, fr. 124a–b Maehler and (much later) *Isthmian* 2.

134   EWEN BOWIE

Second, although neither this nor any other fragment talks about
Simonides' journey to his hosts' establishment, we may be invited to see
the sea-voyage to the *locus amoenus* of the luxuriant island as a mirror
of the journey undertaken by Simonides to Thessaly. Just as Simonides
and Echecratidas will weave and wear fresh garlands, and sing with the
clear voice of desire, so at its first performance Simonides is presumably
singing, garlanded, in a symposium organised by his hosts. The trip to the
isles of the blest becomes one of many Simonidean journeys, one that he
would gladly make, but can no more do in real life than he can shed his
wrinkles.

The third and most discussed product of the 1992 publications is the
elegiac poem narrating the preliminaries to, and presumably thereafter
(in lines we have lost) the actual engagement of, the battle of Plataea
in 479 BC (fr. 10–17 West²). The opening hymnic address to Achilles
(for whatever reason it began the poem) allows Simonides to stress that
the κλέος enjoyed by the heroes of the Trojan War was bestowed upon
them thanks to Homer knowing about the war from the Pierian Muses
and thus making the short-lived generation of heroes famous among later
men (fr. 11.15–18 West²). So too he, with the Muse's aid, will create 'this
honey-minded adornment of our song' (καὶ τόνδ[ε μελ]ίφρονα κ[όσμον
ἀο]ιδῆς [ἡμετ]έρης. In a self-referential trope that goes back as early as
Solon (fr. 1.2 West), the poet reminds his audience that they are getting
an ambitious song: the preceding comparison with Homer has hinted just
how ambitious it is. The manoeuvre is not far distant from Ibycus' in his
Polycrates poem (S151 Davies): there his poem's ability to confer κλέος is
juxtaposed with the knowledge of the valour and beauty of the heroes at
Troy which his audience knows chiefly from Homeric epic (to which the
poem repeatedly alludes). What matters to the self-presentation of Ibycus
in S151 and of Simonides in frr. 10–17 West² is neither whence the poet has
come, nor in what social capacity, but that his skill allows him to compete
with epic.[67]

I close discussion of Simonides with a brief glance at his epigram for
the seer Megistias, quoted by Herodotus 7.228.3–4. Herodotus notes that
it was the Amphictyons who honoured the Thermopylae dead as a group
and the Spartan dead with *stēlai* and epigrams (Ἀμφικτύονές εἰσί σφεας
οἱ ἐπικοσμήσαντες), other than the epigram for the seer, but that it was
Simonides who inscribed the epigram for the seer Megistias because of

---

[67] There is no space here to address the problem of whether this poem was conceived for performance
in a public festival, where competition would carry particular point, or in a symposium.

Wandering poets, archaic style 135

their *xenos*-relationship (τὸ δὲ τοῦ μάντιος Μεγιστίεω Σιμωνίδης ὁ Λεω-πρέπεός ἐστι κατὰ ξεινίην ὁ ἐπιγράψας).[68] Whatever this implies about the authorship of the other epigrams, this seems to me to indicate that in the case of Megistias Simonides composed the epigram, waived any fee there may have been (and there may have been none), and covered the cost of inscription κατὰ ξεινίην. This in turn suggests that (still?) in the immediate aftermath of the Persian Wars the status of ξένος was of great importance in the provision of poetry.

SOME CONCLUSIONS

Travelling poets have been found to be in three broadly separable categories. The first comprises poets whose travel is perceived as that of a member of a group: Archilochus in his *iamboi* and perhaps in martial elegiacs; Tyrtaeus and Mimnermus in their elegiac evocation of their city's settlement; just possibly Anacreon. The best populated category is of solitary travellers who give evidence of performing in a context outside their polis, either manifestly in a symposium, as in the case of many poems of Anacreon, or almost certainly so, as for several pieces in the *Theognidea*. Within this category is a substantial group of poems where the travelling singer moulds his composition to honour, praise or thank his host. Already there in the iambic fragments of Semonides frr. 22–3 West (? *c.* 630 BC), this function is also fulfilled by lyrics of Alcaeus and elegiacs of Solon in the 580s. In none of these cases have we any hint that the travel is undertaken *in order to* sing. The third category is of poets whom later tradition, at least, represents as professional and who *are* travelling in order to sing. I have questioned the applicability of this category to Ibycus and Anacreon; and even if they fall into it, they clearly share much with singers in the second category, as indeed does Simonides whose candidature for membership of the third category is strongest. In different ways all three behave as sympotic guests, praising the beauty of boys, in Ibycus' case also vaunting his poetic skill, in Simonides' case also adopting the rôle of discursive moral instructor common in sympotic elegy. The demand for *epinikia* may have changed the ground-rules, but it is certainly far from evident that Ibycus was rewarded with anything more than hospitality, for them or for any of his other poems; and in Simonides' case, even if evidence as early as Aristophanes points to payment for *epinikia*, it should not be immediately inferred that all his other poetry was either 'commissioned' or remunerated. The

---

[68] Cf. Petrovic (this volume).

136   EWEN BOWIE

all-singing (and in one documented case, Hippocleides, all-dancing) itinerant aristocrat who first emerges in seventh-century elegy remains an important figure at the end of the sixth century, and is indeed still documented
in the fifth.[69]

---

[69] Cf. *Theognidea* 783–8 discussed at the start of this paper; and for a travelling symposiast (who would
presumably sing) Dionysius Chalcous fr. 4 West, certainly from the mid-fifth century. The Clearistus
of *Theognidea* 511–21 and the addressee of *Theognidea* 691–2 are not precisely dateable.

CHAPTER 6

Defining local identities in Greek lyric poetry

Giovan Battista D'Alessio

The formative period of the Greek *poleis* overlaps with the earliest phase of the development of archaic lyric poetry. The two phenomena are not unrelated, as both the sympotic songs of solo lyric and public choral songs were among the most effective media used for negotiating the position of individuals and groups within the community, and for staging shared identities. Poetic discourse in the context of public festivals and other social gatherings was a privileged occasion for parading, reinforcing and redefining collective local identities and, strange as it may seem at first sight, in this process a very important rôle was played by itinerant and/or foreign poets: the construction of a *local* identity was in fact often voiced through the articulation of a *foreign* poet. I hope that the following exploration of some case studies of public poetic discourse as a means for defining and promoting civic identities in the archaic and classical periods, and of the different strategies by which such a poetic communal self-definition was constructed, may help us to shed some light also on this aspect of the issue.

A SONG WITHOUT A CITY: EUMELUS' DELIAN PROSODION FOR THE MESSENIANS

One of the most impressive examples of a song being crucial for defining civic identity is provided by what purports to be the most ancient preserved quotation of Greek choral lyric, or, indeed, of Greek poetry *tout court*.

In two passages of the Messenian book of his *Periēgēsis* (4.4.1 and 4.33.2) Pausanias refers to what he defines as a prosodion performed on the island of Delos and composed by the Corinthian poet Eumelus for the Messenians at the time of king Phintas. Pausanias even adds that this prosodion was thought to be the only genuine verses (ἔπη) attributed to Eumelus (4.4.1).

I am grateful to M. Cannatà Fera, A. C. Cassio, L. Prauscello, and to participants in the Cambridge conference for helpful suggestions and comments on previous drafts and on the oral version of this paper.

138   GIOVAN BATTISTA D'ALESSIO

Several chronographic sources agree in placing Eumelus before or slightly
after the mid-eighth century, making him a contemporary of the founder of
Syracuse, his fellow citizen Archias. In Pausanias' narrative, the performance
of the prosodion takes place some time before the outbreak of the First
Messenian War, under Phintas' successor. The dating and the interpretation
of this historical event is a notorious crux for modern scholars, some of
whom have even denied it took place altogether, or have supposed that it
should in fact be dated only to a later period (as late as the sixth century), and
that Pausanias, and other sources, may have been misled by the existence of
competing and diverging chronological systems.[1] We are not concerned here
with the historical event as such, as there is no doubt that Pausanias (and his
source) firmly thought that the Delian prosodion for the Messenians was
to be dated much earlier than the sixth century. This date may have been
'false', as we shall see, but certainly does not depend on a misunderstanding
of different chronological systems. Eumelus' early dating is in line with the
relative chronology of his Messenian patron, King Phintas, within the list
of the early kings of Messene provided by Pausanias himself (and which
clearly derives from earlier sources). In this list, Phintas falls in the sixth
generation after the first Heracleid king of Messenia, Cresphontes, and in
the seventh (the eighth within an inclusive reckoning) after Temenos. This
brings us to a date even earlier than that given for Archias, who, according
to chronographic sources (Eusebius), belonged to the tenth generation after
Temenos. If we project these data onto our chronological systems, it emerges
that Pausanias and his sources thought that the prosodion was to be dated as
early as the first half of the eighth century. Pausanias and his sources clearly
imagined that such an event did belong to a period not much later than
four centuries after the Fall of Troy, and this cannot depend only on the
misunderstanding of a different reckoning of the series of the Olympiads. I
suggest that, rather than than rationalising Pausanias according to our ideas
about chronological verisimilitude, we should try to understand him on
his own terms: Pausanias' Eumelus stands at the very beginning of Greek
poetic tradition.

    The fact itself that such a song should have been thought important
enough to preserve and to quote around a thousand years after its supposed
remote origin is extremely remarkable, even more so if we take into account
the difficulties its historical context would entail. Pausanias, either directly
or through his sources, had access to at least part of the poem, and is able to

---

[1] Cf., most recently and drastically, Shaw 2003: 100–44, 129–30, 245, who places also Eumelus at a date
   around 590. For a discussion of the problems involved by her thesis, cf. Huxley 2006.

Defining local identities in Greek lyric poetry

quote a couple of its lines in order to prove that in archaic times a musical competition took place on Mount Ithome (*PMG* 696):[2]

τῶι γὰρ Ἰθωμάται καταθύμιος ἔπλετο Μοῖσα
ἁ καθαρὰ καὶ ἐλεύθερα σάμβαλ' ἔχοισα.

For the god of Ithome took (or takes) pleasure in the Muse who is pure and wears free sandals.[3]

The theme of these verses is a frequent one in archaic and classical lyric poetry: the praise of the musical tradition and activities of a local community, and it is usual in such songs to refer to a sort of personification of the 'local' Muse.[4] The most 'ancient' occurrence after the Eumelus passage is, interestingly enough, attributed to another ghostly figure of early archaic lyric poetry, the Lesbian poet Terpander. The praised community is, in this case, Messenia's arch-enemy, Sparta itself (fr. 5 Gostoli):

ἔνθ' αἰχμά τε νέων θάλλει καὶ Μῶσα λίγεια
καὶ Δίκα εὐρυάγυια, καλῶν ἐπιτάρροθος ἔργων

There the spear of the young men flourishes and the clear-voiced Muse and Justice who walks in the wide streets, that helper in fine deeds. (tr. Campbell)

Plutarch quotes these lines along with other very similar ones from a lost Pindaric poem in praise of the same community (fr. 199 S–M):

ἔνθα βουλαὶ <μὲν> γερόντων
καὶ νέων ἀνδρῶν ἀριστεύοισιν αἰχμαί,
καὶ χοροὶ καὶ Μοῖσα καὶ Ἀγλαΐα

there excel the counsels of the elderly ones,
and the spears of the young men,
and choirs and Muse and Feast.

Pindar himself uses similar expressions when praising Corinthian traditions in *Olympian* 13.22–3 (particularly close: the Muse, Ares and 'the spears of the young men'). He also praises in slightly different terms the Locrian Muse in *Olympian* 10.13–5 (where Calliope is singled out among her sisters), the Ceian Muse in *Paean* 4 (another processional song to be performed in

---

[2] Pausanias is clearly drawing on some source on Messenian antiquities: he says that Eumelus' prosodion is only one among various elements which can prove the early existence of the music competition, but does not dwell on the others.

[3] The epic aorist ἔπλετο is capable of conveying both a past and a present reference (by indicating the result of a process). Bowra 1963 has argued that it must have a past value here, but I do not find his arguments cogent: the lines may be read as referring to the musical activities in Messene both as a past and as a present event.

[4] Cf. Kienzle 1936: 74–6 (who omits Eumelus and Pind. *Isth.* 9, quoted later on in the text).

Delos, to which I shall return), and the Aeginetan Muses in the fragmentary *Isthmian* 9.[5] These passages demonstrate that the idea was a sort of commonplace, but also that it was a deeply felt one for most audiences. In all these cases, it must be noticed, local communities had their traditions in songs and music promoted through the songs composed by or attributed to a foreign poet. The similarity between Pindar's and Terpander's praise of Sparta is remarkable[6] and may be interpreted in several ways. Wilamowitz argued that the lines attributed to Terpander are in fact a third-century forgery based on Pindar;[7] Gostoli, on the other hand, thinks that it was Pindar who imitated the genuine Terpander.[8] In both cases, the fact either that Terpander's praise was preserved for such a long time and that Pindar paid homage to it or that somebody had reasons to invent Terpander's song at a later stage testifies to the high importance attributed to such songs for the promotion of local self-definition throughout the entire existence of the Greek polis.

The fragment attributed to Eumelus is a sort of Messenian parallel to (?)Terpander's praise of Sparta, and raises a number of problems. Both in the archaic period and later, processional songs to be performed during *theōriai* abroad in pan-Hellenic sanctuaries were common and formed an ideal venue for giving voice to the local communities: we shall focus on some cases presently. What sort of Messenian community would have been involved in this sort of activity in the eighth century? Hiring a foreign poet, training a chorus and financing a *theōria* at a considerable distance is a costly enterprise, which presupposes a community able to take collective decisions and motivated to promote itself within a broader horizon. Several modern historians are sceptical about the possibility that eighth-century Messene might have been such a developed kind of community. More importantly, according to the available historical and archaeological evidence the possibility that a Peloponnesian community might have been interested in expensive cultic and self-promotional activities in far-away Delos would be remarkable indeed. The remains of Geometric pottery and bronze offerings in Delos are revealing: in the whole Geometric period there is no sign of objects with a Peloponnesian provenance. The vast majority of the ceramic remains come from the Cyclades, with more or less

---

[5] In *Isthmian* 9 and *Paean* 4 the praise of the local Muse is accompanied by that of success in athletic competitions. A further instance of praise of musical activities is provided by *Pyth.* 5.114–15 (where it refers not to the whole community but to the local king Arkesilas).

[6] This is not the only contact point between Pindar and the scanty fragments attributed to Terpander: cf. also the echo between fr. 4.2 Gostoli and Pind. *Paean* 7b.10, discussed in D'Alessio 1992a: 359–60.

[7] Wilamowitz 1903: 64–5 n. 1.

[8] Gostoli 1990: 141, and cf. already Janni 1965: 93.

Defining local identities in Greek lyric poetry

substantial proportions originating from Rhodes, Attica, Cyprus and Crete (in decreasing order).[9] The Geometric and Orientalising bronze objects from Delos have been carefully studied by C. Rolley, who has noted the important implications of the total absence of Peloponnesian tripods in the second half of the eighth century.[10] This cannot be taken as a proof that a Peloponnesian community *could* not have sent *theōriai* with offerings or choruses to Delos in the eighth century, but it certainly does prove that such an event would have been an exceptional one. Even if we admit the possibility, we should ask why a hypothetical Messenian community would have been interested in investing so much in a venue which at the very least was peripheral from a Peloponnesian point of view.[11]

A further, important question to ask is how we should suppose that such a song was preserved through the long period when the community of the Messenians, if ever it had existed as such before, had disappeared, and the whole territory was under Spartan control. Martin West's answer is that 'it is imaginable that the song was preserved orally as an anthem of independence down to the fourth century, and that the most basic facts about its author were remembered with it until some historian wrote them down'.[12] On this hypothesis, we should imagine that for an important part of its history, the hymn, after its original public Delian performance, was clandestinely performed and remembered, until it finally gained pride of place in newly founded Messene.[13] Others scholars, such as Bowra, have argued that a copy of the poem may have been preserved at Delos.[14] The idea that Delos may have served as a depository of written copies of songs

---

[9] Cf. Dugas and Rhomaios 1934.

[10] Cf. Rolley 1973: 506 and 524, Rolley 1983, Morgan 1990: 205–7.

[11] The idea that the Messenians might have received a *Delian* oracle on the occasion of their participation in the foundation of Rhegium depends entirely on modern conjecture (Ganci 1998: 131–4, Debiasi 2004: 47). The ancient tradition (which may well not antedate the sixth or fifth century, cf. Asheri 1983: 32; for a less radical approach, cf. Luraghi 1994: 187–206) does not mention Delos at all. The same can be said of the alleged Delian rôle for Chalcis' involvement. More generally the evidence (where little can be added to the data discussed by Càssola 1954: 358–67) for oracles attributed to *Delian* Apollo regarding historical events (as opposed to oracles given to mythical characters) is very thin at best (cf. Càssola 1954: 359).

[12] West 2002: 110.

[13] It seems unlikely that the 'Messenians' performed this song at the Ithomaia during the later archaic period. Luraghi 2002: 59 has argued that 'archaeological evidence from Archaic and Early Classical Messenia looks thoroughly Lakedaimonian and should most probably be connected with [perioikic] presence' (cf. also Luraghi 2001: 299–301). On the archaeological evidence for the cult at Mt Ithome in the archaic period, cf. Cartledge 1979: 193. A fragment of a leg of a geometric bronze tripod, found close to the top of Mt Ithome and now in the Kalamata museum, has been published by Maass 1978: 33 and Plate 67; there is no new archaeological information in Themelis 2004. For some speculations on the origin and meaning of the Ithomaia, cf. Robertson 1993: 219–31.

[14] On Delos as the place where the song was preserved, cf. Bowra 1963 ('inscribed after performance and preserved, possibly at Delos'), referring to Wilamowitz 1900: 38 (who, in fact, only suggested

142   GIOVAN BATTISTA D'ALESSIO

performed by foreign communities before the late sixth century, however, is
unlikely in itself, and certainly not corroborated by the anecdote concerning
the copy of the *Homeric Hymn to Apollo* (the *Hymn* itself not being more
ancient than the second half of the sixth century) allegedly preserved in the
local Temple of Artemis. The fact that there was no independent Messenian
community that may have promoted re-performances of the song at Delos
from the mid-eighth to the mid-fifth century makes this hypothesis even
more unlikely.

From a linguistic and metrical point of view, the two lines are of some
interest. Apart from the proper noun Ithome and the preservation of the
long alphas, lexicon and morphology belong to the epic *koinē*,[15] with the
remarkable exception of Μοῖσα, a form usually connected to the dialect
of Lesbos and to the poetic diction of archaic choral poetry.[16] It is in fact
attested also in mainland inscriptions from the seventh century, both in
verse and in proper nouns arguably belonging to earlier poetic tradition.
The most convincing explanation of the feature is that it reflects the prestige
of Lesbian poetic tradition in mainland Greece.[17] It is usually thought that
this started with the influence of Terpander, who reputedly was active both
at Delphi and at Sparta in the early seventh century. If the prosodion
really dates from the mid-eighth century or before, it would precede both
Terpander and the earliest occurrences of this feature, which was retained
by Greek 'choral' poets well into the fifth century.

The metrical structure, a dactylic hexameter followed by a dactylic pentameter, is in line with the practice attributed to the most ancient lyric
poets, who were thought by Heracleides Ponticus and others to have worked
mostly in the same metres as epic poets did.[18] It is remarkable, however,
that the same sequence was used by Aeschylus in the opening lines of the
grand parodos of his *Agamemnon* in 458. As Eduard Fraenkel has argued in
an important paper, this and other Aeschylean choral songs were conscious

---

     that Pausanias knew this poem thanks to a collection of *Dēliaka*), and Debiasi 2004: 41 n. 121, who
     refers to the story about the *Homeric Hymn to Apollo*. Pavese 1987: 54 thinks that a more or less
     authentic text was first orally transmitted, and later recorded either at Delos or in Messenia, and
     that it got to Pausanias through a grammatical source.

[15] The meaning of the adjective καταθύμιος, though, diverges from that attested in its three Homeric
     occurrences: Aristarchus (cf. in particular the scholia on *Il.* 17.201d) noted the difference between its
     meaning in Homer (ἐνθύμιος, κατὰ ψυχήν) and the later meaning (ἀρεστός); Bowra 1963 recognises
     this same meaning in *Od.* 22.392, but the context is different, and Aristarchus' interpretation seems
     more appropriate there also: cf. Lehrs 1865: 146.

[16] The restitution of the same feature, instead of the transmitted ἔχουσα, in the next line is due to a
     conjecture of Dindorf.

[17] Cf., most recently, Cassio 2005.

[18] Cf., above all, Ps. Plut. *de musica* 1132b-d with Heracleides Ponticus fr. 157 Wehrli.

Defining local identities in Greek lyric poetry 143

attempts at evoking the metres of the archaic citharodes.[19] The parody of this and other passages in the *Frogs* shows that a fifth-century audience was well able to perceive the archaising implication of such metres.

The most striking feature of the two lines, however, is that, in spite of their alleged very early date, they obviously presuppose a situation in which Messenia has already suffered the loss of its freedom. If the Muse of Mount Ithome is praised for being 'pure' and 'wearing free sandals', the implication is that both issues were felt as being problematical.[20] Several scholars have, therefore, questioned Pausanias' relative chronology of Eumelus' song, and have proposed a date after the end, or at least the beginning, of the Messenian War.[21] The prosodion, however, according to Pausanias, is firmly linked to both Phintas and Eumelus, two characters who on any chronographic account *must* antedate the Messenian Wars.[22] We should not assume that any historical problem connected with the two lines depends on a mistake of Pausanias or of his source: the two lines either actually belong to that context, or were later deliberately attributed to that context. Accepting Pausanias' attribution, while situating it in a different historical period, is not really being more faithful to ancient sources than accepting his information wholesale, while questioning its 'veracity'. Once

---

[19] Fraenkel 1918: 321–3 = 1964: 202–3. Fraenkel does not mention Eumelus' lines in this context.

[20] For a 'political' interpretation of the phrase in Eumelus, cf., Bowra 1963, Càssola 1964: 271–2, De Martino in De Martino and Vox 1996: 117, Debiasi 2004: 45 n. 147. It is very aptly compared to Hor. *carm.* 1.37.1–2 *pede libero* by Nisbet and Hubbard *ad loc.* (recalled also by Debiasi *loc. cit.*). Pavese 1972: 256 n. 86 (followed by Grandolini 1987–8: 29–33) argues that 'pure' refers here to the sound of the voice of the singers, and that 'free' merely indicates that the feet of the Muse were free of physical impediments to the dance (or of foreign thoughts: Pavese 1987: 55), ruling out any political implication. For this alleged meaning of ἐλευθερία Pavese quotes Pind. *Isth.* 8.15, a passage where all other readers have argued for a 'political' reading (correctly, in my opinion). Eumelus' text does not support Edmonds' contention (accepted by Untersteiner) that these lines are hinting at the poet's own literary originality. Croiset 1914: ii.52 n. 3 (quoted by Untersteiner 1951–2: 13) dubiously suggested that the adjective implies that the performers were of free status, as opposed to being slaves, but this was true for any civic celebration.

[21] Scholars who date the prosodion *before* the outbreak of the war (either denying its 'political' implications or without discussing the problem) include: Dunbabin 1948: 67, Untersteiner 1951–2, Campbell 1988, Pavese (1987: 57, one generation before 743; 1972: 256, second half of the eighth century) and Grandolini 1987–8: 29–33. Other scholars placed Eumelus' prosodion *after* the outbreak of the Messenian wars but still at a very early date: Bowra 1963 (later eighth century); Andrewes *ap.* Bowra 1963 (at the time of the colonisation of Rhegion; followed, with modifications, by De Martino in De Martino and Vox 1996:113 and Debiasi 2004: 46–8); West 2002 (mid-seventh century). Shaw 2003 places Eumelus in the early sixth century but dates also the Messenian war at a later period (cf. above, n. 1). Vitalis 1930: 39 somewhat naïvely argued that the prosodion was composed after the very first tensions between Messene and Sparta (which, according to Pausanias, preceded the outbreak of the war), and took the adjective as implying that 'Messenians were free and so they should remain in the future'.

[22] No ancient chronographic source offers a date for Eumelus later than 738/7 (perhaps even 744/3, cf. Mosshamer 1979: 198–203).

we abandon the Phintas-Eumelus time frame, the prosodion can be dated any time before Pausanias' source.[23]

An obvious possibility is that the song belongs to the period after the re-foundation of Messene, when the city was in need of constructing not only its walls but also an historical, musical and poetic tradition.[24] Lyric songs played an important rôle at the moment of the foundation itself: on that occasion, in 369, songs and music by Sacadas of Argos and Pronomus of Thebes were performed (Paus. 4.27.7), and Pronomus is known also as the author of another Delian prosodion, for Chalcis (on which more later).[25] Incidentally, the mention of Sacadas and Pronomus provides us with further evidence on the 'ethnic' and political implications of lyric traditions, as the foundation of Messene took place under the aegis of Argos and Thebes. A more attractive scenario, however, would be provided if we suppose that the poem was in fact 'forged' in the fifth century by the Messenian refugees resident in Naupactus under Athenian protection.[26] As I have argued above, both linguistic and metrical features are fully compatible with fifth-century archaising lyric poetry. In this period (particularly, but not only, after 424), Delos was an important focal point for Athens and its allies, and several choral poems are preserved, which seem to have been composed for performance on the island. The group includes Bacchylides 17 and Pindar, *Paean* 4 (for the Ceians), *Paean* 5 (for an unknown Ionian polis, or for Athens itself), and perhaps Pronomus' prosodion for Chalcis (if it does not fall after Athens' defeat in 404): to two of them, I shall return. The Messenians at Naupactus certainly had many more reasons to send a *theōria* to Delos than eighth-century 'Messenians' might ever have had.[27] They were, moreover, obviously very much interested in furthering the traditional

[23] I fully agree with Robertson 1993: 224 n. 14 that, once 'Pausanias' account of how and when the choir was sent' is discarded, 'there is little reason to follow Pausanias in other details, such as the early date or the ascription to Eumelus'.

[24] Pohlenz 1955: 190; cf. also Raaflaub 1981: 192 and 351.

[25] Wilamowitz 1900: 38–9 n. 1 (unnecessarily, in my opinion) argues that Pausanias may have drawn all his information on these Delian poems from a single, Delian source (cf. n. 14, above).

[26] This was first argued by de Schoeffer 1889: 7–8; some of his linguistic arguments (suggested to him by H. Diels) are not quite cogent, but the historical scenario still seems to me to offer the most plausible explanation. His suggestion has been largely neglected, though Robertson 1993: 224 and n. 14, apparently without knowledge of de Schoeffer, also mentions a fifth-century date as an alternative to the possibility that the Messenian refugees at Naupactus may have preserved the old processional hymn.

[27] On the Messenians at Naupactus, cf. Deshours 1993, Figueira 1999, Luraghi 2001 and 2002, Alcock 2002. None of these interesting papers focusing on Messenian identity (and the other ones included in the recent volumes by Powell and Hodkinson 2002 and Luraghi and Alcock 2003) has anything to say about Eumelus' prosodion. The dedication by the Messenians from Naupactus of Paeonius' Nike at Olympia (on which, cf. Luraghi 2001: 294) is a(nother?) remarkable sign of their attempt to draw pan-Hellenic attention to their community.

Defining local identities in Greek lyric poetry 145

cult of Zeus Ithomatas: according to Pausanias, the famous bronze statue of the god, attributed to the artist Hageladas, had been commissioned by the Messenians at Naupactus.[28] After Messene's foundation in 369 it became the cult statue on Mount Ithome itself. It is probably no coincidence that this information is provided by Pausanias immediately before his quotation of the two lines from the prosodion.

Two factors may have contributed to the choice of Eumelus as the author of the Messenian prosodion: on the one hand, the famous names of the seventh century were too strongly linked to Sparta,[29] while, on the other hand, an eighth-century name was needed, because the event described *had* to precede the First Messenian War (and because this would give Messenia the edge over Sparta, where the earliest lyric tradition goes back to the later Terpander).

We have really no way to say for sure whether the prosodion was a surprising relic from the eighth century, or a late 'forgery'. Based on the evidence available, I would decidedly incline towards this latter solution. On both accounts, however, the story of the prosodion demonstrates the great importance attributed to the lyric tradition in shaping local identities. Incidentally, it also illustrates the issues which might have been at stake in the tradition of a choral poem: an ancient song might have been perceived in a different light through re-performance in different contexts; a newer one might have presented itself as the re-performance of an original song projected to a foundational past.[30]

DELIAN PROSODIA

Leaving aside for a moment the issue of whether Eumelus' poem should be dated well into the eighth century or considered a later creation, its presentation as a processional song to be performed on Delos has interesting implications for the expected context of such a choral self-presentation. This pan-Hellenic venue seems to have long been crucial for the Ionian communities, and, perhaps, for Eastern Greeks more generally, as a place

---

[28] There are problems also with this attribution, as other evidence suggests that Hageladas (or an earlier artist with this same name) was active in the last quarter of the sixth century, while the Messenians moved to Naupactus only around the mid-fifth century.

[29] Cf. the information about the Helots not being allowed to sing the songs of Terpander in Plut. *Lycurg.* 28.10 (= Test. 57 Gostoli).

[30] For another interesting fifth-century case of choral celebrations presented as going back to a foundational event, cf. Thuc. 5.16.3, where the Spartans 'recalled Pleistoanax with the same choruses and sacrifices (τοῖς ὁμοίοις χοροῖς καὶ θυσίαις) as when the Spartans established the kingship at the founding of Sparta', with Hornblower 2004: 312–13 (I owe the reference to S. Hornblower).

146 GIOVAN BATTISTA D'ALESSIO

for displaying and enjoying their musical and poetic traditions, as the *Homeric Hymn to Apollo* vividly evokes. We know of several processional songs performed by choruses for various *poleis* in the island, and we can even read, though in a fragmentary state, the remains of two or three of them.[31] Pindar's *Paean* 4 probably is, as I have argued elsewhere, the same poem referred to by the scholia to *Isthmian* 1 as a 'processional paean for the Ceians to be performed on Delos',[32] and, as we shall see later on, the identity of this Ionian community and its past are at the centre of the song. The community itself speaks in the first person throughout the ode (even if the text is the work of a foreign poet, Pindar of Thebes). *Paean* 5, the next ode in the collection of Pindar's *Paeans*, belongs within a section, which seems to have included songs labelled as 'processional paeans' by ancient sources or compatible with such a definition. This short song certainly was meant for a performance at Delos and its last section preserves the final part of a history of the foundation of Euboea and the Cyclades by the Ionians. It very clearly emerges how in both the Delian processional odes of Pindar the self-definition of the Ionian communities was an important feature. The possible chronological frame of the two paeans is compatible with their having been performed in the period when the Delian league was under Athenian control. The Athenian point of view might have been an important issue in *Paean* 5, though this is far from certain. It apparently is not in the case of *Paean* 4, and we have no reason to believe that the crucial function of the Delian festival in putting civic identities on parade only started under the aegis of Athens.

Interestingly enough, the next Delian prosodion known to us, the processional song Pronomus composed for Chalcis in Euboea (Paus. 9.12.6), was also the work of a Theban poet for an Ionian polis. I have argued elsewhere that already in the fifth century Thebes may have had interests at stake in the Delian sanctuary, as is suggested by Pindar's *First Hymn*, and by the Theban involvement in the sanctuary of Delion near Tanagra.[33] In the last stages of the Peloponnesian War, Chalcis moved away from Athenian influence, and in the early years of the fourth century was much closer to Thebes. We know too little of the chronology of Pronomus' career to say

---

[31] Cf. also *Paean* 12 S-M, which was, as I have argued in D'Alessio 1997: 28, in fact a prosodion for the Naxians to be performed on Delos. For other fragments possibly belonging in this context, cf. D'Alessio 1997: 28–9.

[32] D'Alessio 1994: 64.

[33] Cf. D'Alessio 2007. For Boeotia and Delos in the Hellenistic period: Reger 1994. On cultic links between Boeotia and Delos, cf. also Schachter 1999.

Defining local identities in Greek lyric poetry   147

anything about the date of the prosodion for Chalcis.[34] In the late fifth
century this poet and music-performer was certainly popular at Athens, as
is shown both by his depiction on a famous Athenian vase and by the anecdote about his rôle as Alcibiades' teacher of *aulos*-playing.[35] It is conceivable
that the Chalcidians may have requested him to compose the prosodion
when the polis was under Athenian control, and when Pronomus was one
of the most popular artists on the Athenian market. On the other hand,
Pausanias' story about Pronomus' music being performed on the occasion
of the foundation of Messene in 369 clearly shows that the Thebans did
attach political implications to his work, and I would not rule out the possibility that the prosodion may date from the period when Thebes had an
important political influence on Chalcis.[36]

   The last Delian prosodion mentioned by our sources, the one composed
by Amphicles of Rheneia for the Athenians in the second century BCE, also
has obvious political implications.[37] In 167, the Athenians took control of
the island: they expelled the local population and established a *klērouchia*.
An honorary decree from 165/4 (*ID* 1497) mentions one Amphicles son of
Philoxenos, from Rheneia, a μουσικὸς καὶ μελῶν ποιητής ('a musician
and melic poet') who had composed a Delian prosodion praising the city
of Athens: καὶ προσόδιον γράψας ἐμμελὲς εἰς τὴν πόλιν τούς τε θεοὺς
τοὺς τὴν νῆσον κατέχοντας καὶ τὸν δῆμον τὸν Ἀθηναίων ὕμνησεν,[38]
ἐδίδαξεν δὲ καὶ τῶν πολιτῶν παῖδας πρὸς λύραν τὸ μέλος ᾄδειν ἀξίως
τῆς τε τῶν θεῶν τιμῆς καὶ τοῦ Ἀθηναίων δήμου ('and, having written a
harmonious processional song for the city, he sang the gods who rule the
island and the *dēmos* of the Athenians, and he instructed the sons of the
citizens to sing the song to the accompaniment of the lyre in a manner
worthy of the honour of the gods and of the *dēmos* of the Athenians'). The
Athenian cleruchs seem to have followed the ancient tradition of the Delian
prosodia, and the poem featured the praise of the city, which had sent the
chorus. This time, however, the 'visiting' city has taken the place of Delos

---

[34] On Pronomus, cf. also Berlinzani 2004: 127–9 and the forthcoming papers of the Oxford Pronomus
Conference (September 2006).

[35] On Pronomus, Alcibiades and the *aulos*, cf. Cordano 2004: 316–22.

[36] In the same passage, Pausanias says that in the Theban *agora* the statue of Pronomus was located
close to that of Epameinondas, who was celebrated in an accompanying epigram as the founder of
Messene.

[37] On Athenian *theōriai* to Delos, cf. Rutherford 2004a: 82–9 (no reference to Amphicles: his *prosodion*,
however, seems to have been performed by the Athenian cleruchs rather than by a theoric chorus),
Rutherford (this volume) p. 245.

[38] Cf. also the *enfant prodigue* and epic poet Ariston of Phocaea, who according to a later Delian
inscription, (*ID* 1506; Chaniotis 1988b: 340–1, 146–4 BCE) ὕ]μνησεν τόν τε ἀρχηγέτην Ἀπόλλ[ωνα
καὶ τ]οὺς ἄλλους θεοὺς τοὺς κατέχον[τας τὴν ν]ῆσον καὶ τὸν δῆμον τὸν Ἀθηνα[ίων.

148   GIOVAN BATTISTA D'ALESSIO

itself: the Athenians were playing both rôles, visitors of the sanctuary and
new citizens of the island. It is worth noting that this same Amphicles is
styled as Delian in a nearly contemporary honorary decree from Oropus
(*IG* VII 373). It is possible that the Oropus inscription is to be dated before
the expulsion of the former Delians in 167, and/or that his Athenian patrons
would not officially recognise his former citizenship, which now belongs to
the Athenians οἱ ἐν Δήλωι κατοικοῦντες ('the ones resident on Delos').[39]
It is somewhat ironical that the first Delian composer of a Delian prosodion
we hear of was a foreigner in his own homeland.

A CITY WITHOUT A SONG: 'THE POETICS OF PLACE' VS. 'THE POETICS OF COMMONPLACES' AT NEPHELOKOKKYGIA

The performance and transmission of choral songs was an important issue
for establishing and promoting civic self-presentation both at home and
abroad. A city needs its own songs, and professional poets to compose them.
More often than not, they did not belong to the community they praised.
There were several reasons for this, the most obvious one being that poets, as
other skilled craftsmen, would produce more goods than a single medium-
sized community may usually have needed. Another important factor is
that the evidence tends to record exceptional cases, involving communities
which had sought the best poets on the market. There may be, however, at
least in some cases, a more profound reason for the circumstance that the
poets best suited for speaking on behalf of a whole community were not
usually members of that community. Before moving to this, however, let
us consider a possibly not too exceptional case, which would certainly have
gone unrecorded had it not taken place in Nephelokokkygia.[40]

As soon as Euelpides and Peisetairos have given a name to their new city
among the clouds and the birds, the birds express their intention to perform
a prosodion (851–8). A sacrificial procession starts, led by a bird-priest,
soon substituted by Peisetairos himself (863–903). It is exactly during this
procession that a poet arrives (904) singing the praise of the newly founded
city. After what we have just seen about the close link between public, cultic
poetry and the promotion of civic identity, the poet's arrival at this moment
and his praise of the city does not come as a surprise. He is ready to supply
the new polis with an item crucial for its identity. The very first word he sings
on his arrival is the name of the new city (904), for which he has composed
a whole array of poems: choral circular songs (the κύκλια, indicating not

---

[39] Cf. also Chaniotis 1988b: 349–50, Reger 1994: 77–8.
[40] For its relevance in this context, cf. also Chaniotis 1988b: 375. For two recent readings of this part of
Birds cf. Catenacci 2007 and Martin (this volume).

Defining local identities in Greek lyric poetry 149

only dithyrambs but several kinds of choral dances and songs, performed by a circular chorus),[41] *partheneia* ('maiden songs'), and poems à la Simonides (perhaps *enkōmia*? *thrēnoi* do not seem suited in this context). The situation must have been all too typical. Nephelokokkygia, just founded, is a city without poems. It needs them as much as it needs its identity, and there comes a wandering poet, with his merchandise, a whole series of ready-made songs (including a Pindaric poem in praise of the foundation of another city, Aetna). We have already had occasion to notice, when examining the praise of the musical traditions in songs for Messene, Sparta and Corinth, how lyric self-presentations of the polis were centred on recurring motifs. This paradox is at the core of the comic scene in *Birds*, where the poet would in fact supply the new city with a second-hand identity, entirely made up out of commonplaces and recycled cyclic songs. Important as the rhetoric of civic identity was, the danger of a shift from the poetics of place into the poetics of commonplaces was obviously round the corner. This should not be taken as a sign that the days of choral self-celebrations were over, at Athens or elsewhere, as the case of Amphicles and many other epigraphically attested poets certainly show. It suggests, however, that its very popularity had exhausted the potentialities of this communication medium. In its later forms, it seems to have somewhat lacked the impact and sophistication it apparently had in the early centuries of polis formation. At another level, it also suggests that an exceptional city, as Nephelokokkygia is, needs an exceptional poet, like Aristophanes himself, and a different poetic form of self-expression. The ways in which Athenian dramatic literature competes with and appropriates the lyric discourse of civic identity is a subject at which I can here only hint.[42] Nevertheless, when it comes to the chorus of the *Birds* themselves to sing *their* praises of their newly founded city, they cannot but recur to the very same commonplaces of the choral lyric tradition, as happens in 1318–22:

> τί γὰρ οὐκ ἔνι ταύτηι
> καλὸν ἀνδρὶ μετοικεῖν;
> Σοφία, Πόθος, ἀμβρόσιαι Χάριτες,
>   τό τε τῆς ἀγανόφρονος Ἡσυχίας
> εὐήμερον πρόσωπον

> for what beauty is not available in it
> to people who come to dwell here?
> There are Wisdom, Desire, the immortal Graces,
>   and of gentle Tranquillity
> the prosperous countenance

---

[41] Cf. D'Alessio, forthcoming.
[42] On this passage, cf. Paduano 1973: 130, Toscano 1991, Dougherty 1994a: 35–6.

Verses 1321–2 strongly recall a famous passage from a Theban *hyporkhēma* by Pindar (fr. 109 S-M).[43]

Incidentally, the *Birds* situation raises another important issue. The discourse of poetic self-definition of the polis would often include foundation histories, though this may not always have been the core of the narration. From this point of view, it is remarkable that 'colonial' foundations tend to follow the same pattern of the metropoleis. A 'new' city needs a new poetic tradition, but it shares the same rhetorical strategies adopted in the case of the ancient foundations. Cyrene and Abdera need to stage their own past and their own identity as much as Sparta, Athens and Ceos.

In the next section we shall have occasion to deal with three cities with a different background: Sparta, whose mythical and historical identity goes back to the foundation by the Heracleids; Abdera, a seventh-century Ionian colony which had been effectively re-founded by Teos in the mid-sixth century; and Ceos, which traces back its local identity to the mythical time of Minos and earlier.

'I' AND THE CITY: LYRIC DISCOURSE, CHORAL CIVIC IDENTITY AND THE *EPITAPHIOS LOGOS*

In order to assess the relevance and impact of lyric discourse as an important medium for expressing a communal image of the polis, we have, luckily enough, not to rely only on the indirect information about such songs as the Delian prosodia of Eumelus, Pronomus and Amphicles, and the poor attempts of the wandering poet in Nephelokokkygia. We do have, though in a fragmentary form, important remains of some of the poems, which did actually play a more important rôle in shaping this communication context. In this section, I shall examine poems which give voice to the community itself. The voice singing during their performance did not sound as that of the praising poet, nor as that of the particular group of the actual performers. It offered, instead, a paradigmatic discourse, in which every member of the polis is represented as expressing communal civic identity.

Tyrtaeus' 'choral' elegy

For obvious contextual reasons, choral lyric would seem to be the most appropriate medium to convey such a discourse, and two of the most

---

[43] On the apparent contradiction between this passage and the representation of the new city elsewhere in the play, cf. Paduano 1973: 140 and Dunbar 1995 *ad loc.*

Defining local identities in Greek lyric poetry

interesting cases in which it is used are, indeed, choral poems, Pindar's *Paeans* 2 and 4.[44] Its first occurrence, however, is to be found in a different performance context, that of the Spartan elegies of Tyrtaeus, another immigrant poet, according to the prevalent later tradition. It is a striking feature of Tyrtaeus's elegy that all first-person statements in what survives of his poems are hardly ever to be understood as an expression of the voice of a single individual, as opposed to other members of a group, or even as that of a representative of a particular group opposed to other ones within the polis, as is usual in archaic sympotic poetry. It is not just a matter of expressing a communal *ideology*, which may have been true for other kinds of poems as well. It is a matter of communicative strategy: these lines are formulated in such a way that anyone belonging to the community could identify himself in the poetic voice. It is as much a collective discourse as it is in the case of the two Pindaric paeans to be examined presently. The only difference we can discern in some poems is that the speaker is sometimes represented as addressing a group of younger citizens, or as articulating the audience in various groups with different military duties.[45] Equally often, however, no distinction is made between 'us' and 'you'. When Tyrtaeus addresses his audience as the 'progeny of unvanquished Heracles' in fr. 11.1 West (8 G-P) the whole text makes clear that he is not opposing a group of the élite to the rest of the youths, but representing the entire community of the young warriors as descendants of the hero.[46] It has recently been argued that Tyrtaeus, in this poem and elsewhere, addresses and represents only a restricted group that claimed Heracleid ancestry.[47] Such an interpretation, however, is contradicted by the very fact that in fr. 2.14–15 West (= 1ª G-P) Tyrtaeus uses the first person plural ('we came') to describe the people who moved to the Peloponnese from central Greece *together with* the Heracleids. Once again, a clear strategy emerges that produces a voice ideologically inclusive of the whole community: no sharp difference is made between those who may have claimed such heroic ancestry and the rest of the population.

[44] Traces of the same kind of discourse articulated through a first-person perspective can be found also in *Pythian* 5 and in fr. 215 S-M.

[45] This happens in fr. 11 West (8 G-P) where an address to the νέοι in line 10 is followed by another one to the γυμνῆτες in line 35. In fr. 23 West (10 C col. 2 G-P) the articulation into different groups seems to have involved the use of the first person (cf. Tarditi 1983), instead of the second. The text, however, is too fragmentary to allow any firm conclusion, and the preserved portion does not suggest that there was any ideological opposition among the groups.

[46] Cf. Huttner 1997: 44–8, with previous bibliography (and add Callimachus fr. 617 Pf. to the passages that imply that the whole Spartiate community might have been described as formed from descendants of Heracles) and Meier 1998: 22.

[47] Quattrocelli 2006.

152   GIOVAN BATTISTA D'ALESSIO

This communal voice is very unusual in archaic elegiac production, and, more generally, in archaic sympotic poetry, where individual egos abound, and where even when the content may be perceived as representing a shared ideology, it is formulated in such a way as to bear the imprint of an oppositional point of view, and of a particular voice.[48] Later and even contemporary performers may have impersonated Theognis, Archilochus, Mimnermus, Solon.[49] Judging from what is preserved of his poetry, nobody needs to have impersonated 'Tyrtaeus'. It is, rather, Tyrtaeus who impersonates 'the Spartan citizen'. This raises a very interesting issue, that of the relation between performance context and communal discourse. It has been suggested that Tyrtaeus' *Eunomia* may not have been meant for performance in a sympotic context, but for a public festival.[50] Later sources, however, suggest a closer link between performance context and communicative strategy. In the fourth and third centuries, the orator Lycurgus and the historian Philochorus give us interesting details about the occasions on which Tyrtaeus' poems were performed, at least in later times. According to Philochorus, after the Spartan victory in the Second Messenian War, the Spartans instituted the custom of singing Tyrtaeus' poems during their military campaigns in post-prandial competitions, where the polemarch acted as judge. According to Lycurgus, such performances took place during military campaigns, when everybody was summoned to the tent of the king in order to listen to them.[51] It is commonly assumed that this custom presupposes an organisation of Spartan symposia later than the time of Tyrtaeus' poems. Sympotic practice in seventh-century Sparta may have provided several possible models, perhaps in fluid evolution.[52] I would emphasise, however, that the obvious difference between the communal

[48] When Bowra 1961: 240 contrasts Sappho and Archilochus with Tyrtaeus and Solon, he overlooks this important difference between Tyrtaeus and Solon. Very useful insights on this subject are to be found in Jaeger 1932, and Steinmetz 1969. Cf. also Stehle 1997: 53–4, on the lack of authoritative stance in Tyrtaeus and in Alcman's partheneia: an important difference, however, is that Alcman's first-person statements are descriptive and focus on the performers themselves, involving only a group within the community, while in Tyrtaeus they are usually representative and inclusive, applying to any member of the 'political' male community.

[49] For some recent stimulating approaches to Solon's poetic ego cf. the papers in the first section of Blok and Lardinois 2006.

[50] Cf. Bowie 1986: 27–34. The subjunctive in 2.10 suggests a hortatory context, which would be unexpected in a festival performance. Cf. below on Bowie's hypothesis that the passage may have been part of a speech of some historical character.

[51] Bowie 1990a: 224–8 has reasonably argued that Lycurgus' and Philochorus' accounts complement and do not contradict each other.

[52] Cf. Bowie 1990a: 225 n. 16 (sixth century); Rösler 1990; Nafissi 1991: 173–226 has a very detailed discussion (on Tyrtaeus and the symposion: 92–3). Cf. also Meier 1998: 170–83, 216–21, who (p. 221) sees a convergence between the institution of the new *syssitia* and the ideology of Tyrtaeus' exhortations, though without addressing the relation between the communication context and the

Defining local identities in Greek lyric poetry 153

voice of the elegies of Tyrtaeus and other sympotic poetry finds an impressive match in the difference between the usual aristocratic symposia, which gave voice to competing *groups*, and the communal meals of the Spartan 'equals'. Whether, in this case, the medium has shaped the message, or the reverse, is very difficult to tell. That there is a relation between them seems very likely. The message would certainly have been more effective had its first-person narrative been performed by the citizens themselves, and the peculiar structure of Spartan *syssitia* would have been ideally suited for this sort of 'choral' elegy.

The remains of Tyrtaeus' elegies represent the most impressive and articulated case (at least at a verbal level) of self-representation of a Greek polis before the fifth century.[53] Particularly important are the fragments attributed or attributable to the *Eunomia* elegy (1–7 West = 1–5 G-P), where the history of the community is described in the first person. This features:

1 'our' arrival in the Peloponnese, which Zeus himself has granted to those who came under the guidance of the Heracleids (2 West = 1ᵃ G-P);
2 the oracle of Apollo, which has sanctioned the internal order of the city and, perhaps, prophesied its final victory (4 West = 1ᵇ G-P);
3 the conquest of Messenia by 'the fathers of our fathers' during a twenty years long campaign, led by 'our king Theopompus, dear to the gods' (5 West = 2–4 G-P);
4 the description of the status of the vanquished Messenians in opposition to that of their 'masters' (6–7 West = 5 G-P).

The elegy seems also to have included hortatory passages with reference to the present situation. Fr. 2 West is preceded in a papyrus by a fragmentary section, where oracles are mentioned, and where the speaker says: 'let us obey' (line 10). Similar exhortations in the first person plural occur in 10.13–4 West (= 6 G-P) and in another papyrus fragment, 19.11–12, 20.15 (10.19–20 and 43 G-P), where the future is used: 'we shall obey'.

The representation of the remote past in a first-person narrative may have already been a traditional feature by Tyrtaeus' time. It occurs in a fascinating and tantalising fragment of Mimnermus, where the arrival of the Ionians from Pylos to Asia Minor is narrated in the first person (fr. 9 West = 3 G-P).[54] In both cases, it has been argued that the speaker must (or

---

communication strategy. On the evidence provided by the fragments of Terpander and Alcman, cf. most recently Quattrocelli 2004.

[53] I take it for granted, of course, that Tyrtaeus is *not* to be dated in the fifth century.

[54] On the historical self-consciousness in Mimnermus and Tyrtaeus, cf. the excellent treatment in Steinmetz 1969.

154   GIOVAN BATTISTA D'ALESSIO

might) have been a character within a narrative.[55] This is, in my opinion, next to impossible in the case of the Tyrtaeus passage. Fr. 2 West (1a G-P) is quoted by Strabo in order to show that Tyrtaeus himself was a Spartan, introducing it with the words: 'he says that he is from Sparta in the elegy entitled *Eunomia*'. It is hardly believable that as careful an author as Strabo, who had access to the complete elegy and who was discussing precisely the issue of Tyrtaeus' origin, would use the reported speech of a different character for this purpose. It may be added that, as we have seen, the passage in Tyrtaeus fr. 2 is preceded by a hortatory section quite similar to those apparently involving the actual audience in other fragments, and that there would be no space for the introduction of a different speaker in the single intervening line.[56] Once we accept this was the case for Tyrtaeus, there is no reason to suppose that Mimnermus' structurally similar narrative must have been part of a reported speech.[57]

It is interesting, however, that in the only other fragment we possess from an historical narrative by Mimnermus (fr. 14 West = 23 G-P) the first person is not a collective one, but is clearly individualised, with the speaker actually mentioning something he has personally heard from those who witnessed the achievements of a character of the past. We have no reason to believe that the pervasive communal ego of Tyrtaeus' elegy was equally relevant for other archaic elegists. It does not seem to have been a prominent feature in later 'historical' elegy either, if we may judge from the remains of Simonides' 'Plataea poem', where no such first-person communal narrative occurs.

It is certainly paradoxical that later tradition should have thought that the author of these elegies, where every first-person statement refers to the 'Spartan citizen', was not a Spartan himself. As we have already seen, Strabo even quotes the historical passage of fr. 2 West to this effect. The whole issue of Tyrtaeus' origin is shrouded in the mist of reshaping in transmission, and of propaganda. That he may actually not have been a native Spartan, however, is less improbable than is usually assumed. Later biographical traditions on archaic poets were often based on naïve or pseudo-naïve

---

[55] Bowie 1986: 31 (after Tsagarakis 1966: 50–3, and 1977: 22–4) argues that the first-person statements in Tyrtaeus 2 West are from 'a speech made by one of the founding generation of Spartans'; he expresses a similar opinion about Mimnermus fr. 9 West on p. 30 n. 90, again after Tsagarakis 1966: 53–4, 1977: 27–8, and Gentili 1968: 67 (cf., however, Bowie's sensible qualification on p. 31 n. 95). Bowie is followed by Stehle 1997: 52 and n. 80.

[56] This section is known from *P. Oxy.* 2824, which was published in 1971, only after Tsagarakis 1966.

[57] Rösler 1990: 235 (after Zimmermann) aptly quotes Ar. *Lys.* 1247–70 for another case of such a 'historical we'.

Defining local identities in Greek lyric poetry

readings of their works. The fact itself that everything in Tyrtaeus' poems would have suggested that he *was* a Spartan is one of the reasons why this ancient tradition should be taken seriously. In fact, the pervasive use of an all-inclusive communal ego should be seen not as a biographical element, but as the result of a precise communicative strategy. As we shall see, exactly the same communicative structure underlies the two Pindaric paeans for Ceos and Abdera, and this would never be taken as evidence that the two poems were composed by a Ceian or an Abderite poet. 'Tyrtaeus', whoever he was, seems to have given voice not to 'himself', but to the construction of Sparta's communal 'I'.[58]

Aristotle in the *Politics* offers an interesting piece of information about the historical circumstances of the *Eunomia* (fr. 1 West). From this poem, Aristotle says, it emerges that Sparta was divided by internal strife (στάσις), as a consequence of the war with the Messenians. Tyrtaeus is only one of the seventh-century poets known by later traditions to have resolved a situation of civil strife in Sparta.[59] Another famous case is that of Terpander, whom we have had already occasion to mention. According to several sources (test. 12, 14a–c, 15, 19, 20, 21, 60f, 60i Gostoli),[60] some of them going back at least to the fourth century, Terpander had been invited to Sparta during a period of political unrest (στάσις), to which his poems and his music put an end. One of the sources (test. 14a–c, from Philodemus, *On Music*, going back to Diogenes of Babylon) places the performance of his poems in the context of the communal *syssitia/phiditia*.[61] A similar story was told of another, later choral poet active in seventh-century Sparta, Thaletas of Gortyna (test. 4, 5 (both mentioning a plague), 6 Campbell (mentioning a στάσις, as in another Philodemus passage omitted in Campbell)).[62] The same pattern applies also to later poets, such as Stesichorus and Pindar.[63]

---

[58] Luraghi 2003: 111 n. 5 notes that Strabo's inference rests on a shaky premise: this requires, however, some qualification, in the sense that Tyrtaeus' first person is not quite a typical case in archaic elegiac and/or sympotic poetry.

[59] Cf., most recently, van Wees 1999.

[60] Cf. also Gostoli 1988. Some of these sources may ultimately derive from the Aristotelian *Constitution of the Spartans*.

[61] Cf. also Quattrocelli 2004.

[62] Nagy 1990a: 366–9 connects the function of choral lyric, as a means to put an end to στάσις, with the structure of the chorus itself, which represents the internal articulations of the polis and brings them into a new unity. This is an important insight, but the phenomenon is not limited to *choral* poetry: neither the poems of Terpander nor those of Tyrtaeus were meant for choral performance.

[63] Aelian, *VH* 12.50 (Terp. test. 21 Gostoli) adds to the list of the foreign poets invited by the Spartans to solve their public problems (ἢ νοσήσαντες ἢ παραφρονήσαντες ἢ ἄλλο τι δημοσίαι παθόντες) Alcman and the otherwise unknown Nymphaios of Kydonia.

156   GIOVAN BATTISTA D'ALESSIO

In all these cases, with the exception of Pindar in Thebes, the most recent
one, the pattern always implies that the poet who puts an end to the civic
disorder does not himself belong to the community he 'cures'.[64] Later
authors have sometimes sought an explanation for these anecdotes in a
pervasive anti-Spartan attitude of the sources: Spartans did not practise
poetry themselves, and so they needed to look for poets abroad. This may
have played a rôle at some later stages (it clearly was Aelian's opinion),
but our early sources are all but hostile towards Sparta and its culture. I
think that the explanation of this recurrent pattern is rather to be sought in
the nature of the political circumstances themselves. Internal strife, στάσις,
usually implies a harsh confrontation between groups competing for power.
Authoritative members of the polis itself, as a rule, would belong to one or
the other of those groups. They may function as mediators (see, for example,
the case of Solon), but on most occasions they could have hardly have
represented a discourse of the *unified* community. Somewhat paradoxically,
an authoritative voice impersonating an undivided polis would often have
more easily been the product of a foreign personality, not directly implicated
in any of the competing political groups. The rôle of the foreign poet,
providing a unified discourse of identity for the community, comes to be
typologically close to that of the foreign αἰσυμνῆται, who, according to
several ancient sources, played an important function in putting an end to
archaic στάσεις.[65]

                    A reading of Pindar, Paeans *2 and 4*

Two Pindaric poems are the best-preserved instances of lyric self-
representation of a local community through a communal voice. *Paean* 2
and *Paean* 4, though partly fragmentary, provide an invaluable opportunity to analyse the actual verbal articulation of local identities within the
medium of choral performance.[66] As we shall see, στάσις and the quest for

---

[64] In the case of Pindar, the information refers to the lost *hyporkhēma* for the Thebans (fr. 109 S-M;
Pythian 11 provides further evidence for Pindar giving voice to a communal discourse for his polis).
There is, however, abundant evidence for the pervasiveness of the *stasis*-theme in Pindaric poems
for other *poleis*.

[65] Cf. Gehrke 1985: 261–2, 266, on the αἰσυμνῆται, and the remarks about the traditions on Alcman's
foreign origin in Diels 1896: 363 and Janni 1965: 100–5. For a similar view of the Hesiodic *persona* as
that of an 'immigrant poet' (*metanastēs*), cf. Martin 1992, in particular p. 29 (though I do not myself
see the case of Hesiod as relevant to the context I am discussing here).

[66] For a recent survey of the political functions of ancient Greek choral performances, focusing more
on the performance situation and on the ritual background than on the textual articulation of the
discourse as here, cf. Kowalzig 2004.

Defining local identities in Greek lyric poetry

internal political stability are a central issue in these poems, as indeed they are in many of Pindar's cultic poems.[67]

Abdera and Athens

Paean 2, composed by Pindar for the city of Abdera in Thrace, is an extraordinary poem, whose literary importance has partly been overshadowed by its contextual obscurity.[68] It is an actual case of a polis performing its civic identity, and provides a crucial link between the Tyrtaean tradition and Athenian self-representation in the Funeral Oration. By focusing almost exclusively on the two most idiosyncratic political traditions, that of 'egalitarian' Sparta and post-Cleisthenic democratic Athens, historians have overlooked this fascinating case of a city performing its communal historical past (as opposed to its mythical foundation) in a ritual context.

Space precludes here a detailed reading of the ode.[69] Its ritual context is a festival in honour of the eponymous hero Abderos. There is no reason to suppose that he was celebrated as the city's founder, as is alleged in a tradition attested only later.[70] His function emerges quite clearly from the text itself. He is a warrior, wearing a bronze breastplate (v. 1). He is invoked to protect the army of the Abderites, who rejoice in horses, in the final war (v. 104). He is the son of Poseidon (v. 2), exactly as the horses of Abderite horsemen are said to be Ποσειδάνιον γένος ('offspring of Poseidon', v. 41) in the community's self-description. This heroic figure has been seen by some modern scholars as hardly compatible with that known from later mythology, where Abderos is a boy loved by Heracles, and killed by the man-eating horses of Diomedes. It has even been argued that the Abderite Abderos had nothing to do with this later ἐρώμενος of Heracles.[71] From a typological point of view, however, the two are really two sides of the same coin. Abderos is the young soldier, or, more precisely in the case of Abdera,

---

[67] Cf. fr. 109, Paean 2.48, 4.53, 9.15, and 1.1–4, where the word is lacking, but the concept is clear; Dith. 3.3 (not necessarily a Corinthian poem, as it is often stated!) and the prosodion *Paean. 14.13. On stasis and the dithyramb, cf. Wilson 2003b.

[68] For a recent assessment of the historical and archaeological evidence for Abdera, cf. Veligianni-Terzi 2004: 37–46.

[69] A stimulating and very useful treatment of communal poetry from the point of view of its performance context is to be found in Stehle 1997: 119–69. My emphasis is somewhat different from hers: as I argue below, Pindar's text does not suggest that the performers as such may be singled out as particularly significant in poems such as Paean 2 and 4; Lefkowitz: 1963 and 1991, on the other hand, sees these poems as exclusively focused on the chorus' self-description.

[70] Abderos is presented as founder of the city only in Ps. Scymnus 667–8 (who, as I argue in D'Alessio, in progress, may perhaps be based on Ephorus). Malkin 1987, Rutherford 2001 (more hesitantly), and Veligianni-Terzi 2004: 40–1 take for granted or argue that he must have been the city founder also for Pindar.

[71] Cf. Raven 1967: 293–4; Rutherford 2001: 265.

158 GIOVAN BATTISTA D'ALESSIO

horseman, killed in action, a typical heroic figure connected in ritual and myth with Heracles.[72]

It is a common mythical narrative pattern that Heracles' adolescent companions meet a premature death. They are portrayed as his ἐρώμενοι, as his younger relatives, even as his sons, and are sometime celebrated in funerary rituals, which are crucial for the articulation of military life in the ancient Greek city. Similar rites are attested in Thebes, where external traditions knew of the killing of Heracles' innocent children by the father himself, while Pindar and Theban cultic practice imagine them as 'eight bronze-clad dead', χαλκοαρᾶν ὀκτὼ θανόντων (*Isth.* 4.63). Important civic festivals and athletic competitions took place in their honour at the Herakleion outside the Elektrai Gates.[73] It was the focal point for rites involving the Theban army, as part of the community. It has been argued that it may have been at this festival that tribute was paid to the fallen Theban warriors.[74] Iolaos, another young companion of Heracles, is a central figure in the Theban festival, which may have been known also as Iolaeia. It was at his burial place that Theban soldiers of the ἱερὸς λόχος swore the famous oath between the ἐραστής and the ἐρώμενος (Arist. fr. 97 A Rose = 1008 Gigon).[75] Another place where a festival in honour of Heracles plays a crucial rôle as a venue for articulating the city into its military structure is much closer to Abdera. From a fourth-century inscription we know that on Thasos the sons of fallen soldiers received a complete panoply from the polemarchs at the local Herakleia. It has also been argued that on this occasion athletic competitions in honour of the fallen warriors were held, but this is more doubtful.[76] Athletic contests in honour of Abderos are known only from a much later source, Philostratus *Imag.* 2.25.2, who attributes their foundation to Heracles. Luckily enough, however, we do happen to know that in the early fifth century the Herakleia were among the most important civic festivals both at Abdera and at its mother-city Teos. They were, together with the Dia and the Anthesteria,

---

[72] Dougherty 1994b: 209 suggests that the myth may 'predicate the founding of Abdera upon Greco-Thracian hostilities'. As I argue below, the myth has more to do with a ritual (and mythical) pattern typical of military integration within the community.

[73] Cf. Schachter 1986: 14–30; Krummen 1990: 59–79. The site of the Herakleion is currently being excavated by V. Aravantinos.

[74] Cf. Krummen 1990: 71–4; Schachter 1999: 173.

[75] The festival in honour of Iolaos and Heracles in Sicilian Agyrion presents similar features. For this and other examples of such a mythical and ritual pattern, cf. Jourdan-Annequin 1989: 372–5.

[76] Cf. Pouilloux 1954: 371–9, Salviat 1958: 228–32, 254–9, Sokolowski 1962: 122–3, no. 64, Bergquist 1973: 80, n. 170, Pouilloux 1974: 314, Jourdan-Annequin 1989: 368–9, Krummen 1990: 71 ff. Salviat argues that the contests belong not to the Herakleia, but to the Sōteria, which were also in honour of Heracles, and that the cult of the Ἀγαθοί (the fallen warriors) belongs to the Heroxeinia, though he stresses the similarity to the ritual banquets of the Herakleia: the inscription on the Ἀγαθοί, however, mentions only the Herakleia. Cf. also Frisone 2000: 136.

Defining local identities in Greek lyric poetry

the festivals in which the public curses regulating political life were regularly recited.[77] I think it may be safely argued that Abderos at Abdera played a rôle similar to that of Iolaos and the Alkaidai at Thebes, and, perhaps, to that of Perinthos, another companion of Heracles, in Thracian Perinthos, where other Herakleia were celebrated.[78]

This premise is important for placing Abdera's self-representation in its probable ritual context. A typical venue for the shaping of civic identity is that of the celebration of fallen soldiers: this is famously true for the Athenian *Funeral Oration*, which was recited on the occasion of games in honour of the Ἀγαθοί.[79] There is no evidence that this was actually the case also at Abdera. Celebrations in honour of Abderos are, however, typologically, celebrations in honour of the prototype of the young fallen warrior, and *Paean* 2 has very much in common with the Athenian *epitaphios logos*. Both are obviously indebted to the tradition of Tyrtaean elegy, but the historical context and the articulation of the texts invite a closer comparison between Athens and Abdera. The great influence of Tyrtaeus on Athenian patriotic oratory has been the object of an important study by Werner Jaeger, and finds its own place in Loraux's monumental work on this subject. The relationship with Pindar's poetry, on the other hand, has more often been seen as a contrastive one, with the discourse of 'the poet, invested with a divine, all-powerful mission, who must account only to the Muses' strongly opposed to that of the communal voice of the *Funeral Oration*.[80]

It is, however, precisely in the communicative strategy that a poem such as *Paean* 2 emerges as the closest predecessor of the Athenian *Funeral Oration*. The voice of the chorus is not that of the *maître de vérité*, nor is it that of a particular group of performers. It presents itself as the voice of the polis, reconstructing its own past.[81] In both cases the city sees itself as a city of

[77] Cf. Meiggs-Lewis, 30, B 31–4 and *SEG* 31 (1981), n. 985.

[78] On Perinthos, cf. *RE* 19 (1937), 808 and Wilamowitz's conjecture in sch. Ap. Rhod. *Arg.* 1.1207b; Veligianni-Terzi 2004: 50–1.

[79] Cf. Hornblower 1991: 315 (*ad* 2.46.1). Amandry 1971: 612–26 tentatively argues that the Herakleia at Marathon may also have been held in honour of the fallen soldiers. On the issue, cf., most recently, Jung 2006: 28–38 and 61–6 (sceptical on the identification).

[80] Loraux 1986 recurrently stresses the view that the tradition of the Athenian funerary speech is antithetical to the 'Pindaric' one: cf. Loraux 1986: 53 on the 'Pindaric' voice of the 'master of praise', that privileges individuality and myth vs. the Athenian communal discourse, which privileges anonymity and history; this latter definition, however, applies, almost exactly, to the Pindaric *Paean* 2 as well. Other points of contrast stressed by Loraux (cf. 1986: 236–7 with 434, n. 87, quoting Detienne 1967: 59 = 1996: 75) do not apply to 'Pindaric' discourse in general, as the example of *Paean* 2 eloquently shows. More relevant is Loraux's observation of the lack of any supernatural presence in the Athenian *epitaphios logos*, as this may be effectively contrasted with the reference to Hecate in *Paean* 2: for the Athenian attitude to the issue, cf., however, the divine epiphanies mentioned in A. *Persians*. On Tyrtaeus' rôle, cf. Jaeger 1932.

[81] Stehle's idea (1997: 130–1) that in v. 28 'the chorus-members designate themselves female (since the word *city* is female in Greek)' is based on a misunderstanding: νεόπολις in νεόπολίς εἰμι (translated

160 GIOVAN BATTISTA D'ALESSIO

soldiers (in Abdera more specifically as a city of cavalrymen). In both cases, the reconstruction of the past is functional to a pragmatic purpose: fostering internal cohesion in face of impending new military confrontation. The motifs are the same, though focus and perspective considerably diverge. Nevertheless, Pindar's Abderite paean does not find a place in any recent study of the prehistory of the *Funeral Oration*.[82]

Common elements are the praise of the land and that of the ancestors. The latter, in the case of Abdera, seems to be limited to the last few generations, just as in Pericles' *Funeral Speech*. Later specimens of the Athenian genre devote a much larger space to the mythical antecedents. Another common feature is the comparison between the capacities of the citizens and those of the enemy. In the case of the paean, this part is almost totally lost in a lacuna in the papyrus, though its general content may partly be recovered thanks to the scholia on v. 41. There are even some more or less close verbal similarities between the paean and the funeral speech in Thucydides. When Pericles illustrates the feats of the previous generation (2.36), he remarks how (οἱ πατέρες ἡμῶν) κτησάμενοι (. . .) πρὸς οἷς ἐδέξαντο ὅσην ἔχομεν ἀρχὴν οὐκ ἀπόνως ἡμῖν τοῖς νῦν προσκατέλιπον ('our fathers . . . having acquired, not without toil, in addition to what they had inherited, the empire we rule now, have left it to us of the present generation'). This closely matches the section of lines 57–70 in our paean.[83] Note, in particular, τοὶ (sc. our fathers) σὺν πολέμωι κτησάμ[ενοι] χθόνα πολύδωρον, ὄλ[βον] ἐγκατέθηκαν ('our fathers . . . having acquired through war a land rich of gifts, accumulated prosperity'), followed by the description of their πόνοι: [βαρεῖα μὲν] ἐπέπεσε μοῖρα ('[harsh] fate fell upon them'), τλάντων ('having suffered'), πονή[σ]αις ('after the effort'). Verbal similarity in this case should not necessarily suggest direct dependence. Both passages belong together with the descriptions of the conquest of Messenia by 'the fathers of our fathers' in Tyrtaeus 5 West, and the motif of the sufferings of the fathers being crowned by their final success recurs also in *Ol.* 2.8–11 about Akragas, (note καμόντες οἳ πολλὰ θυμῶι, 'having much suffered in their hearts'). Another verbal similarity may perhaps be detected in the passage on the disappearance of φθόνος ('envy') towards the dead of past generations (vv. 55–6), to which Thuc. 2.45.1 has been compared:[84]

by Stehle as 'I am a new city': rather 'I belong to a new city', or 'My city is new'), is not a noun, but an adjective, and is no more feminine than δικαιόπολις is.

[82] Cf. for example, more recently, Porciani 2001: in particular 101–17, on the novelty of the *Funeral Oration* for the evolution of an historical discourse, where no mention is made of *Paean 2*.

[83] The two passages, however, are not quoted in the relevant commentaries on the two texts.

[84] Cf. Méautis 1962: 452; Bona 1988: 42–3. I am not certain, however, that the two passages carry the same implication, as in the Pindaric passage another interpretation may be that the envy was that 'of the dead towards each other'.

Defining local identities in Greek lyric poetry   161

φθόνος γὰρ τοῖς ζῶσι πρὸς τὸ ἀντίπαλον, τὸ δὲ μὴ ἐμποδὼν ἀναν-
ταγωνίστωι εὐνοίαι τετίμηται ('for those who are living there is envy
against one's opponent, but whoever is out of the way receives honours
with benevolence and without rivalry').

Leaving aside the issue of possible verbal contacts, the most striking
similarity is that of structure and function.[85] The whole poem can be seen
under many respects as the Abderite equivalent of the Athenian *epitaphios
logos*. Another remarkable similarity, long taken as being a peculiar feature
of the Athenian *Funeral Speech*, is the fact that no individual is singled out
or named when the city is praised.

The differences too can be instructive. (1) The *epitaphios logos* was
pronounced by an Athenian citizen. The paean was sung by a chorus
of Abderites, but its composition had been entrusted to a foreign poet.
Some of the extant or fragmentary Athenian funeral speeches are the work
of non-Athenian writers, like Lysias and Gorgias; the speech in Plato's
Menexenus is even presented as the work of a non-Athenian *woman*. It is
doubtful, however, that any of them was ever delivered at the public festival.
(2) The ritual context is conspicuously inscribed in the text of the paean,
while it is usually obliterated in the Athenian speeches. (3) The paean gives
prominent space to an obscure oracle on military matters, a feature alien
to the Athenian speeches, but conspicuous in Tyrtaeus' *Eunomia*, where
not only the Delphic 'constitutional' oracle was quoted (fr. 4 West = 1[b]
G-P), but also θεοπροπ[and μαντεῖαι occur in the lacunose context of fr.
2.2–4 West (2 G-P), while the expression τερ]άεσσι Διός ('prodigies sent
by Zeus') appears in the Berlin papyrus, fr. 18.7 West (10.7 G-P), in a section describing the moment preceding an actual fight. (4) In the Abderite
poem there is no space, of course, for the Athenian imperial perspective, or
for the idealised self-portrait of its civic life, though the mention of αἰδώς
('shame/respect') and εὐβουλία ('good counsel') in vv. 50–1 can be compared to the passage on the δέος ('fear/reverence'), which leads to obedience
to the laws, and the ὁμολογουμένη αἰσχύνη ('acknowledged shame') in
Thucydides 2.37.3. The Athenian *logos*, in presenting a united city, covers up
any sign of internal divisions. In Pindar's paean, too, the voice of the chorus
is presented as that of a unified city: it does not efface, however, traces of the
internal negotiation which lies behind it.[86] The relevant passage is largely

---

[85] Hornblower 2004: 181–2, has argued that Thucydides, with his biographical Thracian connections,
may have been familiar with this particular poem, though he does not address at all the problem of
its relevance to Pericles' Funeral Speech. *Paean 2* is possibly to be dated later than the institution
of the *Funeral Speech* at Athens, and it may be argued that either the Abderites or Pindar had been
influenced by it. Neither hypothesis, however, is necessary for my interpretation.
[86] Cf. also Stehle 1997: 129 and 132.

162   GIOVAN BATTISTA D'ALESSIO

lost in a lacuna in the papyrus. The scholia on this passage are particularly obscure, but they make clear that a situation of στάσις was mentioned and that it had to do with the problem of citizenship attribution. I have argued elsewhere that the two sets of the so called *Dirae Teiae* may be of some help in trying to guess what was actually going on in early fifth-century Abdera.[87] What is important for my present argument, however, is that the issue was mentioned at all. Conventional as is the language of choral lyric at Abdera, it seems to have been less opaque than that of the rhetoric of Athenian democracy. (5) Another difference, probably not unrelated to our last item, may be seen in the large space the poem gives to the Abderite cavalry. This may be due to the rôle Abderos obviously had in this partic-ular context. It is likely, however, that such apparent hierarchy within the Abderite army may have also reflected the internal social articulation of the polis, where cavalrymen seem to have played a prominent rôle.[88]

Ceos

Pindar's Abderite paean is not likely to have been a unique case. It rather belongs to the same kind of public discourse of civic self-representation, which can be traced back to Tyrtaeus' elegy, and forward to the Athenian *Funeral Speech* and beyond. The medium changes, from communal elegy, to choral song, to public oratory: each of them was effective in its own context. Other Pindaric poems fall into the same category, and offer a welcome glimpse of the ways cities other than Athens portrayed themselves. Other poems of this kind must have left no trace. At a later date, Callimachus' second *Hymn* belongs in this tradition.

Another fairly well-preserved Pindaric paean is entirely centred on com-munal self-representation. Though sharing some important features with the Abderite paean, *Paean* 4, composed for the Ceians, shows how a great poet might have been able to deal with similar stock-motifs in radically different ways when facing different local contexts: from this point of view,

---

[87] Cf. D'Alessio 1992b.
[88] We may even toy with the idea that the paean might have been performed by a group of young Abderite cavalrymen. On cavalry in the Ionian cities of Asia Minor and Thrace, cf. Worley 1994: 36 (Colophon, Thasos). Cavalry was very important for Abdera's Thracian neighbours, as was apparently stated in the poem itself (sch. *ad* v. 41); for Thracian mounted arms, cf. Spence 1993: 62 and n. 113, with reference to Xen. *Anab.* 7.3.40 (ἱππεῖς τεθωρακισμένοι: cf. Abderos χαλκοθώραξ in Pindar). The figure of Abderos as a hero of the cavalrymen may also have played a pivotal rôle in interacting with Thracian religious imagery, where the, later ubiquitous, horseman hero originated: cf. Kazarow 1938 (and already Perdrizet 1910: 20 and n. 3, who established a connection to the hero Rhesus); Venedikov 1976. The material is being collected in the series of the *Corpus Cultus Equitis Thracii* (*CCET*), Leiden 1979–, which, however, does not yet cover the North-Aegean zone. The first iconographic attestation in Abdera itself seems to go back to the third century: cf. Avezou and Picard 1913: 118–21.

Defining local identities in Greek lyric poetry

Abdera and Ceos have been better served than Nephelokokkygia. *Paean* 2, just like the Athenian epitaph, seems to have addressed in the very first place an internal audience. Several obscure references that trouble modern readers would have posed no problem to the Abderite citizens. I have argued elsewhere that *Paean* 4 was meant for a performance abroad, belonging to the same category of Delian prosodia we have already examined.[89] Other scholars, including Ian Rutherford, have opted for a main performance in Ceos.[90] Anyway, unlike the Abderite poem, *Paean* 4 is certainly accessible also for a non-Ceian audience. There is no space here for a close reading, and I shall dwell only on some interesting features.

After the initial section, which places the poem in its performance context and is largely lacunose, a self-description of the territory follows in both poems. Physical details of its landscape apart, the Abderite poem entirely focuses on its peculiar relation to its mother city and on its exploitation of the territory, which leads to its military history. The description of the physical features of the Aegean island, on the other hand, is charged with evaluative overtones, based on the opposition between 'local', marked as poor and positive, and 'foreign', marked as rich, and negative. After a reference to agricultural production and husbandry,[91] the Ceian chorus focuses only on its Μοῖσα, their musical tradition, and their successful involvement in pan-Hellenic games: both elements are topical in such contexts. No space is devoted to a narrative of the island's recent history, which takes the best part of *Paean* 2. Instead, two mythical examples develop the motif of the preference for local poverty over foreign wealth. The second example provides a subtle equivalent for the first-person historical narrative of *Paean* 2, which projects the foundational events of the island's identity into Minoan time. The chorus, who gives voice to the whole community, quotes with approval the narrative of the mythical Ceian hero Euxantius, son of Minos, who refused to leave the poor island in order to inherit his portion of wealthy Crete, his father's estate. The two speeches, the one of the civic chorus and the one of the chorus impersonating (and impersonated by) Euxantius, mirror each other in many respects. In this case, too, the issue of στάσις and internal stability is crucial. The chorus invokes ἡσυχία ('tranquillity') for the island (7) while praising their austere lot.[92] Euxantius remarks that, by renouncing the wealth of Crete for poor

---

[89] D'Alessio 1994: 64.   [90] Rutherford 2000.

[91] Interesting information about husbandry techniques on the island is provided by Aeschylides *ap.* Ael. *NA* 16.32.

[92] I have to rectify what I wrote in D'Alessio 1991: 91; on closer inspection of the papyrus with the binocular microscope, the tip of the lower end of the sigma is preserved, and the reading ἡ]συχίαν is virtually certain.

164 GIOVAN BATTISTA D'ALESSIO

Ceos, he did not have a share in sorrows and strife: οὐ πενθέων ἔλαχον, <οὐ> στασίων ('but I did not partake in sorrows, nor in strife', 53). This is not only a deft rhetorical strategy for extolling Ceos before other famous cities (Babylon and Crete are mentioned), in spite of its marginal economic importance.[93] The message has also, perhaps more importantly, an internal target. In a small community with limited resources, the drive towards the acquisition of new wealth may be dangerously subversive: while praising Ceos as a whole for its being content with little, its citizens are subtly persuaded to be content with their *status quo*, a favourite Pindaric motif.[94] It is easy to overlook how fragile internal stability may have been in a community such as Ceos. Several sources (ultimately going back to the Aristotelian *Constitution of the Ceians*, composed perhaps just a little more than a century after Pindar's paean) offer a striking piece of information on the ways internal stability on the island was preserved:

προσέταττε γὰρ, ὡς ἔοικεν, ὁ νόμος τοὺς ὑπὲρ ἑξήκοντα ἔτη γεγονότας κωνειάζεσθαι τοῦ διαρκεῖν τοῖς ἄλλοις τὴν τροφήν

the law, it seems, ordered those who were older than sixty years to drink hemlock, so that there may be enough food for the rest (Strabo 10.5.6).[95]

Perhaps we should not read this curious passage as evidence for the actual circumstances in fifth-century Ceos (this was most effectively done in a wonderful poem by Giovanni Pascoli, *I vecchi di Ceo*, inspired by the recent discovery of the Bacchylides papyrus), though it certainly can help us to place the rhetorical strategy of *Paean 4* in its historical context.[96]

Euxantius' speech is interrupted by a lacuna in the papyrus, and seems to have eventually linked Ceos' Minoan past with its subsequent history. In its preserved part it is an effective piece of patriotic oratory. Once again, communal lyric poetry can be seen as the closest antecedent of civic rhetoric. It is by looking in this direction that we may solve an interpretative problem of the text. Euxantius tells how the gods had destroyed the whole island, saving only his mother's household. This gives the hero the reason why he cannot abandon the island (47–8):

---

[93] The whole poem can be read in rhetorical opposition to colonisation stories: cf. D'Alessio, in progress.

[94] Cf. e.g. *Paean* 1.1–4.

[95] Strabo had just quoted Men. fr. 879 K-A ('there is a good law of the Ceians, Phanias, according to which he who is unable to live well should not live miserably'). Other sources are Heracl. Lemb. *Excerpt. Const.* = Aristot. *Const.* 77 Gigon, Ael. *VH* 3.37, Strab. 11.517, Steph. Byz. *s.v.* Ἰουλίς, Val. Max. 2.6.8.

[96] On poverty and the islands, within the same historical context, L. Kurke reminds me of the famous reply of the Andrians (another member of the Delian league) to the Athenians in Hdt. 8.111.

Defining local identities in Greek lyric poetry 165

ἔπειτα πλούτου πειρῶν μακάρων τ' ἐπιχώριον
τεθμὸν π[ά]μπαν ἐρῆμον ἀπωσάμενος
μέγαν ἄλλοθι κλᾶρον ἔχω;

shall I then, in pursuit of wealth and <u>thrusting away</u>
<u>into utter abandonment the local *tethmos* of the blessed ones,</u>
have a great estate elsewhere?

In the first part of this sentence the reason for leaving Ceos is presented as a drive towards wealth, which, in the whole poem, as we have seen, is marked as negative and dangerous. The second part is usually not properly understood. Most critics understand the τεθμός of the blessed ones as a 'decision' or 'decree' of the gods regarding the island. It is not clear in what sense Euxantius might have thrust this decree into desolation, and various explanations have been sought. Only Farnell, while taking into consideration this same explanation, had tentatively advanced an alternative interpretation, according to which the τεθμός of the blessed ones would be 'the rites in honour of the blessed ones'.[97] This is a meaning the word has elsewhere in Pindar (cf. *Ol.* 6.69, 13.40, *Nem.* 10.33) and it is the meaning required here. The appeal not to abandon the local cult places is an important motif of civic rhetoric, which appears several times in later Athenian literature. One of the most relevant passages is the speech of the Plataeans to the Spartans in Thucydides 3.58:

ἀποβλέψατε γὰρ ἐς πατέρων τῶν ὑμετέρων θήκας, οὓς ἀποθανόντας ὑπὸ Μήδων καὶ ταφέντας ἐν τῆι ἡμετέραι ἐτιμῶμεν κατὰ ἔτος ἕκαστον δημοσίαι ἐσθήμασί τε καὶ τοῖς ἄλλοις νομίμοις (. . .) ὑμεῖς δὲ εἰ κτενεῖτε ἡμᾶς καὶ χώραν τὴν Πλαταιίδα Θηβαΐδα ποιήσετε, τί ἄλλο ἢ ἐν πολεμίαι τε καὶ παρὰ τοῖς αὐθένταις πατέρας τοὺς ὑμετέρους καὶ ξυγγενεῖς ἀτίμους γερῶν ὧν νῦν ἴσχουσι καταλείψετε; πρὸς δὲ καὶ γῆν ἐν ἧι ἠλευθερώθησαν οἱ Ἕλληνες δουλώσετε, <u>ἱερά τε θεῶν οἷς εὐξάμενοι Μήδων ἐκράτησαν ἐρημοῦτε</u> καὶ θυσίας τὰς πατρίους τῶν ἐσσαμένων καὶ κτισάντων ἀφαιρήσεσθε.

Look at the tombs of your fathers, who were killed by the Medes and were buried in our land, and whom we honour every year with public ceremonies, presenting them with clothes and other ritual offerings (. . .) But you, if you kill us and make the land of Plataea under Theban control, what else will you be doing if not abandoning in an enemy country and to the hands of their murderers your fathers and relatives, depriving them of the honours that they receive now? Even more, you are going to enslave the country where the Greeks conquered freedom, <u>and you are making desert the temples of the gods to whom you addressed your prayers</u>

---

[97] Cf. Farnell 1932: 398. This interpretation has found very few followers. For other interpretations of the passage, cf. Rutherford 2001: 290. According to Call. fr. 75.33–7 (whose main source is the fifth-century Ceian historian Xenomedes) the Euxantiads were hereditary priests of Zeus Ikmios.

before you won over the Medes, and deprive your ancestral sacrifices of those who founded and instituted them.[98]

The same motif appears in the allegations against Leocrates of Lycurgus (38):

καὶ εἰς τοσοῦτον προδοσίας ἦλθεν, ὥστε κατὰ τὴν αὐτοῦ προαίρεσιν ἔρημοι μὲν ἦσαν οἱ νεῴ [τῶν ἱερέων], ἔρημοι δὲ αἱ φυλακαὶ τῶν τειχῶν, ἐξελέλειπτο δὲ ἡ πόλις καὶ ἡ χώρα

and he got to such an extreme of treachery that, had things gone according to his design, the temples would have been deserted, the defence of the walls would have been deserted, and the city and its territory would have been abandoned.

Euxantius' behaviour is the opposite of that of Leocrates, who, according to Lycurgus, did in fact abandon his fatherland in order to pursue great wealth abroad. The presence of the same motif also helps to explain a passage in Aristophanes, *Plut.* 445–8, where Chremylus is exhorting Blepsidemus not to abandon the god:

καὶ μὴν λέγω, δεινότατον ἔργον παρὰ πολὺ
ἔργων ἁπάντων ἐργασόμεθ', εἰ τὸν θεὸν
ἔρημον ἀπολιπόντε ποι φευξούμεθα
τηνδὶ δεδιότε, μηδὲ διαμαχούμεθα.

I say that we'll be doing by far the most terrible
thing ever done, if we run away
leaving the god abandoned
because we are frightened of her (Poverty), and won't fight till the end.

This is particularly close to Euxantius' rhetorical strategy. The general context is, however, ironically, completely subverted. While in Pindar the pursuit of wealth is conducive to the abandonment of the local cults of the gods, in Aristophanes the god who should not be abandoned is Wealth, Ploutos himself.

CONCLUSIONS

Public poetic performance, as it emerges from this survey, was one of the privileged media for Greek cities to give voice to their 'identities' from the archaic age onward. Even communities that did not enjoy a properly independent political status till a later age, as in the case of Messenia, felt the necessity of establishing the foundational memory of their identity by

---

[98] For a vivid depiction of a city whose local cult places have been abandoned (ἐρημία and cognate terms are used) by men and gods after its destruction, cf. Eur. *Tro.* 15–16, 26–7, 95–6.

Defining local identities in Greek lyric poetry

linking it to a purportedly ancient choral song. The practice of providing ancient and new cities with 'ancient' or new songs expressing their 'identities' remains alive and kicking well into the classical and the Hellenistic periods.

More easily than other available media (such as, for example, dances, ritual enactments, or the visual arts), 'lyric' poetry provided the possibility to articulate local identities within an explicit and rhetorically effective first-person discourse, in which every member of the political community was invited to recognise his own voice. The most common venues for the staging of such a discourse were communal choral performances, but in some contexts, as in the case of Tyrtaeus' elegies at Sparta, this seems to have happened in a particular sympotic setting. The Athenian *Funeral Speech*, as I have argued here, shares several features with this lyric tradition, and can well be seen as belonging to it, while modifying it in some important respects (not least that of performance).

More often than not, local communities seem to have entrusted the task of self-representation to foreign poets, as if the divided polis could find a communal voice more easily through external authoritative figures than partisan members of its élite. On the other hand, it was exactly the circulation of songs and poets that contributed, in its turn, to the shaping and the spreading of a common supra-local background for the individual patterns of political self-representation. Throughout this paper I have used the term 'self-representation' without qualifications. It should be clear by now that several are needed. The lyric discourse of communal 'self-presentation' in the period covered in my survey can be seen very rarely as the product of a spontaneous narrative internally originated within the concerned group. Its structure and *topoi* are the results of a complex network of relationships, which includes issues of stability within the community itself and a confrontational aspect, by which a community is defined against other ones. This latter aspect includes both analogy ('commonplaces') and opposition (by which a tradition is defined as antagonistic to another one). Several factors have contributed to the formation of a common language for self-presentation of the different *poleis*. Meeting at supra-local festivals was an important one. The circulation of wandering poets and continuously re-performed songs was certainly another.

CHAPTER 7

Wandering poetry, 'travelling' music: Timotheus' muse and some case-studies of shifting cultural identities

Lucia Prauscello

From Homer onwards, the composition, performance and dissemination of poetry are inextricably linked to stories of migration and wandering, rejection and assimilation.[1] Welcomed or stigmatised as wandering poets may have been, the process of self-definition of many Greek local communities is in part also the history of different responses, in terms of integration or resilience, towards *poeti vaganti*, their poetry and their music. To sketch a map of the physical journeys of travelling poets is also, to a certain extent, to trace the mental routes by means of which different conceptualisations of 'Greekness' and other, competing forms of cultural identity took shape.[2] The aim of the present paper is to investigate one of these routes, focusing on the various ways of exploitation and re-interpretation on the part of Greek micro-cultures to which the songs of a *poeta vagante* of iconic status such as Timotheus of Miletus may be open. In doing so, I shall be concerned with whether and to what extent re-performances, both those historically attested and those merely fictionalised,[3] and musical re-settings, staged at times and places different from the original ones, may have affected the generic boundaries of the text itself and its reception among the intended audience.

A dynamic tension between tradition and innovation, the latter often being disguised as the re-emergence of a past open to varying degrees of

---

I should like to thank all the participants in the Cambridge conference for inspiring comments on the oral version of this contribution and especially the following for having so generously criticised and, I hope, improved the paper in its final written version: G. B. D'Alessio, A. H. Griffiths, R. Hunter, L. Kurke, D. J. Mastronarde, I. C. Rutherford. A major debt of gratitude is wholeheartedly owed to I. C. Rutherford and R. Hunter for inviting me to deliver this paper at the *Poeti Vaganti* conference.

[1] See Graziosi 2002: 35–6 and Cassio 2003.
[2] Cf. Martin 1992: 19 on Hesiod's 'metanastic' stance and his reception among later Athenian audiences.
[3] As we shall see, even misrepresentations (Timotheus performing the *Birthpangs of Semele* at the Spartan festival of the Eleusinian Demeter) may indeed be as significant as 'true' ones, at least in terms of the social imagery of the recipient.

re-appropriation,[4] frames the history of Greek music from its earliest time onwards. Far from imposing once and for all an ultimate and straightforward teleological model on the meandering paths of song, the Greeks seem to have considered the inherent fluidity across geographic and temporal boundaries triggered by this process of transmission and reception as a valuable tool by means of which to assert (and differentiate) cultural identities.

If history itself is a 'heuristic discourse' engendering distinctions between 'us' and 'others', past and present,[5] music or, to put the issue at its strongest from the very outset, the virtually open-ended process of inventing (and constantly re-fashioning) a self-reflexive narrative about music as conveyor of a broader set of underlying cultural practices and beliefs out of which musical performance itself is produced, may likewise be rightly considered as a prominent feature in the rhetoric of self-construction of Greek cultural identities, local and supra-local as well.[6]

It is within these guidelines that special attention will be paid here to the intriguing case represented by Timotheus' lyric poetry and the contested process of cultural re-appropriation (sometimes by way of rejection) which his poetry (and music) underwent in the Hellenistic and early imperial period on the part of different local communities – in Sparta, Arcadia and Crete.[7] The contested nature of Timotheus' poetry from his own times onwards, the disruptive novelty of his music, his own strongly appropriative strategy in relation to the past citharodic tradition[8] and, to quote Wilson's formulation, his 'poetic and political self-positioning' at the end of the *Persians* (his most ambitious and pan-Hellenic poem)[9] as an anti-Spartan

---

[4] Cf. D'Angour 1997: 337 n. 42 on the importance of musical history as a theoretical paradigm for a proper understanding of the notion of innovation in Greek culture.

[5] See Kennedy 1993: 7 and more recently Flower 2002 (primarily focused on Spartan history, but with valuable general observations on the Hobsbawmian concept of 'invention of tradition').

[6] See most recently Murray and Wilson 2004: 1–6, Csapo 2004: 235–48 (on the social and political topography of ancient 'musical' utopianism) and Wilson 2004. On the ideological value ascribed to diverging musical genealogies and *aitia*, often by-products of a contested negotiation between competing political strands within the social body of the polis itself, see Martin 2003. For the role of music in shaping civic identities at home and abroad, see Rutherford 2004a.

[7] The principal texts are as follows: Spartans: the so-called 'forged' Laconian decree transmitted by Boeth. *De inst. mus.* 1.1; Arcadians: Polyb. 4.19–21, Plut. *Philop.* 11, Paus. 8.50.3; Cretans: *ICret* V.viii.11 (Knossos) and xxiv.1 (Priansos).

[8] Cf. the much-discussed sphragis of the *Persians* (*PMG* 791. ll. 202–36), where Timotheus criticises Spartan musical conservatism and promotes his own poetry as the 'true' heir of the most celebrated lyric poets of the tradition, Orpheus and Terpander; see Nieddu 1993: 526, Hunter 2001: 244 and Wilson 2004: 204–6.

[9] For the generally pan-Hellenic veneer of the *Persians* see recently Hall 1994. The pan-Greek aspirations of the poem do not preclude, however, a more specific Athenian interest, cf. Wilson 2004: 305–6 and van Minnen 1997.

'democratic citharodos in tune with the finest tradition of Athenian democratic culture'[10] are all features that make Timotheus' poetic experience a
privileged test-bed for the present analysis.

As we shall see, the different outcomes of this process of cultural
re-negotiation coalescing around Timotheus' poetry find their common
ground, first of all, in the poet's widely recognised status already during his own lifetime as a professional travelling performer. Timotheus,
it has been noted, represents one of the most symptomatic cases of a literary figure who crossed and re-crossed the alleged boundaries between
'poeti vaganti' and 'literary poets'.[11] Explicit emphasis on a cash-based relationship with local communities (the 1,000 shekels won in a poetic contest advertised by the Ephesians for the (re)-dedication of their temple of
Artemis)[12] and his exile-like wandering through various places (culminat-
ing in his death in Macedonia)[13] are features around which the subsequent
Nachleben of the icon 'Timotheus' revolves. Mapping the different cultural patterns into which Timotheus' poetry has variously been framed
and customised in antiquity is thus all the more interesting if we keep
in mind the fact that already from an early time a somewhat uncom-
fortable phenomenon of 'displacement' has been traditionally associated
with Timotheus' fictionalised *persona*. One may think of the contrasting reactions of integration and rejection the Milesian poet experienced
from the Athenian audience,[14] the polemic with the musically conservative Spartan tradition (the episode of the cutting of the strings by the
ephors at the Carnean games),[15] his link with the foreign 'Asian cithara'[16]
and the somewhat obscure *magadis*,[17] and the late Macedonian connection

---

[10] Wilson 2004: 306. On the pun on the Spartan political keyword εὐνομία in *PMG* 791, l. 240, re-
functionalised by Timotheus in a polemically anti-Spartan sense, see Bassett 1931: 163, van Minnen
1997: 253 n. 38, Csapo 2004: 240 n. 133. Cf. also Hansen 1984: 137–8 and more diffusely van Minnen
1997: 251–7 on the political attitude displayed by Timotheus towards Sparta in the *Persians*.

[11] See Cairns 1992: 15–16.

[12] Cf. Macrob. *Sat.* 5.22.4ff. quoting Alexander Aetolus' *Musae* (fr. 4 Magnelli): for a thorough discussion see Brussich 1990 and Magnelli 1999 *ad loc.*

[13] On this tradition see Hordern 2002: 5.

[14] Cf. Eur. *TGrF* T 87a = Satyr. *Vit. Eur. P. Oxy.* 1176 fr. 39 col. xxii: Euripides comforting Timotheus
after he was booed on the Athenian stage. On Timotheus being rejected and ridiculed in Athens as
an outsider, see Dobrov and Urios-Aparisi 1995: 148.

[15] Attested, with a varying range of contrasting details, at least since the second century BC; see
Artemon of Cassandrea, *FHG* IV. 342 (= Athen. 14.636e). For the several adapted versions of this
anecdote (Plut. *Agis* 10, *Apophth. Lac.* 220c, *Inst. Lac.* 238c) see below.

[16] For the 'New Music' overtones evoked by this association see Wilson 2004: 305 n. 82, who rightly
claims that this aspect is not to be considered as mutually exclusive of a ritual interpretation (emphasised by Cassio 2000).

[17] Athen. 14.636e (quoting Artemon of Cassandrea: see n. 15 above). For the nature of the *magadis*,
already a matter of debate in Aristoxenus' time, see Barker 1988, 1998 and Rocconi 2003: 26 n. 117.

Wandering poetry, 'travelling' music 171

with Archelaus, perhaps favoured by the problematic relationship between Athens and Miletus in the last part of the fifth century BC (Miletus joined the revolt of Athenian allies in 412).[18] Finally, Timotheus' apparently uninterrupted fame throughout antiquity (at least until the third century AD)[19] allows one to test how these overlapping layers of anecdote and belief may have affected the way of preserving or altering the identity of a text over time.

Many interlocking questions immediately arise. How may we account for the process of transformation from Timotheus the radical and thought-provoking innovator (apparently still perceived as such by the intended recipients of the second-century AD 'forged' Laconian decree transmitted by Boethius, cf. below) into Timotheus the classic (see the Arcadians' fondness for Timotheus as reported by Polybius 4.19–21)? Is this only a matter of relative chronology and historical oblivion, with time levelling original differences?[20] Or can we still detect, under certain circumstances, some traces of a deeper cultural self-awareness in this apparently politically uncharged use of Timotheus' poetry? What function does a 'customised' Timotheus perform in the recipient's social and political context? Finally, and at an even more speculative level, are we to assume in such an appropriative process a complete effacement of the original musical aspect? Does Timotheus' unchanging fame through antiquity entail also an equally unchanging survival of his own music? And, if some kinds of musical re-setting are in fact attested, how, if at all, do they affect the cultural authority of Timotheus' poetry? Can a musical setting different from the putatively 'authorial' one be still perceived, at least loosely speaking, as Timotheus' own? There are of course no easy and standardised solutions to these questions, and almost invariably questions outnumber answers. Nevertheless, let us start by considering an often neglected piece of evidence for Timotheus' long-lasting influence as cultural icon in shaping the self-perception of local identities in second-century AD Sparta.

---

[18] See Hordern 2002: 5–7. During the Ionian war Miletus was actually the main Peloponnesian bulwark in Asia Minor: see Greaves 2002: 133. On Archelaus' role in appropriating and disseminating the *avant-garde* of the Athenian poetry of the late fifth century BC (Euripides, Agathon, Timotheus) through the Greek world, see Revermann 1999–2000.

[19] An inscription from Didyma dating to *c.* 213/250 AD (*IDid* 181) demonstrates Timotheus' long-lasting popularity: Aurelios Hierocles won at the Great Didymeia performing as τιμοθεαστής and ἡγησιαστής. For the so-called Themison Inschrift (= *SEG* 11.52c: second century AD) see n. 114. A survey of Timotheus' *Nachleben* in the Hellenistic and early imperial period can be found in Hordern 2002: 73–9.

[20] See e.g. Wallace 2003: 91–2 on the 'Arcadian' musical training that transformed 'Athens' late fifth-century musical revolutionaries' into 'inspirational classics in rural Arcadia'. For a different perspective cf. Goldhill 2002.

172   LUCIA PRAUSCELLO

BOETHIUS, *DE INST. MUS.* I.I: CIVIC RELIGIOSITY AND ELITE
SELF-FASHIONING IN ROMAN SPARTA

Sparta's well-known musical conservatism may be considered to a great
extent the joint product of two competing strands of tradition. To paraphrase Cartledge,[21] the alleged musical insularity of ancient Sparta is at the
same time the collaborative output of the 'partly distorted, partly invented
image' of the antidemocratic musical utopia *par excellence* as created by and
for non-Spartans (that is, basically, nostalgic Athenian oligarchic élites),[22]
and the ideal portrait that Spartans themselves shaped for their own use
and actively disseminated.[23] One of the main staples of these interlocking
traditions of Sparta as the entitled guardian of proper cithara-playing[24] is,
of course, the famous episode of the ephors censuring Timotheus' performance at the Carneia by cutting the additional strings of his eleven-string
cithara.[25] The number of the strings and the very target of the musical
censure (Timotheus, Phrynis, once even Terpander as well) oscillate in the
ancient sources. Be this as it may, it is however the link with Timotheus
that ultimately imposed itself as the vulgate version through antiquity;[26] the
putatively original connection of the episode with Timotheus was probably
suggested by the Spartans' hostile treatment alluded to by the poet himself
in the *Persians* at ll. 206–12.[27] The same can be said about the commonly
alleged venue of Timotheus' Spartan performance. Putting aside the likely
historical spuriousness of this account,[28] as far as we know the occasion of

---

[21] Cartledge 1987: 118.   [22] See most recently Wilson 2003a and Csapo 2004: 241–8.

[23] For Spartans' involvement in inventing their own tradition, see generally Flower 2002. More specifically, on the role played by the Spartans in creating the 'myth' of an uncorrupted, genuine Spartan
music, see e.g. Athen. 14.628b (Spartans' claims that they saved music three times from being
corrupted: cf. Csapo 2004: 243 n. 149). For the 'first' (Carneia) and 'second' (Gymnopaideia) musical καταστάσεις at Sparta by Terpander and Thaletas and their political relevance as means of
reasserting social control in periods of internal crisis, see van Wees 1999: 4–6, and 36 n. 74.

[24] For Sparta's close association with lyre-playing in antiquity see Wilson 2004: 269–71 and 280 with
n. 27.

[25] Artemon of Cassandrea, *FGH* IV.342 (= Athen. 14.636e), Plut. *Agis* 10 (extending the same stricture
also to Phrynis), *Apophth. Lac.* 220c (only Phrynis), *Inst. Lac.* 238c (Terpander and Timotheus),
Paus. 3.12.10, Dio Chrys. 32.67 and 33.57. A complete collection of ancient sources (Greek as well as
Latin) reporting different variants of this anecdote can be found in Palumbo Stracca 1999: 130–2.

[26] On Timotheus as the original target of the fictional episode, later developed into a 'stock literary
anecdote', see Hordern 2002: 7–8.

[27] ὁ γάρ μ᾽ εὐγενέτας μακραί-ων Σπάρτας μέγας ἀγεμὼν/ βρύων ἄνθεσιν ἥβας/ δονεῖ λαὸς ἐπι-
φλέγων/ ἐλᾷ τ᾽ αἴθοπι μώμῳ/, ὅτι παλαιοτέραν νέοις/ ὕμνοις μοῦσαν ἀτιμῶ ('for Sparta's great,
well-born, ancient leader, the people abounding with the flowers of youth, drives me about blazing
with hostility and hounds me with glaring blame, because I dishonour the older muse with my new
songs').

[28] The desire to create a straightforward polarisation with Terpander, the putative founder and first
victor of the musical contest at the Carneia (676 BC: Hellanicus *FGrH* 4 F 85a), not to say the
leading figure of the first re-organisation of Spartan music, is clearly operating here.

Wandering poetry, 'travelling' music

Timotheus' scandalous citharodic performance, when recorded by ancient sources, is traditionally associated with the most important among the Dorian musical festivals, the Carneia.[29]

To sum up, the picture we gain from the literary sources is of a Timotheus performing monodically to his eleven-string cithara (most likely a citharodic nomos) at the Spartan Carneia. Of course, this anecdote may well not reflect historical truth,[30] but what is indeed telling is that it sheds light on the (re)-telling and (re)-shaping of the story in reception, showing that the image of the lyre with too many strings had become 'a potent symbol . . . of the breaking of all the aesthetic and social boundaries'.[31] It is thus easy to see why traditional Spartan *xeno-* and *kaino*-phobia easily transformed the narrative of the otherwise acclaimed fifth-century poet Timotheus being censured at the Carneia into the paradigmatic hallmark of its musical and political conservatism.

How does the 'forged' Laconian decree preserved by Boethius, *De inst. mus.* 1.1 enter into this picture? Modern scholarship has variously credited the decree with being the learned forgery of a later grammarian keen on dialectal antiquarianism,[32] a didactic 'Illustration zu der Musikgeschichte' used in peripheral and less cultivated areas of the second-century BC Hellenised world[33] and, most recently, the product of the neo-Pythagorean renaissance via Nicomachus of Gerasa.[34] As we shall see, none of these explanations is entirely satisfactory, inasmuch as they fail to provide a general interpretation of the decree which at the same time accounts for the seemingly indistinct array of contrasting details scattered all over the text.[35] But are these the only possible explanations? And, above all, is there some other way of working out a coherent sense from the apparently idiosyncratic

---

[29] For the prominent role of the Carneia in shaping Dorians' self-definition of their own ethnic identity see recently Robertson 2002 (esp. 15 with n. 21). For the Carneia as the alleged venue of Timotheus' Spartan performance, see Plut. *Inst. Lac.* 238c and Paus. 3.12.10.

[30] See Palumbo Stracca 1999: 132 with n. 4 and Hordern 2002: 7. [31] Wilson 2004: 287.

[32] Cf. Thumb and Kieckers 1932: 80, who considered both the Laconian decree and Cheilon's letter to Periander (Diog. Laert. 1.73) 'Falschungen von Grammatikern' that 'kommen nur als Zeugnisse für die Kenntnis der jung-lakonischen Mundart in Betracht'.

[33] Wilamowitz 1903: 70 'ich nehme also an, dass in Gegenden und Kreisen, die dem Peloponnes und der Grammatik fern standen, als Illustration zu der Musikgeschichte das Dokument verfertig ist'.

[34] Palumbo Stracca 1999: 153–5, according to whom Nicomachus would have legitimated the forgery by integrating it authoritatively into his musical treatise. Nicomachus of Gerasa is commonly considered the main source of the first four books of Boethius's *De inst. mus.*: see Pizzani 1965 (esp. 156–64 as regards the relative autonomy of Boethius' proem from Nicomachus) and 1981.

[35] Cf. e.g. Palumbo Stracca 1999: 134, who speaks of 'acritico affastellamento degli argomenti impiegati nel decreto per motivare la condanna di Timoteo'.

174 LUCIA PRAUSCELLO

misrepresentations offered by the decree? Let us thus turn directly to the
text transmitted by Boethius:[36]

ἐπειδὴ Τιμόθεορ ὁ Μιλήσιορ παραγινόμενορ ἐττὰν ἀμετέραν πόλιν τὰν
παλαιὰν μῶαν ἀτιμάσδη καὶ τὰν διὰ τᾶν ἑπτὰ χορδᾶν κιθάριξιν ἀποστρε-
φόμενορ πολυφωνίαν εἰσάγων λυμαίνεται τὰρ ἀκοὰρ τῶν νέων, διά τε τὰρ
πολυχορδίαρ καὶ τὰρ καινότατορ[1] τῶ μέλιορ ἀγεννῆ καὶ ποικίλαν ἀντὶ
ἁπλόαρ καὶ τεταγμέναρ ἀμφιέννυται τὰν μῶαν ἐπὶ χρώματορ συνιστά-
μενορ τὰν τῶ μέλιορ διασκευὰν ἀντὶ τᾶρ ἐναρμονίω[2] ποττὰν ἀντίστροφον ἀμοιβάν, παρακληθεὶς δὲ καὶ ἐν τὸν ἀγῶνα τᾶρ Ἐλευσινίαρ Δάματρορ
ἀπρεπῆ διεσκευάσατο τὰν τῶ μύθω διασκευάν – τὰν γὰρ Σεμέλαρ ὠδῖνα[3] οὐκ
ἔνδικα[4] τὼρ νέωρ διδάκκη – δεδόχθαι †φα†[5] περὶ τούτοιν τὼρ βασιλέαρ καὶ
τὼρ ἐφόρωρ μέμψαττι Τιμόθεον, ἐπαναγκάσαι δὲ καὶ[6] τᾶν ἕνδεκα χορδᾶν
ἐκταμόνταρ[7] τὰρ περιττὰρ ὑπολιπομένωρ[8] τὰρ ἑπτά, ὅπωρ ἕκαστορ τὸ τᾶρ
πόλιορ βάρορ ὁρῶν εὐλαβῆται ἐττὰν Σπάρταν ἐπιφέρην τι τῶν μὴ καλῶν
ἠθῶν[9], μήποτε ταράρρηται κλέορ ἀγώνων

> [1] καινότατορ Wilamowitz: ΚΑΝΟΤΑΤΟΡ C: ΚΕΝΟΤΑΤΟΡ cett. [2] post ἐναρμονίω
> lacunam susp. Wilamowitz supplens e.g. <ἀπολελυμένα τε ποιῶν ἀντὶ τᾶρ ποτ-
> τἀντίστροφον ἀμοιβᾶρ> [3] ὠδῖνα Wilamowitz, Palumbo Stracca: ΩΔΙΝΑΡ codd.
> [4] ἐν δίκα<ι> Bergk II, 541 n. 58, Palumbo Stracca [5] ΦΑ codd.: supplendum videtur ὁ
> δᾶμος Friedlein: Τ(ΥΧΑΙ) Α(ΓΑΘΑΙ) Wilamowitz: ΘΑ(ΛΙΑΙΑΙ) Palumbo Stracca (i.e.
> τᾶ ἁλιαίᾳ) [6] post δὲ καὶ lacunam statuit Palumbo Stracca supplens e.g. <ἀπίμεν>
> coll. Boeth. p. 182 l. 3–4 Friedlein exigere de Laconica consultum de eo factum est
> [7] ἐκταμέν{ταρ} Wilamowitz [8] ὑπολιπομένων Friedlein: ΥΠΟΛΙΠΟΜΕΝΩ codd.:
> ὑπολειπόμενον Wilamowitz [9] ΗΘΩΝ P5marg: ΝΕΤΟΝ hklomnP6: ΝΗΤΟΝ V:
> ΝΕΤΩΝ P7CP2P3P4: ΗΤΟΝ P1: ΗΕΤΩΝ QP8: ἐόντων Friedlein, Wilamowitz[37]

Since Timotheus of Miletus, having come to our city, dishonours the ancient muse
and by turning away from the seven-stringed cithara and introducing a variety of
tones he corrupts the ears of the youth; and since by means of the multiplicity of
the strings and the novelty[38] of his song in place of her simple and well-ordered
garments he clothes the muse in ignoble and intricate ones by composing the frame

[36] The text reproduced here is, with slight divergences, that of Palumbo Stracca's most recent edition
(1999: 141: for a brief outline of the status quaestionis concerning the manuscript tradition of Boethius'
De inst. mus. see pp. 137–41). As to the editorial criteria adopted by Bower 1989: 4–5 (text) and 185–9
(critical apparatus and an English translation by T. Burgess [1821]), see Palumbo Stracca's criticism
in 1999: 140–1 n. 23. For the present purpose I have recorded in the apparatus only the main variants.

[37] The reading of P5marg gives perfect sense and it seems appropriate to end the decree with such a
general statement. Yet one might perhaps wonder whether νητῶν (i.e. 'not to introduce any of
the unpleasant high-pitched notes': Timotheus was traditionally associated with the exploitation of
exceedingly high-pitched notes, the range of pitch covered by a system of two disjoint tetrachords
featuring now the νήτη ὑπερβολαίων: cf. West 1992: 362) despite its technicality could be right in
such a bizarre decree.

[38] Marzi's defence of the reading κηνότατορ (1988: 267–8, followed by Csapo 2004: 228–9 with
n. 95 and 243) is unconvincing. Pace Marzi, an alleged expression such as 'the emptiness of melody'
(κενόταρ τῶ μέλιορ) cannot refer to 'impressionistic' and 'swollen up' melodies. On the contrary,
κενός and similar words, when used to qualify a sound, voice or song, mean the virtual absence,
interruption or suspension of that sound. It is not a coincidence that κενὸς χρόνος is a technical

Wandering poetry, 'travelling' music

of his melody according to the chromatic genre instead of the enharmonic one to the antistrophic responsion; and since being further invited to the musical contest at the festival honouring the Eleusinian Demeter he arranged the story improperly, for he did not instruct becomingly the youth about the *Birthpangs of Semele*; be it resolved *** that the kings and ephors shall censure Timotheus for these two reasons and, after having cut the superfluous among the eleven strings and leaving the seven, shall also enforce[39] that anyone who sees the grave dignity of the city will be deterred from introducing into Sparta any unpleasant (musical) ethos and the glorious fame of the contests may not be affected.

Modern scholarship has almost exclusively considered our decree a curious object of interest for linguistic archaeology,[40] focusing primarily on its dialect and trying thus to gain from the linguistic evidence a relatively stable criterion by means of which to date the text itself. In this regard, the comparison of the most striking linguistic features of the decree (consistent rhotacism of final sigma,[41] occasional substitution of sigma for theta,[42] occasional omission of intervocalic sigma to reproduce the Laconian aspirate,[43] the spelling of zeta as /σδ/[44]) with Laconian epigraphic evidence of imperial date (especially that from the sanctuary of Artemis Orthia at Sparta)[45] has allowed scholars to date our decree with a reasonable degree of confidence

---

term used in musical treatises to indicate the so-called *leimma*, a marker of rhythmic pause in musical scores: cf. e.g. Arist. Quint. 38.28–9 W-I κενὸς μὲν οὖν ἐστι χρόνος ἄνευ φθόγγου πρὸς ἀναπλήρωσιν τοῦ ῥυθμοῦ. For the reading καινότατορ, καινός being a keyword of the New Musical manifesto, see Palumbo Stracca 1999: 140 with n. 22 and Brussich 1999: 35.

[39] A problematic line: after ἐπαναγκάζω one should expect an acc. + inf. construction, whereas according to the manuscript tradition what we have is two accusative plural participles followed by ὅπως + subj. Wilamowitz emended ἐκταμόνταρ and ὑπολιπομένωρ respectively into ἐκταμέν (inf.) and ὑπολειπόμενον (referring thus to Timotheus), but already Bourguet 1927: 157–8 objected that 'le blâme est pour Timothée, mais l'obligation de couper les cordes superflues pour tout le monde'. The lacuna posited by Palumbo Stracca 1999: 144–5 after δὲ καί is perhaps unnecessary. Since we already have βάρος meaning Lat. *gravitas*, it may be that this is a further instance of the interference of Latin linguistic structures: by analogy with verbs of command such as ἀξιόω, διακελεύω etc., ἐπαναγκάζω has taken the ὅπως construction by the 'extension of finite (subjunctive) clauses introduced by final conjunctions . . . at the expense of infinitival structures', as a consequence of the influence of Lat. *ut* + subj., a process which had already begun anyway in the Hellenistic period (Horrocks 1997: 75).

[40] Cf. Wilamowitz 1903: 70–1 with n. 1, Bourguet 1927: 154–9 (esp. 158–9), Thumb and Kieckers 1932: 80, Palumbo Stracca 1999.

[41] With some hypercorrection: cf. ταράρρηται convincingly argued by Palumbo Stracca 1999: 151 against Wilamowitz's Boeotian form ταράττηται (Wilamowitz, 1903: 71 n. 1)

[42] Cf. the following exceptions (already pointed out by Palumbo Stracca 1999: 150): Τιμόθεορ, κιθάριξιν, παρακληθείς, μύθω.

[43] Cf. e.g. μῶα but Μιλήσιορ, Ἐλευσινίαρ, βασιλέαρ.

[44] The form ἀτιμάσδη is discussed by Palumbo Stracca 1999: 150.

[45] The agonistic inscriptions in honour of Artemis Orthia are the only ones which exhibit the phenomenon of rhotacism: see Brixhe 1996: 98 and 101, Palumbo Stracca 1999: 151.

176   LUCIA PRAUSCELLO

to the beginning of the second century AD,[46] a period whose inscriptional evidence records a remarkable increase in the display of dialectal features.[47]

More to the point, recent studies of the agonistic inscriptions of Artemis Orthia[48] have compellingly argued that the archaising linguistic surface of this epigraphic material (mostly sickle dedications) should be interpreted neither as an 'ennobled patois' preserving with slight variations much of the Laconian fifth-century dialect[49] nor as a living language (a kind of 'peasant' Laconian).[50] What we have is not a fully revitalised Laconian dialect in itself with some *koinē*-like veneer[51] but instead 'the conversion of koinè into laconising forms'.[52] Kennell's comparative analysis of Laconian 'civic' (devoid of archaising features) and 'agogic' (with rhotacism and so forth)[53] inscriptions from the sanctuary has allowed him to draw the compelling conclusion that the artificial use of a hybrid Laconian in these ephebic dedications has most likely to be filtered through an ideological frame: they are part of a desire to revive the traditional Lycurgan ἀγωγή. To quote Kennell's words, 'Spartan archaism, or, more accurately laconism, was rooted in a desire to recreate the city's famous traditions in a vision that

[46] See already Bourguet 1927: 158–9, who dated the decree to Hadrian's time. Wilamowitz's dating to the second century BC for stylistic reasons (Wilamowitz 1903: 70) is thus to be definitely rejected (a Hellenistic date is still accepted by West 1992: 362 n. 23).

[47] For the revival of antiquarian interests and emergence of archaising features in the cultural life of Sparta during the Greek Renaissance, see Spawforth in Cartledge and Spawforth 2002: 106–8, 176–7, 190–211.

[48] For a broader cultural analysis of the entire epigraphic corpus, see Kennell 1995: 87–92. A collection (with commentary) of the inscriptions of the sanctuary of Artemis Orthia can be found in Dawkins *et al.* 1929.

[49] The stance argued by Bourguet 1927: 25 (followed by Horrocks 1997: 37).

[50] Cassio 1986: 144–5 and 158–9 rightly recognises the truly archaising nature of the revival of the Laconian dialect from Trajan's time onwards while denying a similar development for the Aeolic of Asia Minor, where, however, the evidence does not present, from a linguistic point of view, a real gap between the classical and Hellenistic period.

[51] Kennel 1995: 92 with n. 122 correctly points out that the only instance of 'a proper Laconian dialectal variant' out of 151 'agogic' inscriptions is ποδδεξαμένων for προσδεξαμένων in *IG* V 1, 653a, II AD (= no. 142 in Dawkins *et al.* 1929). Phonetical mispellings and orthographical oddities like κασσηρατόριν for καθθηρατόριον, Ἰούλιρ for Ἰούλιος, or ἰερεύρ for ἰαρεύς are most likely to be explained as 'an unlikely alliance between koinè and Laconian' (Kennell 1995: 91). The same conclusion has independently been drawn also by Brixhe 1996: 97–8 (see esp. his analysis of ὠτῶ for αὐτῶ in *IG* V 1, 305 l. 10).

[52] Kennell 1995: 90. In the same direction see also Brixhe 1996: 98–9, who speaks *à propos* of a 'koinè à coloration laconienne' with strongly north-western features and with some isolated hyperdialectalism confined to the domain of religion (the same position is stated by Brixhe in Brixhe and Vottero 2004: 27; see also Kennell 1995: 92, who ascribes the blurred mixture of artificiality and orality exhibited by the agogic inscriptions to the 'ceremonial occasion').

[53] As observed by Brixhe 1996: 97–9 and 101–2, the archaising features of the sickle dedications co-exist with standard *koinē* forms which are only superficially doricised.

Wandering poetry, 'travelling' music 177

nonetheless conformed to contemporary cultural notions.'[54] But what if we shift our attention from the merely dialectal data and try to recover, as far as we can, the possible cultural scenario that produced the 'decree'? How may the comparison with the inscriptional evidence from the sanctuary of Artemis Orthia provide us with a useful template for grasping the cultural background of Boethius' pseudepigraphon?[55] And what is signified, in terms of a discursive strategy of representation, by the choice of the formal layout of a decree or, to use Kennell's distinction,[56] by the choice of a 'civic' inscription (and not of an 'agogic' one, the category to which the sickle dedications from Artemis Orthia all belong) as a medium to celebrate a utopian continuity with the past? As we shall see, closer attention to some hitherto neglected details in the narrative may reveal clues that, if projected into the wider context of the self-fashioning of Greek élites in second-century Sparta,[57] may aid to work a coherent sense out of the apparent inconsistencies with which the decree itself is strewn.

Let us then turn back to the text itself. We have already seen that linguistic oddities strongly argue against the likelihood that we are dealing with the erudite product of a grammarian.[58] At the same time the marked local veneer confirmed by comparison with the epigraphic evidence from Artemis Orthia rules out the hypothesis of an extra-Peloponnesian provenance for our text.[59] Nor does the decree's clumsiness in dealing with the most technical aspects of musical practice suggest a strictly 'musical' or in any case 'professional' origin,[60] which indeed we should expect if a skilled theoretician like Nicomachus were actually the author. Furthermore, even

---

[54] Kennell 1995: 92. See also Spawforth in Cartledge and Spawforth 2002: 206. The Laconian decree against Timotheus is mentioned only very cursorily by Kennell 1995: 92, as a concoction of 'Laconian forms with slightly more verve and imagination'.

[55] Brixhe, the first to recognise the common provenance of the Laconian 'archaising' inscriptions from a unique source, i.e. the sanctuary of Artemis Orthia at Sparta (Brixhe 1996: 98), did not establish any link between them and the 'decree' preserved by Boethius. Palumbo Stracca 1999: 151–3 acknowledges the similarity between the two sets of documents but does not ask herself what that could mean in terms of social imagery and cultural practice.

[56] Kennell 1995: 87.

[57] On the increasing vitality of Sparta's agonistic life under the Romans, mostly the by-product of the unceasing efforts, on the part of Greek élite, both to assert its own local identity and to please the Roman social hierarchy, see Spawforth in Cartledge and Spawforth 2002: 93–104, 160–4, and van Nijf 2001: 320 (the institution of the new festivals Kaisarea and Kommodeia).

[58] Cf. Cassio 1986: 158–9. Against the 'grammatical' origin of the decree see already Wilamowitz 1903: 70 and, on a different basis, Palumbo Stracca 1999: 153–4.

[59] A stance argued by Wilamowitz 1903: 70. As to the content of the decree, the presence of patently contradicting pieces of information (on which see below) seems to make unlikely the use of this decree as a didactic 'Illustration zu der Musikgeschichte'.

[60] Already Wilamowitz 1903: 71 n. 1 pointed out the second-hand nature of sentences such as ἐπὶ χρώματορ συνισταμενορ τὰν τῶ μέλιορ διασκευὰν ἀντὶ τᾶρ ἐναρμονίω ποττὰν ἀντίστροφον ἀμοιβάν, rightly observing that 'die Responsion hat mit der Tonart nichts zu tun'. See also Bourguet

178   LUCIA PRAUSCELLO

if ancient sources acknowledge a link between Pythagoras and Sparta,[61] Pythagoreans were certainly not particularly interested in defending the traditional seven-stringed lyre, since Pythagoras himself was credited with having added an eighth string to the seven and having invented the octochord, traditionally perceived as the distinctive hallmark of Pythagorean musical practice.[62] The musically conservative Pythagoreans would certainly have welcomed the *Stimmung* of our decree, and Nicomachus of Gerasa may well have reported the present text in his treatise,[63] particularly given his penchant for dialects.[64] Yet to claim a direct neo-Pythagorean descent for the decree against Timotheus is to go a step too far and leaves unexplained the most idiosyncratic features of the narrative.

Let us focus first on some formal features of our decree, which provide the broader frame within which to contextualise it. One most obvious aspect, in terms of rhetorical strategy, is that the decree, while presenting itself as a punitive, censorial document, closely resembles, from a formal point of view, the general structure and diction of the Hellenistic decrees honouring 'poeti vaganti'. We find not only the usual bipartition between the motivation for the honours granted and the actual granting of those honours (in our case, of course, reversed into punishment), but we can also detect traces of well-established formulae. In particular, the sequence 'ἐπειδή clause followed by participle of arrival in the city (usually παραγίγνομαι)' is the standardised beginning of many decrees praising wandering poets, and it is exactly echoed in the ἐπειδή . . . παραγινόμενορ of our decree.[65]

Within this general frame, the first part of the decree certainly does not stand out for its originality: what we have is a collection of commonplaces about the corrupted nature of Timotheus' songs and of the New Music

---

1927: 156, who wondered whether we could be sure that 'l'auteur de ce faux, dans l'étalage des termes techniques dont il use, ne s'attachait pas surtout à faire parade de sa science'.

[61] See Rawson 1969: 99–100, 110.

[62] This difficulty is not ignored by Palumbo Stracca 1999: 137 n. 13, who mentions the generally conservative attitude of the Pythagorean school in matters of musical taste. This is certainly true, yet our decree makes of the seven-string cithara a staple too important to be dismissed in such a way. For Pythagoras as the inventor of the octochord and the eight-note octave system see Nicom. *Ench.* 5 pp. 244–5 Jan (on which cf. Bower 1989: 32–3 with n. 107) and Iambl. *Vit. Pyth.* 26.119.

[63] Cf. Pizzani 1965: 162.

[64] See Cassio 1988 on Nicomachus' manipulation of the dialectal veneer of Archytas fr. 1 D-K. More generally, on the hyper-archaising features of pseudopythagorean writings see Centrone 1990: 49–50.

[65] The epigraphic instances are too many to be quoted here exhaustively, but cf. e.g. the expression ἐπειδή . . . παραγενόμενος in Guarducci no. 12 ll. 4–6, no. 13 ll. 2–3, no. 17 ll. 3–4 (ἐπειδή . . . πα[ρα]γ[ε]νομ[έ]να), no. 21 l. 3, no. 22 ll. 5–6, no. 25 l. 6 ἐπεὶ παραγενόμενος, no. 28 l. 1, no. 29 ll. 3–5, no. 32 ll. 3–5 ἐπειδή . . . παραγενόμενοι, and above all no. 33 ll. 2–5 ἐπ[ειδή] . . . παραγενηθε[ε]ῖσα . . . [καὶ παρακληθεῖ]σα and no. 35 ll. 4–6 ἐπεὶ . . . [παραγ]ενηθεὶς . . . καὶ παρακληθείς for which see παρακληθεὶς δέ of our decree.

Wandering poetry, 'travelling' music 179

in general (polychordy, polyphony, avoidance of strophic responsion, use of the chromatic genos, intricate melodic frame),[66] a *résumé* which has been embellished with quotations from Timotheus' own works.[67] Even the charge of 'corrupting the ears of the youth' (λυμαίνεται τὰρ ἀκοὰρ τῶν νέων)[68] suits perfectly what we know to have been the accusations raised by traditionalists against the corrupting moral effects of the New Music,[69] and at the same time generally echoes the charges against another corrupter of youth and protagonist of an actual early fourth-century Athenian show-trial, namely, Socrates.[70] Nor should the image of Timotheus 'clothing' the muse with ignoble garments (ἀγεννῆ καὶ ποικίλαν ἀντὶ ἁπλόαρ καὶ τεταγμέναρ ἀμφιέννυται τὰν μῶαν) seem puzzling, at least not to a closer inspection. It clearly recalls the language and imagery of Aristophanes' *Frogs*, where the disreputable Muse of Euripides is mocked for the unworthy clothes in which the tragedian dressed his characters (*Frogs* 1058ff.).[71] Furthermore, Timotheus' concern for the Muse's clothes may also be understood as an involuntarily ironic echo of Music's complaint of having been stripped by the Milesian poet himself (cf. Pherecr. 155. 25 K-A ἀπέδυσε κἀνέλυσε χορδαῖς δώδεκα).[72]

What strikes the reader at once in our document is the second part of the decree. The content of the first lines is still compatible with what we know about Timotheus' citharodic performance at the Carneia, the traditionally alleged venue for the cutting of the strings.[73] Yet later on (παρακληθεὶς δὲ

---

[66] For the inherently political overtone of New Music's 'language of plurality, complexity and liberation' see Csapo 2004: 229–30 and 237.

[67] τὰν παλαιὰν μῶαν ἀτιμάσδη of the decree imitates 791. 211–2 *PMG* παλαιοτέραν . . ./ μοῦσαν ἀτιμῶ.

[68] Cf. Dio Chrys. 32.67 ὡς ἂν μὴ διαφθαρῶσιν αἱ ἀκοαί (for Dio Chrys.'s account closely echoing in some points our decree see Palumbo Stracca 1999: 145 n. 30).

[69] The main source for such a traditional accusation is of course Old Comedy: suffice it here to quote, e.g., Aristoph. 225 K-A.

[70] Hordern 2002: 8–9 has correctly pointed out the generic resemblance of the charges against Timotheus with those of the decree against Socrates (Diog. Laert. 2.40): Socrates added *new* gods, just as Timotheus is accused of adding *new* strings. Alan Griffiths suggests to me that under the expression παραγινόμενον ἐττὰν ἀμετέραν πόλιν may possibly be lurking also some oblique allusion to 'traditional' *xenoi* like Protagoras and other subversive immigrant sophists; cf. above p. 2. Furthermore, as Richard Hunter reminded me, Socrates' conduct (his stubborn refusal to leave Athens) can well be seen as the counter-model of a prototypical 'wandering poet'.

[71] I owe this point to A. H. Griffiths and D. J. Mastronarde. One could as well think of the make-up of Pindar's Muse in *Isthm.* 2.8 ἀργυρωθεῖσαι πρόσωπα . . . ἀοιδαί.

[72] [Plut.] *De mus.* 1141c explicitly mentions that Music entered the stage ἐν γυναικείῳ σχήματι (i.e. 'wearing a female dress'). The simplicity (ἀντὶ ἁπλόαρ) referred to in the decree is certainly that of the genuine and uncorrupted music (cf. [Plut.] *De mus.* 1135c–d, where ἁπλότης is associated to ὀλιγοχορδία). Yet it may be worth observing that ἁπλοῦς is also a technical textile term; see Casson 1983: 193–9.

[73] I am grateful to G. B. D'Alessio for this observation.

180 LUCIA PRAUSCELLO

καί) we learn also of a second, 'diverted' place of performance (no longer the
Carneia but a musical contest at the extra-urban sanctuary of the Eleusinian
Demeter at Therai)[74] and of an equally 'perverted' performance (at least
if compared with the vulgate version) ascribed to Timotheus himself – no
longer a citharodic, that is, a soloist piece, but a dithyramb, and a very
precise one: *The Birthpangs of Semele*).[75] Besides, to puzzle the reader to an
even greater extent, this is somehow linked with the cutting of the strings
of Timotheus' lyre,[76] although the dithyramb, at least from the end of the
sixth century BC onwards, was a choral piece sung to the accompaniment
of the *aulos*.[77] To solve the riddle, one could think of an inert projection
of contemporary musical practice into the past, as citharodic, that is solo,
performances of originally dithyrambic pieces are occasionally attested from
the Hellenistic period onwards.[78] Yet this does not seem to be the case here:
in our decree we are explicitly told about a singing chorus of young people
(τὼρ νέωρ διδάκκη),[79] the verb διδάσκω being a technical term referring
to the activity of instructing a chorus (χοροδιδασκαλία).[80]

---

[74] Cf. παρακληθεὶς δὲ καὶ ἐν τὸν ἀγῶνα τᾶρ Ἐλευσινίαρ Δάματρορ (the 'displaced' venue is emphasised again at the end of the decree: cf. μήποτε ταράρρηται κλέορ ἀγώνων). For the identification of Pausanias' Therai (Paus. 3.20.5), the site of the Eleusinium, with the modern 'Kalyvia tes
Sokhas' cf. Stibbe 1993: 77–83. As to the geographic location of the sanctuary see Guettel Cole 1994:
208–9.

[75] Cf. τὰν γὰρ Σεμέλαρ ὠδῖνα οὐκ ἔνδικα τὼρ νέωρ διδάκκη. For the dithyrambic nature of this
poem as recoverable from ancient sources (Athen. 8.352a, *Anth. Pal.* 16.7.2–3, Dio Chrys. 78.32) see
Hordern 2002: 10 and 249.

[76] It is true that the structure of the decree is quite bipartite (one could still think of the Carneia as
regards the first lines), yet the cutting of the strings by the kings and ephors is somehow linked by
our decree also to the Eleusinian context: cf. περὶ τούτοιν and the final words κλέορ ἀγώνων.

[77] For the classical 'historical' dithyramb as a choral song performed by a circular chorus to the
accompaniment of the aulos and not of the cithara, see Hordern 2002: 18–9 and 23–4. For
the much debated nature of Arion's 'mythical' dithyramb, whether citharodic or aulodic, see
Ieranò 1992: 44–5, and the still valuable observations of Privitera 1957 (to be supplemented
now by Privitera 1991). Most recently, in favour of an archaic citharodic dithyramb see Franklin
forthcoming a.

[78] See e.g. *IG* II² 3779 l. 6 (dating to the middle of the third century BC), where the well-known citharode Nicocles of Taras is said to have performed (and won) at the Lenaea by playing a dithyramb: see
Hordern 2002: 23–4 and Wilson 2000: 318–9, n. 79. On this 'perverted' performance of dithyrambs
in Hellenistic time (especially by the *technitai* of Dionysus), see more generally Bélis 1995: 1053–5
(even if the instance of Pylades is wrong) and the Tean inscriptions now re-edited by Le Guen 2001:
I, 241–2 (cf. also Wilson 2000: 391 n. 155).

[79] The late evidence of Clem. *Strom.* 1.16.79, according to which Timotheus νόμους τε πρῶτος ᾖσεν
ἐν χορῷ καὶ κιθάρᾳ is most likely due to scholarly confusion, even if a certain overlap between
dithyramb and nomos, at least from a classificatory perspective, may have been already an ancient
feature; see Hordern 2002: 26–7, Rutherford 1995: 356 n. 11 and D'Alessio forthcoming b. There is
thus no need to assume that the *The Birthpangs of Semele* was a citharodic dithyramb, as suggested
by Brussich 1999: 37.

[80] See already Hordern 2002: 11 in this direction. Hordern's remark that nevertheless we cannot be
sure that the author of the decree was aware of the choral nature of the *Birthpangs of Semele*, since

Wandering poetry, 'travelling' music

Now, did such a competitive tradition which somehow embeds Timotheus' performance at the Eleusinium within the narrative of the cutting of the strings exist before the composition of our decree?[81] The key for understanding these peculiarities is to be sought, I believe, in both the local history of the Spartan Eleusinium and the broader cultural context underlying the strategies of self-representation of local élites in second-century AD Sparta.

Let us start from what we know about the Spartan Eleusinium from ancient literary sources, that is, basically, the report of Paus. 3.20.5–7:[82]

(5) Ταλετοῦ δὲ τὸ μεταξὺ καὶ Εὐόρα Θήρας ὀνομάζοντες Λητώ φασιν ἀπὸ τῶν ἄκρων τοῦ Ταϋγέτου ***[1] Δήμητρος ἐπίκλησιν Ἐλευσινίας ἐστὶν ἱερόν· ἐνταῦθα Ἡρακλέα Λακεδαιμόνιοι κρυφθῆναί φασιν ὑπὸ Ἀσκληπιοῦ τὸ τραῦμα ἰώμενον· καὶ Ὀρφέως ἐστὶν ἐν αὐτῷ ξόανον, Πελασγῶν ὥς φασιν ἔργον. καὶ τόδε δὲ ἄλλο δρώμενον ἐνταῦθα οἶδα· (6) ἐπὶ θαλάσσῃ πόλισμα Ἕλος ἦν . . . (7) ἐκ τούτου δὴ τοῦ Ἕλους ξόανον Κόρης τῆς Δήμητρος ἐν ἡμέραις ῥηταῖς ἀνάγουσιν ἐς τὸ Ἐλευσίνιον.

> [1] post Ταϋγέτου lacunam susp. Bekker, alii alia suppl.

Between Taletum and Euoras there is a place called Therai, where they say that Leto from the peaks of Taygetus *** there is a sanctuary of Demeter named Eleusinian. Spartans say that here Heracles was hidden by Asclepius while being healed of the wounds. In this sanctuary there is also a wooden image of Orpheus, which is, they say, a piece of work of the Pelasgians. I know also of the following rite which is celebrated here: by the seashore there was a city, Helos . . . From this Helos, on fixed days, they bring up to the Eleusinium the wooden statue of Kore, the daughter of Demeter.[83]

Unfortunately, the text is seriously corrupt and a lacuna has necessarily to be posited between Ταϋγέτου and Δήμητρος. The details of Leto descending (?) 'from the top of mount Taygetus' can only be guessed; nevertheless what is clearly recoverable from the text, damaged as it may be, is that, at least

---

the parallel charges of the decree against Socrates may have influenced our text, cannot be ruled out *a priori*. Yet it seems to me unlikely: ancient evidence referring to Timotheus' *Semele* shows that awareness of the dithyrambic nature of this poem was prevalent in antiquity even at a late stage: see Athen. 8.352a (Stratonicus' criticism of the exceedingly mimetic music of Timotheus), *AP* 16.7.2–3 (= *HE* 54–61, Alcaeus of Messene) and Dio Chrys. 78.32 (ὥσπερ αὐλοῦντα τὴν τῆς Σεμέλης ὠδῖνα).

[81] This, of course, is not to deny that Timotheus ever performed a dithyramb at the Eleusinia, which might well have been the case. What is at stake here is the fact that, notwithstanding its bipartite structure, our decree links this dithyrambic performance to the cutting of the strings.

[82] The source of this passage is most likely the third-century BC Laconian antiquarian and historian Sosibius; see Immerwahr 1889: 110 and 112.

[83] For this 'ritual enactment of a seasonal epiphany', see Parker 1988: 103. As for the link between the hereditary priesthood at Helos and landed interest in this part of Laconia from the Spartan élite (the families of Pomponii and Brasidas) see Spawforth in Cartledge and Spawforth 2002: 138.

182   LUCIA PRAUSCELLO

to a second-century AD visitor like Pausanias, some kind of connection
between Leto and the Eleusinian Demeter still existed and was rooted in
the local history of the sanctuary itself. The most reasonable explanation for
such a connection was given more than one hundred years ago by Wide.[84]
If we keep in mind that Artemis was worshipped by Greeks as a goddess
of childbirth and fecundity[85] and that a Laconian Demeter was addressed
as ἐπιπολαία and ἐπίασσα ('she who comes timely': the Doric form for
the Attic ἐπιοῦσα),[86] quite apart from the primary or derivative origin
of this cultic overlap,[87] a link between Leto and Artemis as Εἰλείθυια is
readily explicable, especially given the active rôle traditionally ascribed to
Eileithyia in easing Leto's birthpangs at Delos.[88] To sum up, whatever the
etymology (pre-Greek or Mycenean) of Eileithyia may be, and quite apart
from the primary or secondary nature of her connection with the Eleusinian
Demeter,[89] what emerges from Pausanias' account is that in second-century
Roman Sparta the cult of Eleusinian Demeter presented itself to the eyes
of a foreign beholder as the output of a multilayered archaism (the link
with Leto, the ξόανον of Orpheus, Heracles healed by Asclepius) which
still shaped its cultic reality.[90] In this context, it is in fact not too difficult

[84] Wide 1893: 175–6, followed by Stibbe 1993; see also Hupfloher 2000: 63–4.
[85] Cf. Guettel Cole 1994: 201–4. More generally, on the kourotrophic function of Artemis see Vernant
     1991: 198–201.
[86] Respectively Hesych. s.v. ἐπιπολαία (ε 5080 Latte)· οὕτως ἐν Λακεδαίμονι ἡ Δημήτηρ ἱδρυμένη
     τιμᾶται, and Hesych. s.v. ἐπίασσα (ε 4617 Latte)· Δήμητρος ἐπώνυμον. Furthermore, archaeolog-
     ical evidence has recently confirmed that within the τέμενος of Artemis Orthia there was a space
     reserved for the worship of Eileithyia; see Kilian 1978.
[87] A huge bibliography exists on the alleged connection between Eleusis, Eileithyia and the Spartan
     Eleusinian Demeter, and its nature (i.e. whether primary or secondary): see e.g. Nilsson 1950: 518–21,
     Willetts 1958, Heubeck 1972, Parker 1988, Stibbe 1993: 84–8, and for an extremely sceptical (and often
     misleading) view see more recently Robertson 1996: 377–8, 1998: 569–72 and 1999: 25–8. Heubeck
     1972: 93–5 (apparently unknown to Parker 1988) convincingly argues for a Mycenean origin of
     Eileithyia stemming from the form e-re-u-ti-ja attested in the Knossos tablets.
[88] Cf. Hymn. Hom. 3.115ff. Wide 1893: 176 (followed by Stibbe 1993: 84–6, the latter believing in the
     pre-Doric origin of Eileithyia) suggests that Leto 'der Demeter Eleusinia . . . ein Opfer dargebracht,
     einen Tempel gestiftet oder anderes dergleichen getan hat'.
[89] Nilsson 1950: 523 is most probably right in asserting the originally distinct nature of the two goddesses
     and in supposing that only at a later stage 'Demeter Eleusinian superseded Eleuthyia and appropriated
     her cult as Apollo did with Hyakinthos'. See recently Sourvinou-Inwood 2003: 39 on the not
     'inconceivable' fact that Demeter Eleusinia 'could have been influenced by – and even in very broad
     terms reflected – the Eleusinian cult'.
[90] This aspect is well emphasised by Stibbe 1993: 83–4, 86–7 (who also points out that the Eleusinion
     seems to have been located very close to another sanctuary of Dionysos, that at Bryseai, cf. Paus.
     3.20.3: access to the temple was restricted to women) and above all by Hupfloher 2000: 36–7 and 64–5
     (esp. as regards the link with Asclepius and Orpheus). Hupfloher's discussion is a most welcome
     reassessment of the question, especially after Robertson's strong denial of any link between the
     Eleusinion and Eleusis (2002: 17 n. 24 with further bibliograpical references).

Wandering poetry, 'travelling' music   183

to envisage the sanctuary of Eleusinian Demeter as the venue, fictional or otherwise, for a dithyramb entitled the *Birthpangs of Semele*.[91]

All this is still more interesting if we cast a glance at the archaeological evidence of the Roman period for the Eleusinium of 'Kalyvia tes Sokhas', a site which was properly excavated by British scholars in the late forties of the previous century.[92] Archaeological data confirm the existence of the sanctuary at least from the sixth century BC onwards,[93] and most of the terracotta figurines date to the fourth century BC, but it is especially during the second century of the Roman empire that the cult of Demeter at 'Kalyvia tes Sokhas' seems to have enjoyed a thriving revival and prosperity.[94] Apart from some terracotta figurines and ceramic vessels, the findings mostly consist of first-, second- and third-century inscriptions and votive sculptures set up either by the city of Sparta or by male relatives to celebrate female devotees and officials of the cult (addressed as θοιναρμόστρια, that is, 'mistress of the banquet' or ἑστία πόλεως),[95] all of them being almost invariably upper-class women of senatorial rank.[96] All this strongly suggests that, at least in its 'revitalised' imperial version, the worship of Demeter Eleusinia was mainly a concern of women and thus strictly associated with fertility and childbirth.[97]

Let us now turn to the expression ἐν τὸν ἀγῶνα τᾶρ Ἐλευσινίαρ Δάμα-τρορ. As far as the archaeological evidence goes, we have no positive proof that contests, either athletic or musical, took place at the sanctuary, at least not in imperial times.[98] On the contrary, if we cast a glance at the literary

---

[91] For the birth of Dionysus and Semele's birthpangs as an appropriate subject for a dithyramb, see Ieranò 1997: 160–2, 164–6. The fact that Timotheus 'worked up a story composition which was inappropriate' (ἀπρεπῆ διεσκευάσατο τὰν τῶ μύθω διασκευάν) does not necessarily refer to the choice of the subject itself but to the way of treating the myth.

[92] For a general survey see Cook 1950. See now also Walker 1989: 131–2.

[93] Recently Stibbe 1993: 88 has argued that a group of late-geometric fragments might suggest dating the first appearance of the Eleusinium back to the 700s BC.

[94] See Parker 1988: 101, Walker 1989: 132, Spawforth in Cartledge and Spawforth 2002: 194.

[95] For an up-to-date study of the cultic tasks underlying these labels see Hupfloher 2000: 34–65.

[96] For a prosopographic analysis of the likely hereditary priesthood at the Spartan Eleusinium see Walker 1989 (focusing on the so-called Aberdeen reliefs of the second century AD, i.e. on Claudia Ageta, identified as the grand-daughter of the Spartan senator Tiberius Claudius Brasidas) and Spawforth 1985 on the family of the Memmii and their 'mythical' pedigree. A list of the inscriptions can be found in Cook 1950: 263.

[97] See Walker 1989: 134, Hupfloher 2000: 55 and Spawforth in Cartledge and Spawforth 2002: 194. Robertson 1996: 378, 1998: 571 and 1999: 28 with n. 99 argues in favour of both female and male actively taking part in the cult. This might well have been the case, yet this cannot be inferred by Pausanias' ἀνάγουσιν (Paus. 3.20.7), as suggested by Robertson 1998: 571 ('In saying "they bring up" . . . Pausanias appears to mean a general procession of men as well as women').

[98] See Hordern 2002: 8 n.16.

and epigraphic side, a gloss in Hesychius[99] tells us that the Eleusinia was a
Laconian musical festival (θυμελικὸς ἀγών)[100] in honour of Demeter, and
an inscription dating to 450/31 or to the first part of the fourth century BC[101]
tells us that the Spartan Damonon won several times at the Ἐλευhύνια as
charioteer.[102] Now, what these two pieces of information seem to suggest,
if compared with the archaeological vacuum, is that at a relatively early
stage (fifth/fourth century BC) the Spartan Eleusinia must have entailed
athletics and/or musical contests of some kind[103] but later these contests
were possibly abandoned. The information about Timotheus performing a
dithyramb at the Eleusinia may thus possibly rely on ancient material, but
apart from this late inscription we do not know of any other source which
frames this performance within the episode of the cutting of the strings, nor
is there evidence for a survival of the musical contest beyond the Hellenistic
period (if we accept that Hesychius is here probably drawing on Sosibius).[104]
As regards ritual dynamics, it has recently been stressed that 'continuity in
use of the same space does not necessarily mean its identical use'.[105] Now,
the fact that the cult of Demeter Eleusinia knows a true 'revival' in the
second century AD in forms and ways partially different from the original ones (i.e. in athletic and/or musical contests) is perfectly in keeping
with the pragmatics of (re-)founding (or renewing) alleged ancient festivals
alluding to Sparta's glorious past by the Spartan élites under the Roman
empire and thus integrating the city into the new reality of Roman
power.[106] Actually, it is hardly a coincidence that the inscriptions from
'Kalyvia tes Sokhas', while reasserting the continuity of a long-standing local
tradition and its connection with a distinctively Spartan past,[107] are at the

---

[99] Hesych. *s.v.* Ἐλευσίνια (ε 2026 Latte)· ἀγὼν θυμελικὸς ἀγόμενος Δήμητρι παρὰ Λάκωσιν· καὶ ἐν
Σικελίᾳ τιμᾶται Ἄρτεμις καὶ Ζεὺς Ἐλευσίνιος παρ᾽ Ἴωσιν. On the necessity of punctuating after
Λάκωσιν and not after Δήμητρι, see Wide 1893: 119–20.

[100] For θυμελικὸς ἀγών (as distinct from σκηνικός) meaning, at least from the fourth century BC
onwards, purely musical (that is, not dramatic) entertainments or competitions, see Lloyd-Jones
1963: 82 and Wörrle 1988: 227.

[101] For the latter date see Jeffrey 1988: 179–81. Cf. also Nafissi 1991: 64 n. 137, 166 n. 54.

[102] *IG* V 1, 213 l. 11 (= *GDI* 4416); see Parker 1988: 101 with n. 24.

[103] Hupfloher 2000: 63–4 rightly points out that the musical and athletic contests could belong to
different historical stages. Robertson 1999: 26 with n. 86 does not seem to be aware of this possibility:
he conflates together the gloss of Hesychius, the *Damonon-Inschrift* and the text of Paus. 3.20.7
by reconstructing an atemporal pattern of procession, musical and equestrian contests going on
uninterruptedly from the fifth century BC onwards till Pausanias' time.

[104] See D'Alessio forthcoming b.   [105] Chaniotis 2005b: 150.

[106] This process is discussed at length by Spawforth in Cartledge and Spawforth 2002: 104–8, 192 (the
Leonidea, refounded in the reign of Trajan, in memory of the Spartan hero of the Thermopylae),
195 (the Urania). For a broader contextualisation of the Spartan reality see also Spawforth 1989.

[107] On the importance of local fabulous pedigrees exhibited by these epigraphs as means of asserting
a pure Spartan descent, see Spawforth 1985: 193.

Wandering poetry, 'travelling' music   185

same time framed by constant references to the social structures of Roman power.[108]

Summing up, if we keep in mind the revival of the cult of Eleusinian Demeter in second-century AD Sparta as suggested by both archaeological and epigraphical evidence, then the emphasis of our decree on the local dimension of the episode (the mention of a very distinct title, that is, the *Birthpangs of Semele*, as the piece allegedly performed by Timotheus), the partially 'misplaced' venue of the contest (perhaps facilitated also by the fact that the Carneia are attested only until the Augustan period),[109] the artificially archaising language (though one still influenced by the Roman language of power, cf. τὸ τᾶρ πόλιορ βάρορ),[110] are all elements which strongly suggest that we contextualise the document within the Spartan ruling class's broader attempts at re-asserting its own Greek local identity under the Roman empire. In a period when re-creating a Lycurgan past was itself perceived 'as a valid form of cultural activity',[111] to re-affirm the strictures against Timotheus' corrupting muse means a desire both to display an image of the whole Spartan civic body as faithful to a long unchanging tradition and, at the same time, to manipulate the present.[112]

If projected onto the broader horizon of the contemporary Greek festive culture in the Roman Mediterranean, this revived censure against Timotheus' alleged 'original' music may seem to be, on closer inspection, quite out of place, if not entirely pointless. A contemporary inscription from

---

[108] See e.g. *IG* V 1, 592 (second century AD) praising Poplius Memmion Deximachos for being φιλοκαίσαρα καὶ φιλόπατριν (cf. also 631 l. 2), 596 ll. 11–2 honouring the husband of the dedicatee as φιλόπολις and ἱππεὺς Ῥωμαίων, or 590 ll. 11–13 where Tiberius Claudius Eudamos is praised as ἀρχιερεὺς τῶν Σεβαστῶν καὶ τῶν θείων προγόνων αὐτῶν (the same formula also in 595 ll. 9–11). Furthermore, as pointed out by Spawforth 1985: 192, and Walker 1989: 132, the female merits praised in these inscriptions testify to the reception of specifically Roman values like the *ius liberorum* and, more generally, of Roman domestic virtues like chastity, *philandria*, *sophrosyne* and *eusebeia*.

[109] See Spawforth in Cartledge and Spawforth 2002: 193. Robertson's use of the evidence is misleading in this regard (Robertson 2002: 43 n. 101): *IG* V 1, 497 ll. 11–13 (middle of the second century AD) simply mentions the hereditary priesthood of Carneios βοικέτας and δρομαῖος, any reference to the festival being lacking. The latest mention of the Carneia attested by epigraphical evidence goes back to the first century BC (= *IG* V 1, 209 l. 20).

[110] For βάρος as a semantic borrowing from Latin *gravitas* see Hiltbrunner 1967: 408–9 and Dubuisson 1985: 76–8 (which needs partial correction: already Polybius used this Latinism, see the fragment of Polybius transmitted by *Suda* s.v. βάρος 121 = Polyb. 30.10.4).

[111] Spawforth in Cartledge and Spawforth 2002: 210. The importance of the new-founded Panhellenion in favouring this 'archaeological' quest for a truly Greek pedigree has rightly been emphasised also by Whitmarsh 2001: 23.

[112] As to the 'Roman dimension' underlying the marked reference to the civic past from the Spartans' aristocracy cf. Spawforth in Cartledge and Spawforth 2002: 107–8.

186   LUCIA PRAUSCELLO

Miletus (*SEG* XI 52c, first half of the second century AD)[113] informs us
that the local musician Gaios Aelios Themison was praised by the δῆμος
for 'having set to music by himself' (ἑαυτῷ μελοποιήσαντα)[114] Euripides,
Sophocles and Timotheus (ll. 7–9). Timotheus' 'original' music then, whatever this label may have meant to an ancient Greek, must not have been
a great danger any longer, the melodic frame of his poems being variously
adapted if not entirely re-invented.[115] It is thus within the peculiar local
dynamics of Roman Sparta that our decree acquires an historically deeper
dimension and a coherence of its own: in a sense, it is much more a commentary on the civic life of Roman Sparta and only secondarily also on the
relation of Sparta with the outside, non-Spartan world. This local dimension does not of course exclude inner tensions and minor inconsistencies,
which once again reflect the complexity of 'being Greek under Rome'.
In order to claim an unchanging continuity with her uncorrupted and
semi-mythical past, Sparta, which still in the second century AD proudly
exhibited the monuments which celebrated her decisive rôle in the war
against the Persians (the tomb of Eurybiadas, the memorials for the dead
at Thermopylae etc.),[116] is also the very same city that severely censures the
author of the song which, throughout the Hellenised Mediterranean, had
become the manifesto *par excellence* of Greek freedom from the barbarians,
The Persians.[117]

Finally, let us consider the purportedly official format of the text, or, to
put it better, the choice of a 'civic' decree (and not of an 'agogic' inscription
like those from the sanctuary of Artemis Orthia) as a vehicle to re-create
a 'Lycurgan' façade in the contemporary civic life of second-century AD
Sparta. What does it mean? Can the comparison with the agogic inscriptions
from Artemis Orthia help us once again to understand, this time by means of
contrast, the strategy of representation enacted by our decree? We know that

---

[113] For the discovery of this honorary inscription (the base of a statue found in the Isthmian walls) and
its dating, on letter style, to the first half of the second century AD see Broneer 1953: 192–3. Latte
1954, 125 has accepted this date too.

[114] For the interpretation of this much-debated expression see Latte 1954: 125–6 and Tabachovitz 1946:
303, 1955: 77–8. See also *IDid* 181 (*c.* 213/250 AD): the Milesian δῆμος honours Aurelios Hierocles,
winner at the Great Didymeia as τιμοθεαστής, that is for having composed songs 'in the manner
of Timotheus': for this meaning of τιμοθεάζειν see Rehm 1954: 179.

[115] This practice, of course, is not exclusively a late one. *Suda s.v.* Τιμόθεος (τ 620) tells us that already
the Milesian poet had composed διασκευαί, probably 'musical re-arrangements' of traditional
pieces: see Hordern 2002: 10. On the meaning of διασκευή see Veyne 1989.

[116] For Roman Sparta's active involvement in emphasising her role during the Persian war according to
the guidelines of Roman propaganda depicting the Parthian and Sassanians as the 'new' Persians,
see Spawforth in Cartledge and Spawforth 2002: 190–2.

[117] Cf. τὰν παλαιὰν μῶαν ἀτιμάσδη of the decree which is an echo of *PMG* 791. 211–2
παλαιοτέραν . . ./ μοῦσαν ἀτιμῶ.

Wandering poetry, 'travelling' music

during the Roman period a special relevance among the ephebic contests performed at the sanctuary of Artemis Orthia was ascribed to the so-called μῶα and κελοῖα, both of them solo musical competitions[118] which were intended to revive Sparta's ancient musical tradition.[119] The precise nature of these performances is mostly obscure,[120] but their main function was clearly that of integrating the youth into the civic community by means of renewing the Lycurgan *agōgē*.[121] Even more importantly, the agonistic inscriptions of Artemis Orthia are mostly sickle dedications on the part of winners. That is, within the competitive economy of the élite's struggle for honour, they work as a visible sign of the social capital acquired and displayed by the single individual before the eyes of all the beholders, local and extra-local as well.[122] Thus these inscriptions, while engendering distinctions by praising individualist values, contribute to establishing and, at the same time, visualising social hierarchy within the community to which they were addressed.[123] On the contrary, a 'civic' decree, even one that clearly reflects the élite's cultural propaganda, addresses the whole local community with virtually no distinction. What is offered to the eye of fellow citizens and, secondarily, to non-citizens as well is the image of a compact civic body which recognises itself in its past glorious tradition. In

---

[118] See Woodward in Dawkins *et al.* 1929: 287 against Tillyard's suggestion of team competition (Tillyard 1905–6: 354).

[119] For Alcman and Thaletas, together with the paeans of an unknown Dionysodotus the Laconian, sung at the Gymnopaidiai (probably later 'amalgamated' with the Parparonia, from 370/69 BC onwards: cf. Parker 1989: 167 n. 39 and more generally Wilson 2000: 393 n. 178), see Sosibius *FGrH* 595 F 5.

[120] Woodward in Dawkins *et al.* 1929: 288 inclines to consider both contests as merely vocal and not instrumental, whereas according to Rose in Dawkins *et al.* 1929: 406 (followed also by Chrimes 1949: 119–20) the μῶα was probably 'a contest of song' and the κελοῖα (alternatively spelt κελέα, κελῆα, κελεῖα, κελῦα, καιλῆα) a competition of 'oratory or declamation', the latter inference being drawn from *IG* V 1, 264, ll. 6–10 (= no. 4 Dawkins; Augustan period) where the victor says that he dedicates the prize of 'the sweet sound of a nimble tongue' (εὔστομον εὐτροχάλου γλώσσης τόδ᾽ ἄεθλον ἀείρας). Yet the conclusion drawn by Rose is unnecessary. If it is true that the expression εὐτρόχαλος γλῶσσα may refer to rhetorical skill in speech (cf. e.g. Eur. *Ba.* 268, Plut. *Per.* 7.1), the adjective εὐτρόχαλος can be used also of a song and/or melody, cf. e.g. Apoll. Rhod. 4.907 κραιπνὸν εὐτροχάλοιο μέλος κανάχησεν ἀοιδῆς, where εὐτρόχαλος is here likely 'purely instrumental': see Hunter 1996b: 146 with n. 20. Furthermore, from Hesych. *s.v.* μῶά (μ 2018 Latte)· ᾠδή ποιά nothing can be gained in terms of musical performance (that is, vocal or instrumental): Hesych. employs ᾠδή for both kinds of performances, see e.g. Hesych. *s.v.* ἡδύκωμος (η 139 Latte) [instrumental] and *s.v.* ἱμαλίς (ι 600 Latte) [vocal]. For an even more speculative reconstruction of κελοῖα ('hunting cries') see Kennell 1995: 52.

[121] Cf. Kennell 1995: 126–7.

[122] By the first century AD the sanctuary of Artemis Orthia at Sparta had already become the centre of an intense 'touristic' pilgrimage: see Chaniotis 2005b: 155 and König 2005: 92 on the ritual of the καθθηρατόριον (a kind of initiatory hunting-game).

[123] For an analogous function accomplished by the athletic inscriptions from Oinoanda dating to the imperial period see the valuable discussion of van Nijf 2001.

188   LUCIA PRAUSCELLO

our case, the underlying process of social negotiation that such a filtered
image implies is mostly lost, but some bits of it may still be recovered, even if
only partially and fragmentarily, by cross-examination of the archaeological
and epigraphical evidence from 'Kalyvia tes Sokhas'.

Finally, such reflections may make us re-think the cultural premises
underlying the label of 'forgery' commonly ascribed to our decree. As we
have seen, the spuriousness of the text is beyond doubt and in this sense
the decree is certainly 'inauthentic'.[124] But was this 'inauthentic' document
intended to deceive the would-be audience?[125] This is very slippery ground.
Yet if we turn our attention to the archaising inscriptions of Artemis Orthia,
it is quite clear that they did not intend to be seen as 'old': they celebrated
young men who wanted to be recognised as winners by their contemporary
fellow-citizens. Now, our decree mentions of course the old dual kingship
and the ephors (τὼρ βασιλέαρ καὶ τὼρ ἐφόρωρ), yet the overall emphasis
put on the local dimension of the event (re-asserted in the very final line:
μήποτε ταράρρηται κλέορ ἀγώνων) and the remarkably diverging variants which it introduces as regards the well-known episode of the cutting of
the strings seems indeed to suggest that what is actually at stake here is more
the desire to celebrate the present by referring to an illustrious past oppor-
tunely 'customised' rather than to falsify seriously the past *per se*. This is of
course not to deny that a manipulation of the past was actually arranged,
and intentionally so. What I would like to emphasise here is that the revival
of the censure against Timotheus' polychordy and its particular setting was
primarily intended to be a homage to the revived cult of Demeter at the
Spartan Eleusinium: the intended audience might have been aware or not
of the spuriousness of such an invented tradition,[126] but – either way – they
willingly participated in this shared process of re-shaping civic religiosity.

CUSTOMISING TIMOTHEUS AMONG THE ARCADIANS

Let us now jump backwards to the second century BC and turn briefly to
another instance of identity socially constructed by means of 'inventing'
an *ad hoc* musical pedigree. Once again, it is Timotheus' iconic status that
will provide our starting point.

---

[124] The somewhat 'paradoxical' nature of our decree is even more apparent if we keep in mind Lycurgus'
alleged prohibition of written laws (on Sparta's attitude towards written records see Thomas 1989:
31–2). A by-product of the Roman fondness for written legislation?

[125] For the cultural implications of 'Fälschung' and 'forgery' in the ancient world see recently Barnes
1995.

[126] We know that Hellanicus of Lesbos wrote a victor list recording the names of the winners at the
Carneian games (= *FGrH* 4 F 85a).

Wandering poetry, 'travelling' music

Polybius' account in 4.20–1 of the savage and uncivilised nature (ἀγριότης) of the Cynaetheans, the only people among the Arcadians to have abandoned the practice of musical education as introduced by their ancestors (τὰ καλῶς ὑπὸ τῶν ἀρχαίων ἐπινενοημένα καὶ φυσικῶς συντεθεωρημένα), includes a long and significant digression on the rôle of music in shaping human characters and, consequently, national identities in relation to natural environmental conditions.[127] It is within this ancient version of environmental determinism that the Arcadian Polybius gives us a full account of the importance of musical training in Arcadia as a means of 'a state-run system of musical socialisation'.[128] Since the harshness of the climate and the roughness of the territory where Arcadians live (τὸ τῆς φύσεως αὔθαδες καὶ σκληρόν at 4.21.3) do not represent a naturally favourable base on which to graft a regulated and well-ordered form of socialisation, it is the social potential inherent in music, and especially in its choral dimension, that constitutes 'an essential community bond', social and choral order being virtually identified.[129] It is at this point of Polybius' narrative of the Arcadians' invented 'community poetry'[130] that we find the mention of Timotheus' music (together with Philoxenus') as a standard example of 'the true and real music' (τήν γε ἀληθῶς μουσικήν),[131] or, to put it differently, as a canonical part of this civic musical training. The passage deserves to be quoted at length (Polyb. 4.20.8–12).

ταῦτα γὰρ πᾶσίν ἐστι γνώριμα καὶ συνήθη, διότι σχεδὸν παρὰ μόνοις Ἀρκάσι πρῶτον μὲν οἱ παῖδες ἐκ νηπίων ᾄδειν ἐθίζονται κατὰ νόμους τοὺς ὕμνους καὶ παιᾶνας, οἷς ἕκαστοι κατὰ τὰ πάτρια τοὺς (9) ἐπιχωρίους ἥρωας καὶ θεοὺς ὑμνοῦσι· μετὰ δὲ ταῦτα τοὺς Φιλοξένου καὶ Τιμοθέου νόμους μανθάνοντες πολλῇ φιλοτιμίᾳ χορεύουσι κατ᾽ ἐνιαυτὸν τοῖς Διονυσιακοῖς αὐληταῖς ἐν τοῖς θεάτροις, οἱ μὲν παῖδες τοὺς παιδικοὺς ἀγῶνας οἱ δὲ νεανίσκοι (10) τοὺς τῶν ἀνδρῶν λεγομένους. ὁμοίως γε μὲν καὶ παρ᾽ ὅλον τὸν βίον τὰς ἀγωγὰς τὰς ἐν ταῖς συνουσίαις οὐχ οὕτως ποιοῦνται διὰ τῶν ἐπεισάκτων ἀκροαμάτων ὡς δι᾽ αὑτῶν, ἀνὰ μέρος (11) ᾄδειν ἀλλήλοις προστάττοντες . . . (12) καὶ μὲν ἐμβατήρια μετ᾽ αὐλοῦ καὶ τάξεως ἀσκοῦντες, ἔτι δ᾽ ὀρχήσεις ἐκπονοῦντες μετὰ

---

[127] On the 'impact of state organization on collective behaviors' as a means of shaping national characters in Polybius' narrative see most recently Champion 2004: 79–82.

[128] Wilson 2000: 300. This is what is clearly meant by Polybius when, while objecting to Ephorus' censure of music as γοητεία and ἀπάτη, he reports that 'the early Arcadians [did not act randomly] in bringing music into their whole constitution to such an extent that not only boys but young men up to the age of thirty must practise it constantly' (4.20.7).

[129] Kowalzig 2004: 42.

[130] For a definition of 'community poetry' as 'poetry composed for the setting and function of community performance' see Stehle 1997.

[131] For the overtly Platonic overtones of this expression and, generally speaking, of the whole passage, see Kowalzig 2004: 42. For ἀλήθεια referring to music performances within Plato's ideal state, see also Wohl 2004: 340–1 with n. 7.

190   LUCIA PRAUSCELLO

κοινῆς ἐπιστροφῆς καὶ δαπάνης κατ' ἐνιαυτὸν ἐν τοῖς θεάτροις ἐπιδείκνυνται
τοῖς αὐτῶν πολίταις οἱ νέοι.

For it is a well-attested fact and familiar to everyone that in the first place (and
almost exclusively among the Arcadians) the boys from their very childhood are
used to sing in measure[132] the hymns and paeans by means of which the various
communities[133] separately celebrate the local heroes and gods according to their
traditional customs. Later on, learning the nomoi of Philoxenus and Timotheus,
they zealously compete every year in the theatre in choral contests[134] to the accompaniment of professional *aulos*-players, the boys in the boys' contest and the young
men in the so-called men's contest. Similarly, through all their life they enter-
tain themselves at symposia not by means of hired musicians but by performing
themselves, calling for a song from each in turn . . . furthermore the young men
practise military tunes to the *aulos* while parading, train themselves hard at dancing
and give annual performances in the theatres, to their citizens, all this under state
control and at the public expense.

What at once strikes the reader's attention in Polybius' account is, at least
from a historical perspective, the composite, heterogeneous nature of the
musical curriculum proudly displayed by the Arcadians. Now, the whole
system purports to be ancient (or at least what would seem so to a second-
century observer): we have just been told that this very same institutionalised use of music had been introduced by their forefathers (cf. τὰ καλῶς
ὑπὸ τῶν ἀρχαίων ἐπινενοημένα at 4.20.3, τοὺς πρώτους Ἀρκάδων at
4.20.7 and οἱ πάλαι at 4.21.1). Besides, the ancestral musical customs of
Crete and Sparta have just been mentioned as a proper touchstone for the
antiquity of the Arcadian traditions.[135] The first part of the account thus
well suits the archaic and law-abiding nature of this noble inheritance:
the boys, from their very childhood, learn traditional songs (hymns and
paeans) to praise local gods and heroes κατὰ τὰ πάτρια.[136] Immediately
after this information, which could be regarded as perfectly in keeping with
a strongly conservative musical attitude such as that displayed by Plato in
his *Republic* or *Laws*,[137] we learn quite surprisingly that the second stage

---

[132] This is also Paton's translation of κατὰ νόμους (Paton 1922); cf. Walbank 1957: 467 *ad loc.*
[133] For the political fragmentation of the 'Arcadian nation' into individual communities, see Nielsen
1999: 47 and 51–5.
[134] For this meaning of χορεύουσι, see Walbank 1957: 468.
[135] Cf. 4.20.6 on the introduction of the *aulos* in war training by 'the ancient Cretans and Spartans'
(τοὺς παλαιοὺς Κρητῶν καὶ Λακεδαιμονίων). The antiquity of Arcadia's musical tradition is
echoed also by [Plut.] *De mus.* 1142e, where the Mantineans are said to have developed from
ancient times onwards (τὸ παλαιόν) a system of musical training in order to shape properly the
characters of the youth.
[136] For the importance of local compositions within the economy of the communal poetry also in the
Hellenistic period, see Stehle 1997: 57.
[137] For Plato's 'choral kosmos' see Kowalzig 2004: 44–9.

of this traditional curriculum involves the (apparently choral) performance of Timotheus' and Philoxenus' *nomoi*, that is, the contested *avant-garde* of fifth-century Athenian music. As we proceed, our puzzlement grows: annual contests of male choruses are said to take place to the accompaniment of 'hired *aulos* players' (τοῖς Διονυσιακοῖς αὐληταῖς). This time it is the irruption of the Διονυσιακοὶ τεχνῖται, that is, professional musicians belonging to an organised guild, into this otherwise fifth-century polis-like picture skilfully portrayed by Polybius that startles us.[138] And equally surprising is the manner of this annual performance: Timotheus' *nomoi* are performed *chorally* to the accompaniment of the *aulos*, although the *nomos* was usually a monodic piece.[139] And the astonishment at the miscellaneous nature of Arcadia's educational system only increases when we learn of Arcadians preserving the aristocratic practice of themselves performing at symposia (not by accident a custom to which the musically conservative Spartans also proudly claimed to be faithful).[140] Now, what does this mixed array of sixth-, fifth- and fourth-century musical practices in Polybius' account mean? Whom is Polybius addressing? And what function does this apparently 'tamed' Timotheus perform in the recipient's social and political context?

Let us start from the question of the addressee. Goldhill has rightly underlined that Polybius' digression at 4.20–1 is to be understood mostly as 'a piece of Greek cultural polemic'.[141] Polybius' passionate defence of Arcadian musical training is part of his broader strategy of constructing a Greek cultural identity under Rome, a 'Greekness' able to keep pace with the new historical conditions (among which, of course, the reality of Roman power has to be listed first). To quote Goldhill, Polybius is constructing here an *ad hoc* image of *paideia* for his own region

out of a long intellectual tradition back to Plato at least . . . This musical education is said to be traditional and ancient – but it includes the New Music. It says a lot about how Polybius is constructing an Arcadia in the image of the polis of the fifth

---

[138] As pointed out by Guarducci 1929: 645, at Polybius' time Arcadia greatly contributed to providing the guilds of the *technitai* with local musicians. For the puzzling presence of the Artists of Dionysus in this context see already Goldhill 2002.

[139] For this passage as pointing out 'how classificatory names based on different points of view were interfering within the same "dithyrambic" semantic field' see D'Alessio forthcoming b.

[140] See Walbank 1957: 468 quoting Philocorus (via Athen. 14.630f) as regards the Spartan custom, in war periods, of performing Tyrtaeus' hymns in turn at the end of the dinner. On the Spartans' hostility towards hired musicians and incoming professionals, both at private and public performances, see e.g. Athen. 14.633a–b (on which cf. Wilson 2000: 115). More to the point, for the persistence of this hostility, see also Xen. *Ages.* 2.17 (Agesilaos singing the paean during the Hyakinthia of 391 BC and taking part actively in the chorus).

[141] Goldhill 2002: 4.

192   LUCIA PRAUSCELLO

century and the philosophical schools rather than a rural world of προσέληνοι . . .
It is an image to set not just against other Greek cities or other images of Arcadia,
but also against Rome.[142]

The Arcadia depicted by Polybius is thus an Arcadia that consciously places
itself at the centre of an enlarged world of culture, an Arcadia that has to find
a compromise between old ancestral customs and increasingly sophisticated
stimuli.[143]

So why is our Timotheus included in such a peculiar pedagogical
curriculum? In what sense could Timotheus' *nomoi* be perceived by the
Arcadians as the proper constituent of an educational system which aimed
at 'softening and tempering the stubbornness and harshness of nature'[144]
and consequently at shaping national ethnic identity?[145] Are we simply
dealing here with the familiar phenomenon by which innovators, whatever
their field, are regarded by later generations as 'a pillar of the old order'?[146]
Of course, this is certainly one element of the process that is operating here.
Two roughly contemporary Cretan inscriptions (*ICret* V.viii.11 from Knossos and xxiv.1 from Priansos)[147] inform us that, in order to gain a renewal
of the asylia previously granted to his city, the Tean ambassador Menecles,
most likely an artist of the Dionysiac guild settled at Teos from about 220
BC,[148] repeatedly performed to the cithara poems of Timotheus, Polyidos
and ancient local Cretan poets,[149] as well as a collected anthology of Cretan

---

[142] Goldhill 2002: 4.
[143] On the Arcadians' privileged link with music see Nielsen 1999: 74 n. 188 (= Nielsen 2002: 79 n.
204).
[144] Cf. 4.21.3 βουλόμενοι δὲ μαλάττειν καὶ κιρνᾶν τὸ τῆς φύσεως αὔθαδες καὶ σκληρόν, τά τε
προειρημένα πάντα παρεισήγαγον.
[145] Cf. 4.21.2 where different atmospheric conditions are explicitly said to be the main source of ethnic
and cultural distinctions. Polybius' awareness of the distinct ethnic identity of the Arcadian nation
is set out at once at 4.20.1 (τὸ τῶν Ἀρκάδων ἔθνος). For Arcadians perceiving themselves, from an
early date onwards, as a distinct ethnic group among the Greeks and ethnic identity being 'a focus
of self-ascription and identification' see Nielsen 1999.
[146] See Wallace 2003: 91–2 according to whom 'Athens' late fifth-century revolutionaries ended as
inspirational classics in rural Arcadia' and Wilson 2000: 300 who claims that 'poetic innovation
was probably not especially important to the choral contests of this period. The antiquity of these
poet-musicians of old Greece in itself guaranteed their value as vehicles of tradition, even though
they had been known in their own age as controversial innovators'.
[147] Gathered together in Guarducci 1929, no. 36. The date of the inscriptions of the so-called 'second
asylia series' prompted by the Teans is a much-debated issue, hypotheses having variously ranged
down to 131 BC: the only certain datum is that they are to be dated after 170 BC; see Curty 1995:
n. 46 and Rigsby 1996: 289–90 (apparently inclined to date the inscriptions back to 203 BC).
[148] For the guild of the *Technitai* of Ionia and Hellespont having its headquarters at Teos, see Le Guen
2001: II, 27ff. As to Menecles, see Stephanis 1988, no. 1650.
[149] See *ICret* V.viii.11 ll. 7–12 ἀλλὰ καὶ ἐπε-/δείξατο Μενεκλῆς μετὰ κιθάρας πλεονάκις τά τε/
Τιμοθέω καὶ Πολυίδω καὶ τῶν ἁμῶν ἀρχαίων ποι-/ητᾶν καλῶς καὶ ὡς προσῆκεν ἀνδρὶ

Wandering poetry, 'travelling' music

mythology.[150] In this case, Timotheus' music is, at least to the Tean ambassadors and their intended audience, nothing more than a traditional piece of the classical citharodic repertoire, a piece which is perceived as perfectly equivalent to and interchangeable with the classical Cretan 'greatest hits', that must most likely have included Thaletas' songs, as two contemporary inscriptions from Mylasa strongly suggest (*IMyl* 652 and 653).[151] The combining of Timotheus and Thaletas, almost a heretical combination to a Spartan,[152] was evidently routine for the Artists of Dionysos in the second century BC: historical differences or even rivalries[153] are erased and they can both be properly considered as belonging to the common pan-Hellenic inheritance. But is this exactly the case also for our passage? The mention of Philoxenus alongside Timotheus might suggest so; yet if we look more closely at what was probably the historical origin of this Arcadian musical systematisation another explanation may also be taken into account.

Stehle has already observed that 'Polybius thinks that the purpose (sc. of such a musical training) was to "soften" and civilize the Arcadians, but more mundane considerations may have moved the Arcadians also. One of them was probably the fostering of Arcadian ethnic identity after the restoration of independence in 370.'[154] Perhaps we can go even a step further. We know that in 370 BC the Arcadians founded a federal state predicated on an exclusively ethnic basis and animated from the very beginning by a strong hostility towards Sparta,[155] and it is precisely after the foundation of the Arcadian confederacy and the liberation of Messenia that the construction of 'a common Arcadian prehistory' notably increased.[156] That is, a distinctively Arcadian, shared cultural background was actively constructed mostly in the fourth century 'since it provided the Arcadians with a

---

πεπαιδευμέ-/νωι, and xxiv.1 ll. 4–9 ἀλλὰ/ καὶ ἐπεδείξατο Μενεκλῆς μετὰ κιθάρας τά τε Τι-/ μοθέου καὶ Πολυίδου καὶ τῶν ἁμῶν παλαιῶν ποι-/ητᾶν καλῶς καὶ πρεπόντως.

[150] xxiv.1 ll. 9–13 εἰσ(ή)νεγκε δὲ κύκλον/ ἱστορημέναν ὑπὲρ Κρήτας κα[ὶ τ]ῶν ἐν [Κρή]ται γε-/ γονότων θεῶν τε καὶ ἡρώων, [ποι]ησάμενο[ς τ]ὰν / συναγωγὰν ἐκ πολλῶν ποιητᾶ[ν] καὶ ἱστοριαγρά-/φων. For this interpretation of κύκλον ἱστορημέναν see Guarducci 1929: 647 and Chaniotis 1988a: 154 (*pace* Hordern 2002: 12–13, who speaks of 'a citharodic cycle of poems').

[151] On these two asylia decrees for Mylasa from two unknown Cretan cities (dating to the second century BC) see Chaniotis 1988a. As in the Tean case, the ambassadors perform here, among other pieces, also those of Thaletas the Cretan (Θαλήτα τῶ Κρητός).

[152] See Plut. *Agis* 10.3–4 where Thaletas is becomingly matched with Terpander and Pherecydes as one of the pillars of the Spartan musical tradition and is contrasted with Timotheus and Phrynis' debauched muse.

[153] Polyidos probably represented a musical trend 'apparently opposed to the developments of the New Music': see Hordern 2002: 5 on [Plut.] *De mus.* 1138b.

[154] Stehle 1997: 66.

[155] Cf. Nielsen 1999: 44–5. Megalopolis itself had been founded as a 'bulwark against Sparta': see Nielsen 2002: 106–7.

[156] Nielsen 1999: 36–7.

194   LUCIA PRAUSCELLO

tradition of active hostility toward Sparta which corresponded to the actual
historical situation after 370'.[157] If we think of the long-lasting tradition
of Spartan rejection of Timotheus' Muse and, even more, of Timotheus'
strong criticism of Sparta at the end of the *Persians*, it is not so difficult to
understand why Timotheus was happily welcomed by the forefathers of the
Arcadian nation, notwithstanding the non-traditional features exhibited by
his music. This is even more the case if we pay attention to other pieces of
evidence for the Arcadians' long-standing fondness for Timotheus, namely
Plut. *Philop.* 11 and Paus. 8.50.3. Both passages report Philopoemen's tri-
umphal epiphany at the celebration of the Nemean games of 206/5 BC, that
is, shortly after the defeat of the Spartans at Mantinea. Just as Philopoemen,
the present victor against the Spartans and future dismantler of the Lycurgan ἀγωγή,[158] enters the stadium accompanied by his soldiers, Pylades of
Megalopolis, one of the most famous citharodes of that time, is singing 'by
chance' (κατὰ τύχην in Plut. *Philop.* 11. 2) the opening verse of Timotheus'
Persians (*PMG* 788).[159] The reaction of the audience is immediate: all the
beholders turn their eyes upon Philopoemen and applaud him as the new
leader of Greek freedom.[160] On this occasion the anti-Spartan potential
lurking within the *Persians* is re-enacted by the Arcadian Pylades, with the
Spartans defeated at Mantinea as the new barbarians.

    This is, of course, not to deny that Timotheus' music 'ended as inspira-
tional classic(s) in rural Arcadia' as has recently been asserted:[161] it is instead
an attempt to recover some of the meandering byways by which Timotheus'
music acquired an iconic status among the 'Arcadian nation'.

---

[157] Nielsen 1999: 36.
[158] For Philopoemen's abolition of the Lycurgan constitution at Sparta in 188 BC (formally re-
    established by the Romans in 146 BC), see Cartledge in Cartledge and Spawforth 2002: 77–9,
    80.
[159] κλεινὸν ἐλευθερίας τεύχων μέγαν Ἑλλάδι κόσμον.
[160] Cf. Plut. *Philop.* 11.3, Paus. 8.50.3.   [161] Wallace 2003: 92.

CHAPTER 8

Epigrammatic contests, poeti vaganti *and local history*

Andrej Petrovic

This paper addresses the role of wandering poets as local historians. There will be two principal limitations to my enquiry: first, the enquiry will be restricted to the period up to the end of the Hellenistic epoch, and secondly, I will examine only the activity of wandering poets as authors of poems written for public monuments. The first section discusses the fact that composing public epigrams, i.e. epigrams set up in public spaces[1] by groups, political institutions, ruling élites or the polis as a whole, was in a number of cases a task fulfilled by wandering poets. The second section is concerned with the procedure through which texts for public monuments were chosen, and it will be proposed that the procedure was occasionally agonistic. A closer look at the contexts of such epigrammatic competitions suggests that they took place in (a) the framework of public festivals, and (b) the framework of public commissions.

In the third section I will demonstrate that poems composed by wandering poets for local public monuments, even though they may reflect the patron's view or version of historical events, still had an impact which surpassed the boundaries of the polis, local group or political élite that sponsored them. Therefore, I will argue for a supra-local reception of poetry composed for local addressees. In this sense it will be suggested that one of the first media through which such poems were diffused were the earliest epigrammatic collections, which were organised on the principle of interest in local history.

I would like to express my gratitude to the editors and the organisers of the conference, Richard Hunter and Ian Rutherford, as well as to the audience for their contributions to this paper. I am especially indebted to Ewen Bowie, Paola Ceccarelli, Angelos Chaniotis, Jon E. Lendon, Ivana Petrovic and David Sider for numerous helpful suggestions. I am also grateful to Lilah G. Fraser and Alan Sheppard for polishing my English.

[1] On public space in archaic and early classical Greek *poleis* see Hölscher 1998.

196 ANDREJ PETROVIC

WANDERING POETS AS COMPOSERS OF PUBLIC EPIGRAMS

That wandering poets were involved in composing public epigrams can be shown with certainty for the early fourth century, and we may, albeit rather tentatively, suppose the same already for the late sixth century.

If we take a glance at verse-inscriptions from public monuments from the archaic to Hellenistic periods,[2] we will soon notice that the names of their authors do not often accompany the poems.[3] In regard to the names of the authors of both public and private epigrams, the stones remain silent for all of the archaic period and a great part of the classical period. It is only at the beginning of the fourth century BC that authors' names start emerging, carved upon the stone along with the epigrams; even then names do not occur in great numbers.[4] Therefore, the little we know about the epigrammatists in the archaic and classical periods stems from literary sources, some of which are not entirely trustworthy in the matter of ascriptions.[5]

Symmakhos of Pellana and an anonymous paidotribas at the court of Arbinas: not wandering poets?

The first secure occurrence of a poet's name on a stone comes with a base dedicated by the late fifth- / early fourth-century BC Xanthian dynast Arbinas. The rectangular base (inv. No. 6121), excavated during French excavations in the Letoon in 1973,[6] bore a statue of the dynast dedicated to Leto. All four of its faces are inscribed. On two faces appear Greek poems (A+B), the other two (C+D) display texts in Lycian. The poem on face A (= CEG 888 vv. 1–19) is usually considered a long epigram (consisting of seventeen hexameters followed by an elegiac couplet) with a roughly twofold subject:[7] for the most part the poem summarises the military exploits of Arbinas (with an emphasis on his subjugation of Xanthos, Pinara and

---

[2] Editions: the verse-inscriptions until the end of the fourth century BC are collected in Hansen *CEG*. There is no systematic collection of Greek epigrams on stone for the period third to first centuries BC. This period has been partly covered by Peek *GVI*, Pfohl 1967 and Page *FGE*. Merkelbach-Stauber *SGO* I–V limit their collection to the Greek East and provide with it a bibliography, translations and commentary.

[3] This has been observed on numerous occasions ever since Kaibel 1873: 436. Cf. recently Gutzwiller 1998: 48, Fantuzzi 2004: 299–91 and Meyer 2005: 98 n. 265.

[4] *Pace* Page 1981: 120, n. 2 who argued that it was only in Hellenistic times that we encounter poets' names on stone.

[5] On signatures cf. Parsons 2002: 114–15.

[6] Bryce 1986: 95. On the history of excavations and the base in general cf. Bourgarel/Metzger (*FdX* IX, 1): 149–54.

[7] For the full text see *FdX* IX, 1: 156 and *CEG* 888, with restorations p. 283. All translations, unless otherwise stated, are mine.

Epigrammatic contests and local history

Telmessos, i.e. the establishment of his rule over the Lycians)[8], but it also deals with the appearance of, and the grounds for the dedication of, the statue of Arbinas (vv. 8–10). It is in this context that we learn that the dedication of his statue to Leto was prompted by the Delphic oracle: v. 9 Πυθῶι ἐρωτήσας Λητῶι με ἀνέθηκεν ('Having inquired of the Delphic Oracle, he [sc. Arbinas] dedicated me . . .').

The last two verses, physically separated from the rest of the text, state explicitly that the poem's author comes from the Peloponnese, vv. 18f.:

Σύμμαχος Εὐμήδεος Πελλανεὺς μάντις ἀ[μύμων]
δῶρον ἔτευξε ἐλεγῆια Ἀρβίναι εὐσυνέτως.

Symmakhos of Pellana, son of Eumedes, blameless (?) seer fashioned with good understanding[9] elegiac verses as a gift for Arbinas.

Poem B (*CEG* 888 vv. 19–53) from the same base is apparently not a single poem, but represents a set of five 'eulogies', in character very close to the Symmakhos-epigram, and only loosely bound together (if at all) by particles. Bousquet comments on the structure of the verse-inscription B as follows:[10] 'Comme il arrive fréquemment, surtout dans les épitaphs, l' "éloge" du prince est fait de plusieurs versions, ou variants, mises bout à bout.'[11] This possibility could, and in my opinion should, be entertained: on metrical grounds alone one may read five separate poems, since the inscription uses sequences both of elegiac couplets and of hexameters.[12] As far as we can discern from the fragmentary lines, the content too suggests a division into separate verse-inscriptions, since a number of elements keep recurring in (arguably) separate poems: as in the poem of Symmakhos (A 16), at least three of the poems involved an apostrophe of Arbinas,[13] and all of them seem to have had, in one way or another, the very same subject – the praise of Arbinas, especially of the military ventures he conducted as a young man[14] and of the piety he displayed by dedicating the statue.[15] Therefore on the Letoon-base inv. No. 6121 we seem to have a dossier of six Greek verse-inscriptions, one of which is inscribed alone, on a single face,

---

[8] On this cf. Savalli 1988: 103–23. [9] On the meaning of εὐσυνέτως cf. below pp. 214–15.

[10] For this and the text see *FdX* IX, 1: 159. Hansen (*CEG* 889, iii) prints Bousquet's text, albeit without many comments on the proposed division.

[11] Variation on a theme in epitymbic/commemorative epigrams is known since the early classical period (cf. e.g. *CEG* 174, 578, 593). On this cf. Fantuzzi forthcoming; for the Hellenistic period cf. Kirstein 2002.

[12] *FdX* IX, 1: 159: 'J'ai cru déceler la répartition: I: 1–7 (et probablement 8 ou 10 vers): hexamètres, II: 8–13: trois distiques élégiaques, III: 14–19: trois distiques élégiaques, IV: onze hexamètres, V: 31–4: deux distiques élégiaques.'

[13] *FdX* IX, 1: 157–8 poem B. Apostrophe: vv. 19, 20, 28, 32 (= *CEG* 888 iii 37, 47, 51).

[14] Cf. *FdX* IX, 1: 156 v. 5, 157 vv. 4, 15. [15] *FdX* IX, 1: 156, vv. 8–10; 157, vv. 10 (?), 15–16, 32–4.

198 ANDREJ PETROVIC

and accompanied by the name of its author, and five further anonymous epigrams inscribed together on a different face.

Symmakhos of Pellana is however not the only author of a public inscription whose name was recorded on a stone in Lycia. In the Letoon stood one further base also bearing an epigram and containing information about its author. This second base (inv. Nos. 271 + 453[16]), which also bore a dedication of Arbinas, is preserved in a much more battered shape. The poem consists of four elegiac couplets accompanying a dedication by Arbinas to Artemis. The first three couplets dealt with the military victories of Arbinas (stressing yet again his triumph over Xanthos, Telmessos and Pinara and his rule over Lycians),[17] while the last couplet stated the name of the poet (vv. 7–8.):

> παιδοτρίβας επ[
> δῶρ' ἐποίησε ελ[
>
> *paidotribas* . . .
> fashioned as a present el[egiac verses?

Whereas in the case of the *paidotribas*, it is not possible to infer much about the author of the dedicatory epigram, the information on Symmakhos is remarkable in more than one sense. It is noteworthy that the author comes from the Peloponnese since he states that his fatherland is Pellana; secondly, he states that the poem was a gift; thirdly, it is said that he is a *mantis a[mūmōn]*.

Even though at present we can not infer much about the relationships between the last Xanthian dynasts and the Greek world, it would be a fair guess that Symmakhos belonged to the group of wandering professionals. The contacts between the Greek world and Lycian dynasts, on a political level, have been newly reassessed by Keen[18] who accepted that the evidence for direct contacts between Sparta or the Peloponnese and Lycia in general do not exist, at least as far as the end of the fifth and the beginning of the fourth century are concerned.

About the origin of the anonymous Greek who composed the dedicatory epigram of Arbinas not much can be deduced, but since he seemingly had the profession of *paidotribas*, perhaps he was yet another wandering professional. As we saw, his poem appears also to have been a present for the dynast, just like the poem of Symmakhos. Furthermore, the authors of both poems seem to have been fully aware and perhaps even proud of their skill,

---

[16] *CEG* 889, *FdX* IX, 1: 159, C.   [17] vv. 3–4.
[18] Cf. Keen 1998: 140. Keen however does not exclude the possibility of some contact between Lycians and the Greek world.

Epigrammatic contests and local history

as the position of their names on the stone implies: the names of the authors are marked out by being physically separated from the rest of the poems.[19] The question therefore arises as to what kind of wandering professionals we should recognise in Symmakhos and the anonymous *paidotribas*. The case of the *paidotribas* is somewhat simpler than the case of Symmakhos: since his profession is clearly stated, one might imagine some sort of a *Gastarbeiter*, a professional instructor engaged to see to the prince's physical development, rather than a genuine 'wandering poet' in the narrow sense of the phrase.[20]

The case of Symmakhos is more complex, due to the fact that his profession is labelled as μάντις ἀμ[ύμων] and to his emphasis on the poem as a present (δῶρον). Another instance where we can recognise the relationship of *xenia* between poet and addressee of the poem, and the poem as a present, is the well-known epigram of Simonides for the seer Megistias who fell together with Leonidas' three hundred.[21] Herodotus states in the passage following the Thermopylae epigrams that it was Simonides who wrote the epigram, *kata xeiniēn*, thus implying that the poem was a gift for his deceased friend, as opposed to the rest of the epigrams on the Thermopylae memorial which were financed by the Amphictiony.[22]

It is important to stress these two elements, since they involve several difficulties. How are we to interpret the *sphragis* in vv. 18–19? Is μάντις ἀμ[ύμων] an indication of Symmakhos' profession as a seer[23] or does he see himself in the tradition of a poet-prophet, a tradition familiar from the Roman *vates* and which is at least conceivable also in the poetry of the classical period?[24] As things stand, both possibilities must remain open

---

[19] Cf. the photos at *FdX* IX, 2 pl. 72.2 (Symmakhos) and pl. 74 (*paidotribas*).

[20] The fact that he was the prince's instructor does not necessarily, of course, exclude the possibility that the man in question was a poet or even a poet of rank; Himerius, *Or.* 29.24 tells the story of Polycrates summoning Anacreon to Samos to instruct his son in music and poetry. The Greek in Lycia was however a *paidotribas*, a *gymnastic* teacher who presumably spent a longer time at Arbinas' court and this does exclude him from the category of *wandering* poets as defined below.

[21] Hdt. 7.228: μνῆμα τόδε κλεινοῖο Μεγιστία, ὅν ποτε Μῆδοι / Σπερχειὸν ποταμὸν κτεῖναν ἀμειψά-μενοι, / μάντιος ὅς τότε Κῆρας ἐπερχομένας σάφα εἰδώς / οὐκ ἔτλη Σπάρτης ἡγεμόνας προλιπεῖν. ('This is the gravestone (*mnēma*) of the famed Megistias whom the Medes once killed after they passed over the river Spercheios, of the seer, who at that point knew very well that doom was about to fall, but could not find it in his heart to desert the Spartan leaders.')

[22] Cf. Molyneux 1992: 175–9.

[23] Since the dedication of his statue was incited by a visit to Delphi (cf. above p. 197), one could imagine that Symmakhos was given the task of interpreting the answer of the oracle. For *manteis* and *exēgētai* cf. Garland 1984: 75–123.

[24] Even though a solid parallel is lacking, one could imagine a similar development in Greek poetry: cf. Pind. fr. 150 Sn-M, μαντεύεο, Μοῖσα, προφατεύσω δ᾽ ἐγώ. For προφάτας cf. *Paean* 6.6; Bacch. 9.3. Cf. also Pl. *Ion* 532d. It is notable, however, that Greek poets are inclined to take the role of a *prophētēs*, but not that of a *mantis*. On *mantis* vs. *prophētēs* cf. Nagy 1990b: 56–61, and 64.

200   ANDREJ PETROVIC

and we can gain no certainty about the exact content of the label *mantis*. Both as a poet and as a seer Symmakhos could have belonged to a group of wandering professionals able to find a home with Arbinas.[25]

It seems therefore that the Greek epigrams in Lycia were written by professionals, but not necessarily by professional wandering poets, since Symmakhos and the *paidotribas* were presumably in the service of their non-Greek employers for a longer time. If one makes a survey of the epigraphic evidence pertaining to Greek epigrams outside Greece, i.e. the commissions of Greek poets for non-Greek cities up to the Hellenistic period, it becomes obvious that there is no strong evidence that genuine wandering poets went beyond the limits of the Greek world. This statement is valid, of course, only if we define wandering poets in quite narrow terms, i.e. as poets who do not spend long at the place where they performed and as poets whose services were in some way reimbursed.[26]

Ion of Samos at Delphi: a wandering poet

If therefore we can not securely classify these occurrences of the poets' signatures on the Lycian public monument as belonging to wandering poets, we should do so in the case of the epigrams of Ion of Samos. Probably no more than a decade after the poem of Symmakhos of Pellana was carved upon the monument in Xanthos, poems of Ion of Samos were inscribed upon a dedication of the Lacedaemonians in Delphi. Pausanias records these offerings and says that Spartans set up statues of the Dioscuri, Zeus, Apollo, Artemis,

---

[25] It is unnecessary to list here instances of the patronage of wandering poets by local rulers; that wandering *manteis* could also have been endorsed by wealthy sponsors is well known. Cf. Pl. *Rep.* 2.364b. Poems of Greek professionals working for non-Greek patrons are attested. The poems of Symmakhos and the *paidotribas* remind us of the epigram for the Greek architect Mandrocles who built the bridge over Bosporus in 514. This epigram also involves praise of his employer, the Persian king Darius (Hdt. 4.88; A.P. 6.341 (vv. 1–3); Pseudo-Symeon, *Chron.*, T73; Dion. *Byz.* II 42): Βόσπορον ἰχθυόεντα γεφυρώσας, ἀνέθηκε / Μανδροκλέης Ἥρῃ μνημόσυνον σχεδίης, / αὑτῷ μὲν στέφανον περιθείς, Σαμίοισι δὲ κῦδος, / Δαρείου βασιλέος ἐκτελέσας κατὰ νοῦν ('After he had bridged Bosporus, rich with fish, Mandrocles has dedicated to Hera a reminder of the overpass. He was crowned with a wreath, and the Samians with glory, when he accomplished the intentions of king Darius'). The evidence for commissions of wandering poets outside the Greek world before the Hellenistic period is scanty; notable is the case of Timocreon of Ialusos, for whom one can find no evidence that he was active as a poet at the court of Xerxes (unless one regards the personally motivated invectives against Themistocles as Persian commissions). On the other hand, Greek seers abroad or in the service of foreigners are well attested: cf. *mantis* Arexion (Xen. *An.* 6.4.13; 6.5.2; 6.5.8; Hofstetter No. 32); Basias (Xen. *An.* 7.8.10; Hofstetter No. 65); *mantis* Hegesistratos (Hdt. 9.37.4; Hofstetter No. 134); *mantis* Hippomachos (Hdt. 9.38.7; Hofstetter No. 160); *chrēsmologos / diathetēs chresmōn* Onomakritos (Hdt. 7.6.11; Hofstetter No. 239).

[26] On the label 'professional poets' cf. Hardie 1983: 15–36 and below pp. 213–15.

Epigrammatic contests and local history 201

Poseidon and Lysander, who was depicted as being crowned by Poseidon.[27]
The epigrams for the Dioscuri and Lysander are partially preserved:[28]

[παῖ Διός, ὦ] Πολύδευ[κ]ες, Ἴων [?καὶ τοῖσ]δ' ἐλεγείοι[ς]
[?λαϊνέαν] κρηπῖδ' ἐστεφάνωσ[ε ?τεά]ν,
[ἀρχὸς ἐπ]εὶ πρῶτος, πρότερο[ς δ' ἔ]τι τοῦδε ναυάρ[χου],
[?ἔστας ἀγ]εμόνων Ἑλλάδος εὐρυχόρου.

εἰκόνα ἑὰν ἀνέθηκεν [ἐπὶ] ἔργωι τῶιδε ὅτε νικῶν
ναυσὶ θοαῖς πέρσεν Κε[κ]ροπιδᾶν δύναμιν
Λύσανδρος, Λακειδαίμονα ἀπόρθητον στεφανώσα[ς]
Ἑλλάδος ἀκρόπολ[ιν, κ]αλλίχορομ πατρίδα.
ἐξάμο ἀμφιρύτ[ας] τεῦξε ἐλεγεῖον : Ἴων.

[Child of Zeus], Polydeuces, [with these] elegiacs Ion crowned [your stone] base,
because you were the principal [commander], taking precedence even over this
admiral, among the leaders of Greece with its wide dancing places.

Lysander set up this image of himself on this monument when with his swift ships
he victoriously routed the power of the descendants of Kekrops and crowned the
invincible Lacedaimon, the citadel of Greece, the homeland with the beautiful
dancing-places. Ion of sea-girt Samos composed these elegiacs. (*CEG* 819 ii–iii,
trans. M. Fantuzzi)

Even though the wording of the signature is to some extent similar to that
of Symmakhos' epigram (τεῦξε ἐλεγεῖον),[29] we can find no support here for
the assumption that Ion of Samos was already a professional in the service
of the Lacedaemonians – the poem is not a gift, and Ion does not state that
he has any other profession. In short, we might register Ion of Samos as the
first epigraphically recorded case of a wandering poet commissioned by a
polis to compose an epigram. It is quite remarkable how the poet's name,
Ion, could be seen as corresponding to the nature of his profession.[30]

The first recorded case of this kind will presumably not have been the
earliest instance of this practice, and we have no reason to suppose that it
was very unusual to engage a wandering poet to compose a public epigram.
In fact, a random examination of the poetic signatures on stone suggests
that, when a poet's name is recorded, the author is, more likely than not, a
foreigner and thus, possibly, a wandering poet, as table 1 shows:

[27] Pausanias 10.9.7–10.   [28] On these poems cf. Fantuzzi 2004: 290–1.
[29] Notable also is the position of the *sphragis* which corresponds to that of Symmakhos, albeit it occupies
only a pentameter. Should one accept the reading [π]έμψας μοι πρόπολον Σ[ύμμαχον in *CEG*
888.28 (proposed by Bousquet, cf. *CEG* 888:284), its position would be comparable to that of Ion
in 819 ii, 1.
[30] Perhaps one might recognise a pun in the poet's name – Ἴων as Ἰών; or in the fact that a poet named
Ionian writes ἐλεγεῖον. Cf. further above p. 6, n. 25.

202   ANDREJ PETROVIC

Table 1 *Poets' signatures on stone (until III c. BC): Thessaly, Delphi, Lycia*

Poet and his provenance	Date	Sponsor or beneficiary	Epigram found at	Edition
1 Symmakhos of Pellana	early IV BC	Arbinas of Xanthos	Xanthos, Lycia	*CEG* 888
2 Anonymous *paidotribas*; Attika(?)	early IV BC	Arbinas of Xanthos	Xanthos, Lycia	*CEG* 890
3 Ion of Samos	405–350 BC (?)	Spartans/ Lysandros (son of Aristokrites)	Delphi	*CEG* 819
4 Ion of Samos	405–350 BC (?)	Spartans	Delphi	*CEG* 819
5 Aphthonetos (?)	III BC (?)	Group of soldiers	Phallana, Thessaly	*ISE* p. 74
6 Herakleides, son of Trallianos	III BC	A family	Larisa, Thessaly	*IG* IX 2, 637

In only one out of six cases do we find a patronymic indicating that the poet in question might be a local. In the first four cases it is certain that the poets were foreigners. In the case of Aphthonetos it is quite difficult to determine whether he was a foreigner or not – we read only Ἀφθονήτου τὸ ἐλεγεῖον, there is no indication of his provenance nor do we find a patronym.[31] One could argue that he was either a prominent citizen of Phallana or a well-known poet.[32] Aphthonetos is not a unique case among the *epigrammatopoioi*. There is a further attestation for the practice that only a name without further specification is inscribed. The third-century BC poet Eukleides, who composed a dedicatory epigram, offers a parallel case:

τῷ σφε καὶ Εὐκλείδης Μούσαι[ς φίλος, ἱ]ερ[ὸ]ς [– X]
κοσμεῖ ἀειμνήστοις εὐλογίας ἔπεσιν.

Therefore, Eukleides, friend of Muses, the sacred [. . .], adorns them with ever-memorable words of eulogy (*IG* IX 1, 131, vv. 5f.)

---

[31] Aphthonetos' poem is most readily accessible at *ISE* I p. 74.

[32] As a parallel case, one could perhaps think of Callimachus in Athens. Cf. *Ath. Ag.* XVI, 213, col. I, 70 and Oliver 2002: 6–8. We actually know an example, also from the Hellenistic period, of the practice that when a poet's current citizenship was unclear, only his name, without patronym or ethnonym, was recorded. Consider Diodorus of Sinope, who at the end of his life became Diodorus of Athens (cf. *IG* XI 105, 21 and *SEG* 33, 106).

Epigrammatic contests and local history

Even if we did not have the names of wandering poets recorded on some public monuments, one might assume that the texts set up in the public space of a polis were not haphazardly chosen nor indiscriminately carved upon the stone. What exactly the procedure for choosing a poet was and what steps it included is a question well worth raising. Secondly, since we can observe that, at least in a number of cases, wandering poets had been involved in composing such texts, then the model we should propose must have allowed at least some access for non-citizens.

EPIGRAMMATIC CONTESTS

Turning now to the process of choosing epigrams for public monuments, I will argue that possibly already in the classical epoch, and quite probably in the Hellenistic period, some of the poems carved upon public monuments were chosen by means of epigrammatic contests.

The sources on this subject are neither very copious nor very detailed, yet there is some suggestion of agonistic contexts already for the early fifth century. I begin with a passage from the *Vita Aeschyli*, where the author explains the reason why Aeschylus left Athens.

ἀπῆρεν δὲ ὡς Ἱέρωνα [. . .] κατὰ δὲ ἐνίους ἐν τῷ εἰς τοὺς ἐν Μαραθῶνι τεθνηκότας ἐλεγείῳ ἡσσηθεὶς Σιμωνίδῃ· τὸ γὰρ ἐλεγεῖον πολὺ τῆς περὶ τὸ συμπαθὲς λεπτότητος μετέχειν θέλει, ὃ τοῦ Αἰσχύλου, ὡς ἔφαμεν, ἐστὶν ἀλλότριον.

He [Aeschylus] went away to Hieron . . . since, as some say, he was defeated by Simonides in the epigram-contest for the fallen of Marathon. For the epigram demands a lot of refinement when it comes to sympathy and this is alien to Aeschylus as already mentioned. (*Vit. Aesch.* 8[33])

The noun ἐλεγεῖον has been translated as 'epigram' because, as Martin West has argued, the substantive, when used in the singular, denotes an elegiac couplet and, quite often, an epigram; even when used in the plural, it might denote an epigram, as we saw in the case of Ion of Samos, and later it could even be used for an epigram which was not written in elegiac couplets at all.[34]

An epigrammatic contest, on the other hand, could be implied by the verb ἡσσηθείς which is well known from agonistic contexts,[35] and therefore the interpretation 'epigram-contest' seems possible. What this seems

---

[33] *TrGF* iii, 33–4. On this passage cf. Oliver 1933:480; Podlecki 1984: 185, Molyneux 1992: 148–53, Boedeker 1995: 225, Obbink 2001: 79. Already Oliver argued that the term might denote an epigram.

[34] Cf. West 1974: 3 The term was probably coined by the end of the fifth century BC, cf. Bowie 1986: 25–7.

[35] Cf. LSJ *s.v.*; *Passow Wörterbuch der griechischen Sprache, s.v.*, p. 1362: 'in einem Wettstreite verlieren'.

to imply is that, at some stage of the process of choosing an epigram to be publicly displayed either the texts or their authors were in some respect assessed. Yet this is certainly not much more than just one possible way of understanding the passage, and I am not really inclined to give it much weight. The author of the *Vita* could, as Mary Lefkowitz argued,[36] have inferred information about the authors from their own poems or the texts of other poets – the *Vita* is much influenced by Aristophanes.[37] The information about the poets concerned is certainly quite precarious and the reasons for distrusting it outweigh those for confidence in it. If however we decide to accept the possibility that behind this the passage lies a contemporary – classical? – practice of organising epigrammatic contests, we will find confirmation of this assumption in epigraphic evidence.[38] I do not claim, of course, that this is the case for all public epigrams, but I do think it plausible that some were composed by wandering poets who were not necessarily appointed and commissioned, but had to take part and be victorious in a competition in order to have their epigram inscribed in public space.

This notion could be important for several reasons. Epigrams' supposed 'writtenness' is often taken to be an essential feature of the genre's pre-Hellenistic history, and is taken to imply that it was only in the Hellenistic period that epigrams emerged as a full literary form, since until the Hellenistic period the epigram was 'excluded from the arena of oral discourse where poetry could obtain rank and status by performance, and reperformance, before a collective audience'.[39] If we can show that in the Hellenistic period, certainly, and possibly in the classical period as well, epigrams, even those inscribed on monuments, were not necessarily excluded from the arena of oral performance, then some aspects of our understanding of the epigram's early history and its place among the literary genres would have to be accordingly redefined.[40]

The two basic starting-points for my suggestion are as follows. First I refer to an *a priori* reason. If we bear in mind how the designs for statues

---

[36] Lefkowitz 1981.   [37] Lefkowitz 1991: 119–22. See also Radt 1981: 1–7.

[38] Lefkowitz 1991: 121 speaks of an 'elegiac competition' and emphasises that 'the notion of *contest* matters more than its subject or the identity of his [sc. Aeschylus'] opponents'.

[39] Gutzwiller 1998: 2–3. A further feature which influenced the modern conception of the pre-Hellenistic epigram as a second-class poetry is certainly its anonymity and/or the fragility of its ascriptions. On the lack of authorial authority and on how poems of dubious authorship quickly turn into bad poems cf. Hunter 2002.

[40] Cf. also Fantuzzi 2004: 290, in the context of the importance of authorial identity: 'The epigrams of Ion [of Samos, for the text see above p. 201], on the contrary, suggest that verse inscriptions had already followed their autonomous course towards literary pretension and an authorial awareness, when the high period of the "literary" epigram dawned.'

Epigrammatic contests and local history

which were set up in public space were chosen, one will remember that ever since the fifth century BC we have an agonistic setting: Pliny's report on the sculptors' competition to make an Amazon for the temple of Artemis in Ephesus is just one of the sources for this.[41] Further cases of sculptors' competitions are also known from epigraphic evidence. If such a procedure is attested since the fifth century for statues set in the public space, for other products of figural arts and for the production of Panathenaic amphorae, then I can see no reason why contests for public epigrams should not be conceivable.[42]

Secondly, there is a direct source for an epigrammatic contest. The following inscription (*IG* IX 2, 531, see ll. 48f.) was found in the Jewish cemetery in Larisa and is now in the Louvre. It is a list of victors in athletic and literary contests which were organised in 172 BC in honour of those who fought in the battle of Thermopylae. I print the full text:

Φίλωνος τοῦ Φίλωνος | τοῦ ταγεύοντος τὴν| πρώτην χώραν ἐν στρα-|τηγῷ Ἡγησίᾳ, τιθέντος | 5 τὸν ἀγῶνα τοῖς προκε-|κινδυνευκόσιν κατὰ τὸ|γενόμενον ὑπὸ τοῦ δή-|μου ψή[φισμα π]ερὶ τῆς | ἀνανεώ[σεω]ς τοῦ ἀγῶ-|10 νος. οἱ νενεικηκότες |ταυροθηρίᾳ· Μάρκος Ἀρρό(ν)τιος.| καταλογ[ῇ π]αλαιᾷ· Φίλων Φίλωνος |ὁ νεώτερος. προσδρομῇ | ἱππέων· Δημήτριος Δημητρίου.|15 προσ-δρομῇ πεζῶν· Δημήτρι-|ος Ξένωνος. προσδρομῇ συ-|νωρίδι· Τειμασίθεος Γοργώπα.|ἀφιππολαμπάδι· Μάρκος Ἀρρόντιος.|σαλπιστάς· Λυσικλῆς Λεπτίνου.|20 κήρυκας· Πετάλων Διονυσίου.|παῖδας στάδιον· Γάϊος Κλώδιος Γα[ΐ]-|ου. ἄνδρας στάδιον· Δημήτριος | Δημητρίου. παῖδας δίαυλον· Ν[εο-]|μένης Ἀρίστωνος. ἄνδρας |25 δίαυλον· Ἀριστόμαχος Ἑρμίου|παῖδας λαμπαδιστάς· Ἐμπεδίων | Ὁμήρου. παῖδας πύκτας·|Δημόνεικος Εὐδή-μου. ἄνδρας |πύκτας· Δημήτριος Δημητρί-|30 ου, παῖδας παγκράτιον· Φί-|λων Φίλωνος ὁ νεώτερος.|δευτέρας κρίσεως, παῖδας |παγκράτιον· Εὐπαλίδης Θε-|μιστογένους. ἄνδρας |35 παγκράτιον. Ἀσκληπιάδης |Ἀσκληπιάδου. ὁπλίτην· Κτή-|σων Παυσανίου. ἀφιππο-|δρομάν. Ἀρισ-τομένης Ἀσανδρίδου.|ἀποβατικῷ· Λάδαμος Ἀργαίου.|40 σκοπῷ πεζῶν· Ἀλέξανδρος Κλέω-|νος. τόξῳ· Ὀνόμαρχος Ἡρακλείδου.|σκοπῷ ἱππέων· Ἀριστομένης Ἀσαν-|δρίδου. ἐγκωμίῳ λογικῷ·|Κόϊντος Ὄκριος Κοΐντου. ἐγκω-|45 μίῳ ἐπικῷ· Ἀμώμητος Φιλοξ(ε)νί-|δου. καταλογῇ νέᾳ·|Φίλων Φίλωνος ὁ νεώτερος.|ἐπιγράμματι· Ἀμώμη-|τος Φιλοξενίδου.

(1–5) When Philon, son of Philon was *tāgos* in the first division, and Hegesias was general, a competition was organised for those (6–10) who ran into peril and those who fell, as is decided by the decree of the polis, regarding the reinstallation of the

---

[41] Pliny *NH*, 34, 53.

[42] The evidence for contests in painting, drawing and sculpture at festivals (in Asia Minor) is collected in Donderer 1996: 329–38. Note the existence of the contests in painting in fifth century BC (Corinth, Delphi, Samos); Pliny *NH*, 35, 38, Donderer 1996: 333–4 with notes 27–33 (scholarship on authenticity). Cf. also *SEG* 37.626; *SEG* 46.2289; amphorae: *IG* II² 6320.

206   ANDREJ PETROVIC

competition. The winners (11–15): in Bull-chasing (*taurothēria*) Marcus Arrontius.
In the Old Catalogue (*katalogē palaia*) Philon Junior, son of Philon. In the Charge
of Cavalry (*prosdromē hippeōn*) Demetrius, son of Demetrius. In the Charge of
Infantry (*prosdromē pezōn*), Demetrius, son of Xenon. (16–20) In the Charge of
Chariots (*prosdromē synōridi*), Timasitheus, son of Gorgopas. In the Torch-race on
Horseback (*aphippolampadi*), Marcus Arrontius. Among the Trumpeters (*salpistas*), Lysicles, son of Leptines. Among the Shouters (Heralds; *kērykas*), Petalon, son
of Dionysios. (21–5) In the Stadium-race for juniors Gaius Clodius, son of Gaius.
In the Stadium-race for seniors, Demetrius, son of Demetrius. In the Double-
course race (*diaulon*) for juniors, Neomenes, son of Ariston. In the Double-course
race for seniors, Aristomachus, son of Hermias. (26–30) In the Torch-race for
juniors Empedion, son of Homer. In the Boxing for juniors: Demoneicus, son
of Eudemos. In the Boxing for seniors, Demetrius, son of Demetrius. In Boxing and Wrestling (*pankration*) for juniors, Philon Junior, son of Philon. In the
second division, Boxing and Wrestling (*pankration*) for juniors, Eupalides, son
of Themistogenes. In the Boxing and Wrestling (*pankration*) for seniors, Asclepiades, (36–40) son of Asclepiades. In the Race under Arms (*hoplitēn*), Kteson, son
of Pausanias. In the Horse-race, Aristomenes, son of Asandrides. In the Chariot-
leaping (*apobatikōi*), Ladamus, son of Argaeus. In Scouting-on-foot (*skopōi pezōn*),
Alexander, son of Cleon. (41–5) Among archers, Onomarchus, son of Heracleides.
In Scouting-on-horseback (*skopōi hippeōn*), Aristomenes, son of Asandrides. In
the Prose-encomium, Quintus Ocrius, son of Quintus. In the Verse-encomium,
Amometos, son of Philoxenides. (46–9) In the New Catalogue (*katalogē nea*),
Philon Junior, son of Philon. In the epigram (*epigranmati*), Amometos, son of
Philoxenides.

Generically, the inscription belongs to the same class as *IG* IX 2, 525–37 –
that is to lists of victors in literary and musical competitions. The lists attest
the existence of two different festivals held at Larisa, one international
(the penteteric *Eleutheria* festival) and one local.[43] For the international
festival, which as far as we can see included gymnastic, equestrian and
musical disciplines (note that, apart from *aulōidia*, 'literary' disciplines are
missing), the élite was gathered: *stratēgoi*, sons of *stratēgoi*, and high-born
ladies entered their horses in races and so on. We also notice that contestants
came from all over the Greek world – even when local contestants were
victorious, their provenance was stated.[44]

The above-cited inscription is one of five texts documenting the local
festival,[45] and unlike the rest of the dossier it is preserved in excellent

---

[43] See Gallis 1988: 217–18. *Pace* S. G. Miller 2004: 86.
[44] *IG* IX 2, 528 states that 'Stratios, son of Melanthios, Thessalian from Kierion' was victorious as
salpistas (trumpeter); another Thessalian was the best among the *kērukes*; but the best piper came
from Ephesus; the best cithara-player came from Antiochia upon Maiandros; the best citharode
came from Naples.
[45] Local festival: IX 2, 527, 531–3. A further text which supposedly also pertains to the local contest is
published in *Arkhaiologikon Deltion* 16 (1960) 185.

Epigrammatic contests and local history

condition. As we can see from the lines introducing the list of victors, the festival was probably neither penteteric, like the above-mentioned *Eleutheria* in Larisa, nor was it organised by the Thessalian *koinon*. It was based on the *psēphisma* of the *dēmos*, and *tāgoi* were responsible for its organisation. Louis Robert argued that the inscription bears witness to the festival held to commemorate the fallen and the fighters of the battle in 172/171 BC, when the Thessalian cavalry fought with the Romans against Perseus during the third Macedonian War. The wording of the opening clause (ll. 6–10 κατὰ τὸ γενόμενον ὑπὸ τοῦ δήμου ψή[φισμα π]ερὶ τῆς ἀνανεώ[σεω]ς τοῦ ἀγῶνος) shows that for some reason or other the festival ceased to exist at one point in time and was subsequently reintroduced, probably in the late second or early first century BC.[46] Due to the poor condition of the surviving inscriptions we can tell relatively little about its dynamic, at least as far as the variation, i.e. inclusion or exclusion of literary disciplines, is concerned. Only *IG* IX 2, 531 provides a full list of victors and disciplines. Be that as it may, the impression one gains on the basis of this text is that the festival in question was essentially a commemorative one, viz. that it presented some sort of a Thessalian *agōn epitaphios*.[47] Its structure is quite remarkable since it resembles the structure of the actual battle with its prelude and ending – essentially the festival is a symbolic re-enactment of the combat and related events: if we assume that the sequence of disciplines in the list corresponds to the sequence of events in the festival, then we can discern the following groups of events: (a) sacrifice (*taurothēria* / battlefield sacrifice[48]); (b) pre-battle speech/*katalogē palaia*;[49] (c) battle/military contests (*prosdromai*); (d) funeral games (sports, military skills and literary contests).

The literary disciplines are, like some of the athletic contests, referred to in the dative with instrumental connotation – that is to say 'by means of' or 'due to his skill in': we read that a Kointos (i.e. Quintus) Okrios was victorious in the competition called *enkōmion logikon*; Amometos, son of Philoxenides, won the competition of epic encomion (that is to say an encomium in hexameters as opposed to *enkōmion logikon*, the encomium in prose); Philon junior, son of Philon, won in a discipline called *katalogē*

---

[46] The date of the inscription is held to be uncertain by some scholars. It is however to some extent secured by the mention of Amometos, son of Philoxenides (ll. 48f. *IG* IX 2, 531) in a further document (a manumission record; cf. *SEG* 35.599). Helly 1983: 363–5 argues that the extant lists pertaining to the local festival indicate three different stages in its development after its reintroduction, starting with IX 2, 533, which he dates to 100 BC.

[47] For the individual components of an *agōn epitaphios* cf. Pl. *Menex.* 249B, Jacoby 1944: 37–66, Clairmont 1983: 23, Pritchett 1979–85: IV, 106.

[48] On the religious character of *taurothēria* cf. *RE s.v.* ταυροκαθαψία. Heliodor. *Aeth.* 10.30 witnesses that the final destination of the bull is the altar. On battlefield sacrifice Pritchett 1979–85: III: 83.

[49] On both *katalogai* cf. below pp. 208–9.

208   ANDREJ PETROVIC

nea, which, at the moment at least, remains mysterious, whereas the same
Amometos, who won in the epic *enkōmion*, also won with an *epigramma*.
All of the disciplines, military, sports and literary, are connected with the
praise of the fallen and fighting soldiers. The relevance of the disciplines
connected with horse riding and with battle situations is obvious at first
glance – the fact that no less than three *prosdromai* are organised speaks for
itself.

The commemorative character of the literary disciplines is discernable
as well. We find an *epigramma*, a hexametric and a prose *enkōmion*, and a
katalogē nea (ll. 43–9), all of these being introduced by *katalogē palaia* (l. 12).
It goes without saying that three of these disciplines simply do not occur
as a frequent part of literary contests – unlike *enkōmia*, both *katalogai* and
epigramma are, to my knowledge, not otherwise attested in the epigraphic
evidence. The commemorative character of these genres is unmistakable
for both types of *enkōmia* (which possess a long tradition and are attested
in the inscriptional material).[50]

More elusive is the exact nature of the *katalogai*. On its own, the term
might recall Archilochean and dramatic *parakatalogē*, which is usually taken
to be some kind of a performer's rap – a technique of rhythmic recital
accompanied by music.[51] Even though in the case of our *katalogē* we are
clearly not dealing with a technique, but with a genre, it seems plausible
that its nature is illuminated by the term *parakatalogē* and that some type
of recital is meant. This impression is confirmed by a lemma in Hesychius
(κ 1244 Latte) to which LSJ and Pickard-Cambridge refer:[52] καταλογή·
τὸ τὰ ἄισματα μὴ ὑπὸ μέλει λέγειν, 'to recite the poems without music'.
A further lemma in Hesychius (κ 1213 Latte) might reveal the contents of
this recital: notably, the verb καταλέγεσθαι is followed by the clarification
ὀδύρεσθαι τὸν τεθνεῶτα. Therefore, to put together Hesychius' entries,
we would seem to have some kind of lamentatory recital, which is attested
in two distinct types, an old and a new. It is not necessary, however, to
link the distinction between these two types to their generic characteristics

---

[50] *IG* VII 419, 9–10. Cf. Cameron 1995: 47–8, for the evidence and esp. 48: 'It is logical to assume that
competitions for epic eulogies were widespread long before they were added to the sacred festivals.'
[51] On *parakatalogē* cf. Arist. *Pr.* 19.6; Mathiesen 1999: 73: '*parakatalogē* . . . seem[s] to refer to the
practice of using a vocal tone that combines speaking and singing in order to provide a particularly
tragic effect at important points within composition'. On dramatic *parakatalogē* cf. West 1992: 40
with n. 6 and Sommerstein 2003: 14.
[52] LSJ *s.v.*, Pickard-Cambridge 1968: 156–7, with n. 7 referring to *IG* IX 2, 531. Gallis' explanation
(1988: 228) of the terms is unacceptable: he assumes that the competition in poetic composition was
divided into two categories (*palaia* and *nea katalogē*), 'the old and the new languages' and notices
that 'it seems that the Greeks had the problem of two languages – ancient and modern Greek – even
in antiquity'.

Epigrammatic contests and local history 209

and to assume a distinction parallel to that between Old and New comedy or the like. If we look at the victors' list again, we notice that the old and new *katalogē* are not placed next to each other,[53] but that one opens the contests, and the other, in a sense, closes them. This might be taken as a hint at their different subject matter, and I would tentatively suggest that the *katalogē palaia* is to be compared to a pre-battle oration, whereas the *katalogē nea* might in its essence resemble *epitaphios logos*. *Katalogē palaia* could have, I suppose, included lists of names of the warriors of old, and could have presented a reminder of virtuous deeds accomplished before the battle against Perseus, whereas the new *katalogē* possibly glorified the new generation of heroes whose virtue was displayed in the combat commemorated by the festival.[54] It is neither surprising nor unattested that lists of fallen warriors should be the subject of a recital, viz. poetry,[55] and this type of recital, together with a competition in epigram-composition, seems quite fitting as a closing act of a commemorative festival.

Now that we have established public festivals as a context for epigrammatic contests, one could ask whether we should suppose that there were also further occasions on which epigrams (which were subsequently inscribed) could have been performed and could have competed with each other.[56] It would be logical to suppose that, apart from competitions within festivals, there were also competitions which were organised by the state or ruling élite for public commissions. The supposition that contests for public commissions were organised, as speculative as it may be, could explain some apparent oddities: (a) the existence of wandering poets as authors of public epigrams, and (b) some difficult contradictions pertaining to problems of authorship of some epigrams.

(a) The motivation of the wandering poets can, in my opinion, be summed up in three words: privileges, money and fame. The evidence

---

[53] As is usual in different types of the same *genus*, cf. the position of both encomia.

[54] For the evidence on the six classical funeral orations and recent scholarship cf. van Henten and Avemarie 2002: 17–18; Sourvinou-Inwood 1996: 191–3. For *epitaphios logos* see Loraux 1986. The existence of pre-battle orations has been taken as questionable by some scholars, yet the practice is still generally accepted.

[55] The obvious parallel are the oral traditions with strong genealogical elements, well attested in South-Slavic and Central-Asian oral epics, cf. Foley 2002: 199–203. Illuminating also are vv. 302–30 of Aeschylus' *Persians* which might give us an idea of what the *katalogai* could have looked like (I am indebted for this parallel to Leslie Kurke). The list of the Persian war-dead is modelled after Athenian casualty-lists, as Ebbot 2000 shows. The existence of this genre might, perhaps, help explain better Herodotus' statement that he 'learned the names of all the three hundred' fallen at Thermopylae (7.224).

[56] As remarked in the beginning of this paper, I will not consider epigrams which were solely meant for the oral arena: sympotic epigrams, quite agonistic in their essence, will therefore not be taken into account.

210   ANDREJ PETROVIC

for privileges and fame is well known and there is no need to repeat it here. The financial part is, as often, somewhat more elusive, but as far as we can tell, writing a commissioned epigram seems to have been a desirable and rewarding task. Since most of the public epigrams stood in very prominent areas of a polis it does not cause surprise that they were often incised with considerable care. The verses on these monuments were usually cut by professional stone masons (however hard it may be in some cases to believe so), and copies of the incised verses were preserved, so that in the event of a stele being damaged or destroyed, the epigram could be republished. This kind of care for these texts can be seen as an indicator of their pecuniary value: bearing in mind that a relatively modest marble stele of the Hegeso-type could cost as much as a simple house in fourth-century Attica,[57] an assumption of a significant price for the poems inscribed on public monuments seems plausible. Actually, there are further indications that a public epigram could have cost a small fortune: the sepulchral epigram from the grave of the famous astrologist and *mantis* Petosiris (third century BC) is relevant here:[58]

> Πετόσειριν αὐδῶ τὸν κατὰ χθονὸς νέκυν,
> νῦν δ᾽ ἐν θεοῖσι κείμενον· μετὰ σοφῶν σοφός.
> κεφάλαιον τούτων τῶν ἰαμβείων
> εἰς ἀργύριον λόγον ±,ητογ´
> τούτου δὲ αὐτοῦ, βψκ´

I speak of Petosiris, the corpse in the earth, but now laid among the gods: sage among sages.
The total sum of these iambic verses is 8373 silver drachmas; and the total sum of this is 2720.

The iambic lines of the epigram are apparently followed by an addendum (written by another hand) explaining the costs of the epigram. The figures were calculated by reading each letter of the epigram (from Πετόσειριν to σοφός) as a number, and then by doing so again with the author's own remark in lines 3–4. It is tempting to understand these lines as an ironic comment on the substantial amounts paid to the authors of public epigrams.

(b) There is also a second advantage in accepting the possibility of contests for public commissions: such a procedure could help explain

---

[57] For the Hegeso-stele cf. Breuer 1995: 66. Prices: Bäbler 1998: 59 n. 288; Nielsen *et al.* 1990. Inflation between fifth and fourth century: Loomis 1998: 240–50, 255–8; costs of engaging an epigram's inscription: ibid., 121, Nolan 1981 (*non vidi*).

[58] *GVI* 1176; *IMEGR* 125. See esp. Bing and Bruss 2007: 16 who draw attention to a passage from Athenaeus (5.209b) stating that Hieron II paid the poet Archimelus 1,500 bushels of wheat for a single epigram.

Epigrammatic contests and local history

some inconsistencies. The famous epigram on the tyrant-killers which was inscribed on a statue-base in the Athenian agora is attributed to Simonides by Hephaestion (*Ench.* 4, 6), a reliable source for Simonidean attributions.[59] The authorship has been doubted many times because Simonides was connected to the Peisistratids, and therefore it has seemed unlikely that the poet could have been the author of an epigram celebrating the murderers of his former patron, or that the Athenians were ready to engage someone connected to the regime which allegedly inflicted so many terrors on them.[60] I am not inclined to muse here on the fragility of the morals of poets living in societies governed by terror, but it is conceivable that Simonides somehow discovered a soft spot for the new regime(s).[61] More serious is the problem of the aversion Athenians could have had towards the poet at the moment when the epigram was to be chosen[62] – this makes a direct and unmediated commission quite unlikely. If however we allow for the existence of a public contest for a commission, then there is much less reason to reject the authorship of Simonides.

There is also a further reason why one might conceive of this type of contest: since the fifth century BC, we encounter parallel-epigrams, basically variations on a theme, epigrams dedicated to the same subject and sometimes even written on the same stone. It is interesting to note that, more frequently than not, we are dealing with public epigrams (as with poem B of Arbinas' dedication) and that only in the fourth century and especially in the Hellenistic period do we find such variations attested for private contexts (private dedicatory and, particularly, sepulchral epigrams). Perhaps this phenomenon should lead us to recognise the existence of epigrammatic contests and to assume that in cases where the victory was indecisive or the competition ended in a close call, a decision was made to publish not only the victorious epigram, but all the best ones.[63] Subsequently, what was originally a public practice found its place in private contexts and is also reflected in the endless variations of the Hellenistic 'book-epigram'.[64]

---

[59] For the text of the epigram see Petrovic 2007: 113–31.

[60] Cf. Molyneux 1992: 73 with further bibliography.

[61] Cf. Shear 1937: 352: 'Simonides was a poet by profession, who wrote poetry for financial remuneration, and it would have been good business policy for him to dissociate himself from the party of tyrants if he hoped to continue to receive commissions from the Athenians.'

[62] There is no consensus on the date of the first group (Antenor's composition). The scholarship on this subject is vast; useful recent bibliography can be found in Rausch 1999: 43.

[63] On the variations in inscribed epigram in archaic and classical epoch Fantuzzi forthcoming, above p. 197.

[64] One might be attracted by the idea that, in return, the public epigrammatic competitions reflect the practice of private or half-private contexts, i.e. that they spawned from sympotic competitions in the composition of *skolia*. On verse and *skolia*-competitions see most recently Collins 2005: 54.

212   ANDREJ PETROVIC

To sum up: two general contexts for epigrammatic competitions can be suggested – that of public festivals, and that of public commissions. Even though the existence of epigrammatic contests on the occasion of public festivals (an *agōn epitaphios*) is first attested in the Hellenistic period, one might suppose that the commemorative epigrams inscribed on battlefields or city memorials since the Persian Wars could have been selected in this manner as well.

It is certainly very tempting to suppose that the epigrams which were victorious in public festivals (presumably on the occasion of the introduction of a festival)[65] are the ones which were actually inscribed, especially since we know that, also in the case of the competitions of lyric poets, their victorious poems were inscribed on stone – Philodamos of Scarpheia and Aristonoos of Corinth are cases in point.[66] If, therefore, we take a look at the battlefield and home memorials including epigrams, from the time of the Persian Wars onwards, we should probably imagine that these epigrams might just present those which were victorious in commemorative contests (i.e. *epitaphioi agōnes*) and were subsequently inscribed.[67] Nothing demonstrates that the elective procedure of public epigrams is a pre-Hellenistic practice more clearly than the passage of Demosthenes accompanying the epigram for the fallen in the battle of Chaeronea. In a direct address to Aeschines, Demosthenes (*Cor.* 289) reminds him of the virtue of the fallen and says, before quoting the epigram[68] (bear in mind that it was Demosthenes who delivered the *epitaphios logos* for the fallen at Chaeronea): λέγε δ' αὐτῷ τουτὶ τὸ ἐπίγραμμα, ὃ δημοσίαι προείλεθ' ἡ πόλις αὐτοῖς ἐπιγράψαι. 'Read for his sake this epigram, which the state had publicly chosen to have inscribed for them'. On which occasion, other than the public funeral of the fallen at Chaeronea, at which the *epitaphios logos* of Demosthenes was delivered as well, could this epigram have been 'publicly chosen' by the Athenian polis?[69]

---

[65] For a similar view in regard to the Plataea elegy of Simonides cf. Boedeker 1995: 223.

[66] Cameron 1995: 47.

[67] The number of epigrams which can be connected to public burial and (afterwards) to *patrios nomos* and festival (*epitaphios agōn*, be it a part of *patrios nomos* or not) both in and outside Attica is itself remarkable. See Clairmont 1983: 22–8.

[68] For the text cf. Clairmont 1983: 218–19.

[69] Cf. Yunis 2001 *ad loc.*· 267–8: 'προείλεθ' . . . implies that they chose the epigram deliberately, as in choosing policy'. Yunis connects δημοσίαι with ἐπιγράψαι, which is unnecessary since public epigrammatic competitions are, as we have seen, attested. There is intense debate as to whether the epigram quoted by Demosthenes is authentic, but this is irrelevant for the present discussion. See Wankel 1976 and Yunis 2001.

LOCAL HISTORY, SUPRA-LOCAL RECEPTION

Public epigram, being an occasional genre par excellence, can nicely illu-
minate what we are actually talking about when we talk about local history.
At first glance, it might seem a strange phenomenon to engage wandering
poets to compose texts which are not only to occupy the most significant
places within public space, but should also reflect a local sense of history
and local perception of a historical event.[70] Now, the key phrase 'local
sense of history' leads us back to Athens from the end of the sixth century
and to the public monuments which can illustrate what was emphasised in
the presentation of an event. I will be able to show only in a very cursory
manner what kind of local knowledge Simonides possibly possessed as he
composed the epigram for the tyrant-killers; then I will return, also in a
very cursory manner, to Symmakhos, and I will try to work up some aspects
of the presentation of an historical event by a foreigner in Lycia.

Before discussing these aspects, however, we should turn back to the question of professionalism to take a closer look at the class of 'professional' wandering poets, who composed public epigrams: when did professional poets
start composing public epigrams, i.e. when did epigram-composition start
being a *technē*?[71] There are several difficulties, arising from the nature of our
evidence, which impede an unambiguous and simple answer. Since authors'
names simply did not accompany epigrams on stone until the fourth century, in most cases the authorship of archaic and classical authors, claimed
by later sources, is precarious, so much so that in the case of epigrams
attributed to Simonides some editors accept only one poem as authentic.
But even if the attributions are as unreliable as they are claimed to be,
one might assume that the mercenary Muse of Simonides was certainly
quite willing to be hired to compose an epigram. If my reasoning concerning fees paid for the composition of public epigrams is correct, and if
the numerous anecdotes pertaining to Simonides' appreciation of adequate
payment have any foundation in historical reality, it should not surprise
that antiquity saw him as one of the first great poets of public epigrams.[72] Be
that as it may, the first secure clue that a poet could be engaged to compose
an epigram (in this case a private *epitymbion*) comes with Euripides' *Troades*
(vv. 1188–91). The engagement of poets for the composition of epigrams,

---

[70] This matter is obviously related to the phenomena discussed by D'Alessio (this volume).
[71] On definition and features of a professional Greek poet cf. Hardie 1983: 15ff.
[72] On financial aspects cf. above p. 210; on Simonides and money cf. Bell 1978: 29–86 and Carson
2002: 24–7. On finances and itinerant poets cf. Hardie 1983: 16.

214   ANDREJ PETROVIC

even if we discard the evidence concerning Simonides, is therefore attested
from the fifth century BC on.[73]

It is small surprise, if a surprise at all, that in public epigrams which
were composed by professional poets one observes the presentation of an
event shaped by the ideology of the group which had the epigram carved
upon a monument. Probably no other epigram could demonstrate this
more clearly than that of Simonides on the tyrant-killers:[74] this poem acts
not only as a propagandistic tool of Cleisthenes,[75] but is also very different
from the view any contemporary Athenian could have had about the event.

If we take another look at the Greek epigrams composed for Arbinas
of Xanthos, we can also find local elements. As problematic as their exact
meaning may be, the texts in Lycian do contain motifs very similar to those
in the epigrams of Symmakhos and the *paidotribas*. In both cases we have
a short history of the military endeavours and victories of Arbinas. Further
on, Symmakhos claims that he produced the elegiac couplets '*eusunetōs*',
whatever we might understand by this term. One could translate it with the
adjective 'skilfully', but this is not quite what the word denotes. Its primary
meaning is 'easy to understand' and should we ask why someone would
employ such a word, we could presume that it pertains to the numerous
homerisms in the poem.[76]

The homerisms are worthy of closer inspection: Symmakhos, by calling
himself a *mantis amūmōn*, is obviously presenting himself as Calchas (*Iliad*
1.92), as is noted by Bousquet.[77] Bousquet plausibly argues that Symmakhos
knew by heart whole passages from the *Iliad* pertaining to Lycia and that
a significant number of his verses were formulated exactly after the Lycian
passages of the *Iliad*.[78] Therefore we are dealing here with the presentation

---

[73] τί καί ποτε / γράψειεν ἂν σοι μουσοποιός ἐν τάφῳ; / τὸν παῖδα τόνδ᾽ ἔκτειναν Ἀργεῖοί ποτε /
δείσαντες; αἰσχρὸν τοὐπίγραμμα γ᾽ Ἑλλάδι. Herodotus' ascription of the Megistias-epigram is
earlier, of course, but due to textual problems allegedly uncertain in respect to its exact meaning.
On that see Petrovic 2004.

[74] *IG* I³ 502 vv. 2, 4; Heph. *Ench.* 4.6, (S. 14–15 ed. Consbruch) vv. 1–2; Eustathius, *Hom.* 984.12–13.

[75] There is a long and animated discussion concerning the question of who exactly commissioned
Antenor's group. For an overview cf. Rausch 1999: 43 and Page *FGE*: 187. I adopt the view that it
was Cleisthenes' circle. On epigram and propaganda cf. Cameron 1995: 291.

[76] One is tempted to see a pun in the fact that a *mantis* feels a need to stress that his poem is 'easy to
understand' as opposed to his usual utterances.

[77] Bousquet sees a parallel between Symmakhos/Arbinas and Calchas/Agamemnon. Bousquet 1992:
163: 'Symmachos est le confident d'Arbinas comme Calchas est le confident d'Agamemnon.' I am
not entirely convinced that intentionally evoking this very parallel would be good for Symmakhos'
business-ventures. By the wording *mantis amūmōn*, Symmakhos is perhaps alluding to the parallel
between his journeys and those of Calchas (perhaps even a legendary ancestor of Symmakhos?). For
Calchas' journeys along the coast of Asia Minor, all the way to Pamphylia, Cilicia and Syria, cf. Hdt.
7.91. On business-strategies cf. Martin (this volume).

[78] Bousquet 1992: 163–5.

Epigrammatic contests and local history 215

of events modelled on the view of the ruling élite, but formulated in the poetic *lingua franca* of the Greek world. The local élite, Xanthians who could understand Greek, would probably agree with *what* is being said, whereas an educated Greek in Xanthos could (also?) agree with *how* it is being said. Something for all tastes.

Thus Arbinas certainly had a reason to be satisfied with Symmakhos. Honorific inscriptions, on the other hand, tell us a lot about the contentment of the Greek commissioners of poems dedicated to local history, sometimes even in detail. Long before the bunch of 'new Homers' and 'new Nestors' were praised for their compositions in the imperial period, we find hints which tell us pretty clearly what really mattered when history (that is, an event) was remembered by means of a poem. To reflect local perception was in this respect essential: to stress the supremacy of a ruler, to honour the achievements of a polis, to celebrate and disseminate the values of the élite.

The honours given to the poets, on the other hand, are especially well documented for the *epopoioi*, the poets who wrote local epics; an inscription from Lamia dated to the third or second century BC is very informative in this respect. (*IG* IX 2, 63):

[ἀγαθᾶι τύχα]ι· ἔδοξε τᾶι πόλει· | [ἐπειδὴ Πολ?]ίτας Πολίτα Ὑπαταῖο[ς]| [ποιητὴς ἐ]πῶμ παραγενόμενο[ς]||[ἐν τὰμ] πόλιν δείξεις ἐποιήσατ[ο]|5 [ἐν αἷς] τᾶς πόλιος ἀξίως ἐπεμνάσ[θη],||[εἶν]αι αὐτὸν πρόξενον τᾶς πόλιος καὶ| [ε]ὐεργέταν, δεδόσθαι δὲ αὐτῶι καὶ πο-|λιτείαν τὸμ πάντα χρόνον καὶ γᾶ[ς]| καὶ οἰκίας ἔγκτησιν καὶ ἐπινομίαν| 10 καὶ ἀσφάλειαν καὶ κατὰ γᾶν καὶ κατὰ | θάλασσαν καὶ πολέμου καὶ εἰράνας κα[ὶ]|αὐτῶι καὶ ἐκγόνοις καὶ χρήμασιν τὸν|ἄπαντα χρόνον καὶ ὅσα τοῖς ἄλλοις|προξένοις καὶ εὐεργέταις δίδοται πά[ν]-|15 τα. ἀρχόντων Θεομνάστου, Ζεύξιος, Δε[ξι]-|[κ]ράτεος, στραταγέοντος Φιλίππου τοῦ Δε[ξι]-|[κρ]άτεος, ἱππαρχέοντος Μενεφύλου, ἔγγ[υος]||τᾶς προξενίας Φίλιππος Δεξικράτεο[ς].

With good fortune, the polis decided: Since Politas from Hypate, son of Politas, an epic poet, came to the city and made performances, in which he recalled the city appropriately, may he be pronounced a *proxenos* of the city and a benefactor, and may citizenship for all times be given to him, and the right of possessing land and of owning a house, and the right of pasture, and safety both on sea and land, in peace and war, to him and his descendents, and their property, for all times, and all that is given to other *proxenoi* and benefactors. Archons were Theomnastes, Zeuxis, Dexicrates, the general was Philipp, son of Dexicrates, *hipparchos* was Menephylos, and Philipp, son of Dexicrates, is certifying the right of proxeny.

Politas son of Politas from Hypate is being praised, because he (ll. 4–5) δείξεις ἐποιήσατ[ο]||[ἐν αἷς] τᾶς πόλιος ἀξίως ἐπεμνάσ[θη]. Obviously,

216 ANDREJ PETROVIC

the small city of Lamia was more than happy that it was mentioned in the *epideixeis* of Politas[79] 'in a proper way'[80] by the poet, so happy, actually, that the poet was declared *proxenos* and *euergetēs* of the city, obtained life-long citizenship, the right to hold property and use public pasture-land, and his security was guaranteed both on land and sea, both in war and peace times. His *epideixis* was 'worthy of the city' and the praise he received is a consequence of the praise he gave.[81]

The reason for such forms of gratitude was certainly the knowledge that by means of a song, especially a hexameter encomium, a polis could be known and celebrated.[82] Yet is the same valid for public epigrams, inscribed on stone, set firmly in place and time? Could they have the same or similar impact? I believe that at least since the Hellenistic period they did, and I believe that the principles of organisation of the early epigrammatic collections are in this respect important. If we seek traces of organisational principles, which could be either conjecturally or safely traced back to the fourth century, we might observe that a number of epigram collections were organised upon the principle of interest in local history, in public monuments and events in and anecdotes about a given city. It is very remarkable indeed that a significant number of Hellenistic epic poems and epigram collections bear very similar names.[83] Rhianus of Crete is in this respect a case in point, as the titles of Rhianus' poems *Achaika, Messeniaka, Thessalika* and *Eliaka* resemble titles of epigram collections from the fourth century BC and later. Obvious instances are the *epigrammata Attika* of Philochoros,[84] the *epigrammata Thebaika* of Aristodamos,[85] and the *Peri tōn kata poleis epigrammatōn* of Polemon.[86] Interest in local history is obviously present both in the case of epics and the collections of public epigrams. These inscriptions were not only read by local recipients, but were handed down at the latest by the end of the fourth century in collections which were organised on the principle of their interest for local history.

---

[79] The term is well defined in Pallone 1984: 165: 'esibizioni in pubblico finalizzate principalmente a mettere in evidenza la capacità del singolo poeta e a cantare le glorie di un determinato popolo o de origini di una città'.

[80] Similar formulations are frequent; cf. Hardie 1983: 19–20, and Introduction, above p. 3. On this inscription and honours cf. also Cameron 1995: 48.

[81] On honours cf. Hardie 1983: 18–19 and 26ff.   [82] Cf. *FD* III: 1: 223.

[83] For the titles of the Hellenistic agonistic epics cf. Pallone 1984, Fantuzzi 1988: xxvff., Cameron 1995: 262.

[84] Harding 1994: 32–34.   [85] *Schol.* A. R., 2.904; *Schol.* Theoc. 7.103.

[86] *FGrHist* 328 T. There is a discussion concerning the exact title of the collection. Cf. Cameron 1993: 5.

CHAPTER 9

World travellers: the associations of Artists of Dionysus

Sophia Aneziri

Patterns of mobility on the part of poets and musicians in any society and in any given period are likely to be determined by three factors: first, key features of the society they are operating in, such as its cultural and political divisions, and conditions of travel and communication; second, the existence of opportunities for performance that might attract performers, such as festivals and competitions; and third, aspects of the professional organisation of poets and musicians: are we dealing with individuals or groups, with people who normally live at home or with professionals who are continuously on the move? The present paper explores these issues for the Artists of Dionysus operating in the Mediterranean world during the Hellenistic and imperial periods. I shall show that in both these periods the volume of travel was very great, as the result of the explosion in festival culture that took place at the beginning of the Hellenistic period and continued in the Roman empire. At the same time, I shall suggest that the general pattern exhibited by the movements of the Artists was very different in the two periods: in the Hellenistic period, travel is focused through a number of regional associations of artists, which themselves comprised poets and musicians from a wide variety of places; whereas in the Roman empire, these regional associations fall away, and eminent artists are designated as belonging to the *oikoumenē* ('the inhabited world' within the boundaries of the Roman empire). Thus, in the imperial period the Association of the Artists of Dionysus achieved the status of an empire-wide network.

EVIDENCE FOR THE ASSOCIATIONS

From the third century BC people were moving to and fro with ever increasing frequency and intensity for commercial and more generally professional

---

I would like to thank A. Doumas for the translation of this text into English, and Dr. E. Stavrianopoulou (Heidelberg) and Dr. I. Kralli (Corfu) for fruitful discussion.

217

218   SOPHIA ANEZIRI

purposes, for worship, education or travel, as well as for a thousand other
reasons. There were many who travelled in order to take part in festivals
and contests, as official envoys representing cities and kingdoms, merchants
and pedlars, pilgrims, ambassadors and other official emissaries, physicians,
intellectuals and, of course, artists and athletes.[1] Honorary inscriptions for
artists of various specialities, from both the Hellenistic and the imperial
period, enumerate their victories in many contests held throughout the
Graeco-Roman world, and are therefore indirect evidence for constant
movement.[2]

These movements took place within a world that was no longer composed of city-states but had powerful umbrella structures: the Hellenistic
kingdoms, the federal states that emerged from the uniting of cities within
a wider geographical region or the political organisation of nations (ethnē),
and later the *imperium Romanum*.[3] Consequently, people in Hellenistic and
Roman times were not merely citizens of their native city: they were at the
same time members of federations (which continued to exist during the
imperial era and retained mainly their religious character), or subjects of
regional kingdoms and eventually of the Roman empire.

Within this changing world of expanding frontiers the associations
offered artists an identity beyond that of citizen of a particular city and
subject of a monarch or an emperor. It is surely not fortuitous that, according to the available evidence, these associations came into being in the
early third century BC, that is in the period when the new conditions
arising from the geographical expansion of the Hellenic world, in conjunction with the intensification of travel, were crystallising and becoming
clear.

Hellenistic period

In the Hellenistic period, poets, musicians, dancers, actors and in general
those persons necessary for staging performances of drama and music in the

[1] Casson 1974, Giebel 1999: 131–85, Ferrandini Troisi 2006. For travel for purposes of pilgrimage see
   Elsner and Rutherford 2005: 13–14.
[2] Among the numerous examples, see two cases of κιθαρωιδοί who were honoured at Athens and at
   Smyrna (*IG* II² 1839, third century BC, and *IGR* IV 1432, second–third century AD), and also that of a
   flute player who accompanied a chorus (χοραύλης) honoured at Delphi (*FD* III 4, 476, second–third
   century AD). For similar cases involving athletes see e.g. *IAG* 77, 79, 81. Another characteristic piece
   of evidence for these movements is the funerary inscription found in Cologne of a sixteen-year-old
   choraulēs from Mylasa, whose father was both an Alexandrian and an Athenian (*ILS* 9344).
[3] For political structures that transcend the Greek cities, see Funke 1994 and several contributions in
   Buraselis and Zoumboulakis 2003.

World travellers

framework of Greek festivals and contests were organised in associations that are described as Κοινά or Σύνοδοι τῶν περὶ τὸν Διόνυσον τεχνιτῶν ('Guilds of the Artists devoted to Dionysus'). Information about the existence and activity of the associations of Artists of Dionysus comes mostly from inscriptions. These are primarily decrees of the Hellenistic cities and leagues regarding the privileges of the associations and their participation in the organisation and conduct of festivals and contests;[4] epistles of Hellenistic kings and Roman officials;[5] decrees of the Senate concerning the granting of privileges and the settlement of disputes between associations or between association and city;[6] and lists of competitors or victors in musical (thymelic and dramatic) contests.[7] Other important testimonies are the decrees through which the associations themselves agree to participate in festivals and contests[8] or honour their prominent members or officials of the cities in which they are based.[9]

The earliest evidence comes from the Σύνοδος τῶν ἐν Ἀθήναις περὶ τὸν Διόνυσον τεχνιτῶν ('*Synodos* of the Artists of Dionysus at Athens') and is dated to the years 279/8 or 278/7 BC.[10] The Κοινὸν τῶν περὶ τὸν Διόνυσον τεχνιτῶν τῶν εἰς Ἰσθμὸν καὶ Νεμέαν συμπορευομένων/συντελούντων ('*Koinon* of the Artists of Dionysus who travel together/contribute towards Isthmos and Nemea')[11] was created as early as the first half of the third century BC. It participated, as can be deduced from its title, in the games held at the Isthmos and at Nemea (the Isthmia and the Nemeia) and had branches in cities of the Peloponnese, Euboea and central and north

---

[4] Decrees of the Delphic Amphictiony: *IG* II² 1132 (= *CID* IV 12, 114, 116), and *CID* IV 70–2, 97, 117, 120. Decrees of the Aetolians: *IG* IX 1², 192. Decrees of cities: *FD* III 2, 47, 49, 50; Tracy 1975: 60–7 no. 7h; *Syll.³* 457, 460; *IG* II² 1134 ll. 64–76; Bringmann, Ameling and Schmidt-Dounas 1995: no. 262[E]; Rigsby 1996: no. 134; *I. Magnesia* 89.

[5] Letters of Hellenistic kings: *SEG* XLI 1005 ll. 11–16; *RC* 53. Letters of Roman officials: *RDGE* 44, 49; Roesch 1982: 198–202 no. 44.

[6] *RDGE* 15 – in lines 10, 12, 20–1, 36–8 of this decree, reference is made to other decrees of the Roman Senate relating to the same issue.

[7] For the lists of participants in the Sōteria of Delphi, see Nachtergael 1977: 407–24 nos. 3–5, 7–10. For the lists of victors in the Mouseia of Thespiai, see Roesch 1982: 188–94 nos. 32–9.

[8] Note the Isthmian-Nemean Guild for the Mouseia of Thespiai (*Syll.³* 457 + Feyel 1942: 92–3 col. B) and the Ionian-Hellespontine Guild for the Leukophryena of Magnesia ad Maeandrum (*I. Magnesia* 54).

[9] Key examples of related decrees are: for the Athenian Guild *IG* II² 1320, 1338 and 3211; for the Isthmian-Nemean Guild *Syll.³* 704B, *IG* IV 558 and *IG* XII 9, 910; for the Ionian-Hellespontine Guild Daux 1935: 210–30, and *CIG* 3068; for the Egyptian association *OGIS* 50–1.

[10] This is a decree through which the Delphic Amphictiony grants privileges to the Athenian Guild of Artists. Three copies of it are preserved, two at Athens (*IG* II² 1132, *CID* IV 116) and one at Delphi (*CID* IV 12).

[11] *Syll.³* 460 and *IG* XI 4, 1059.

220   SOPHIA ANEZIRI

Greece.[12] In Asia Minor the earliest evidence dates from the second half of the third century BC and concerns the Κοινὸν τῶν περὶ τὸν Διόνυσον τεχνιτῶν τῶν ἐπ' Ἰωνίας καὶ Ἑλλησπόντου ('*Koinon* of the Artists of Dionysus (who are active) in or (who travel) to Ionia and the Hellespontine region').[13] For almost a century (from the mid-third century to 146 BC) the Association's seat was at Teos, but because of a dispute with this city it was moved subsequently to Myonnesos and then to Lebedos.[14] After 188 BC it joined forces with a corresponding association based in Pergamon and was henceforth known as the Κοινὸν τῶν περὶ τὸν Διόνυσον τεχνιτῶν τῶν ἐπ' Ἰωνίας καὶ Ἑλλησπόντου καὶ περὶ τὸν Καθηγεμόνα Διόνυσον ['*Koinon* of the Artists of Dionysus (who are active) in or (who travel) to Ionia and the Hellespontine region and (those who) are devoted to Dionysus Kathegemon'].[15] In addition to these three associations, we may also cite the *synodos* of the Artists in Egypt,[16] with a branch in Cyprus,[17] as well as smaller associations that were active in south Italy and Sicily.[18]

Imperial period

Evidence for the Hellenistic associations continues until the first half of the first century BC. The organisation of Artists of Dionysus in associations continued in other forms during the imperial period too.[19] Most of the evidence in the imperial period consists of honorary decrees for emperors, presidents of the games (*agōnothetai*), benefactors and members of the associations and in general artists of various specialisations,[20] epistles and rescripts of emperors and officials, as well as letters, petitions and

---

[12] Epigraphic evidence for these branches: *IG* IV 558; *IG* VII 2484–6; *IG* IX 1, 278; *IG* XII 9, 910; *I.Olympia* 405; Roesch 1982: 189–90 no. 33, 191–2 no. 37, 196–7 no. 42. For the structure of the association in question, see Aneziri 2003: 56–65.

[13] The inscriptions from the third century BC are: *FD* III 3, 218B ll. 5–8; Bringmann *et al.* 1995: no. 262[E]; *SEG* XLI 1003, 1005; *IG* IX 1², 192; *CID* IV 97; Rigsby 1996: 295–6 no. 134; *Iscr. Cos* ED 79; *I. Magnesia* 54.

[14] Strabo 14.1.29. For this change of headquarters, cf. Le Guen 2001: II 33–4; Aneziri 2003: 80–4.

[15] The relevant inscriptions are: Daux 1935: 210–30; *CIG* 3068; *RC* 53; *I. Iasos* 152; Roesch 1982: 199–200 no. 44; *I. Lindos* II 264; *Iscr. Cos* ED 7.

[16] *OGIS* 50–1.   [17] Aneziri 1994; Aneziri 2003: 119–20.   [18] Aneziri 2001–2.

[19] The presentation of the Roman associations here is more extensive than those of the Hellenistic period because there is no previous synthesis of the material for the Roman period.

[20] *SEG* VI 58–9; *SEG* VII 825; Rouaché 1993: 226–7 no. 88 III; Rey-Coquais 1973: 47–64 no. 10; *I. Ephesos* 22, 1618; *I. Erythrai* 60; *I. Tralleis* 50, 65; *IG* XIV 2495; *I.Side* 147; Pekary 1965: 121–2 no. 5; *CIG* 3082.

World travellers

applications of the associations and their members regarding matters of concern to them, especially their privileges.[21]

Already from the early imperial period, there is evidence from the cities of Asia Minor for groups of victors in sacred contests (*hieronīkai*). In several cases it is not clear whether these are artists or athletes, or whether the two groups coexisted.[22] The sacred victors appear in diverse ways in various inscriptions.[23] The existence of decrees of sacred victors passed in conjunction with the council, the assembly of citizens and the council of elders (*gerousia*)[24] suggests that in some cities at least there was a solid organisation of sacred victors (artists and/or athletes) whose members were active in a manner comparable to that of other organisations of citizens.[25]

The status of the victors in sacred contests was extremely high and entailed significant privileges (e.g. exemption from public burdens and liturgies) and honours (e.g. front seat in the theatre, wearing of a wreath), acknowledged initially by the cities and subsequently by the Romans.[26] Furthermore, cities granted financial support to their citizens who were victors in sacred contests.[27] Through these honours and privileges they recompensed those who as victors in prestigious contests contributed – through

---

[21] *P. Oxy. Hels.* 25 (= Frisch 1986: no. 4); *BGU* 1073–4 (= Frisch 1986: nos. 1–2); *P. Oxy.* 2475–6 (= Frisch 1986: no. 3), 2496, 2610 (= Frisch 1986: no. 5); Oliver 1989: nos. 29, 32, 47, 97–104; *I. Tralleis* 105; *RDGE* 57; Roueché 1993: 164–8 nos. 50–1.

[22] *I. Tralleis* 105 (Aydin); *I. Smyrna* 217 (Smyrna); *RDGE* 57 (Ephesos); *I. Ephesos* 14 ll. 20–7, 18c l. 22, 27 ll. 437, 456–7, 475, 561 (Ephesos). Athletes (with or without other groups) are certainly found in the inscriptions *I. Erythrai* 429, *IAG* 59 (Miletus), and 62 (Magnesia ad Maeandrum), Merkelbach 1975: 146–8 (Elaia).

[23] From Ephesos alone there are the following versions: 'sacred victors apart from those crowned in the Great Sebasta Epheseia' (*I. Ephesos* 14 ll. 25–7: ἱερονεικῶν χωρὶς τῶν στεφανουμένων τὰ μεγάλα Σεβαστὰ Ἐφέσηα); 'sacred victors dedicated to Artemis' (*I. Ephesos* 18c l. 22: τοὺς ἱερονείκας, ὅσοι ἱεροὶ τῆς Ἀρτέμιδος); 'the priests and sacred victors who wear golden ornaments for the goddess' (*I. Ephesos* 27 ll. 437, 456–7, 475, 561: οἱ χρυσοφοροῦντες τῆι θεῶι ἱερεῖς καὶ ἱερονεῖκαι); 'those, who carried the golden ornaments of the Great Goddess Artemis, i.e. the priests of the gods, who are the head of the city, and the sacred victors' (*I. Ephesos* 276: οἱ τὸν [χρύ]σεον κόσμον βαστά[ζον]τες τῆς μεγάλης θεᾶς [Ἀρτέ]μιδος πρὸ πόλεως ἱερεῖς [καὶ] ἱερονεῖκαι); 'the priests of the gods, who are the head of the city, and tbe sacred victors' (*I. Ephesos* 3005: τῶν πρὸ τῆς πόλεως ἱερέων καὶ ἱερονεικῶν).

[24] See e.g. *I. Tralleis* 112, 133; Roueché 1993: 236–7 no. 93; Judeich 1898: 84 no. 36.

[25] The occurrence of the expression ἀπὸ τῆς οἰκουμένης ἱερονῖκαι στεφανῖται ('sacred wreath-crowned victors of the *oikoumenē*') possibly indicates a central association of victors in sacred contests (cf. Pleket 1973: 199–200).

[26] The evidence from the Hellenistic period has been collated by Herrmann 1967: 68–9, notes 38–40; see also L. Robert, *BE* 1977: no. 420 and Parker 2004: 12, note 10. There is a letter from Mark Antony concerning the privileges of the sacred victors from as early as the first century BC (*RDGE* 57).

[27] See Méautis 1918: 152–5, 199–203; Mitteis and Wilcken 1912: I.2. 157; Pleket 1973: 204 n. 27 and Pleket 1975: 62–3. Cf. *IG* XII 2, 68 l. 11.

their *ethnikon* – to promoting their native city beyond its borders.[28] The
status of sacred victors became even more important in the imperial period
when, according to the Roman legal and social system, those who competed
for money or appeared on stage for remuneration were of inferior legal and
social status and were considered of very low prestige (ἄτιμοι, *infames*).[29]
This is the reason why the qualification ἱερονίκης στεφανίτης[30] was an
integral part of the full title of the association of artists in the imperial
period: ἡ ἱερὰ σύνοδος τῶν ἀπὸ τῆς οἰκουμένης περὶ τὸν Διόνυσον καὶ
αὐτοκράτορα . . . τεχνειτῶν ἱερονεικῶν στεφανειτῶν καὶ τῶν τούτων
συναγωνιστῶν ('the sacred *synodos* of sacred wreath-crowned victors of the
oikoumenē devoted to Dionysus and the emperor . . . and of their fellow-
competitors').[31] Through these titles, the members of the world-wide Guild
escaped the stigma of paid musicians and actors.[32] In practice, of course, the
distinction was not strictly observed, since the wreath awarded to victors in
sacred contests was frequently accompanied by money,[33] while the artists
and athletes described as *hieronīkai stephanītai* also took part in games with
financial prizes (*themat ītai* or *chrematītai*).[34]

The world-wide Guild of artists that bears this prolix title[35] is distinguished from the aforementioned organisations of sacred victors as follows:
(1) it includes only artists and not athletes, (2) it encompasses not only those

[28] The glory accruing to a city from the victory of an artist or athlete bearing its *ethnikon* is noted by
Robert 1967: 17–18, 22–7 and Robert 1968: 195–8.

[29] See in detail Leppin 1992: 71–7. Cf. also Lebek 1996: 39–40; Vendries 1999: 285–9, 316–18.

[30] *Hieronīkēs* is synonymous with *stephanītēs*. The term ἱερονίκης στεφανίτης corresponds fully to the
description of the contests in question as ἱερῶν καὶ στεφανιτῶν ('sacred crown-games'); on the
terminology see Aneziri 2003: 328–30.

[31] This is the exact title of the world-wide guild recorded in the inscription Rey-Coquais 1973: 47–64
no. 10 from the reign of Hadrian.

[32] The qualification *hieronīkai stephanītai* was added precisely to secure the prestige and distinction of
the artists of the world-wide guild over other artists who represented specialisations that, while very
popular with the general public, had long been excluded from the programme of sacred musical
contests of the Greek type (e.g. pantomimists, performers of mime). In the West performers of
mime had long had their own associations (see e.g. *CIL* III 3980; VI 10109, 10188; XIV 2408). On
the exclusion of the pantomimists and mime performers from the contests of the Greek type and
primarily from the sacred contests, see Robert 1930: 119–22, and Slater 1995: 271–2, 281–2, 289–90.

[33] See Pleket 1975: 54–71.

[34] In honorific inscriptions for artists and athletes, victories in the sacred games are enumerated first,
followed by a general statement of the number of victories won in the other games (e.g. Carratelli
1952–4: 293–5 no. 67; *IAG* 77, 79, 127). Although participation in games with financial prizes did
not prevent, *a priori*, an artist from competing in sacred games, a professional boxer from Alexandria
was dismissed from Olympia in the imperial period because he did not arrive at Olympia in time,
since he was collecting money from games held in Ionia (Paus. 5.21.12–14).

[35] In fact, in some inscriptions and papyri the additional epithets περιπολιστική, θυμελική or μουσική
are encountered, as well as the name of the emperor used as an epithet (e.g. Ἀδριανή, Ἀντωνιανή,
Σεπτιμιανή, Γαλλιηνή) defining the world-wide guild. See *SEG* VI 58, *I. Ephesos* 22 ll. 35–9 + Clerc
1885: 126 ll. 73–7, *P. Oxy. Hels.* 25 ll. 15, 17, 22–3, 25–6, 28–9, 33, 41.

World travellers

specialisations for which prizes were awarded in contests and which could therefore be victors (e.g. poets, leading actors, musicians of dithyrambic and lyric choruses), but also their fellow-competitors (*synagōnistai*) of these – that is, the specialisations that were essential to the production but were not awarded prizes (e.g. musicians of dramatic choruses, trainers of choruses and producers of plays, dancers and persons who hired out costumes and provided the artists with all necessary equipment).[36]

The organisation of the world-wide Guild (*oikoumenikē synodos*) largely eludes us. There were central facilities in Rome and branches in eastern provinces of the empire.[37] In at least one case the fellow-competitors (*synagōnistai*) formed a separate association from the world-wide Guild of artists.[38] There is also evidence for local associations, some of which seem to be continuations of associations of the Hellenistic period.[39] However, our incomplete knowledge about the organisation of the world-wide Guild often makes it difficult to distinguish this guild and its branches from local associations, especially in those cases where the title appears in abbreviated form.[40]

MANAGING THE ARTISTS TRAVELLING TO THE FESTIVALS

Hellenistic period

During the Hellenistic period there was a significant increase in the number of newly founded or re-organised festivals and contests.[41] On the one hand new festivals and contests appeared, many of which were no longer organised by the cities – which had traditionally played this rôle – but by Hellenistic kings, as well as by political confederations and religious

---

[36] Aneziri 2003: 324–31. The *synagōnistai* were also members of the Hellenistic associations, but separate mention of them in the titles of these associations was not necessary because the artists were not qualified as *hieronīkai stephanītai*.

[37] *I. Ephesos* 22, esp. in ll. 17, 24, 68, leaves no doubt about the facilities in Rome.

[38] We have a decree of this association: *IG* XIV 2495 (Nicaea, reign of Hadrian). The decree is discussed by Lavagne 1986: 137–9 and Ghiron-Bistagne 1990–1, 64–7, who interpret the *synagōnistai* differently.

[39] This is certainly the case with the Ionian-Hellespontine *Koinon*: *CIG* 3082; *I. Tralleis* 50; *I. Ephesos* 1618.

[40] The associations that defined themselves as local, at Sardis and Miletus, were perhaps branches of the world-wide Guild (*I. Sardis* 13; Pekary 1965: 121–3 no. 5), whereas the association in Side was probably a separate one (*I. Side* 147–8). The *synodos* of the musical artists accompanying the God of the Dance (σύνοδος τῶν περὶ τὸν Χορεῖον τεχνειτῶν μουσικῶν) in Athens was perhaps also a separate association (Oliver 1989: nos. 97–104).

[41] On the increase of festivals in the Hellenistic period see Robert 1984: 36–7, Chaniotis 1995, Köhler 1996: 89–90. Contests were not only organised in the context of periodical festivals, but were also held as isolated events to celebrate an anniversary or a victory (e.g. Plut. *Luc.* 29.4; Athen. 14.615 b–d; Diod. 20.108.1).

224   SOPHIA ANEZIRI

associations, such as the Delphic Amphictiony.[42] On the other hand, existing contests were re-organised and upgraded as sacred crown-games.[43] Con-
currently, there was an increase in the importance that the political powers
of the period – both the politically emasculated cities[44] and the flourishing Hellenistic kingdoms[45] – attached to these events as sites of political
influence and propaganda.

Precisely because of the increase in the number of contests and of their
geographical expansion, it became increasingly difficult to organise them
successfully. This required frequent movements of artists and careful coordination in order to meet the minimum needs of contests, which frequently
coincided in date; I define as 'minimum needs' the participation of at least
two competitors per event.[46] At the same time, developments in the domain
of drama, mainly with the introduction of performances of Old Tragedy
and Comedy, and changes in the content and composition of the dramatic choruses gave the theatrical groups greater flexibility and made them
independent of the city in which the performance was staged.[47]

Under these conditions the Hellenistic associations of Artists of Dionysus
came to provide their own mechanisms for the success of the contests, the
organisation of which was no longer in the hands of the city-states, or
whose prestige and spectacle were now beyond their capabilities. In a period
when sacred embassies (*theōriai*) of cities and those organising festivals
crisscrossed the Hellenic world from end to end, addressing themselves
to cities, confederacies and Hellenistic monarchs, in order to secure the

---

[42] See the festivals organised by Alexander in the course of his campaign (Athen. 12.538f; Plut. *Alex.*
29.6). For the numerous festivals founded by the Ptolemies in Egypt (*Ptolemaia, Dionysia, Basileia,
Genethlia*) see Weber 1993: 169–79, and Perpillou-Thomas 1993: esp. 151–62.

[43] A case in point is the Leukophryena of Magnesia ad Maeandrum (*I. Magnesia* 16; *SEG* XXXII 1147).
The Mouseia of Thespiai (Knoepfler 1996: 141–67) and other Boeotian contests, such as the Ptoia
of Akraipheia, the Charitesia-Homoloia of Orchomenos and the Herakleia of Thebes were also
reorganised and (partly) upgraded (Roesch 1982: 219; Schachter 1981–94: I 142–3 and II 29). Other
examples are assembled by Robert 1984: 37. Reservations about Robert's list of games have been
expressed by Parker 2004: 14.

[44] For Athens in particular, see Habicht 1995: 105–11, 140–1, 173–5, 238–43. For the characteristic case
of the Leukophryena of Magnesia ad Maeandrum, see Dunand 1978: 206–9. An overview is given
by Gauthier 1993: 226–7, Giovannini 1993: 265–6, Chaniotis 1995: 151–63.

[45] Dunand 1981, Weber 1993: 169–82, 323–7, Leuteritz 1997: 119–21, Bloedow 1998. For the festivals
and the contests dedicated to ruler cults, see Habicht 1970: 147–53.

[46] Under these circumstances, it is no surprise that there are occasions when there are no athletes or
artists participating in certain events (see Robert 1978: 282–4). For unopposed victories in athletic
contests see Crowther 2004: 281–95 (pp. 291–2 for contests with no competitors).

[47] Performances of Old Tragedy are attested at Athens already from 387/6 BC and were systematised
c. 341–339 BC, while Old Comedy made its appearance in 340/39 BC and was included in the annual
Dionysia in 311 BC (*IG* II² 2318 ll. 202–3, 317–18). On this, see Pickard-Cambridge 1968: 99–100
and Wilson 2000: 33 with n. 58. On the dramatic choruses during the Hellenistic period see Sifakis
1962–3, Pöhlmann 1988: 41–55, Slater 1993: 192–9.

World travellers   225

greatest possible participation of official emissaries (*theōroi*), merchants and visitors to their festivals,[48] the associations offered a rich pool of artists and met – at a basic level at least – the needs for recruiting and mobilising competitors in the music (thymelic and dramatic) contests of each festival.

This very process is recorded in a long inscription from Chalkis dating from between 294 and 288 BC.[49] Although this does not yet speak of an association, it implies an important gathering of artists in the city, which is later[50] one of the headquarters of the Isthmian-Nemean Guild of Artists. Ambassadors of the Euboean cities of Histiaia, Eretria, Chalkis and Karystos addressed themselves to the artists congregated in Chalkis, requesting a certain number of artists with specific specialisations to take part in the Dionysia and the Demetrieia of these cities. This practice evidently changed little when informal unions of artists were replaced by formally constituted associations. We know for example that Delphi and Thespiai, together with the Boeotian League, as well as Iasos and Magnesia ad Maeandrum, approached the associations, requesting their contribution for the winter Sōteria, the Mouseia, the Dionysia and the Leukophryena respectively.[51] In my opinion, other evidence for the associations' activities away from their headquarters testifies indirectly to similar appeals and acceptances.[52]

There are two clear pieces of evidence that in games in which associations played the rôle of (co-)organiser, they themselves carried out the distribution or enrolment of the artists (νέμησις and καταλογή respectively) – that is, they determined the specific artists who would take part in the contest.[53]

---

[48] One consequence of the large number of festivals and games, and also their supra-local character, in the Hellenistic period, was an increase in the number of embassies to announce festivals and games. The evidence is collected in Boesch 1908. See also Perlman 2000, 14–16.

[49] *IG* XII 9, 207 add. p. 176 + *IG* XII Suppl. p. 178 (*SEG* XIII 462; XXX, 1095). This inscription is analysed by Stephanis 1984: 499–564 (*SEG* XXXIV 896). Cf. Le Guen 2001: I no. 1.

[50] *IG* XII 9, 910, second century BC.

[51] *Syll.³* 690 (winter Sōteria); *Syll.³* 457 + Feyel 1942: 92–3 col. B (Mouseia); *I. Iasos* 152 (Dionysia); *I. Magnesia* 54, 89 (Leukophryena). In each case, however, the nature of the contribution is different: in the Mouseia of Thespiai it is full co-organisation, in the winter Sōteria of Delphi and the Dionysia of Iasos it is dispatching artists *gratis*, in the Leukophryena it is a mission of official emissaries, observance of a truce and participation in the procession and in the contest (*I. Magnesia* 54 ll. 17–21).

[52] See e.g. the participation of the Isthmian-Nemean Guild in the Sōteria of Delphi (above note 8) and the delegation of official emissaries of the Ionian-Hellespontine Guild to Samothrace (*IG* XII 8, 163).

[53] *CID* IV 71 ll. 34–6: 'if any of the flute-players, the dancers, the performers of tragedy or comedy who were distributed/assigned to the Trieterides by the artists do not compete in the Trieterides . . .' (the *Trietērides* here are the Dionysia of Thebes, in the joint organisation of which the Isthmian-Nemean Guild took part); *IG* II² 1330 ll. 41–2: 'the epimeletēs' (of the Artists) 'shall enrol those who will offer their performances as first fruits to the god' (this refers to the annual competition that the association of Athens decided to hold in honour of Ariarathes V, the king of Cappadocia). Cf. Piolot 2001: 299–300; Aneziri 2003: 282.

At the same time the associations probably drew up the competing theatrical and music groups, since many musical and dramatic performances relied not on individuals but on groups; this applies to all performances of tragedy, comedy and satyr plays, as well as to musical spectacles including dance.

Beyond ensuring a sufficient number of competitors, forming the relevant groups and – in many cases – sending them to a place away from their headquarters, the associations served the organisers by fulfilling another basic requirement for ensuring the success of the contests. The prestige and splendour of the games – especially the pan-Hellenic ones – was measured in large part by their power to attract participants from various regions of the Hellenic world. Since all the associations were heterogeneous – that is their members included artists from different cities and regions – the dispatch of members of an association to a certain contest largely met the need for participants bearing a diversity of *ethnika*.[54] This does not mean, of course, that the embassies of the organisers did not approach more than one association of artists – especially in cases of pan-Hellenic or supra-local games – or that their embassies announcing the festivals did not appeal directly to (individual?) artists from other cities.

It is particularly interesting, in the light of the above, that the movement of artists to places where contests were held or their activity within a wide geographical area are mentioned in the titles of two large Hellenistic associations, and constitute precisely that part of the title that differentiates these associations from the rest. The associations in question are: the '*Koinon* of the Artists of Dionysus who travel together/contribute towards Isthmos and Nemea' and the '*Koinon* of the Artists of Dionysus (who are active) in or (who travel) to Ionia and the Hellespontine region'. Both associations define themselves by the places to which or within which their members move.[55] In the former case, the two places refer directly to the Isthmia and the Nemeia, festivals in which the artists of the association were obviously active. Both contests were surely the most significant and prestigious activities of the association, which extended however to the Peloponnese, Boeotia, Euboea, Lokris and Macedonia (areas in which branches of the association are attested). Indeed it is possible that participation in these

[54] For the heterogeneous nature of the associations see Le Guen 2001: II 41–6, and Aneziri 2003: 227–43. The most characteristic cases are those of the *Koinon* of Artists of Isthmos and Nemea, which attracted mainly artists from the Peloponnese, central Greece, Macedonia (without excluding other regions), and the Asia Minor *Koinon*, the members of which came mainly from Asia Minor and the neighbouring islands.

[55] ἐπί + the genitive may also denote both the main region of activity for the association and the direction of its artists to the specific regions (Ionia, Hellespont) and their games.

sacred pan-Hellenic games was the reason artists from so many different regions joined together in one association. The same logic can be seen in the titles of some branches of this association: *Koinon* of the Artists of Dionysus who contribute towards Isthmos, Nemea and Pieria (τὸ Κοινὸν τῶν περὶ τὸν Διόνυσον τεχνιτῶν τῶν εἰς Ἰσθμὸν καὶ Νεμέαν καὶ Πιερίαν συντελούντων), Artists of Dionysus from Isthmos and Nemea who travel together to Elis (τεχνῖται περὶ τὸν Διόνυσ[ον ἐξ Ἰσθμοῦ κ]αὶ Νεμέας οἱ εἰς Ἦλιν συμπορευόμενοι), Artists who contribute towards Helikon (τεχνῖται οἱ συντελοῦντες εἰς Ἑλικῶνα).[56] This form of title thus concerns regions that were at the epicentre of the specific associations' activities, though this does not mean, of course, that their activity was confined to these regions.

Imperial period

Evidence dating from the imperial period relating to the world-wide Guild, as well as to local associations of artists, comes from all regions of the empire: from numerous cities in Asia Minor, Egypt, Greece, Italy, Gaul. The density and spread of the associations correspond directly to the increase in festivals and contests, and specifically to the plethora of sacred crown-games:[57] cities in all parts of the empire enriched their festive calendar with contests, which were modelled on the Pythian, Nemean or the Olympic games (*agōn isopythios, isonemeios, isolympios*), and aspired to attract participants from regions as distant as possible, in order to secure their presence and prestige in the Roman *oikoumenē*.[58] Thus, the associations were called upon to cover the increasingly complex needs of coordination in organising the contests and the participation of artists in them. A recently published letter from the emperor Hadrian to the world-wide Guild of the Artists gives an insight into the effort he made to contribute to this difficult task of coordinating the exact dates and the duration of the contests, so as to facilitate the 'circulation' of participants and particularly competitors in them.[59]

The constant movement of artists to the venues of festivals and contests is expressed more generally, though indirectly, in the title of the Guild of Roman imperial times through the epithet περιπολιστική, which means 'travelling around, circulating'.[60] The other epithet, οἰκουμενική ('of the

---

[56] Roesch 1982: 189–92, 197–8 nos. 33, 37, 43; *I. Olympia* 405. The later variation τὸ Κοινὸν τῶν περὶ τὸν Διόνυσον τεχνιτῶν τῶν ἐξ Ἰσθμοῦ καὶ Νεμέας ('*Koinon* of the Artists of Dionysus from Isthmos and Nemea') probably reflects the consolidation of the association (*IG* XI 4, 1059; *RDGE* 15 l. 53).

[57] Herz 1990: 177–83 (esp. nn. 16–18).   [58] Pleket 1975: 61–71.

[59] Petzl and Schwertheim 2006.   [60] Poland 1934: 2515; Pickard-Cambridge 1968: 291.

228   SOPHIA ANEZIRI

inhabited world'), ascribes to the guild its geographical dimension. This epithet is undoubtedly associated with the description of the sacred wreath-crowned victors as 'of the inhabited world' (ἀπὸ τῆς οἰκουμένης ἱερονῖκαι στεφανῖται).[61] The exact meaning of this adjectival phrase has generated much scholarly debate: according to one view it pertains to the places where the said artists carried off victories in sacred contests and had been crowned with a wreath,[62] while according to another it is associated with the origin of the victors.[63]

The extension of the qualification 'of the inhabited world' (ἀπὸ τῆς οἰκουμένης) in expressions which do not contain the epithets *hieronīkai stephanītai* (e.g. 'artists/athletes of the inhabited world')[64] rules out, in my opinion, the interpretation that involves victories won in contests through-out the world. Nor is the interpretation of *oikoumenē* as a comprehensive term embracing the numerous places of origin of the artists very con-vincing, principally because origin was of little importance within each association, since the basic identity of the artist was that of member. In the titles of the associations of the Hellenistic period there is no hint of the members' origin, while, on the contrary, the principal region of their activity is defined.[65] The answer lies presumably in the partial conflation of both explanations: the qualification ἀπὸ τῆς οἰκουμένης signifies place of origin (second view), which, however, is defined on the basis of the place of activity (first view) rather than that of birth. This interpretation seems to be confirmed by the appearance of the analogous expression in the title of the local Ionian-Hellespontine Guild during the imperial period:[66] τῶν ἀπὸ Ἰωνίας καὶ Ἑλλησπόντου τεχνιτῶν ('artists from Ionia and the Hellespontine region') instead of τῶν ἐπὶ Ἰωνίας καὶ Ἑλλησπόντου τεχ-νιτῶν ('artists (who are active) in or (who travel) to Ionia and the Helle-spontine region') found in the title of the Hellenistic association.[67] This change is surely to be attributed to the influence of the formula ἀπὸ τῆς οἰκουμένης ἱερονῖκαι στεφανῖται and confirms furthermore the equiva-lence of both expressions (ἐπί + genitive and ἀπό + genitive) as denoting the regions of activity in these particular cases.

[61] For this description see e.g. *I. Erythrai* 429 (athletes), *IAG* 59, 62; *Syll.*[3] 494; *SEG* VI 58–9; *SEG* VII 825.
[62] Cf. Keil 1911: 130, Poland 1934: 2515, San Nicolò 1972: I 64 n. 1, Forbes 1955: 241.
[63] This is the view of Pleket 1973: 200–1. The issue is left open by Öhler 1913: 1535.
[64] *I. Ephesos* 22 ll. 17, 24; *I. Erythrai* 429; *I. Olympia* 436 (οἱ ἀπὸ τῆς οἰκουμένης τεχνῖται and οἱ ἀπὸ τῆς οἰκουμένης ἀθληταί).
[65] Aneziri 2003: 227–43. Cf. above pp. 226–7.   [66] *CIG* 3082; *I. Tralleis* 50.
[67] The Hellenistic title is also preserved, however, in an inscription of the imperial period (*I. Ephesos* 1618).

World travellers   229

The movement and activity of the world-wide Guild of artists and its members throughout the Roman empire is thus expressed in the epithets περιπολιστική and οἰκουμενική in the title of the guild. These define the scope of the activities of the association and reinforce its prestige, but provide no clarification regarding its organisation. In the many cases where the full title of the world-wide Guild of artists appears, there is usually no indication that it is a section or a branch of it, even when it is clear from the find-spot of the inscription or the subject of its text that this cannot concern or – in the case of a decree – derive from the total of its members.[68] The sole exception to date is the decree in honour of Titus Aelius Alcibiades, which specifies that it was issued by the members of the world-wide Guild, who met in Ephesos for the quinquennial contest of the Great Ephesea.[69]

The vagueness and the difficulty in understanding the organisation of the world-wide Guild[70] stems in my opinion from the fact that it was a centrally organised association, which was active in all regions of the empire, but which did not give prominence to its local branches. In this respect the oecumenical association of the imperial period is the antithesis of the Hellenistic *Koinon* of Isthmos and Nemea, the branches of which existed in their own right and are reflected in the title of the *Koinon*. On the other hand, its organisation is similar to that of the Hellenistic association of artists in Egypt, the allocation of which to cities and festivals does not seem to have acquired an institutional form, while the guild as a whole was structured around the central Ptolemaic authority.[71] As I see it, the similarities emerge from the fact that both the Hellenistic Egyptian association and the imperial world-wide Guild thrived in centralist political systems, although they were called upon – like all the other associations of artists – to cover the needs of a wide or even very wide geographical space, which made the mobility of the members and the diffusion of their activities an inherent element of their existence.

THE IMPORTANCE OF MEMBERSHIP IN AN EXPANDING WORLD

Membership of a guild offered artists a privileged legal and, by extension, social status. Indeed, bearing in mind that artists were not necessarily

---

[68] The most characteristic examples are the association's decrees from cities of Asia Minor honouring a local president of games (*agōnothetēs*) or a benefactor: e.g. *SEG* VI 58–9 (Ankyra); *SEG* VII 825 (Gerasa).
[69] *I. Ephesos* 22 ll. 35–43.   [70] See also above p. 223.
[71] On the organisation of the Isthmian-Nemean and the Egyptian guilds see Aneziri 2003: 56–65, 112–15.

230   SOPHIA ANEZIRI

citizens of the city in which their association had its seat,[72] the special
importance of membership can be appreciated. When account is taken of
the fact that the guilds exchanged embassies and letters/decrees with cities,
kings and later emperors, sent their own emissaries (*theōroi*) to festivals, and
in general had the features of an organisation that functioned as a state, it
may be said that the membership of a guild corresponded in a way with
citizenship and offered artists an alternative identity.[73]

The status of member was linked with highly significant privileges,
such as inviolability (*asylia*), security (*asphaleia*), immunity from taxation
(*ateleia*), exemption from liturgies, contributions, billeting (*aleitourgēsia,
aneisphoria, anepistathmeia*), the right to front seats in theatres or in the
public assemblies (*proedria*), priority in litigation (*prodikia*), priority in
consulting the oracle (*promanteia*) etc. During the Hellenistic period cities,
kings, the Delphic Amphictiony and Roman officials collectively acknowledged these privileges and honours for the members of the associations,[74]
advancing as a basic argument the artists' need to be left undistracted in
the service of the gods and to perform, when required, the honours and
sacrifices entrusted to them.[75] In the imperial period the world-wide Guild
of artists was careful to secure recognition of its members' privileges, as is
implied by the imperial letters attached to the documents of acceptance of
its new members.[76] These efforts to establish documentation that would
strengthen their privileges are possibly at the same time a consequence of
the converse endeavours by the imperial central administration to limit the
numbers of those entitled to them.[77]

Some basic privileges granted to the members of the associations, in
both Hellenistic and Roman times, related directly to their travels and their
movements in general. These were, principally, inviolability and security

---

[72] See above n. 54.

[73] The analogies between the guilds in question and the Greek cities are further supported by the
evidence for a synoecism between the Ionian-Hellespontine Guild of the Hellenistic period and the
city at which it had its headquarters, Teos (see Aneziri 2003: 100–4), and also by the issuing of a
coin by this same association (Lorber and Hoover 2003).

[74] The relevant sources and discussion of the privileges and honours have been collected by Le Guen
2001: I nos. 2, 6, 10, 11, 13, 14, 17, 26 bis, 34, 38, 56 and Aneziri 2003: 243–52, 347ff. nos. A5–A7, A10,
A11, B1, B6–D15, D1, D3–D6, D18, Dubia 2.

[75] The culmination of this argument is the characterisation of the artists as 'sacred' (ἱεροί): *IG* II² 1132
ll. 15–19, 84–5. Similar documentation, more succinctly formulated, is to be found in the relevant
letters of Roman officials: *RDGE* 44 ll. 3–4; 49b ll. 4–6.

[76] *P. Oxy.* 2475, 2476; *P. Oxy. Hels.* 25; *BGU* 1074; *P. Lond.* 1178 (cf. Frisch 1986: no. 1–4, 6; Oliver 1989:
nos. 24, 96, 212). For the privileges of the victors of sacred contests see *I. Tralleis* 105 and *RDGE* 57.
For the privileges of artists who were members of local guilds see Oliver 1989: nos. 29, 32.

[77] In the Codex Justinianus (10.54) it is stipulated, *inter alia*, that athletes entitled to privileges must
have been victorious in at least three sacred games in Rome or 'Old Greece'. Similarly, the cities
sought to limit the pensions paid to victors of sacred contests, as can be seen from the correspondence
between Trajan and Pliny (Plin. *epist.* 10.118–19; cf. Sherwin-White 1966: 728–31).

World travellers

(ἀσυλία, ἀσφάλεια), privileges that protected the artists and their property from uncontrolled acts of reprisal,[78] which fell within the widespread practice of συλᾶν (right of seizure and reprisal), and – primarily – from attacks by brigands or pirates.[79] Furthermore, thanks to these privileges no one could take the artists to court for anything they might have done; the only exceptions were debts owed to a city or breach of contract.[80]

In Hellenistic times these privileges were very important, as wars became more frequent and larger-scale, while there was an escalation of brigandage and piracy.[81] The artists of the Hellenistic period lived in a fragmented world, a world convulsed by tensions and containing many dangers for travellers. In these circumstances, wide participation in festivals and contests, and therefore the success of these, was an issue that went far beyond the artists, as it presupposed securing access to and accommodation in the sanctuaries and other venues of the celebratory events, not only for participants in the contests but also for official envoys of cities or kingdoms, merchants and even ordinary visitors. As a result, numerous Hellenistic decrees of cities and of the Delphic Amphictiony, as well as letters of kings, recognise the inviolability (*asylia*) of the sanctuary and, by extension of the whole city in which it is located,[82] or guarantee a truce (*ekecheiria*) for the duration of the preparation and celebration of a specific festival. It is noteworthy that competitors in the contests were protected by inviolability and security (*asylia* and *asphaleia*), which concerned them individually as members of associations. However, it was very useful that they were further protected by guarantees of security relating to the place and/or duration of the festivals and the contests, since they thus acted in protected space and time.[83]

The situation changed in the imperial period, when peace prevailed and piracy had been largely curtailed.[84] In these circumstances, it is difficult to explain the granting of inviolability and security to victors of sacred contests and to artists generally. Moreover, the continuing recognition of the

---

[78] The view that security (*asphaleia*) related to persons and inviolability (*asylia*) to goods is particularly widespread (held, among others, by Ghiron-Bistagne 1976: 170–1). According to Bravo 1980: 750, *asphaleia* and *asylia* are synonymous. More persuasive is the view that *asphaleia* pertained to times of war and *asylia* to times of peace (Gauthier 1972: 219–20).

[79] Victims of pirates recorded in the literary sources include the artist Phrygon in the middle of the fourth century BC (Aesch. *Emb.* 12) and the boxer Atyanas in 72 BC (Cic. *pro Flacco* 13.31).

[80] *IG* II² 1132 ll. 19–22, 82–5; *CID* 71 ll. 34–9. The lifting of inviolability was essential in order to punish artists who did not meet their obligations and it obtained until they gave account or until they paid the fine imposed on them (see *IG* XII 9, 207 ll. 42–9).

[81] On war in the Hellenistic period, see Chaniotis 2005a. On piracy see Brulé 1978 and Souza 1999: 43–96 (cf. also pp. 97–148). Of the examples of festivals and games that were not held because of war, the majority date from between the third and first century BC (Habicht 2006: 156–64).

[82] Gauthier 1972: 226–30 analyses the inviolability (*asylia*) of the sanctuaries and cities. All this material has been collected by Rigsby 1996 (see the comments of Buraselis 2003 on the views of Rigsby).

[83] Cf. *CID* 70 ll. 17–24. [84] Souza 1999: 179–214.

232   SOPHIA ANEZIRI

inviolability of the sanctuaries and the truce of the festivals comes up against
the same interpretative problem.[85] Possibly these are privileges which,
beyond their now limited practical efficacy (there were surely still smaller-
scale conflicts, robberies and clashes in general), reinforced and consoli-
dated the prestige of a sanctuary, of a contest or of a particular professional
group, like the artists and the athletes, in some cases also enhancing the
continuity with the Hellenistic past.[86] With regard to artists in particular,
the link with the past and continuity are cogent arguments, since the documentation relating to the acceptance of new members to the world-wide
Guild was usually accompanied by a statement of the earlier recognition
of privileges.[87]

In my view, another basic privilege of the artists, immunity (*ateleia*),
is also linked in part with their movements. In the Hellenic world the
terminology of economic obligations (*phoros, telos, eisphora, leitourgia*),
and by extension of economic privileges (*aphorologēsia, ateleia, aneisphoria,
aleitourgēsia*), remains vague in several cases, since the terms acquire a precise
meaning only in the context of a particular economic and political system.
Immunity (*ateleia*), however, seems to have exempted those who travelled
frequently from, *inter alia*, all kinds of dues levied on the use of harbours
and in general the entry and exit of persons and goods to and from the
territory of a city. Such taxes, and also sales- and purchase-taxes, were levied,
logically, on those who attended festivals and who had not been granted
the relevant privileges.[88]

                              CONCLUSION

The associations of Artists of Dionysus can be understood within the changing political and social conditions of the Hellenistic and imperial periods.
Movement, in many forms, played a vital rôle in the foundation and func-
tioning of these associations. On the one hand, the organisers of games

---

[85] Cf. Rigsby 1996: 11–12.
[86] From the second century BC onwards, the privileges of the Hellenistic associations (including
inviolability and security) were also recognised by Roman officials (*RDGE* 44, 49; Roesch 1982:
198–202 no. 44; *Corinth* VIII 3, 40). Moreover, in the second half of the first century BC, from
which dates the first evidence for the granting of privileges to the *synodos* of sacred victors by Mark
Antony (*RDGE* 57), inviolability was still very useful against the background of the Roman civil
wars.
[87] Imperial letters of the early years of the empire are incorporated, for example, in later documents
accepting new members into the association (see above note 76).
[88] For these taxes and the immunity of the festival (*ateleia* of the *panēgyris*), see Ligt 1993: 45–8, 225–34,
244–5 and Chandezon 2000: 85–92. The fact that the artists were paid in coins that circulated widely
and could easily be exchanged seems also to have been intended to facilitate their movements (Psoma
forthcoming).

World travellers

needed to mobilise artists from various parts of the Greek world to the places in which the games were held. Their objective – that is, the success of the particular music competition and by extension of the festival during which it was held – depended in large measure on securing adequate, wide participation of artists in it. The attainment of this objective became more difficult and more complicated as the number of competitions increased rapidly during the Hellenistic and imperial period, and many of them acquired a pan-Hellenic character.

On the other hand, movement from place to place, an activity exposed to great difficulties, was an inevitable feature of the life of the participants in competitions. These difficulties were mainly due to the burden of taxes and duties levied in ports and on entrance to cities in general, as well as dangers arising from warfare, piracy and brigandage, mainly in the Hellenistic period. Membership of an association and the basic privileges of inviolability, security and immunity that accompanied it thus provided the artists with a passport that facilitated their movement. At the same time, enriched by a large number of privileges, some of which were of a purely honorary character, membership provided artists with an alternative identity which enjoyed prestige and recognition beyond the borders of the city from which they came and/or where their association was based.

The most characteristic examples of the concept of the cosmopolitan, citizen of the world[89] seem to have been found in the artists' associations. Moving amongst other cosmopolitan groups, such as merchants, orators, philosophers and ambassadors, the Artists of Dionysus were the only professionals in the Hellenistic period who, through their associations, gave their cosmopolitanism substance and identity. Later, in the imperial period, this cosmopolitanism of the artists acquired a new dimension and an oecumenical character:[90] artists no longer operated as members of (supra-)local associations in a politically fragmented world, but as members of a unified world-wide guild within the Roman empire. They moved in a world in which the dangers attendant on travel had been reduced and the infrastructure for it (roads, staging posts) had improved significantly compared with the previous period, since it now formed a necessary condition for the unhindered administration of the empire (imperial post, travel by administrative officials and journeys by the emperors themselves).

---

[89] For cosmopolitanism in the Hellenistic and early imperial period, see Chrysipp. Stoic. *frgm. moralia* III p. 82 (ed. J. von Arnim. Stuttgart 1978–9) and Philo Alex. *de mundi opificio* I.3 p. 1, I.142–3 p. 50 (ed. L. Cohn and P. Wendland. Berlin 1896–1915). Cf. Svencickaya 1996: esp. 611–14.

[90] Philo states: 'for he [i.e. the cosmopolitan] is a world citizen and in the cause of this not member of any city in the inhabited world, rightly so because he has received no mere piece of land but the whole world as his portion' (Philo Alex. *de vita Mosis* 4.1 p. 157). In another passage of his work, he is 'someone who took the world for his city and native country' (Philo Alex. *de confusione linguarum* 106).

234   SOPHIA ANEZIRI

To draw a somewhat schematic picture, it may be said that the organisation of the artists in associations in each of the two periods – Hellenistic and
imperial – corresponds to the degree of political unification attained during
the period in question. In the Hellenistic period, local artists' associations –
with the exception of Athens – were, just like the kingdoms and federations
of cities, based in more than one city or within a large region, even when, as
in Egypt, these were under the unifying authority of a Hellenistic dynasty.
In the imperial period, the world-wide Guild (*oikoumenikē synodos*) corresponded fully to the geographical extent and political unity of the empire.
The fact that in the same period a number of local associations continued
to exist confirms the lack of strict central planning or of the imposition of
homogeneity from above – a phenomenon already familiar in the relative
autonomy enjoyed by cities, their mints, and so forth.

If this correspondence between political organisation and the organisation of the associations reveals very clearly the close dependence of the
artists and their guilds on their social and political environment, the reverse
course followed by this mutual influence is equally interesting, if less evident. The efforts of the Greek cities after the classical period to play their
part in the world and indeed to create this world, transcending their geographical boundaries, are manifested, *inter alia*, in the sphere of festivals
and competitions, and are what to some extent dictated the patterns of
mobility of the artists. Already in the Hellenistic period, peripatetic artists
reinforced the tendency to unification in the Greek world at the ideological
and cultural level, through their physical presence, their activities and their
dramatic and musical repertoire, and they played a crucial rôle in creating a
unified Greco-Roman culture, long before it acquired a political dimension
in the context of the Roman empire.[91]

Concordances

The following catalogue gives the numbers in Le Guen 2001 and Aneziri
2003 of inscriptions dating from the Hellenistic period relating to the
associations of Artists of Dionysus.

[91] For such phenomena in a context of globalisation Appadurai uses the term 'ideoscape', which is
one of the five dimensions of global cultural flows: 'Ideoscapes are also concatenations of images
but they are often directly political and frequently have to do with the ideologies of states and
counterideologies of movements explicitly oriented to capturing state power or a piece of it. These
ideoscapes are composed of elements of the Enlightenment worldview, which consists of a chain of
ideas, terms and images, including *freedom, welfare, rights, sovereignty, representation*, and the master
term *democracy*' (Appadurai 2003: 36).

Bringmann, Ameling and Schmidt-Dounas 1995: no. 262[E] = Le Guen
2001: I no. 39; Aneziri 2003: 375–6 no. D2

CID IV 12 = Le Guen 2001: I no. 2 (cf. Aneziri 2003: 347–50 no. A5a)

CID IV 70 = Le Guen 2001: I no. 20, ll. 10–29; Aneziri 2003: 359 no.
B3b

CID IV 71 = Le Guen 2001: I no. 20, ll. 30–9; Aneziri 2003: 359–60 no.
B3c

CID IV 72 = Aneziri 2003: 358–9 no. B3a

CID IV 97 = Aneziri 2003: 379 no. D5

CID IV 114 = Le Guen 2001: I no. 6 (cf. Aneziri 2003: 347–50 no. A5c)

CID IV 116 (cf. Aneziri 2003: 347–50 no. A5c)

CID IV 117 = Le Guen 2001: I no. 11; Aneziri 2003: 368–70 no. C1a

CID IV 120 = Le Guen 2001: I no. 12E; Aneziri 2003: 371 no. C1c

CIG 3068 = Le Guen 2001: I nos. 33, 44, 48; Aneziri 2003: 386–7 no.
D11-B5

Daux 1935: 210–30 = Le Guen 2001: I no. 45; Aneziri 2003: 383–6 no.
D10

FD III 2, 47 = Le Guen 2001: I no. 10; Aneziri 2003: 350–1 no. A6

FD III 2, 49 = Le Guen 2001: I no. 13; Aneziri 2003: 353–4 no. A10

FD III 2, 50 = Aneziri 2003: 351–2 no. A7

FD III 3, 218B = Le Guen 2001: I no. 38, ll. 5–8; Aneziri 2003: 375 no.
D1

Iscr. Cos ED 7 = Le Guen 2001: I no. 56; Aneziri 2003: 394–5 no. D18a–b

Iscr. Cos ED 79 = Le Guen 2001: I no. 43; Aneziri 2003: 380 no. D7

IG II² 1132 = Le Guen 2001: I no. 7 Aneziri 2003: 28–9, 347–50 no. A5a

IG II² 1134 = Le Guen 2001: I no. 12E; Aneziri 2003: 370 no. C1b

IG II² 1320 = Le Guen 2001: I no. 3; Aneziri 2003: 343–4 no. A1

IG II² 1338 = Le Guen 2001: I no. 15; Aneziri 2003: 356–7 no. A12

IG II² 3211 = Le Guen 2001: I no. 3 bis; Aneziri 2003: 344 no. A2

IG IV 558 = Le Guen 2001: I no. 36; Aneziri 2003: 364–6 no. B9

IG VII 2484 = Le Guen 2001: I no. 27; Aneziri 2003: 367 no. B12

IG VII 2485 = Le Guen 2001: I no. 28; Aneziri 2003: 367 no. B13

IG VII 2486 = Le Guen 2001: I no. 30; Aneziri 2003: 368 no. B15

IG IX 1, 278 = Le Guen 2001: I no. 31; Aneziri 2003: 366–7 no. B11

IG IX 1², 192 = Aneziri 2003: 378 no. D4

IG XI 4, 1059 = Le Guen 2001: I no. 18; Aneziri 2003: 358 no. B2

IG XII 8, 163 = Le Guen 2001: I no. 57; Aneziri 2003: 395 no. D19

IG XII 9, 910 = Le Guen 2001: I no. 32; Aneziri 2003: 366 no. B10

I. Iasos 152 = Le Guen 2001: I no. 53; Aneziri 2003: 392–3 no. D13

I. Lindos II 264 = Aneziri 2003: 394 no. D17

I. Magnesia 54 = Le Guen 2001: I no. 40; Aneziri 2003: 380–1 no. D8

I. Magnesia 89 = Le Guen 2001: I no. 41; Aneziri 2003: 381–3 no. D9

I. Olympia 405 = Le Guen 2001: I no. 37; Aneziri 2003: 368 no. B16

Nachtergael 1977: 407–12 nos. 3–5 = Le Guen 2001: I no. 24A–C; Aneziri 2003: 403–5 no. Ga1–Ga3

Nachtergael 1977: 413–24 no. 7–10 = Le Guen 2001: I no. 24D–G; Aneziri 2003: 405–12 no. Ga4–Ga7

OGIS 50 = Le Guen 2001: I no. 60; Aneziri 2003: 395–6 no. E1

OGIS 51 = Le Guen 2001: I no. 61; Aneziri 2003: 396–7 no. E2

RC 53 = Le Guen 2001: I no. 47; Aneziri 2003: 387–91 no. D12

RDGE 15 = Le Guen 2001: I no. 12; Aneziri 2003: 372–4 no. C2

RDGE 44 = Le Guen 2001: I no. 34, 51; Aneziri 2003: 361–2 no. B6

RDGE 49 = Le Guen 2001: I no. 56; Aneziri 2003: 394–5 no. D18

Rigsby 1996: 295–6 no. 134 = Aneziri 2003: 379 no. D6

Roesch 1982: 188–94 nos. 32–9 = Le Guen 2001: I no. 23A–H; Aneziri 2003: 412–16 no. Gb1–Gb8

Roesch 1982: 196–202 nos. 42–4 = Le Guen 2001: I nos. 29, 30, 51; Aneziri 2003: 362 no. D15, 367–8 no. B14–B15

SEG 41, 1003, 1005 = Le Guen 2001: I no. 42; Aneziri 2003: 376–8 no. D3

Syll.[3] 457 = Le Guen 2001: I no. 22; Aneziri 2003: 360–1 no. B4A

Syll.[3] 460 = Le Guen 2001: I no. 17; Aneziri 2003: 357–8 no. B1

Syll.[3] 690 = Le Guen 2001: I no. 26; Aneziri 2003: 362–3 no. B7

Syll.[3] 704B = Le Guen 2001: I no. 35A; Aneziri 2003: 363–4 no. B8

Tracy 1975: 60–7 no. 7h = Le Guen 2001: I no. 14; Aneziri 2003: 354–6 no. A11

CHAPTER 10

Aristodama and the Aetolians: an itinerant poetess and her agenda

Ian Rutherford

THE ARISTODAMA DECREES

The poetess Aristodama, daughter of Amyntas, was most likely born in the third quarter of the third century BCE in Smyrna on the west coast of Asia Minor. Many Greeks believed that Homer had been born in Smyrna, and even if Aristodama's Smyrna was a recreated city – Homer's Smyrna was destroyed in the early sixth century BCE and it was not refounded until about 300 BCE – still it must have had a strong sense of its literary past.[1] Aristodama is known to us for one reason only: around 220 BCE she visited central Greece, where she performed her poems, and was honoured for her poetic accomplishments by two cities.[2]

The two decrees are as follows. In 218/217 BCE, the city of Lamia passed a decree in her honour (*IG* IX 2, 62 = G(uarducci)17), framed as a decree of the Aetolian League, which controlled most of central and west Greece from the early third century BCE till well into the second.

(After the introductory formula . . .)
Since Aristodama, daughter of Amyntas, from Smyrna in Ionia, an epic poetess, came to our city and made many displays of her own poems in which she commemorated the *ethnos* of the Aetolians and the ancestors of the people making her *apodeixis* (performance) with complete enthusiasm . . . she should be *proxenos* of the city and benefactor and that an award should be made of citizenship, possession of land and home, *epinomia*, inviolability, safety both by land and sea, in war and peace to her and her children and her property for all time, and everything that is given to *proxenoi* and benefactors. Her brother and his children also are to have *proxenia*, citizenship, inviolability.
(Concluding formula)

Thanks particularly to Lucia Prauscello, and also to Angelos Chaniotis, Giovan Battista D'Alessio, Simon Goldhill and Richard Hunter.

[1] Smyrna: see Rigsby 1996: 95–105.

[2] Basic bibliography on Aristodama: Hiller von Gaertringen 1903; Guarducci 1929, no. 17 and no. 17*; Snyder 1989, 97; Pomeroy 1975, 126; Pomeroy 1977, 55; Ferrandini Troisi 2000, nos. 2.2 and 2.3; in Stephanis 1988 she is no. 326.

237

238   IAN RUTHERFORD

Lamia was the principal city of Malis, one of the ethnic groups that made
up the Delphic Amphictiony, and this is one of two decrees for itinerant
poets it passed, a surprising fact considering the small size of the dossier;
the other was for Politas of Hypata (G9), capital of Ainis, a neighbouring
territory. The reason Lamia gave for honouring Aristodama is that she
recalled the race of the Aetolians and the ancestors of the *dāmos*, which
could either be the Aetolians again or Lamia itself. She is awarded a mostly
conventional set of honours:[3] she is to be *proxenos* of the city and to receive
citizenship; she is to receive land and a home, as well as *epinomia*, which
means 'right of pasturage'; she gets inviolability and safety both by land
and sea, in war and peace. All of these things come to her and her children
and her property for all time, as well as everything that is given to *proxenoi*
and benefactors, and her brother Dionysius (presumably her chaperone)
receives honours as well. No husband is specified for Aristodama, a fact that
might suggest she was still a girl (the 'children' referred to are presumably
potential children). The decree does not, however, specify that she was a
pais, as some inscriptions for others do.[4]

The Lamian decree for Aristodama is highly unusual, however, in so far
as she is awarded citizenship of the city. Like other benefactors, poets are
frequently rewarded with grants of citizenship, particularly in the Roman
period, and the successful ones collected citizenships like a modern rockstar
collects gold records.[5] But granting citizenship to a woman is conceptually
highly awkward in a society which does not, generally speaking, allow that
women can be citizens at all.[6] Thus, though Aristodama was described as
'Smyrnaean', the chances are that she was not a citizen of Smyrna in the
sense that she enjoyed full political rights there. Thus, the possibility arises
that in virtue of her profession she might have come to enjoy in the broader
Greek world a political status denied to her in her own community.[7] We
shall come back to this.

The second decree for Aristodama, which is undated, is a Delphic copy
of a decree originally emanating from the west Lokrian city of Khalaion
just to the south of Delphi on the Gulf of Krisa (*FD* 3.2.145 = G17*). We
know from the decree itself that two copies were set up, one at the local
sanctuary of Apollo Nasiōtas in Khalaion, and the other in Delphi:

---

[3] For such decrees cf. above p. 3.
[4] So Ariston of Phokaia was honoured as a child-poet by Delos in 146–144 BCE (*ID* 1506 = G12), and
a child-poet from Skepsis was honoured by Delphi in 132 BCE (*FD* 3.1.273 = G4).
[5] See below p. 244.   [6] See Pomeroy 1975: 126, Vatin 1970: 267, Ferrandini Troisi *ad loc.*
[7] Chaniotis 1988b: 385 on the difference between *Wander-Historiker* and *Bürger-Historiker*.

Aristodama and the Aetolians

Aristodama daughter of Amyntas from Smyrna in Ionia, epic poetess, arrived here and commemorated [our city]. So that we are seen to honour her appropriately, (it is resolved) to praise her for the piety which she has to the god and for her good-will to the city and to crown her with a garland of sacred laurel from the god, as is traditional for Khaleion. The proclamation about the garland is to be made at the *Poitropia*. And there should be sent to her from our city a prerogative from Apollo's sacrifice, a share of [meat to the hearth] of Smyrna. She should be *proxenos* and benefactor of the city. And there should be given to her and her offspring from the city possession of land, immunity, inviolability by war and peace by land and sea and everything else that goes to other proxenoi and benefactors. And there should be sent to her one hundred drachmas as a guest-gift. Her brother Dionysius should have proxenia, citizenship, immunity. So that it is manifest to all who arrive in the sanctuary that the city of Khaleion values highly those who choose to speak or write about the god, the decree is to be written up by the *epidāmiorgos* Arkhagoras with the scribe Philios and one copy is to be set up in the shrine of Apollo Nasiōtas, the other in Delphi.

This decree, which is much longer than the one from Lamia, shows that Aristodama performed at Khalaion as well, 'remember[ing] the ancestors of the city'. And here too Aristodama and her brother get a long list of honours, including a garland of laurel, to be proclaimed at the *Poitropia* festival (apparently a local version of the Delphic festival of the same name), and a share of a sacrifice to Apollo which is to be sent all the way to Smyrna – an itinerant slice of meat for an itinerant poetess.[8] Perhaps the most striking thing about the decree from Khalaion is that, unlike the one from Lamia, it does not mention the gift of citizenship to Aristodama, although her brother is given it.[9]

Like most of the *poeti vaganti* decrees, the decrees for Aristodama tell us little about her poems, the nature of their performance, or her professional status. If the context was a competition at a festival, it is not mentioned, and Aneziri has recently argued that women-performers did not take part in competitions at least until the late Hellenistic period.[10] Aristodama herself may have been a member of one of the associations of Tekhnitai, and, as a native of Smyrna, the association she is likeliest to have belonged to was that of Ionia and the Hellespont, based at this time in Teos.[11] Central Greece seems to have been dominated by the Association of the Isthmos and Nemea at this time, but that would not have stopped Artists from other

---

[8] Parallels for this practice are pointed out by Daux 1922: 448–9.   [9] Vatin 1970: 267.

[10] Aneziri 2003: 221–3; on festivals, see Petrovic (this volume).

[11] Why would the decree ignore the professional status of the poet? Is it perhaps because the city wanted to pretend that visiting poets and musicians were not professionals, but citizen amateurs, so that conditions had not changed a great deal since the fifth century BCE? On the Tean association cf. Aneziri (this volume).

240   IAN RUTHERFORD

associations from participating.[12] Her poems seem to have been hexameter
compositions, probably city encomia (of the sort now familiar to us from
the so-called 'Pride of Halicarnassos').[13] This is the form of poetry most
commonly mentioned in the *poeti vaganti* decrees, and most fully described
in the Knossian decree for Dioscourides of Tarsus (G16), which refers to
an 'an *enkōmion* of our race in the manner of 'the poet' (i.e. Homer)'.[14]
This 'city *enkōmion*' genre is not unrelated to another genre that was very
much in vogue in the Hellenistic period, the regional history, such as the
Messēniaka of the Cretan poet Rhianus, which gave literary form to the story
of the Messenian diaspora;[15] in Alan Cameron's words, 'the regional epic
is surely a more systematic version of the prize poems that made worthy
mention of the gods, myths, temples and ancestors of the cities . . .'.[16]
Similar compositions and performances could probably be produced in
prose. For example, the city of Larisa in Thessaly honoured an orator called
Bombos (the name means 'humming', a good name for an orator) from
Alexandria Troas; Bombos made *epideixeis* for several days in the *gumnasion*,
recalled the glorious history of Larisa and increased friendship between the
two cities, making mention of the goodwill that Aeolians had for Larisa,
praising Larisa and generally encouraging goodwill between Larisa and
the 'Aeolians', where 'Aeolians' presumably means Aeolians in Asia Minor,
particularly Alexandria; there is no reference to poetry here, so one imagines
this is oratory.[17]

OTHER ITINERANT POETESSES

If itinerant poetesses are unusual in ancient Greece, that is partly because
the profession or pursuit of poetry was comparatively rarely practised by
women.[18] But another factor may be that women in general travelled less
than men, so that women poets tended to stay close to home.[19] So Sappho
stayed on Lesbos, as far as we know, although her brother travelled, as

---

[12] Aneziri 2003: 281.   [13] Isager 1998.
[14] Guarducci *ad loc.* compares the description of Crete at Homer, *Odyssey* 19, 172ff.
[15] Rhianus' son may have been *thearodokos* for Delphi at Keraia in Crete, raising the possibility that
Rhianus himself had this position before him (see Rigsby 1986: 350–5). Was Rhianus honoured
by Delphi for his poetic performances there? On poetry and the Messenian diaspora, see further
D'Alessio (this volume).
[16] Cameron 1995: 298.
[17] Chaniotis 1988b: 310, actually classes this among the historians.
[18] On women poets in the ancient world, see Snyder 1989, Greene 2005. We get some sense of the
proportion of women poets and other performers from Stephanis 1988: 593–4, who lists about a
hundred women poets, musicians and other performers among a total of over 3,000.
[19] For women and travel, see Dillon 1997: 183–99.

Aristodama and the Aetolians 241

did the poet Alcaeus;[20] some of Sappho's women-friends left Lesbos in consequence of marriage. There is no sign that Corinna, whatever her date, ever left her native Tanagra. Telesilla of Argos is famous for having organised the defence of Argos against military attack from Sparta but not for any activities outside Argive territory.[21] But at least from the Hellenistic period there are signs that some poetesses enjoyed a degree of interstate mobility.

The case most readily compared to Aristodama's is probably that of Alkinoe, a woman from Thronion, in east Lokris. She was awarded a decree by the civic authorities of the island of Tenos for some service to the gods there (G18) and another one by her own city (G18*) in the late third century. The decree from Tenos, which lauds her as an 'Aetolian woman', is restored so that it refers to the composition of a hymn, though the remains of the stone are worryingly slight.[22] It may be observed that the area of Lokris was reputed to be one where women held an usually high degree of political power.[23]

We may also mention Glauke of Chios, a *kitharōidos* of the early Hellenistic period, who seems to have been based in Alexandria, since she is supposed to have been the mistress of Ptolemy Philadelphos. How she came to Alexandria, and whether she journeyed elsewhere is not recorded.[24] A less certain case is that of Aristomache of Erythrai, who is reported by Polemo Periegetes to have dedicated a golden book at Delphi, in the treasury of the Sicyonians, after winning two victories with an epic poem at the Isthmian Games. Her date is unknown, except that she predated Polemo (early second century BCE), and it is not even certain that she was an historical person.[25]

The celebrated epigrammatist Anyte of Tegea also deserves mention here, not because she is known to have travelled to perform poetry, but because of an anecdote told about her. According to Pausanias (10.38.13 = *SH* 80), she was sent on a mission to Naupactus by the god Asclepius, who gave her a sealed tablet and instructed her to take it to a man called Phalysios there who was suffering from blindness. The tablet turned out to contain instructions that he pay Anyte two thousand staters of gold, and Phalysios,

---

[20] Cf. Bowie (this volume) pp. 118–22.   [21] Plutarch, *Mul. Virt.* 4, 245c–f; Paus. 2.20.8–10.

[22] G18 = *IG* XII 5, 812, edited with bibliography in Ferrandini Troisi 2000: no. 2.1. Another *poeti vaganti* decree from Tenos, *IG* XII 5, 813, has been of use in reconstructing it. Bouvier 1980 doubted that Alkinoe was a poetess, though see J. and L. Robert at *Bulletin Epigraphique* 1981, n. 362 (reference from *SEG* 30 (1980), 1066). Thronion produced another poet in this period, the citharode Nikon, cf. Stephanis 1988, n. 1877.

[23] Lokris: see Polybius 12.5.3–11.   [24] P. Maas, article 'Glauke', n. 13, *RE* 7, 1396–7.

[25] *Sum. Probl.* 5.2 (675b) = Polemo Periegetes fr. 27 Preller, *FHG* 3.123. Daux 1943: 115 reports a suggestion of M. Bourguet that Plutarch either wrote or meant to write Aristodama, but that seems highly unlikely.

242   IAN RUTHERFORD

cured, founded a temple of Asclepius at Naupaktos. It is as the aetiology
of that temple that Pausanias relates the story, though it would also have
made a good *iama*-narrative at Epidauros.[26] In any case, it seems possible
that some aspect of the story (the rededication of the gold somewhere?)
was the theme of a poem by Anyte.

Besides these four cases, mention may be made here of a few performers
who were not strictly poets, but worked in the related fields of acting and
music. For example, there is the case of Aristodemis of Paphos, a *lusiōidos*
(a practitioner of a type of gender-transgressive mime), probably of the
second century BCE, for whom Antipater wrote an epigram (*Anth. Pal.*
9.567), describing how she crossed to Italy 'so that by her softening charm
she may make Rome cease from war and lay down the sword' (ἵνα πτολέ-
μοιο καὶ αἰχμῆς | ἀμπαύσηι Ῥώμην μαλθακίνηι χάριτι).[27] Like travel-
ling poets in archaic Greece, Aristodemis brings an end to internal political
discord, except that the tawdry associations of *lusiōidia* are ridiculously
inappropriate for the world of international diplomacy. Again, honorary
decrees from Delphi survive for two female musicians, one from Kyme
whose name is lost (134 BCE), and a Polygnota of Thebes (86 BCE), both
decrees included in Guarducci's dossier (G33 and G34). Both had performed
as *khoropsaltriai*, i.e. played some sort of harp while a chorus danced, a designation which has no masculine equivalent and which is attested only in
the second–first centuries.[28]

A few other cases are attested from the period of the Roman empire.
Three notable ones are:

Hedea of Tralles. A decree from Delphi dated to the middle of the first
century CE (*FD* 3.1.533–4; *Syll*[3] 3.802) honouring Hermesianax of Tralles
along with his three daughters records that the daughters were victorious
in athletic competitions, particularly the *stadion*. One of the daughters,
Hedea, besides victories in the *stadion* at the Nemean Games at Sicyon
and the armed chariot race at the Isthmian Games, had won in the boys'
kitharōidia event at the Athenian Sebasteia.[29] The rôle of the proud father
Hermesianax here resembles that of Dionysius in the Aristodama-decrees.
This is an extraordinary document, because apart from this virtually nothing is known about girls entering athletic competitions, and we are not even

---

[26] See Merkelbach, 1973: 53, referring to Dieterich 1911: 246. Cf. Nikagora of Sicyon who introduced
the cult of Asclepius from Epidauros there: Paus. 2.10.3; Dillon 1997: 199.
[27] See Garton 1982: 593–4.
[28] Another case from Iasos in the early second century is Kleino, cf. *IIasos* 165.
[29] See Lee 1988; Mantas 1995: 132–3; Golden 1998: 138–9; Weir 2004: 138–9. For Hedea and the
kitharōidia competition at Athens, see the excellent discussion of Lee 1988: 108–10.

Aristodama and the Aetolians 243

sure whether the competitions referred to here were mixed-gender or for girls only. This text forces us to acknowledge the degree of our ignorance about the movement of competitors between cities in this period.[30]

Anonymous of Alexandria and Cos. Dimitris Bosnakis has recently published a decree from Roman Cos (first century CE) which honours a poetess, probably specialising in ancient comedy, described as both 'Alexandrian' and 'Coan', who had won a number of competitions, including one in Pergamon. The decree refers to a statue of an earlier poetess from Cos, Delphis, daughter of Praxagoras, an *elegeiographos*. The chances are that this is an Alexandrian poetess who had performed on Cos.[31]

Auphria of unknown city. A Delphic decree survives from the Roman period bestowing citizenship on a certain Auphria in recognition of educational performances staged by her there: λόγους τε πολ[λοὺς καὶ κ]αλοὺς καὶ ἡδί[στους ἐν]τῆι Π[υ]θικῆι συ[νόδωι τῶν] Ἑλ[λήν]ων δ[ιέθετο . . .]. These performances were not specified as poetic, and it is more likely that Auphria made a rhetorical display with historical or cultural significance.[32]

A catalogue of itinerant poetesses of this period would not be complete without reference to Julia Balbilla, who commemorated her visit to the Colossi of Memnon at Thebes in Egypt with Hadrian in 130 CE with four elegiac poems which were inscribed on the statues. Julia Balbilla was certainly not a professional poet in the conventional sense, but a well-connected aristocrat of royal pedigree.[33] And we may perhaps now add the name of Damo, who had a short poem in aeolic dialect inscribed on the Colossi; Corey Brennan has recently suggested that she be identified with a certain 'Claudia Damo known as Sunamate' attested from Roman Athens, and that the additional name 'Sunamate' signifies 'Companion' (i.e. of Hadrian on his grand tour).[34]

In the cases of the Aristodama decrees, I observed that the most striking feature is the award to her by Lamia of citizenship. What parallels do we find for this in the cases I have listed from the Hellenistic and Roman periods? To begin with, it should be observed that we would know about grants of citizenship only in cases for which we have an honorary decree, or similar epigraphic document; so in the case of Glauke of Chios, Aristomache of Erythrai, Anyte of Tegea and Aristodemis the *lusiōidos* the question cannot be answered. As for the rest, Alkinoe of Thronion was not awarded

[30] For a good survey, see Mantas 1995.   [31] Bosnakis 2004.
[32] Auphria: *FD* 3.4.79; not in Chaniotis 1988b, apparently.
[33] A. and E. Bernand 1960, nos. 28–31; Brennan 1997–8; Ippolito 1996.
[34] Brennan 1997–8: 227–33. Cf. the case of Paion of Side, another *poeta vagante* who left poems at Memnon: Robert 1980: 19–20, above p. 8.

244   IAN RUTHERFORD

citizenship either by Tenos or by Thronion itself; and the two *khoropsaltriai* were not awarded citizenship by Delphi. However, in the other three cases, there is reference to citizenship:

Auphria of unknown city: the decree for Auphria appoints her a citizen of Delphi.[35]

Anonymous of Alexandria: the poetess honoured in the decree published by Dimitris Bosnakis is styled 'Alexandrian and Coan', which Bosnakis plausibly suggests is an example of the multiple citizenships acquired by successful poets and performers in the Roman period.[36]

Hedea of Tralles: the Delphic decree for Hermesianax and his daughters has been restored, probably rightly, to describe Hermesianax as a citizen of two cities besides Tralles, and his daughters as 'having the same citizenships as well'. This again is a case of the multiplicity of citizenships earned by successful performers in the Roman empire, though it is surprising that it has been extended to girls.

All of these cases are from the Roman period, and this evidence would seem to suggest that conventions about citizenship were beginning to change by then. The case of Aristodama and Lamia on the other hand is somewhat anomalous for its period, and it is rather uncertain how we are to interpret it. Was Lamia perhaps a city where women enjoyed privileges denied them in other parts of Greece, although there is no evidence for that for Malis, unlike the famous case of Lokris?[37] Or was Aristodama's performance there so extraordinary and significant that Lamia (and the Aetolian League as well?) voted her an honour that transgressed the usual conventions of Greek society?

ARISTODAMA AND THE AETOLIANS

The key to understanding Aristodama is perhaps to understand the poetic service that she carried out. As we see elsewhere in this volume, itinerant poets sometimes served a political purpose.[38] In some cases, diplomats in the Hellenistic period actually used poems to get their message across.[39] In other cases there might have been a political agenda behind the commissioning and performance of some of the poems, in which case the poets will have played a political rôle. One example is the Athenian decree for Amphicles of Rheneia, for a Delian *prosodion*, which dates from 165 BCE, the year after the island passed back into Athenian possession, thanks to Roman

[35] Thanks to Bosnakis 2004: 101 n. 11.   [36] Bosnakis 2004: 101 n. 8.
[37] Lokris: see n. 23 above.   [38] Cf., e.g., D'Alessio (this volume).
[39] Cf. Prauscello and Chaniotis (this volume).

Aristodama and the Aetolians

intervention.[40] For almost two hundred years the Athenians had had to suffer the indignity of an independent Delos on their doorstep, like a sort of Hellenistic Cuba. Now it was over, and the *prosodion* was part of the Athenian propaganda drive at that time, and its principal talking points would have been: (a) Athens is great; (b) Rome is also pretty great; and (c) Delos belongs to Athens, and has done since mythological times. So it is, in a sense, all about creating a sense of common identity.

In the case of most of the *poeti vaganti* decrees, analysis is hampered by the non-survival of the poems, but sometimes we can glimpse a political agenda behind one of them. Take, for example, the case of the two Chiote poets who doubled as delegates to the Delphic Amphictiony. These were Amphiklos, who wrote for Delos in the mid-third century BCE but showed up at Delphi as a *hieromnēmon*, and Hermocles, son of Phainomenos, who was honoured by Delphi in a decree dated to the late third century BCE for his service as a *hieromnēmon*, and the decree lists various other services he performed including writing a hymn. This decree praises Chios for, above all else, 'struggling intensely and eagerly over common freedom'. It sounds like the decree is a response to a minor chapter in a Hellenistic war, one of the numerous conflicts involving Macedonia, Aetolia and Rome that took place in this period. So was that a theme of the hymn? The decree also specifies that Hermocles went to the assembly of the Delphians and made a speech about 'the relationship (*oikeiotēs*) existing from Ion to the god and the city' (or something like that). This must mean that Hermocles gave an account of the genealogical relationship between Delphi and the Ionians, including his home island of Chios. This is the rhetoric of *sungeneia* that we find so often in Hellenistic diplomacy.[41] If Hermocles spoke this way in his speech to the Delphic assembly, did his hymn perhaps cover similar ground? Certainly, a hymn could accommodate genealogical material as well, as we can see from the case of the *Homeric Hymn to Aphrodite*. Perhaps, then, the composition of the hymn and the delivery of the speech had in common the quasi-diplomatic force of corroborating what seems already to have been an existing political relationship.

Another case where a *poeti vaganti* decree conceals an international political agenda may be the Samothracian decree in honour of Dymas from the Carian town of Iasos, honouring him for composing a drama about Dardanos (early second century BCE). This was a critical period in the history of Samothrace, when Rome had been drawn into the geo-politics of the Aegean and Greek cities were scrambling to establish relations with her.

---

[40] See D'Alessio (this volume) pp. 147–8.   [41] Cf., e.g., Chaniotis (this volume).

246   IAN RUTHERFORD

Lampsacus in the Troad is already establishing diplomatic connections with
Rome based on genealogy or '*sungeneia*' in 196 BCE.[42] Now, the common
factor between Rome and Lampsacus is, precisely, the royal line of Troy,
which takes us right back to Samothrace. Against that background, it is
tempting to see Dymas' drama as part of the same movement, reflecting a
heightened appreciation of Samothrace in view of its importance in establishing relations with Rome. So the overt reason for the poem's existence
would have been to honour the traditions of Samothrace, but the covert
one would have been to celebrate the broad community of states with an
interest in the cult of Samothrace. While there is no evidence that Dymas'
poem was in itself part of a diplomatic mission, it seems to reflect a diplomatic agenda that might reasonably have been thought to be in the air at
the time.[43]

Aristodama herself may well have taken part in poetic competitions, but
it seems unlikely that she was doing that at Lamia or Khalaion. So what
was she doing? One factor might be *sungeneia*-diplomacy, since in some
traditions at least Smyrna was regarded as an Aeolian foundation, and one
could imagine it wanting to forge links with Aeolian cities on the mainland,
just as Bombos of Alexandria Troas sought to consolidate his city's relation
with Larisa. But in the case of Aristodama the diplomatic agenda could be
of a different sort. The Lamian decree praises Aristodama for recounting
'the race of the Aetolians', which suggests here that the idea was to compose
a sort of pan-Aetolian poem. If that is right, then it is possible to imagine
the motivation for it coming from the Aetolians themselves, who may
have been interested in creating a new Aetolian metanarrative.[44] We might
ask, why engage a poet from Smyrna rather than a home-grown Aetolian
poet, someone in the tradition of Alexander of Pleuron, surnamed 'the
Aetolian', who had achieved some celebrity in Alexandria in the first quarter
of the third century BCE? The answer to that might be partly that they
will have encouraged local poets too (cf. the case of Alkinoe *Aitolissa apo
Throniou*, cited above), and partly for the purposes of pan-Hellenic cultural
dissemination, it was perhaps better to have someone from outside Aetolia
who had already achieved a supraregional or pan-Hellenic reputation.[45]

In fact, another foreign poet may have been hired by the Aetolians to do
exactly the same thing. Nicander of Colophon is known today as the author
of two didactic poems, the *Alexipharmaka* and the *Thēriaka*, versified lists of

---

[42] Curty 1995, n. 39; Jones 1999: 95–6.   [43] See Rutherford 2007: 289.
[44] On Aetolian propaganda, Antonetti 1990.
[45] For the cultural authority often ascribed to experts who come from a distance, see, e.g., Helms 1988
and D'Alessio (this volume).

Aristodama and the Aetolians 247

pharmaceutical lore, but his lost works included an *Aitolika*, presumably a regional epic of some sort. One fragment of this poem offers a contribution to the age-old debate about why Delos was called 'Ortygia'; Nicander seems to have said that it was so termed after a place in Aetolia and that all three of the celebrated Ortygias – Delos, the one in Ephesos and the one in Syracuse – derived their names from this Aetolian original. So in Nicander's Aetolian reworking of Greek mythology, Aetolia is revealed not as a marginal backwater of Greek civilisation, but as its forgotten centre. Nicander is also supposed to have been the author of the *Heteroioumena*, a poem that recounted a series of metamorphoses, known to us largely from Antoninus Liberalis' metamorphosis stories, some of which purport to be largely taken from Nicander:

Antoninus Liberalis 2: Oeneus of Calydon, Meleagrides
Antoninus Liberalis 4: Cragaleus of Dryopis and the ownership of Ambracia
Antoninus Liberalis 12: Cycnus of Calydon
Antoninus Liberalis 22: Cerambus of Mount Othrys in Malis
Antoninus Liberalis 32: Dryope of Oeta

The location of the stories seems to be significant: most of them are in the area of greater Aetolia, including many in areas covered by the member-states of the Delphic Amphictiony, and in particular Malis, the territory of Lamia.

There even seems to be a piece of evidence that links Nicander with Aetolian Delphi itself. This is a decree awarding proxenia and the usual series of honours to 'Nicander, son of Anaxagoras, of Colophon, the epic poet', passed during the Delphic archonship of Nikodamos (G2). There are, however, a couple of problems here. First, the date of that decree is very uncertain, because the date of the archonship of Nikodamos, like those of many Delphic archons in this period, is uncertain. Some people place the decree in the mid-third century, others attribute it to the late third, roughly between 225 BCE and 210 BCE. Secondly, it is by no means certain that this is the same Nicander of Colophon as the one credited with the authorship of the *Aitolika* and the other poems. We have reason to think that there was another Nicander, operating in the second century, perhaps towards its end. One theory is that he was the grandson of the first, and that his father Damaios – a name found primarily at Delphi – was the son of the first Nicander by a Delphian woman.[46]

---

[46] Archons: Gauthier 1989; Nicander generally: Cameron 1995, index *s.v.* Nicander.

248   IAN RUTHERFORD

While there is a chance that the Aetolian works of 'Nicander' date from the late second century BCE, they would better suit a date around 225–210 BCE, if not earlier, because we might expect these to come from the period when the Aetolian League was most powerful, and this did not extend very far into the second century. If that is right, it has the interesting consequence that the decree for Nicander was passed within eight years of those for Aristodama. So I would endorse the hypothesis that the Aetolians somehow engaged Nicander and Aristodama, and possibly other poets and writers of the period, to write about Aetolia, thus creating a sort of pan-Aetolian poetic tradition, again forging a political community through song. For the Aetolian League, this will not have been a trivial matter of academic concern only, but a vital dimension of their supraregional political agenda in the highly-charged diplomatic environment of Greece in the last quarter of the third century BCE. Thus, the Aetolian League will have attached extraordinary significance to the works of these poets, and it is surely this factor more than anything else that will have been behind the extraordinary award of citizenship to a women poet.[47]

[47] Poetry and Aetolian propaganda: see Scholten 2000: 5 n. 15, Antonetti 1990: 114–18; this is implied as early as Hiller von Gaertringen 1903.

CHAPTER II

Travelling memories in the Hellenistic world

Angelos Chaniotis

A DRAMATIC PERFORMANCE OF ENVOYS IN THE ASSEMBLY OF XANTHOS

Those citizens of Xanthos who attended the assembly on 2 Aoudnaios of the year 206 BC, a winter morning, late in November, were unexpectedly rewarded for their willingness to fulfil their citizen duties. For a rather uncommon event awaited them – not the usual agenda of honouring a benefactor or deciding about how to cover a deficit, but the appearance of three men from a distant place most of them had never heard of: Kytenion in Doris. These three men, Lamprias, Ainetos and Phegeus, equipped with two letters of recommendation by the Dorians and the Aetolians, but also equipped with their eloquence, fascinated the Xanthians with their lecture so much that the decree voted on by the assembly gives an unusually lengthy report of their oral presentation, thus providing an interesting insight into oral performances in the popular assembly.[1] The three envoys of Kytenion requested financial aid for the reconstruction of the fortification wall of their city. They supported this request with a common argument of Hellenistic diplomacy: kinship.[2]

The oral presentation of the envoys is referred to with the terms *apologizesthai* ('to give an account') and *dialegesthai* (here not in the sense 'to hold converse with someone', but rather 'to present a discourse, to give a lecture'). The latter meaning of *dialogos* and *dialegesthai* is attested, e.g., in connection with the rhetorical competition which took place during the festival of the Eleutheria and to which I shall return later. The oral presentation of the envoys included at least five sections:

[1] The text: *SEG* XXXVIII 1476: Main commentaries: Bousquet 1988; Curty 1995: 183–91 no. 75; Hadzis 1997; Jones 1999: 61–2, 139–43.
[2] Kinship between communities is a subject to which Olivier Curty (Curty 1995; cf. Curty 1999 and 2005, for response to some criticism of his book) and Christopher Jones (Jones 1999) have dedicated two profound studies, extensively discussing this document.

249

1 an account of recent events (lines 10–13: 'they brought a decree of the Aetolians and a letter of the Dorians, with which they gave an account (*apologizesthai*) of what had befallen their fatherland; they gave a lecture (*dialegesthai*) in accordance with what was written in the letter ');

2 a mythological narrative treating the birth of Artemis and Apollo in Lycia and the birth of Asklepios in Doris (lines 16–20: 'they said that Leto, the patron/leader of our city, gave birth to Artemis and Apollo amongst us; from Apollo and Koronis, the daughter of Phlegyas, a descendant of Doros, Asklepios was born, in Doris');

3 a heroic genealogy (lines 20–4: 'besides their kinship with us, which derives from these gods, they gave an additional account (*prosapologizesthai*) of the intertwining of kinship which derives from the heroes, putting together (*synistasthai*) the genealogy which goes back to Aiolos and Doros');

4 a foundation legend which, according to the plausible analysis by Christopher Jones, concerned the foundation of the Lycian cities (lines 24–30: 'besides, they demonstrated (*paradeiknysthai*) that the colonists, sent out from our land by Chrysaor, the son of Glaukos, the son of Hippolochos, received protection from Aletes [the Wanderer], one of the descendants of Heracles; for Aletes, starting from the land of the Dorians, came to their aid when they were being warred upon. Putting an end to the danger by which they were beset, he married the daughter of Aor [the Sword], the son of Chrysaor [the Golden Sword]');

5 a genealogy of the Ptolemies (lines 47–9: 'for King Ptolemy as a descendant of Heracles is a relative of the kings who descended from Heracles'; cf. lines 109–10: 'for King Ptolemy is our relative on account of his kinship with the kings', i.e. the Argeads).

Other historical narratives are alluded to in the phrase 'they indicated with many other proofs the goodwill that they had customarily felt for us from ancient times because of the tie of kinship' (lines 30–2).

The interest of the commentators of this text has been monopolised by its reference to myths. This is quite natural, since the myth of Aletes and Aor is otherwise unattested and has essential elements of a Hellenistic soap opera: a wandering hero with the characteristic name Aletes, a typical Heraclid, follows his destiny which brings him to Lycia in a crucial moment of its early history. Here, colonists are under attack, certainly by anonymous barbarians. In this moment of despair, Aletes appears, defeats the enemies and marries the daughter of Aor, presumably a beautiful princess – by the

Travelling memories in the Hellenistic world 251

way, the only anonymous person in this narrative. The story has the happy end we know from other *ktisis*-legends.[3]

The interest of recent scholarship in this mythological narrative may be justified, but the focus on this narrative does no justice to the dramatic qualities of another oral account of the envoys: the narrative of a recent war. It is summarised in the decree of Xanthos and in the letter of the Kytenians:

It occurred that in the time when king Antigonos had invaded Phokis [228 BC] parts of the city walls of all the cities had collapsed because of the earthquakes and the younger men had marched to the sanctuary of Apollo in Delphi in order to protect it. When the king arrived in Doris he destroyed the walls of all our cities and burned down our houses.

Even these few lines give us a sense of the dramatic narrative the envoys of Kytenion presented in Xanthos. After earthquakes had destroyed parts of the fortification walls, the enemy exploited this moment of weakness to invade Phokis. The cities of Doris lacked not only the *promakhōnes* of their fortifications, but also the *promakhoi*, the young warriors, their usual defenders in such situations. The young men, in accordance with a pattern we find both in real life and in literature, had marched to Delphi, in order to defend it. The irony of the situation must have been observed by the more attentive Xanthians in the audience. An earthquake had saved the sanctuary of Delphi from invading barbarians twice, from the Persians in 480 (Herod. 8.36–9) and from the Galatians two centuries later (Paus. 10.23.1–10; cf. Iust. 24.8). Ironically, this time it was an earthquake that weakened the defenders of Apollo. The defence of the cities of Doris was left to the old men and the women; the enemy prevailed, taking the cities, destroying what had been left of the city walls and burning the houses.

It is a real pity that this narrative of a recent war has not survived, but similar narratives in contemporary historiography, e.g., Phylarchos' descriptions of the attack of Pyrrhos against Sparta (Plut., *Pyrrhos* 28.4–5) and of the sack of Pellene by the Aetolians (Plut. *Aratos* 31–2), as well as Polybius' narrative of the sack of Abydos (16.30–4), may give us an impression of the possible content of the narrative of the Kytenian envoys.[4] Hellenistic audiences loved these stories, full of suspense, dramatic changes

---

[3] E.g. the legend of Leukippos and Leukophryene (Parthenios *Mythogr. Gr.* 2.1.5). See Prinz 1979: 111–37.
[4] Chaniotis 2005a: 198–9, 208.

252 ANGELOS CHANIOTIS

and tragic ironies. Such stories filled them with compassion and entertained them, even when the bad guy prevailed – e.g. Philip V in the case of Abydos. This sense of suspense and compassion is evident not only in the historiography of this period, but also in the Hellenistic decrees which describe attacks, battles and campaigns. One of the best examples is the long decree of Chersonesos for Diophantos.[5] But even a short phrase in a list of magistrates in Tenos (*IG* XII Suppl. 315), which mentions the most important event during their term in office, can give us an impression of the oral narratives of war: 'when some men noticed those who had sailed against (the city) and had climbed up the walls and had occupied the lower parts of the town, Onesas and the guards (?) formed themselves in battle-order within the city and threw the enemies out by storm'.

The narrative of the Kytenian envoys ended with a dramatic appeal to their distant relatives in Xanthos not to show indifference: 'they ask us to bring to our memory our kinship to them, which originates in the gods and the heroes, and not to remain indifferent to the fact that the walls of their fatherland have been razed to the ground' (lines 14–17); and a few lines later: 'they requested us not to look on the elimination of the largest city among the cities of the Metropolis (the Mother-City) with indifference (περιιδεῖν)'. This dramatic appeal, recalling the greatness of the city – an exaggeration, of course – the collapsed towers and the burned houses, brings to mind the lament for destroyed cities, e.g., for Corinth two generations later (*Anthologia Graeca* 9.151):[6]

Dorian Corinth, where is your admired beauty, where are the crowns of your towers, where is your old wealth? Where are the temples of the Blessed? Where are the palaces? Where are the wives, and the myriads of men, the descendants of Sisyphos? Not a single trace has been left of you, most miserable. For war has seized and devoured everything.

The dramatic narrative and the emotional appeal were effective. We may detect compassion in the answer of the Xanthians: 'we should respond that all the Xanthians felt the same grief with you (*synachthesthai*) for the misfortunes (*aklērēmata* – a unique attestation of this word in a non-literary context) which have befallen your city' (lines 42–4).

---

[5] *IOSPE* I² 352; Bagnall and Derow 2004: no. 56; commentary: Chaniotis 2005a: 210–11.

[6] Cf. a decree of Maroneia (*SEG* LIII 659 A 9–11): ὑπομείνας ἐπιδεῖν κατασκαφὴν μὲ[ν τῆς ἑξήκον]|τασταδίου τὸ περίμετρον πόλεως, τέκνων δὲ ἀπολήας καὶ λε[ηλασίαν | κ]αὶ αἰχμαλ-ωσίαν καὶ τὰς ἄλλας τὰς κατὰ μέρος συμφοράς.

Travelling memories in the Hellenistic world 253

'MNEMOPOIESIS' IN THE HELLENISTIC WORLD

The travels and the performances of epic, tragic and choral poets in the Hellenistic period – the subject of this volume – are part of a more general phenomenon: the mobility of culture, the mobility of texts, images and performances. This chapter focuses on the impact this cultural mobility had on the shaping of memory in the Hellenistic world. For this reason, more emphasis is given to the contribution of orators, historians and envoys than to that of poets.

The inscription of Xanthos is the best introduction to the question of how lectures, poetic performances and orations by itinerant scholars, poets and envoys contributed to shaping a collective memory in the Hellenistic world. The few lines which I have discussed represent in an exemplary way essential features of what we are accustomed to call 'memory' (or 'historical memory') in the Hellenistic period and which is a mixture of a constructed image of the past ('cultural memory') and of personal experiences of recent history or of stories narrated by eye-witnesses ('collective memory'; see below).

The performance of the Kytenian envoys in the assembly at Xanthos reminds us that in the Hellenistic period (and beyond) the transmission of 'memory' was to a great extent oral. In this particular case, the lecture of the Kytenian envoys is summarised in just a few lines, but it must have had a substantial duration and dramatic qualities. The oral transmission did not end with the popular assembly. Some of those citizens who had attended the lecture of the Kytenians must have talked immediately about it to those who did not, possibly also later. More examples of oral transmission of 'memory' will be presented later.

Regardless of whether it is transmitted orally or in writing, 'historical memory' is always subject to selection. In this particular example, only the sections of the lecture referring to the earliest and latest events were selected to be written down. The early period is represented by the theogony myths of Apollo, Artemis and Asklepios, by the heroic genealogy of Aiolos, Doros, and the Heraclids, and by the foundation legend. After a brief allusion to the following period ('they indicated with many other proofs the goodwill that they had customarily felt for us from ancient times'), a huge leap brings us from the time of the legendary founders to the present. This focus on contemporary history, on the one hand, and the history of beginnings, on the other, corresponds to a distinction between 'collective' and 'cultural memory', to which I shall return later.

254   ANGELOS CHANIOTIS

'Historical memory' was not exclusively transmitted by historians – or
scholars for that matter. In the case of Kytenion, we will never know who
composed the text which the envoys orally performed in the assembly of
Xanthos and all the other cities they visited. He may have been a local
scholar, a grammarian, or a foreign scholar engaged for this purpose by the
Kytenians, possibly recruited among the many scholars who visited Hellenistic Delphi; or he may have been one of the envoys.[7] We will never know
to what extent this anonymous author exploited existing traditions and to
what extent he invented 'memories'. At any rate, he was not only concerned
with local traditions. He also knew of the claim of the Lycians that Apollo
and Artemis were born in Lycia; and he had heard of the colonisation legends of the Carians and Lycians, with which he associated the Dorian hero
Aletes. These stories, no matter by whom collected or composed and how,
were not transmitted through a historiographical treatise (or not exclusively
through such a treatise), but through the lecture of the envoys.

'Historical memory' travels, and indeed it travels through unusual channels. In the classical period, and to some extent in the Hellenistic period
as well, historiography (Momigliano's 'great historiography') was primarily
the work of historians who lived in exile; their displacement made historical
memory mobile.[8] In addition to the circulation of written narratives and
to the lectures of itinerant historians, in the Hellenistic world 'memory'
travelled following the steps of diplomats, of poets treating recent history,
of singers of hymns with a mythological content, of pilgrims to sanctuaries,
of mercenaries who had visited the tourist attractions of their places of service and were only too happy to narrate their journeys to foreign countries
and their adventures in great and small battles.

Finally, 'memory' is to a large extent constructed and continually
reshaped. For this phenomenon I propose the term 'mnemopoetic', a neo-
logism (from *mnēmē* and *poiēsis*) that alludes both to the constructed nature
of Hellenistic images of the past (*poiēsis* as making) and to the aesthetic
qualities of narratives of the past (*poiēsis* as poetry).

The lecture of the Kytenians in Xanthos impressed the assembly so much
that the relevant dossier of documents was engraved on stone and set up in
a public space, for future generations to read. This turned the narrative of
the mythological war of Aletes from oral to written, albeit in an abridged
form. In this way, the mythological war of Aletes, a largely (or entirely)

---

[7] For the employment of local and foreign scholars in similar situations see Chaniotis 1988a: 128–30.
For 'intentional history' see Dillery 2005: 519–22 with further bibliography.
[8] Momigliano 1972 and 1978: 20–1; Dillery 2007. Cf. Chaniotis 1988a: 125.

Travelling memories in the Hellenistic world   255

newly invented foundation legend with dramatic qualities, became part of the common cultural memory of Xanthians and Kytenians.

'COLLECTIVE MEMORY' AND 'CULTURAL MEMORY'

The 'historical memories' presented by the envoys of Kytenion were in part *memories* in the literal sense of the word, i.e. accounts of events that most of the citizens of Kytenion had experienced two decades ago, and in part *memories* of narratives concerning a remote past. The fundamental difference between these two types of memory makes a distinction between *collective* and *cultural* memory necessary.[9] The *collective memory* refers to what a community had jointly experienced, i.e., to events of the recent past; by contrast, the *cultural memory* of a community consists of events of the mythical or remote past, the knowledge of which is obscured by time. This distinction between 'collective' and 'cultural' memory corresponds to changes in the commemoration of events. The killing of Hipparchos in 514 BC, for example, was part of the collective memory of the Athenians until the Persian Wars. As such it was subject to political exploitation, but also to controversy. Three generations later, exactly the same event had become part of the Athenian tradition concerning the establishment of democracy. It was an uncontroversial part of the Athenian cultural memory.[10] Only a historian (Thuc. 6.54–9) could recognise this evolution. Another example: the invasion of the Celts in 278 BC was part of the collective memory of the Greeks in the third century, both in mainland Greece and in Asia Minor, even in an island community that was not threatened by the invasion, such as Cos (*Syll.*[3] 398). In Pergamon, this event developed into part of the *local* cultural memory, as it was important for the legitimacy of the Pergamene dynasty. But unlike the Persian Wars, the wars against the Celts never became part of a *Hellenic* cultural memory. The rescuers of the Hellenes, the Aetolians and Antigonos Gonatas, were the enemies of the Greek *poleis* that transmitted cultural memory.[11]

---

[9] On this distinction see Chaniotis 2005a: 215–16. With the notion of 'cultural memory' (*kulturelles Gedächtnis*) I follow and in part modify Jan Assmann's theoretical definitions (Assmann 1992; cf. Assmann and Harth 1991). The bibliography on the complex issue of how memory is generated, stored, transmitted etc. is vast; on this debate see esp. Halbwachs 1925 and 1950, Bartlett 1932, Lowenthal 1985, Casey 1987, Le Goff 1988, Burke 1989, Fentress and Wickham 1992, Irvin-Zarecki 1994, Gedi and Elam 1996, Confino 1997, Olick and Robbins 1998, Connerton 1999, Namer 2000, Gehrke 2001, Alcock 2002: 1–35, Welzer 2002, Fried 2004.

[10] Taylor 1992.

[11] For the commemoration of the wars against the Galatians see Chaniotis 2005a: 220–1, 223, 228, 233, 235–6, 239–40 (with further bibliography).

Cultural memory is usually expressed through a few keywords, as an anecdote concerning the negotiations between Sulla and the Athenians in 87 BC shows (Plut., *Sulla* 13). Plutarch presents the Athenian envoys proudly referring to Theseus (an allusion to his victory over the Amazons), Eumolpos (an allusion to the unsuccessful Thracian invasion under Eumolpos) and to the Persian Wars. These three Athenian victories over barbarians were stereotypically narrated from the fourth century onwards as significant pillars of Athenian self-representation.[12] It sufficed for Plutarch to mention Theseus, Eumolpos and the Persian Wars, with no further details, expecting his readers to understand the allusion to the most glorious chapters of Athenian military history. If in Plutarch's anecdote Sulla was not moved by this oration, it is because he did not share in the Athenian (and Hellenic) cultural memory, but rather represented the last in a long line of non-Greek aggressors.

The Athenian cultural memory was transmitted to the citizens through a variety of media: historiography, mythography, drama and other literary genres, monuments, works of art, and rituals such as festivals, commemorative anniversaries and the ritualised visits of the ephebes to the tombs of the war dead. It was also transmitted to the other Greeks through similar channels: festivals, such as the Eleutheria of Plataia (see below), historiographical works and oral presentations of Athenian envoys in the assembly of other cities or during diplomatic negotiations. When the Athenians negotiated with Sparta in 371 BC, the main argument in favour of a peace treaty used by Callias, one of the Athenian envoys, was the myth of Triptolemos, who had taught the mysteries of Demeter and agriculture to Heracles and the Dioscuri, first among the rest of the Greeks (Xen. *Hell.* 6.3.3). Precisely the same tradition was presented in detail by a delegation of the Athenian Artists of Dionysus to Delphi more than two and a half centuries later, around 115 BC:[13] the Athenian *dēmos* had been the originator of all good things, bringing humans from animal life to civilisation; the Athenians had established bonds of community among the humans by introducing the tradition of the mysteries; thus, they had taught the Greeks that the greatest benefit for humans is intimacy and trust among each other; after receiving from the gods as gifts the cultivation of crops and the laws concerning humanity and education, the Athenians shared these presents with

---

[12] Plato *Menexenos* 239 b–240 e; Ael. Arist. *Panath.* 1.83–113.

[13] Most recent editions of these texts: Le Guen 2001: 11 and 12E; *CID* IV 117 and 120; Aneziri 2003: nos. C1Ab and C1Ba. The anonymous author of the 'aretalogy' of Isis in Maroneia (late first century BC) refers to the same tradition in his praise of Isis/Demeter and Athens (*SEG* XXVI 821 lines 35–41 (new edition of this text and bibliography in Loukopoulou *et al.* 2005: 383–5 no. E205).

Travelling memories in the Hellenistic world

the Greeks. The orations of Callias and of the Athenian Artists of Dionysus reveal three further essential elements of cultural memory: continuity,
consistency and standardisation. The myth narrated by Callias in Sparta in
371 BC was the same as the one narrated by the *tekhnītai* in Delphi in 115
BC. We have already observed here a similar continuity of traditions in the
case of the three victorious wars against invading barbarians.

In the case of Athens we are in a position to observe a continuity of cultural memory because of the abundance of sources. Lindos on Rhodes offers
a good example of an analogous continuity and consistency. In Lindos, the
miracles of Athena Lindia were an important constituent of local cultural
memory.[14] The so-called 'Lindian Chronicle', an inscription containing a
list of the legendary and historical dedications to Athena and narratives of
her epiphanies, mentions the written sources used by the scholars who com-
piled this work. The miracle of Athena during the attack of the Persians in
the spring of 490 BC was referred to, e.g., by Eudemos in his *Lindiakos*, by
Ergias and Polyzalos in the fourth book of their *Histories*, by Hieronymos in
the second book of the *Heliaka*, by Myron in the thirtieth book of *Rhodou
Enkomion*, by Timokritos and Aristion in the first book of the *Chronikai
Syntaxeis*, by Hieron in the first book of *Peri Rhodou*, and by Xenagoras
in the fourth book of his *Chronicle*. From the abundance of references we
infer that this miracle was a standard constituent of local pride. Similarly,
a dedication of Artaphernes was mentioned by Eudemos in the *Lindiakos*,
by Myron in the *Enkomion* of Rhodos, by Timokritos and Aristion in their
Chronicle, by Polyzalos in his *Histories*, and by Hieronymos in the *Heliaka*.
A dedication by the Egyptian king Amasis was mentioned by the historians Herodotus and Polyzalos, in the chronicles of Agelochos, Aristion,
Aristonymos, Onomastos and Xenagoras, by Hieron in *Peri Rhodou* and
in a letter of Hieroboulos to the magistrates (*mastroi*). The narratives concerning the relations of Lindos to Amasis and the unsuccessful attack of the
Persians under Artaphernes were the 'highlights' of local history that could
not be omitted by any local historian or orator – or by a foreign historian
for that matter.

If we take a close look at the historical periods to which the selected
dedications to Athena and Athena's miracles belong, we recognise a particular pattern. The dedications and the miracles are connected with local
heroes (the eponymous hero Lindos, the Telchines, the legendary king
Tlepolemos), great personalities of Greek myth, the heroes of the Trojan

---

[14] On the Lindian *anagraphē* as a document of cultural memory see Chaniotis 1988a: 52–7; Higbie
2003: 204–42; Chaniotis 2005a: 222–3, 235; Dillery 2005: 514–19.

258   ANGELOS CHANIOTIS

War, personalities of the Archaic period (the colonists of Cyrene, legendary
Archaic tyrants, the Pharaoh Amasis), and the Persian Wars. Then there is a
'black hole' after the Persian Wars, and the references to historical personalities and events start again with Alexander the Great and the Successors, i.e.
with another period that we may characterise as a period of 'founders' and
'beginnings'. The cultural memory of the Lindians consisted of the memory
of myths, especially those connected with Troy, the period of colonisation,
the Persian Wars, the reign of Alexander the Great and the formation of
the Hellenistic World.

   This is exactly the pattern we have already observed in the case of the
accounts of the Kytenian envoys, who treated myths and foundation legends and then, after a gap, recent history. We recognise the same pattern
also when we study Athenian honorary inscriptions for ephebes in the Hellenistic period. These documents highlight the visits of ephebes to war
monuments and their participation in rituals that transmitted the local
cultural memory to the youth. One of these texts honours the ephebes of
the year 122 BC and describes their various activities (*IG* II² 1006).[15] They
attended the procession for Artemis Agrotera on 6 Boedromion, which was
at the same time the anniversary of the battle of Marathon; they sacrificed
to Athena Nike, the patron of military victory; at the funeral contest in
honour of the war dead (*Epitaphia*) they held a race in armour, starting at
the *polyandreion*, the common burial place of the Athenians who had died
in the sea-battle of Salamis; at the Theseia they honoured Theseus as the
legendary founder of the Athenian state and as archetypical ephebe; they
visited the tomb at Marathon, crowned it and sacrificed to the dead of the
battle of Marathon, in a ritual which must have included some oral reference to the historical events; in the sanctuary of Amphiaraos, the ephebes
testified to (*historēsan*) the ancestral claim of their city to this sanctuary;
they sailed to the trophy erected by the Athenians after the sea-battle at
Salamis and sacrificed to Zeus Tropaios; at the Aianteia they honoured Ajax,
the hero of Salamis, organised a regatta, a procession, and a sacrifice. As
in the anecdote concerning Sulla, the allusions to the past primarily refer
to the founders' times (e.g., Ajax and Theseus) and to the Persian Wars.
Similarly, in an inscription that concerns the restoration of sanctuaries in
Attica[16] one observes a preference for events that marked the beginning
of new eras (Theseus, Solon, the Persian Wars), as well as a preference for

---

[15] Chaniotis 2005a: 51–3. For the memorials of the Persian Wars in the Roman period see Alcock 2002:
74–86.
[16] *IG* II² 1035; *SEG* XXVI 121; Chaniotis 2005a: 239–40.

Travelling memories in the Hellenistic world   259

wars against barbarians (Persians, Galatians) and for victories that legitimised claims (the occupation of Salamis).

In the Hellenistic period both collective and cultural memories travelled and were to a great extent orally transmitted. It is to these oral memories and to the three most important means of their mobility that I now turn: public lectures of historians and other scholars, lectures of envoys in diplomatic missions, and rituals.

THE WINGS OF ITINERANT MEMORIES: LECTURES, EMBASSIES, RITUALS

Public lectures

The tradition of public historical lectures goes back to the fifth century (at the latest), but a culture of *akroaseis* (public lectures) grew in the Hellenistic period, continuing until the second century AD.[17] The lectures by itinerant historians are primarily attested through honorary decrees.[18] A good example concerns an anonymous teacher in Amphipolis in the third century BC.[19] The verb *parepidēmein* shows that he was a foreigner who stayed for some time in Amphipolis, perhaps as a teacher in the gymnnasium. During his stay he read the existing works of historiography and poetry and collected information relevant to Amphipolis. From the reference to 'old authors of histories' (*archaioi historiographoi*) we may infer that the material did not concern recent or contemporary history, but probably early history (foundation myths, possibly the history down to the Peloponnesian War). The anonymous historian also wrote a treatise about Artemis Tauropolos, i.e. he treated the relevant myths, possibly also the miracles of the goddess. This material was presented in *akroaseis*, in public lectures, probably not in the context of competitions, but in the gymnasium.

The second example concerns Mnesiptolemos of Kyme, a historian of the Seleucids.[20] He was honoured in Delos in the late third century

---

[17] For *akroaseis*, in general, see Robert 1946: 35–6; historians: Chaniotis 1988a: 367–8; Dillery 2005: 521 with n. 63; doctors: Samama 2003: 197–8 no. 98, 439–42 no. 341.

[18] Honorary decrees for historians: Chaniotis 1988a: 290–326, 365–82.

[19] *SEG* XXVIII 534; Chaniotis 1988a: 299 E6: [. . .] παρεπιδημῶ[ν – – –] καὶ παιδεύων καλῶ[ς – – –] ἐξετάσας καὶ συνα[γαγὼν τὰ παρὰ τοῖς ἀρ]χαίοις ἱστοριογράφοις [καὶ ποιηταῖς? γεγραμ]μένα περὶ τῆς πόλεως [ἡμῶν πλείονας ἐποιή]σατο ἀκροάσεις περὶ τού[των? – – – ἐν αἶς] καὶ εὐδοκιμήκει· συνετ[άξατο δὲ βιβλίον?] καὶ περὶ τῆς Ταυροπόλου [– – –] ('– – – during his stay – – – educating in a good manner – – – having examined and collected the things that the old historians and poets have written concerning our city, he gave many lectures on these subjects – – – with great success; he also composed a book concerning (Artemis) Tauropolos').

[20] *IG* XI 4 697; Chaniotis 1988a: 303 E10.

260   ANGELOS CHANIOTIS

as a *historiographos* ([ἐπαινέσαι Μνησιπτόλεμον Κ]αλλιάρχ[ου τὸν
ἱ]στοριογ[ρά]φ[ον]) and this shows that the honour was the result of
this activity. From Athenaeus (10.432b: ἀνάγνωσιν ποιησαμένου τῶν
ἱστοριῶν) we know that Mnesiptolemos used to read from his historiographical work. His lectures in Delos may have had contemporary history
as their subject.

Contemporary history was also the subject of the public lectures of Aristotheos of Troizen in another pan-Hellenic sanctuary, this time Delphi.[21]
As we learn from the honorary decree of Delphi, Aristotheos presented his
treatises in lectures for many days, and in addition to this he also read encomiastic orations for the Romans, the common benefactors of the Greeks.
The subject matter of Aristotheos' historical treatises is not known; but
a good guess – given the subject of his orations – is that he was a historian of contemporary history, possibly of the Third Macedonian War. We
may assume that in both Delos and Delphi, two of the most important
international sanctuaries of this period, the lectures were attended by a
pan-Hellenic audience.

A third pan-Hellenic sanctuary which became the venue of the lectures
of another historian of contemporary history is Epidauros. It is here that at
the very end of the Hellenistic period a statue of Philippos of Pergamon, a
historian of the contemporary wars of the late Republic, was erected. The
inscription on the statue base reads (in a rather free translation):[22]

I (the statue), Philippos, son of Aristeides from Pergamon, the master of divine
history, have been dedicated by Epidauros; but all the Greeks honoured me (or
took delight in me), when with loud voice I recited the written account of wars,
treating the world of the mortals.

---

[21] *FD* III.3, 124; Chaniotis 1988a: 309 E17: ἐπειδὴ Ἀριστόθεος Νικοθέου [Τρο]ζάνιος ἱστοριογράφος
παραγενόμενος [ἐ]ν τὰν πόλιν τάν τε ἀναστροφὰν ἐπ[οιά]σατο ἀξίως τοῦ τε ἱεροῦ καὶ τᾶς ἰδίας
πατρίδος· ἐποιήσατο δὲ καὶ ἀκροάσεις ἐπ[ὶ π]λείονας ἁμέρας τῶν πεπραγματευμένων αὐτῶι·
παρανέγνω [δὲ καὶ] ἐν[κώ]μια εἰς Ῥωμαίους, τοὺς κοινοὺς τῶν Ἑλλάνων εὐεργέτας ('because
Aristhotheos, son of Nikotheos, from Troizen, a historian, has come to our city and conducted his
stay in a manner worthy of the sanctuary and his own fatherland; he also gave lectures for many
days presenting his treatises; in addition to this he read out praises for the Romans, the common
benefactors of the Greeks').

[22] *IG* IV² 1 687; Chaniotis 1988a: 314 E23: ἄνθετο μέν μ' Ἐπίδαυρος Ἀριστείδαο Φίλιππον |
Περγαμόθεν, θείας κοίρανον ἱστορίας· ἀγλάϊσαν δ' Ἕλλανες, ἐπεὶ πολεμόγραφον αὐδὰν |
ἔκλαγον ἀμερίων κόσμον ἐπερχόμενος. ἐγὼ παντοίων παθέων καὶ ξυνεχέος ἀλληλοφονίης
ἀνά τε τὴν Ἀσίην καὶ τὴν Εὐρώπην καὶ τὰ Λιβύων ἔθνεα καὶ νησιωτέων πόλιας καθ'
ἡμέας γεγενημένων ὁσίῃ χειρὶ τὴν περὶ τῶν καινῶν πρήξεων ἱστορίην ἐξήνεγκα ἐς τοὺς
Ἕλληνας, ὅκως καὶ δι' ἡμέων μανθάνοντες, ὁκήσα δημοκοπίη καὶ κερδέων ἀ[μετρησίη] καὶ
στάσιες ἐμφύλιοι καὶ πιστίων καταλύσιες γεννῶσιν κακά, παρατηρήσει παθέων ἀλλοτρίων
ἀπενθή[τους] ποιέωνται τὰς τοῦ βίου διορθώσιας. For an analysis of this text see Goukowsky
1995; Chaniotis 2005a: 16–17, 240–1.

Travelling memories in the Hellenistic world 261

There can be little doubt that the expression *polemographos audā* refers to oral reciting of a written historiographical work dealing with wars. The beginning of this historical work is quoted on the statue base:

With my pious hand I delivered to the Greeks the historical narrative of the most recent deeds – all sorts of sufferings and a continual mutual slaughter having taken place in our days in Asia and Europe, in the tribes of Libya and in the cities of the islanders; I did this, so that they may learn also through us how many evils are brought forth by courting the mob and by love of profit, by civil strifes and by the breaking of faith, and thus, by observing the sufferings of others, they may live their lives in the right way.

In the second century (*c.* 160–150 BC), Bombos of Alexandria in the Troad visited the city of Larisa in Thessaly. His activity is described in a decree issued to honour him:[23]

Bombos, son of Alkaios, an Aiolian from Alexandreia, coming to our city and giving performances in the gymnasium, commemorated both in his treatises and in his lectures the glorious events that have occurred with regard to the Lariseans and renewed the kinship and the friendship between the two cities.

The 'glorious events' (*endoxa*) treated by Bombos must have included the contribution of the Lariseans to the Aeolian colonisation but probably also recent wars, e.g., the Thessalian contribution to the Roman victory over Perseus.[24] I should draw attention to three aspects of Bombos' historical contribution: the oral character of his presentation, the addressees of his performance – the youth that exercised and learned in the gymnasium – and the encomiastic character of his treatise. The encomiastic character of Hellenistic historiography, criticised by Polybius, has already been observed in the case of Aristotheos of Troizen (above).

Unfortunately, no historical lecture of the Hellenistic period is preserved. From references in honorary decrees we may assume that the subjects treated in these lectures were 'deeds of glory' (*endoxa*), i.e., wars, foundation myths, and miracles of local gods.[25] It is only by coincidence that a small fragment of an *enkōmion* for Athens survives. It is a fragment of an oration delivered

---

[23] Helly 2006 (new critical edition with detailed commentary), lines 12–19: ὁπειδὴ [Β]όμβος Ἀλκαί[οι] Α[ἰολεὺς ἀπ' Ἀλεξαν]δρείας παρεπιδαμείσας ἐν τᾶ πόλε[ι καὶ ποιεισάμε]νος ἐπιδείξις ἐν τοῦ γ[υμ]νασί[ου συνεμνεμονεύσατο? ἔ]ν τε τοῖς πεπραγματευμένοις αὐτοῦ καὶ ἀκροάσεσσιν τοῦν γεγενημένουν ἐνδόξουν Λαρισαίοις καὶ τάν τε συγγένειαν καὶ φιλίαν ταῖς πολίεσσι π[ὸ]θ' εὔτὰς ὀνενε[ούσατο]. Cf. Chaniotis 1988a: 310 E18, Rutherford (this volume) p. 240.

[24] Chaniotis 2005a: 224. I understand *endoxa* as neuter; Helly 2006: 173, who translates 'des personnages qui ont été fameux chez les Lariséens', thinks of references to glorious men, e.g., Aleuas (cf. Helly 2006: 198). But the text reads τοῦν γεγενημένουν ἐνδόξουν Λαρισαίοις and not τοῦν γεγενημένουν ἐνδόξουν Λαρισαίουν.

[25] *endoxa*: Chaniotis 1988a: 310 no. E18; 312 no. E20; 372–7.

by Hegesias, a local historian of Rhodes and an orator (Strabo 9.1.16 C 396): 'I see the acropolis and, there, the sign of the miraculous trident; I see Eleusis, and I have been initiated in the sacred rites; the Leokorion is there, here Theseus' sanctuary. I cannot describe everything in detail, for Attica belongs to the gods, who laid claim on the land, and to the ancestors, who are honoured as heroes.' The orator alludes with a few words to standard elements of Athenian cultural memory: foundation myths (i.e., the contest between Athena and Poseidon, the synoecism of Athens by Theseus), the Eleusinian mysteries, deeds of self-sacrifice – the Leokorion was the monument for the daughters of a king who sacrificed themselves to save Athens from hunger, but also the place where Harmodios and Aristogeiton were remembered as tyrannicides – and the heroic deeds of the ancestors. He could afford to be merely allusive in his references, precisely because the sites, persons and events to which he referred were parts of the Athenian cultural memory.

These historical lectures correspond to the pattern I have already sketched: they deal either with contemporary history ('collective memory' in the narrow sense of the word) or with narratives of legend and early history, which contribute to the construction of an identity (i.e., with 'cultural memory'). The same pattern can be recognised in oral presentations which are connected with diplomatic activities.

Diplomatic missions

In the late third or more plausibly in the early second century BC – possibly during the War of Antiochos – the poet Hermocles of Chios came to Delphi as one of the *hieromnēmones* sent by Ionian Chios to the Amphictiony. During his stay he composed a hymn praising Apollo.[26] He also appeared in front of the assembly presenting an account (*apologizesthai*) of the friendship (*oikeiotēs*) between Delphi and the Ionians, the roots of which he discovered in the myth of Ion and his childhood in Delphi. The decree of the Delphians

---

[26] *FD* III.3, 224; Chaniotis 1988a: 304 no. E11: . . . καὶ ὕ[μνον γέγραφε τῶι θεῶι καὶ τὰν ἐπιδαμίαν ἐποιήσατο ἀ]ξίως τοῦ τε ἱεροῦ καὶ τῶν ἀποστειλάντων [αὐτόν· καὶ ἐπελθὼν ποτὶ τὰν ἐκκλησίαν τὰν οἰκειότ]ατα τὰν ὑπάρχουσαν ἀπὸ Ἴωνος ἀπελογίξατο [ποτί τε τὸν θεὸν καὶ τὰν πόλιν] . . . ἐπαινέσαι μὲν τὰν πόλιν τῶν [Χίων ἐπί τε τᾶι λοιπᾶι αἱρέσει καὶ ἐπὶ τῶι ἀγωνίζεσθ]αι ὑπὲρ τᾶς κοινᾶς ἐλευθερίας ἐκτενέως κα[ὶ προθύμως] ('he wrote a hymn for the god and conducted his stay in a manner worthy of the sanctuary and those who have sent him. And he appeared in front of the assembly and presented an account of the friendship which exists towards the god and the city, originating in Ion . . .; we should praise the city of the Chians for its whole attitude and in particular for zealously and willingly fighting for the common freedom'). For the date see Lefèvre 2002: 242.

Travelling memories in the Hellenistic world   263

to his honour praises not only him, but also the city of the Chians, for being a 'zealous and willing combatant for the common freedom'. This phrase seems to allude to the fact that during the War of Antiochos Chios had taken the side of the Romans. Based on this observation, I suspect that Hermocles had also treated recent history in his lecture.

One of the best documented diplomatic enterprises in Greek history was Magnesia's effort to upgrade the local *agōn* of Artemis Leukophryene and to have the inviolability of city and sanctuary recognised by kings, federal states and cities.[27] More than eighty cities received embassies of the Magnesians. One of the strategies of persuasion used by the envoys was the presentation of historical lectures. Many responses of the recipients of this embassy describe the performances of the envoys. Their presentation in each city they visited included the narrative of a recent miracle (*epiphaneia*) of Artemis, which had caused the Magnesians to reorganise their festival. The rest of their lecture was adapted to the interests of their audience. Exactly as Teian and Mylasean envoys to Crete sung Cretan songs in the assembly of Cretan cities,[28] the Magnesian envoys presented a mythical or historical narrative that demonstrated the relation of their fatherland to the city they were visiting. In Kephallenia, for example, they referred to foundation legends, narrating the myth of Kephalos, the eponymous hero, who was the son of the brother of their own eponymous hero, Magnes.[29] In Megalopolis they recalled that Magnesia had contributed 300 *dareikoi* for the fortification of the city (*c.* 370 BC).[30] We observe, again, a familiar pattern: both in Kephallenia and in Megalopolis the lecture included references to *ktiseis*. In Epidamnos the envoys of Magnesia gave an account of their contribution to the defence of Delphi, mentioning 'the military assistance offered to

---

[27] Rigsby 1996: 179–279; Chaniotis 1999; Kassel 2003.   [28] Chaniotis 1988b.

[29] *I. Magnesia* 35 = *IG* IX² 1, 1582: ἐμφανιξάντων δὲ καὶ περὶ τᾶς οἰκειότατος τᾶς ὑπαρχούσας Μαγνήτοις ποτὶ Κεφαλλᾶνας κατὰ τὰν συγγένειαν τὰμ Μάγνητος καὶ Κεφάλου τοῦ Δηίονος . . . ('they presented the friendship between the Magnesians and the Kephallenians on account of the kinship between Magnes and Kephalos, son of Deion').

[30] *I. Magnesia* 38: τῶν δὲ Μαγνήτων τῶν ἀπὸ Μαιάνδροι ἐκ παλαιῶν μὲν χρόνων ἔχοντες εὐνόως πρὸς ἄμμε, συμφανὲς δὲ ποιησάντων τὰν ἔχοιεν ἐκτένοιαν καὶ αἵρεσιν, ἀνάκα παρεγένετο πὸς αὐτὸς πρεσβεύοντες Πρόξενος, Ἆγις, Ἀριστοπάμων· εὐνόως τε γὰρ προσ[ε]δέξαντο οἱ Μάγνητες καὶ ἔδωκαν ἰν τὸν τειχισμὸν τᾶς πόλιος δαρεεικὸς τριακοσίος, τὸς ἐκόμισεν Ἀγαμήστωρ ('the Magnesians have been benevolent towards us from old times; and they made clear their zeal and their goodwill when Proxenos, Agis and Aristopamon came to their city as envoys; for the Magnesians received them with benevolence and gave three hundred *dareikoi* for the construction of the city wall, which Agamestor brought to us'). Roy 2003 has argued that the relevant decree is that of Mantineia, and not Megalopolis. None of the names that appear in this decree (Agis, Aristopamon, Arkesilas, Nikeratos, Proxenos, Sthenolas) is, however, attested in Mantineia, while almost all of them are independently attested in Megalopolis (Agis, Aristopamon, Nikeratos, Proxenos; for Arkesilas cf. Arkesilaos).

264 ANGELOS CHANIOTIS

Delphi by their ancestors, when they defeated in battle the barbarians who had campaigned in order to plunder the property of the god.'[31] They also mentioned a recent event: ten years earlier they had arbitrated in a Cretan war. In Crete they must have mentioned this event, but also the help offered by the Cretans to the mythical founder of Magnesia, Leukippos, when he stopped at Crete, coming from Thessaly and on his way to Asia.

As I have argued elsewhere,[32] the envoys must have taken along in their journey an anthology of poems and a historiographical work, the *praxeis tōn Magnētōn*, from which they recited passages in their lectures in the assembly. I suspect that one of these envoys was actually the author of the work. This travelling memory was in part 'collective memory' (the miracle of Artemis, the activities of the Magnesians as peace-makers), in part local 'cultural memory' (the foundation myth of Magnesia), in part the 'cultural memory' of their partners (the foundation myth of Kephallenia, the *ktisis* of Megalopolis), in part the 'cultural memory' of the Panhellenes (the victory over the Gauls in Delphi). The travelling memories of the Magnesians contributed to shaping the memories of their partners.

This is not an isolated case. In the second century, envoys of Apollonia on the Rhyndakos, on the south coast of the Black Sea, came to Miletus in order to establish relations based on kinship. The relevant document explains:[33]

The Milesians listened to the envoys favourably and, after examining the historical narratives about this issue as well as the other documents, they responded that our city (Apollonia) has truly been a colony of their city. Their ancestors did this, when they sent an army to Hellespontos and to Propontis, defeated in war the barbarians that inhabit these places and founded the other Greek cities and our own; Apollo of Didyma was their leader in this campaign.

---

[31] *I. Magnesia* 46: ἐμφανίξ[αντες τὰν] τᾶς Ἀρτέμι[δος ἐπιφάν]ειαν καὶ τὰν γεγενημέν[α]ν βοάθειαν ὑπὸ τ[ῶ]ν π[ρ]ο[γόνων α]ὐτῶν [εἰ]ς τὸ ἱερὸν τὸ ἐν Δελφ[οῖς], νικασάντων μάχαι τοὺς βαρ[β]άρους το[ὺ]ς ἐπιστ[ρατεύ]σαντας ἐπὶ διαρπαγᾶι τῶ[ν το]ῦ [θ]εοῦ χρημάτων, καὶ τὰν εὐε[ργ]εσίαν, ἃν [συ]νετελέσαντο εἰς τὸ κοινὸ[ν] τῶν Κρηταιέ[ων] δι[α]λύσαντες τὸν ἐμφύλιον πόλεμον. ἐνεφάνιξαν δὲ καὶ τὰς εἰς τοὺς ἄλλους ["Ελ]λανας γεγενημένας εὐε[ρ]γεσίας διά τε τῶν τοῦ θεοῦ χρησμῶν καὶ διὰ τῶ[ν π]οιητᾶν καὶ διὰ τῶν ἱ[σ]τορ[ι]αγράφων τῶν συγγεγραφότ[ων] τὰς Μαγνήτων πρ[άξ]ει[ς] ('they presented the miracle of Artemis, the help that their ancestors have given to the sanctuary at Delphi, when they defeated in a battle the barbarians who had campaigned in order to plunder the property of the god, and the benefaction they did to the league of the Cretans, when they put an end to the civil war; they also presented their benefactions to the other Greeks by means of the oracles of the god, the poets and the historians who have written down the deeds of the Magnesians').

[32] Chaniotis 1988a: 128–30. [33] Curty 1995: 143–5 no. 58. Milet I.3 no. 155.

Travelling memories in the Hellenistic world

It is, again, an oral presentation and discussion in the assembly – accompanied by a study of written documents – that brought an old war back to memory. The event concerns, as in many other cases, a war against barbarians in the founders' time.

The aforementioned examples of oral narratives concern wars of the remote past. Oral accounts of recent wars were also common, playing a prominent part in honorary decrees. The proposals, orally presented in the assembly, included a justification (*narratio*) which often took the form of a more or less detailed narrative of heroic deeds in battles.[34] If these oral reports have survived, it is because many decrees were inscribed on stone upon approval. In many cases the honours were periodically announced in the theatre or in athletic competitions, thus perpetuating the memory of the military achievements. A decree of Apollonia in honour of Histria is an instructive example of this practice:[35]

It occurred that the inhabitants of Mesembria carried out an undeclared war against us, occupied our territory beyond the sea, committed many and great acts of sacrilege against the sanctuary of Apollo, and brought our city to the greatest dangers. But the Histrians, who are our relatives and friends and have a favourable disposition towards our people, sent ships and soldiers to help us.

The decree included a narrative that presented the enemy in the darkest colours as a cowardly, unjust and impious aggressor. It was not only to be inscribed on the base of the statue of the victorious general; but it was also to be read aloud during the contests that took place in Histria for ever (ἀεί).

The embassy of Magnesia (208 BC) took place only two years before the embassy of the Kytenians (206 BC). The envoys of Magnesia certainly visited Aetolia, perhaps they made a stop in Doris. It can hardly be a coincidence that the embassy of the Kytenians follows – probably intentionally imitates – the Magnesian pattern. In both cases we find a reference to kinship originating with gods and heroes; Aletes, the wandering warrior, and Aor's daughter, are modelled after Leukippos, Magnes and his daughter Leukophryene; the young Kytenians who march to Delphi to defend the sanctuary recall the ancestors of the Magnesians who defeat the Gauls near Delphi; as for foundation myths, the very name Metropolis (the 'mother city') alludes to them. The travelling memories of the Magnesians showed the Kytenians how they should construct and present their own travelling memories. In both cases the Hellenes were the virtual audience of the 'mnemopoetic' activities of the envoys.

[34] Chaniotis 2005a: 209–11.   [35] *ISE* 129; Curty 1995: 39–41 no. 21; Chaniotis 2005a: 226.

Rituals

The mobility of worshippers and ritual performers was part of Greek cult practice from an early period, at the latest from the archaic period onwards. The establishment of new festivals and *agōnes*[36] and the professional specialisation of the performers of the theatre,[37] in addition to other factors (euergetism, royal patronage, etc.), increased mobility in Hellenistic cult practice. This increased mobility resulted in manifold ways by which memories, both 'cultural' and 'collective' memories, travelled. The worshippers in the pan-Hellenic sanctuaries, the participants in the contests and the official *theōroi* brought the news of recent political developments, the pilgrims to Asklepios' sanctuaries or to oracles presumably passed the time waiting for a miracle or an oracular response not only by giving accounts of their diseases and their other troubles, but also by telling stories. In one of Theophrastus' *Characters* (8.4), the imaginary informant of the 'newsmaker' is the slave of the piper Asteios, a man with an itinerant life exactly because of his profession. During their stay in a sanctuary the visitors were offered explanations by *exēgētai* that undoubtedly referred to myths and history, old and recent.[38] But here I should be more concerned with the more institutionalised channels of commemoration than with the occasional story-telling and gossiping about 'world history' – although their significance for the shaping of 'memory' should not be underestimated.

The ritual context of festivals was possibly the most significant context for the oral presentation of travelling memories.[39] There are two reasons. First, the celebration of a festival is connected with a large variety of oral performances, such as acclamations, prayers, dramatic performances, the singing of hymns and choric songs, in addition to lectures and concerts at the initiative of scholars and artists. The ritual performative texts, especially the hymns, drew heavily upon myth, and this applies also to the tragedies performed in the thymelic competitions. Limenios' song for Apollo in Delphi (128 BC), for example, refers to the god's birth, his first visit to Athens, and his victories over Python, Tityos and the Gauls,[40] and in Epidauros, Isyllos' paian to Apollo and Asklepios (early third century?)

---

[36] Chaniotis 1995.   [37] Le Guen 2001, Aneziri 2003, cf. Chaniotis 1990.

[38] For the Roman imperial period see Jones 2001.

[39] Unavoidably, this section heavily relies on my earlier work, on Hellenistic festivals (Chaniotis 1995), commemorative anniversaries (Chaniotis 1991), and the commemoration of war (Chaniotis 2005a: 214–44).

[40] Furley and Bremer 2001: I 137–8; II 92–100. Bélis 2001 has argued that the aim of this composition, which continued to be performed until 97/6 BC, was to demonstrate the musical excellence of the Athenian *technitai* and to associate the myths of Apollo with Athens.

Travelling memories in the Hellenistic world

contains a detailed account of Asklepios' genealogy and birth.[41] The tragic poet Dymas of Iasos composed for a theatrical festival in Samothrace a drama treating the deeds of Dardanos, a local hero, thus satisfying the feelings of local pride.[42] The treatment of recent history, or brief allusions to it, was not standardised, but not uncommon. Two Delphic hymns, probably composed on the occasion of the Athenian Pythais of 128 BC,[43] refer to the invasion of the Gauls,[44] and Isyllos' paian in Epidauros treats a recent incursion of Philip II or III in the Peloponnese.[45]

The second reason why Hellenistic festivals contributed to the dissemination of 'collective' and 'cultural memory' is simply the fact that in the Hellenistic period the presence of foreign participants in festivals, whether as spectators or as performers, was stronger than in any preceding period of Greek history. Festivals were celebrated in the presence of foreigners, foreign residents, official guests, foreign competitors in the musical and athletic contests, traders, and spectators. They could, therefore, present an ideal stage for Greek communities to construct and demonstrate identity and otherness.

A ritual in Athens which brought this city into connection with Priene presents a good example. In the late fourth century the citizens of Priene decreed to send to Athens on the occasion of the Great Panathenaia an armour, as a votive offering to Athena, and to have a delegation participate in the Panathenaic procession (*I. Priene* 5). The decree characterises the procession and the dedication as 'a reminder (*mnēmeion*) of the relations of kinship and friendship that exist between us and the Athenians'. These relations, based on myths and memories of the Ionian colonisation, must have been refreshed during the festival by the Prienian envoys who brought their city's offering.

Naturally, commemorative anniversaries, a particular type of celebration, were full of historical memories presented not only to the citizens, but also to foreign guests. The Cretan cities in the Hellenistic period regularly

---

[41] Kolde 2003. Further examples of late classical and Hellenistic hymns with mythological references are the hymn of Aristonoos to Apollo (Furley and Bremer 2001: I 119–21; I 45–52) and Philodamos' paian to Dionysos (Furley and Bremer 2001: I 121–8; II 52–84).

[42] *IG* XII 8 p. 38; Chaniotis 1988a: 345–6 no. E68. Cf. further Rutherford 2007, Rutherford (this volume).

[43] On the date see more recently Bélis 2001.

[44] Furley and Bremmer 2001: I 136; II 85 (Athenaios): 'likewise the foreign horde of Gauls which brutally attacked this land perished in the wintry snowstorms'; I 138; II 93 (Limenios): 'Then, Apollo, you protected Earth's sacred navel, when a foreign army brought sacrilegious plunder to your wealthy seat of prophecy but perished in a storm of freezing rain.'

[45] Furley and Bremer 2001: I 230–6, Kolde 2003.

268   ANGELOS CHANIOTIS

invited delegations of their allies to attend important festivals.[46] The city
of Lyttos invited its allies to particular festivals, both of them important
local commemorative anniversaries:[47] one of them commemorated the
re-foundation of the city after its destruction during the 'Lyttian War'
(*c.* 220 BC), the other commemorated the destruction of the neighbouring
city of Dreros (late third/early second century). During these festivals, the
foreign guests became the audience of the Lyttian commemoration of their
past.

    The rôle of orations during such celebrations is best known in connection
with the most important commemorative anniversary of the Greek world,
that of the battle at Plataia (478 BC) which continued to be celebrated
by a pan-Hellenic council until Plutarch's time.[48] The festival included a
rhetorical competition (*dialogos*, 'debate') between the two leading powers
of the Greeks during the Persian Wars, Athens and Sparta. The representative of Athens tried to prove that the contribution of his native city to the
victory was more significant than that of Sparta, and the representative of
Sparta tried to prove the opposite. A pan-Hellenic jury decided who had
brought the most convincing arguments, the winner was honoured by his
countrymen and his city had the privilege to lead the procession (*propom-
peia*).[49] This rhetorical contest was introduced in the second century, and
continued to take place even in the Roman period. An inscription found
in Athens preserves a fragment of a speech delivered on this occasion (late
second century AD).[50] In the course of time the focus of the celebration
could change, shifting for instance in the third century BC from the idea
of freedom to the idea of concord.[51] Commemorative anniversaries of wars
could be continually adapted to new circumstances and were one of the
occasions on which Hellenistic statesmen urged their countrymen to learn
from history.

            WHEN GREEK POETIC MEMORIES TRAVEL TO ROME

Not only travelling memory changes, its audience changes as well. We tend
to regard the imperial period as a direct continuation of the Hellenistic
world, and this is to a great extent justified. The presence of the Romans

---

[46] Chaniotis 1996: 123–33.
[47] These festivals of Lyttos are known from a still unpublished inscription of the late second century, a
    treaty between Lyttos and Olous, which was presented by Charalambos Kritzas at the Congress of
    Cretan Studies (Chania, October 2006).
[48] Chaniotis 1991, Alcock 2002: 79–81, Chaniotis 2005a: 228–31, Jung 2006.   [49] Robertson 1986.
[50] *IG* II² 277; Chaniotis 1988a: 42–8.   [51] Thériault 1996: 102–22, Chaniotis 2005a: 229–30.

Travelling memories in the Hellenistic world

may not have made all the difference in the world, but it did make a difference. It changed the recipient of the collective memory of the Greeks. Sulla, one of the early recipients, reacted with indifference, because what the Athenian envoys presented to him was hard to digest. Two centuries later things had changed.

An inscription recently bought by the Louvre,[52] preserves a letter of Hadrian to Naryx, in which the emperor recapitulates what the envoys of Naryx had undoubtedly presented to him, only shortly before his death (AD 138):

I think that no one will dispute the fact that you have a polis and the rights of a polis, for you contribute to the Koinon of the Amphiktyones and to the Koinon of the Boiotoi, you elect a Boiotarches and a representative to the Panhellenion, you send a priest, you have a council, magistrates, priests, Greek tribes and the laws of the Opountians and you pay the tribute together with the Achaioi.

Through the establishment of the Panhellenion the Roman emperor had found himself in the position of a judge of Greekness and Greek cultural memory. After the Narykians in the land of the Opountian Lokroi had proven their Greekness and their status as a polis, they had something else to offer:

And some of the most famous poets, both Romans and Greeks, have mentioned you as Narykeians; and they explicitly name some of the heroes as originating in your city.

Hadrian, quoting the ambassadors, refers to the Lokrian hero Ajax; the Roman poets are Virgil and Ovid; one of the Greek poets was Callimachus.[53]

What I find striking in this context is the reference to Roman and Greek poets. The Teian envoy of the second century had sung the songs of Cretan poets; the Magnesian envoys presented the words of poets and historians – Greek poets and historians. The envoys of Naryx had to present their cultural memory, not to the fellow Greeks, but to a Roman. To their standard set of quotations from Greek literature they had to add quotations from Roman poetry. And this makes a difference.

---

[52] *SEG* LI 641, Knoepfler 2005: 66–73, Knoepfler 2006, Jones 2006.   [53] Jaillard 2000.

Bibliography

Acosta-Hughes, B. 2002. *Polyeideia: The Iambi of Callimachus and the Archaic Iambic Tradition*. Berkeley.

Albinus, L. 2000. *The House of Hades: Studies in Ancient Greek Eschatology*. Aarhus.

Alcock, S. E. 2002. *Archaeologies of the Greek Past: Landscape, Monuments, and Memories*. Cambridge.

Alfieri, N. 1979. *Spina. Museo archeologico nazionale di Ferrara, I*. Bologna.

Alfieri, N., Arias, P. and Hirmer, M. 1958. *Spina*. Florence.

Allen, T., Sikes, E. E. and Halliday, W. R. (eds.) 1936. *The Homeric Hymns*. Oxford.

Amandry, P. 1971. 'Collection Paul Canellopoulos (I)', *Bulletin de Correspondance Hellénique* 95: 585–626.

Aneziri, S. 1994. 'Zwischen Musen und Hof: Die dionysischen Techniten auf Zypern', *Zeitschrift für Papyrologie und Epigraphik* 104: 179–98.

    2001–2. 'A different guild of artists: τὸ Κοινὸν τῶν περὶ τὴν Ἱλαρὰν Ἀφροδίτην τεχνιτῶν', *Archaiognosia* 11: 47–56.

    2003. *Die Vereine der dionysischen Techniten im Kontext der hellenistischen Gesellschaft*. Stuttgart.

Annus, A. 2002. *The God Ninurta in the Mythology and Royal Ideology of Ancient Mesopotamia*. Helsinki.

Antonetti, C. 1990. *Les Étoliens: Images et Religion*. Paris.

Appadurai, A. 2003. *Modernity at Large: Cultural Dimensions of Globalization*. Minneapolis and London.

Archi, A. 1973. 'Fêtes de printemps et d'automne et réintégration rituelle d'images de culte dans l'Anatolie Hittite', *Ugarit-Forschungen* 5: 7–27.

    1983. 'Die Adad-Hymne ins Hethitisch übersetzt', *Orientalia* 52: 20–30.

    2001. 'Text forms and levels of comparison: the rituals of Emar and the Syrian tradition', in Richter *et al.* 2001: 19–28.

    2004. 'The singer of Kaneš and his gods', in Hutter and Hutter-Braunsar 2004: 11–26.

Ardzinba, V. G. 1982. *Ritualy i mify drevnej Anatolii*. Moscow.

Arnott, R. 1996. 'Healing and medicine in the Aegean Bronze Age', *Journal of the Royal Society of Medicine* 89: 265–70.

Asheri, D. 1983. 'La diaspora e il ritorno dei Messeni', in *Tria corda: Scritti in onore di Arnaldo Momigliano*, ed. E. Gabba (Como) 27–42.

Bibliography

Asper, M. 1997. *Onomata allotria: Zur Genese, Struktur und Funktion poetologischer Metaphern bei Kallimachos.* Stuttgart.

Assmann J. 1992. *Das kulturelle Gedächtnis: Schrift, Erinnerung und politische Identität in frühen Hochkulturen.* Munich.

Assmann, A. and Harth, D. (eds) 1991. *Mnemosyne: Formen und Funktionen der kulturellen Erinnerung.* Frankfurt.

Aurigemma, S. 1960. *Scavi di Spina, I: La necropoli di Spina in Valle Trebba, I.* Rome.

Austin, C. and Bastianini, G. 2002. *Posidippi Pellaei quae supersunt omnia.* Milan.

Austin, J. L. 1975. *How to Do Things with Words,* 2nd edn. Cambridge, MA.

Avezou, C. and Picard, C. 1913. 'Inscriptions de Macédoine et de Thrace', *Bulletin de Correspondance Hellénique* 38: 118–21.

Bäbler, B. 1998. *Fleissige Thrakerinnen und wehrhafte Skythen.* Stuttgart/Leipzig.

Bachvarova, M. R. 2002. 'From Hittite to Homer: the role of Anatolians in the transmission of epic and prayer motifs from the Ancient Near East to the Ancient Greeks', Diss., Chicago.

2005. 'The eastern Mediterranean epic tradition from *Bilgames and Akka* to the *Song of Release* to Homer's *Iliad*', *Greek, Roman and Byzantine Studies* 45: 131–54.

forthcoming. 'Milesian tales at a Theban feast: hunting, courting and long-distance elite interactions in the Linear B tablets from Thebes', in *Mycenaeans and Anatolians in the Late Bronze Age: the Ahhiyawa Question,* ed. A. Teffeteller.

Bader, F. 1989. *La langue des dieux, ou l'hermétisme des poètes indo-européens.* Pisa.

Bagnall, R. S. and Derow, P. 2004. *Historical Sources in Translation: The Hellenistic Period.* 2nd edn. Oxford.

Barker, A. 1984. *Greek Musical Writings,* vol. I. Cambridge.

1988. 'Che cos'era la magadis?', in *La musica in Grecia,* ed. B. Gentili and R. Pretagostini (Rome/Bari) 96–107.

1998. 'Telestes and the "five-rodded joining of strings"', *Classical Quarterly* 48: 75–81.

2004. 'Transforming the nightingale: Aspects of Athenian musical discourse in the late fifth century', in Murray and Wilson 2004: 185–204.

Barnes, T. D. 1995. '"Fälschung" and forgery', *Historia* 44: 497–500.

Barron, J. P. 1961. 'The son of Hyllis', *Classical Review* 11: 185–7.

1964. 'The sixth-century tyranny at Samos', *Classical Quarterly* 14: 210–29.

1984. 'Ibycus: Gorgias and other poems', *Bulletin of the Institute of Classical Studies* 31: 13–24.

Bartlett, F. C. 1932. *Remembering.* Cambridge.

Bassett, S. E. 1931. 'The place and the date of the first performance of the *Persians* of Timotheus', *Classical Philology* 26: 153–65.

Bastianini, G. and Gallazzi, C. 2001. *Posidippo di Pella: Epigrammi (P. Mil. Vogl. VIII 309).* Milan.

Becker, O. 1937. *Das Bild des Weges und verwandte Vorstellungen im frühgriechischen Denken.* Berlin.

Beckman, G. 1983. 'Mesopotamians and Mesopotamian learning at Hattuša', *Journal of Cuneiform Studies* 35: 97–114.

Bibliography

Beckman, G., Beal, R. and McMahon, G. (eds.) 2003. *Hittite Studies in Honor of Harry A. Hoffner, Jr.: On the Occasion of his 65th Birthday*. Winona Lake, IN.

Bélis, A. 1995. 'Cithares, citharistes, citharôdes en Grèce', *Comptes rendus des Séances de l'Académie des Inscriptions et Belles-Lettres* 1995, 1025–65.

2001. 'Esthétique musicale du péan à travers l'example des Hymnes delphiques à Apollon', in *Chanter les dieux: Musique et religion dans l'Antiquité grecque et romaine. Actes du colloque des 16, 17 et 18 décembre 1999 (Rennes et Lorient)*, ed. P. Brulé and C. Vendries (Rennes) 97–114.

Bell, J. M. 1978. 'Simonides in the Anecdotal Tradition', *Quaderni Urbinati di Cultura Classica* 28: 29–86.

Bergquist, B. 1973. *Herakles on Thasos*. Uppsala.

Berlinzani, F. 2004. *La musica a Tebe di Beozia tra storia e mito*. Milan.

Bernand, A. and E. 1960. *Les inscriptions grecques et latins du colosse de Memnon*. Paris.

Bertolini, F. 1995. 'Muse, re e aedi nel proemio della *Teogonia* di Esiodo', in *Studia Classica Iohanni Tarditi oblata*, ed. L. Belloni, G. Milanese and A. Porro (Milan) 127–38.

Beschi, L. 1991. 'La prospettiva mitica della musica greca', *Mélanges de l'École francaise de Rome* 103: 35–50.

Bickerman, E. 1967. *Four Strange Books of the Bible*. New York.

Bing, P. 2005. 'The politics and poetics of geography in the Milan Poseidippus, Section One: On Stones (AB 1–20),' in *The New Posidippus: A Hellenistic Poetry Book*, ed. K. Gutzwiller (Oxford) 119–40.

Bing, P. and Bruss, J. S. 2007. 'Introduction', in *Brill's Companion to Hellenistic Epigram, Down to Philip*, ed. P. Bing and J. S. Bruss (Leiden/Boston) 1–26.

Blok, J. H. and Lardinois, A. P. M. H. (eds.) 2006. *Solon of Athens: New Historical and Philological Approaches*. Leiden.

Bloedow, E. F. 1998. 'The significance of the Greek athletes and artists at Memphis in Alexander's strategy after the Battle of Issus', *Quaderni urbinati di cultura classica* 58: 129–42.

Blum, H., Faist B. and Pfälzner, P. (eds.) 2002. *Brückenland Anatolien: Ursachen, Extensität und Modi des Kulturaustausches zwischen Anatolien und sein Nachbarn*. Tübingen.

Boedeker, D. 1995. 'Simonides on Plataea: Narrative elegy, mythodic history', *Zeitschrift für Papyrologie und Epigraphik* 107: 217–29.

Boedeker, D. and Sider, D. (eds.) 2001. *The New Simonides: Contexts of Praise and Desire*. Oxford.

Boesch, P. 1908. Θεωρός. *Untersuchung zur Epangelie griechischer Feste*. Berlin.

Bolton. J. D. P. 1962. *Aristeas of Proconessus*. Oxford.

Bona, G. 1988. *Pindaro. I peani. Testo, traduzione, scoli e commento*. Cuneo.

Bonatz, D. 2002. 'Fremde "Künstler" in Ḫattuša: zur Rolle des individuums beim Austausch materieller Kultur in der späten Bronzezeit', in Blum *et al.* 2002: 69–84.

Bibliography

Bonnet, A. 2001. 'En parcourant le Val des Muses. Remarques sur un concours musical de l'Antiquité: les *Mouseia* de Thespies', in *Musique et Poésie dans l'Antiquité. Actes du colloque de Clermont-Ferrand Université Blaise Pascal 23 mai 1997*, ed. G.-J. Pinault (Clermont-Ferrand) 53–70.

Borgna, E. 2004. 'Aegean feasting: a Minoan perspective', in Wright (ed.) 2004b: 127–60.

Borthwick, E. K. 1970. 'P. Oxy. 2738: Athena and the Pyrrhic dance', *Hermes* 98: 318–31.

Bosnakis, D. 2004. 'Zwei Dichterinnen aus Kos: Ein neues inschriftliches Zeugnis über das öffentliche Auftreten von Frauen', in *The Hellenistic Polis of Kos. State, Economy and Culture*, ed. K. Höghammar (Uppsala) 99–107.

Bosnakis, D. and Hallof, K. 2003. 'Alte und neue Inschriften aus Kos I' *Chiron* 33: 203–62.

Bourguet, É. 1927. *Le dialecte laconien*. Paris.

Bousquet, J. 1988. 'La stèle des Kyténiens au Létôon de Xanthos', *Revue des Études Grecques* 101: 12–53.

1992. 'Les inscriptions gréco-lyciennes. Les inscriptions du Létôon', in *Fouilles de Xanthos*, IX, 2 (Paris) 154–79.

Bouvier, H. 1980. 'Une intruse dans la littérature grecque', *Zeitschrift für Papyrologie und Epigraphik* 40: 36–8.

1985. 'Hommes de lettres dans les inscriptions delphiques' *Zeitschrift für Papyrologie und Epigraphik* 58: 119–35.

Bower, C. M. 1989. *Fundamentals of Music*. New Haven.

Bowie, E. L. 1986. 'Early Greek elegy, symposium, and public festival', *Journal of Hellenic Studies* 106: 13–35.

1989. 'Poetry and poets in Asia and Achaia', in *The Greek Renaissance in the Roman Empire: Papers from the Tenth British Museum Classical Colloquium*, ed. S. Walker and A. Cameron (London) 198–205.

1990a. 'Miles Ludens? The problem of martial exhortation in early Greek elegy', in Murray (ed.) 1990: 221–9.

1990b. 'Greek poetry in the Antonine age', in *Antonine Literature*, ed. D. A. Russell (Oxford) 53–90.

2001. 'Early Greek iambic poetry: the importance of narrative', in *Iambic Ideas: Essays on a Poetic Tradition from Archaic Greece to the Late Roman Empire*, ed. A. Cavarzere, A. Barchiesi and A. Aloni (Lanham, MD) 1–27.

2007. 'Early expatriates: displacement and exile in archaic poetry', in *Writing Exile: The Discourse of Displacement in Greco-Roman Antiquity and Beyond*, ed. J. F. Gaertner (Leiden) 21–49.

2008. 'Sex and politics in Archilochus' poetry', in *Archilochus and his Age: Proceedings of a Conference on Paros in October 2005*, ed. J. Petropoulos *et al.* (Athens).

Bowra, C. M. 1961. *Greek Lyric Poetry: From Alcman to Simonides*. Oxford.

1963. 'Two Lines of Eumelus', *Classical Quarterly* 13: 145–53 (= *On Greek Margins*, Oxford 1970: 46–58).

Brandt, P. 1888. *Corpusculum poesis epicae graecae ludibundae* I. Leipzig.

Bravo, B. 1980. 'Sulān: Représailles et justice privée contre des étrangers dans les cités grecques', *Annali della Scuola Normale Superiore di Pisa*, 3 ser., 10, 3: 675–987.

Bremer, J. M. 1991. 'Poets and their Patrons', in *Fragmenta Dramatica*, ed. H. Hofmann and A. Harder (Göttingen) 39–60.

Bremmer, J. N. 2001. 'The scapegoat between Hittites, Greeks, Israelites and Christians', in *Kult, Konflikt und Versöhnung: Beiträge zur kultischen Sühne in religiösen, sozialen und politischen Auseinandersetzungen des antiken Mittelmeerraumes*, ed. R. Albertz. Alter Orient und Altes Testament 285 (Münster) 176–86.

2002. *The Rise and Fall of the Afterlife*. London/New York.

2006. 'The myth of the golden fleece', *Journal of Ancient Near Eastern Religions* 6: 9–38.

Brennan, T. C. 1997–8. 'The Poets Julia Balbilla and Damo at the Colossus of Memnon', *Classical World* 91: 215–34.

Breuer, C. 1995. *Reliefs und Epigramme griechischer Privatgrabmäler. Zeugnisse bürgerlichen Selbstverständnisses vom 4. bis 2. Jh. v. Chr.* Cologne/Weimar/Vienna.

Brillante, C. 1991. 'Le Muse di Thamyris', *Studi Classici e Orientali* 41: 429–53.

Bringmann, K., Ameling, W. and Schmidt-Dounas, B. 1995. *Schenkungen hellenistischer Herrscher an griechische Städte und Heiligtümer 1: Zeugnisse und Kommentare*. Berlin.

Brixhe, C. 1996. 'Les IIe et Ier siècles dans l'histoire linguistique de la Laconie et la notion de koina', in *La koiné grecque antique, vol. II: La concurrence*, ed. C. Brixhe (Nancy) 93–111.

Brixhe, C. and Vottero, G. 2004. 'L'alternance codique ou quand le choix du code fait sens', in *La koiné grecque antique, vol. V: Alternances codiques et changements de code*, ed. R. Hodot (Nancy) 7–43.

Broneer, O. 1953. 'Isthmia excavations 1952', *Hesperia* 22: 182–95.

Brown, C. 2003. *Stagolee Shot Billy*. Cambridge, MA.

Brown, M. K. 2002. *The 'Narrationes' of Konon*. Munich and Leipzig.

Brulé, P. 1978. *La piraterie crétoise hellénistique*. Paris.

Brussich, G. F. 1990. 'L'inno ad Artemide di Timoteo', *Quaderni Urbinati di Cultura Classica* 34: 25–38.

1999. 'Il decreto spartano contro Timoteo e la σφραγίς dei *Persiani*', in *Per Carlo Corbato: Scritti di filologia greca e latina offerti da amici e allievi*, ed. B. Gentili, A. Grilli and F. Perusino (Pisa) 31–46.

Bryce, T. R. 1986. *The Lycians I: The Lycians in Literary and Epigraphic Sources*. Copenhagen.

1998. *The Kingdom of the Hittites*. Oxford.

1999. 'Anatolian scribes in Mycenaean Greece', *Historia* 48: 261–4.

Budin, S. L. 2003. *The Origin of Aphrodite*. Bethesda, MD.

Bundrick, S. 2005. *Music and Image in Classical Athens*. Cambridge.

Bibliography

Bunnens, G. 2004. 'The Storm-God in northern Syria and southern Anatolia from Hadad of Aleppo to Jupiter Dolichenus', in Hutter and Hutter-Braunsar (eds.) 2004: 57–81.

Buraselis, K. 2003. 'Zur Asylie als aussenpolitischem Instrument in der hellenistischen Welt', in *Das antike Asyl. Kultische Grundlagen, rechtliche Ausgestaltung und politische Funktion*, ed. M. Dreher (Cologne/Weimar/Vienna/Böhlau) 143–58.

Buraselis, K. and Zoumboulakis, Kl. (eds.) 2003. *The Idea of European Community in History. Conference proceedings II: Aspects of Connecting Poleis and Ethne in Ancient Greece*. Athens.

Burke, P. 1989. 'History as social memory', in *Memory: History, Culture and the Mind*, ed. T. Butler (Oxford) 97–113.

Burkert, W. 1972. 'Die Leistung eines Kreophylos: Kreophyleer, Homeriden und die archaische Heraklesepik', *Museum Helveticum* 29: 74–85.

1975. 'Apellai und Apollon', *Rheinisches Museum* 118: 1–21.

1979a. 'Kynaithos, Polycrates, and the Homeric Hymn to Apollo', in *Arktouros: Hellenic Studies Presented to B. M. W. Knox* (Berlin) 53–62. Reprinted in Riedwig (ed.) 2001: 189–97.

1979b. *Structure and History in Greek Mythology and Ritual*. Sather Classical Lectures 47. Berkeley, Los Angeles, London.

1983. 'Itinerant diviners and magicians: a neglected element in cultural contacts', in *The Greek Renaissance of the Eighth Century B. C.: Tradition and Innovation*, ed. R. Hägg (Stockholm) 115–200.

1987a. 'The making of Homer in the sixth century B. C.: rhapsodes versus Stesichoros', in *Papers on the Amasis Painter and his World: Colloquium Sponsored by the Getty Center for the History of Art and Humanities and Symposium Sponsored by the J. Paul Getty Museum* (Malibu, CA) 43–62. Reprinted in Riedwig (ed.) 2001: 198–217.

1987b. 'Oriental and Greek mythology: the meeting of parallels', in *Interpretations of Greek Mythology*, ed. J. N. Bremmer (London) 41–59.

1992. *The Orientalizing Revolution*. Cambridge, MA.

2004. *Babylon, Memphis, Persepolis: Eastern Contexts of Greek Culture*. Cambridge, MA.

2005. 'Near Eastern connections', in *A Companion to Ancient Epic*, ed. J. M. Foley (Malden, MA) 291–301.

Burnett, A. P. 2004. *Pindar's Songs for Young Athletes of Aigina*. Oxford.

Burr, V. 1944. *ΝΕΩΝ ΚΑΤΑΛΟΓΟΣ. Untersuchungen zum homerischen Schiffskatalog*. Klio Beiheft 49. Leipzig.

Buxton, R. 1980. 'Blindness and limits: Sophokles and the logic of myth', *Journal of Hellenic Studies* 100: 22–37.

Cadoux, C. J. 1938. *Ancient Smyrna*. Oxford.

Cairns, F. 1992. 'Theocritus, Idyll 26', *Proceedings of the Cambridge Philological Society* 38: 1–38.

Calame, C. 1983. *Alcman*. Rome.

276   *Bibliography*

Cameron, A. 1965. 'Wandering poets: a literary movement in Byzantine Egypt',
    Historia 14: 470–509.
    1993. *The Greek Anthology from Meleager to Planudes.* Oxford.
    1995. *Callimachus and his Critics.* New York.
Campbell, D. A. 1982. *Greek Lyric Poetry: A Selection of Early Greek Lyric, Elegiac
    and Iambic Poetry.* London.
    1988. *Greek Lyric, Vol. II: Anacreon, Anacreontea, Choral Lyric from Olympus to
    Alcman.* Cambridge, MA.
    1992. *Greek Lyric, Vol. IV: Bacchylides, Corinna, and Others.* Cambridge,
    MA.
Carratelli, G. 1952–4. 'Supplemento epigrafico rodio', *Annuario della Scuola arche-
    ologica di Atene* n.s. 14–15: 247–316.
Carruba, O. 1995. 'Poesia e metrica in Anatolia prima dei Greci', in *Studia classica
    Iohanni Tarditi oblata*, ed. L. Belloni, G. Milanese and A. Porro (Milan)
    567–602.
    1998. 'Hethitische und anatolische Dichtung', in *Intellectual Life of the Ancient
    Near East: Papers Presented at the 43rd Rencontre Assyriologique Internationale.
    Prague, July 1–5, 1996*, ed. J. Prosecký (Prague) 67–89.
Carson, A. 2002. *The Economy of the Unlost.* Princeton.
Carter, C. W. 1988. 'Athletic contests in Hittite religious festivals', *Journal of Near
    Eastern Studies* 47: 185–7.
Cartledge, P. A. 1979. *Sparta and Lakonia: A Regional History 1300–362 BC.* London.
    1982. 'Sparta and Samos: a special relationship?' *Classical Quarterly* 32:
    243–65.
    1987. *Agesilaos and the Crisis of Sparta.* London and Baltimore.
Cartledge, P. A. and Spawforth, A. J. 2002. *Hellenistic and Roman Sparta: A Tale
    of Two Cities*, 2nd edn. London and New York.
Casey, E. S. 1987. *Remembering: A Phenomenological Study.* Bloomington.
Cassio, A. C. 1986. 'Continuità e riprese arcaizzanti nell'uso epigrafico dei dialetti
    greci: il caso dell'eolico d'Asia', *Annali dell'Istituto Universitario Orientale di
    Napoli . . . Sezione linguistica* 8: 131–46.
    1988. 'Nicomachus of Gerasa and the dialect of Architas, fr. 1', *Classical Quarterly*
    38: 135–9.
    2000. 'Esametri orfici, dialetto attico e musica dell'Asia Minore', in *Synaulía:
    Cultura musicale in Grecia e contatti mediterranei*, ed. A. C. Cassio, D. Musti
    and L. E. Rossi (Naples) 97–110.
    2003. 'Ospitare in casa poeti orali: Omero, Testoride, Creofilo e Staroselac
    ([Herodot.] *vita Hom.* 190 ss. Allen; Plat. *resp.* 600b)', in *ΡΥΣΜΟΣ. Studi di
    poesia, metrica e musica greca offerti dagli allievi a Luigi Enrico Rossi per i suoi
    settant'anni*, ed. R. Nicolai (Rome) 35–45.
    2005. 'I dialetti eolici e la lingua della lirica corale', in *Dialetti e lingue letterarie
    nella Grecia arcaica*, ed. F. Bertolini and F. Gasti (Pavia) 13–44.
Càssola, F. 1954. 'La leggenda di Anio e la preistoria delia', *Parola del Passato* 9:
    345–67. Reprinted in *Scritti di storia antica. Istituzioni e politica I: Grecia*,
    Naples 1993, 43–64.

Bibliography

1964. Ἐλεύθερος- Ereutero', in *Synteleia Vincenzo Arangio-Ruiz* (Naples) I 269–79 (reprinted in *Scritti di storia antica. Istituzioni e politica* I: *Grecia*, Naples 1993, 121–32).

Casson, L. 1974. *Travel in the Ancient World*. London.

1983. 'Greek and Roman clothing: some technical terms', *Glotta* 61: 193–207.

Catenacci, C. 2007. 'L'iporchema di Pindaro e gli Uccelli di Aristofane', in *Dalla lirica corale alla poesia drammatica: Forme e funzioni del canto corale nella tragedia e nella commedia greca*, ed. F. Perusino and M. Colantonio (Pisa) 233–58.

Ceccarelli, P. 1998. *La pirrica nell'antichità greco romana: studi sulla danza armata*. Pisa.

Centrone, B. 1990. *Pseudopythagorica ethica: I trattati morali di Archita, Metopo, Teage, Eurifamo*. Naples.

Champion, G. B. 2004. *Cultural Politics in Polybius's Histories*. Berkeley, Los Angeles and London.

Chandezon, Ch. 2000. 'Foires et panégyries dans le monde grec classique et hellénistique', *Revue des Études Grecques* 113: 70–100.

Chaniotis, A. 1988a. 'Als die Diplomaten noch tanzten und sangen: Zu zwei Dekreten kretischer Städte in Mylasa', *Zeitschrift für Papyrologie und Epigraphik* 71: 154–60.

1988b. *Historie und Historiker in den griechischen Inschriften: epigraphische Beiträge zur griechischen Historiographie*. Wiesbaden.

1990. 'Zur Frage der Spezialisierung im griechischen Theater des Hellenismus und der Kaiserzeit', *Ktema* 15: 89–108.

1991. 'Gedenktage der Griechen: Ihre Bedeutung für das Geschichtsbewußtsein griechischer Poleis', in *Das Fest und das Heilige: Religiöse Kontrapunkte zur Alltagswelt*, ed. J. Assmann (Gütersloh) 123–45.

1995. 'Sich selbst feiern? Städtische Feste des Hellenismus im Spannungsfeld von Religion und Politik', in *Stadtbild und Bürgerbild im Hellenismus*, ed. M. Wörrle and P. Zanker. Vestigia 47 (Munich) 147–72.

1996. *Die Verträge zwischen kretischen Poleis in der hellenistischen Zeit*. Stuttgart.

1999. 'Empfängerformular und Urkundenfälschung: Bemerkungen zum Inschriftendossier von Magnesia am Mäander', in *Urkunden und Urkundenformulare im klassischen Altertum und in den orientalischen Kulturen*, ed. R. G. Khoury (Heidelberg) 51–69.

2005a. *War in the Hellenistic World: A Social and Cultural History*. Oxford.

2005b. 'Ritual dynamics in the eastern Mediterranean: case studies in ancient Greece and Asia Minor', in *Rethinking the Mediterranean*, ed. W. V. Harris (Oxford) 141–66.

Chrimes, K. M. T. 1949. *Ancient Sparta: A Re-Examination of the Evidence*. Manchester.

Cillo, P. 1993. 'La "cetra di Tamiri": mito e realtà musicale', *Annali di archeologia e storia antica, Istituto Universitario Orientale di Napoli* 15: 205–4.

Clairmont, C. W. 1983. *Patrios Nomos: Public Burial in Athens during the Fifth and Fourth Centuries B.C.* (2 vols.). Oxford.

Bibliography

Clay, D. 2004. *Archilochos Heros: The Cult of Poets in the Greek Polis.* Washington DC.

Clerc, M. 1885. 'Inscriptions de Nysa', *Bulletin de Correspondance Hellénique* 9: 124–31.

Cohen, M. E. 1993. *The Cultic Calendars of the Ancient Near East.* Bethesda, MD.

Cole, S. Guettel 1994. 'Demeter in the ancient Greek city and its countryside', in *Placing the Gods: Sanctuaries and Sacred Space in Ancient Greece*, ed. S. E. Alcock and R. Osborne (Oxford) 199–216.

Collins, B. J. 1995. 'Ritual meals in Hittite cult', in *Ancient Magic and Ritual Power*, ed. M. Meyer and P. Mirecki (Leiden/New York/Cologne) 77–92.

    2006. 'Pigs for the gods: sacrifice east and west', *Journal of Ancient Near Eastern Religions* 6: 155–88.

Collins, D. 2005. *Master of the Game: Competition and Performance in Greek Poetry.* Cambridge, MA.

Cook, J. M. 1950. 'Laconia. Kalyvia Sokhas', *Annual of the British School at Athens* 45: 261–81.

Confino, A. 1997. 'Collective memory and cultural history: problems of method', *American Historical Review* 102: 1386–404.

Connerton, P. 1999. *How Societies Remember.* Cambridge.

Connolly, A. 1998. 'Was Sophocles heroised as Dexion?', *Journal of Hellenic Studies* 118: 1–21.

Cordano, F. 1994. 'La città di Camarina e le corde della lira', *Parola del Passato* 49: 418–26.

    2004. 'La musica e la politica, ovvero gli *auloí* ad Atene', in *Sviluppi recenti dell'antichistica: Nuovi contributi*, 'Quaderni di *ACME*' 68, ed. V. de Angelis (Milan) 309–25.

Croiset, A. 1914. *Histoire de la littérature grecque.* Paris.

Crowther, N. B. 2004. *Athletika: Studies on the Olympic Games and Greek Athletics.* Nikephoros Beihefte 11. Hildesheim.

Csapo, E. 2004. 'The Politics of the New Music' in Murray and Wilson (eds.) 2004: 207–48.

Currie, B. 2004. 'Reperformance scenarios for Pindar's odes,' in *Oral Performance and its Context*, ed. C. J. Mackie (Leiden) 49–69.

Curty, O. 1995. *Les parentés légendaires entre cités grecques.* Geneva.

    1999. 'La parenté légendaire à l'époque hellénistique: précisions méthodologiques', *Kernos* 12: 167–94.

    2005. 'Un usage fort controversé: la parenté dans le langage diplomatique de l'époque hellénistique', *Ancient Society* 35: 101–17.

D'Alessio, G. B. 1991. 'Osservazioni e paralipomeni ad una nuova edizione dei frammenti di Pindaro', *Rivista di Filologia e di Istruzione Classica* 119: 91–117.

    1992a. 'Pindaro, *peana* VIIb (fr. 52 h Sn.M.)', in *Proceedings of the XIX International Congress of Papyrology* (Cairo 2–9 September 1989), vol. I: 353–73.

    1992b. 'Immigrati a Teo e ad Abdera (*SEG* XXXI 985; Pind. fr. 52b Sn.-M.)', *Zeitschrift für Papyrologie und Epigraphik* 92: 73–80.

Bibliography

1994. Review of L. Käppel, *Paian: Studien zur Geschichte einer Gattung*, Berlin 1992, *Classical Review* 44: 62–7.

1997. 'Pindar's *Prosodia* and the classification of Pindaric papyrus fragments', *Zeitschrift für Papyrologie und Epigraphik* 118: 23–60.

2007. 'Per una ricostruzione del *Primo Inno* di Pindaro: la "Teogonia" tebana e la nascita di Apollo', *Seminari Romani* 10: 101–17.

forthcoming. 'The name of the dithyramb', in *Song Culture and Social Change: The Contexts of Dithyramb*, ed. B. Kowalzig and P. Wilson (Oxford).

in progress. *Pindar's Fragments: Introduction, critical text and commentary.*

Danek, G. 1998. *Epos und Zitat*. Vienna.

D'Angour, A. 1997. 'How the dithyramb got its shape', *Classical Quarterly* 47: 331–51.

Dardano, P. 2006. *Die hethitischen Tontafelkataloge aus Ḫattuša (CTH 276–282)*. Studien zu den Boğazköy-Texten 47. Wiesbaden.

Daux, G. 1922. 'Inscriptions de Delphes', *Bulletin de Correspondance Hellénique* 46: 439–66.

1935. 'Craton, Eumène II et Attale II', *Bulletin de Correspondance Hellénique* 59: 210–30.

1943. *Fouilles de Delphes* 3, Épigraphie 3. Chronologie delphique. Paris.

Dawkins, R. M. *et al.* (eds.) 1929. *The Sanctuary of Artemis Orthia at Sparta*. London.

Debiasi, A. 2003. '*POxy* LIII, 3698. Eumelii Corinthi fragmentum novum', *Zeitschrift für Papyrologie und Epigraphik* 143: 1–5.

2004. *L'epica perduta*. Rome.

del Monte, G. F., and Tischler, J. 1978. *Die Orts- und Gewässernomen der hethitischen Texte. Répertoire géographique des textes cunéiformes* 6. Wiesbaden.

De Jong, I. J. F. 2001. *A Narratological Commentary on the Odyssey*, Cambridge.

de Martino, F. 1995. 'La voce degli autori', in *Lo spettacolo delle voci. I*, ed. F. de Martino and A. Sommerstein (Bari) 17–59.

de Martino, F. and Vox, O. 1996. *Lirica greca, I*. Bari.

de Martino, S. 2002. 'Songs and singing in the Hittite literary evidence', in *Studien zur Musikarchäologie III: Archäologie früher Klangerzeugung und Tonordnung: Musikarchäologie in der Ägäis und Anatolien*, ed. E. Hickmann, A. D. Kilmer and R. Eichmann (Rahden) 623–9.

Deshours, N. 1993. 'La légende et le culte de Messène ou comment forger l'identité d'une cité', *Revue des Études Grecques* 106: 39–60.

1999. 'Les Mességens, le règlement des mystères et la consultation de l'oracle d'Apollon Pythéen à Argos', *Revue des Études Grecques* 112: 463–84.

Detienne, M. 1967. *Les maîtres de vérité dans la Grèce archaïque*. Paris = (1996) Engl. trans. *The Masters of Truth in Archaic Greece*. New York.

Dickie, M. 1998. 'Poets as initiates in the mysteries: Euphorion, Philicus and Posidippus', *Antike und Abendland* 44: 49–77.

Diels, H. 1896. 'Alkmans Partheneion', *Hermes* 31: 339–74.

280 *Bibliography*

Dieterich, A. 1911. 'Weitere Beobachtungen zu den Himmelsbriefen', in *Kleine Schriften* (Berlin) 242–51.

Diggle, J. 1994. *Euripidea: Collected Essays.* Oxford.

Dillery, J. 2005. 'Greek sacred history', *American Journal of Philology* 126: 505–26.

2007. 'Exile: The making of the Greek historian', in *Writing Exile: The Discourse of Displacement in Greco-Roman Antiquity and Beyond*, ed. J. F. Gaertner (Leiden) 51–70.

Dillon, M. 1997. *Pilgrims and Pilgrimage in the Ancient World.* London.

Dinçol, A. M. 1989. 'Ein hurro-hethitisches Festritual: (Ḫ)išuwaš (I)', *Belleten* 53: 1–50.

Doan, J. 1985. *The Romance of Cearbhall and Fearbhlaidh.* Mountrath, Ireland.

Dobrov, G. W. and Urios-Aparisi, E. 1995. 'The maculate music: gender, genre, and the *Chiron* of Pherecrates', in *Beyond Aristophanes*, ed. G. W. Dobrov (Atlanta) 139–74.

Doherty, L. 1991. 'The internal and implied audiences of *Odyssey* 11', *Arethusa* 24: 145–76.

Donderer, M. 1996. 'Zeugnisse Kleinasiens für Agone in den Bildenden Künsten', in *Fremde Zeiten I: Festschrift J. Borchhardt* (2 vols.) (Vienna) 329–338.

Dougherty, C. 1994a. 'Archaic Greek foundation poetry: Questions of genre and occasion', *Journal of Hellenic Studies* 94: 35–46.

1994b. 'Pindar's second paean or civic identity on parade', *Classical Philology* 89: 205–18.

Dübner, F. 1877. *Scholia Graeca in Aristophanem.* Paris.

Dubuisson, M. 1985. *Le latin de Polybe: Les implications historiques d'un case de bilinguisme.* Paris.

Dugas, C. and Rhomaios, C. 1934. *Exploration archéologique de Délos, XV: Les vases préhellénique et Géométriques.* Paris.

Dunand, F. 1978. 'Sens et fonction de la fête dans la Grèce hellénistique', *Dialogues d'histoire ancienne* 4: 203–13.

1981. 'Fête et propagande à Alexandrie sous les Lagides', in *La fête, pratique et discours: D'Alexandrie hellénistique à la mission de Besançon* (Paris) 13–40.

Dunbabin, T. J. 1948. 'The early history of Corinth', *Journal of Hellenic Studies* 68: 59–69.

Dunbar, N. 1995. *Aristophanes: Birds.* Oxford.

Dunkel, G. E. 1993. 'Periphrastica Homerohittitovedica', in *Comparative-historical Linguistics: Indo-European and Finno-Ugric: Papers in Honor of Oswald Szemerényi, III*, ed. B. Brogyanyi and R. Lipp (Amsterdam/Philadelphia) 103–18.

Durante, M. 1976. *Sulla preistoria della tradizione poetica greca, vol. II.* Rome.

Easterling, P. 1998. Review of Lloyd-Jones (1996), *Journal of Hellenic Studies* 118: 212–13.

Ebbott, M., 2000. 'The list of the war dead in Aeschylus' "Persians"', *Harvard Studies in Classical Philology* 100: 83–96.

Edwards, A. T. 2004. *Hesiod's Ascra.* Berkeley.

Eichner, H. 1993. 'Probleme von Vers und Metrum in epichorischer Dichtung Altkleinasiens', in *Die epigraphische und altertumskundliche Erforschung*

Bibliography

Kleinasiens: Hundert Jahre Kleinasiatische Kommission der Österreichischen Akademie der Wissenschaften. Akten des Symposiums vom 23. bis 25. Oktober 1990, ed. G. Dobesch and G. Rehenböck. Österreichische Akademie der Wissenschaften. Philosophisch-Historische Klasse Denkschriften 236 (Vienna) 97–169.

Elsner, J. and Rutherford, I. (eds.) 2005. *Pilgrimage in Graeco-Roman and Early Christian Antiquity: Seeing the Gods.* Oxford.

Erlmann, V. 1983. 'Marginal men, strangers and wayfarers: Professional musicians and change among the Fulani of Diamare (North Cameroon)', *Ethnomusicology* 27: 187–225.

Fantuzzi, M. 1988. 'Epici ellenistici', in *L'epos ellenistico*, ed. K. Ziegler (Bari) i–xci.
  2004. 'The epigram', in Fantuzzi and Hunter 2004: 283–349.
  forthcoming. 'Typologies of variation on a theme in archaic epigraphic epigrams', in *Archaic and Classical Greek Epigram: Contextualisation and Literarisation*, ed. M. Baumbach, A. Petrovic and I. Petrovic (Cambridge).

Fantuzzi, M. and Hunter, R. 2004. *Tradition and Innovation in Hellenistic Poetry.* Cambridge.

Faraone, C. A. 2004. 'Orpheus' final performance: necromancy and a singing head on Lesbos', *Studi italiani di filologia classica* 97: 5–27.

Farnell, L. R. 1932. *The Works of Pindar. Translated with Literary and Critical Commentaries. vol. II: Critical Commentary.* London.

Fauth, W. 1974. 'Der Schlund des Orcus: Zu einer Eigentümlichkeit der römisch-etruskischen Unterweltsvorstellung', *Numen* 21: 105–27.

Fentress, J. and Wickham, C. 1992. *Social Memory: New Perspectives on the Past.* Oxford.

Ferrandini Troisi, Fr. 2000. *La donna nella società ellenistica: testimonianze epigrafiche.* Bari.
  2006. 'Professionisti "di giro" nel Mediterraneo Antico. Testimonianze Epigrafiche', in *Le vie della Storia: Migrazioni di popoli, viaggi di individui, circolazione di idee nel Mediterraneo antico*, ed. M. G. A. Bertinelli and A. Donati (Rome) 145–54.

Ferri, S. 1931. 'Χορòς κυκλικός. Nuovi documenti archeologici e vecchia tradizione letteraria', *Rivista del R. Istituto d'Archeologia e Storia dell'Arte* 3: 299–301.

Feyel, M. 1942. *Contribution à l'Épigraphie béotienne.* Le Puy.

Figueira, T. 1999. 'The evolution of the Messenian identity', in *Sparta: New Perspectives*, ed. S. Hodkinson and A. Powell (London) 211–44.

Finnegan, R. 1970. *Oral Literature in Africa.* Oxford.

Fisher, N. 2001. *Aeschines 'Against Timarchos'.* Oxford.

Fleming, D. 1996. 'The Emar festivals: city unity and Syrian identity under Hittite hegemony', in *Emar: The History, Religion and Culture of a Syrian Town in the Late Bronze Age*, ed. M. W. Chavalas (Malibu) 81–122.

Flower, M. A. 2002. 'The invention of tradition in classical and Hellenistic Sparta', in *Sparta Beyond the Mirage*, ed. A. Powell and S. Hodkinson (London) 191–217.

Foley, J. M. 2002. *How to Read an Oral Poem.* Urbana/Chicago.

282   *Bibliography*

Fontenrose, J. 1959. *Python: A Study of Delphic Myth and Its Origins*, Berkeley.
Forbes, C. 1955. 'Ancient athletic guilds', *Classical Philology* 50: 238–52.
Ford, A. L. 1988. 'The classical definition of ΡΑΨΩΙΔΙΑ', *Classical Philology* 83:
   300–7.
   1992. *Homer: The Poetry of the Past*. Ithaca NY and London.
   2002. *The Origins of Criticism*. Princeton.
Forrer, E. 1924a. 'Die Griechen in den Boghazköi-Texten', *Orientalische Liter-*
   aturzeitung 27: 113–18.
   1924b. 'Vorhomerische Griechen in den Keilschrifttexten von Boghazköi', *Mit-*
   teilungen der Deutschen Orient-Gesellschaft 63: 1–22.
Fowler, R. 2000. *Early Greek Mythography I: Texts.* Oxford.
Fraenkel, E. 1918. 'Lyrische Daktylen', *Rheinisches Museum* 72: 161–97, 321–52 =
   Kleine Beiträge zur klassischen Philologie (1964) I: 165–239.
Franklin, J. C. forthcoming a. '"Songbenders of circular choruses": dithyramb
   and the "demise of Music"', in *Song Culture and Social Change: the Contexts*
   of Dithyramb, ed. B. Kowalzig and P. Wilson. Oxford. (pdf available at the
   website http://www.kingmixers.com/cv.html#Publications)
   forthcoming b. *The Middle Muse: Mesopotamian Echoes in Archaic Greek Music.*
   Oxford.
Fraser, P. M. 1972. *Ptolemaic Alexandria.* Oxford.
Fried, J. 2004. *Der Schleier der Erinnerung: Grundzüge einer historischen Memorik.*
   Munich.
Frisch, P. 1986. *Zehn agonistische Papyri.* Papyrologica Coloniensia 13. Cologne.
Frisone, F. 2000. *Leggi e regolamenti funerari nel mondo greco. I: Le fonti epigrafiche.*
   Galatina.
Froning, H. 1971. *Dithyrambos und Vasenmalerei in Athen.* Würzburg.
Funke, P. 1994. 'Staatenbünde und Bundesstaaten', in *Unity and Units of Antiquity:*
   Papers from a Colloquium at Delphi, 5–8.4.1992, ed. K. Buraselis (Athens) 125–
   36.
Furley, W. D. 1994. 'Apollo humbled: Phoenix' Koronisma in its Hellenistic literary
   setting,' *Materiali e Discussioni* 33: 9–31.
Furley, W. D. and Bremer, J. M. 2001. *Greek Hymns. Vol. I: The Texts in Translation.*
   Vol. II: Greek Texts and Commentary. Tübingen.
Gaertner, J. F. 2007. *Writing Exile: The Discourse of Displacement in Greco-Roman*
   Antiquity and Beyond. Leiden.
Gallis, K. 1988. 'The games in ancient Larisa: an example of provincial Olympic
   games', in *The Archaeology of the Olympics: The Olympics and Other Festivals*
   in the Antiquity, ed. W. J. Raschke (Madison, WI) 217–35.
Gallo, I. 1976. 'Solone a Soli', *Quaderni Urbinati di Cultura Classica* 21: 29–36.
Ganci, R. 1998. *Uno ktisma, tre memorie storiche: il caso di Reggio.* Rome.
Garland, R. S. J., 1984. 'Religious authority in archaic and classical Athens', *Annual*
   of the British School at Athens 79: 75–123.
   1992. *Introducing New Gods: The Politics of Athenian Religion.* Ithaca, NY.
Garton, C. 1982. 'A revised register of Augustan actors', in *Aufstieg und Niedergang*
   der römischen Welt, ed. H. Temporini and W. Haase (Berlin/New York) II
   30.1, 580–609.

Bibliography

Garvie, A. 1998. *Sophocles: 'Ajax'.* Warminster.

Gaster, T. H. 1961. *Thespis: Ritual, Myth and Drama in the Ancient Near East.* Garden City, N.Y.

Gates, C. 1995. 'Defining boundaries of a state: the Mycenaeans and their Anatolian frontier', in *Politeia: Society and State in the Aegean Bronze Age, Proceedings of the 5th International Aegean Conference/ 5e Rencontre Egéenne Internationale, University of Heidelberg, Archäologisches Institut, 10–13 April 1994* (AEGAEUM 12) ed. R. Laffineur and W.-D. Niemeier. (Liège) 289–98.

Gauthier, Ph. 1972. *Symbola: Les étrangers et la justice dans les cités grecques.* Annales de l'Est 42. Nancy.

1989. *Nouvelles inscriptions de Sardes II.* Geneva.

1993. 'Les cités hellénistiques', in *The Ancient Greek City-State: Symposium on the Occasion of the 250th Anniversary of The Royal Danish Academy of Sciences and Letters, 1–4 July 1992.* Historisk-filosofiske Meddelelser 67, ed. M. H. Hansen (Copenhagen) 211–31.

Gedi, N. and Elam, Y. 1996. 'Collective memory: What is it?', *History and Memory* (Fall 1996), 30–50.

Gehrke, H.-J. 1985. *Stasis: Untersuchungen zu den inneren Kriegen in den griechischen Staaten des 5. und 4. Jahrhunderts v. Chr.* Munich.

2001. 'Myth, history, and collective identity: uses of the past in ancient Greece and beyond', in *The Historian's Craft in the Age of Herodotus*, ed. N. Luraghi (Oxford) 286–313.

Gentili, B. 1968. 'Epigramma e elegia', in *L'épigramme grecque*, Entretiens Hardt XIV (Vandoeuvres/Geneva) 37–90.

1988. *Poetry and its Public in Ancient Greece: From Homer to the Fifth Century.* Baltimore.

Gentili, B. and Catenacci, C. 2007. *Polinnia: Poesia Greca Arcaica.* 3rd edn. Messina/Florence.

Gentili, B. and Lomiento, L. 2003. *Metrica e Ritmica: Storia delle forme poetiche nella Grecia antica.* Milan.

Ghiron-Bistagne, P. 1976. *Recherches sur les acteurs dans la Grèce antique.* Paris.

1990–1. 'Les artistes dionysiaques de Nîmes à l'époque impériale', in *Realia: Mélanges sur les realités du théâtre antique.* Cahiers du GITA 6, ed. P. Ghiron-Bistagne (Montpellier) 57–78.

Giebel, M. 1999. *Reisen in der Antike.* Düsseldorf/Zurich.

Gilan, A. 2001. 'Kampfspiel in hethitischen Festritualen: eine Interpretation', in Richter *et al.* (eds.) 2001: 113–24.

2004. 'Sakrale Ordnung und politische Herrschaft im hethitischen Anatolien', in Hutter and Hutter-Braunser (eds.) 2004: 189–205.

Giovannini, A. 1993. 'Greek cities and Greek commonwealth' in *Images and Ideologies: Self-definition in the Hellenistic World*, ed. A. Bulloch, E. S. Gruen *et al.* (Berkeley/Los Angeles/London) 265–86.

Glocker, J. 1997. *Das Ritual für den Wettergott von Kuliwišna: Textzeugnisse eines lokalen Kultfestes im Anatolien der Hethiterzeit.* Florence.

Golden, M. 1998. *Sport and Society in Ancient Greece.* Cambridge.

284 *Bibliography*

Goldhill, S. 2002. 'What is a sociology of Greek music and Greek music theory?' at http://www.dismec.unibo.it/musichegreci/web2002/pdfgoldhill.

Gostoli, A. 1988. 'Terpandro e la funzione etico-politica della musica', in *La Musica in Grecia*, ed. B. Gentili and R. Prestagostini (Rome) 232–7.

1990. *Terpandro: Introduzione, testo critico, testimonianze, traduzione e commentario*. Rome.

Goukowsky, P. 1995. 'Philippe de Pergame et l'histoire des guerres civiles', in *Hellenika Symmeikta II (Études d'archéologie classique* 8), ed. C. Brixhe (Paris) 39–53.

Gow, A. S. F. and Page, D. L. 1968. *The Greek Anthology: The Garland of Philip*. Cambridge.

Graf, F. and Johnston, S. Iles. 2007. *Ritual Texts for the Afterlife*. London/New York.

Grandolini, S. 1987/1988. 'Osservazioni sul prosodio', *Annali della Facoltà di Lettere e Filosofia dell'Università degli Studi di Perugia*, 25, n.s. 11, 1, Studi Classici: 29–52.

1996. *Canti e aedi nei poemi omerici*. Rome/Pisa.

Graziosi, B. 2002. *Inventing Homer: The Early Reception of Epic*. Cambridge.

Greaves, A. M. 2002. *Miletos: A History*. London.

Green, A. R. W. 2003. *The Storm-god in the Ancient Near East*. Winona Lake, IN.

Green, J. 2002. 'Towards a reconstruction of performance style' in *Greek and Roman Actors: Aspects of an Ancient Profession*, ed. P. Easterling and E. Hall (Cambridge) 93–126.

Greene, E. 2005. *Women Poets of Ancient Greece and Rome*. Norman, OK.

Griffith, M. 1978. 'Aeschylus, Sicily and Prometheus', in *Dionysiaca*, ed. R. D. Dawe, J. Diggle and P. Easterling (Cambridge) 105–39.

Grottanelli, C. 1982. 'Healers and saviours of the eastern Mediterranean in pre-Classical times', in *La soteriologia dei culti orientali nell'Impero Romano: Atti del Colloquio Internazionale, Roma 24–28 Settembre 1979*, ed. U. Bianchi and M. J. Vermaseren (Leiden) 649–70.

Guarducci, M. 1929. *Poeti vaganti e conferenzieri dell' età ellenistica: ricerche di epigrafia greca nel campo della letteratura e del costume* (Atti della R. Accademia nazionale dei Lincei. Classe di scienze morali, storiche e filologiche, serie 6: vol. 2, 9) (Rome) 629–65.

1961. 'Ancora sul poeta L. Settimio Nestore' *Rivista di Filologia e di Istruzione Classica* 89: 180–3.

Güterbock, H. G. 1974. 'Appendix: Hittite parallels', *Journal of Near Eastern Studies* 33: 323–7.

1983a. 'A Hurro-Hittite hymn to Ishtar', *Journal of the American Oriental Society* 103: 155–64. Reprinted in Hoffner and Diamond (eds.) 1996: 65–74.

1983b. 'The Hittites and the Aegean world. Part 1: The Ahhiyawa problem reconsidered', *American Journal of Archaeology* 87: 133–8. Reprinted in Hoffner and Diamond (eds.) 1997: 199–204.

1986. 'Troy in Hittite texts? Wilusa, Ahhiyawa, and Hittite history', in *Troy and the Trojan War: A Symposium Held at Bryn Mawr College, October 1984*, ed.

Bibliography

M. Mellink (Bryn Mawr, PA) 33–44, reprinted in Hoffner and Diamond (eds.) 1996: 223–8.

1987. 'Hittite liver models', in *Language, Literature, and History: Philological and Historical Studies Presented to Erica Reiner*, ed. F. Rochberg-Halton (New Haven) 147–53, reprinted in Hoffner and Diamond (eds.) 1996: 157–60.

Güterbock, H. G., and Hoffner, H. A., Jr. (1989–). *The Hittite Dictionary of the Oriental Institute of the University of Chicago*. Chicago.

Gulizio, J., Palaima, T. G. and Pluta, K. 2001. 'Religion in the Room of the Chariot Tablets', in Laffineur and Hägg (eds.) 2001: 453–61.

Gutzwiller, K. J. 1998. *Poetic Garlands: Hellenistic Epigrams in Context*. Berkeley/Los Angeles/London.

Haas, V. 1975. 'Jasons Raub des goldenen Vliesses im Lichte hethitischer Quellen' *Ugarit-Forschungen* 7: 227–33.

1978. 'Medea und Jason im Lichte hethitischer Quellen', *Acta Antiqua Academiae Scientarum Hungaricae* 26: 241–53.

1981. 'Zwei Gottheiten aus Ebla in hethitischer Überlieferung', *Oriens Antiquus* 20: 251–7.

1988. 'Betrachtungen zur Rekonstruktion des hethitischen Frühjahrsfestes (EZEN *purulliyaš*)', *Zeitschrift der Assyriologie und vorderasiatische Archäologie* 78: 284–98.

1993. 'Ein hurritischer Blutritus und die Deponierung der Ritualrückstände nach hethitischen Quellen', in Janowski *et al.* (eds.) 1993: 67–85.

1994. *Geschichte der hethitischen Religion*. Handbuch der Orientalistik. Erste Abteilung. Der Nahe und Mittlere Osten 15. Leiden/New York.

2003. 'Betrachtungen zur Traditionsgeschichte hethitischer Rituale am Beispiel des "Sündenbock"-Motivs', in Beckman *et al.* (eds.) 2003: 131–41.

Habicht, Chr. 1970. *Gottmenschentum und griechische Städte*. Zetemata 14, 2nd edn. Munich.

1995. *Athen: Die Geschichte der Stadt in hellenistischer Zeit*. Munich.

2006. 'Versäumter Götterdienst', *Historia* 55: 153–66.

Hadzis, C. D. 1997. 'Corinthiens, Lyciens, Doriens et Cariens: Aoreis à Corinthe, Aoroi à Corcyre, Aor, fils de Chrysaōr et Alétès fils d'Hippotès', *Bulletin de Correspondance Hellénique* 121: 1–14.

Halbwachs, M. 1925. *Les cadres sociaux de la mémoire*. Paris.

1950. *Mémoires collectives*. Paris.

Haldane, J. 1963. 'A paean in the *Philoctetes*', *Classical Quarterly* 13: 53–6.

Hale, T. A. 1998. *Griots and Griottes: Masters of Words and Music*, Bloomington, IN.

Hall, E. 1989. *Inventing the Barbarian: Greek Self-definition through Tragedy*. Oxford.

1994. 'Drowning by nomes: the Greeks, swimming and Timotheus' *Persians*', in *The Birth of the European Identity: The Europe-Asia Contrast in Greek Thought, 490–322 B.C.*, ed. H. Akbar Khan (Nottingham) 44–89.

286   *Bibliography*

2000. 'Female figures and metapoetry in Old Comedy', in *The Rivals of Aristophanes: Studies in Athenian Old Comedy*, ed. D. Harvey and J. Wilkins (London) 407–18.

Hallo, W. W. and Younger, K. L., Jr. (eds.) 2002. *The Context of Scripture. Vol. III: Archival Documents from the Biblical World*. Leiden/New York/Cologne.

Hansen, M. H. and Nielsen, T. H. 2004. *An Inventory of Archaic and Classical Poleis: An Investigation Conducted by The Copenhagen Polis Centre for the Danish National Research Foundation*. Oxford.

Hansen, O. 1984. 'On the date and place of the first performance of Timotheus' *Persae*', *Philologus* 128: 135–8.

Hardie, A. 1983. *Statius and the Silvae*. Liverpool.

2004. 'Muses and mysteries' in Murray and Wilson (eds.) 2004: 11–37.

Harding, P. E. 1994. *Androtion and the 'Atthis'*. Oxford.

Harrison, E. 1905. *Studies in Theognis*. Cambridge.

Hauser, F. 1905. 'Nausicaa: Pyxis in Fine-Arts-Museum zu Boston', *Jahreshefte des Österreichischen archäologischen Instituts in Wien* 8: 18–41.

Hazenboos, J. 2003. *The Organization of the Anatolian Local Cults during the Thirteenth Century B. C.* Leiden/Boston.

Heath, M. 2004. *Menander: A Rhetor in Context*. Oxford.

Helly, B. 1983. 'Les Italiens en Thessalie au IIe et au Ier s. av. J.-C.', in *Les "bourgeoisies" municipales Italiennes aux IIe et au Ier s. av. J.-C*, ed. M. Cébeillac-Gervasoni (Paris/Naples) 355–80.

2006. 'Décret de Larisa pour Bombos, fils d'Alkaios, et pour Leukios, fils de Nikasias, citoyens d'Alexandrie de Troade (ca. 150 av. J.–C.)', *Chiron* 36: 171–203.

Helms, M. W. 1988. *Ulysses' Sail: An Ethnographic Odyssey of Power, Knowledge, and Geographical Distance*. Princeton.

Hendriks, I. H. M., Parsons, P. J. and Worp, K. A. 1981. 'Papyri from the Groningen Collection I: Encomium Alexandreae', *Zeitschrift für Papyrologie und Epigraphik* 41: 71–83.

Henten, J. W. van, and Avemarie, F. 2002. *Martyrdom and Noble Death: Selected Texts from Graeco-Roman, Jewish and Christian Antiquity*. London/New York.

Herington, C. J. 1986. *Aeschylus*. New Haven/London.

Herman, G. 1987. *Ritualised Friendship and the Greek City*. Cambridge.

Herrmann, P. 1967. 'Antiochos der Grosse und Teos', *Anadolu* 9: 29–160.

Herz, P. 1990. 'Die musische Agonistik und der Kunstbetrieb der Kaiserzeit', in *Theater und Gesellschaft im Imperium Romanum*, ed. J. Blänsdorf (Tübingen) 175–95.

Heubeck, A. 1972. 'Etymologische Vermutungen zu Eleusis und Eileithyia', *Kadmos* 11: 87–95.

Higbie, C. 2003. *The Lindian Chronicle and the Greek Understanding of their Past*. Oxford.

Hiller von Gaertringen, F. 1903. 'Aristodama', *RE* Suppl. 3: 158.

Hiltbrunner, O. 1967. 'Vir gravis', in *Römische Wertbegriffe*, ed. H. Oppermann (Darmstadt) 402–19.

Bibliography

Hoffner, H. A., Jr. 1992. 'Syrian cultural influence in Hatti', in *New Horizons in the Study of Ancient Syria* (Bibliotheca Mesopotamica 25), ed. M. W. Chavalas and J. L. Hayes (Malibu) 89–105.

1998a. *Hittite Myths*, 2nd edn. Writings from the Ancient World 2. Atlanta, GA.

1998b. 'Hurrian civilization from a Hittite perspective', in *Urkesh and the Hurrians: Studies in Honor of Lloyd Cotsen* (Bibliotheca Mesopotamica 26), ed. G. Buccellati and M. Kelly-Buccellati (Malibu) 167–200.

Hoffner, H. A., Jr. and Diamond, I. L. (eds.) 1997. *Perspectives on Hittite Civilization: Selected Writings of Hans Gustav Güterbock.* Assyriological Studies 26. Chicago.

Hölscher, T. 1998. *Öffentliche Räume in frühen griechischen Städten.* Heidelberg.

Hordern, J. H. 2002. *The Fragments of Timotheus of Miletus.* Oxford.

Hornblower, S. 1991. *A Commentary on Thucydides*, I. Oxford.

2004. *Thucydides and Pindar: Historical Narrative and the World of Epinikian Poetry.* Oxford.

Horrocks, G. 1997. *Greek: A History of the Language and its Speakers.* London/New York.

Houwink ten Cate, Ph. H. J. 1992. 'The Hittite Storm God: his role and his rule according to Hittite cuneiform sources', in *Natural Phenomena: Their Meaning, Depiction and Description in the Ancient Near East*, ed. D. J. W. Meijer (Amsterdam) 83–148.

2003. 'A new look at the outline tablets of the AN.TAH̬.ŠUM^[SAR] festival: the text-copy VS NF 12.1', in Beckman *et al.* (eds.) 2003: 177–204.

Hunter, R. 1992. 'Callimachus and Heraclitus', *Materiali e Discussioni* 28: 113–23.

1996a. 'Callimachus swings (frs. 178 and 43 Pf.)', *Ramus* 25: 17–26.

1996b. *Theocritus and the Archaeology of Greek Poetry.* Cambridge.

2001. 'The poet unleaved', in *The New Simonides: Contexts of Praise and Desire*, ed. D. Boedeker and D. Sider (Oxford/New York) 242–54.

2002. 'The sense of an author: Theocritus and [Theocritus]', in *The Classical Commentary: Histories, Practices, Theory*, ed. R. K. Gibson and Chr. Shuttleworth Kraus (Leiden/Boston/Cologne) 89–108.

2003. *Theocritus, Encomium of Ptolemy Philadelphus.* Berkeley/Los Angeles.

(ed.) 2005. *The Hesiodic Catalogue of Women: Constructions and Reconstructions.* Cambridge.

Hupfloher, A. 2000. *Kulte in kaiserzeitlichen Sparta: Eine Rekonstruktion anhand der Priesterämter.* Berlin.

Hutchinson, G. O. 2001. *Greek Lyric Poetry: A Commentary on Selected Larger Pieces.* Oxford.

Hutter, M. 2001. 'Luwische Religion in den Traditionen von Arzawa', in *Akten des IV Internationalen Kongresses für Hethitologie. Würzburg, 4.-8. Oktober 1999* (Studien zu den Boğazköy-Texten 45), ed. G. Wilhelm (Wiesbaden) 224–34.

2002. 'Das H̬ii̯ara-Fest in H̬attuša: Transformation und Funktion eines syrischen Festes', in *Silva Anatolica: Anatolian Studies Presented to Maciej Popko on the Occasion of his 65th Birthday*, ed. P. Taracha (Warsaw) 187–96.

288   *Bibliography*

Hutter, M. and Hutter-Braunsar, S. (eds.) 2004. *Offizielle Religion, lokale Kulte und individuelle Religiosität: Akten des religionsgeschichtlichen Symposiums 'Kleinasien und angrenzende Gebiete vom Beginn des 2. bis zur Mitte des 1. Jahrtausends v. Chr.' (Bonn, 20.–22. Februar 2003)*. Münster.

Huttner, U. 1997. *Die politische Rolle der Heraklesgestalt im griechischen Herrschertum*. Stuttgart.

Huxley, G. 1969. 'Choerilos of Samos', *Greek, Roman and Byzantine Studies* 10: 12–29.

  2006. 'Olympiad dating' (review of Shaw 2003). *Classical Review* 56: 148–51.

Hyde, D. 1903. *Abhráin atá Leagtha ar an Reachtúire (Songs Ascribed to Raftery)*, reprinted with intro. by D. Daly. Shannon, Ireland (1973).

Ieranò, G. 1992. 'Arione e Corinto', *Quaderni Urbinati di Cultura Classica* 41: 39–52.

  1997. *Il ditirambo di Dioniso: Le testimonianze antiche*. Pisa/Rome.

Immerwahr, W. 1889. *Die Lakonika des Pausanias auf ihre Quellen untersucht*. Berlin.

Ippolito, A. 1996. 'Tecnica compositiva e modelli letterari degli epigrammi di Giulia Balbilla', *Sileno* 22: 119–36.

Irvin-Zarecki, I. 1994. *Frames of Remembrance: The Dynamics of Collective Memory*. New Brunswick, NJ.

Isager, S. 1998. 'The Pride of Halikarnassos: Editio Princeps of an inscription from Salmakis', *Zeitschrift für Papyrologie und Epigraphik* 123: 1–23.

Isager, S. and Pedersen, P. (eds.) 2004. *The Salmakis Inscription and Hellenistic Halikarnassos*. Odense.

Jacoby, F. 1944. 'Patrios Nomos: State burial in Athens and the public cemetery in the Kerameikos' *Journal of Hellenic Studies* 64: 37–66.

Jaeger, W. 1932. 'Tyrtaios ueber die wahre ἀρετή', *Sitz. Ber. Akad. Wiss*. Phil.-Hist. Kl., 23: 537–68 (= *Scripta minora*, II, Rome 1960: 75–114).

Jaillard, D. 2000. 'A propos du fragment 35 de Callimaque', *Zeitschrift für Papyrologie und Epigraphik* 132: 143–4.

Jakobson, R. 1956. 'Two aspects of language and two types of aphasic disturbances', in *Fundamentals of Language*, ed. R. Jakobson and M. Halle (The Hague) 49–73. Reprinted in *Language in Literature* (1987), Cambridge, MA: 95–119.

Janko, R. 1982. *Homer, Hesiod and the Hymns: Diachronic Development in Epic Diction*. Cambridge.

Janni, P. 1965. *La cultura di Sparta arcaica. Ricerche I*. Rome.

Janowski, B., Koch, K. and Wilhelm, G. (eds.) 1993. *Religionsgeschichtliche Beziehungen zwischen Kleinasien, Nordsyrien und dem Alten Testament: Internationales Symposium Hamburg 17.–21. März 1990*. Göttingen.

Janowski, B. and Wilhelm, G. 1993. 'Der Bock, der die Sünden hinausträgt', in Janowski *et al*. (eds.) 1993: 109–70.

Jeffrey, L. H. 1988. 'The development of Laconian lettering: a reconsideration', *Annual of the British School at Athens* 83: 179–81.

Johnstone, H. 1997. 'A fragment of Simonides', *Classical Quarterly* 47: 293–5.

Jones, C. P. 1999. *Kinship Diplomacy in the Ancient World*. Cambridge, MA/London.

Bibliography

2001. 'Pausanias and his guides', in *Pausanias: Travel and Memory in Roman Greece*, ed. S. Alcock, J. F. Cherry and J. Elsner (Oxford) 33–9, 268–70.

2006. 'A letter of Hadrian to Naryka (Eastern Lokris)', *Journal of Roman Archaeology* 19: 151–62.

Jourdan-Annequin, C. 1989. *Héraclès aux portes du soir*. Paris.

Judeich, W. 1898. *Altertümer von Hierapolis*. Berlin.

Jung, M. 2006. *Marathon und Plataiai: Zwei Perserschlachten als 'Lieux de mémoire' im antiken Griechenland*. Göttingen.

Kaibel, G. 1873. 'Quaestiones Simonideae', *Rheinisches Museum* 28: 436–60.

Kaimio, M. 1999. 'The citizenship of theatre-makers in Athens', *Würzburger Jahrbücher für Altertumswissenschaft* 23: 43–61.

Kanne, J. 1798. *Cononis narrationes L. ex Photii Biblioteca edidit et adnotationibus illustravit Io. Arnoldus Kanne*. Göttingen.

Käppel, L. 1992. *Paian: Studien zur Geschichte einer Gattung*. Berlin.

Kassel, R. 2003. 'Gesandtschaft nach Ithaka', *Zeitschrift für Papyrologie und Epigraphik* 144: 77–8.

Kazarow, G. 1938. *Die Denkmäler des thrakischen Reitergottes in Bulgarien*, Textband und Tafelband, Diss. Pann., ser. II. fasc. 14. Budapest.

Keen, A. G. 1998. *Dynastic Lycia: A Political History of the Lycians and their Relations with Foreign Powers, c. 545–362 B.C.*. Leiden.

Keil, J. 1911. 'Die Synodos der ökumenischen Hieroniken und Stephaniten', *Jahreshefte des Österreichischen Archäologischen Institutes in Wien* 14 Beibl.: 123–34.

Kennedy, D. F. 1993. *The Arts of Love: Five Studies in the Discourse of Roman Love Elegy*. Cambridge.

Kennell, N. M. 1995. *The Gymnasium of Virtue: Education and Culture in Ancient Sparta*. Chapel Hill, NC.

Kiechle, F. 1960. 'Pylos und der pylische Raum in der antiken Tradition', *Historia* 9: 45–67.

Kienzle, E. 1936. *Der Lobpreis von Städten und Ländern in der älteren griechischen Dichtung*. Basel.

Kilian, I. 1978. 'Weihungen an Eileithyia und Artemis Orthia', *Zeitschrift für Papyrologie und Epigraphik* 31: 219–22.

Kirk, G. 1985. *The 'Iliad': A Commentary. Volume I, books 1–4*. Cambridge.

Kirstein, R. 2002. 'Companion Pieces in the Hellenistic Epigram (Call. 21 and 35 Pf.; Theoc. 7 and 15 Gow; Mart. 2.91 and 2.92; Ammianos AP 11.230 and 11.231)', in *Hellenistic Epigrams*, ed. M. A. Harder, R. F. Regtuit and G. C. Wakker (Leuven) 113–35.

Klengel, H. 1965. 'Der Wettergott von Ḫalap', *Journal of Cuneiform Studies* 19: 87–93.

Knoepfler, D. 1996. 'La réorganisation du concours des Mouseia à l'époque hellénistique: esquisse d'une solution nouvelle', in *La montagne des Muses* (Recherches et Rencontres 7) ed. A. Hurst and A. Schachter (Geneva) 141–67.

2005. *Apports récents des inscriptions grecques à l'histoire de l'Antiquité*. Paris.

290   *Bibliography*

2006. 'L'inscription de Naryka (Locride) au Musée du Louvre: La dernière lettre publique de l'empereur Hadrien', *Revue des Études Grecques* 119: 1–34.

Köhler, J. 1996. *Pompai: Untersuchungen zur hellenistischen Festkultur*. Europäische Hochschulschriften, 38 ser., 61. Frankfurt/Bern/New York/Paris.

Kolde, A. 2003. *Politique et religion chez Isyllos d'Epidaure*. Basel.

Koller, H. 1963. *Musik und Dichtung im alten Griechenland*. Munich.

König, J. 2005. *Athletics and Literature in the Roman Empire*. Cambridge.

Kovacs, D. 1994. *Euripidea*. Leiden/New York/Cologne.

Kowalzig, B. 2004. 'Changing choral worlds: song-dance and society in Athens and beyond', in Murray and Wilson (eds.) 2004: 39–65.

Krummeich, R. 2002. '"Euaion ist schön": zur Rühmung eines zeitgenössischen Schauspielers auf attischen Symposiengefäsen', in *Die Geburt des Theaters in der griechischen Antike*, ed. S. Moraw and E. Nölle (Mainz) 141–5.

Krummen, E. 1990. *Pyrsos Hymnon: Festliche Gegenwart und mythisch-rituelle Tradition als Voraussetzung einer Pindarinterpretation (Isthmie 4, Pythie 5, Olympie 1 und 3)*. Berlin/New York.

Kugelmeier, C. 1996. *Reflexe früher und zeitgenössischer Lyrik in der alten attischen Komödie*. Stuttgart.

Kümmel, H. M. 1967. *Ersatzrituale für den hethitischen König*. Studien zu den Boğazköy-Texten 3. Wiesbaden.

Kurke, L. 1991. *The Traffic in Praise: Pindar and the Poetics of Social Economy*, Ithaca, NY/London.

1999. *Coins, Bodies, Games, and Gold: The Politics of Meaning in Archaic Greece*. Princeton.

Laffineur, R. and Hägg, R. (eds.) 2001. *Potnia: Deities and Religion in the Aegean Bronze Age*. Liège/Austin, TX.

Lammers, J. 1931. *Die Doppel- und Halbchöre in der antiken Tragödie*. Paderborn.

Lardinois, A. P. M. H. 2006. 'Have we Solon's verses?' in *Solon of Athens: New Historical and Philological Approaches*, ed. J. H. Blok and A. P. M. H. Lardinois (Leiden) 15–35.

Laroche, E. 1965, 1968. 'Textes mythologiques en transcription', *Revue Hittite et Asianique* 23, 26: 61–178, 5–90.

1971. *Catalogue des textes hittites*. Paris.

Latacz, J. 2004. *Troy and Homer: Towards a Solution of an Old Mystery*, 4th edn., trans. by K. Windle and R. Ireland. Oxford.

Latte, K. 1954. 'Zur Geschichte der griechischen Tragödie in der Kaiserzeit', *Eranos* 52: 125–7.

Latte, K. and Erbse, H. (eds.) 1965. *Lexica Graeca Minora*. Hildesheim.

Lavagne, H. 1986. 'Rome et les associations dionysiaques en Gaule', in *L'association dionysiaque dans les sociétés anciennes: Actes de la Table ronde organisée par l'École française de Rome*, May 1984 (Rome) 129–48.

Lavecchia, S. and Martinelli, M. 1999. '*P. Oxy.* XXXV 2736. Quattro *Fragmenta Dubia* di Pindaro', *Zeitschrift für Papyrologie und Epigraphik* 125: 1–24.

Leaf, W. 1900. *The 'Iliad'*. London.

Lebek, W. D. 1996. 'Moneymaking on the Roman stage', in *Roman Theater and Society. E. Togo Salmon Papers I*, ed. W. J. Slater (Michigan) 29–48.

Bibliography

Lebrun, R. 1980. *Hymnes et prières hittites*. Louvain-la-Neuve.

Lee, H. M. 1988. 'SIG³ 802: did women compete against men in Greek athletic festivals?', *Nikephoros* 1: 103–17.

Lefèvre, F. 2002. *Corpus des Inscriptions de Delphes. Tome IV. Documents amphictioniques avec une Note d'architecture par Didier Laroche et des Notes d'onomastique par Olivier Masson*. Paris.

Lefkowitz, M. 1963. 'ΤΩ ΚΑΙ ΕΓΩ: The first person in Pindar', *Harvard Studies in Classical Philology* 67: 177–253.

　1981. *The Lives of the Greek Poets*. London.

　1991. *First-Person Fictions: Pindar's Poetic 'I'*. Oxford.

Le Goff, J. 1988. *Histoire et mémoire*. Paris.

Le Guen, B. 2001. *Les Associations de technites dionysiaques à l'époque hellénistique* (2 vols.). Nancy.

Lehrs, K. 1865. *De Aristarchi studiis Homericis*. Leipzig.

Leppin, H. 1992. *Histrionen: Untersuchungen zur sozialen Stellung von Bühnenkünstlern im Westen des römischen Reiches zur Zeit der Republik und des Prinzipats*. Bonn.

Lesky, A. 1951. 'Die Maske des Thamyris', *Anzeiger der Österreichischen Akademie der Wissenschaften, Wien* 100: 101–11.

Leuteritz, E. 1997. *Hellenistische Paideia und Randgruppen der Gesellschaft: Herrscher und Frauen, 'Bildungpolitik' und Eukosmia*. Munich.

Lightfoot, J. L. 1999. *Parthenius of Nicaea*. Oxford.

Ligt, L. de 1993. *Fairs and Markets in the Roman Empire: Economic and Social Aspects of Periodic Trade in a Pre-industrial Society*. Amsterdam.

Lloyd-Jones, H. 1963. 'The Seal of Posidippus', *Journal of Hellenic Studies* 83: 75–99.

　1994. 'Notes on fragments of Sophocles', *Studi Italiani di Filologia Classica* 12: 129–48.

　1996. *Sophocles: Fragments*. Cambridge, MA.

Loomis, W. T. 1998. *Wages, Welfare Costs and Inflation in Classical Athens*. Ann Arbor.

Loraux, N. 1986. *The Invention of Athens: The Funeral Oration in the Classical City*. Cambridge, MA/London.

Lorber, C. and Hoover, O. 2003. 'An unpublished tetradrachm issued by the Artists of Dionysos', *The Numismatic Chronicle* 163: 59–68.

Loscalzo, D. 2005. 'Vestire il poeta (Aristoph. *Av.* 904–959)', in *Lirica e teatro in Grecia: il testo e la sua ricezione*, ed. S. Grandolini (Naples) 221–34.

Loukopoulou, L., Zournatzi, A., Parisaki, M. G. and Psoma, S. 2005. Ἐπιγραφὲς τῆς Θράκης τοῦ Αἰγαίου. Athens.

Lowenthal, D. 1985. *The Past is a Foreign Country*. Cambridge.

Luraghi, N. 1994. *Tirannidi arcaiche in Sicilia e Magna Grecia da Panezio di Leontini alla caduta dei Dinomenidi*. Florence.

　2001. 'Der Erdbebenaufstand und die Entstehung der messenischen Identität', in *Gab es das Griechische Wunder? Griechenland zwischen dem Ende des 6. und Mitte des 5. Jahrhundert v. Chr.* ed. D. Papenfuß and M. Strocka (Mainz) 279–301.

　2002. 'Becoming Messenian', *Journal of Hellenic Studies* 122: 45–69.

2003. 'The imaginary conquest of the Helots', in Luraghi and Alcock (eds.) 2003: 109–41.

Luraghi, N. and Alcock, S. E. (eds.) 2003. *Helots and Their Masters in Laconia and Messenia: Histories, Ideologies, Structures.* Washington, DC.

Maas, M. and Snyder, J. 1989. *Stringed Instruments of Ancient Greece.* New Haven, CT.

Maass, M. 1978. *Die geometrischen Dreifüsse von Olympia.* Berlin.

MacDowell, D. 1995. *Aristophanes and Athens.* Oxford.

Mace, S. 2001. 'Utopian and erotic fusion in a new elegy by Simonides' in Boedeker and Sider (eds.) 2001: 185–207.

Magnelli, E. 1999. *Alexandri Aetoli testimonia et fragmenta.* Florence.

Malkin, I. 1987. *Religion and Colonisation in Ancient Greece.* Leiden.

Mantas, K. 1995. 'Women and athletics in the Roman East', *Nikephoros* 8: 125–44.

Markwald, G. 1986. *Die homerischen Epigramme: sprachliche und inhaltliche Untersuchungen.* Königstein.

Martin, R. 1989. *The Language of Heroes: Speech and Performance in the 'Iliad'.* Ithaca, NY.

1992. 'Hesiod's Metanastic Poetics', *Ramus* 21: 11–33.

1997. 'The Scythian accent: Anacharsis and the Cynics', in *The Cynics*, ed. B. Branham and M.-O. Goulet-Cazé (Berkeley) 136–55.

2001. 'Rhapsodising Orpheus', *Kernos* 14: 23–33.

2003. 'The pipes are brawling: conceptualizing musical performance in Athens', in *The Cultures within Ancient Greek Culture: Contact, Conflict, Collaboration,* ed. C. Dougherty and L. Kurke (Cambridge) 153–80.

Marzi, G. 1988. 'Il "decreto" degli Spartani contro Timoteo (Boeth., *De Instit. Mus.* I, I)', in *La musica in Grecia*, ed. B. Gentili and R. Pretagostini (Rome/Bari) 264–72.

Mathiesen, Th. J. 1999. *Apollo's Lyre: Greek Music and Music Theory in Antiquity and the Middle Ages.* Lincoln/London.

Méautis, G. 1918. *Une métropole égyptienne sous l'empire romain: Hermoupolis la Grande.* Lausanne.

1962. *Pindare le dorien.* Neuchâtel/Paris.

Meier, M. 1998. *Aristokraten und Damoden.* Stuttgart.

Melchert, H. C. 1993. *Cuneiform Luvian Lexicon.* Chapel Hill, NC.

1998. 'Poetic meter and phrasal stress in Hittite', in *Mír Curad: Studies in Honor of Calvert Watkins* (Innsbrucker Beiträge zur Sprachwissenschaft 92) ed. J. Jasanoff, H. C. Melchert and L. Oliver (Innsbruck) 483–94.

Merkelbach, R. 1973. 'Zwei Texte aus dem Sarapeum zu Thessalonike', *Zeitschrift für Papyrologie und Epigraphik* 10: 45–54.

1975. 'Der griechische Wortschatz und die Christen', *Zeitschrift für Papyrologie und Epigraphik* 18: 101–48.

Merro, G. 2006. 'Apollodoro, Asclepiade di Tragilo ed Eschilo in *Scholl. Eur. Rh.* 916 e 912', *Rivista di Filologia e di Istruzione Classica* 134: 26–51.

Meyer, D. 2005. *Inszeniertes Lesevergnügen: Das inschriftliche Epigramm und seine Rezeption bei Kallimachos.* Stuttgart.

Bibliography

Meyer, J.-W. 1987. *Untersuchungen zu den Tonlebermodellen aus dem Alten Orient.* Alter Orient und Altes Testament 39. Kevelaer/Neukirchen-Vluyn.

Miller, A. 1993. 'Pindaric mimesis: the associative mode', *Classical Journal* 89: 21–53.

Miller, J. 2002. 'The *katra/i-* women in the Kizzuwatnean ritual from Ḫattuša', in *Sex and Gender in the Ancient Near East: Proceedings of the 47th Rencontre Assyriologique International, Helsinki, July 2–6, 2001,* ed. S. Parpola and R. M. Whiting (Helsinki) 423–31.

    2004. *Studies in the Origins, Development and Interpretation of the Kizzuwatna Rituals.* Wiesbaden.

Miller, S. G. 2004. *Arete: Greek Sports from Ancient Sources.* Berkeley/Los Angeles.

Mitteis, L. and Wilcken, U. 1912. *Grundzüge und Chrestomathie der Papyrusurkunde.* Berlin.

Molyneux, J. H. 1992. *Simonides: A Historical Study.* Wauconda, IL.

Momigliano, A. 1972. 'Tradition and the classical historian', *History and Theory* 11: 279–93.

    1978. 'Greek historiography', *History and Theory* 17: 1–28.

Montiglio, S. 2005. *Wandering in Ancient Greek Culture.* Chicago.

Morgan, C. 1990. *Athletes and Oracles: The Transformation of Olympia and Delphi in the eight century BC.* Cambridge.

Morris, S. P. 1995. 'The sacrifice of Astyanax: Near Eastern contributions to the siege of Troy', in *The Ages of Homer: A Tribute to Emily Townsend Vermeule,* ed. J. B. Carter and S. P. Morris (Austin, TX) 221–45.

    2001a. 'Potnia Aswiya: Anatolian contributions to Greek religion', in Laffineur and Hägg (eds.) 2001: 423–34.

    2001b. 'The prehistoric background of Artemis Ephesia: a solution to the enigma of her "breasts"?' in *Der Kosmos der Artemis von Ephesos* (Österreichisches Archäologisches Institut Sonderschriften 37), ed. U. Muss (Vienna) 135–53.

Mosshamer, A. A. 1979. *The Chronicle of Eusebius and Greek Chronographic Tradition.* London.

Moyer, I. 2006. 'Golden fetters and the economies of cultural exchange', *Journal of Ancient Near Eastern Religion* 6: 225–56.

Murray, O. (ed.) 1990. *Sympotica: A Symposium on the Symposion.* Oxford.

Murray, P. and Wilson, P. (eds.) 2004. *Music and the Muses: The Culture of Mousike in the Classical Athenian City.* Oxford.

Musti, D. and Torelli, M. 2000. *Pausania: Guida della Grecia, Libro IV: La Messenia,* 4th edn. Milan.

Nachtergael, G. 1977. *Les Galates en Grèce et les Sôtéria de Delphes: recherches d'histoire et d'épigraphie hellénistiques.* Brussels.

Nafissi, M. 1991. *La nascita del kosmos: Studi sulla storia e la società di Sparta.* Naples.

Nagy, G. 1979. *The Best of the Achaeans.* Baltimore/London.

    1990a. *Pindar's Homer.* Baltimore.

    1990b. 'Ancient Greek poetry, prophecy and concepts of theory', in *Poetry and Prophecy,* ed. J. L. Kugel (London) 55–64.

294   *Bibliography*

1996. *Poetry as Performance: Homer and Beyond*. Cambridge.

2000. 'Homeric *humnos* as a rhapsodic term', in *Una nueva visión de la cultura griega antigua hacia el fin del milenio*, ed. A. M. González de Tobia (La Plata) 385–401.

Nagy, J. F. 1985. *The Wisdom of the Outlaw: The Boyhood Deeds of Finn in Gaelic Narrative Tradition*. Berkeley.

Nagy, J. F. and Jones, L. E. (eds.) 2005. *Heroic Poets and Poetic Heroes in Celtic Tradition: A Festschrift for Patrick K. Ford*. Dublin.

Nakamura, M. 2002. *Das hethitische nuntarriyašḫa-Fest*. Leiden.

Namer, G. 2000. *Halbwachs et la mémoire sociale*. Paris.

Naoumides M. 1968. 'New fragments of ancient Greek poetry', *Greek, Roman and Byzantine Studies* 9: 267–90.

Neu, E. 1996. *Das hurritische Epos der Freilassung I: Untersuchungen zu einem hurritisch-hethitischen Textensemble aus Hattuša*. Studien zu den Boğazköy-Texten 32. Wiesbaden.

Nieddu, G. F. 1993. 'Parola e metro nella *sphragis* dei *Persiani* di Timoteo (*PMG* fr. 791, 202–236)', in *Tradizione e innovazione nella cultura greca da Omero all'età ellenistica. Scritti in onore di Bruno Gentili*, ed. R. Pretagostini, vol. II (Rome) 521–9.

Nielsen, T. H. 1999. 'The concept of Arcadia: the people, their land, and their organisation', in *Defining Ancient Arcadia. Symposium, April, 1–4 1988. Acts of the Copenhagen Polis Centre*, vol. VI, ed. T. H. Nielsen and J. Roy (Copenhagen) 16–79.

2002. *Arkadia and its Poleis in the Archaic and Classical Periods*. Göttingen.

Nielsen, T. H., Bjertrup, L., Hansen, M. H., Rubinstein, L. and Vestergaard, T. 1990. 'Athenian grave monuments and social class', *Greek, Roman and Byzantine Studies* 30: 411–20.

Niemeier, W.-D. 1998. 'The Mycenaeans in western Anatolia and the problem of the origins of the Sea Peoples', in *Mediterranean Peoples in Transition Thirteenth to Early Tenth Centuries BCE: In Honor of Professor Trude Dothan*, ed. S. Gitin, A. Mazar and E. Stern (Jerusalem) 17–65.

1999. 'Mycenaeans and Hittites in war in western Asia Minor', in *Polemos: Le contexte guerrier en Égée à l'âge du bronze: Actes de la 7e Rencontre égéenne internationale Université de Liège, 14–17 avril 1998* (Aegaeum 19) ed. R. Laffineur (Liège) 141–56.

Nilsson, M. P. 1950. *The Minoan-Mycenaean Religion and its Survival in Greek Religion*. Lund.

1972. *Cults, Myths, Oracles, and Politics in Ancient Greece with Two Appendices: The Ionian Phylae, the Phratries*. New York.

Noegel, S. B. (ed.) 2000. *Puns and Pundits: Word Play in the Hebrew Bible and Ancient Near Eastern Literature*. Bethesda, MD.

Nolan, B. T., 1981. Inscribing Costs at Athens in the Fourth Century B.C. University of Michigan, Diss., Ann Arbor.

Noussia, M. 2001. *Solone, frammenti dell'opera poetica*. Milan.

Obbink, D. 2001. 'The genre of Plataea', in Boedeker and Sider (eds.) 2001: 65–85.

Bibliography

Oettinger, N. 1989/1990. 'Die "dunkle Erde" im Hethitischen und Griechischen', *Die Welt des Orients* 20/21: 83–98.

O'Flynn, C. 1998. *Blind Raftery*. Inverin.

Öhler, J. 1913. Ἱερονῖκαί, *Paulys Realencyclopädie der classischen Altertumswissenschaft* VIII 2 (Stuttgart) 1535–6.

Ó hÓgáin, D. 1985. *The Hero in Irish Folk History*. Dublin.

(ed.) 1991. *Myth, Legend, and Romance: An Encyclopedia of the Irish Folk Tradition*. New York.

Olick, J. K. and Robins, J. 1998. 'Social memory studies: from "collective memory" to the historical sociology of mnemonic practices', *Annual Review of Sociology* 22: 105–40.

Oliver, G. J. 2002. 'Callimachus the poet and benefactor of the Athenians', *Zeitschrift für Papyrologie und Epigraphik* 140: 6–8.

Oliver, J. H. 1933. 'Selected Greek inscriptions', *Hesperia* 2: 480–513.

1989. *Greek Constitutions of Early Roman Emperors from Inscriptions and Papyri*. Philadelphia.

Osborne, R. G. 2001. 'The use of abuse: Semonides 7', *Proceedings of the Cambridge Philological Society* 47: 49–64.

Paduano, G. 1973. 'La città degli Uccelli e le ambivalenze del nuovo sistema etico-politico', *Studi Classici e Orientali* 22: 115–44.

Page, D. 1955. *Sappho and Alcaeus*. Oxford.

1959. *History and the Homeric Iliad*. Berkeley/Los Angeles.

1981. *Further Greek Epigrams*. Oxford.

Palaima, T. G. 2004. 'Sacrificial feasting in the Linear B documents', in Wright (ed.) 2004b: 97–126.

Pallone, M. R. 1984. 'L'epica agonale in età ellenistica', *Orpheus* 5: 156–66.

Palumbo Stracca, B. M. 1999. 'Il decreto degli Spartani contro Timoteo (Boeth. *De instit. mus.* I. 1)', in *KATA ΔΙΑΛΕΚΤΟΝ. Atti del III Colloquio Internazionale di Dialettologia Greca, Napoli-Fiaiano d'Ischia, 25–8 settembre 1996* [= *Annali dell'Istituto Universitario Orientale di Napoli . . . Sezione filologico-letteraria 19*], ed. A. C. Cassio (Naples) 129–60.

Parker, R. 1988. 'Demeter, Dionysus and the Spartan pantheon', in *Early Greek Cult Practice: Proceedings of the Fifth International Symposium at the Swedish Institute at Athens, 26–29 June 1986*, ed. R. Hägg, N. Marinatos and G. C. Nordquist (Stockholm) 99–103.

1989. 'Spartan religion', in *Classical Sparta: Techniques Behind Her Success*, ed. A. Powell (London) 142–72.

1996. *Athenian Religion: A History*. Oxford.

2004. 'New "panhellenic" festivals in hellenistic Greece', in *Mobility and Travel in the Mediterranean from Antiquity to the Middle Ages*, ed. R. Schlesier and U. Zellmannn (Münster) 9–17.

Parsons, P. 2002. 'Callimachus and the Hellenistic epigram', in *Callimaque*, Entretiens de la Fondation Hardt XLVIII. (Vandoeuvres/Geneva) 99–141.

Paton, W. R. 1922. *Polybius, The Histories*, vol. II. Cambridge, MA/London.

Pavese, C. O. 1972. *Tradizioni e generi poetici della Grecia arcaica*. Rome.

296   *Bibliography*

1987. 'Il più antico frammento di lirica corale greca', in *Filologia e forme letterarie: Studi offerti a F. Della Corte* (Urbino) I: 53–7.

Pearson, A. 1917. *The Fragments of Sophocles*. London.

Pecchioli Daddi, F. 1982. *Mestieri, professioni e dignità nell'Anatolia ittita*. Rome.

1987. 'Aspects du culte de la divinité hattie Teteshapi', *Hethitica* 8: 361–80.

Pekary, T. 1965. 'Inschriftenfunde aus Milet 1959', *Mitteilungen des deutschen archäologischen Instituts (Abteilung Istanbul)* 15: 118–34.

Perdrizet, P. 1910. *Cultes et mythes du Pangée*, 'Annales de l'Est' 24. Paris/Nancy.

Perlman, P. 2000. *City and Sanctuary in Ancient Greece: The "Theorodokia" in the Peloponnese*. Hypomnemata 121. Göttingen.

Perpillou-Thomas, F. 1993. *Fêtes d'Égypte ptolémaïque et romaine d'après la documentation papyrologique grecque*. Studia Hellenistica 31. Leuven.

Peterson, I. V. 1983. 'Lives of the wandering singers: pilgrimage and poetry in Tamil saivite hagiography' *History of Religions* 22.4: 338–60.

Petrovic, A. 2004. 'Ἀkoὲ e autopsía. Zu den Quellen Herodots für die Thermopylai-Epigramme (Hdt. 7,228)', in *Studia humanitatis ac litterarum trifolio Heidelbergensi dedicata. Festschrift für E. Christmann, W. Edelmeier, R. Kettemann*, ed. A. Hornung, Ch. Jäkel and W. Schubert (Frankfurt) 255–73.

2007. *Kommentar zu den simonideischen Versinschriften*. Leiden/Boston.

Petzl, G. and Schwertheim, E. 2006. *Hadrian und die dionysischen Künstler: Drei in Alexandria Troas gefundene Briefe an die Künstlervereinigung*. Asia Minor Studien 58. Bonn.

Pfohl, G. 1967. *Greek Poems on Stone*. Leiden.

Philippaki, B. 1988. 'ΑΠΟΛΛΩΝΟΣ ΕΧΙΛΑΣΜΟΣ', in *Studies in Honour of T. B. L. Webster*, vol. II, ed. J. Betts, J. Hooker and R. Green (Bristol) 89–95.

Pickard-Cambridge, A. 1968. *The Dramatic Festivals of Athens*, 2nd edn. Oxford.

Piolot, L. 2001. 'Le recrutement des musiciens pour les fêtes à l'époque hellénistique: le cas messénien', in *Chanter les dieux: Musique et religion dans l'Antiquité grecque et romaine. Actes du colloque des 16, 17 et 18 décembre 1999 (Rennes et Lorient)*, ed. P. Brulé and Chr. Vendries (Rennes) 279–305.

Pirenne-Delforge, V. 2004. 'Image des dieux et rituel dans le discours de Pausanias', *Mélanges de l'École française de Rome* 116: 811–25.

Pizzani, U. 1965. 'Studi sulle fonti del *De Institutione Musicae* di Boezio,' *Sacris Erudiri* 16: 5–164.

1981. 'Il *quadrivium* boeziano e i suoi problemi,' in *Atti del Congresso Internazionale di Studi Boeziani*, ed. L. Orbetello (Rome) 211–26.

Pleket, H. 1973. 'Some aspects of the history of the athletic guilds', *Zeitschrift für Papyrologie und Epigraphik* 10: 197–227.

1975. 'Games, prizes, athletes and ideology', *Stadion* 1: 49–89.

Podlecki, A. J. 1984. *The Early Greek Poets and their Times*. Vancouver.

Poe, E. W. 1995. 'The Vidas and Razos', in *A Handbook of the Troubadours*, ed. F. Akehurst and J. Davis (Berkeley) 185–97.

Pohlenz, M. 1955. *Griechische Freiheit: Wesen und Werden eines Lebensideals*. Heidelberg.

Bibliography

Pöhlmann, E. 1988. *Beiträge zur antiken und neueren Musikgeschichte.* Quellen und Studien zur Musikgeschichte von der Antike bis in die Gegenwart 17. Frankfurt/Bern/New York/Paris.

Poland, F. 1934. 'Technitai', in *Paulys Realencyclopädie der classischen Altertumswissenschaft* V 2, 2nd edn. Stuttgart: 2473–578.

Pomeroy, S. B. 1975. *Goddesses, Whores, Wives and Slaves: Women in Classical Antiquity.* New York.

1977. '*Technikai kai Mousikai*: the education of women in the fourth century and the Hellenistic period', *American Journal of Ancient History* 2: 51–68.

Popko, M. 1975. 'Zum hethitischen ᴷᵁˢ *kurša-*', *Altorientalische Forschungen* 2: 65–70.

Porciani, L. 2001. *Prime forme della storiografia greca: Prospettiva locale e generale nella narrazione storica*, 'Historia' Einzelschriften 152. Stuttgart.

Pouilloux, J. 1954. *Recherches sur l'histoire et les cultes de Thasos*, I. Paris.

1974. 'L'Héracles thasien', *Revue des Études Anciennes* 76: 305–16.

Powell, A. and Hodkinson, S. (eds.) 2002. *Sparta: Beyond the Mirage.* London.

Prauscello, L. 2004. 'A note on *Tabula defixionis* 22(A).5–7, Ziebarth: when a musical performance enacts love', *Classical Quarterly* 54: 333–9.

2006. *Singing Alexandria: Music between Practice and Textual Transmission.* Leiden.

Prechel, D. 1996. *Die Göttin Išḫara: Ein Beitrag zur altorientalischen Religionsgeschichte.* Münster.

Prinz, F. 1979. *Gründungsmythen und Sagenchronologie.* Munich.

Pritchett, W. K. 1979–85. *The Greek State at War* (4 vols.). Berkeley.

Privitera, G. A. 1957. 'Archiloco e il ditirambo letterario pre-simonideo', *Maia* 9: 95–110.

1991. 'Origini della tragedia e ruolo del ditirambo', *Studi Italiani di Filologia Classica* 9: 184–95.

Psoma, S. forthcoming. 'Profitable networks: coinages, panegyreis, profit and the Dionysiac Artists', in *Networks in the Greek World* (Mediterranean Historical Review, supplementary volume) Tel Aviv.

Puech, B. 2002. *Orateurs et sophistes grecs dans les inscriptions d'époque impériale.* Paris.

Puhvel, J. 1983. 'Homeric questions and Hittite answers', *American Journal of Philology* 104: 217–27.

1988a. 'An Anatolian turn of phrase in the *Iliad*', *American Journal of Philology* 109: 591–3.

1988b. 'Hittite athletics as prefigurations of Ancient Greek games', in *The Archaeology of the Olympics: The Olympics and Other Festivals in Antiquity*, ed. W. J. Raschke (Madison) 26–31.

1991. *Homer and Hittite.* Innsbrucker Beiträge zur Sprachwissenschaft, Vorträge und kleinere Schriften 47. Innsbruck.

1992. 'Shaft-shedding Artemis and mind-voiding Ate: Hittite determinants of Greek etyma', *Historische Sprachforschung* 105: 4–8.

1993. 'A Hittite calque in the *Iliad*', *Historische Sprachforschung* 106: 36–8.

298   *Bibliography*

Quattrocelli, L. 2004. 'Poesia e convivialità a Sparta arcaica: Nuove prospettive di studio', *Cahiers du Centre Gustave-Glotz* 13: 7–32.

   2006. 'Tirteo: poesia e ἀνδρεία a Sparta arcaica', in *I luoghi e la poesia nella Grecia antica: Atti del Convegno. Università 'G. D'Annunzio' di Chieti-Pescara, 20–22 aprile 2004*, ed. M. Vetta and C. Catenacci (Alessandria) 133–44.

Raaflaub, K. 1981. 'Zum Freiheitsbegriff der Griechen: Materialien und Untersuchungen zur Bedeutungsentwicklung von ἐλεύθερος/ἐλευθερία in der archaischen und klassischen Zeit', in *Soziale Typenbegriffe im alten Griechenland und ihr Fortleben in den Sprachen der Welt*, 4, ed. E. C. Welskopf (Berlin) 180–405.

Rabe, H. 1908. 'Euripideum', *Rheinisches Museum* 63: 419–22.

Race, W. H. (ed.) 1997a. *Pindar: Olympian Odes, Pythian Odes*. Cambridge, MA.

   (ed.) 1997b. *Pindar: Nemean Odes, Isthmian Odes, Fragments*. Cambridge, MA.

Radt S. L. 1981. 'Vita Aeschyli 6', *Zeitschrift für Papyrologie und Epigraphik* 42: 1–7.

Rausch, M. 1999. *Isonomia in Athen*. Frankfurt.

Raven, E. J. P. 1967. Review of J. M. F. May, *The Coinage of Abdera, 540–354 B.C.*, London 1966, in *Numismatic Chronicle* 7: 289–97.

Rawson, E. 1969. *The Spartan Tradition in European Thought*. Oxford.

Reger, G. 1994. 'Some Boiotians in the Hellenistic Kyklades', *Boeotia Antiqua* 4: 71–99.

Rehm, A. 1954. 'Neue Wörter aus Didyma', *Indogermanische Forschungen* 61: 170–86.

Renfrew, C. 1985. *The Archaeology of Cult: The Sanctuary at Phylakopi*. London.

Restani, D. 1995. 'Introduzione' in *Musica e mito nella Grecia antica*, ed. D. Restani (Bologna) 7–35.

Revermann, M. 1999–2000. 'Euripides, tragedy and Macedon: some considerations of reception', *Illinois Classical Studies* 24–5: 451–60.

Rey-Coquais, J.-P. 1973. 'Inscriptions grecques d'Apamée', *Annales archéologiques arabes syriennes* 23: 39–84.

Richter, T. 2002. 'Zur Frage der Entlehnung syrisch-mesopotamischer Kulturelemente nach Anatolien in der vor- und frühen althethitischen Zeit (19.–16. Jahrhundert v. Chr.)', in *Brückenland Anatolien: Ursachen, Extensität und Modi des Kulturaustasches zwischen Anatolien und sein Nachbarn*, ed. H. Blum, B. Faist and P. Pfälzner (Tübingen) 295–322.

Richter, T., Prechel, D. and Klinger, J. (eds.) 2001. *Kulturgeschichten: Altorientalistische Studien für Volkert Haas zum 65. Geburtstag*. Saarbrücken.

Riedwig, C. (ed.) 2001. *Walter Burkert: Kleine Schriften I: Homerica*. Göttingen.

Riemschneider, K. K. 2004. *Die akkadischen und hethitischen Omentexte aus Boğazköy*. Dresdner Beiträge zur Hethitologie 12. Dresden.

Rigsby, K. J. 1986. 'Notes sur la Crète hellénistique', *Revue des Études Grecques* 99: 350–60.

   1996. *Asylia: Territorial Inviolability in the Hellenistic World*. Berkeley/Los Angeles/London.

Robert, L. 1930. 'Pantomimen im griechischen Osten', *Hermes* 65: 106–22 (= *Opera Minora Selecta* I: 654–70).

Bibliography

1946. 'Décret de Delphes', in *Hellenica* 2: 34–6.

1967. 'Sur des inscriptions d'Éphèse: Fêtes, athlètes, empereurs, épigrammes', *Revue de Philogie* 16, 3 ser.: 7–84.

1968. 'Les épigrammes satiriques de Lucillius sur les athlètes: Parodie et réalités', in *L'épigramme grecque*. Entretiens Hardt XIV (Geneva) 179–295.

1978. 'Catalogue agonistique des Romaia de Xanthos', *Revue archéologique* 1978: 277–90.

1980. 'Deux poètes grecs à l'époque impériale' in Στήλη. Τόμος εἰς μνήμην Νικολάου Κοντολέοντος (Athens) 1–20.

1984. 'Discours d'ouverture', in Πρακτικά του Η' Διεθνούς Συνεδρίου Ελληνικής και Λατινικής Επιγραφικής, Αθήνα, 3–9 Οκτωβρίου 1982 (Athens) 35–45 (= *Opera Minora Selecta* VI: 709–19).

Robertson, N. D. 1986. 'A point of precedence at Plataia: the dispute between Athens and Sparta over leading the procession', *Hesperia* 55: 88–102.

1993. *Festivals and Legends: The Formation of Greek Cities in the Light of Public Ritual.* Toronto/Buffalo/London.

1996. 'New light on Demeter's mysteries: the festival *Proerosia*', *Greek, Roman and Byzantine Studies* 37: 319–79.

1998. 'The two processions to Eleusis and the program of the mysteries', *American Journal of Philology* 119: 547–75.

1999. 'The sequence of days at the *Thesmophoria* and at the Eleusinian mysteries', *Études du Monde Classique* 18: 1–33.

2002. 'The religious criterion in Greek ethnicity: the Dorians and the festival *Carneia*', *American Journal of Ancient History* 1.2: 5–74.

Rocconi, E. 2003. *Le parole delle Muse: La formazione del lessico tecnico musicale nella Grecia antica.* Rome.

Roesch, P. 1982. *Études béotiennes.* Paris.

Rogers, B. B. 1906. *The Birds of Aristophanes.* London.

Rolley, C. 1973. 'Bronzes géométriques et orientaux à Délos', *Bulletin de Correspondance Hellénique* Suppl. 1, *Études Déliens*: 491–524.

1983. 'Les grands sanctuaries panhelléniques', in *The Greek Renaissance of the 8th century BC; Tradition and Innovation*, ed. R. Hägg (Stockholm) 109–14.

Röllig, W. 1992. 'Achäer und Trojaner in hethitischen Quellen?', in *Troia: Brücke zwischen Orient und Okzident*, ed. I. Gamer-Wallert (Tübingen) 183–200.

Rose, M. A. 1993. *Parody: Ancient, Modern and Post-modern.* Cambridge.

Rösler, W. 1990. 'Mnemosyne in the Symposion', in Murray (ed.) 1990: 230–7.

Roueché, Ch. 1993. *Performers and Partisans at Aphrodisias in the Roman and Late Roman Periods (Journal of Roman Studies* Monographs 6). London.

Roy, J. 2003. '"The Arkadians" in Inschriften von Magnesia 38', *Zeitschrift für Papyrologie und Epigraphik* 145: 123–30.

Russell, D. and Wilson, N. (eds.) 1981. *Menander Rhetor.* Oxford.

Rutherford, I. 1995. 'Apollo's other genre: Proclus on *nomos* and his source', *Classical Philology* 90: 354–61.

300   *Bibliography*

2000. 'Keos or Delos? State-pilgrimage and the performance of *Paean 4*', in
   Poesia e religione in Grecia. Studi in onore di G. A. Privitera, ed. M. Cannatà
   Fera and S. Grandolini (Naples) 605–12.

2001. *Pindar's Paeans: A Reading of the Fragments with a Survey of the Genre*.
   Oxford.

2004a. 'Χορὸς εἶς ἐκ τῆσδε τῆς πόλεως . . . (Xen. *Mem.* 3.3.12): song-dance and
   state-pilgrimage at Athens', in Murray and Wilson (eds.) 2004: 67–90.

2004b. 'Women singers and the religious organisation of Hatti: on the interpretations of CTH 235.1 & 2 and other texts', in Hutter and Hutter-Braunsar
   (eds.) 2004: 377–94.

2007. '*Theoria* and theatre at Samothrace: the Dardanos by Dymas of Iasos' in
   Wilson 2007b (ed.): 279–93.

Rutherford, W. G. 1896. *Scholia Aristophanica*, vol. I. London.

Salmen, W. 1960. *Der fahrende Musiker im europaischen Mittelalter*. Kassel.

Salviat, F. 1958. 'Une nouvelle loi thasienne: institutions judiciaires et fêtes
   religieuses à la fin du IVe siècle av.J. C.', *Bulletin de Correspondance Hellénique*
   82: 193–26.

Samama, É. 2003. *Les médecins dans le monde grec: Sources épigraphiques sur la
   naissance d'un corps médical*. Geneva.

Sandbach, F. H. 1942. 'ΑΚΡΑ ΓΥΡΕΩΝ once more', *Classical Review* 56: 63–5.

San Nicolò, M. 1972. *Ägyptisches Vereinswesen zur Zeit der Ptolemäer und Römer*
   (2 vols). Münchener Beiträge zur Papyrusforschung 2, 2nd edn. Munich.

Sasson, J. M. 1973. 'The worship of the golden calf', in *Orient and Occident: Essays
   Presented to Cyrus H. Gordon on the Occasion of his Sixty-Fifth Birthday*, ed.
   H. A. Hoffner, Jr. Kevelaer/Neukirchen-Vluyn: 151–9.

(ed.) 1995. *Civilizations of the Ancient Near East*. New York.

Savalli, I. 1988. 'L'idéologie dynastique des poèmes grecs de Xanthos', *Antiquité
   classique* 47: 103–23.

Scarpi, P. (ed.) 2004. *Le Religioni dei Misteri, Vol. II: Samotracia, Andania, Iside,
   Cibele e Attis, Mitraismo*, 3rd edn. Milan.

Schachter, A. 1981–94. *Cults of Boeotia. Bulletin of the Institute of Classical Studies*
   Suppl. 38 (4 vols.). London.

1986. *Cults of Boiotia. Vol. 2: Herakles to Poseidon*. London.

1999. 'The Nyktophylaxia of Delos', *Journal of Hellenic Studies* 119: 172–4.

Schadewaldt, W. 1965. *Von Homers Welt und Werk*, 4th edn. Stuttgart.

Schlesier, R. and Zellmann, U. (eds.) 2004. *Mobility and Travel in the Mediterranean
   from Antiquity to the Middle Ages*. Münster.

Schoeffer, V. de 1889. *De Deli insulae rebus. Berliner Studien für classische Philologie
   und Archaeologie* 9.1. Berlin.

Scholten, J. B. 2000. *The Politics of Plunder: Aitolians and their koinon in the early
   Hellenistic era, 279–217 B.C.* Berkeley.

Schuol, M. 1994a. 'Die terminologie des hethitischen SU-Orakels: Eine Untersuchung auf der Grundlage des mittelhethitischen Textes KBo XVI 97 unter
   vergleichender Berücksichtigung akkadischer Orakeltexte und Lebermodelle,
   I', *Altorientalische Forschungen* 21: 73–124.

Bibliography

1994b. 'Die terminologie des hethitischen SU-Orakels: Eine Untersuchung auf der Grundlage des mittelhethitischen Textes KBo XVI 97 unter vergleichender Berücksichtigung akkadischer Orakeltexte und Lebermodelle, II', *Altorientalische Forschungen* 21: 247–304.

Schwemer, D. 2001. *Die Wettergottgestalten Mesopotamiens und Nordsyriens im Zeitalter der Keilschriftkulturen: Materialien und Studien nach den schriftlichen Quellen*. Wiesbaden.

Scodel, R. 1998. 'Bardic performance and oral tradition in Homer', *American Journal of Philology* 119: 171–94.

Scullion, S. 2003. 'Euripides and Macedon, or the silence of the *Frogs*', *Classical Quarterly* 53: 389–400.

Séchan, L. 1967. *Études sur la tragédie grecque dans ses rapports avec la céramique*. Paris.

Shaw, P.-J. 2003. *Discrepancies in Olympiad Dating and Chronological Problems of Archaic Peloponnesian History*, 'Historia' Einzelschriften 166. Stuttgart.

Shear, T. L. 1937. 'The Campaign of 1936', *Hesperia* 6: 333–81.

Sherwin-White, A. N. 1966. *The Letters of Pliny: A Historical and Social Commentary*. Oxford.

Shirane, H. 1998. *Traces of Dreams: Landscape, Cultural Memory and the Poetry of Basho*. Berkeley.

Sifakis, G. M. 1962–3. 'High stage and chorus in the hellenistic theatre', *Bulletin of the Institute of Classical Studies* 9–10: 31–45.

1967. *Studies in the History of Hellenistic Drama*. London.

Simms, Ronda R. 1988. 'The cult of the Thracian goddess Bendis in Athens and Attica', *Ancient World* 18: 59–76.

Singer, I. 1983. *The Hittite KI.LAM Festival: Part I*. Studien zu den Boğazköy-Texten 27. Wiesbaden.

1984. *The Hittite KI.LAM Festival: Part II*. Studien zu den Boğazköy-Texten 28. Wiesbaden.

2002. *Hittite Prayers*. Writings from the Ancient World 11. Atlanta.

Slater, W. J. 1969. *Lexicon to Pindar*. Berlin.

1993. 'Three problems in the history of drama', *Phoenix* 47: 189–212.

1995. 'The pantomime Tiberius Iulius Apolaustus', *Greek, Roman and Byzantine Studies* 36: 263–92.

Snyder, J. M. 1989. *The Woman and the Lyre: Women Writers in Classical Greece and Rome*. Bristol.

Sokolowski, F. 1962. *Lois sacrées des cités grecques: Supplément*. Paris.

Sommer, F. 1932. *Die Ahhijavā-Urkunden*. Abhandlungen der Bayerischen Akademie der Wissenschaften. Philosophisch-historische Abteilung 6, N. F. Munich.

Sommerstein, A. H. 2003. *Greek Drama and Dramatists*. London.

Souček, V. and Siegelová, J. 1974. 'Der Kult des Wettergottes von Ḫalap in Ḫatti', *Archív Orientální* 42: 39–52.

Sourvinou-Inwood, Chr. 1996. *'Reading' Greek Death*. Oxford.

302   *Bibliography*

2003a. 'Festival and mysteries: aspects of the Eleusinian cult', in *Greek Mysteries: The Archaeology and Ritual of Ancient Greek Secret Cults*, ed. M. B. Cosmopoulos (London/New York) 25–49.

2003b. *Tragedy and Athenian Religion*. Lanham/Boulder/New York/Oxford.

Souza, Ph. de 1999. *Piracy in the Graeco-Roman World*. Cambridge.

Spawforth, A. J. 1985. 'Families at Roman Sparta and Epidaurus: some prosopographical notes', *Annual of the British School at Athens* 80: 191–258.

1989. 'Agonistic festival in Roman Greece', in *The Greek Renaissance in the Roman Empire: Papers from the Tenth British Museum Colloquium* (= *Bulletin of the Institute of Classical Studies* Suppl. 55), ed. S. Walker and A. Cameron (London) 193–7.

Spence, I. G. 1993. *The Cavalry of Classical Greece*. Oxford.

Starke, F. 1985. *Die keilschrift-luwischen Texte in Umschrift*. Studien zu den Boğazköy-Texten 30. Wiesbaden.

1997. 'Troia im Kontext des historisch-politischen und sprachlichen Umfelds Kleinasiens im 2. Jahrtausend', *Studia Troica* 7: 447–87.

Stehle, E. 1997. *Performance and Gender in Ancient Greece: Non-Dramatic Poetry in Its Setting*. Princeton.

Steiner, D. 2005. 'Nautical matters: Hesiod's Nautilia and Ibycus fragment 282 *PMG*', *Classical Philology* 100: 347–55.

Steinmetz, P. 1969. 'Das Erwachen des geschichtlichen Bewusstsein in der Polis', in *Politeia und res publica. Beiträge zum Verständnis von Politik, Recht und Staat in der Antike dem Andenken R. Starks gewidmet* (Wiesbaden) 51–78.

Stephanis, I. E. 1984. 'Ὁ Εὐβοϊκός νόμος για τη μίσθωση των Διονυσιακών τεχνιτών (*IG* XII 9, 207)', *Epistemonike Epeteris Thessalonikes* 22: 499–564.

1988. Διονυσιακοὶ Τεχνῖται. Συμβολὲς στὴν προσωπογραφία τοῦ θεάτρου καὶ τῆς μουσικῆς τῶν ἀρχαίων Ἑλλήνων. Heraklion.

Stephens, S. A. 2003. *Seeing Double: Intercultural Poetics in Ptolemaic Alexandria*. Berkeley.

Stibbe, C. M. 1993. 'Das Eleusinion am Fusse des Taygetos in Lakonien', *Bulletin Antieke Beschaving* 68: 71–105.

Stocker, S. R. and Davis, J. L. 2004. 'Animal sacrifice, archives, and feasting at the Palace of Nestor', in Wright (ed.) 2004b: 59–76.

Sutton, D. F. 1984. *The Lost Sophokles*. New York/London.

Svencickaya, I. 1996. 'Der Stadtmensch der hellenistischen Zeit: Erscheinungsbild und Lebensweise', in *Hellenismus: Beiträge zur Erforschung von Akkulturation und politischer Ordnung in den Staaten des hellenistischen Zeitalters*. Akten des Internationalen Hellenismus-Kolloquiums, Berlin, 9.-14. März 1994, ed. B. Funck (Tübingen) 611–27.

Swinnen, W. 1970. 'Herakleitos of Halikarnassos, an Alexandrian poet and diplomat?' *Ancient Society* 1: 39–52.

Tabachovitz, D. 1946. 'Ein paar Beobachtungen zum spätgriechischen Sprachgebrauch', *Eranos* 44: 296–305.

1955. 'ἑαυτῷ = αὐτός = "selbst"', *Eranos* 53: 76–8.

Bibliography

Talamo, C. 1975. 'Il mito di Melaneo, Oichalia e la protostoria eretriese', in *Contribution à l'étude de la société et de la colonisation eubéennes* (Cahiers du Centre Jean Bérard 2, Naples) 27–36.

Tambiah, S. J. 1968. 'The magical power of words', *Man*, n. s. 3: 175–208.

Taplin, O. 1993. *Comic Angels*. Oxford.

Taracha, P. 2000. *Ersetzen und Entsühnen: das mittelhethitische Ersatzritual für den Großkönig Tuthalija (CTH*448.4) und verwandte Texte*. Culture and History of the Ancient Near East 5. Leiden/Boston/Cologne.

2004. 'Fremde Gottheiten und ihre anatolischen Namen. Betrachtungen zur hethitischen Religion der Großreichzeit', in Hutter and Hutter-Braunsar (eds.) 2004: 451–60.

Tarditi, G. 1983. 'Tirteo: momenti di una campagna di guerra', *Aevum* 57: 1–13.

Tassignon, I. 2001. 'Les éléments anatoliens du mythe et de la personnalité de Dionysos', *Revue de l'histoire des religions* 218: 307–37.

Taylor, M. W. 1992. *The Tyrant Slayers: The Heroic Image in Fifth Century B.C. Athenian Art and Politics*. Salem.

Themelis, P. 2004. 'Cults on Mount Ithome', *Kernos* 17: 143–54.

Thériault, G. 1996. *Le culte d'Homonoia dans les cités grecques*. Lyon/Québec.

Thiel, H.-J., and Wegner, I. 1984. 'Eine Anrufung an den Gott Teššub von Ḫalap in hurritischer Sprache', *Studi micenei ed egeo-anatolici* 24: 187–213.

Thomas, R. 1989. *Oral Tradition and Written Record in Classical Athens*. Cambridge.

Thumb, A. and Kieckers, E. 1932. *Handbuch der griechischen Dialekte*, vol. I, 2nd edn. Heidelberg.

Tillyard, H. J. W. 1905–6. 'Excavations at Sparta, 1906: inscriptions from the Artemisium', *Annual of the British School at Athens* 12: 351–93.

Toscano, F. 1991. 'Figure di poeti negli "Uccelli" di Aristofane', *Giornale Italiano di Filologia* 43: 71–9.

Tracy, S. 1975. *The Lettering of an Athenian Mason*. Hesperia Suppl. 15. Princeton.

Trendall, A. and Webster, T. 1971. *Illustrations of Greek Drama*. London.

Tsagarakis, O. 1966. *Die Subjektivität in der griechischen Lyrik*, Diss. Munich.

1977. *Self-expression in Early Archaic Lyric Elegiac and Iambic Poetry*. Wiesbaden.

Tsiafakis, D. 1998. *Η ΘΡΑΚΗ ΣΤΗΝ ΑΤΤΙΚΗ ΕΙΚΟΝΟΓΡΑΦΙΑ ΤΟΥ 5ΟΥ ΑΙΩΝΑ Π.Χ.* Komotini.

Untersteiner, M. 1951–2. 'Eumelo di Corinto', *Antiquitas* 6–7: 3–13 = *Scritti minori. Scritti di letteratura e filosofia greca*, Brescia 1971, 165–79.

van den Hout, T. P. J. 1991–2. 'Some remarks on the third tablet of the Hittite KI.LAM festival', *Jaarbericht van het Vooraziatisch-Egyptisch Genootschap Ex Oriente Lux* 32: 101–18.

1998. *The Purity of Kingship: An Edition of CHT 569 and Related Hittite Oracle Inquiries of Tuthaliya IV*. Documenta et Monumenta Orientis Antiqui 25. Leiden/Boston/Cologne.

Van der Valk, M. (ed.) 1971–87. *Eustathii Commentarii ad Homeri Iliadem pertinentes ad fidem codicis Laurentiani editi*. Leiden.

Van Groningen, B. 1966. *Théognis: Le premier livre*. Amsterdam.

304 *Bibliography*

Van Minnen, P. 1997. 'The performance and readership of the *Persai* of Timotheus', *Archiv für Papyrusforschung* 43: 246–60.

Van Nijf, O. 2001. 'Local heroes: athletics, festivals and elite self-fashioning in the Roman East', in *Being Greek Under Rome: Cultural Identity, the Second Sophistic and the Development of Empire*, ed. S. Goldhill (Cambridge) 306–34.

Van Vleck, A. 1991. *Memory and Re-Creation in Troubadour Lyric*. Berkeley.

Van Wees, H. 1999. 'Tyrtaeus' *Eunomia*: nothing to do with the Great Rhetra', in *Sparta: New Perspectives*, ed. S. Hodkinson and A. Powell (London) 1–42.

Vatin, C. 1970. *Recherches sur le mariage et la condition de la femme mariée a l'époque hellénistique*. Paris.

Veligianni-Terzi, Ch. 2004. Οι Ελληνίδες πόλεις και το βασίλειο των Οδρυσών από Αβδήρων πόλεως μέχρι Ίστρου ποταμού. Thessaloniki.

Vendries, Ch. 1999. *Instruments à cordes et musiciens dans l'empire romain*. Paris and Montréal.

Venedikov, I. 1976. 'The Thracian horseman', in *Thracian Legends*, ed. A. Fol, I. Venedikov, I. Marazov and D. Popov (Sofia) 9–37.

Vernant, J.-P. 1991. *Mortals and Immortals: Collected Essays*, ed. F. I. Zeitlin. Princeton.

Vetta, M. 2003. 'L'*epos di Pilo* e Omero: Breve storia di una saga regionale', in *PYΣMOΣ: studi di poesia, metrica e musica greca offerti dagli allievi a Luigi Enrico Rossi per i suoi settant'anni*, ed. R. Nicolai (Rome) 13–33.

Vetta, M. and Catenacci, C. (eds). 2006. *I luoghi e la poesia nella Grecia antica*. Alessandria.

Veyne, P. 1989. 'ΔΙΑΣΚΕΥΑΙ: le théâtre grec sous l'empire (Dion de Pruse, XXXII, 94)', *Revue des Études Grecques* 102: 339–45.

Vitalis, G. 1930. *Die Entwicklung der Sage von der Rückkehr der Herakliden (untersucht im Zusammenhang mit der politischen Geschichte des Peloponnes bis auf den I. Messenischen Krieg)*, Diss. Greifswald.

Von Reden, S. 1995. 'Deceptive readings: poetry and its value reconsidered', *Classical Quarterly* 45: 30–50.

Walbank, F. W. 1957. *A Historical Commentary on Polybius*, vol. I. Oxford.

Walker, S. 1989. 'Two Spartan women and the Eleusinion', in *The Greek Renaissance in the Roman Empire: Papers from the Tenth British Museum Colloquium* (= *Bulletin of the Institute of Classical Studies* Suppl. 55), ed. S. Walker and A. Cameron (London) 130–41.

Wallace, R. W. 1998. 'The sophists in Athens', in *Democracy, Empire, and the Arts in Fifth-Century Athens*, ed. D. Boedeker and K. Raaflaub (Cambridge, MA) 203–22.

2003. 'An early fifth-century Athenian revolution in aulos music', *Harvard Studies in Classical Philology* 101: 73–92.

Wankel, H. 1976. 'Das Chaironeia-Epigramm *GV* 29 Peek', *Zeitschrift für Papyrologie und Epigraphik* 21: 97–115.

Watkins, C. 1970. 'Language of gods and language of men: remarks on some Indo-European metalinguistic traditions', in *Myth and Law among the Indo-Europeans*, ed. J. Puhvel (Berkeley) 1–17. Reprinted in *Selected Writings*

(Innsbrucker Beiträge zur Sprachwissenschaft 80) ed. L. Oliver (1994) Innsbruck: 456–72.

1986. 'The language of the Trojans', in *Troy and the Trojan War*, ed. M. J. Mellink (Bryn Mawr) 45–62. Reprinted in *Selected Writings* (Innsbrucker Beiträge zur Sprachwissenschaft 80) ed. L. Oliver (1994) Innsbruck: 700–17.

1992. 'Le dragon hittite Illuyankas et le géant grec Typhōeus', *Comptes rendus des Séances de l'Académie des Inscriptions et Belles-Lettres* 1992, 2: 319–30.

1995. *How to Kill a Dragon: Aspects of Indo-European Poetics*. Oxford.

1998. 'Homer and Hittite revisited', in *Style and Tradition: Studies in Honor of Wendell Clausen*, ed. P. Knox and C. Foss (Stuttgart/Leipzig) 201–11.

2000. 'A distant Anatolian echo in Pindar: the origin of the aegis again', *Harvard Studies in Classical Philology* 100: 1–14.

2001. 'L'Anatolie et la Grèce: résonances culturelles, linguistiques et politiques', *Comptes Rendus des Séances de l'Académie des Inscriptions et Belles-Lettres* 2001, 3: 3–18.

Weber, G. 1993. *Dichtung und höfische Gesellschaft*. Stuttgart.

Webster, T. 1969. *An Introduction to Sophocles,* 2nd edn. London.

Wegner, I. and Salvini, M. 1991. *Die hethitisch-hurritischen Ritualtafeln des (ḫ)išuwa-Festes*. Corpus der hurritischen Sprachdenkmäler I/4. Rome.

Wegner, M. 1949. *Das Musikleben der Griechen*. Berlin.

Weiler, I. 1974. *Der Agon im Mythos*. Darmstadt.

Weir, R. 2004. *Roman Delphi and its Pythian Games*. Oxford.

Weiss, P. 1990. 'Mythen, Dichter and Münzen von Lykaonien', *Chiron* 20: 221–37.

Welzer, H. (2002) *Das kommunikative Gedächtnis. Eine Theorie der Erinnerung*. Munich.

West, M. L. 1966. *Hesiod 'Theogony'*. Oxford.

1970. 'Melica', *Classical Quarterly* 20: 205–15.

1974. *Studies in Greek Elegy and Iambus*. Berlin/New York.

1983. *The Orphic Poems*. Oxford.

1985. *The Hesiodic Catalogue of Women*. Oxford.

1988. 'The rise of Greek epic', *Journal of Hellenic Studies* 107: 151–72.

1990. 'Ringing welkins', *Classical Quarterly* 40: 286–7.

1992. *Ancient Greek Music*. Oxford.

1997. *The East Face of Helicon*. Oxford.

1999. 'The invention of Homer', *Classical Quarterly* 49: 364–82.

2002. '"Eumelos": a Corinthian epic cycle?', *Journal of Hellenic Studies* 122: 109–33.

2003. *Homeric Hymns, Homeric Apocrypha, Lives of Homer*. Cambridge, MA.

2005. '*Odyssey* and *Argonautica*', *Classical Quarterly* 55: 39–64.

Whallon, W. 1964. 'Blind Thamyris and blind Maeonides', *Phoenix* 18: 9–12.

White, J. W. 1901. 'Tzetzes's notes on the *Aves* of Aristophanes in Codex Urbinas 141', *Harvard Studies in Classical Philology* 12: 69–108.

Whitmarsh, T. 2001. *Greek Literature and the Roman Empire*. Oxford.

Wide, S. 1893. *Lakonische Kulte*. Leipzig.

Bibliography

Wilamowitz Möllendorff, U. von 1900. *Die Textgeschichte der griechischen Lyriker.* Berlin.

1903. *Timotheos: Die Perser.* Leipzig.

Willetts, R. F. 1958. 'Cretan Eileithyia', *Classical Quarterly* 8: 221–3.

Wilson, N. G. 1999. 'Travelling actors in the fifth century', *Classical Quarterly* 49: 625.

Wilson, P. 1999. 'The aulos in Athens,' in *Performance Culture and Athenian Democracy*, ed. S. Goldhill and R. Osborne (Cambridge) 58–95.

1999/2000. 'Euripides' tragic muse' in *Euripides and Tragic Theatre in the Late Fifth Century*, ed. M. Cropp, K. Lee and D. Sansone. *Illinois Classical Studies* 24–5: 427–50.

2000. *The Athenian Institution of the Khoregia: The Chorus, the City and the Stage.* Cambridge.

2003a. 'The sound of cultural conflict: Kritias and the culture of mousikē in Athens', in *The Cultures within Ancient Greek Culture: Contact, Conflict, Collaboration*, ed. C. Dougherty and L. Kurke (Cambridge) 181–206.

2003b. 'The politics of dance: dithyrambic contest and social order in ancient Greece', in *Sport and the Festival in the Ancient World*, ed. D. J. Phillips and D. Pritchard (Swansea) 163–96.

2004. 'Athenian strings', in Murray and Wilson (eds.) 2004: 269–306.

2007a. 'Sicilian choruses' in Wilson (ed.) 2007b: 3511–77.

2007b (ed.) *The Greek Theatre and Festivals.* Oxford.

Wohl, V. 2004. 'Dirty dancing: Xenophon's *Symposium*', in Murray and Wilson (eds.) 2004: 337–63.

Worley, L. J. 1994. *Hippeis: The Cavalry of Ancient Greece.* Boulder/San Francisco/Oxford.

Wörrle, M. 1988. *Stadt und Fest im kaiserzeitlichen Kleinasien. Studien zu einer agonistischen Stiftung aus Oinoanda.* Munich.

Wright, D. P. 1987. *The Disposal of Impurity: Elimination Rites in the Bible and in Hittite and Mesopotamian Literature.* Dissertation Series/Society of Biblical Literature 101. Atlanta, GA.

Wright, J. C. 2004a. 'The Mycenaean feast: an introduction', in Wright (ed.) 2004b: 1–12.

(ed.) 2004b. *The Mycenaean Feast.* Hesperia 73:2. Princeton.

Wyatt, W. 1989. 'The Intermezzo of *Odyssey* 11 and the poets Homer and Odysseus', *Studi micenei ed egeo-anatolici* 27: 235–53.

Yunis, H. 2001. *Demosthenes: On the Crown.* Cambridge.

Zaccagnini, C. 1983. 'Patterns of mobility among ancient Near Eastern craftsmen', *Journal of Near Eastern Studies* 42: 245–64.

Zinko, C. 2001. 'Bemerkungen zu einigen hethitischen Pflanzen und Pflanzennamen', in *Akten des IV Internationalen Kongresses für Hethitologie: Würzburg, 4.-8. Oktober 1999* (Studien zu den Boğazköy-Texten 45), ed. G. Wilhelm (Wiesbaden) 739–59.

Zunino, M. 1997. *Hiera Messeniaka: la storia religiosa della Messenia dall'età micenea all'età ellenistica.* Udine.

Index

Abaris 16
Abdera 119–21, 128, 157–62
Abderos 157–8
Achaea, cheese from 110
aegis 29
Aeschylus 12, 59, 62
   Bassarai 47
   Women of Aitna 33
   Life of 203
Aesop, Life of 3
Aetolians 237–48
Africa 15, 93
Ahhiyawa 36
Ainos 121–2
Alcaeus 19, 118–22
   fr. 45 121–2
   fr. 140 122
   fr. 307(a) 120–5
   fr. 307(b) 120–2
   fr. 325 119
   fr. 327 119
   fr. 347(a)V 118–19
Alciphron 12
Alcman 11, 68
Aleppo, storm god of 34–5
Alexander Aetolus 246
Alexander the Great 18, 258
Alexandria 4–5, 12, 241, 243
Alkinoe 241
Amphicles of Rheneia 147–8, 149,
   244
Amphiklos of Chios 3, 245
Anacharsis 81
Anacreon 11, 16, 18, 127
   fr. 346 128
   fr. 347 128–9
   fr. 352 128
   fr. 354 128
   fr. 357 128
   fr. 358 128
   fr. 359 128

   fr. 366 128
   fr. 372 128
   fr. 388 128
   fr. 417 128
   fr. 448 130
   fr. 463 127
   fr. 471 128
   fr. 490 127
   fr. 505(a) 127, 130
Andania 52
Antiphanes 60
Anyte of Tegea 17, 241–2
Aphrodite 29–31, 115
Apollo 23, 37, 40–1, 44, 54–5, 64, 73, 76,
   119–21, 251
Apollo Karneios 53
Apollonia on the Rhyndakos 264–5
Apollonius of Rhodes 7
Apollonius of Tyana 16
Aratus 12
Arcadia 171, 188–91
Archias of Antioch 4
Archilochus 107–10, 112
   fr. 9 110
   fr. 11 110
   fr. 19 108, 110
   fr. 21 108
   fr. 22 108, 110
   fr. 23 110
   fr. 102 108
   fr. 105 109–10
   fr. 116 108
   Ades. Eleg. 61 112
   Ades. Eleg. 62 112
   Mnesiepes inscription 89
Argonauts 1
Arion 11, 92
Aristeas 16
Aristodama 237–48
Aristodemis of Paphos 242
Aristomache of Erythrai 241

Aristophanes
  Birds 148
  Birds, 904–56 81–3, 101–2, 103–4
    941–5 93–5
    948 97
    1318–22 149
  Frogs 1030–2 1–3
  Frogs 1058ff. 179
Aristotheos of Troizen 260
Artemis 35, 182
  Artemis Orthia 175–7
Artists of Dionysus 4, 191, 217–34, 239–40,
  256–7, 266–8
Asklepiades of Tragilos 62
Athenian *mousikē* 60
Athens 11, 13–14, 18, 104, 130, 245, 255–9, 260,
  262, 267, 268
audience 105
aulos 119, 120–1, 124, 147, 191
Auphria 243

Bacchylides, exile of 16
  Ode 3.90–8 88–9
  Ode 5.7–14 86–7
  Ode 17 144
Basho 14
Bendis 35–6
blame 98
blinding 56–7, 61, 95
Boeotia 119
Boethius 172–88
Bombos 240, 261
Bronze Age 11, 15, 35–6

Callimachus 5–6, 19, 101, 115, 269
  Aitia fr. 178.32–3 5
  Epigrams 17
  fr. 203.11–14 6
  Hymn 2 162
Callinus 114
  fr. 2 114
  fr. 2a 114
cannabis 67–8
Carneia 173, 179
Ceos 162–6
Chios 262
Choerilos of Iasos 18
Choerilos of Samos 18
choral
  elegy 153
  lyric 150–1
  performance 124, 163–6
Cicero, *Pro Archia* 4
cithara *see* kithara
citizenship 238, 239, 243–4

Clazomenae 111
codes, poetic 86
comedy, Athenian 74
comic poets 14
commissions 17–18, 106, 209–12
competitions, musical and poetic 6, 18, 59, 187,
  195, 203–12, 239
  sacred 221
concord 268
contest of Homer and Hesiod 7, 89
Corinna 241
cosmopolitan 233
Cratinus 74
Crete 19, 23, 31, 91, 192–3, 263–4,
  267
Crinagoras of Mytilene 19
curse 98, 159

death, symbolic 54
Delos 6, 11, 39, 137, 238–47, 259
  Delian League 146
  Delian maidens 23, 89
Delphi 3, 37, 45, 119–21, 200–3, 238, 241, 242,
  243–4, 254, 256–7, 260, 262
  Amphictiony 218–30, 238–47, 262
  archonship 247
  defence of 251, 263–4, 265
  hymns 266–7
  oracle 161, 197
  Poitropia festival 239
  records 59
  Sōtēria 6
Delphis 243
Demeter 28, 180–5
dēmiourgoi 10, 23, 46, 50
Demodokos 10, 50, 58, 77
Demosthenes 212
Demoteles of Andros 3
dialect, poetic 19, 39, 142, 175–6, 243
dialogos 249, 268
Dio Chrysostomus 8–9
Dionysia 6, 38
Dionysus 3, 28, 47
  Artists of *see* Artists of Dionysus
Dioscuri 200
Dioscourides of Tarsus 240
diplomacy 19, 36–43, 244, 246, 249, 254,
  256–8, 259–62, 262–5
dithyramb 6, 14, 64, 65, 92, 101–2, 149, 180,
  181–2
drama 6, 40, 46–79, 104, 149, 218, 224,
  246
dress of poets 92
drōmena and *legomena* 32, 44
Dymas of Iasos 245, 267

Index

economy 93–104
  of Bronze Age 15
  competitive 187
  market 15
Egypt 8, 19, 99, 220, 229, 243
Eiresiōnē 98
ekphrasis 122
elegiac 112–18
Eleusis 38
Empedocles 2
encomium
  city 240, 261
  logikon 207–8
enlightenment, as journey 16
Ephebes 256–8
Ephesus 111–12, 114
epic 10, 24–5, 46, 70, 98, 241
  enkōmion 207–9, 240
  koinē 137–42, 161
  local and regional 19, 216, 240,
    247
  metre 137–42
  poets 18, 215
  poetess 239
  recitation of 6
Epidauros 6, 260
epideixis 240
epidēmia 257–8, 259
epigram 196–200
  public 196–203
  parallel 211
  collections 215–16
epinikia 86, 104, 135
epitaph 98
epitaphios logos 150, 157, 159–61
Euboia 225
Eumelus of Corinth, prosodion 137–45
  metrical structure of 142–3
Euripides 12, 33
  Bacchae 3
  Rhesos 924 60
  Tr. 1188–91 213
  epinikion 104
exchange, sociopoetic 85
exchange relationship 13, 92–3
exēgētai 266
exile 16, 85, 106, 118, 120–1, 170,
    253–4

fame: see *kleos*
festivals 18, 32, 35, 38–42, 50, 158, 206, 223,
    265–6
  festival culture 217
  foreign participants at 267
foundation legend 250, 263

Gastarbeiter 199
genealogical poetry 20, 245
genealogy 250
generic *polyeideia* 98, 101
geography, sacred 5–6, 15
Glauke of Chios 241
Golden Fleece 28
Greekness 269
griots 15, 93

Hadrian 227, 243, 250, 269
Hausa 93
Hedea of Tralles 242
Hegemon of Thasos 14
Hegesias 262
Hephaestus, festival of 73
Heraclitus of Halicarnassus
    17
Heraclitus Homericus 109
Heracleides Ponticus 58
Hermocles of Chios 245,
    262
Herodotus
  1.24 11
  3.39 126
  3.121 127
  5.113 115
  7.228 134
Hesiod
  as metanastic poet 80–1
  name of 87
  Theogony 70
  Works and Days 26 18
    582–96 119
    648–53 5
    654–7 6
Hesiodic *Catalogue* 48
hieromnēmon 245
hip-hop 95
Hipponax 6, 92, 101, 111–12
  fr. 1 111
  fr. 26 112
  fr. 50 112
  fr. 42 111
historiography 259–61
Hittites 23–45
Homer 20, 90–1, 95–7, 100
  Catalogue of Ships 19, 20
  Il. 2.484–92 56–7
  Il. 2.591–600 47–8, 77–8
  Il. 2.730 53
  Od. 1.326–7 10
  Od. 8.64 50
  Od. 8.487–91 10
  Od. 9.19–20 10

Homer (*cont.*)
  Od. 11.333–84 94
  Od. 17.380–91 10, 23, 46, 85
Homer, Lives of 6–7, 95–7, 98–9, 102–3
Homeric *Epigram* 12 100
Homeric hymns
  to Apollo 6, 10, 23, 37, 89–90,
    146–64
  to Aphrodite 245
Homeridai 51
Homerisms 214
Hurrian 32, 34–5, 41

iambos 107–12
Ibycus 11, 122–7
  epinician 124
  PMG 282.45–7 89
  PMG 289 123
  PMG 321 123
  PMG 323 123
  S151 122–3, 125, 126, 134
  S166 122
  S220 122–8
  S221 124
  S222 124
  S227 122–30
ideology 151–2
India, poetry 15
Indo-European poetry 41, 43,
  88
inscriptions
  CEG 819 200–1
  CEG 888 196
  FD 3.1.533–4 242
  FD 3.2.145 238
  GVI 1176 210
  ID 1497 147
  IG II² 1006 258
  IG II² 1283 36
  IG VII 373 148
  IG IX 1, 131 200–2
  IG IX 2, 62 237
  IG IX 2, 63 215–16
  IG IX 2, 531 205–9
  IG XII Suppl. 315 252
  SEG 38.1496 249–52
invitation 18
invocation 26
Ion of Chios 14, 101
Ion of Samos 200–3
Ionians 146, 245, 267
Irish literature 93, 98, 99–100

Japanese poetry 14, 16
Julia Balbilla 8, 19, 243

katalogē 208–9
Kharites 85
khoropsaltriai 242
Kinesias 91–2
kinship *see sungeneia*
kithara 63, 75–6, 170, 172
kitharists 77
kitharōidia 53, 57–8, 64, 65, 69, 74, 75, 194,
  242
Kleochares of Athens 3
kleos 2, 6–7, 10, 89–90, 94, 125, 171,
  207–9
koinē, pan-Hellenic 19, 176
ktiseis 263
kuklia 148
kursa 28–9
Kytenion 249–53, 265–6

landmarks 111
Larisa 205–9
lectures, public 259–62
Limenios 266
Lindos 257–69
  Lindian Chronicle 257–8
lingua franca, poetic 215
local cult places 165
local history 98, 195–216
Longianus, C. Julius 8
Lucian 2
lusiōidos 242
Luwian 32–3
Lycia 196–200
lyric 118–35
Lycurgus of Sparta 185, 186

Magnes of Smyrna 2, 8–9
Magnesia on the Maeander 263, 265
Megara 106
Melanippides 14
memory
  collective 20, 253–4, 255–9, 264, 266,
    269
  cultural 253–4, 255, 262, 264, 266
  historical 253–4
  travelling 266
Menander 12, 14
Menander Rhetor 9, 84
Messenia 52–6, 137–45, 193
metanastic poetics 80–1
Middle Ages, poetry of 14–15
Miletus 264
mimesis 90
Mimnermus 113
  fr. 9 113–14
  fr. 14 154

Index

311

miracles 257–9, 263–4, 266
mnemopoiesis 253–5
Mnesiptolemus of Kyme 257–9
mobility
 of cult-practice 266
 of culture 253
 of memory 253–4
motivation of wandering poets
 209
mousikē, Athenian 60
Muses 56–7, 63, 64, 70–3
music, poetry set to 186
musical instruments 65–6
musical tradition 57–8
Mycenae 44
mystery-cult 55–6
Mytilene 118, 120–5

name of poet 201–2
Naryx 269
Neo-Pythagorean 173
Nestor of Laranda 8
New Music 70–9, 178
Nicander of Colophon 246–8
Nicolaus of Damascus 2–3

Odysseus 1, 18
Oikhalia 52–5, 56–7
Olen of Lycia 10
Opountian Lokris 269
orality 261, 265
Orientalising Period 23–4
Orpheus 1–2, 4, 47, 55, 181

paean 37, 120–1
paidotribas 198–9
Paion of Side 8
pan-Hellenic
 audience 260
 cycles of myth 20
 perspectives 20
Panhellenion 269
para-poetic traditions 89
parainetic 98
parody 87
Paros 108, 109, 112
partheneia 101, 149
Parthenius of Nikaia 17
Pausanias
 3.20.5–7 181
 4.4.1 137–42
 4.33.2 137–42
 4.15.6 113
 9.30.5 1
 10.38.13 241

performance 107
 oral 266
performance tradition 56–7
Petosiris 210
Phemios 10
Philammon 54, 78
Philippos of Pergamon 260–1
Philopoemen 194
Philostratus, *Vit. Soph.* 2, 16
Philoxenus of Cythera 17, 188–91
Phrygian mode 65, 66
pilgrimage 15
pilgrims 218, 254, 266
Pindar 12–13, 17, 20, 103–4, 133,
 156
 Isth. 1 12
 Isth. 4.63 158
 Isth. 9 140
 Nem. 5, 1–5 7
 Nem. 9.1–3 13
 Ol. 1.115–7 89
 Ol. 10.13–15 139
 Ol. 13.22–4 139–49
 Ol. 2.8–11 160
 Pyth. 2.1–4 13
 Pyth. 4, 275–80 84–6
 fr. 105 13, 93–5
 fr. 106 95
 fr. 109 150
 fr. 199 139–62
 dithyrambs 14
 Paean 2 155–62
 Paean 4 139, 144, 146, 156, 162–6
 Paean 4.47–8 164–5
 Paean 5 144, 146
planetic poetics 81, 95, 98
Plataia, Battle of 268
Plato
 Ion 541b8 6
 Laws 13–14
 Prot. 315.a7–b1 2
 Rep. 1.3281–4 36–43
 Rep. 3.398a 9, 10
poeti vaganti, Hellenistic 3–4, 17,
 178, *passim*
poetry, definition 26
Politas of Hypate 215–16, 238
Polybius 171, 189–92
Polycrates of Samos 11, 125, 127, 129
Polygnota of Thebes 242
Polymnestos of Colophon 11
Posidippus of Pella 5
praise 98
Praxeis tōn Magnētōn 264
'Pride of Halicarnassus' 19, 240

Priene 267
privileges for Artists 230–2, 238, 239,
    247
professional poets 16, 213
Pronomos of Thebes 144,
    146–7
propemptic 98
prosodion 137–48
Protagoras 2
Pythagoras 178
Pythian Games 41
Python's *Agēn* 19

Raftery 100
rap 208
reading, act of as movement 6
reception, supra-local 213–16
religious cults, relocation of 11
reperformance 107
return 117
Rhegium 122, 123–5
Rhianus 19, 216, 240
rhapsodes 6
rituals 256–7, 266–8
Rome 269

Sacadas of Argos 144
Sack of Oikhalia 56–7
Samos 110, 125, 127
Samothrace 245
Sappho 240
    fr. 2V 29–31
    exile of 16
seer 199
Semonides 107, 110
    Frr. 22–3 110, 117, 135
Simonides 11, 14, 101, 130–5, 213,
    211, 214
    epigram for Megistias 134,
        199
    Epinikia 130, 133
    fr. 10–17W 134
    fr. 11W 131, 154
    fr. 19–20W 132
    fr. 22W 132–3
    PMG 310 131
    PMG 313 131
    PMG 410 131
    PMG 519 131
    PMG 520 130
    PMG 531 131
    PMG 541 131
    PMG 542 131
    Threnoi 130
Smyrna 113–14, 237

Soloi 115
Solon of Athens 16, 114–15
    fr. 1 134
    fr. 19 12, 115
Sophocles 33
    Paean 33
    Thamyras 60–79
Sparta 169–70, 172–88, 268
    war memorials at 186
sphragis 74, 199
stasis 118, 155–62, 164
statues 204–5
Stesichorus 69, 123–5
sungeneia 245–6, 249
Symmakhos of Pellana 196–200,
    214–15
symposium location 122, 135
sympotic poetry 151–2, 153
syncretism 36–43

technē 213
Telesilla 241
Telipinu 26–8, 29–31
Tenos 109, 252
Teos 127
    Teian Dirae 162
Terpander 69, 139–40, 142, 155
Thaletas of Gortyn 11, 37, 155,
    193
Thamyris/Thamyras 46–79
thamyrists 51, 76
Thasos 107–9, 158
Thebes 146–7
Theocritus 5, 12
Theognis and *Theognidea* 115–17
    11–14 116
    237–40 7, 17
    773–82 106
    879–84 117
    1087–90 116
    1123–8 116
Theophrastos 266
theōria 140–1, 144, 217–34, 266
therapōn 86–7, 91
Thrace 61–2
Thucydides 160–1, 165
Timotheasts 76
Timotheus 168–94
    Persians, opening 194
    Persians 206–12 172
    Birthpangs of Semele 175, 180, 185
tourist attractions 254
tragedy 32, 39, 74
    tragic lyric 59
    tragic poets 14

Index

Triptolemos 256–7
troubadours, Provençal 89
Typhon 40–1
Tyrtaeus 113, 150–6
 Eunomia 151–2, 153, 155, 161
 fr. 2 113, 151, 153
 fr. 5W 160
 fr. 11 151–2
 origin 154–5

verbal art 26
Virgil, *Georg.* 4.516–20 1

wandering 16
wandering hero 250
women
 performers 39, 239, 240–4
 and ritual 100, 183
 sexuality of 119
 and citizenship 248
worldwide guild 222–3, 227–9
writtenness 204

Xanthos 196–200, 249–54
xenia 13–14, 23, 124, 133, 135, 199